Come Retribution

COME

UNIVERSITY PRESS OF MISSISSIPPI
JACKSON AND LONDON

RETRIBUTION

The Confederate Secret Service
and the Assassination of Lincoln

WILLIAM A. TIDWELL
with James O. Hall *and* David Winfred Gaddy

Copyright © 1988 by the University Press of Mississippi
Manufactured in the United States of America

91 90 89   4 3 2

The paper in this book meets the guidelines for permanence
and durability of the Committee on Production Guidelines for
Book Longevity of the Council on Library Resources.

Designed by John A. Langston

Library of Congress Cataloging-in-Publication Data

Tidwell, William A.
  Come retribution.

  Includes index.
  1. United States—History—Civil War, 1861–1865—
Secret service. 2. Lincoln, Abraham, 1809–1865—
Assassination. 3. Intelligence service—Confederate
States of America—History. I. Hall, James O.
II. Gaddy, David Winfred. III. Title.
E608.T53 1988   973.7'86   88-5463
ISBN 0-87805-347-6 (alk. paper)
ISBN 0-87805-348-4 (pbk. alk. paper)

Seek the truth
Come whence it may
Cost what it will

—Inscription at the door
of the Bishop Payne Library,
Virginia Theological Seminary

Contents

Acknowledgments

This book is a group effort in more ways than one. Not only did three of us participate in the writing of it, but many other people helped to make it possible.

First were our wives, who endured our absences and preoccupation over many years. Then were the people who with remarkable insight helped us locate and recognize the information we have used to develop the story of Confederate intelligence and its role in the Lincoln assassination. In addition, many people have given invaluable advice on statistical and other technical matters. Finally, a small host of people have helped with the preparation of the manuscript.

Among the many people who have assisted us, we wish particularly to thank the following. Michael P. Musick archivist at the Military Reference Branch in the U.S. National Archives was especially helpful in facilitating our research. Linda McCurdy showed remarkable talent in locating pertinent material in the Southern Historical Collection at the University of North Carolina and at Duke University. Paul Scheips, Wallace Winkler, John Stanton, and members of the Surratt Society of Clinton, Maryland, especially Joan Chaconas and John Brennan, provided help and information in a variety of ways. Terry Alford of the Northern Virginia Community College gave us essential encouragement. None of them should be held accountable for our conclusions; some of them, indeed, will be surprised.

Special recognition is due to Seetha Srinivasan and others at the University Press of Mississippi who perceived the value of the manuscript in spite of its blemishes and to Trudie Calvert, the copyeditor, who helped smooth them away.

Harry Cummins prepared the maps, and Cynthia Bryan was the last of a long line who typed and retyped drafts of the manuscript.

We thank them all.

William A. Tidwell
James O. Hall
David Winfred Gaddy

A Word to the Reader

This book is a history of Confederate intelligence and covert operations and a case study of one ambitious, complex covert operation that had an unexpected outcome. We also trust it will provide new insight on a much studied topic.

The leaders of the Confederacy were reasonably knowledgeable about intelligence and clandestine operations, and they concerned themselves personally with the secret collection of information and the mounting of clandestine operations. The operation that involved John Wilkes Booth and resulted in the assassination of President Abraham Lincoln is a classic example of one that was too closely tied to critical government decisions, influenced by unexpected circumstances beyond the control of those responsible for it, and had an impact quite unlike that anticipated when the operation was planned.

Relatively little serious scholarship has been devoted to the study of Civil War intelligence activity. There have been a number of accounts of spies and spy activity, but some of these have been sensationalized and only a few reflect the effort required to contribute to an understanding of the total structure of intelligence in the Civil War.[1]

It is important to keep in mind three distinct phases in the history of the Confederate intelligence effort. First, during the war, many intelligence-related activities such as scouting and interrogating local inhabitants were treated as normal combat functions, and little effort was made to conceal them. Spying while wearing civilian clothes or the enemy's uniform, however, was something to avoid talking about, if there was a chance that one might be caught.

xi

During the Civil War, several activities that we might treat more casually today were considered especially sensitive. For instance, people assigned to the Confederate Torpedo Service took a special secrecy oath and generally avoided discussion of their assignments. Other examples of secret activities were the procurement of warships and weapons abroad, which the Confederates referred to as "secret service" or "special service."

Other areas in which security was high throughout the war included the use of ciphers, counterintelligence, sabotage, and the general field of covert political or military-political activity conducted outside of Confederate lines. Some of the results of political action became known, but most of the organization that initiated and carried out these operations was and has been kept well hidden.

A second historical phase, immediately following the war, influenced the testimony of persons with knowledge of Confederate intelligence activities following the assassination of President Lincoln. With the Union victorious, there was no Confederate government to defend the individuals who had carried on clandestine activities. Some of these people had been involved with Booth in one way or another and were afraid that they would be tried by peacetime standards for what they had done in the war. In this second phase, a strong attempt was made to hide questionable activities or to reinterpret wartime experiences to fit innocent explanations. In this period, little firsthand information was published bearing on Confederate covert operations.

The third phase began after many of the principal members of the Union and Confederate governments had died and a new generation had grown up that had no personal involvement in the war. About twenty to twenty-five years after the war, personal accounts of involvement in various aspects of Confederate clandestine activity began to appear. These accounts tended to emphasize the romantic aspects of a bygone war that was now something of a curiosity.

An important example is that of Captain Thomas Nelson Conrad, whose story of his adventures as a cavalry scout and master spy was first published in a Philadelphia newspaper in 1887 and then in book form in 1892. Conrad retold his story in several different ways: sometimes he rearranged and distorted the events in which he participated so that his chronology is not always to be trusted; and it now seems clear that he also knew many things that he did not tell in his books. Conrad's story was followed in 1893 by the publication of a book by Thomas A. Jones, the Confederate Signal Corps agent at Popes Creek, Maryland. His account is relatively straightforward, but again, it is clear that he knew more than he told.[2]

In 1906, John W. Headley, a former lieutenant in Confederate operations guided from Canada, published a book about Confederate operations in Canada and New York, many of them conducted in 1864. In 1911 and 1912, one volume of the ten-volume *Photographic History of the Civil War* was titled *Soldier Life and the Secret Service*. In this work, Headley wrote an article on the Secret Service of the Confederacy. Captain John B. Castleman published his version of these activities, *Active Service* in 1917.[3]

These revelations led to some excellent work on specific examples of the Confederate covert operations run from Canada, but the main framework of Confederate intelligence remained untouched. It has only been in recent years that the existence of the Confederate War Department Secret Service Bureau has been confirmed. The total organization of the Confederate intelligence and covert effort has not yet been described. One purpose of this book is to attempt such a description.

Another purpose is to probe Confederate involvement in the Lincoln assassination. There is no documentary evidence that directly proves Confederate involvement, and there probably never was any such evidence. There is some personal testimony—some of it in the form of statements by persons who were under arrest. Such testimony had obvious biases and selective recall. Some of it exists in memoirs written long after the event. There is very little hearsay evidence. Circumstantial evidence, however, abounds. No activity as important and as complex as an attempt to capture a president of the United States could exist without affecting the actions of large numbers of people. The biggest problem is to find the evidence in the mounds of archival material and to recognize its pertinence.

The evidence presented in this book is largely circumstantial. Basically, we are trying to tell our story by putting together many small pieces of information. Each item is well documented. By assembling enough of such pieces we hope that we can shed some new light on the events of 1865 for those persons who are interested in the truth.

This is a tricky game to play, and one can easily misinterpret a given piece of indirect evidence. The strength of the procedure, however, is that if one finds enough items to form a consistent pattern, the outcome does not depend on correct interpretation of one or two items but of the overall pattern.

In studying the Confederate intelligence effort, it is often difficult to formulate the correct hypothesis to investigate because of the emotional impact of issues involved in the assassination of President Lincoln. The emotion comes from the self-inflicted wound of the Civil War.

When Lincoln was assassinated, many southerners felt that the bullet was well deserved. It soon became obvious, however, that it was not wise to expound that view in public. The remains of the Confederate army evaporated within a few months (the last southern unit crossed into Mexico in July 1865), and the South was left in the power of a hostile occupying army.

Many southerners were, of course, genuinely horrified by the assassination. It was not only murder, but it was the first murder of a president in the short life of the American republic. Within a few days, the futility of the act began to be obvious, and many people could see that as bad as they thought Lincoln might have been, the situation without him could be much worse.

It was widely believed in the North that the Confederate government might have been involved in the assassination of Lincoln, and the federal government launched a frantic campaign to prove that theory. In the rush, federal officers did a slipshod job of investigating the ramifications of Booth's group. The net result of the haste was to discredit those who believed in Confederate involvement. As a result of northern misinterpretation and southern defense, the world is now convinced that Booth was a murderer because he was mentally unbalanced.

Fortunately, modern America will not be much affected if Jefferson Davis and his colleagues now accept their responsibility for a covert operation that did not produce the intended result. From the perspective of the latter half of the twentieth century, with its revelations of the workings of secret warfare and the trauma of the assassinations of political figures, we can look in more detached and objective fashion at the leaders of the Confederacy in their struggle for survival. Perhaps we can now study their use of intelligence and covert action objectively, admire their ingenuity and their successes, and gain valuable vicarious experience from their failures. Knowing the control he sought to maintain over military affairs and the "imperial presidency" he represented in matters of state, we should not be surprised to see the evidence build toward a central role for Jefferson Davis in the clandestine warfare of the 1860s—and the fateful act that ended it.

Notes

1. One of the most constructive of the few exceptions is H. V. Canan, "Confederate Military Intelligence," *Maryland Historical Magazine* 59 (March 1964): 34–51.

2. Thomas Nelson Conrad, *A Confederate Spy* (New York: J. S. Ogilvie, 1892); Thomas A. Jones, *J. Wilkes Booth* (Chicago: Laird & Lee, 1893).

3. John W. Headley, *Confederate Operations in Canada and New York* (New York: Neale, 1906); Francis Trevelyan Miller, ed., *The Photographic History of the Civil War*, 10 vols. (New York: Review of Reviews, 1912). The volume *Soldier Life and the Secret Service* has an article entitled "The Secret Service of the Confederacy" by Headley; John B. Castleman, *Active Service* (Louisville: Courier-Journal Job Printing Co., 1917).

Come Retribution

Introduction: The Logic Trail

The assassination of President Lincoln by the actor John Wilkes Booth on the night of 14 April 1865 has fascinated generations of Americans and provided the basis for hundreds of books, pamphlets, and articles purporting to explain how and why it happened. Unfortunately for explanations, Booth was killed by his pursuers on 26 April 1865 and was thus unable to clarify his motives or answer questions that subsequently arose.

The federal government tried immediately to prove that the assassination was the responsibility of the leaders of the Confederate government and a group of Confederate agents in Canada known to have been engaged in clandestine operations against the North during the Civil War. In their haste to satisfy the popular demand for vengeance, the Union prosecutors were unable to prove their case against the Confederacy. The chaotic state of Confederate records precluded the definitive evidence they sought and continued to seek after the execution of Booth's associates. Convinced of the conclusion but unable to demonstrate it with hard evidence, the Union prosecutors resorted to some witnesses, such as James B. Merritt and Charles A. Dunham, alias Sandford Conover, whose testimony was questionable at best and in many instances outright perjury. This weakness in the Union case allowed other theories to flourish. As time went by, many writers of various degrees of sophistication and integrity made attempts to develop a convincing explanation for the assassination. Most of them accepted the view that John Wilkes Booth was the primary mover of the action and that he and a small group of associates whom he had gathered in Washington were solely responsible for the deed.

Those who believed Booth was primarily responsible developed

3

elaborate rationales to explain why he could have killed a man so obviously great and good. They tried to explain that he must have been mentally unbalanced to consider such an odious act. One "long-range psychiatrist" concluded that Booth hated his father and killed the president as a father substitute. Another said that Booth was losing his stage voice and struck out in frustration over a failing career as an actor. The peculiarities of Booth's eccentric family were cited as evidence of family instability to support the view that John Wilkes Booth was "mad."[1]

Others were not satisfied that an unstable Booth was responsible for the assassination. They tried to blame it on conspiracies by Catholics or by moneyed interests seeking to control government policy. One of the most persistent themes in recent years has been the idea that the Union secretary of war, Edwin M. Stanton, was secretly behind the conspiracy.

While these various theories were being propounded, John Wilkes Booth became something of a cult hero in some circles. It was rumored that he had escaped the Union pursuit and lived for many years in Texas, or in Canada, or in India, or somewhere else. These ideas were combined with the Stanton theory to claim that the wrong man was intentionally shot in the pursuit and that the real Booth had been permitted to escape and was subsequently hidden by his secret sponsors.

This morass of explanations generated over the years was examined in 1983 in *The Lincoln Murder Conspiracies*, by William Hanchett of San Diego State University. Hanchett provided a critical analysis of the various published theories about the assassination. Although he advanced no theory of his own, his work brings out two significant problems in trying to unravel the mystery of the assassination.[2] First, it is clear that many, if not all, of the theories regarding the assassination rest on unwarranted and unsupported speculation. Authors faced with inadequate evidence have relied upon their beliefs and values to fill objective gaps. Hanchett's work clearly demonstrates the weakness in this form of argumentation. A second problem highlighted by Hanchett's work is that no plausible theory exists to explain the events of 1865. Even those who believe that Booth acted alone are left with no satisfactory explanation of his motive.

Unfortunately, the most logical theory to explain the assassination, and the one best supported by objective evidence, has never been explicitly stated and was, therefore, not covered in Hanchett's critique. This theory was derived by treating the assassination as an intelligence problem and approaching it with the objective handling of information and analytical tools that a modern intelligence officer would use. The theory is a variant of the federal government's initial case, but one that can now be supported by much more evidence than the government had available in 1865. Furthermore, it is a theory that is not clouded by the emotions and prejudices of the Civil War era. Briefly, the theory is that leaders in the Confederate government tried to capture President Lincoln as a hostage, and when that effort failed they decided to attack Union leaders to disrupt command and control of the Union forces. Events in April 1865 moved so fast that John Wilkes Booth thought that he was acting in accordance with Confederate interests even though, as we can see in retrospect, the actual need for such action had been obviated by General Robert E. Lee's surrender of the Army of Northern Virginia. Hanchett showed flaws in the government's initial case, but the variant case depends on circumstantial and factual evidence and not on the evidence of fallible witnesses.

Let us briefly outline the logic behind the explanation that we are advancing.

The activities of Booth after the assassination have been examined by professional and amateur scholars in minute detail. In the course of his flight, until he was killed at the Garrett farm in Caroline County, Virginia, Booth was helped in various ways by a number of different people. These included John Lloyd at Surratt's tavern in what is now Clinton, Maryland; Dr. Samuel Mudd, who set Booth's broken leg; a black farmer named Oswell Swann, who guided him to the home of Samuel Cox near the present village of Bel Alton, Maryland; Cox and his son, who hid Booth and his companion, David Herold, in a thicket; Thomas Jones, who fed Booth and Herold for several days and eventually put them into a boat to cross the Potomac River; Colonel John J. Hughes, who lived near Nanjemoy Creek in Maryland and gave them food; Thomas Harbin and Joseph Baden, who met Booth and Herold in Virginia; Mrs. Elizabeth Quesenberry, who sent food to the two fugitives; William Bryant, a farmer, who took the two men to the home of Dr. Richard Henry Stuart in King George County, Virginia; Dr. Stuart, who gave them a meal; Charles Lucas, a free black, who took them by wagon to Port Conway on the Rappahannock River; William Rollins, a fisherman at Port Conway, who let them wait for the ferry at his home; three Confederate soldiers, Lieutenant Mortimer B. Ruggles, his cousin Private Absalom R. Bainbridge, and Private Willie Jett, who put Booth on Ruggles's horse and escorted the fugitives to the Garrett farm and arranged for Booth to stay there until ready for the next move.

These people who helped Booth and Herold have been treated as unrelated individuals, and their assistance to Booth has been treated as coincidental, but it is instructive to look at what they have in common. John Lloyd was the manager of Surratt's tavern, a well-known way station for Confederate agents. Dr. Samuel Mudd was an ardent pro-Confederate reported to have earlier provided assistance to Walter Bowie, a famous Confederate agent. Oswell Swann was a free black farmer of southern Maryland. Samuel Cox, another ardent pro-Confederate, had been involved in organizing prosecession activity in Maryland in 1861 and later. Thomas Jones was the principal agent for the Confederate Signal Corps "mail" system north of the Potomac River. John J. Hughes lived on a farm near where the conspirators had hidden a boat to be used to carry a captive President Lincoln across the Potomac. Thomas Harbin, an agent of the Secret Service of the Confederate War Department, was involved with Booth in planning the capture of President Lincoln. Joseph Baden, a private in the Confederate army assigned to the Signal Corps camp in King George County, Virginia, had worked with Harbin in various operations. Elizabeth Quesenberry, widow of a Virginia farmer, was the sister of Mrs. John Tayloe, whose husband, a Confederate captain, may have been involved with Confederate clandestine operations. William Bryant, a Virginia farmer, was a neighbor of Mrs. Quesenberry. Dr. Richard Henry Stuart, a leading Confederate citizen of King George County, Virginia, knew about the activities of the Confederate Signal Corps in his area. Charles Lucas, a free black, was the son of William Lucas, who lived on Dr. Stuart's plantation. William Rollins was the Confederate Signal Corps agent responsible for expediting passage of the Rappahannock River for Confederate agents and mail. Lieutenant Mortimer B. Ruggles was the son of Confederate General Daniel Ruggles and second in command to Confederate agent Captain Thomas N. Conrad, who had scouted President Lincoln's movements in planning his capture. Absalom R. Bainbridge, a private in Mosby's Rangers and a cousin of Ruggles, had just returned to his home after the breakup of Mosby's command. Willie Jett was also a member of Mosby's Rangers and had just returned from the breakup of the command.

Booth's escape appears to have involved the main Confederate underground network leading into the North. If one omits Swann, Bryant, and Lucas as playing only subordinate roles in Booth's flight, the remainder of those on the list share two attributes: all had strong, pro-Confederate feeling or connections, and all were associated with official Confederate underground operations or with people engaged in that work.

The second of these attributes immediately raises a question—particularly in the minds of those familiar with the history and conduct of clandestine operations. It would violate nearly every principle of good security to allow individuals connected with a clandestine organization to associate themselves with any activity not approved by the organization. Casual activity, not officially sponsored, could involve individuals in dangerous and politically explosive enterprises. Helping the escape of an unsponsored assassin is exactly the kind of activity that a clandestine operator would want to avoid in normal circumstances. In the light of this understanding of normal clandestine security and discipline, can one assume that these people were all acting on their own initiative out of sympathy for John Wilkes Booth? Or should we assume that there was an official connection and that the Confederate clandestine organization felt a responsibility to keep Booth from falling into the hands of his Union pursuers?

It seems clear to us (as it did to Union authorities at the time) that the second assumption is much more realistic. But if one assumes that the Confederate government's clandestine organization felt an official responsibility to help Booth escape, a number of additional questions become relevant: How was Confederate clandestine activity organized, and what did it do? What was Booth's relationship to the Confederate clandestine organization? What objective would Confederate decision makers have had in mind in working with Booth? What could be the nature of a clandestine operation that would advance Confederate objectives and also require the assistance of John Wilkes Booth?

This book is divided into three parts to examine these questions: "The Confederate Intelligence Machinery," a description of the various components of Confederate intelligence and undercover activity; "Using the Machinery against President Lincoln," an examination of various efforts to take clandestine action against Lincoln and how these eventually coalesced into a major operation supported by the highest levels of the Confederate government; and "A Desperate Plan to Win the War, No Holds Barred," describing how the Confederate high command planned to force a decision in 1865, and how that operation against Lincoln was incoporated to support the campaign.

The first part will show that the Confederacy had considerable ability in clandestine operations and that it became increasingly capable of performing with a high degree of sophistication for that era. The second part will show that the Confederates began to investigate the possibility of mounting a serious effort to capture President Lincoln as a hostage in 1864. The third part will show how this operation came to play a role in Confederate plans for the spring campaign of 1865. Finally, it will show that in support of these plans, the Confederates had reason to consider direct action against leading Union officials to disrupt Union command and control and create confusion to the advantage of Confederate arms.

The success of the unexpected Union flanking attack at Five Forks on 1 April 1865 forced the premature abandonment of Richmond by Confederate authorities and upset the timetable for the Confederate campaign. A week later, surrounded and frustrated in his aims, General Lee was forced to surrender the Army of Northern Virginia, the principal (but by no means the only) Confederate army in the field. But the poor communications of that era did not allow people to form a true picture of day-to-day developments over a wide area. As a result, John Wilkes Booth acted on 14 April in accordance with Confederate objectives as he had understood them to be two weeks earlier. Because the ex post facto knowledge of the true military situation was better than Booth's, his act has appeared to the world as a "last-gasp" assassination rather than as a wartime attack against the enemy command, undertaken as a part of a concerted plan.

Having developed the idea that there might have been official Confederate interest in John Wilkes Booth and that this interest was evidenced by persons connected to one degree or another with Confederate underground activity, the problem arose of how to investigate this idea. The Union prosecutors in the 1860s had tried a direct approach. They had tried to find evidence of an organization and a plan to kill President Lincoln. This approach had two basic weaknesses. First, if such a plan had existed, prudence would have dictated that little direct evidence be created. Nothing would have been put in writing, or if writing had existed it would have been destroyed when Richmond was evacuated. The persons directly involved and having personal knowledge of the plan would have been kept to a minimum, and those few would have been under extreme pressure to keep silent to save their own lives and those of their colleagues. Second, the direct approach assumed that the assassination of the president was the central focus of the supposed plan. No allowance was made for the evolution of a plan with a different initial focus or for the death of President Lincoln as a by-product of a plan with a completely different focus. The first of these weaknesses was what caused the Union prosecutors to make tactical errors in trial procedure and to use questionable testimony. The second weakness prevented the prosecutors from recognizing the pertinence of information that was available and that bore on the operation that led to the assassination.

To avoid these traps, it appeared to us that the logical tack to take was to avoid the direct approach. Instead, it seemed wise to develop the institutional context in which a Confederate plan could have been developed that somehow resulted in the death of President Lincoln. Having developed the context, we should then proceed to investigate what could be found out about Confederate plans that might have involved clandestine activity and that could be established to have existed at the time of the assassination.

These were ambitious objectives. The assassination had been investigated many times before. What sources had not been thoroughly exploited already? Because of the inadequacies of the previous research, we determined that we would focus primarily on original records and other primary source material even if it had already been reviewed by others.

The need to investigate the institutional context of Confederate clandestine activity led initially to the records of the state of Virginia. Few scholars seem to have considered that these records might shed any light on matters pertinent to Confederate undercover operations, but for two months in 1861 the state of Virginia was operating independently with all of the defense and intelligence problems of a nation. Virginia had seceded from the Union but had not yet become an operating member of the Confederacy. During this interregnum, Governor John Letcher was advised in military matters by General Robert E. Lee, commander of the Virginia army, and by a special council that included Colonel Francis H. Smith, the superintendent of the Virginia Military Institute, and Lieutenant (later Commodore) Matthew Fontaine Maury, formerly of the U.S. Navy. With the guidance of this council, the state of Virginia established its own military forces and sought to prepare itself against the expected Union attack. Several important facts emerged from the Virginia records. We learned that the state of Virginia had its own secret service funds, which were controlled by Governor Letcher. The council devoted considerable effort to helping the prosecession element in Maryland, which sought to induce that state to secede from the Union. This effort included the clandestine shipment of weapons to Maryland and the organization of military units made up of men from Maryland. The first underground line into Maryland for messages and agents was established by Major William S. Barton of the Virginia militia in April 1861. This appears to have been the forerunner of the clandestine line whose members were involved in helping John Wilkes Booth to escape from Union pursuit. An elaborate signal system was established to communicate news of Union intrusions into Virginia territory. Rose Greenhow and her espionage organization in Washington were recruited by Thomas Jordan, an army officer who resigned from federal service to be commissioned in the Virginia forces. The initiative for the organization of Greenhow's activity appears to have come from the state of Virginia rather than from the Confederate government.

Particularly impressive about this information was the amount of time that senior men—Governor Letcher and the members of his council—devoted to clandestine operations at this most critical point in the affairs of Virginia. Like their revolutionary war forefathers, they must have felt that such activity could make a real contribution to the safety of the state.

When we went on to study *The War of the Rebellion: A Compilation of the Official Records of the Union and Confederate Armies* and other source material dealing with the Civil War, we found that when the Confederacy took command of the Virginia forces in June 1861 and pulled together a Confederate army on Virginia soil, Colonel Jordan was assigned to the headquarters of General P. G. T. Beauregard, the Confederate commander. He and other officers of the staff of what was to become the Army of Northern Virginia continued to direct the activities of Rose Greenhow and her associates. After her arrest by Union authorities, other members of the Greenhow organization continued in contact with Jordan and his successors.

This contact appears to have evolved eventually into a previously undiscovered system operated for the remainder of the war by Major Cornelius Boyle, the post commander at Gordonsville, Virginia. Other clandestine elements reporting through Maryland were taken over by the Confederate Signal Corps.

In addition to having its own espionage organization, the Army of Northern Virginia, particularly after General Lee took command, developed an impressive intelligence-collecting capability by using cavalry scouts. The cavalry did conventional tactical reconnaissance using patrols, pickets, and observation posts, but it also developed a corps of bright, aggressive men who could operate on their own in no-man's-land or behind enemy lines. Sometimes the activities of these men were almost indistinguishable from those of the organizations charged to carry out espionage against the Union. This intelligence-collecting activity was the responsibility of General J. E. B. Stuart, who reported to General Lee. After Stuart's death, General Lee appears to have tried to give more of his own time to the direction of this activity.

While the Army of Northern Virginia continued to operate its own agents and to collect information on the enemy, the Confederate government appears to have developed two distinct Secret Services at the department level. These were the War Department Secret Service and the State Department Secret Service. It is not entirely clear just how these activities were organized, but we have uncovered direct reference to both and have identified some of the people involved in them.

For a time, at least, the Confederate War Department Secret Service appears to have operated with or under the control of the Signal Corps. Possibly the Signal Corps was the cover for the Secret Service. If so, it was an unusual and sophisticated organizational structure. The Signal Corps, which had an overt responsibility to provide communication services to the troops in the field, also had a clandestine mission to operate a courier and agent line behind enemy lines. This overt-covert organization also may have served as a cover for clandestine operations even more secret than the "Secret Line" into Maryland.

The Signal Corps came into being in part because of Jefferson Davis's familiarity with experimental work on signaling done by the United States Army before 1861. As an administrator and wartime leader, Davis ran a tight ship. He controlled many operations personally, and the Signal Corps was in his direct service. Thus we have a sophisticated, technical, intelligence-related organization operating clandestine missions and reporting directly to President Jefferson Davis.

These Confederate secret operations were accompanied by innovations in related fields. Under the leadership of Commander Maury and others, the Confederates explored the possibilities of underwater explosives early in the war. Both the Confederate army and navy developed organizations to build and emplace underwater mines and mine fields. Later the army also developed mines for use on land, and Special Service companies were organized to plant explosives and other sabotage devices behind enemy lines. Some of these operations were very successful—the USS *Cairo*, now raised and on display at Vicksburg, Mississippi, was the victim of one such operation. The most spectacular, however, was the explosion of a large part of General Ulysses S. Grant's supply base at City Point, Virginia, in 1864.

In surveying Confederate knowledge or use of other intelligence-related activities, we found that they were aware of most of the intelligence or clandestine operations technology and culture that existed in the mid-nineteenth century. Early in the war, President Davis made General John H. Winder responsible for defending the Richmond area against Union agents. Winder organized a group of detectives whose activities sometimes overlapped those of the Secret Services. Because Winder was responsible for internal security, and because the first substantial number of Union prisoners of war were sent to Richmond, Winder was charged with their care. This task outgrew its beginnings as the number of prisoners reached astronomical proportions, and eventually Winder was relieved of his other duties and charged solely with operating military prisons.

We also learned that the Confederate leaders knew the value of prisoners of war as sources of information about the enemy. Even more important, they learned that prisoners could be recruited as agents or that agents could be disguised as prisoners and then exchanged to enter Union territory with a false identity and good bona fides. We even found one case when this maneuver was directed by President Davis.

In addition to the operations of the Special Service companies behind enemy lines, we found that the Confederacy had at various times actively encouraged irregular warfare behind enemy lines or in areas over which Union control was weak. This activity included the formation of guerrilla bands—armed persons who appear to be civilians but who gather for clandestine raids or ambushes and then disperse to appear as civilians once more—and other more organized efforts. General Lee, in particular, followed the precedent of General George Washington and General "Lighthorse Harry" Lee and established a unit to operate as partisans, (regular soldiers operating in small units and conducting raids or ambushes) behind enemy lines. This unit was headed by Colonel John S. Mosby. Mosby is often referred to as a guerrilla in both Confederate and Union sources, but in fact his troops were regularly enlisted soldiers under military discipline. Such misconceptions may have contributed to Union difficulties in defending against Mosby, who caused the Union much hardship. He was a source of information useful to General Lee, and Lee paid a great deal of attention to Mosby's operations.

The Confederacy was displeased with the results of undisciplined operations by some guerrilla units and eventually tried to divert most of this manpower into more conventional military units. This displeasure, in part, reflected the Confederate government's normally correct attitude toward matters of legality and morality. One unconventional operation, however, shows that the leaders of the Confederacy were capable of making daring decisions regarding secret operations.

In the summer of 1864, the Union had collected several thousand Confederate prisoners of war in a camp at Point Lookout, on the southernmost tip of Maryland, where the Potomac River enters Chesapeake Bay. The Confederates decided to send a pair of fast armed ships loaded with troops and spare rifles into Chesapeake Bay to free the prisoners and lead them through southern Maryland until they could cross back into Virginia. This joint operation of some eight hundred soldiers, sailors, and marines was to coincide with General Jubal Early's raid into Maryland from the Shenandoah Valley, and the prisoners were to attempt to join him.

This plan had the personal approval of General Lee and President Davis. It was a daring maneuver from a military standpoint, but it also took political courage. The captain of the lead ship was British Captain Charles Augustus Hobart-Hampden, previously the commander of Queen Victoria's private "yacht." To involve the British in this operation meant that Davis was willing to take political as well as military risks.

The ships left their port in North Carolina and then were recalled. Word of the plan had leaked in Richmond, and Davis was afraid that the essential element of surprise had been lost. This, however, was only one example of the ambitious operations attempted by the Confederates. They gave secret help to antiwar elements in the North and tried to get them to revolt. They made other attempts to free Confederate prisoners, tried biological warfare, burned boats on the Mississippi, tried to burn New York City, and raided St. Albans, Vermont. Not many of these operations achieved tactical success, but the overall strategy showed some successes in that a few Confederate agents were able to tie up a larger number of federal troops and spread alarm on the northern home front.

Coordination of clandestine activities became a problem, and the Confederacy hit upon a most imaginative solution. In late 1864 legislation was secretly introduced to establish a Special and Secret Service Bureau to oversee the various clandestine operations and to develop or encourage the invention of new weapons and to employ them against the enemy. Clearly these were to be weapons for sabotage or other secret employment behind enemy lines. This bureau was the Confederate version of a Central Intelligence organization.

The legislation was not enacted until March 1865, and there is almost no information about its formal implementation. The time was too short before the end of the war, and events were too disruptive for much information to be preserved, but the care and effort devoted to the formulation and passage of the legislation indicated a positive attitude about the future and is clear evidence of the importance the Confederate government gave to its clandestine activities. Judging from the precedent of the Signal Corps, which operated for about a year before it was made "official," it is probable that the Special and Secret Service Bureau was already carrying out most of its assigned duties before the legislation was enacted.

The organization and breadth of the Confederacy's secret operations clearly show that it had the technical knowledge, experienced personnel, and operational precedent to have organized a clandestine operation against the president of the United States.

In seeking evidence of an official Confederate operation against President Lincoln, it is necessary to ask precisely, evidence of what? There was an assassination, and evidence taken shortly thereafter established that Booth and his associates had spent several months planning to capture Lincoln and take him to the Confederacy. What we needed to know is whether any connection existed between this plan and the Confederate government. We had already concluded that we are not likely to find evidence of President Davis ordering John Wilkes Booth to shoot President Lincoln. Such an order probably never existed, and if it had, it is highly unlikely that there would be any record of it. What, then, should we be looking for?

Anybody who has studied clandestine operations widely or who has had personal experience with them knows that such operations take much time, effort, money, and often other specialized resources. It is highly unlikely that an individual citizen would get up some morning and decide on his own to organize a few associates to kidnap a president—even under the conditions of the 1860s. No matter how determined a man might be—whether a John Wilkes Booth or a John Brown—he is nearly always found to have some association with a larger group that provides money and moral support.

In the circumstances of 1865, the most obvious group with the resources and the motivation to recruit and support Booth was the Confederate government, but it would have done little good to ask Booth's associates if they were sponsored by the Confederate government. Regardless of what they were told by Booth, the individuals involved would have assumed that they were acting in the interest of the Confederacy and that when they arrived in Confederate territory they would be well received. If, on the other hand, they *were* sponsored by the Confederates, they would have had little need to ask questions. As long as Booth acted with confidence and provided money as needed, knowledge of sponsorship was not an operational imperative.

The theories that were discussed at the beginning of this chapter were put forward in the absence of firm knowledge about Booth's backers. We may never know the absolute truth, but if we explore the most likely relationship—the Confederacy as Booth's sponsor—and find that the Confederate leaders were taking actions in parallel with Booth that they would have done if they were sponsoring the operation, we can strengthen the supposition that they were his sponsors. This assumption can be clarified by examining how clandestine operations develop and what events in the Confederacy might be related to an operation against President Lincoln.

The development of an operational plan can follow any one of several courses. There is no rigid pattern that such planning must take, but there are some features that occur often enough to sound familiar to those who have been involved in conceiving and carrying out operations involving secrecy and military action.

First, there must be an objective to achieve—a target—and a motive for reaching the target. The objective must be important enough to justify the effort of planning and the likely future expenditure of assets such as money, time, weapons, lives, and goodwill. Additional objectives may be added, motives may alter, and the relative priority of objectives may change over time. Changes in focus that could have occurred in any Confederate operation involving Lincoln might complicate any effort to reconstruct its history.

Objective
↓
Concept

Once an objective is formulated and accepted by those in power, a concept must be developed of how to achieve that objective. There may be competing concepts, and the development of a plan may represent compromises between parties advocating different concepts. A concept for the operation must be based on credible information and must seem practicable to the planning group, who must reach sufficient agreement to permit planning to go ahead. The idea of capturing a senior enemy official such as the president had occurred to a number of Confederates at various times during the war, so agreement on the concept of capturing him in the outskirts of Washington should have been relatively easy to achieve.

One of the most common errors in planning military or clandestine operations is to overlook the complexities and restrictions that technical matters nearly always introduce into those operations. One may assume that a plan can be easily changed to suit a new development, but if one is not aware of the technical factors involved, one can think it easy when in fact it is very hard. The following checklist gives an idea of the questions that should be taken into account in planning almost any operation that one hopes will surprise an enemy:

1. What are the key tasks to be performed and who will do them?
2. Will the key people be made available?
3. What special equipment will be needed, and where will it be procured?
4. Will the equipment be available in time?
5. What troops will be employed? Will they be available, or must special arrangements be made to get them released for use in the operation?
6. Once the troops are assured, where will they be based so that they can have any necessary training and in the meantime stay out of trouble?
7. What arrangements must be made to feed them?
8. Are any special weapons needed, and if so, what must be done to make sure that they will be available when needed?
9. Are there adequate maps of the operating area, and if not, can they be made in time to be of use?
10. Where will the funds to cover the expenditures involved in the above items come from? Which items can be covered by routine accounts already available, and which will require special authorizations?

In addition to the foregoing questions, there are others of a more operational nature:

1. How will the information needed to mount and carry out the operation be obtained and still keep the operation secret?

2. What will be said publicly about various parts of the operation if a public explanation is needed? "Public" in this case may have several definitions—the public at large, the military establishment, the army as a whole, the participating troops, or the people providing logistic support—depending on circumstances. Several explanations may be needed, each for a different audience.

3. How will the operation be supported logistically once it has been launched?

4. How is the enemy likely to react to the operation?

This list is merely a sample of the questions that have to be formulated and answered for every operation of any consequence. Even if they are all answered thoroughly and the operation is managed correctly, mass confusion may result. War and clandestine operations have in common that the best laid plans can go awry.

Staffs nowadays are organized and trained to cope routinely with many of these questions. Staffs in the era of the Civil War were less well structured and trained. Whether the person responsible for the operation employed a staff or performed the planning function himself, he had to answer these questions or the operation was almost certain to fail. There is a logic in technical matters that prevails even if the technical question is not recognized by those affected.

Any operation as ambitious as the capture of the president of the United States would have had to deal with questions like these. Any such operation could not be kept entirely secret; it would have to be disguised as something else. The activities associated with a major operation are bound to leave a trail. The problem is to recognize the traces though they are obscured by the original cover stories and the passage of time.

Once a concept for an operation has been formulated and some of the basic technical questions have been answered, it is necessary to put together a first draft of the plan. At that point the planners should meet with those in power to see if they approve the plan or if it needs to be reworked. Approval at that point does not mean that the first draft becomes the final plan. It means that the powers approve the plan as a basis for moving through the next phase— assembling the assets (money, equipment, weapons, manpower, and so forth) and refining the plan as new information comes in or new problems are uncovered.

Finally, there comes a point when the planning has been done and the force to carry it out is complete. At that point the powers in charge would need to have a final opportunity to say "go" or "don't go." At that point the expected consequences of implementing the plan have to be evaluated, and commanders have to make that final judgment.

In the Confederate context, only President Davis had that power.

If there was a Confederate plan to capture President Lincoln, the process used in developing it must have been something like the process described above, even allowing for differences between their times and ours. Our next logical step was to look for evidence of events that might fit into such a planning sequence.

First, a motive had to be ascertained. Lincoln was widely blamed in the South for bringing on and sustaining the war with its accompanying destruction. There were people in the South who made no secret of their desire to kill him. But it appeared to us that the so-called Dahlgren's raid of February and March 1864 provided the motive that could have persuaded the Confederate government to consider retaliation against Lincoln personally. The Confederates had evidence that persuaded them that he had issued explicit orders to a Union raiding force to kill Jefferson Davis and the leading members of the Confederate government and to lay waste to Richmond. Such drastic measures had to be answered, and a strong party in the South wanted to answer them in kind. If President Lincoln wanted to attack the person of President Davis, they reasoned, then President Lincoln was a fair target for retaliation.

Alternative concepts for retaliation might have ranged from assassination at one emotional extreme to a deliberate, judicial trial for crimes committed against the people of the South at the other extreme. To carry out any of these alternative schemes would probably have involved getting access to President Lincoln, and most of them would have required having possession of his person. A "war crimes" trial in absentia would not be particularly satisfying and would put a severe limit on any negotiation that the Confederacy might wish to carry out subsequently. If Lincoln were under the physical control of the Confederacy, however, the situation would be radically different. If he were a captive in the South, the Confederacy could negotiate with him, use him as an asset in negotiations with the residual Union government, or bring him to trial. One or more of these options could be tried, depending on how the situation looked at the time.

These are examples of the rationalizations that might have influenced a decision by the Confederate government finally to consider seriously the idea of capturing President Lincoln by clandestine action and bringing him into the Confederacy. The idea had been advanced previously, but the Confederate leaders had not warmed to it. Now, however, there was pressure to act, the action might be feasible, and successful action might benefit the southern cause.

What events took place after the Dahlgren raid that might be evidence of a plan against President Lincoln? There might be alternative explanations for these events, but are there enough of them to provide a pattern that would fit into the sequence of a planning process? The answer again is yes.

First, there was an increase in Confederate clandestine activity designed to encourage the antiwar faction in the North to organize and revolt. Senior political figures, energetic agents, and a large allocation of Secret Service funds were assigned to undercover activity in the North and in Canada aimed against the North. This is not evidence of a plan against President Lincoln, but it is evidence of a willingness on the part of the Confederates to put extra efforts into clandestine operations at a time when an operation against Lincoln would have been considered.

At about this same time, an element in the Confederate cavalry began to plan a raid into Maryland and the District of Columbia to capture Lincoln at his summer residence at the Soldiers' Home, north of the city of Washington. This plan came to nothing, but in late June 1864 General Jubal Early led an army into Maryland with a view to capturing Washington, and with it, Lincoln. This effort failed, and in late July and August a series of events began to occur that can be interpreted as part of the planning process discussed above.

On 26 July 1864 John Wilkes Booth was in a hotel in Boston with four men whose true identity has not been established, but one has been identified as having been in Canada before and later. It has the appearance of a secret meeting, possibly to recruit Booth for an action assignment. There is some evidence that Booth was already a Confederate agent involved in other activity.

Somebody reviewed available personnel and selected Captain Thomas Nelson Conrad, chaplain of the Third Virginia Cavalry and a cavalry scout, to be brought to Richmond in connection with an assignment that later turned out to involve the Lincoln matter. The orders directing Conrad to Richmond were dated on 9 August, but the staff work leading to their issuance probably began in July.

One of the best of the junior Confederate engineer officers,

Lieutenant B. Lewis Blackford, was recalled from his post in North Carolina in August 1864 and given the task of mapping Stafford County and a large area in Prince William and Fauquier counties, Virginia. Although beyond the arena of military operations at that date, these were areas in which military action might be necessary if a raiding party with a captive Lincoln were threatened with hot pursuit. At that point in the development of a presumed plan, it would still have been an open question whether such a raiding party should go north and west of Washington to cross the Potomac and exit southward through territory controlled by Colonel Mosby, or go southeasterly from Washington through southern Maryland near the established Signal Corps route. If the route through Mosby country were followed, the Union might well try to get ahead of the raiders by moving into Stafford County.

By Special Order 187 issued by the Confederate adjutant and inspector general on 9 August 1864, Conrad was instructed to report to Richmond for temporary assignment to duty. He drew rations for his horse in Richmond for 12–15 September 1864. It is known that he met with the secretary of war during this time. General Lee was in Richmond; presumably he also saw the secretary of war, but it is not known if he saw Conrad.

In September 1864 either George N. Sanders, a Confederate agent in Canada under Jacob Thompson and Clement C. Clay, the Confederate commissioners there, or his son and assistant, Lewis Sanders, appears to have made a secret trip to Richmond. Sanders had been associated with European democratic radicals in the 1850s and had advocated assassination as a way to deal with tyrants. Lewis Sanders worked closely with his father and might have represented him. Whichever Sanders made the trip could have been present for discussions of a plan against President Lincoln.

On 15 September 1864 the Confederate secretary of war issued an order directing Colonel Mosby, the partisan leader in northern Virginia, and Lieutenant Charles H. Cawood, the commander of the Signal Corps camp in King George County, Virginia, to cooperate with Captain Conrad on his mission. Conrad was given $400 in gold by Secretary of State Judah Benjamin with President Davis's approval and left on 17 September for the Northern Neck of Virginia (the area between the Potomac and Rappahannock rivers) with a party of Secret Service and Signal Corps personnel.

It would appear that there were discussions with Conrad in Richmond during 12 to 15 September 1864 of a plan to capture President Lincoln. This could well have been the meeting that approved a draft plan, and Conrad's mission to Washington could have been part of the next phase to make the plan more specific.

On 13 September Mosby organized a new company in his battalion of partisans and appointed one of General Lee's principal agents, Walter Bowie, as a lieutenant in the company. In late September he sent Bowie with twenty-five men to conduct an unprecedented raid into southern Maryland, crossing in the vicinity of Cawood's Signal Corps camp.

The Bowie operation was so out of character for Mosby that it may have been a deliberate test of the feasibility of moving a small armed unit through southern Maryland. This was one of the routes that any party with a captive Lincoln would have had to take. Exiting on the west of the District of Columbia, the party ran into trouble and Bowie was killed.

Conrad was in Washington by late September and devoted considerable time and effort to observing the movements of President Lincoln and ascertaining the best location to seize him and the best route to follow with him as a captive.

John Wilkes Booth began in September to recruit a team to help him capture Lincoln. In mid-October he went to Montreal, Canada, where he met Confederate agents who may have played some role in the direction of the action part of the plan against Lincoln. In November Booth returned to Washington. There is no indication that he and Conrad met, but they were in Washington simultaneously for several days before Conrad left to report his findings to Richmond.

In late September an Episcopal minister, the Reverend Doctor Kensey Johns Stewart, made a trip from Canada into the Confederacy. Stewart was related by marriage to the Lee family. He had served as a chaplain under General Winder, who managed one of the Confederate organizations involved in clandestine operations. In 1863 Stewart had gone to England and later to Canada. His correspondence and other documents reveal that he was involved in some secret activity with President Jefferson Davis and other Confederate agents in Canada. In October 1864 he left Canada and went to Baltimore, traveled through southern Maryland, and crossed the Potomac in a makeshift boat at the spot that Booth later planned to use as the crossing with a captive Lincoln. He went to Cawood's Signal Corps camp, where he wrote to General Lee. He later went to Richmond, conferred with Davis, visited Lee, and returned to Canada after having been allocated $20,000 in Secret Service funds by Davis. Because of Stewart's past association with some of the critical geography involved in Booth's planned escape route, and because of his high-level contacts, it is possible that he may have been involved in planning part of the Lincoln operation.

On 23 September 1864 Colonel Edwin Gray Lee, a cousin of General Robert E. Lee, was promoted to brigadier general. Lee had been involved in clandestine operations earlier in the war, and in December 1864 he was sent to Canada to take over some of the Confederate undercover work from Jacob Thompson and Clement C. Clay, the commissioners who had been operating there since the spring of that year. One cannot eliminate the suspicion that his promotion may have been related to decisions made at the presumed meeting of 12–15 September in Richmond.

On 20 October 1864 Brigadier General G. W. C. "Custis" Lee, General Robert E. Lee's oldest son, was promoted to major general. Custis had been one of the leaders of the abortive Point Lookout raid in July. Now he was given command of another ad hoc task force, a "synthetic" division, made up of various reserve units in Richmond and some troops in a quiet part of the defensive line east of Richmond. Some of these troops appear to have been used later to provide security for the escape route that Booth was planning to use. One suspects that Custis Lee's promotion was related to the planning for the Lincoln operation.

Lieutenant Blackford, the engineer, was ordered to Richmond for a meeting during the first week of November 1864. As a result of this meeting, he did not finish mapping some of the area originally assigned but instead began to work on a map of King William County, an area that would have been of importance to a different route for the action party with a captive Lincoln. This change of Blackford's assignment indicates that there had been a change in the plan for the escape route. Instead of going south through territory controlled by Colonel Mosby, the route on which Bowie had run into trouble, the action party would now exit through southern Maryland and possibly go by water up the Rappahannock River. Lieutenant Cawood, the senior officer of the Signal Corps in the Northern Neck, was in Richmond at this time and could have participated in a meeting at which the escape route was discussed.

In November Booth went into southern Maryland and began to organize an escape route through that area.

On 5 November 1864 the Confederate War Department established a fund in the Treasury Department of $250,000 for the purpose of paying officers and soldiers passing through Richmond on furlough. This was enough money to pay the salaries of about fifteen hundred officers and men for six months. No similar fund had been established before. Why was it needed now?

The establishment of this fund followed close on the heels of Custis Lee's promotion to major general. We believe that both actions related to the provision of a security force for Booth's escape route. Naturally, if the Confederates were planning to capture President Lincoln, they would also have to plan to receive him in Confederate territory and defend the action party against pursuit. The escape route that Booth was working on led to the Northern Neck of Virginia. This was a no-man's-land between the Potomac and Rappahannock rivers. The appearance there of organized forces from either side would likely provoke a reaction from the other side. The Confederacy could not overtly establish a security force there without risking increased Union interest in the area. The answer was to establish a security force there covertly. To accomplish this, men from regiments recruited in the Northern Neck were sent home "on furlough." Once at home, as we shall see, they were organized into ad hoc units to patrol the area and to be ready to repel a Union raid. These may well have been the officers and soldiers on furlough to be paid from the special fund.

In late September Union forces had assaulted the Confederate defensive line at Chaffin's Farm, east of Richmond and north of the James River. This assault had been repelled, and Union attention had turned to the lines near Petersburg. The defenses at Chaffin's Farm, however, had been greatly improved to include a deep moat. The area was also heavily mined. In mid-October General Lee had two well-trained individuals give him independent evaluations of the strength of the defenses in that area. Both reported that the defenses appeared to be excellent.

In late December, several regiments recruited in the Northern Neck were moved into the lines at Chaffin's Farm, where they became part of General Custis Lee's division. After the surrender at Appomattox in April 1865, several hundred men from these regiments, including a number of high-ranking officers, signed their paroles at locations near their homes in and around the Northern Neck. Their regiments had never left the army, but the men appear to have been at home on leave instead of with the Army of Northern Virginia. It would thus appear that the Confederates had taken advantage of the new strength of the Chaffin's Farm sector to send many of the men from the defending regiments home on leave—their homes being in the area through which a captive Lincoln was to be led.

At the end of December, several companies of Colonel Mosby's regiment were sent into the Northern Neck to live in small groups in private homes. They too appear to have been part of the security force.

In January Booth's associates were procuring boats in southern Maryland to be used to take President Lincoln across the Potomac. It would appear that his planning of the escape route was almost finished.

Also in January 1865 Captain Conrad and Colonel Mosby were both in Richmond for conferences of an unknown nature, and Conrad was supplied with additional Secret Service funds approved personally by Jefferson Davis. Major William Norris, the chief of the Signal Corps, was also ordered back to Richmond at this time, and the secretary of war personally drafted an order transferring operational control over a number of Signal Corps soldiers in the Northern Neck to Secretary of State Benjamin for secret service. Booth's associate John Harrison Surratt was in Richmond sometime between 25 January and 2 February 1865. On about the first of February, the Confederates adopted the phrase "Come Retribution" as the key for their top cipher system, reflecting some new policy decision and a tightening of security. These actions may have reflected the final review of the planning for the operation to capture Lincoln.

In summary, it is clear that a number of actions were taken in the Confederacy that could have been part of an official clandestine plan to capture President Lincoln and bring him into Confederate control. These actions and those of John Wilkes Booth appear to fit into the same planning sequence.

After the preceding portion of the logic trail had been constructed, we had the good fortune to find two independent pieces of evidence that formed a direct connection between John Wilkes Booth and the confederate clandestine apparatus in Canada. We found that Colonel Robert M. Martin, known to have been assigned to Confederate Commissioner Jacob Thompson in Canada, had told cell mates in prison in 1865 that he had known Booth. We also found that Colonel James Gordon, the husband of Jacob Thompson's niece, stated that while in Canada with Thompson in 1865 he had been engaged in the operation to capture Lincoln and that he had met Booth.

Judging from the circumstances surrounding them, these two

pieces of direct evidence have considerable credibility, and their existence enhances our confidence in the reasoning followed in developing the logic trail.

Thus it is clear that the Confederates had the knowledge, the institutions, and the precedent of previous operations to enable them to mount a secret operation to capture President Lincoln should that have become a desirable objective. It is also clear that they took actions in 1864 and 1865 that could have been associated with planning for such an operation. But what of the context? How would such a plan have fitted into the Confederate concept of ending the war?

Based on an article published in a Richmond newspaper on 8 August 1864, we believe that the planners of strategy in the Confederate government had begun that early to analyze the situation around Richmond and Petersburg and to try to think of ways to exploit the situation to defeat the North. They felt that they could defend against a frontal assault by General Grant but that their weakest point was their southern flank. If Grant tried to go around their northern flank, he would merely force the Confederate army back on its supply lines, but if he could get around their southern flank he could cut those same lines of supply. If the Confederates tried to stretch to match Grant's moves around the flank, they might eventually stretch to the point where they could no longer defend against a frontal attack.

Grant's early moves against the Confederate position involved blowing up their lines ("the Crater") near Petersburg and the assault on Fort Harrison, east of Richmond, in late September 1864. These efforts were examples of the frontal approach. Grant also organized moves against the southern flank, which were countered at first but finally proved successful on 1 April 1865.

The Confederates were successful in defeating Grant's frontal attacks, but beyond the simple strategy of defending in position they were left with two choices. They could try to catch Grant when his forces were extended in one of the attempts against the southern flank and make a frontal assault of their own to cut the northern line in two. As an alternative, they could create as many obstacles as possible along their front and then abandon Richmond and Petersburg and resort to a war of maneuver while Grant's army was still caught in the obstacles.

These alternatives carried great risks. The frontal assault on Grant risked military defeat because the Union would have the same advantages on the defensive that the Confederacy had when the Union attacked. The abandonment of Richmond had to be carried out with skill or it too might be defeated, but it carried serious political risks. The abandonment of the capital of the Confederacy might be widely interpreted abroad and by many at home as a death blow. It could be justified only if it resulted quickly in a serious defeat for the Union.

It is probable that these two alternatives were thought about and discussed privately by the highest makers of strategy, but other events, including the disasters met by the Army of Tennessee and General William T. Sherman's progress through the Carolinas, pre-empted much of the public debate. By January 1865, however, it was obvious that those favoring the abandonment of Richmond were beginning to press their case. In early February 1865 General Lee assumed command of all Confederate armies, putting him in a position to command their cooperation should he have the opportunity to resume the war of maneuver.

In mid-February Lee spent several days in Richmond engaged in serious discussions of strategy with President Davis and General John C. Breckinridge, the new secretary of war. It would appear that these discussions ended with a general agreement on the nature of the strategy to be followed. Lee was to lead his army out of Richmond, join the Confederate army in North Carolina, and use the combined armies to fight either Sherman or Grant—whichever presented the better opportunity.

In reviewing the assets available to support the new strategy, President Davis doubtless considered the effect of the Lincoln operation. It appeared to be nearly ready to go, and if successful, it could have wide-reaching effects on the course of the war. The capture of Lincoln might make it unnecessary to evacuate Richmond, or it might inject enough confusion into the command process in Washington to be of help to the Confederate armies in the field. It would have to be considered as a measure that could benefit the southern cause.

Unfortunately, the agreement on the new strategy apparently did not extend to its timing. Lee and Breckinridge clearly felt that they needed to prepare for the evacuation soon. Davis, however, was more attuned to the political problems caused by this course of action and discouraged early action lest it cause panic among the population and antagonism among the political leaders of the Confederacy. There is no direct evidence that Davis was also thinking about the operation against Lincoln and its possible effect on the military situation, but we know from a letter found among Booth's possessions that during this period he was being pressured to act.

Booth could not capture Lincoln whenever it suited him. He had to find the right opportunity and organize his people to take advantage of it. Furthermore, Booth's helpers were not trained, disciplined operatives. He had his hands full keeping them in line, out of trouble, and in good spirits.

Finally, on 17 March 1865 Booth thought that an opportunity had arisen. He was told that Lincoln was supposed to visit the Campbell Military Hospital in the country north of Washington. Booth and his group waited along the road, but Lincoln did not appear. Later, it was learned that the president had gone elsewhere that afternoon. The members of the group were extremely upset, fearing that they had been given faulty information to cause them to expose themselves. Booth promptly lowered the profile of the group by sending several of them out of town.

In Richmond, time was growing short. The evacuation had to take place about the middle of April at the latest. After that date the ground would be dry enough for Grant to push his flanking strategy, and Lee had to move first. The value of a captive Lincoln as a possible bargaining chip was about over. The only aspect of the operation that could possibly do Confederate military strategy some good now was its potential impact on Union command and control. Confusion in Washington might help to cause confusion in the field. Now, for the first time, there was a clear, logical value that might result from the killing or disabling of the president of the Union, and the imperative of time argued for such drastic action.

The Confederate government appears to have made this very judgment. On 1 April a small team, including Thomas F. (Frank) Harney, an explosives expert, was sent to Colonel Mosby with instructions to infiltrate the team into Washington. Mosby organized a special task force to carry out this mission and sent the men to raid near Burke, Virginia, near Washington, as a cover for the infiltration. There, on 10 April 1865, unaware that Lee had surrendered the day before, the force was surprised by Union cavalry and Harney was captured.

The Mosby raid was so unusual that it was clear that Harney was intended for some very important assignment. One could surmise that it was something as important to the Confederacy as blowing up the White House during a meeting of war leaders. This surmise, moreover, is supported by two pieces of evidence. Lewis Thornton Powell, one of Booth's helpers, had scouted the White House and its surroundings earlier in the year—clearly with a view to learning if action could be taken against President Lincoln. More important, however, it was learned that George Atzerodt, another of Booth's helpers, had made a statement that was preserved by his defense lawyer to the effect that the group had discussed blowing up the White House when a number of high officials were inside.

If Booth learned of Harney's capture on 11 or 12 April, he would have been faced with a difficult situation. His last instructions probably directed him to see that the White House and several senior officials were blown up about the middle of April. The explosion would have occurred at about the time the Confederates planned to evacuate Richmond, though Booth would not likely have been aware of this information. Booth would have been hampered because the explosives expert he needed to carry out his directive was not available. Although Lee had surrendered, the number of troops surrendering with him was so small that many dedicated southerners did not believe at first that the entire Army of Northern Virginia had been involved. Booth probably shared this view. He would have been aware that there was another large Confederate army in North Carolina. He also knew that there were other Confederate armies in the field and could not bring himself (any more than Jefferson Davis, at this stage) to recognize that the Confederacy was a lost cause. If a few key officials could be killed at about the same time, however, it might approximate the impact that would have been caused by blowing up the White House.

Booth seems to have decided to do the best he could do to carry out his mission as he understood it. Originally expecting Lincoln and Grant to be together at Ford's Theatre, Booth shot the president at about ten o'clock on the night of 14 April 1865. At the same time, Powell attacked Secretary of State Seward, and Atzerodt got drunk instead of carrying out his assignment to attack Vice-President Andrew Johnson.

In conclusion, it can be shown that the Confederates had the knowledge and technical skill to mount an operation against President Lincoln; that they engaged in a number of activities in 1864 and 1865 that could have been related to planning such an operation; that John Wilkes Booth was in contact with known Confederate agents; and that the course of the war developed in such a way that an attack on Lincoln was a logical amendment to the original plan to capture him.

Many of the suppositions in this logic trail may never be proven, but there is much firm evidence that supports it. Of all of the theories about the assassination, this one does appear to be the one that can be most strongly supported.

Notes

1. Philip Van Doren Stern, *The Man Who Killed Lincoln* (New York: Literary Guild, 1939); Stanley Kimmel, *The Mad Booths of Maryland* (1940; rpt. New York: Dover, 1969).

2. William Hanchett, *The Lincoln Murder Conspiracies* (Urbana: University of Illinois Press, 1983).

PART ONE

The Confederate Intelligence Machinery

1

The Intelligence Problems of the Confederacy

The Confederacy provides a unique opportunity to study the needs of a modern nation for intelligence and the institutions that can be developed to satisfy these needs. Involved in a war featuring mass armies and the large-scale application of technology and industrial production, the Confederacy made great strides in its four years of existence to develop institutions that provided a remarkable intelligence capability. Many Confederate records were destroyed or lost in the turmoil of 1865, and there was some selective destruction of documents that were believed to be especially sensitive. In spite of these detriments, a great deal of pertinent material has survived.

A good source of easily accessible Confederate records is *The War of the Rebellion: A Compilation of the Official Records of the Union and Confederate Armies,* the main body of which contains both Union and Confederate records of the land war but with a complementary series dealing with the Union and Confederate navies. There are also considerable quantities of additional manuscript materials in the U.S. National Archives, in the Library of Congress, in the possession of state governments, and in various university collections, historical societies, and museums. Some original material remains in the hands of individuals, collectors or the families of participants in the Civil War.

The main challenge in studying the vast amount of historical material is to ask the right questions. If one is researching a specific subject in the Confederate records, one will seldom find the material organized and indexed to provide a direct answer, especially if the question is asked in terms of today's thinking. The raw material is available, however, to provide some insight into almost any subject if the analytical approach is properly conceived and executed.

The surviving Confederate records have another bias that scholars should keep in mind. Because the central Confederate government was intimately involved with the war in Virginia, more material survives on activities in the eastern theater than on the war in Tennessee, along the Mississippi, or the trans-Mississippi. Lack of information on those areas does not necessarily mean that large-scale clandestine activities took place there, but it raises the possibility that there were more than we know of.

The Confederacy was faced with a wide range of military, economic, and political decisions. Because of its success in developing information-gathering institutions, the Confederacy was able to use intelligence as a force multiplier. This is a modern term that describes the Confederates' ability to use information to make their limited forces more effective. With good intelligence, the moves of the Union could be anticipated and the Confederate armed forces could be positioned where they would be most effective.

The Confederates were also able to use clandestine operations, an extension of their intelligence capability, to immobilize large numbers of federal troops that would otherwise have aided the Union in the field of battle. These clandestine operations were not always successful, and part of this book is devoted to a description of the largest and most important of them, which was almost a catastrophe for the Confederacy. Intent on capturing President Lincoln for use as a hostage, the Confederates at last were able only to capture his reputation as a martyr who would have understood the South and treated it more fairly and humanely than was done by the living politicians of Washington.

In the beginning, the leaders of the Confederacy had almost the same sources of information as the leaders of the Union. Before secession many who would become leaders of the Confederacy lived in Washington, where they and their Union antagonists read the same newspapers and books and had access to the same government reports and statistics. With the formation of the Confederacy, some of the access in Washington was lost, but there were other sources to draw upon. The prewar cotton trade to the North and Europe had created a network of people in the North and abroad with whom southerners conducted business and sometimes personal relations.

In addition, the secession movement tended to develop a network for the exchange of information. A great deal of prosecession activity took place in Washington, where the representatives of the various states could meet face to face, but there was also a voluminous correspondence by mail and by travel between representatives in Washington and the state governors and key political leaders at home. The inflammatory nature of the secession movement meant that much of this intellectual and political intercourse had to be kept secret. Because of the quasi-conspiratorial nature of the secession movement, many of the attitudes and practices that are desirable in any clandestine operation were adopted at that time.

Many of the states thought of themselves as truly sovereign and felt a responsibility to keep themselves fully informed on activities that might be injurious. As a result, some states developed their own sources of information in Washington and elsewhere in the North. Some of the contacts and sources developed just before the war were taken over or used by the Confederacy, but many contacts and sources of exchanges of information between North and South were never fully organized. They represented an uncontrolled resource that might produce an information gem at some unpredictable moment.

In addition to the contacts that produced useful information, the South had another asset that is often overlooked: its upper- and middle-class citizens. A sample of tax records in some counties in the South suggests that these classes formed a larger proportion of the total population than in the North or in Europe. Perhaps it was one of the results of slavery that in the economy of the South, a larger proportion of people with a modicum of managerial talent could rise in status. In any case, the South had many talented men, many educated in Ivy League schools, who had traveled and dealt on a broader horizon than their immediate surroundings. These people were available to provide intelligent leadership and manpower for the Confederate officer corps and for the technical jobs that were generated by the demands of war. This pool of talent was also available to be drawn upon for service in intelligence work.

Aside from the educated manpower and the relationships developed by the political and economic leaders, each state had militia or state military forces that provided organized bodies of men with some training or experience in hunting, scouting, or other activities that could be useful in intelligence work. The large cities had their police forces, the counties their sheriffs and deputy sheriffs, and some areas also had bounty-hunters or chasers of runaway slaves whose talents could be adapted to intelligence work.

At the outbreak of the Civil War, many army officers on both sides who had served in the Mexican War knew that adequate provision must be made for intelligence about the enemy. The United States had entered the Mexican War without any institutions to provide intelligence, and cultural and language problems had inhibited the growth of an adequate clandestine information-gathering system. In 1861, no such barrier would prevent penetration of the enemy society. With some fumbling, each side moved quickly to correct its deficiencies in the collection of information about the other.

Jefferson Davis, a West Point graduate, had been a successful troop commander in the Mexican War and shared the determination of many of his former colleagues not to be found deficient through ignorance of the enemy. He was also a successful politician and knew the value of information in that arena as well. At the outbreak of the war, he believed that his future role was to be that of a general officer commanding troops.[1] His election as president of the Confederacy was a surprise to him, but it was an apt choice. He probably had the best combination of skills and technical knowledge of any wartime national leader in the nineteenth century. He knew politics, military affairs, and the value of information about the enemy. Even more significant, he had a good idea of the importance of security and the harm that could be caused by careless talk. Modern game theory and its emphasis on the importance of learning about one's opponent and denying him information about oneself would have come as no surprise to Jefferson Davis. One tries to deny an opponent the knowledge of how one collects information about him and how successful one is at doing so. That makes it difficult for him to counter or manipulate one's information gathering as a means of deception.

Intelligence organizations are created, trained, and operated to make it difficult for an outsider to learn about them and understand their operations. In time of war they tend to reflect the grimness instilled by the death penalty traditionally awarded to spies who are caught. In wartime, intelligence operations are often deadly, serious matters of winning and living or of losing and dying.

In addition to direct threats to individual life and welfare, there are threats to the most private and most vulnerable aspects of the individual ego. The image a person wishes to present to the world may be threatened by the actions he may be involved in during a wartime career in intelligence. The intelligence officer, secret agent, or spy often has to play false roles or carry out acts for which he does not wish to be held personally responsible. It is a dangerous business and one that is filled with emotional traps for people who are sincere in their commitment to a cause. Intelligence work requires people who are patriotic and sincere, and it is exactly these people who can accumulate the most emotional scars in pursuing it.

The Confederacy's main initial requirement was for rapid knowledge of the Union's intentions toward the fledgling nation. That caused a focus on political and military espionage in Washington. This phase was followed by the organization and evolution of the full range of intelligence activities that the Confederacy needed to maintain itself in a deadly combat of some duration. In the first stage, speed was vital. The chosen strategy seemed to be to exploit the sympathy for the South exhibited by the population of Washington and to engage in widespread information gathering. Because of the lack of time or capabilities for training, much of this activity was amateurish, but it was good enough to give the Confederacy the warning it needed. In the second stage, the Confederacy was operating on the basis of some experience and recognized that its intelligence capability had to be built to last for the duration of the war. The intelligence needs recognized by the Confederacy in this stage parallel those of any reasonably modern nation engaged in a war with a powerful enemy.

The first and most obvious need was to collect the information that was openly available, primarily from newspapers and journals. Jefferson Davis, however, could not subscribe to the *Washington National Intelligencer* and expect to have it delivered to his office each day. To get information that was freely available, therefore, it was necessary to set up an elaborate clandestine organization. Arrangements had to be made for people to buy or subscribe to papers from Washington, Baltimore, Philadelphia, and New York. No one person could get them all because it might attract attention and generate suspicion. Furthermore, it was probably wise for two or three people to obtain each publication to ensure against accidental losses or the arrest of individual subscribers. Probably ten to twenty people bought newspapers whose destination was Richmond.

Once the subscribers had been organized, routes had to be determined by which each subscriber could get his papers into the hands of a courier system that could move them quickly and safely across the lines into Confederate territory. The arrangements would differ with the circumstances and location of the subscribers. One might use relays of boys or slaves to carry the papers to an entry point into the courier system. Another might wrap his newspapers in a package and mail it quickly to a safe address in southern Maryland where it could be turned over to Confederate couriers. All of this arranging took time and careful organization. Successful operation of the system took dedicated work and closed mouths on the part of a great many people.

In addition to publications, much valuable information was available by word of mouth. Its collection, however, required people who knew what would be of interest to the Confederacy living where they could hear it. Once known to a sympathetic observer, the information could be sent as a simple personal letter to a safe address within the courier system, but the hard part was to recruit the observer and train him or her on what to listen for.

The personal observer system could be useful in foreign countries as well as in the North. In the absence of diplomatic recognition, agents had to be sent abroad who could organize and maintain a flow of information that would eventually find its way into the Confederacy or support specific Confederate operations abroad. Much of this information, like the newspapers, would be overt, that is, nonsecret. What made it sensitive was its value to the Confederacy, the channels by which it got there, and its ultimate use.

Information of value to the Confederacy could also be collected by visual observation. Such information could be collected openly by trained military personnel who were generally employed as scouts and worked out of the tactical forces. Ideally, these men should have had specialized training, but it was the sort of work that also benefited from natural aptitude and on-the-job experience.

Engineers with the tactical forces might collect information of value such as news on rainfall and its effects on roads. Signal personnel might also provide information through their own observations in addition to their primary function of transmitting messages for others.

One of the fastest and most authoritative ways of finding out about an enemy is to capture one of his soldiers and get the soldier to tell you the information. Obviously, many prisoners would not cooperate, and some would be ignorant of the information desired, but the procedure should work often enough and well enough for it to be considered as a standard source of information. The Confederates took substantial numbers of prisoners, and that source was available to them throughout the war.[2] To get the most from this source, a prisoner had to be interrogated as soon as possible after his capture to acquire any information of immediate tactical value and identify a prisoner who should receive special treatment, either because of what he knew or because of his willingness or unwillingness to cooperate.

It was important to search prisoners thoroughly for letters or documents that contained useful information. The contents of a prisoner's pockets—letters from home, receipts, ticket stubs, coins, pay records, and the like—could be used when equipping an agent with a new identity. Some prisoners were more cooperative than others, and it was important to segregate the willing from the hard-liners to prevent the latter from exerting influence over the more pliable. Some prisoners might even be willing to switch sides and enlist in the Confederate forces, and they needed to be protected from attack by their former comrades. Some cooperative prisoners might even be willing to return to the Union and act as agents for the Confederacy. These people, especially, needed protection from their fellow prisoners. They would need to be trained for their new mission, which could not be done while they were in a conventional prison for captives. In addition to the subtle features of the requirements outlined above, the need to feed, shelter, and guard large numbers of soldiers who did not want to be prisoners meant that their successful exploitation for intelligence purposes proved a tremendous challenge for the Confederacy.

There is no indication that the Confederates thought of information gathering as a systematic staff function to be carried out by what would today be called intelligence officers. The logic of function exerted an inevitable influence, however, and as time went by, many tactical organizations at the division and corps level began to develop staff officers who specialized in the work that modern intelligence officers do. Sometimes these officers were aides-de-camp, sometimes they were assistant adjutants general, sometimes even chaplains. Particularly in the early part of the war, they might have been volunteer aides-de-camp—civilians who were friends of the commander and served without commissions. This latter group was allowed the status and pay of first lieutenants.[3]

An enemy's communications are always a useful target for intelligence collection. Mail may be intercepted intentionally or accidentally, messengers may be captured or subverted, or electronic transmission may be intercepted. During the Civil War, the fluidity of maneuver frequently gave the Union and Confederacy access to the same telegraph lines. Obviously, useful information might be obtained from the opponent's messages.

These threats to the security of communication made it necessary for the Confederacy to develop a system for enciphering its important communications, which would incorporate more than one code or cipher method. There was a need for privacy within the Confederate government. It would not do for many functionaries to have access to some messages. The more people who could read some messages, the greater the risk to security. As a result, several cipher methods were used by different bureaus and departments.

The personnel who enciphered and deciphered the messages had to be trained, and a procedure had to be developed to keep them apprised of changes in the cipher systems. One of the most common items that was changed was the key word or phrase used in the principal Confederate cipher systems. These key words might be compromised if enemies who attempted cryptanalysis succeeded in deciphering them. Key words might also be compromised by the capture and successful interrogation of one of the persons who enciphered or deciphered messages. Because of these dangers, it was common practice to change the key words from time to time. To maintain security, these changes had to be transmitted by special courier.

In addition to the creation and management of a cipher system, there had to be an organized method for carrying messages from point to point. In some cases, the normal mails or commercial telegraph could be used, but in many areas only couriers could provide the necessary service. The most difficult part of the courier service to organize was that part that led across enemy lines. The people engaged in that section of the system had to be recruited carefully to ensure that they were loyal to the Confederacy. They had to be instructed, the type and amount of training depending on the nature of the person's specific job in the courier system. The system also needed to be managed. Performance had to be checked, sick people replaced, and enemy penetrations avoided.

The Confederacy was something of a pioneer in the use of communication on the battlefield. Following the invention of the telegraph in the 1830s, a sizable number of people knew how to use the main telegraphic codes of the time. Messages could be sent visually using a similar code by the use of signal flags or torches. The signal system made it possible to send messages over considerable distances, over obstacles, or over enemy units. The personnel to operate this tactical communications system had to be trained in code and in the use of the signal devices. The signal system also required some administration on the battlefield, which meant that a commander's staff must include someone who understood the technology involved and who could take responsibility for technical management of the system.

A specialized application of tactical signal capability was supplying blockade-running ships with information, advice, and guidance concerning the Union blockading forces, the location of reefs, mines, and obstacles, and other factors that would help them make a safe entry into port. Special signal arrangements had to be made because weather conditions sometimes made it impossible to use the torch system employed by the Confederate army at night.

In addition to the tactical signal system, army telegraphers needed to know telegraphic code. Some trained telegraph operators could be obtained from the civilian telegraph companies, but the needs of the army were too great to be satisfied from that source alone. New operators needed to be trained, perhaps by the telegraph companies, and made available to support Confederate operations in the field.

The technique of determining the organization of enemy forces and keeping track of individual units is commonly called order of battle. The Confederates, like any modern nation facing a large and powerful enemy, would be better able to understand that enemy and the significance of specific maneuvers if they understood the composition and the history of the enemy units involved. For example, it might be important to know that the 139th New York Volunteers were part of Henry's brigade. The order-of-battle files might show that this brigade frequently operated on special assignments. If the 139th regiment was reported to be in a particular area, it might mean that the rest of the brigade was nearby. Such hints could be of immense value in combat. By the end of the war, the Union had developed an outstanding order-of-battle effort. The system used by the Confederacy is less well known and seems to have differed in some respects, but the Confederates were well aware of the Union effort and had a good understanding of the techniques.

Maps are essential to the conduct of modern war, and though the engineers could provide the technical expertise, the production of maps was inescapably an intelligence concern. Maps summarize and display terrain and cultural information that a commander may need to plan and carry out military operations. Maps are not raw data; they are the product of considerable analysis and refinement of large amounts of other information.

In 1861, little of the United States had been mapped at a scale suitable for tactical military use. It was necessary therefore for the Confederates to develop a mapping capability. Furthermore, the territory being mapped was sometimes in a combat area and sometimes behind enemy lines. The need to map territory not under Confederate control required the collection of some of the basic data by clandestine means. A traditional survey involving transits, chains, and plane tables might be impossible, but a reasonable approximation could be achieved by using compass bearings and trigonometry. The taking of compass bearings would be relatively easy to disguise. Landscape painters and photographers could also make a contribution by disguising the collection of map data.

A major problem was that the rate at which maps could be produced would not allow the Confederates to adopt a comprehensive mapping program. Instead, mapping teams could support major military commands by trying to map the areas that a commander might anticipate would be involved in combat. Thus, though much of Virginia was eventually mapped, the actual production of maps would have been related to plans for future combat.

The enemy would be another source of maps and mapping information. With luck, some maps might be captured, or it might be possible to steal them from the enemy's mapping organizations.

In addition to the information that could be collected about the Union and its army from newspapers and other more or less overt sources, it was obvious to Confederate leaders that they would need to use clandestine means to gain access to some secret information. The federal bureaucracy was riddled with southern sympathizers, there was an active Copperhead organization throughout the North, and many other people had ambivalent loyalties. The main target of Confederate espionage would be the federal government in Washington, but there would also be lucrative targets in state capitals and other cities for information on the status of forces being prepared by the states for federal service and for information of an economic and political nature.

There would also be more specialized espionage targets, including Union police, provost marshal, and counterintelligence activities that would be working to uncover Confederate activity and sympathizers. The Union army would have to be an espionage target, but army elements in the combat zone would be difficult targets to work. They could probably be penetrated without too much difficulty, but it would be hard to arrange for Confederate agents in such units to communicate their intelligence in a timely manner. The pace of battle might well move too fast for a communications system that could not depend on local arrangements to handle the agents' messages. Military units not in the combat zone could be penetrated, and satisfactory communications could probably be arranged, but the value of information obtained from those units might not be very great. Overall, the value of the information to be obtained by espionage was so great that the creation of an efficient organization to carry it out must have had a very high priority.

The term "tradecraft" is a modern expression used to describe a wide variety of techniques, habits, practices, gadgets, and organizations used in clandestine operations. The tradecraft involved in the operations of an individual agent or a small clandestine organization has grown up over centuries. It is a body of knowledge that enables a trained agent to organize and operate a clandestine operation with a minimum of risk. It includes techniques for planning, developing a cover story, providing agents with documents and other material to prove their assumed identity, recognition signals, organization of letter drops, safe houses, and a host of similar appurtenances.

In the beginning, the Confederates used more enthusiasm than finesse in their clandestine work. To operate successfully on a large scale, they would have to acquire a command of tradecraft. The only way to do this successfully in a short period was to establish contact with an existing successful intelligence organization that would be willing to provide training. The obvious primary source was British intelligence, which had a long history of successful clandestine work. Although the British might refuse to recognize the Confederacy publicly, it should prove to be far easier to get them to provide assistance in the field of intelligence. That help, by its very nature, would be private and thus far easier for the British government to do. We do not know for certain that British intelligence helped the Confederates, but for them to do so would have made sense. It would be a cheap and relatively safe way of putting the Confederate government in their debt, and it would provide a ready source of inside information for their own use, which would be helpful in deciding British policy toward both North and South.

The Confederacy was fully aware that the Union was equally anxious to keep abreast of plans and events in its opposing camp. One of Jefferson Davis's first acts on arriving in Richmond was to appoint one of his former instructors at West Point, John H. Winder, as provost marshal of the Richmond area.[4] The flow of information to the North had to be stopped, and Union spies had to be exposed.

The most efficient steps for deterring enemy agents—censorship, control of movement of individuals, searching of suspects, clandestine observation of suspects, and the like—are also irritating to the freedom-loving populace, and the white population of the South was every bit as dedicated to personal freedom as their northern cousins. As a result, there was constant friction between the provost marshal's office and the people of Richmond, which inhibited the development of a truly nationwide program of counterintelligence. Much of the effort to defeat Union spies was left to state and local authorities. As a result, the Union remained fairly well informed of events in the Confederacy throughout the war, in spite of the relative inaccuracy of some Union intelligence work.

Another strategy against enemy intelligence that does not depend on ironclad censorship and intolerable population control is to disseminate "disinformation" to the point that the enemy has a hard time distinguishing truth from fiction in the reports of his intelligence apparatus. By deliberately creating false information and feeding it to enemy intelligence, it is often possible to mislead and confuse him. The British have been very good at the game of deceiving an enemy. Their advice would have been very helpful to the Confederates. The disinformation technique depends on the ingenuity and skill of a relatively small number of people and has a less negative effect than other counterintelligence measures. There would always be the problem of misleading one's own people by publishing erroneous information, but in time of war that would usually be easier to manage and less irksome to the populace than counterintelligence measures handled by the police.

The disinformation technique could take several forms. One was to plant erroneous stories in the newspapers. A second was to coach soldiers in a particular story and have them desert to the enemy to give the story to Union interrogators. A third was to infiltrate Confederate agents into Union intelligence and then have them report truthful data carefully blended with false information.

The most important aspect of counterintelligence, particularly in the deception game, was to make commanders and key officials at all levels aware of the existence of Union intelligence and the importance of misleading it. If every military operation were planned with that idea in mind, the chances of success on the battlefield would be enhanced.

The Confederacy was engaged in a life-or-death struggle that would not tolerate the luxury of jurisdictional niceties. If a good Confederate had an opportunity to cause serious damage to the enemy, he was supposed to do it. If an espionage agent suddenly had an opportunity to capture a Union ship, he should probably do so. This pragmatic approach to clandestine operations has made it harder for us to understand the organization of Confederate intelligence, but it was logical.

If the Confederacy had to develop a clandestine organization in the North to support the collection of intelligence, why not use it for other activities as well—activities that might make a more direct contribution to winning the war? Secret operations of a political or military nature would require sending messages back and forth, and the courier system that supported espionage could also carry these messages. Information needed in Richmond about Union military activity could also be used by people who could employ sabotage or launch sneak attacks. Secret activity in the North could do much to help the Confederate war effort.

The military motive for secret operations coincided with the main strategic objective of the Confederacy, which was to convince the North to give up the attempt to restore the Union by force. The South could not win a war of attrition. It had neither the manpower nor the resources to outlast an efficient and determined North. It could outlast the Union, however, if the northern populace could be convinced that the cost of winning would be too high. Obviously, Confederate victories in battle would discourage the public in the North and build support abroad. Judicious political operations might further discourage the public and encourage the growth of the antiwar movement.

The Confederate covert action program tended to have conflicting objectives. Propaganda and bribery might encourage the antiwar movement, but they would not divert troops from the front. Sabotage, guerrilla raids, and the threat of insurrections would drive troops away from combat, but they might frighten the populace and increase hostility to the Confederacy more than they would strengthen the antiwar party. To wage this double-purpose campaign efficiently would require the most careful analysis and the most judicious decision making on the part of the Confederate government. To ensure the most responsible prosecution of this campaign, Davis would have had to have kept the final authority to himself.

If a nation decided to develop a capability for engaging in clandestine operations and to use that capability to cause physical damage to the enemy, the next step is to develop a capability to produce specialized ordnance suitable for clandestine employment. The Confederacy appears to have followed this logic and concluded that it had a major need for such items.

Passive explosive devices such as mines are particularly useful to a nation on the defensive. They can be planted in territory that is about to pass from friendly control and will be there to plague the enemy when he tries to move in. The rivers and estuaries along the southern coastlines were major areas of Union penetration. It was logical that the Confederacy should first turn its attention to the underwater mine, or "torpedo" as it was called, as a means of closing off those avenues. Mines were then employed in a wide variety of operations, some of them in areas not under Confederate control. The full array of clandestine organizations and practice would have to be employed to get mines in place and see that they were set off at the correct moment.

From the underwater mine it was a short step to the land mine or the "subterra torpedo." It would also be logical to develop devices that could be used by individual agents to sabotage Union installations and shipping. The bomb disguised as a lump of coal is a classic example of the devices developed by the Confederates to support their clandestine action programs.[5]

Because of the sensitivity of the new technology of mines and their various fuses and the relationship between these devices and clandestine operations, it was logical for the Confederates to treat their development as a secret activity.

The Confederacy entered the Civil War realizing that it would have to procure many manufactured items from abroad. To do so, however, would involve evading the Union blockade. There were three basic routes that could be followed: by sea, past the blockading Union fleet directly into southern ports; by sea to Mexico and then overland to Texas; or by land, through the Union army, from factories or importers in the North. The route through Mexico was impractical for most of the Confederacy because of the distance involved and the unsettled conditions in Mexico. The routes from the North varied, but on all of them the quantities of goods that could be smuggled in any single operation were restricted. Only the route by sea direct to Confederate ports could be counted on to get large items and sizable quantities into southern territory.

Obviously, the Union would try to reinforce its blockade by monitoring Confederate activity and interfering with it by legal and diplomatic means wherever possible, even by extralegal means. The Confederacy would therefore have to conduct much of its foreign procurement activity secretly. It would also need to collect a considerable amount of intelligence in support of its blockade-running operation. Some of this might be a by-product of normal Confederate intelligence collection, but much of it would have to come from many scattered locations specifically to help the Confederate import effort.

Clandestine organizations tend to differ in their internal operations according to their objectives, the nature of the society in which they operate, their standing vis-à-vis that society, and the nature of the organizations opposing them. In similar circumstances, however, there is a logic to clandestine operations that tends to make them resemble one another.

Confederate clandestine operations across the Potomac would be conducted in a reasonably favorable environment. The populace of southern Maryland and the District of Columbia was mostly favorable to the Confederacy, and many people were strongly so. In Maryland, those who were not pro-Confederacy were not necessarily pro-Union, and those who were pro-Union tended to have ties of blood, friendship, and association with those who were strongly anti-Union. Informers and enemies might be present, but on the whole, the Confederacy could count on most persons either supporting its secret operations if they became known or at least not opposing them to the extent of informing the federal authorities. In addition, the Union did not have the institutions and trained manpower or the technical knowledge to combat clandestine operations efficiently. In this generally benign environment it would be easiest and most efficient for the clandestine organization to reflect the structure of society in creating its own culture within a culture.

Several functions are common to all clandestine organizations operating in a generally favorable society. First, there must be some way for responsible citizens to get in touch with somebody of authority in the organization. This function would be performed by a political front man—somebody widely understood to be able to speak for or to the organization. Next, there must be a local chief of operations who sees that the wheels of the organization turn, that it does the job that it was created to do. This man sees that people are recruited and trained and that they are put in contact with other parts of the organization as required. He receives instructions from outside the local areas and informs his superiors of events in his area that might affect operations.

Third, there must be action officers—people who could be assigned the responsibility for a mission and who would see that it was accomplished. The action officer would have enough authority and knowledge to contact other members of the organization and give them directions within the scope of his mission. He would assemble the forces necessary to accomplish the mission and coordinate his activities with the chief of operations. Next, would come senior agents who headed teams to carry out specific jobs under the supervision of an action officer. These agents would have to have the skill, leadership, training, and cover to enable them to execute the assigned tasks. Under the senior agents, a host of other agents would play various specialized roles. Many of them might be called courier-escorts, who would carry important information and matériel and, when necessary, escort people who were being moved by the organization. They would be the "soldiers" of the organization. Beneath these, there would be a group that might be called courier-messengers. These people would carry the messages, verbal or written, to enable the organization to function. Doctors, ministers, children, and blacks could play this role on occasion. Another group would provide transportation—the wagoners, sailors, oarsmen, and drivers who supported the organization and enabled it to move people from place to place.

In addition to these active people, the organization would have to have "safe houses," that is, places where members of the organization could find shelter and food. Sometimes an agent might provide his own safe house, but in most cases the safe houses were provided by people who, as a security measure, deliberately did not involve themselves in the day-to-day operations of the organization.

The chief of operations would need help from persons trained in ciphers, specialists in training agents how to build and maintain a cover, people knowledgeable about weapons and the myriad skills that make a clandestine organization operate successfully. Such specialists might come from Richmond as needed because people skilled in those specialties were bound to be in short supply.

It is difficult to lay out a clandestine organization in crisp detail. People sometimes changed or combined functions. In some cases, discipline was not observed, and in other cases new objectives caused the organization to be reconfigured. The fluid nature of the organization made it hard for Union counterintelligence people to keep track of Confederate activities, and it makes it hard for the scholar who would reconstruct them through historical research.

In retrospect, it seems clear that Jefferson Davis was his own director of intelligence. There seems to have been no immediate need to set up a monolithic organization encompassing all intelligence activities. Furthermore, the persons needing intelligence support were not all in one place. To be useful, some intelligence activities had to be decentralized.

There was probably no one mysterious master spy of the Confederacy. Instead, there appears to have evolved a loose network of components, each with a set of intelligence-related duties to perform. The entire complex was coordinated through the personal direction of Jefferson Davis and a handful of key officials of the Confederate government. These seem to have included Judah P. Benjamin, the secretary of state; James A. Seddon, secretary of war; Brigadier General John Henry Winder, provost marshal in Richmond and superintendent of military prisons; Colonel Robert Ould, commissioner of prisoner exchanges; General Braxton Bragg, for a time military assistant to the president; and General Robert E. Lee, commander of the Army of Northern Virginia, and, finally, general in chief of Confederate armies. At a somewhat lower level, a number of officers have been identified who seem to have played important roles in intelligence activities. These included Major William Norris, head of the Signal Corps; Jacob Thompson, Clement C. Clay, and General Edwin G. Lee, Confederate commissioners in Canada; John S. Mosby, commander of the Forty-third Battalion of Virginia Cavalry; and Major Thomas P. Turner, commandant of Libby Prison. Additional officers were probably involved at this level in carrying out specific intelligence-related operations who have not yet been identified.

At the close of the Civil War, the Confederates were in the process of pulling this loose network together into a central intelligence organization, but the war ended before this could be fully implemented.

One of the results of the loose organization of intelligence was that it made the personal relationships among the individuals in the components very important. The need for fast results combined with the lack of such modern devices as the polygraph and a trained investigation organization made it necessary for the managers to recruit help from among people they already knew they could trust. That meant that relatives, friends, and neighbors of the people listed above might very likely turn up in some intelligence-related activity. Beyond the ken of personal contact, the managers had to depend on the recommendations of the same people they could trust. As a result, some friends of the managers began to serve as recruiters for jobs involving sensitive responsibilities. Recruitment by personal recommendation and knowledge meant that certain activities might involve people from the same area and of the same social status. Therefore, social and family history can be very important in understanding the history of Confederate intelligence activity and its impact on the course of the Civil War.

Notes

ABBREVIATIONS

NA   National Archives

OR   U.S. War Department, *The War of the Rebellion: A Compilation of the Official Records of the Union and Confederate Armies.* 128 vols. Washington, D.C.: U.S. Government Printing Office, 1880–1901.

ORN   U.S. Navy Department, *Official Records of the Union and Confederate Navies in the War of the Rebellion.* 30 vols. Washington, D.C.: U.S. Government Printing Office, 1894–1914.

RG   Record Group

1. Allen Johnson and Dumas Malone, eds., *Dictionary of American Biography* (New York: Charles Scribner's Sons, 1959), 3:127.

2. William B. Hesseltine, *Civil War Prisons* (New York: Unger, 1930), p. 2; Holland Thompson, "Prisoners of War," in Francis Trevelyan Miller, ed., *The Photographic History of the Civil War,* 10 vols. (New York, Review of Reviews, 1912), 8:50.

3. Confederate Secretary of War to General L. Polk, 31 October 1861, M-524, RG 109, NA.

4. General Samuel Cooper to J. H. Winder, 21 June 1861, John H. Winder Papers, Southern Historical Collection, University of North Carolina, Chapel Hill.

5. J. Thomas Scharf, *History of the Confederates States Navy* (1887; rpt. N.p.: Fairfax Press, 1977), p. 762.

2

The Virginia Connection

When Virginia seceded from the Union on 17 April 1861, the state faced in microcosm nearly all the problems that the Confederacy faced on a larger scale. Two months would pass before Virginia was fully integrated into the Confederacy and the new Confederate government assumed responsibility for the defense of its territory. During those two months the state of Virginia engaged in activities that were to contribute directly to the development of the intelligence and covert action capabilities of the Confederacy.

When Virginia seceded, John Letcher, the state's governor from 1 January 1860 to 1 January 1864, immediately began three simultaneous efforts. First he created a provisional army and navy to protect Virginia's frontiers more effectively than militia forces alone could do. Then he took over the armament belonging to the U.S. government within the state's borders to help build up Virginia's forces and eliminate possible bases for hostile action. Finally, he tried to help the state of Maryland secede from the Union. Maryland was even more exposed to the hostile North than was Virginia, and, understandably, her political leaders could not bring themselves to secede without the means to protect themselves from Union troops stationed in Baltimore and Washington and in the northern states. These efforts were accompanied by the expansion of an already existing intelligence capability.

In the seventeenth century, the king of England ruled five dominions: England, Wales, Ireland, Scotland, and Virginia. For many years afterward, Virginia was the largest, richest, and most populous among the growing number of American colonies. In 1790, nearly one-fifth of all Americans lived in Virginia. New York and Pennsylvania had surpassed Virginia in population by 1810, but

51

Virginians still thought of themselves as the mainstream in the growth of the American nation. They had played a critical part in the American Revolution and for many years thereafter contributed more than their share of leadership to the United States.

When the states in the Deep South began to secede in 1860, Virginia was not particularly enthusiastic. Lukewarm on the slavery issue, most Virginians sympathized with the departing states on constitutional and political grounds but saw no need to follow their path. The majority, however, strongly opposed what they called the policy of coercion—the maintenance of the Union by armed force. Virginians made strenuous efforts to find some compromise solution, and several Virginians earnestly tried to warn Lincoln that the use of force might well lead to the state's secession.

When on 15 April 1861 President Lincoln called for seventy-five thousand volunteers to restore federal authority in the South, sentiment in Virginia was outraged, and on 17 April Virginia seceded from the Union.

John Letcher thus found himself the head of an independent state. He recognized that the secession of Virginia would expose the state to armed attack and that the long, complex northern border would not be easy to defend. At that date the newly formed Confederate government in Alabama could provide little help. Furthermore, it was in complete accord with the Virginia tradition for Virginians to assert themselves in military matters.

On 18 April, Letcher sent Judge William J. Robertson to talk to two Virginians in federal military service, General Winfield Scott and Colonel Robert E. Lee, concerning possible service in the state's armed forces. The aged Scott was unwilling to abandon the United States, but Lee left with the judge for Richmond on 22 April.[1]

On 21 April, Letcher set up an Advisory Council to help him organize Virginia's military effort. He appointed Judge John J. Allen, chief justice of Virginia's Court of Appeals, as president of the council to maintain civilian authority. The other two members were Colonel Francis H. Smith, superintendent of the Virginia Military Institute (VMI); and Lieutenant Matthew Fontaine Maury, the prestigious oceanographer formerly of the U.S. Navy.[2] Both were well qualified by training and character for their responsibilities. Smith was an 1833 graduate of West Point and a close personal friend of Letcher. In early 1860, he had been appointed by Letcher to a commission to procure modern arms for the use of

Virginia's militia. The Virginia Military Institute was also responsible for guarding the state arsenal at Lexington. Maury had an outstanding international reputation as a scientific-minded naval officer and had also written extensively about naval policy and had innovative views about ship design and naval weapons.

Letcher himself had an unusual contribution to bring to this pool of talent. His entire adult life had been spent in Virginia politics. During that time he had supported himself by alternately practicing law and editing a newspaper. He had considerable personal knowledge of the importance of information in making sound decisions, and he had practical experience in how one acquired information. For many years he had subscribed to several newspapers and had many correspondents in Washington and in key areas of Virginia who kept him posted on local events and the views of their neighbors.[3]

Letcher and his council evidently worked intimately together because correspondence addressed to the various members is mixed randomly among the papers addressed to the governor and letters addressed to one appear to have been acted on by another as required. It would thus appear that all members of the group knew what the others were working on.

It would also appear that the files do not contain all of the correspondence received, because there are references to matters that must have been mentioned in letters that are not in the files. A few of these letters are in Letcher's personal papers at the George C. Marshall Research Library in Lexington, Virginia. Special files may have been set up for sensitive operations, and occasionally papers pertaining to them slipped into the main executive file. From the references to sensitive matters that do exist, it would appear that the state of Virginia was providing arms to the pro-secession element in Maryland to help in efforts to cause the state to secede, that Virginia had its own intelligence organization, and that the notorious spy for the Confederacy Rose Greenhow may well have been part of this intelligence network.

Letcher was a member of the U.S. Congress from Virginia from 1853 to 1859 and spent a considerable portion of that time living without his family in Brown's Hotel at Sixth and Pennsylvania Avenue in Washington, D. C. His hotel receipts show that he kept up a moderately active social life, and he appears to have developed several good friends among the politically active residents of Washington. Several of these men corresponded with him at length when he was at home in Lexington between visits to Washington.

They reported in detail on news of both national and Virginia politics, and it is apparent that Washington was a center for the exchange of information about Virginia state affairs. Each faction of consequence in the state appears to have had representatives in the capital city.[4]

After Letcher became governor on 1 January 1860, he continued this style of correspondence and many of the same contacts to keep informed of conditions and political sentiments in Washington and throughout Virginia. Virginia had an active militia, and the John Brown raid in the autumn of 1859 had caused considerable rejuvenation of interest in local defense. New militia units were being formed and old units were gaining new recruits. Soon after taking office, Letcher began to try to improve the defenses of the state. On 30 January 1860 he appointed commissioners to a board to purchase arms. They were Colonel Francis H. Smith; Philip St. George Cocke of Powhatan County, a West Point graduate in 1832 and a progressive planter; and Francis Mallery of Norfolk, president of the Norfolk and Petersburg Railroad, who died on 26 March 1860 without serving on the board. On 27 April the commissioners invited Letcher to accompany them on visits to arms manufacturers in Springfield, Massachusetts, and Chicago.[5]

Within Virginia's borders, stores of arms were located at the U.S. naval base near Norfolk at the mouth of the Chesapeake Bay; Fortress Monroe, across the James River from Norfolk; the federal arsenal at Harpers Ferry, at the junction of the Shenandoah and Potomac rivers; the Virginia State Arsenal at Lexington, near the center of the state; and an arsenal at Richmond. The naval base had not only warships but also large numbers of cannon of various sizes. Fortress Monroe contained primarily the guns that made it a strong fort. Harpers Ferry had a rifle factory and a large store of rifles. A considerable quantity of muskets were stored at the arsenals at Lexington and Richmond, but many of them were old flintlocks.

In a report on the status of weapons in the state on 30 September 1860, William H. Richardson, the adjutant general, noted that in the past accounting year five thousand new percussioned muskets had been procured.[6] It is clear from this report that the great majority of Virginia's weapons were obsolete. Theoretically, more than sixty thousand men could be armed, but fewer than ten thousand would receive modern weapons.

The outline of the original organization of Virginia's defenses reflected the personal knowledge of the members of the governor's

Advisory Council, who had been appointed from among Letcher's friends and associates. Philip St. George Cocke was originally in command of the military operations of the state in the area bounded by the Potomac. Cocke and Colonel Francis Smith, of the Class of 1833, had known each other since cadet days and had served together earlier on Letcher's arms procurement board.

The Potomac line was much too long for one man to command, and the lower part, near Fredericksburg, was split off and put under the command of Colonel Daniel Ruggles, a West Point classmate of Smith. Ruggles shortly became a brigadier general and focused his attention on protecting the northern terminal of the Richmond, Fredericksburg, and Potomac Railroad at Aquia Creek and the strategic bend of the Potomac around Mathias Point in King George County. The section of the Potomac above the mountains fell under the command of Colonel Thomas J. Jackson, a professor at Virginia Military Institute, who was technically a subordinate of Major General Kenton Harper, the militia general who captured Harpers Ferry. The defense of the Kanawha Valley fell to Colonel Christopher Q. Tompkins of the West Point Class of 1836, an acquaintance of Smith since cadet days. Norfolk was assigned to General Walter Gwynn of the West Point Class of 1822, a leading engineer of railroads who had lived in or near Norfolk for much of the time since he left the army in 1832.

Within a few days of its secession, Virginia had begun to put together a defensive organization and had taken possession of Harpers Ferry and the U.S. naval base near Norfolk. Fortress Monroe, however, was too hard a nut to crack, and the Virginia forces never really tried to take it. The two points seized, however, provided a considerable number of additional arms for immediate use.

In the meantime, people in both Maryland and Virginia were trying to arrange for Virginia to help the secessionists in Maryland. These efforts were not well integrated because of the lack of organization among the secessionists in Maryland and their friends in Virginia and poor communications and the need for secrecy.

As deficient as Virginia was in armaments, Maryland was in even worse condition. Baltimore had been plagued by gangs for several years and in 1857 began to take serious measures to restore law and order. The governor of Maryland borrowed weapons from Virginia to arm the Maryland militia called up to police the elections held during that year. These weapons appear to have been returned in due course, but their loan helped set a precedent for later actions.[7]

Virginia's military institutions were the new Provisional Army of Virginia Volunteers and the local militia. There was no statutory provision for men from Maryland to enter units identified with and controlled by Maryland. Many Maryland men were willing to serve in Virginia units, but others wanted to enlist directly under the Confederate government in Maryland units. There was a small Confederate regular army, but the manpower was in the Provisional Army of the Confederate States, whose units were first created by the states and then turned over to the Confederate government. The Confederacy could not legally create a Maryland unit without the sanction of the state of Maryland.

Virginia tried to make it as easy as possible for Marylanders by allowing them to form their own units at the company level, but problems arose when the question of field command came up. Such prestigious jobs obviously had political overtones, and many Marylanders did not like to have their senior officers selected by Virginians.

Major William N. Ward, a West Point classmate of R. E. Lee and an Episcopal minister, organized and trained the Fifty-fifth Virginia Infantry Regiment at Tappahannock, Virginia.[8] At the same location Colonel Richard Henry Thomas (Zarvona) was organizing the Maryland Guerrilla Zouaves as a unit in the Virginia forces. Major Ward referred to his office as "Headquarters, Essex and Maryland Virginia Volunteers, Tappahannock, Virginia," as if Maryland were another Virginia county. That made sense administratively, but it may have galled the more politically minded Marylanders.[9]

The secession of Virginia and the capture of Harpers Ferry by Virginia forces on 18 April excited the prosouthern faction in Maryland. Harpers Ferry, in Jefferson County, Virginia was only a few hours' ride from Baltimore by train, and many county families had relatives or friends in Baltimore, which was their nearest large city.

On 19 April, a force of Massachusetts troops ran into resistance passing through Baltimore on their way to Washington.[10] They finally made it after firing on a mob and suffering some casualties themselves. In the aftermath of this violence, the governor and the mayor of Baltimore jointly sent a telegram to President Lincoln asking that no more troops be sent through the city. In the meantime, railroad bridges north of Baltimore were cut to stop troops already on the way.

Had there been an armed force of any consequence supporting the cause of secession, the prosecession element in the Maryland legislature probably could have taken action. But no such armed force existed. On 21 April a large number of militia companies of forty men each were organized in Baltimore under the command of Colonel Isaac Trimble, but these companies lacked proper arms and training, and they dispersed when the threat of an immediate invasion of Baltimore receded.

The legislature was called to meet in a special session on 26 April, but because Annapolis had been occupied by federal troops, the meeting place was changed to Frederick. In that part of the state there were not many secessionists, and without local support the prosouthern faction could not carry its point of view in the assembled legislature. Finally, on 13 May 1861, federal troops occupied strategic points in Baltimore and any real chance of arranging the secession of Maryland had passed.

Soon after the secession of Virginia, Francis J. Thomas, signing himself "Adjutant General of Maryland," wrote asking the Virginia governor for arms to help the southern faction in Maryland.[11] The letter was forwarded to Governor Letcher through Christopher Q. Tompkins, and Thomas cited Alexander Robinson Boteler as a reference for the project. To understand their relationship, it is important to examine the backgrounds of these three men. Thomas was graduated from West Point in the Class of 1844; Tompkins was a graduate of the Class of 1836. Both had served in the Third U.S. Artillery Regiment at Fort McHenry in Baltimore in 1846, and both had married girls from the Baltimore area.[12] Both had later left the army. Boteler was born in Jefferson County, Virginia, in 1815 but lived for several years in Baltimore and had relatives and friends there.[13] He graduated from Princeton College in 1835 and became a representative from the district including Jefferson County in the Congress of 1859–61. Boteler was acquainted with Governor Letcher and strongly supported the southern cause. He was also a good friend of Rose O'Neill Greenhow, the most notorious Confederate spy of the early days of the war.[14] No record could be found of Thomas as an adjutant general of Maryland. He may have been asked to serve as adjutant to Colonel Trimble's organization or have been sponsored by a political group trying to establish a reliable military force.

An operation sponsored by such men as Thomas, Tompkins, and Boteler was not to be taken lightly. Claims of available manpower in such situations are nearly always overestimated, but Thomas may well have believed that he could muster more men than he finally produced. In any event, Letcher approved the loan of five thousand muskets and six cannons to Maryland from the arsenal at Lexington.[15] The weapons were to be transported to Harpers Ferry, where they could be put on the Baltimore and Ohio Railroad for rapid delivery to Baltimore or elsewhere.

In the meantime, the Baltimore Board of Police had discussed the question of arms with James M. Mason, recently a U.S. senator from Virginia. Board members felt that Mason had assured them they would receive arms, and this understanding caused considerable confusion in the attempt to supply weapons to Maryland.[16]

On 22 April, Governor Letcher's Advisory Council considered a telegram from John S. Barbour, president of the Orange and Alexandria Railroad, who was acting as a "confidential agent of the Government at Alexandria," asking that arms be sent to enable Maryland troops to resist the passage of northern troops through Baltimore. The council responded: "Major General Kenton Harper in command at Harpers Ferry is hereby ordered to deliver to General Stewart at Baltimore one thousand of the arms taken at Harpers Ferry."[17] These weapons were *not* from the Lexington Arsenal, and they were to be delivered to a different recipient. Apparently two different consignments of weapons were involved.

On 26 or 27 April, a consignment of muskets arrived in Baltimore via the Baltimore and Ohio, apparently addressed to the group sponsoring Thomas. The Board of Police had ordered the creation of a division under General George H. Steuart, a West Pointer of the Class of 1848, and felt incensed that somebody else was getting the weapons they thought they had been promised. The police promptly seized the weapons, but Charles Howard, the president of the Police Board, wrote to Senator Mason asking that the matter be clarified. The letter finally reached Mason at his home near Winchester on 7 May. Mason promptly disclaimed any authority in the matter and turned it over to Governor Letcher for resolution.[18]

The situation became even murkier when, on 3 May 1861, John S. Barbour, Jr., telegraphed Letcher: "My messenger to Baltimore has returned. Could not hear of Adjutant General Thomas or of the wire promised to be found for the telegraph to Winchester as per telegram to me last Sunday (28 April). What is now further to be done? Is the whole matter in my hands to manage or not?"[19] Clearly, the whole matter was *not* in Barbour's hands, and in fact, it seems to have been beyond the control of any one pair of hands. Such confusion is all too typical of clandestine operations.

In the meantime, Thomas had gone to Norfolk, where the capture of the Norfolk Navy Yard by Virginia forces had made available a large amount of heavy ordnance. He apparently hoped to acquire some of the cannon for the use of Maryland troops. On 26 April he wrote to General Walter Gwynn, commander of Virginia forces in Norfolk: "Having felt it best to alter my plans with reference to the transportation of my heavy ordnance to Baltimore, I take pleasure in informing you that . . . I have at Fredericksburg a large and swift steamer subject to my orders, and *which* I beg to place at the disposal of the Virginia authorities, should they desire to run guns or other material of war up the Potomac or elsewhere. I do not know what steamer has been sent, but presume the George Peabody."[20] This letter suggests that arms intended for Maryland may already have been shipped by other means. It is more likely, however, that it had been decided to ship the weapons via canal to Lynchburg and then overland to Harpers Ferry and by rail to Baltimore.

Lack of concrete progress in organizing an army in Maryland led the potential forces to trickle away. On 4 May, Edward R. Dorsey, first lieutenant of Company A of the Baltimore City Guard, sent a letter to Governor Letcher via the Baltimore and Ohio Railroad offering his unit for incorporation into the Confederate army (not the Virginia army).[21]

On 8 May, Thomas addressed a letter to Governor Letcher from Frederick, Maryland, telling him that it seemed hopeless to expect the Maryland legislature to pass an act of secession. He offered his services to Virginia and said he believed two thousand to twenty-five hundred men would follow his example. He added: "The heavy guns furnished me by your excellency, I have deemed it imprudent in the present aspect of affairs to bring into Maryland. I have then, for the time being, placed them at the order of Colonel Jackson, the able and efficient Commanding Officer at Harpers Ferry, where they can be made of use."[22] The next day Colonel Jackson asked General Lee to furnish him with a competent ordnance officer so that he could mount the pieces which he identified as having come from "The Virginia Navy-yard."[23]

On 13 May, Governor Letcher received a telegram from the freight agent at Lynchburg saying that someone he did not know had ordered him to stop the shipment of cannon to Harpers Ferry. The same day the post commander at Lynchburg, D. A. Langhorne, sent a telegram to Letcher: "A gentleman representing himself as Soloman Cherry of Norfolk and on business in regard to the movement of cannon claiming to have been the agent in sending twenty

twenty-four pounder cannon from Norfolk [to] this place is here under suspicion and subjected thereby to great annoyance and danger. He says and has paper to show that he has been acting as agent of Colonel Francis J. Thomas of Maryland and in conjunction with Major Gorgas of South Carolina. If you do not remember him he desires to refer you to Colonel F. H. Smith, Colonel Marmaduke Johnson, and Dr. Bisbee." Letcher replied that these guns were orginally intended for Maryland and should be sent on to Harpers Ferry.[24] This shipment must have included cannon shipped from Norfolk or Richmond because the arsenal at Lexington was between Lynchburg and Harpers Ferry, not between Lynchburg and Norfolk.

On 17 May 1861, Thomas wrote to Colonel R. S. Garnett, adjutant-general of Virginia forces, headed "Headquarters Maryland volunteers serving in Virginia." The letter said:

> Pursuant to instructions from Colonel Jackson, based upon a letter to me from Colonel French, aide-de-camp to his excellency Governor Letcher, I have this day assumed command of the Maryland volunteers in this State. Numbers of the men, and especially a large number of the most valuable of the officers, have gone to Richmond and other points in Virginia. As it is desirable that all Maryland men should be together, I respectfully request an order be issued for them to report here. . . . Until better arms can be procured, I shall proceed to arm them with the flint-lock muskets issued to Mr. T. Parkin Scott of Baltimore, by Governor Letcher.

Maryland politics again entered the scene because Colonel Jackson added an endorsement which said: "There are some of the Maryland volunteers who object to serving with Col. Thomas, and in order to secure their services, I would suggest that they be mustered into the service of the Southern Confederacy, and that none except those who muster into the service of Virginia be placed under the command of Col. Thomas."[25]

A few days later, the matter had still not been resolved, and Thomas wrote to Colonel Garnett again on 22 May. About a thousand men were organized in units and were in Virginia, and he claimed that there were an additional fifteen hundred in Maryland waiting to come over. He urged that instructions be issued concerning them. Finally, on 27 May 1861, Garnett signed Special Order 126: "The volunteers from the State of Maryland, accepted into the Service of Virginia, will assemble at Charlestown, Va., and be there organized into regiments by Col. Francis J. Thomas and instructed in their duties. This command will be under the orders of the commanding officer at Harper's Ferry for service on that frontier."[26]

On 31 May, Thomas wrote again to Colonel Garnett, this time from Suffolk, Virginia. He had two companies of Maryland men with him and had been promised some additional troops by the commander at Norfolk. He proposed to launch an amphibious raid on Newport News and asked for General Lee's advice. Garnett replied that his instructions were to prepare the transports but not to act until intelligence had been collected and the operation was coordinated on both sides of the river. Governor Letcher may have been intrigued by the idea of an amphibious raid, for on 18 June he wrote to General Lee: "Oblige me by giving no orders to Company F, 1st Regiment of Virginia Volunteers, I have had a conversation today with Captain Maury, respecting some secret service, and if our plans shall be carried out, I will have need for this company."[27]

This company, a Richmond militia unit, was one of the best manned and trained in the Virginia forces. Initially it had been stationed at Aquia Creek, but on 14 June it was ordered back to Camp Lee in Richmond, where it was eventually incorporated into the Twenty-first Virginia Infantry Regiment.[28] In view of Maury's naval background, the operation he and Letcher had in mind may have been connected with Thomas's proposed amphibious raid.

The attack on Newport News did not materialize, and it was becoming more and more apparent that the secession of Maryland was a lost cause. On 27 June, George P. Kane, the marshal or commissioner of police in Baltimore, was arrested by the Union army and a Union military provost marshal appointed in his place.[29] Kane was one of the strongest supporters of the southern cause in Baltimore, and after his release from prison in late 1862 he found his way to Canada and then to Richmond, where he worked with General Winder, the commander of the Richmond area.

By 9 July, Thomas was back in the Shenandoah Valley. Now, however, instead of commanding troops, he was serving as chief of ordnance under General Joseph E. Johnston at Winchester. On that date, Major M. G. Harmon, the quartermaster at Staunton and a friend of Governor Letcher, telegraphed General Lee saying that Thomas was asking for the remaining three thousand of the five thousand muskets originally promised to Maryland. On the same day General Johnston remarked in a letter to Richmond that "the arms ordered by Colonel Thomas for the militia are not here yet.

The two generals [Harper and Jackson?] expect some 2,200, but at present we cannot arm them all."[30]

On 16 July, Thomas complained to Colonel Samuel Bassett French about the failure to deliver the muskets. Now, however, he merely said that they were needed to arm the militia; nothing more was said about troops from Maryland. In his letter to French, Thomas mentioned that he had just seen his forty-eight-hour-old son. Five days later Thomas was killed at the Battle of Manassas.[31]

The death of Thomas did not mean an end to attempts to operate against the Union in Maryland. There was considerable talk about organizing uprisings in the Maryland countryside, where federal troops were not immediately at hand. Arms were collected and men were recruited throughout the summer of 1861, but nothing came of it, and most of the men crossed the Potomac to join the Confederate army. Some remained to help operate an active underground in Maryland, and some went to Virginia for training and returned as spies and saboteurs. (Some of these activities are discussed in Chapter 6.) The machinations to help Maryland secede had an important impact on subsequent developments. They forced several Virginians who were to fill important posts in the Confederacy to face the importance and the difficulty of having an efficient clandestine capability—both to collect information and to operate against the enemy.

While the maneuvering involving Thomas had been under way, another chain of events had begun which had an even greater effect on the subsequent capability of Confederate intelligence. Clandestine channels for collecting information were being developed, and a signal capability was beginning. On 20 April 1861, Major William S. Barton of the Virginia militia in Fredericksburg telegraphed Governor Letcher: "A line of express may be established to Balta [Baltimore] from opposite Aquia Creek—a reliable man here will assist."[32] This proposal marked the beginning of the development of communications in the area of the lower Potomac that eventually evolved into the formal mechanism of the Confederate Signal Corps and its Secret Line.

On 21 April the Governor's Advisory Council asked Barton to send forces immediately to protect two steamers tied up at the railroad terminus on the north side of Aquia Creek. At about the same time, Barton was assigned Companies E and F of the First Virginia Infantry in Richmond.[33] These were among the best trained and equipped militia units in the state. As a lawyer in Fredericksburg Barton had corresponded with Letcher before the

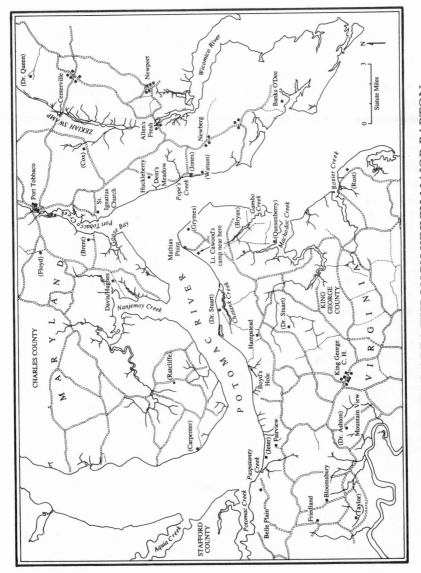

MAP SHOWING AREA THROUGH WHICH MAJOR BARTON
ESTABLISHED HIS SECRET ROUTE TO BALTIMORE. IT WAS
THE FIRST OF MANY CLANDESTINE OPERATIONS TO
TAKE PLACE HERE.

war. His family was well known in the area; one brother had graduated from West Point and another from VMI. He was as well qualified to develop the rudiments of an intelligence system as anyone who could be found at that time.

On 22 April, Brigadier General Daniel Ruggles, the new commander of the Virginia forces in the Fredericksburg area, sent a follow-up telegram to Letcher: "Can I draw on you for one hundred (100) dollars—Secret Service money to send a special messenger to Maryland immediately?" Letcher replied: "You are authorized to draw for the amount mentioned."[34] This exchange indicates that at the outset of the war, Governor Letcher already had in place an arrangement to provide funds for clandestine activity.

Barton or someone else apparently was developing a communication system up and down the Northern Neck as well as across the Potomac. On 24 April 1861, Major Thomas H. Williamson, professor of engineering at VMI, made a report of his examination to plan defenses for the area around Aquia Creek.[35] If the area were to be defended, it would need to be warned of the approach of enemy vessels, and a communication system would be imperative.

On 9 May 1861, the governor's Advisory Council told him that defenses should be improved along the Potomac and Chesapeake by "erecting signal stations along the rivers, and establishing a system for giving warning of the enemy's approach, as well as by signals from station to station as by runners and couriers into the back country."[36]

On 16 May 1861, a Union naval vessel reported that it had found a pole and halyard near Windmill Point on the Rappahannock, which local people had said was part of a signal system that could get messages upriver to Fredericksburg within an hour or two. Presumably a similar system could have been used along the Potomac as well. The system may have been set up in response to the Advisory Council's recommendation of 9 May.[37] Barton's original connection across the Potomac may have been with George W. Carpenter, whose house was on the Maryland shore a short distance above Maryland Point and opposite the mouth of Aquia Creek.[38]

Mail arrangements seem to have evolved elsewhere almost as rapidly as Barton's express line to Maryland. On 13 May 1861, George Thomas of St. Mary's County, Maryland, wrote to Letcher asking his permission to raise a company of Marylanders to be enrolled in the Virginia forces. He ended the letter by asking the governor to respond as soon as possible. "Letters passing through

Washington are *opened*. Anything sent to me should be placed in an office in this county." An endorsement, signed by R. D. Watson, was appended: "You will please direct the answer to this letter which was handed to me by my friend Thomas to Hampstead, King George County, Virginia."[39] The handwriting indicates that this was the same R. D. Watson who wrote a letter on 19 March 1865 summoning John Wilkes Booth's associate John H. Surratt to New York.[40] Watson was the twenty-six-year-old son of Major Roderick Watson, who lived on the Maryland side of the Potomac.

Captain Fleet William Cox of the Fortieth Virginia Infantry, writing to his sweetheart in Maryland on 20 June 1861, instructed her to send letters to him "by your private hand to Dr. Hooe's or to Hamstead [sic] Post Office; King George [County]. I write you a letter a week and send them by public or private conveyance as I can. Mr. Fred Wheelwright was in my room this morning he said I can send letters across at Hooe's Ferry, but I think that Col. Carpenter communicates more frequently with Virginia than any one else from Maryland. Mr. Compton said that he would give a letter to Mr. Carpenter to send to the Fresh [Allen's Fresh post office in Maryland] to you or would take it down himself."[41] Presumably "Col. Carpenter" was the Carpenter involved with Barton.

Cox was a graduate of VMI Class of 1849 and a widower. He had practiced law in Northumberland County, Virginia, and taught school in Westmoreland County before he organized a militia company that became part of the Fortieth Virginia Infantry.

He was stationed in King George County near Mathias Point at the time he wrote. The camp was probably located between the Hampstead Post Office and the Hooe Ferry to Maryland. The ferry, operated by the Hooe family for many years, crossed the river just below the present site of the Route 301 Highway Bridge across the Potomac. The Hooes were prominent people and related to many of the leading families in the Northern Neck. Daniel Ruggles's wife was a Hooe. On 25 June 1861, a landing party from the Union Potomac River Flotilla burned Dr. Abram Barnes Hooe's house, Barnesfield, and he moved to Waterloo, a house on the opposite side of Mathias Point. It was not as good a location as Barnesfield for communicating with Maryland, and his conveyance of mail seemed to have been taken over by Benjamin Grymes, whose house was near Mathias Point.

On 23 July 1861, Cox told his sweetheart: "If you direct your letters to Brooke Station, Stafford County, Va. to the care of Col. Jno. M. Brockenbrough—If they can be placed in the hands of Mr.

George Dent on the Maryland side to be sent over the river to the care of Mr. Ben Grimes [sic] on this side who will place them in the P.O. they will come direct." In addition to Major Roderick Watson, Dent had another neighbor, Thomas A. Jones, who helped him convey mail across the Potomac. On 1 September, Cox instructed his sweetheart to give her letters to "Mr. Jones near Mr. Dent's." In late 1861, both Dent and Jones were arrested and placed in Old Capitol Prison in Washington. Presumably Watson continued the traffic with the help of his daughter Mary, but before Dent and Jones were released in early 1862 Watson died.[42]

While Dent and Jones were in prison, an alternative route appears to have been organized. On 23 November 1861, the Confederate War Department wrote to General Theophilus H. Holmes, who had succeeded Ruggles as commander in the Fredericksburg area: "The Secretary of War directs me to say that, having made arrangements for getting newspapers from the United [sic] to the Confederate States at stated intervals, he desires that you will instruct Captain Beale to receive the packages on the Maryland shore every Tuesday and Thursday and convey them to the Hague, where they will be carried to Carter's Wharf, on the Rappahannock, by expressmen, who you are requested to furnish. At the latter place the packages will be delivered to Mr. J. J. Grindall or his agents for delivery here."[43]

The secretary of war was Judah P. Benjamin, who was involved with clandestine operations throughout his service in the Confederate cabinet. Captain Beale was Richard Lee Turberville Beale, who later became a brigadier general of cavalry. On 1 November 1861, Beale was promoted to major of the Ninth Virginia Cavalry regiment, which was stationed in the Northern Neck. The Hague lies near the head of lower Machodoc Creek, about twenty miles downriver from upper Machodoc Creek, which is near Mathias Point, the scene of the Dent-Watson-Jones mail routes. The Hague is more or less opposite Leonardtown on the Maryland side of the Potomac. The exchange arrangement could undoubtedly work well as long as the Ninth Cavalry was stationed nearby, but once it was transferred out of the area, new arrangements would have to be set up. The situation may have suggested the need for personnel dedicated to the handling of information who did not have to be replaced whenever combat units were moved.

Upon their return from prison, Dent and Jones appear to have continued to handle the mail across the Potomac with Jones as Dent's principal assistant instead of Watson. Jones was later incorporated into the regular Confederate Signal Corps system for the clandestine transfer of mail and dispatches and became its chief agent on the Maryland side, but that system, formalized in the fall of 1862, had its origins in arrangements begun by the state of Virginia in 1861. The Confederate inspector examining the Signal Corps in December 1864 stated that according to his contract Jones was to be paid with Virginia funds.[44]

It is probable that the "express" lines via Carpenter did not outlive the development of the other routes because entry into the Maryland part of the line was not convenient, it was more exposed to Union intervention, and it involved a longer overland route on the Maryland side. It may never have gone completely out of existence, however. Thomas Nelson Conrad described Carpenter's location as his point of entry into a special secret line he had set up. Conrad was captured at Carpenter's house by a landing party from the U.S. Potomac River Flotilla on 17 April 1865.[45]

While these systems for signaling and for passing letters and messages across the lines were being developed, the practice of espionage was also getting under way. For convenience of analysis it is useful to distinguish between "espionage"—the collection of information that the enemy does not want one to have—and "clandestine communications"—the transmission of messages for a wide variety of purposes including those required to operate the clandestine communications system itself as well as the information collected by means of espionage.

One of the officers of the U.S. regular army to offer his services to Virginia was Thomas Jordan of the West Point Class of 1840. Jordan made his offer to Letcher on 8 May 1861 and was nominated to be a lieutenant colonel of infantry in the Virginia Provisional Army on 7 May.[46] The astonishing order of the dates is probably the result of Jordan's written offer being nothing more than the formalization of a prearranged understanding.

Jordan's previous assignment had been in Washington, D.C., and before he left town he made arrangements to establish a flow of information from Washington into Virginia. One of Jordan's principal agents was Rose O'Neill Greenhow, the widow of a State Department official. She knew almost everybody of consequence in Washington and had access to information before her arrest by Union authorities on 23 August 1861. Others were William T. Smithson, president of the Farmers and Merchants Bank; Colonel Michael Thompson, a lawyer from South Carolina; and a young man named George Donnellan, who appears to have been the principal courier for the group. In addition, Benjamin Ogle Tayloe (who lived next door to the house occupied later in the war by Secretary of State Seward on Lafayette Square) had the education, skill, motivation, and opportunity to have been active in Confederate espionage in Washington. Beneath them there were lesser agents, couriers, and informants. In spite of considerable naïveté in their operations, this group collected and delivered to the Virginia, and later the Confederate, forces a considerable amount of useful information about Union military and political activities. Such an organization could not have been put together overnight, and the personnel must have been given some instruction, even if it was minimal and ad hoc.

Governor Letcher had spent a great deal of time in Washington up to 1 January 1860 as a member of Congress. In early 1861, he was back in Washington on a visit that lasted as late as 10 February.[47] Jordan may have been acting for Letcher in organizing the network to procure information that could help Virginia survive in the coming months. Jordan later said that he had adopted the alias of Thomas John Rayford to use in cipher correspondence with Mrs. Greenhow before he left Washington and that the cipher system they used was one he had devised in April 1861. He also noted that it was a poor cipher, hastily conceived, and would have been replaced if Mrs. Greenhow had not been arrested.[48]

As soon as he was commissioned, Jordan was sent to the Virginia forces guarding the Manassas Junction area in northern Virginia. There he found an old acquaintance, Cornelius Boyle, who had been appointed a major of Virginia Volunteers on 29 April 1861. Dr. Boyle had been a physician in Washington for many years and had been the head of the National Volunteers, a politico-military organization in the District of Columbia that sponsored military organizations and political activity favorable to the South.[49] On 16 March 1861, three officers of the National Volunteers, C. K. Sherman, R. Cleary, and William Nelson Barker (later a captain in the Confederate Signal Corps) wrote to Louis T. Wigfall, the former senator from Texas who was acting as an agent for the Confederate government, asking if their organization could be mustered into the Confederate army. On 4 April the new Confederate War Department in Montgomery, Alabama, replied, telling them to contact L. Q. Washington for advice.[50]

Lucius Quintius Washington of King George County, Virginia, was a prominent journalist in Washington, D.C., and a friend and correspondent of Governor Letcher. He had reported information on affairs in Washington to Letcher and to the Confederate secretary of war.[51] Later he moved to Richmond as the chief clerk of the Confederate State Department. He may have been the man who acted for Letcher in helping Jordan set up his spy network. Washington, however, was unable to arrange for arms for the three to four hundred men of the National Volunteers, and they, with the National Rifles, another prosouthern District of Columbia militia company, were too few in numbers to tackle the few regular soldiers, sailors, and marines stationed in Washington.

Dr. Boyle and the National Volunteers could not cope with their exposed situation and retreated to Virginia. There, in spite of a physical disability, Dr. Boyle was commissioned and assigned as commander of the Alexandria Battalion of Virginia Volunteers, and many of his men ultimately became part of Company H of the Seventh Virginia Infantry Regiment.[52] In April 1862, however, in an excess of legalism, the Confederates mustered many Maryland and District of Columbia soldiers out of the Confederate service on the grounds that they were "aliens."

On 11 May 1861, Major Boyle was assigned to command the Manassas Junction post. This was an area command as opposed to a unit command. He was nominally responsible for the police and security of the area and for other administrative duties. In July he was acting as a provost marshal of the troops near Manassas, and eventually he became provost marshal and commandant of the post at Gordonsville, where he stayed for the remainder of the war.[53]

The best clue to Major Boyle's true role in the Confederate army comes from correspondence regarding an incident in November 1863, when General A. R. Lawton, the Confederate quartermaster, asked that Boyle be transferred to the Quartermaster Department. This may have been nothing more than bureaucratic empire-building on Lawton's part, but it stirred up a hornet's nest. Boyle protested the transfer on the grounds that he had been assigned to "*special* duty" for General Johnston and then for General Lee. The transfer was disapproved, and Lee endorsed the document, writing in his own hand: "Major Boyle was commissioned specially for the service on which he is now engaged. I know no one who can take his place."[54] Lee's words carry extra authority because he was working closely with the governor's Advisory Council when Boyle was commissioned.

It seems likely that Boyle's "special" duties involved the reception and forwarding of messages and agents to and from Confederate intelligence operations in northern Virginia and in the Washington area. He clearly worked primarily for the Army of Northern Virginia and not for the Signal Corps. A note from Lieutenant Colonel George W. Lay in Boyle's Compiled Service Record provides some clues. On 5 March 1862, Boyle had asked to be transferred from the Virginia Army to the Provisional Army of the Confederate States. In a note supporting Boyle's request, Lay said that Boyle had been put on detached duty by General Beauregard (the first Confederate commander to take over the army in northern Virginia from the Virginia command) and continued by General Johnston. Lay added: "Major Boyle's duties have to a great extent been performed in connection with this office. . . . His peculiar duties at Manassas covered a great deal of ground."[55]

Colonel Lay's Compiled Service Record helps to put his remarks into context. He was a graduate of West Point in the Class of 1842; among his classmates were several future generals in the Confederate service, including James Longstreet, D. H. Hill, and Earl Van Dorn. He was also a son-in-law of Judge John A. Campbell, the assistant secretary of war in the Confederate cabinet. He complained bitterly about assignments that prevented him from attaining what he felt to be a respectable rank, but he continued to plow ahead at his assigned job. He was appointed a lieutenant colonel of infantry in the Provisional Army of Virginia on 7 May 1861. He appears to have been involved with Colonel Jordan to some extent during the next few months because Jordan sent a note to Mrs. Lay at the Warren Green Hotel at Warrenton in July 1861. On 7 October 1861, Lay was ordered to report to General Joseph E. Johnston, who was commanding the Army of Northern Virginia. In January 1862, Jordan was ordered west with General Beauregard. Lay may have taken over Jordan's intelligence duties at this point. He would then have been responsible for giving Boyle's agents their assignments and reading their reports when they came in.[56]

By Special Order 1/22 published on 2 January 1863, Lay was assigned to be assistant to the chief of the newly organized Conscription Bureau under General Gabriel J. Rains, West Point Class of 1827 (one year ahead of Jefferson Davis and two years ahead of R. E. Lee). Despite the title of his bureau, Rains spent most of his time working with the new, highly secret activity of torpedo development as head of the "Torpedo Bureau."[57]

When Lay left the Army of Northern Virginia in early 1863, his intelligence duties must have been taken over by another officer on General Lee's staff, possibly Lieutenant Colonel Edward Murray of the West Point Class of 1841. There were many other potential recruits for espionage or other clandestine tasks available to Virginia in the opening days of the war. After the first states in the South had seceded, at least twenty-six persons wrote to Governor Letcher offering their services or volunteering information.[58] Among them, George R. Bedinger and John S. Gallaher had connections with people later involved in Confederate intelligence work. Gallaher had worked for the *Richmond Whig* in 1837 and later moved to Jefferson County, Virginia, where he headed the *Free Press* of Charles Town. There he was a friend of Congressman A. R. Boteler. Bedinger was a first cousin of Edwin G. Lee, a brigadier general in the Confederate army and engaged in secret service work as the last Confederate commissioner in Canada. The Boteler, Lee, and Bedinger families were neighbors just outside of Shepherdstown, Virginia. Other neighbors included the Lucas, Yates, and Beall families. Daniel Bedinger Lucas was one of General E. G. Lee's assistants in Canada, and John Yates Beall had a long and active career in irregular warfare before being hanged by the Union as a spy on 24 February 1865.

Gallaher's son John, Jr., was in business in Washington, D.C., with John M. McCalla, a Washington lawyer. McCalla's son Dr. John McCalla, Jr., spent the war in Washington and kept a diary noting some of his social activities. On 4 July 1861, Dr. McCalla visited Dr. C. Duvall of Prince George's County, Maryland, in the company of George M. Emack of Beltsville, Maryland. Emack was the son of Elbert Grandison Emack, who had a large truck gardening farm at Beltsville. The elder Emack had married the daughter of a Maryland congressman and had been a successful grocer on Capitol Hill in Washington before he moved to Beltsville. In the 1830s, he was a neighbor of Rose Greenhow and Duff Green, who became an ardent supporter of the Confederacy.[59]

George Emack was active in the summer of 1861 in recruiting and other clandestine work in southern Maryland. In September he was captured by a group of Union soldiers who started to take him to prison in Washington. When they stopped to rest near a village with the odd name, T.B., in southern Prince George's County, Emack stabbed his guard and escaped to Virginia. In Richmond he was made a lieutenant of infantry and assigned to the guard at Libby Prison, where the Union prisoners of war learned to dislike him intensely.[60] In 1862 he became captain of Company B of the First Maryland Cavalry Regiment. A number of men from that unit were detailed to the Confederate Signal Corps. George's elder brother, James William Emack, appears to have worked as a civilian for General Winder, the provost marshal of Richmond, whose office was responsible for handling prisoners of war (among other things).[61]

Elbert Grandison Emack, the father, was an ardent supporter of the South. His newspapers and newspaper clippings that have survived indicate that he subscribed to the *Baltimore Sun*, the *Philadelphia Inquirer*, the weekly *Constitutional Union* of Washington, *the South* of Baltimore, and *the Prince Georgian*, published in Upper Marlborough, Maryland.[62] He may have subscribed to other Washington papers as well, but no clippings or copies have survived. The assortment of papers suggests, however, that Emack may have been one of the people who provided newspapers to the Confederate courier system.

Dr. Duvall, the friend of Dr. McCalla, was Emack's best friend,[63] and Duvall lived about halfway between Emack and W. W. Bowie, who can be associated with the Confederate courier line. Thomas Jones, the Confederate "mail agent" at Popes Creek, Maryland, included in his published experiences in 1893 the story of George Emack's escape from his captors. Jones also wrote: "Quite a prominent gentleman of Prince George's County, Maryland, was very active as a Confederate mail-agent. He turned his attention to gardening, and as he lived but a short distance from Washington City, would drive his way on into town and get a load of manure in which he would hide the matter destined for the South, and bring it safely out."[64] This "gardener" could well be Elbert Grandison Emack.

We have no way of knowing how many other people may have written to Letcher or to other members of the governor's Advisory Council whose letters were lost, destroyed, or filed with sensitive material that was destroyed or has not yet been found. One such example is Thomas Green of Richmond and Washington. He had been a lawyer, journalist, and land speculator in Richmond, where he probably knew Gallaher. About 1840, he moved to Washington, D.C., to represent the descendants of Virginians who had claims against the U.S. government stemming from the Revolution and the War of 1812. His home was a Federal period mansion on a large lot, occupying nearly the entire block on Constitution Avenue between Seventeenth and Eighteenth Streets N.W. (the Pan American Union headquarters now occupies the site). Green kept a diary for several years, which shows that he knew a number of people who later may have been involved in Confederate intelligence work.[65] These included Dr. Richard Henry Stuart of King George County, Virginia, Beverly Kennon of the U.S. Navy, whose son, Beverly Kennon, Jr., turns up later in this book, and the Barton family of Fredericksburg, who were his cousins. (Again, association with intelligence work seems to run through groups of relatives and friends.)

Thomas Nelson Conrad said that Green provided him with a safe place to stay when he was in Washington. In 1863, Colonel (later brigadier general) Lafayette C. Baker, the Union counterintelligence officer, had Green watched by detectives who reported that a Mrs. Mason lived in his house and traveled frequently to Baltimore and that Green traveled to Baltimore three or four times a week, possibly for the purpose of conveying military information to the rebels.[66] Given the nature of Washington society, Green probably knew Greenhow, Jordan, Smithson, and Boteler. Unfortunately, there is no available evidence on that point. Green later married Anne Corbin Lomax, sister of the Confederate cavalry General Lindsay Lomax. Both Green and his wife were arrested in 1865 for possible complicity in the Lincoln assassination but released for lack of evidence.

Green would have been ideally placed to provide Richmond with information on the Washington scene. He also had the talent to organize and manage espionage activity. He could have been providing information to the governors of Virginia during his entire residence in Washington, but so far no evidence of such activity has turned up.

Even though the people and incidents mentioned here are no doubt only a part of the total, they make it clear that Governor Letcher and his Virginia associates had many opportunities to establish useful intelligence sources in the North. Some of the activities that they started for the state of Virginia seem to have been inherited by the Confederacy. One may presume that the organization recruited originally by Jordan evolved into an espionage network supporting the Army of Northern Virginia.

Little has been known about what happened in Washington after the arrest of "Rebel Rose" and her colleagues, but surely Confederate espionage in the capitol continued. A number of reports in the possession of Lieutenant Colonel Charles Venable of General Lee's staff have been preserved (see Chapter 4). These date mostly from 1863 and 1864 and show that a considerable volume of reasonably accurate information was still flowing from Washington to Richmond at that time.

From a knowledge of how espionage systems usually operate, and various other bits and pieces of information, it is possible to put together a plausible account of the Confederate system and how it probably operated. To begin with, it is likely that Jordan was not the sole organizer of Confederate intelligence in Washington. Governor Letcher visited Washington in February. John Bankhead Magruder, Custis Lee, and R. E. Lee were in the city before they left for Virginia in April. There were also a number of wealthy, influential men in Washington who had strong prosouthern sympathies, including William Wilson Corcoran, Thomas Green, and Benjamin Ogle Tayloe. Given the nature of Washington society, all three of these men probably knew those three Confederate officers.

Mrs. Elizabeth Lomax, mother of Anne and Lindsay Lomax, noted in her diary that Tayloe, Magruder, and Custis Lee had a long conference on the morning of 21 April 1861, the day before Robert E. Lee left Washington for Richmond.[67] Tayloe used the Farmers and Merchants Bank and therefore knew Smithson. It is probable that the espionage organization included all of these men and that only a part of it was crippled by the arrest of Greenhow and Smithson.

Donnellan seems to have continued to act as a courier for some time, organizing a system through southern Maryland, but on 18 March 1862 he was appointed a lieutenant of engineers and assigned to General Magruder's staff.[68] He was doubtless replaced by one or more equally daring operators. It is likely that by early 1864 Lieutenant Walter Bowie held this position. Bowie was a prominent attorney from Upper Marlboro in Prince George's County, Maryland. He seems to have operated in southern Maryland until mid-1864, when he embarked on a short career as one of Mosby's Rangers (see Chapter 6).

Among the Venable papers is a detailed and accurate account, dated 27 April 1864 apparently in Bowie's handwriting and signed simply "B," telling of preparations to reinforce Grant in anticipation of his Wilderness campaign. The report is addressed only to "General," and its use of intimate language indicates that the author was well acquainted with that general. From the text and its presence in Venable's papers, there seems to be little question that the general was Robert E. Lee.[69] The information in the report is too varied to have been collected by one agent operating alone. One can postulate that Tayloe and Green managed a considerable Confederate network in Washington and that Bowie's job was to summarize and report the information they collected. The Washington network probably also included Major Cornelius Boyle, who started at Manassas and eventually became the provost marshal at Gordonsville. He probably maintained the line by which requests for information and other correspondence were sent to the Washington network through northern Virginia.

Among the troops facing Washington, Jordan was undoubtedly the staff officer responsible for receiving the products of the net and passing instructions to its members. When Jordan left to accompany General Beauregard to a new assignment, his place was probably filled by George W. Lay, a West Pointer of the Class of 1842 and an acquaintance of Jordan. Lay appears to have held this position until mid-1862, when he too left to work for Beauregard. Later he served with General Rains, the newly appointed chief of conscription.[70] It seems clear that Rains did not work hard at conscription but did work hard at developing explosive mines, and Lay's experience with clandestine operations may have been useful to Rains in connection with the creation of the Torpedo Bureau.

By the time General Lee took over command of the Army of Northern Virginia in 1862, several men on his staff seem to have been involved with handling intelligence matters. Of these staff officers, Walter H. Taylor, Charles Marshal, and Charles Venable all appear to have had some contact with intelligence. It is probable that Venable was the staff officer responsible for correspondence with the net. One of General Stuart's cavalry scouts, Channing Smith, mentions in a letter dated 10 April 1864 that he is enclosing some stamps (U.S. stamps probably) for Major Venable's use.[71] That would be appropriate if Venable was writing instructions that might be introduced into the U.S. mail at some point.

The principal agents in Washington doubtless worked with many others who collected information from persons in the U.S. government, both willing contributors and those from whom information could be elicited without arousing suspicion. The system appears to have produced useful intelligence for the Confederacy throughout the war. There is no indication that it was ever put out of action. Furthermore, it was probably but one of several espionage systems operated by the Confederacy.

Notes

ABBREVIATIONS

NA   National Archives

OR   U.S. War Department, *The War of the Rebellion: A Compilation of the Official Records of the Union and Confederate Armies.* 128 vols. Washington, D.C.: U.S. Government Printing Office, 1880–1901.

ORN   U.S. Navy Department, *Official Records of the Union and Confederate Navies in the War of the Rebellion.* 30 vols. Washington, D.C.: U.S. Government Printing Office, 1894–1914.

RG   Record Group

1. Douglas Southall Freeman, *R. E. Lee,* 4 vols. (New York: Charles Scribner's Sons, 1935), 1:448.

2. James I. Robertson, ed., *Proceedings of the Advisory Council of the State of Virginia* (Richmond: Virginia State Library and Archives, 1977), p. 1.

3. See Governor John Letcher, Personal Papers, George C. Marshall Research Library, Lexington, Va. The conclusion is based on a review of numerous letters in these files. The official files of the governors of Virginia in the Virginia State Library are useful for this period. The files of incoming materials are intact, although not all incoming material was deposited in these files. The letterbooks containing copies of the governor's outgoing correspondence are missing for the years 1860–65. A few outgoing letters and speeches are reflected in the incoming material in the form of drafts that were filed there because they were not ready to copy in the outgoing letter binders.

4. Numerous letters in Letcher Papers.

5. Theo. P. Mayo to Letcher, 27 April 1860, Executive Files of Governor John Letcher, Virginia State Library and Archives, Richmond.

6. William H. Richardson, Department of Military Affairs, Adjutant General's Correspondence, Virginia State Library and Archives.

The original holdings of the state arsenals were as follows:

Report on Status of Weapons in Virginia in September 1860

	In Militia Units	Lexington	Richmond
Muskets (Rifled)*	400	10	12
Muskets (Percussioned)*	2121	496	42
Muskets (Flint-lock)	5801	27,815	20,372
Rifles (Percussioned)	955	20	45
Rifles (Flint Lock)	1596	1,007	690

*These were muskets that had been altered to the form indicated.

7. A series of documents dealing with this episode in 1857 is in the Adjutant General's Correspondence, Virginia State Library and Archives.

8. Evelyn D. Ward, *The Children of Bladensfield* (New York: Viking Press, 1978), p. 38.

9. William N. Ward to Letcher, 23 July 1861, Letcher Executive Files.

10. The account of events in Maryland given here is based on J. Thomas Scharf, *History of Maryland,* 3 vols. (1879; rpt. Hatboro, Pa.: Tradition Press, 1967), 3:395–431.

11. Thomas to Letcher, April 1861. This letter was in the Executive Files of

Governor Letcher in the Virginia State Library in 1980 but could not be found in 1986.

12. West Point Alumni Foundation, *Register of Graduates and Former Cadets of the United States Military Academy* (West Point, 1962).

13. Information on Boteler comes from *Biographical Directory of the American Congress, 1774–1971* (Washington, D.C.: U.S. Government Printing Office, 1971), and from a fragmentary autobiography published in the *Shepherdstown* (West Virginia) *Register* over a period of several weeks in 1933 and 1934.

14. Several warm letters from Greenhow to Boteler, written in 1863, are in the Alexander R. Boteler Papers, William R. Perkins Library, Duke University, Durham, N.C.

15. Letcher Executive Files.

16. Mason to Letcher, with attachments, 7 May 1861, Letcher Executive Files.

17. Robertson, ed., *Proceedings of the Advisory Council of the State of Virginia,* p. 5.

18. Ibid.

19. Letcher Executive Files.

20. *OR,* Ser. 1, vol. 51, pt. 2, p. 45. The *George Peabody* was a Chesapeake Bay passenger ship.

21. Letcher Executive Files.

22. Ibid. Thomas and T. J. "Stonewall" Jackson had known each other since cadet days at West Point.

23. *OR,* Ser. 1, vol. 2, p. 821.

24. Letcher Executive Files. Letcher endorsed a telegram from J. R. Nicklin dated 13 May 1861 to this effect.

25. *OR,* Ser. 1, vol. 2, p. 856. T. Parkin Scott was apparently the recipient of the muskets sent by Letcher from the arsenal at Lexington.

26. *OR,* Ser. 1, vol. 51, pt. 2, p. 101; ibid., vol. 2, p. 885.

27. Ibid., vol. 2, p. 896; Letcher to Lee, 18 June 1861, Box 18, Folder 14, Letcher Papers.

28. Louis H. Manarin and Lee A. J. Wallace, *Richmond Volunteers, 1861–1865* (Richmond: Western Press, 1963), pp. 231–32.

29. *OR,* Ser. 1, vol. 2, p. 139.

30. Harmon to Lee, 9 July 1861, Letcher Executive Files; Johnston to Cooper, *OR,* Ser. 1, vol. 2, p. 969.

31. Thomas to French, 16 July 1861, Letcher Executive Files; *OR,* Ser. 1, vol. 2, p. 475. French was another acquaintance of Thomas from cadet days at West Point.

32. Letcher Executive Files.

33. Robertson, ed., *Proceedings of the Advisory Council of the State of Virginia,* p. 3; William S. Barton, Compiled Service Record, NA.

34. Letcher Executive Files.

35. Mary Alice Wills, *The Confederate Blockade of Washington, D.C., 1861–1862* (Parson, W.Va.: McClain Printing Co., 1975), p. 21; *ORN,* Ser. 1, vol. 4, p. 771.

36. Robertson, ed., *Proceedings of the Advisory Council of the State of Virginia,* p. 75.

37. *ORN,* Ser. 1, vol. 4, p. 468.

38. The census of 1850 showed Carpenter's real property valued at $7,000, making him one of the most prosperous residents of Charles County, Maryland.

39. Letcher Executive Files.

40. Investigation and Trial Papers Relating to the Assassination of President Lincoln, M-599, reel 3, frame 0114, RG 153, NA.

41. Cox to Mary Turner, 20 June 1861, Fleet William Cox Letters, University of Virginia Library, Charlottesville.

42. Cox to Mary Turner, 23 July, 1 September 1861, Ibid.; Thomas A. Jones, *J. Wilkes Booth* (Chicago: Laird & Lee, 1893), pp. 20–21.

43. *OR*, Ser. 1, vol. 51, pt. 2, p. 389.

44. J. Louis Smith, Captain and Assistant Inspector General, CSA, to James A. Seddon, Secretary of War, 21 December 1864, Letters to the Confederate War Department, RG 109, NA.

45. Thomas Nelson Conrad, *A Confederate Spy* (New York: J. S. Ogilvie, 1892), p. 79; *ORN*, Ser. 1, vol. 5, p. 555.

46. Letcher Executive Files; Robertson, ed., *Proceedings of the Advisory Council of the State of Virginia*, p. 65.

47. Letcher to Greenlee Davidson, 11 February 1861, Letcher Papers.

48. *OR*, Ser. 1, vol. 5, p. 928.

49. Cornelius Boyle, Compiled Service Record, NA; U.S. Congress, House of Representatives, *Alleged Hostile Organization against the Government within the District of Columbia*, 36th Cong., 2d sess., Report 79, 14 February 1861. It is interesting how many physicians became involved in Confederate intelligence work. Their need to call on patients of all walks of life provided a useful cover in dealing with members of a clandestine organization.

50. *OR*, Ser. 1, vol. 53, p. 135; telegram sent by the Confederate War Department, 4 April 1861, M-524, RG 109, NA.

51. Letcher Executive Files; telegrams received by the Confederate War Department, RG 109, NA.

52. Ralph W. Donnelly, "District of Columbia Confederates," *Military Affairs* 23 (Winter 1959–60): 207; see also Robert Underwood Johnson and Clarence Clough Buel, eds., *Battles and Leaders of the Civil War*, 4 vols. (1884–88; rpt. New York: Castle Books, 1956), 1:12–13.

53. Letcher Executive Files; Cornelius Boyle, Compiled Service Record, NA.

54. Boyle to General A. R. Lawton, 16 November 1863, endorsed by General Lee on 26 November 1863, Cornelius Boyle, Compiled Service Record, NA.

55. Boyle to Colonel George W. Lay, 5 March 1862, endorsed by Lay on 16 March 1862, ibid.

56. Ellsworth Eliot, Jr., *West Point and the Confederacy* (New York: G. A. Baker, 1941), p. xxi; George W. Lay, Compiled Service Record, NA.

57. William Davis Waters, "Gabriel J. Rains: Torpedo General of the Confederacy" (M.A. thesis, Wake Forest University, 1971), p. 28.

58. These letters are in Letcher Executive Files.

59. McCalla's diary and other family papers are in the Duke University Library. Other information from Ellen P. Emack of Hyattsville, Maryland, George Emack's niece.

60. William C. Harris, *Prison Life in the Tobacco Warehouse of Richmond* (Philadelphia: George W. Childs, 1862), pp. 133–34.

61. James William Emack to Mother, 7, 21 July 1862, in the possession of Ellen P. Emack. He never says that he is working for Winder, but the context seems to indicate it.

62. The papers, clippings, and family letters are in the possession of E. G.

Emack's granddaughter, Ellen P. Emack, and Elizabeth Cullison of Cabool, Missouri, a granddaughter of George Emack.

63. According to his granddaughter, Ellen P. Emack.

64. Jones, *J. Wilkes Booth*, p. 31.

65. Green's diary is in Virginia Historical Society, Richmond.

66. Alfred Cridge to Baker, 19 June 1863, Office of the Judge Advocate General, Turner-Baker Papers, No. 1528, RG 94, NA.

67. Elizabeth Lindsay Lomax, *Leaves from an Old Washington Diary* (New York: Dutton, 1943), p. 149.

68. George Donnellan, Compiled Service Record, NA.

69. B to General, 27 April 1864, Charles Venable Papers, Southern Historical Collection, University of North Carolina, Chapel Hill.

70. George W. Lay, Compiled Service Record, NA.

71. Smith to General, 10 April 1864, Venable Papers.

3

The Secret Signal Corps

One organization stands out in marked contrast with the improvisation and immaturity that characterized the Confederacy's early efforts at secret warfare—the Confederate army Signal Corps. A tribute to the foresight and imagination of the Confederate leadership and to its prime mover, Edward Porter Alexander, a young West Point-trained Georgian, the Signal Corps consisted from the outset of a small, handpicked group of men, well educated, well disciplined, trained in the arts of secret communication, and sworn by oath to secrecy. As such, it was ideally suited for a covert role, hidden by the overt mission of providing military communications. The North never developed a comparable organization.[1]

In the decade before the war, a medical officer in the U.S. Army, Albert James Myer, had devised a system of visual signals which offered the first practical answer to the age-old problem of battlefield communications for command and control. The morse type of electromagnetic telegraph had been used for strategic communications in Crimea, but it required wire strung on poles, power from the cumbersome wet-cell batteries of the time, instruments to send and receive, and skilled operators. Myer offered a way to communicate using a cheap, lightweight kit that could arch over the battlefield to the limits of vision. In many respects, his system was the forerunner of the military telecommunications made possible by wireless radio a half-century later.

As a youth in New York State, Myer had been an operator on a line that used the Bain system, an early competitor of Morse. (Alexander Bain, a Scottish doctor, used a two-element code, not unlike modern Morse, in contrast to American Morse, which used four elements—dot, space, short dash, long dash.) Myer's interest in telegraphy continued through years of medical school and was evident in his graduation thesis, on a sign language for the deaf. As an assistant surgeon in the army, he was stationed in the West, where the smoke and hand signs of the Plains Indians intrigued less astute observers. His idea took shape: a flag, waved to the left or right of the sender, representing the dot-dash of the Bain code. At night, a torch would replace the flag, with a second torch laid at the feet of the sender to serve as a reference point for the distant viewer.

The genius behind the Myer system was that it was light and easily transportable, it could be improvised in the absence of equipment, it appeared to be secure from unintended eyes, and, aided by telescopes and relays, its range could be extended and networks formed. But Myer had a more revolutionary idea. He wanted to see introduced a separate corps of professional military signalmen, serving at the side of generals as an essential element of each headquarters. And he saw himself, naturally, as the head of such a corps.

Early overtures to Washington did not elicit a response from the army, and the navy indicated that it was content with its time-honored nautical flags. Eventually, though, Myer received a hearing from the army. A review board was set up by Adjutant General Samuel Cooper to evaluate Myer's proposal, and Robert E. Lee was appointed to head it. A second lieutenant of engineers fresh from the military academy, Edward Porter Alexander of Georgia, was detailed to assist Myer, and together they perfected the system to the satisfaction of the army review board. The Senate Military Affairs Committee, chaired by Jefferson Davis of Mississippi, a former secretary of war, conducted hearings, and, although Davis refused to entertain the creation of a separate corps or the elevation of Myer, the system was adopted and Myer designated signal officer of the army. He was promptly sent west to field test the system under campaign conditions. There he was, a one-man signal system, when war erupted and he was hurriedly ordered back east to begin training assistants.

Even as Myer was returning to accept the challenge (and the chance to realize his dream of rank and glory), circumstances conspired to rob him of the honor of being the first to bring his brainchild into battle. Alexander, Myer's brilliant student and colleague, had resigned from the army to serve the South. Jefferson Davis, now president of the Confederacy, received Alexander's proposal to set up signals for the forts guarding the southern coast but instead ordered him to northern Virginia to install a system for General Beauregard.

Alexander, a captain of engineers, went to work with a will. Men detailed to him to learn the mysteries of signaling found the West Pointer a demanding taskmaster. He wanted educated, "sharp" men, quick learners like himself, brave enough to stand exposed to enemy fire, and he was determined to get first-class performance— on the threat of return to infantry ranks for those who failed to meet his exacting standards. After extracting an oath of secrecy, he imparted his variant of the Myer code and drilled the men in the fundamentals. Then, to give them further training, he established signal stations in the Centreville-Manassas area and put them to work. Their schooling was interrupted by the advance of northern forces for what was to become the First Battle of Manassas (or Bull Run). Alexander pulled his men back from Centreville in the face of the advance and permitted most of his detailees to return to their regiments. He remained at his central signal station on an elevation (now known as Signal Hill) which offered an excellent view of the developing battle. Suddenly he spotted the reflection of the sun on bayonets. An attempt was being made to flank the Confederates. Alexander flagged a warning to one of his trainees near the Stone Bridge—look to your left; you are turned! The message was received, and, in the best Hollywood tradition, the threat was averted. Captain Alexander was one of the heroes of the day, and the future of the Myer-Alexander signal system was secure in the Confederate army. (Myer, in chagrin, unable to get into action on the Union side, had to point to southern success to persuade federal authorities to increase their support for him.)

In the aftermath of Manassas, Alexander set about to train, equip, and expand the signal capacity of the Confederate army. He was assisted by William Nelson Barker, a Pennsylvanian by birth and a District of Columbia resident and government worker but a staunch prosecessionist serving as a lieutenant in the First Virginia Infantry Regiment. His brother James Hillhouse Alexander, a detailed private, was put to work developing a manual of instruction, to which was appended a cipher, known as the "court" or "diplomatic" cipher, which was to become the standard cipher of the Confederate army and the government establishment. A Maryland secessionist and former member of the dispersed state legislature, E. Pliny Bryan of Prince George's County, helped to set up a "manufactory" to turn out the flags and torches needed. The cadre of the Confederate army Signal Corps took form, ready for assignment.

The Manassas experience demonstrated more than the ability to transmit information—it showed the contribution a signal officer could make as the "eyes," as well as the long-distance "voice," of a commander. His vantage point, required for line-of-sight signaling, gave the signal officer a natural observation post. The extension of signal stations through relays broadened this information-gathering potential. For a commander, the signal officer was a source of intelligence as well as a means of controlling formations.[2]

The intelligence role for the embryonic Signal Corps would later expand as members learned to intercept and read the signals of their opponents, but it was there from the start. E. Pliny Bryan, something of a daredevil, volunteered to go into Washington as an agent. There he proposed to rent a room with a window that could be visible to Confederate positions across the river. By motions of the shutter or a lamp, he would signal information he had obtained about enemy movements. Before the scheme could be carried out, Confederate forces fell back from their Potomac positions and were no longer in sight of the city.[3]

A young associate of Bryan and a fellow Marylander, Charles H. Cawood of the Seventeenth Virginia, had also been detailed and shared Bryan's earlier adventures with the signal system. Cawood eventually took over the communication with his native state begun by the Virginians under Ruggles and Barton, facilitating the passage of information and people across the Potomac and reporting his observations of enemy movements on and along the river.[4]

While these and other early ventures into military signaling and intelligence-gathering were taking place in northern Virginia, some comparable experience was being gained in the southeastern part of the state. James F. Milligan, an extraordinary "old salt," whose acquaintance with signaling came from naval experience, had established a network of signal stations in the Norfolk-Portsmouth area, on the south bank of the James. Here also communications were combined with observation.[5]

Unlike the Myer system Alexander was using and teaching, which was developed for army use, Milligan applied naval signals on land. He used colored balls hoisted in prearranged fashion on a pole to provide a code that could be read at some distance, although it was a slow means of transmitting. Still, the system worked along the irregular banks of the James, with its peninsulas, islands, and inlets, and Milligan, although serving in the Virginia state navy at the time, was concurrently commissioned captain in the Confederate army and authorized on 22 April 1862 to raise a signal corps, eventually of two companies, for the Department of Norfolk.

Across the James from Milligan on the Peninsula, in the area around Williamsburg and Yorktown, a third major experiment in military signaling and reporting took shape under a volunteer civilian aide serving on the staff of General John Bankhead ("Prince John") Magruder, William Norris—another Marylander. In contrast to the rough-hewn, largely self-educated Milligan, son of an Irish immigrant, Norris was an urbane, cultivated Baltimorean, forty years old, a lawyer educated at Yale, with family ties in Virginia. He had served as judge advocate to the U.S. Pacific Squadron in San Francisco during the Gold Rush days and returned to settle and raise a family at his father's estate near Reisterstown, Maryland. His southern ties determined his course in 1861, and, like thousands of his fellow Marylanders, he crossed the Potomac to serve the Confederacy.[6]

Nautical signals were, of course, no novelty to Norris. He visited Norfolk to see how Milligan's network had been established, then returned to propose a similar network for Magruder. On 28 July 1861 he was authorized to set up a system, devising his code with colored balls and flags hoisted on a pole. He also began to run agents into enemy territory to observe and report their findings, and in this way he earned a reputation with Magruder that won him a commission as captain and signal officer to the commander of the Army of the Peninsula in the fall of 1861.

From these Virginia beginnings in the spring and early summer of 1861, especially Alexander's success at Manassas, the conception of a formal organization matured that winter. The Signal Corps was authorized by Congress on 19 April 1862 and implemented by a general order of 29 May 1862—anticipating by a year similar action on the northern side for poor Myer. The Confederate War Department elected to place its chief signal officer—the head of the corps—under the adjutant and inspector general, in a semi-autonomous role, serving the executive branch of the government. Though offered the position, Alexander declined in favor of field service, and, because he was a West Pointer of promise, his wishes were respected. Alexander had a distinguished war record as an artilleryman in the Army of Northern Virginia and ended the war as a general officer; he later became a writer and historian. Barker was a lieutenant from the First Virginia Infantry Regiment when he began working with Alexander (so long before, in fact, that he had lost any chance of reelection to office when the regiment was reorganized in the spring of 1862). Though next senior in experience, he was junior in rank to Milligan and Norris. Milligan had continued serving in a somewhat cloudy status as an army captain without relinquishing his Virginia navy commission. Magruder's signal officer, on the other hand, was unencumbered; accordingly, Captain William Norris was offered the position of chief, and after little hesitation he accepted it.[7]

Originally the corps was to consist of ten officers, not to exceed the grade of captain (which, naturally, became ten captains, including Norris and Barker), and ten sergeants, with private soldiers to be detailed to assist as required. With the expansion of the corps in November 1862 to a major, ten captains, ten first and ten second lieutenants, and thirty sergeants, Norris was elevated to major, his grade until the closing days of the Confederacy, when he succeeded Robert Ould as commissioner of exchange (of prisoners) as a colonel.

Milligan bitterly contested the selection of Norris, arguing that he was responsible for Norris's success, but the decision prevailed. Thwarted and resentful, Milligan fell back on a claim of oral authority from the secretary of war which predated the act of Congress establishing the corps and gave his signal corps status independent of Norris and the official Confederate Signal Corps. Thus the Independent Signal Corps and Scouts (ISC) was announced by Milligan and accepted by Richmond. After the evacuation of Norfolk in May 1862, Milligan shifted his headquarters to Petersburg, where he held forth in isolation from Norris's corps. The ISC extended signal lines from Fort Darling (Drewry's Bluff), south of Richmond, to Petersburg, down the James, and along the Appomattox, occasionally sending field detachments into southeastern Virginia and North Carolina to support the army as departmental boundaries shifted.

Milligan's ISC adopted the standard Myer-Alexander system (as did the regular Signal Corps) and generally conformed to the requirements of the War Department, but Milligan kept his distance from Norris. Although he obeyed the requirement for quarterly reports as laid down in the general order, Milligan persisted in submitting his directly to the adjutant and inspector general, rather than to or through Norris. He cooperated with Barker, who became Norris's principal officer for instruction and supply, and integrated his lines with signal officers of the Army of Northern Virginia during the siege of Petersburg, but his remnant ISC, thrown into the ranks with the retreating army, kept its independent status to Appomattox.[8]

Arriving in Richmond in the summer of 1862 to set up his headquarters, Norris found that he had inherited an active organization from Alexander's pioneering efforts. Alexander's original trainees, most of them young men, had become the nucleus of the officer corps, eight of them among the first ten captains. The pamphlet of instruction prepared by Alexander and his brother was printed and given limited and controlled distribution—it was sent in numbered copies to named individuals, who were given ten days to digest its contents and return it for accounting. (As a further precaution, although the manual included instructions for the use of cipher, it did not include the essential key to be used—this was separately provided orally by trusted messenger and changed as required.)[9] Barker and Bryan had fabricated an initial supply of signal flags and equipment and devised some mechanical aids for the use of the cipher. When Beauregard was transferred to the Midwest, he took with him several of Alexander's trainees who introduced the signal system in the Mississippi Valley. By the fall of 1862 and the Second Battle of Manassas, trained signalmen were in key positions throughout the army and with departmental headquarters, as well as in Richmond. There, Norris's Signal Bureau, the Office of the Chief Signal Officer, was located throughout the war, near the president and the secretary of war.

In such men as Captain Bryan and Sergeant Cawood (who later became a lieutenant in the corps) Norris inherited some restless souls, burning for adventure, already skilled in running the Potomac line, penetrating into enemy territory, or to assist those who would enter the Confederacy. In February 1862, Bryan was captured on Mason's Neck, downriver from Mount Vernon, and thrown into Old Capitol Prison in Washington. Rose Greenhow and a Maryland secessionist named Thomas A. Jones, among others, were there at the same time. To provide Bryan with appropriate status and cover, a commission as captain in the Signal Corps was arranged on 10 June 1862. As an officer, Bryan was exchanged on 27 August 1862, a move Union authorities may have later had cause to regret exceedingly. Bryan spied in Maryland on personal assignment from General Lee and later went to Charleston to serve on Beauregard's staff, where he applied himself to learning the northern signal code. His southern colleagues exploited this success to anticipate Union moves and conserve their forces. He then turned his attention to torpedoes and became one of the most proficient army officers to work the coastal rivers from Florida to Virginia. Finally, in September 1864, yellow fever did what the Yankees could not. E. Pliny Bryan, a one-man terror for the Union, was dead. Back in Virginia, a young man named Benjamin Franklin Stringfellow, J. E. B. Stuart's famous scout, carried on his tradition. Stringfellow was introduced to "the business" by Bryan and later became a lieutenant in the Signal Corps.

Norris's refugee status, with friends and family members back in Maryland, might well have led him, in conjunction with Joseph H. Maddox, a friend of Governor Letcher, and perhaps others, to make a proposal to the secretary of war on 13 September 1862:

> The verbal suggestion recently made respecting regular and rapid communication with Maryland and the north are [sic] received. Employing eight couriers, and seven seamen, I propose to furnish the Government daily with communications from our friends in Washington, Baltimore, &c &c. and also the northern journals, and perhaps with dispatches from the army.
>
> Even should the present line be uninterrupted it might be judicious to multiply the chances of transmitting army intelligence, and should our forces advance at once the route through lower Maryland would for some time be the most safe, direct, and available.
>
> Trusty messengers and the Federal mail will be the agents relied upon across the Potomac. Mr. Maddox, now raising a regiment of cavalry in Maryland, has with great spirit and self devotion volunteered to execute this part of the duty. His means for obtaining intelligence from men of judgment and position in Washington are peculiarly great, also his facilities for forwarding dispatches. In this connection I beg to suggest for the consideration of the President, a proposition to station a reliable officer in Quebec; his duty to convert into cipher, and the reverse, and forward all dispatches of the President to and from our agents and ministers abroad.
>
> It is believed that this could be accomplished with but little delay beyond that of regular mail time and with no possibility of discovery.
>
> The details of the several plans have been fully matured, and only await your approval to be put into immediate operation.[10]

Two days later a staff officer replied: "I have seen the Secy. He approved at once your proposition, but says that the delay has been occasioned by his being obliged to refer the *Canadian* part of it to the Pres[iden]t. He wishes you *to go at once* with the Baltr & Wash line. Any authority you wish can be had."[11]

This exchange formalized what came to be known as the Secret

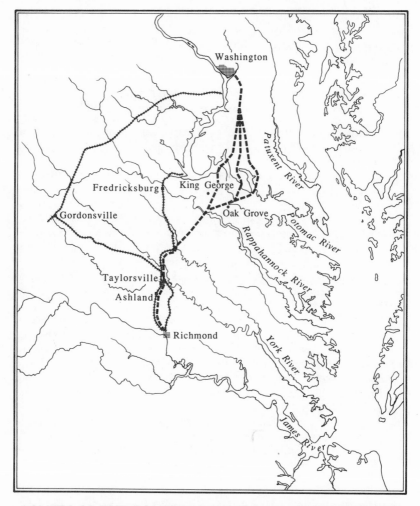

ROUTES OF THE CONFEDERATE SIGNAL CORPS "SECRET
LINE" BETWEEN RICHMOND AND WASHINGTON

Line and, with it, a covert activity of the Secret Service Bureau, run out of the back room of the Signal Bureau by Norris. This enterprise was so secret that even the office files were kept in cipher. It tended to turn Norris's attention from the dull routine of administering a fairly self-sufficient body of signal offices and detachments to the excitement of strategic intelligence and secret operations, causing some to think of him more as the chief of military intelligence than of military communications.[12]

Despite its name, the Secret Line was actually an operation rather than a single line. It entailed three major axes of communication into enemy territory, two across the Potomac into southern Maryland and one across the James and down the Peninsula to Fortress Monroe, opposite Union-held Norfolk, a fort that remained in northern hands throughout the war. Along these lines linking homes, farmhouses, and taverns—"safe houses" in the jargon of espionage today—passed couriers of government correspondence (such as John Harrison Surratt, Jr.), espionage agents (such as Captain Thomas Nelson Conrad), recruits for the southern cause, foreign visitors (such as Fitzgerald Ross), and bearers of contraband or such essentials as technical manuals or northern publications—quasi-military men such as Vincent Camalier of St. Mary's County, Maryland, whose rank and status varied with his mission, but who often feigned smuggling. Their passage was officially authorized over two signatures, those of the chief of the Signal Corps (Secret Service Bureau) and of the secretary of war, and it was officially conducted by Signal Corps personnel, aided by civilian volunteers. (For those lacking official credentials or sanction, free-lance boating operations were also available—some boatmen charged $20 gold for passage—as was the lucrative and illegal smuggling of contraband and luxuries.) Since the Potomac was patrolled by Union gunboats and the northern bank by Union soldiers, the crossing was often hazardous, quite apart from weather and current, but the irregular shoreline on both sides, the inlets and marshes, precluded total control, and the men running the gauntlet knew the area from birth. Their boats were small and were rowed. They could take every advantage offered by season, tide, and night, aided by established habits of the Union patrols or tip-offs of irregular activities received from sympathizers and supporters on both sides of a river that, before the war, had joined, more than separated, friends and families.

The Secret Line was the mainstay of the external or foreign mail service of the Confederate government. Personal messages were handled (whether with official sanction or unofficially as a favor) when possible, contributing to morale and the flow of information, but the purpose of the system was to transmit official correspondence to and from Confederate officials in Canada and abroad, as well as to agents in northern states. As indicated in Norris's original proposal, the Confederates took full advantage of the U.S. postal service and let their enemies handle the bulk of the work gratis. This was done through a simple but effective system of double envelopes and "mail agents" and "mail drops."[13]

They depended on agents in Union territory who were willing to receive and relay rebel correspondence, risking arrest (at the least) if discovered. Friendly postmasters were in an especially good position to handle this mail, and southern Maryland counties were served by postmasters of southern sympathy in the early months of the war, who were willing to cooperate, and country doctors, who could travel about without eliciting suspicion, were in demand as carriers. On the opposite side of the Potomac were the Signal Corps personnel, ready to receive and relay or cross over to accept or turn over shipments. Each of the two major axes of the Secret Line in northern Virginia was anchored on the Virginia side in what was termed a "signal camp." Lieutenant Cawood, officer in charge of the Secret Line on the Potomac, operated the northernmost camp on Mathias Point, opposite Port Tobacco, Maryland. In Charles County, Maryland, his principal agent was Thomas Jones, who had been released from Old Capitol and returned to continue to do his bit to aid the South. Jones operated out of the little post office at Allen's Fresh backed up by "Captain" William Sheirburn of Newport, a sailboat skipper who plied the Potomac. (Sheirburn's involvement was kept so secure that it was not learned until 1978.)[14]

Downstream from Cawood was a second camp, located not far from Oak Grove (and the birthplace of George Washington) in Westmoreland County, Virginia. The principal officer associated with this camp in the last year of the war was Sergeant Harry Hall Brogden, another Marylander. His camp appears to have been oriented toward the eastern shoreline of Charles County and adjoining St. Mary's County, Maryland.

To convey Confederate mail, the agent or official abroad would write his message, frequently in cipher, and seal it inside an envelope with the true address—"Secretary of War, Richmond, Va.," for instance. He would then place it inside another envelope, which he addressed to a Confederate mail agent, whose name he had been provided, for example, "Mr. Thos. Jones, Allen's Fresh, Charles

County, Maryland," and send it through the regular U.S. mail. Upon receipt, Jones would remove the outer envelope and dispose of it, then, through prearrangement, convey the inner envelope and message to Cawood, who would have it couriered to Richmond. Although Union authorities (including the infamous Colonel Lafayette Baker) learned early of the "disloyalty" of many southern Maryland postmasters and how the clandestine mail service worked, they were unsuccessful in putting a halt to it, despite the arrest of some members of the network and the dismissal of others. Through alternative agents or addresses, the Confederates were evidently successful in minimizing the suspicious volumes of mail to one address, and the system continued to the end of the war.

In addition to mail, the Secret Line kept Richmond regularly supplied with northern newspapers and periodicals—a valued source of intelligence on troop movements, commanders, morale, and the like. Newspapers were also used to communicate with agents—for example, through prearranged "open codes" in the personal columns. The procurement of northern newspapers had existed officially since at least November 1861, when the Confederate secretary of war informed the commander in Fredericksburg of arrangements involving the transfer of newspapers across the lower Potomac. More official or specialized publications also came via the Secret Line—copies of U.S. regulations and manuals, technical material much needed by an agrarian economy industrializing "from scratch." And, of course, people moved through the Secret Line. Some of these were government couriers or agents, others were transported "courtesy of the CSA." Some of these individuals are fairly well known to history—Surratt and Captain Conrad; others are obscure figures, their mysterious comings and goings seldom visible then or now. Still others were able to keep their activities so well hidden that they will never be known except through accident or intensive research. Such a man was Vincent Camalier.

Camalier is such a shadowy persona that few, outside of a handful of local historians and buffs, know of his existence.[15] What might today be termed "good cover, low profile," excellent security arrangements—combined with misspellings of his name by contemporaries—concealed the role he played and left it largely to chance that even a sketchy analysis is possible today. And yet, this man, in one case alone, "saved Richmond," according to his chief, Major William Norris.[16]

Vincent Camalier, of French descent, was born in Washington,

D.C., but his family had lived in St. Mary's County, Maryland, for three decades before the war, and Vincent's outlook was totally southern. He was thirty-three years old the first year of the war and determined to aid the South. Sometime around December 1861 to January 1862, he crossed the Potomac to the Northern Neck. Although around Leonardtown, Maryland, his reputation as a secessionist was well established, over on the Virginia side enthusiastic reception of Marylanders had already peaked, and he was greeted with suspicion. Unknown to the locals and having no one to vouch for his loyalty to the Confederacy, he was thrown into jail. When relatives and friends learned of his plight, they sought his release, but to no avail. Then occurred one of those strange and ironic incidents of the war: a Union spy—a Pinkerton detective— came upon the scene. Timothy Webster had already crossed the Potomac several times in this area, and he had firmly convinced southerners on both sides of his unreserved devotion to the cause. Camalier's relatives took advantage of Webster's presence in Leonardtown to plead for his intervention, and Webster agreed—it was a simple matter and one that would further ingratiate him. (Besides, he might have reasoned, he now knew the name and kin of a possible rebel blockade runner.) Webster accordingly wrote to the officer holding Camalier, attesting to his loyalty and requesting his release. As Pinkerton himself later reminisced, "Webster's footing with the rebel authorities was also firmly established, and every one of them with whom he came in contact yielded to the magic of his blandishments and was disposed to serve him whenever possible." Camalier was released and back in Leonardtown a few days later—thanks to the intervention of a Yankee spy![17] (Unfortunately for Webster, there was no reciprocation when his time came. Suspicion by General Winder's detectives was to lead to his arrest in Richmond and his execution as a spy on 29 April 1862, just three months after the freeing of Camalier.)

Camalier's cover as a Confederate agent was that of a blockade runner engaged in the highly lucrative trade in contraband goods.[18] As a cover, it explained his activity, but it lent itself to being misinterpreted as profiteering, and he ran the risk of imprisonment by either side if things went awry. At other times, however, as a slight twist in the cover story, he seems to have posed as a Good Samaritan, ministering to the sick and wounded of both sides equally and without bias—and, of course, freely passing through the lines of either side to get to the other.[19] In a postwar application for a Maryland veteran's group, Norris verified Camalier's service, saying that "he was constantly employed in the secret service department and in the Signal Corps and was one of its most trusted and efficient officers." The same application required an indication of the wartime rank of the applicant, and for this Camalier wrote: "Sometimes as private, sergeant, Lieutenant or Captain, depending on nature of the reconnaissance or duty I had to perform."[20] Despite a claim by William Barker, acting chief in 1864 during Norris's absence, that the bureau ran no agents of its own to collect intelligence but that such acquisition was incidental to their duties, there is no doubt that Norris did run agents specifically for collecting intelligence, whether through direct observation or for the receipt and relay of information, and Vincent Camalier was employed in both ways.

Another Marylander in the Signal Corps was James E. Carey of Baltimore, and the fragments of documentation of his wartime service are intriguing. His prewar occupation was that of bookkeeper, and he was around twenty-nine years of age when he reportedly participated in the stoning of the Sixth Massachusetts Regiment in its contested passage through the city. He was appointed a lieutenant in the Signal Corps in October 1862[21] and appears obscurely in a letter from Secretary of the Navy Stephen Mallory to Secretary of State Benjamin dated 14 November 1862. Mallory's subject was the enigmatic George Sanders and a scheme of his involving a clandestine rendezvous with a ship. The arrangement illustrates how the Confederates treated resignation from military service as a cover for covert activity: "Mr. Sanders desires to leave tomorrow. Mr. [Thomas W.] Benthall, of Baltimore, a master in our Navy and a capable shipmaster and in all respects a judicious and reliable man, will resign his position for a time, proceed at once to Baltimore, purchase a vessel and a portion of a cargo, clear for Boston, and pick up Mr. Sanders near Wolf Trap [Point], in Matthews County, Va., and proceed to Halifax." Lieutenant Carey's role now emerges: "The advance of funds can, I learn, be arranged through Mr. Carey, who is a cashier in a Baltimore bank and is now an officer in our Signal Corps."[22] At some point during this period Carey was sent across the Potomac to meet Thomas Jones and escort the wife of a Maryland lawyer, now in the Confederacy. A return trip, necessitated by the lady's baggage, ran afoul of Union gunboats, and Cary narrowly escaped capture.[23] He was captured, however, on 8 December 1862 in King George County, Virginia—in civilian clothes—and sent to Old Capitol, but exchanged, and he spent most of 1863 at the Signal Bureau, of which he was acting chief that summer during the absence of Major Norris.

In November 1863, Carey received orders to report to Major General William H. C. Whiting at Wilmington, North Carolina, and he served there until June 1864, when he was relieved of duty and ordered to report to the Army of Tennessee as its chief signal officer. On 13 February 1865 he resigned "to enter another branch of the service." Through the recent publication of a delightful memoir of the war years, it is now known that Carey went to Bladensfield, near Warsaw, in Richmond County, Virginia, adjacent to Westmoreland County. His youngest brother, Alec, was one of Mosby's men billeted in private homes in the area, and Carey (described as "a mature man, verging on thirty years old, a Baltimorean exquisite in manners and appearance") gave as his reason for appearing on the scene that he "was made a captain and an aide to General [John Bell] Hood, but became disgusted with Hood's 'unprincipaled career,' and was trying to join Mosby's Partisan Rangers."[24]

In spite of the relative informality of Confederate service at times, this explanation for the casual arrival in the Northern Neck in February 1865 of an experienced signal officer, with a background in covert activity, newly resigned from service as a chief signal officer of the Confederate army, is a bit difficult to accept.

The coincidence becomes even more interesting in considering the posting of Jacob Hite Manning, one of the original ten captains of the Signal Corps, whom Alexander trained in 1861 and who had served in the war up to this point as chief signal officer to General Longstreet and the I Corps. His career appears to have been entirely overt and conventional. He was not a spy but a professional field soldier-technician. But on 20 October 1864 Captain Manning was relieved of his position and ordered to report to Mosby. The assignment is consistent with his origin, for Manning was a native of Loudoun County and knew intimately that section of "Mosby's Confederacy" along the Potomac. He is listed on an inspection report of the I Corps dated 28 February 1865 as "absent . . . by what authority: R. E. Lee." Nothing is known of his assignment, other than that it called for action, for he was severely wounded at Hamilton, near Leesburg, Virginia, a few weeks before Lee's surrender. One of the three senior signal officers of the Army of Northern Virginia (which had no army signal officer, relying instead on the component corps), Manning had been detached by order of the commanding general and sent north to Mosby. Off to the east, another experienced officer—former chief signal officer of the Army of Tennessee—was in casual status at Bladensfield a few months later.[25]

Signal Corps (or Secret Service Bureau) personnel operated at various points along the length of the Northern Neck at various times, but the two Signal Corps camps on the Potomac, Cawood's on Mathias Point and the lower one associated for a time with Brogden, are the best-known activities of the Secret Line. Union authorities knew of their approximate, or even exact, location, at times, but were either unsuccessful in eliminating them, or as some claimed, found more value in tolerating them for Union objectives. An example of the information reaching federal counterintelligence officers (as we would term them today) is the following, which appears to provide an authentic glimpse of the lower camp. The source, a "refugee" described as "a Californian," claimed that he left Richmond on 11 December 1864, with a pass from the secretary of war to go north and directions from the chief signal officer:

> Get off the [railroad] cars at Milford, see Boles [sic: Boulware?] at Bowling Green, Gibbs at Port Royal, Rollins at Port Conway. I went to Oak Grove one and a half miles from the Signal Camp. The Signal Camp is on Bridge[s] Creek. [The description fits Maddox Creek, rather than Bridge's Creek, five miles from its mouth]. At a point on the creek where there was an old bridge which was burned, is where you strike the road that leads to camp, which camp is about three hundred yards from the creek, and on the site of the birth place of Washington. They have a boat there in which they cross the Potomac; it is about twenty-six feet long and capable of carrying about sixteen persons. They keep it about three-quarters of a mile above, on the creek. At the Signal Camp I saw about twelve men, commanded by Sergeant Harry Brogden; they were armed with revolvers. They collect passes that are granted in Richmond, run the mail and Rebel agents North, and back again. They told me they were expecting some twelve or fifteen parties back from Maryland again, very soon.
>
> When I came over in the boat it was manned by four oarsmen and one steersman, and as passengers, Norris, an Englishman, and myself, and brought over a mail. We landed at Cobb Neck. Norris [sic] said he would start back from the other side of the Wicomico.
>
> The following are additional names of members of the Signal Corps:
> —Rowley
> —Reed, formerly a boatman on the Potomac
> —Brockenborough [sic]

These men said they were daily expecting members of Mosby's command on the Neck.[26]

Employing largely volunteers, the Secret Line was run at little expense to the Confederacy. At one point in 1864, for example, Captain Barker requested a minimum of $200 per month to maintain the lines across the Potomac.[27] He preferred, however, that the men involved in Virginia be given military status and later suggested that they, or at least the officers in charge, be given authority to arrest and send to the provost marshal in Richmond all "loiterers without proper papers." This proposal doubtless stemmed from the illegal crossing of the Potomac by a variety of smugglers, deserters, and the like, who complicated life for covert operations. Seeking to regulate the activity better, Barker wrote to Adjutant and Inspector General Cooper on 5 September 1864: "The duties of the Signal Service were incidentally the cause of any secret service being rendered; thus far we have succeeded most admirably, and it only needs proper organization to make it one of the most valuable and effective branches of the service." He went on to propose military status for those involved and higher rank for those already engaged in the work. He recommended Cawood as the best man to head the proposed corps and reminded Cooper that "the agents on this, as well as the Maryland side, were selected for their known loyalty and devotion to the cause."[28]

But even as Barker wrote, complaints were being heard about the signal camps and their personnel, complaints of a sort often heard about irregulars—some doubtless based on envy of their relative freedom from harsh discipline and field duty, some on misperceptions of their duties, and some, perhaps, on abuse of status by some of the personnel involved. As early as 25 April, Thomas Nelson Conrad had filed an official complaint concerning "the inefficiency of Government Agents." He claimed that the officer in charge, Private George H. Norris, had refused him and his companion a crossing, "whilst *ladies are transmitted and parties upon private business also*," and he hinted strongly that "I sincerely believe with *Greenbacks* I could easily effect transit. For I hear they bring over whiskey & retail it, with other articles, at exorbitant prices, whilst the demands of country are little regarded." (By contrast, Conrad termed Lieutenant Cawood "a very efficient officer" and noted that he had made arrangements for Cawood to transmit his dispatches. This is one of several sources that suggests the camps had specialized by this date, with mail being handled at the upper crossing and people at the lower one.] Requested by General Bragg, then serving as military adviser to President Davis, to comment on the charge, the Signal Bureau elicited from Private Norris an indignant explanation that tended to reflect on Conrad's inexperience:

> About a fortnight ago a man named Conrad—representing himself as on business for Genl Bragg—came to my camp and requested to be put across the river. My *orders* required two papers—one from Sec. of War, and one from Chf. Sign. Corps. He had neither of these, nor did he exhibit any papers from Genl. Bragg.
>
> The gentleman and two ladies crossing came to me with proper papers.
>
> Of course I can take no notice of the *insinuations* contained in the letter. My character is too far above suspicion to need any defense. Besides, men are prone to make their own depraved natures the test of the moral rectitude of others.

In his endorsement of the comments, Captain Barker noted:

> Under the circumstances Private Norris would have been guilty of a gross violation of orders to have crossed Mr. Conrad.
>
> The duties required of Priv. Norris are confined to *night* work. There can be no objection *during the day* to his enjoying the recreation of a sail on the waters of a creek entirely out of sight of the enemy. The efficiency of the line depends in a great measure on his friendly relations with the citizens of the neighborhood.
>
> Private Norris' high social and moral character will admit of no such *insinuations* as are contained in [Conrad's] letter.[29]

That fall, Lieutenant Cawood became the target of a similar accusation from a minister, the Reverend Kensey Johns Stewart, a zealot whose services President Davis had been warned against by none other than General Lee, but who nevertheless Davis had sent on a covert mission to Canada. Writing to the president from Toronto on 30 November 1864, Stewart made the following proposal:

> Take steps to discover the party or parties implicated in service of Fed. Govt. as stated below; and after using them to deceive that government, let them be made an example.
>
> 1. 24 hours after an interview with [Pres. Davis] a Fed. detective left Richmond in same train with Dr. S. travelled in the stage with him, & went to Westmoreland Co. stating that he was in the Signal Service. He communicated to the Balt. detectives that a letter addressed to Mrs. H. L. Stewart, Hamilton C[anda] W[est] was *very* important; & had it taken from the Balt. P.O. Every other letter thus directed (say 3) has been taken by Mr. Seward's agents; one of them having been written to trap &

deceive them. A letter to Mrs. Kettlewell care of Br[itish] Vice Consul Balt. Md. placed in hands of Mr. Boulwar Signal Sgt. Bowling Green. & known by him to be important, & sent via Westmoreland, has not been heard from.

2. The Feds. from light boats landed in King-George Co. captured & paroled C. Gryme's son but did not destroy the boat of signal corps; saying "it is of as much use to us as to them" &c. (Mr. G. was obnoxious to Lieut Caywood).

3. Lieut C. is extravagant in $; he borrowed $ Fed. from Dr. Stuart of King-Geo Co. He received $ Fed from Mr. Guildman (Bowling Green) to buy blockade goods which he had no right to deal in & Mr. G. cannot get either the goods or the $.[30]

Charges that Signal Corps personnel engaged in blockade running and transporting unauthorized persons across the Potomac led to an inspection by the Adjutant and Inspector General's Office in December 1864. The inspecting officer reported on 21 December, after having visited both camps on the Potomac and interviewed prominent citizens of the two counties, that he could discover no foundation for such complaints. He thought such stories arose from illegal crossings near the signal camps, giving rise to gossip that the army was involved. "This business I learn," he continued, "is one of steady and profitable employment to parties living on the Potomac shore," and he suggested that detectives or provost marshals be posted to control such activity, a recommendation also made by Captain Barker.[31]

The sources and extent of Signal Corps espionage were carefully guarded during the war (indeed, based on his statement disclaiming any positive efforts to obtain information, one might well wonder if Barker was excluded by Norris from detailed information—Norris did not entertain a high opinion of Barker, who appears to have had a separate office, devoted to training and supplies, when Norris was at the helm). In his report, the inspector called the Secret Line "a regular system of Espionage," employing Marylanders, volunteers for the most part, and uncompensated, with the exception of agents Thomas Jones and old Dr. Dent, both of whom required expenses for transportation. He stated that they operated in Washington, Baltimore, and New York and that "secret information" was generally received on Monday, Thursday, and Saturday of each week and reported to the secretary of war and the general whose army or department was affected. Examples of this reporting are sprinkled throughout the *Official Records*, showing "raw" information of varying quality.[32] There is no evidence that Norris or any other official attempted any systematic assessment of these bits and pieces, and the lack of military experience by many involved must have added to the burden of a Lee, for example, in trying to glean something of value from the reports.

The interception of enemy signals and occasional tapping of telegraph wires provided a more authentic source. The information acquired appears to have had more local or tactical than strategic value, but it nevertheless added to the aura of mystery that accompanied Signal Corps men and telegraphers. General Beauregard, in particular, appreciated the value of such information. While assigned in Charleston to Beauregard's staff to plant torpedoes, Captain E. Pliny Bryan learned of the capture of a signal book from an enemy warship—evidently Myer system signals used for ship-to-shore coordination between the army and the blockade units. All that was missing was an explanation of the way the signals were to be used. As luck would have it, a Union signal officer was captured, and Bryan saw his chance. Posing as a fellow Yank, Bryan had himself placed in a cell with the signal officer and allowed himself to become friendly. He claimed that he had just been assigned to signal duty, so recently, in fact, that he had not had time to learn the system—evidently not an unusual case—before his capture. He then produced the signal book from his boot, saying he had hidden it when he was captured, and proposed that they employ their prison hours teaching him. The federal signal officer agreed, and Bryan shortly became a master of the system. The two were then separated and Bryan turned his information over to the local Signal Corps, which placed daily copies of intercepted messages on Beauregard's desk.[33]

Some of the most dramatic incidents of "wiretapping" involved telegraphers assigned to cavalry generals. Perhaps the best known is "Lightning" George Elsworth, who served with John Hunt Morgan.[34] Another was Charles Gaston, who provided the information that is said to have led to the famous "beefsteak raid," a Confederate cattle rustling straight out of the old West.[35] These telegraphers were usually volunteer aides; some were from the Confederate Military Telegraph, which supplemented the commercial lines. Although some of the Signal Corps personnel were trained in the electromagnetic telegraph, no record of wiretapping by them has as yet been uncovered. But an interesting observation was made by a distinguished Baltimore journalist, who claimed that the Confederates—through means not indicated—gained possession of most telegrams passing in and out of Washington.[36]

Another source of information exploited by the Signal Bureau was the flag-of-truce boat on the James River. This boat operated under a prisoner of war agreement, and it transported prisoners for exchange, plus authorized citizens and special mail. The Confederate commissioner of exchange, Colonel (Judge) Robert Ould handled matters on the southern side, and Major John E. Mulford, was his federal counterpart. Milligan's Independent Signal Corps in Petersburg was assigned certain routine responsibilities involving the boat, including the procurement or exchange of newspapers (a source of information appreciated by both sides), but Major Norris—possibly through his friend Judge Ould—was introduced to Mulford, and the two became the closest thing to friends the war would permit, each undoubtedly rationalizing that whatever he said to the other was more than compensated for by what he learned. In this manner, impressions and facts concerning morale, plans, and the like were gained. And again, no doubt because of the tactics he was employing, Norris found himself misunderstood by an observer, this time a lieutenant in Milligan's Corps, who brought charges accusing Norris of being intoxicated while on the boat on 31 May 1863 and of revealing the Confederate signal code to Mulford. This accusation led to a court-martial of Norris (his rival, Milligan, must have been gleeful), but the charges were found to have been "loosely made without due care and investigation and should not have been entertained." The court censured the lieutenant instead and found that "the private and official character of Major Norris remain unaffected."[37]

But by the following winter, when the inspector general sent his investigator to the Potomac camps, Norris had been "displaced," in the words of a contemporary.[38] Although not officially relieved, so far as the special orders show, he had been sent into exile in April 1864 as a result of a falling-out with Secretary Seddon. Perhaps his proximity to the seat of power—his handling of the confidential cipher correspondence and his being present at times of crisis—and his friendship with Ould, John Taylor Wood (an aide to President Davis), and other movers had prompted him to act beyond the realm of a major, or even a colonel. Whatever the cause (and he had several explanations himself), Norris found himself on inspection tours of the Signal corps activities in the southern states, and he moved his family from Richmond to Raleigh, where they spent the fall and winter of 1864–65.

Perhaps timed to coincide with the pending departure of Seddon from office, on 21 January 1865 Norris received an order to return to Richmond. A very different setting greeted him. That winter the State Department had taken over the running of a section of the Secret Line involving a boat service operated secretly by the department. Two experienced sergeants from the Signal Bureau, Harry Hall Brogden and Alexander Watson Weddell, had been detached to Secretary of State Benjamin. Security was, in this special operation, of supreme importance. When word leaked out about "the secret service of the State Department," Benjamin suspected the Signal Bureau as the source, and Norris took great pains to absolve his men. Then word was received that the cipher key had been learned in some manner in the telegraph office in Atlanta. Official action was taken, and Norris issued a confidential circular to shore up the cipher practices of the government. Stricter security was being emphasized.[39]

From all indications, Norris was settling in again by February 1865. He moved his family back to the capital. His field operations were at their prime—new equipment from England had been procured in 1864 and issued—the "overt" side was healthy. But what of the covert side? The wholesale destruction of some records (including those of the Secret Service, said to have been destroyed personally by Benjamin) and the dispersal of others, combined with the tempo of events in those last weeks in Richmond blocks out an answer. Major Norris continued on the job, and his role was important enough that he was included in the presidential party when it was evacuated southward. Two weeks after Lee's surrender, following a report that Colonel Ould had been captured, Norris was hurriedly appointed colonel and commissioner of exchange by authority of the secretary of war. Starting out under a flag of truce to turn over or exchange a body of Union prisoners, he was arrested by federal authorities, who ignored his flag. Returned eventually to occupied Richmond, he was finally released and, still wearing his Confederate uniform and sword, took the oath on 22 June 1865 and marched off the stage of history.[40]

Norris's place in Confederate history was epitomized by Jefferson Davis in a testimonial of 1870: "Though communicating by signal and in cipher is as old as the time of Polybius its application to military correspondence and message on the field of battle had been so little systematized and developed when you were put in charge of the Confederate Signal Corps, that the art might for practical purposes be regarded as a new one. By judicious arrangement and administration it attained to high efficiency and to you largely belongs the credit for that result." A modern writer on the history of the Signal Corps is even more flattering: "The Confederate States Army Signal Corps was the first independent branch of professional signalmen in the military history of the world."[41] Yet neither noted Norris's role in the capacity in which British observer Colonel Arthur J. L. Fremantle placed him: as chief of the "secret intelligence" services of the Confederacy.[42] Davis would go to his grave, lips sealed concerning the clandestine activities of his government. Norris, too, kept silent concerning covert matters—with occasional lapses: he could not restrain himself when asked to attest to the service of Thomas Jones and Vincent Camalier, and both "civilians" were accorded honorable rank among Maryland's veterans of Confederate military service. But in 1865 the Secret Signal Corps stood ready to play its role in "Come Retribution." Oathbound, disciplined, and experienced in the trappings of intelligence, espionage, and secret communication, its men were prepared to execute orders from Richmond.

Notes

ABBREVIATIONS

NA   National Archives

OR   U.S. War Department, *The War of the Rebellion: A Compilation of the Official Records of the Union and Confederate Armies*. 128 vols. Washington, D.C.: U.S. Government Printing Office, 1880–1901.

ORN   U.S. Navy Department, *Official Records of the Union and Confederate Navies in the War of the Rebellion*. 30 vols. Washington, D.C.: U.S. Government Printing Office, 1894–1914.

RG   Record Group

1. Information about the Signal Corps of the Confederate army is fragmentary. Its founder, Edward Porter Alexander, provides an account of his role, starting with his work with Myer, service at Manassas, and the training and equipping of signalmen in 1861, in his *Military Memoirs of a Confederate* (New York: Charles Scribner's Sons, 1907). The classic Union history, J. Willard Brown's *The Signal Corps, USA, in the War of the Rebellion* (Boston: U.S. Veteran Signal Corps, 1896), devotes chapter 11 to the Confederate Signal Corps, and a modern work, Max L. Marshall, ed., *The Story of the U.S. Army Signal Corps* (New York: Franklin Watts, 1965), includes a chapter by David J. Marshall, "The Confederate Army's Signal Corps." Several members of the corps wrote postwar accounts for magazines and newspapers; one, Charles Elisha Taylor, contributed a pamphlet, *The Signal and Secret Service of the Confederate States* (Raleigh, N.C.: N.C. Booklet Company, 1902), reprinted in slightly edited form in *Confederate Veteran* (August and September–October 1932),

reprinted in facsimile by Toomey Press, Harmans, Maryland, in 1986, with foreword and notes by David Winfred Gaddy. See also David Winfred Gaddy, "William Norris and the Confederate Signal and Secret Service," *Maryland Historical Magazine* 70 (Summer 1975): 167–88, reprinted in Paul J. Scheips, *Military Signal Communications*, 2 vols. (New York: Arno Press, 1980).

2. Although military observer Arthur James Lyon Fremantle, *Three Months in the Southern States, April–June 1863* (New York: John Bradburn, 1864), refers to the chief of the Confederate Signal Bureau only in his "secret intelligence" role (pp. 198–202), and Taylor, *Signal and Secret Service,* clearly identifies the dual mission, it remained for H. V. Canan, "Confederate Military Intelligence," *Maryland Historical Magazine* 59 (March 1964): 34–51, to note the importance of the Signal Corps as a source of military intelligence. See also David Winfred Gaddy, "Gray Cloaks and Daggers," *Civil War Times Illustrated,* July 1975. John Bakeless, *Spies of the Confederacy* (Philadelphia: Lippincott, 1970), considered the Confederate Signal Corps "essentially an espionage service" (p. 6).

3. E. H. Cummins, "The Signal Corps in the Confederate States Army," *Southern Historical Society Papers* 16:95, reprinted in Benjamin La Bree, ed., *The Confederate Soldier in the Civil War* (Louisville: Courier-Journal Job Printing Co., 1895). See also *OR,* Ser. 4, vol. 1, p. 687.

4. Gaddy, "William Norris," p. 178.

5. Ibid., p. 174.

6. Ibid., p. 170.

7. Ibid., p. 172.

8. Ibid., pp. 174–75.

9. Taylor, *Signal and Secret Service,* p. 14.

10. Turner-Baker Papers, Maddox File, M-797, reel 83, NA.

11. Quoted in Gaddy, "William Norris," pp. 177–78.

12. Fremantle, *Three Months in the Southern States,* p. 202.

13. The "senior agent" of the Secret Line on the Maryland side, Thomas A. Jones of Allen's Fresh, Charles County, described the working of the mail system in his *J. Wilkes Booth* (Chicago: Laird & Lee, 1893), pp. 30–32. Union awareness of the system was noted by Lafayette C. Baker, *History of the United States Secret Service* (Philadelphia: Privately printed by Lafayette C. Baker, 1867), p. 114. See also David Winfred Gaddy, "Secret Communications of a Confederate Navy Agent," *Manuscripts* 30 (Winter 1978): 54.

14. David Winfred Gaddy, "Confederate Spy Unmasked: An Afterword," *Manuscripts* 30 (Spring 1978): 94.

15. Camalier is remembered in his home county, St. Mary's, Maryland, by a camp of the Sons of Confederate Veterans bearing his name. Biographical details were provided by the late Edwin W. Beitzell of St. Mary's County in letters of 31 July 1979 and 13 April 1981 to Gaddy.

16. Norris to Camalier, 3 January 1887, Vincent Camalier Papers, Maryland Hall of Records, Annapolis. Norris probably was referring to Camalier's having delivered advance notice of Sheridan's 9–25 May 1864 raid on Richmond.

17. Allan Pinkerton, *The Spy of the Rebellion* (New York: G. W. Carlton, 1883), p. 487.

18. Evidenced among "grocery lists" in the Camalier Papers.

19. See Evelyn D. Ward, *The Children of Bladensfield* (New York: Viking Press, 1978), p. 68.

20. Camalier Papers.

21. James E. Carey, Compiled Service Records, NA.

22. *ORN*, Ser. 2, vol. 2, p. 296.

23. Jones, *J. Wilkes Booth*, pp. 33–36.

24. Ward, *Children of Bladensfield*, pp. 106, 121, and passim.

25. J. H. Manning, Compiled Service Record, NA.

26. Henry B. Smith, *Between the Lines: Secret Service Stories Told Fifty Years After* (New York: Booz Brothers, 1911), pp. 213–18.

27. William N. Barker, Compiled Service Record, NA.

28. Ibid., quoted in Gaddy, "William Norris," pp. 179–80.

29. Conrad to General [Braxton Bragg], 25 April 1864, with endorsements, Jefferson Davis Papers, William R. Perkins Library, Duke University, Durham, N.C.

30. Stewart to Davis, 30 November 1864, chap. VII, vol. 24, pp. 58–65, RG 109, NA.

31. Smith to Seddon, 21 December 1864, Letters Received by the Secretary of War, M-437, reel 151, NA.

32. Ibid., For examples of this reporting see *OR*, Ser. 1, vol. 51, pt. 2, p. 873. See also R. E. Lee, *The Wartime Papers of R. E. Lee*, ed. Clifford Dowdey and Louis H. Manarin (New York: Bramhall House, 1961), pp. 440–41, 692.

33. J. Thomas Scharf, *History of the Confederate States Navy* (1887; rpt. N.p.: Fairfax Press, 1977), p. 699n; "Diary of Lt. Col. John G. Pressley, 25th S. C. V.," *Southern Historical Society Papers* 14 (1886): 51, 55, 56.

34. William R. Plum, *The Military Telegraph during the Civil War in the United States*, 2 vols. (Chicago: Jansen McClung, 1882), 2:193–97. A good example of his work (and humor) is in *OR*, Ser. 1, vol. 16, pt. 1, pp. 774–81.

35. Plum, *Military Telegraph*, 2:264–66.

36. Bayley Ellen Marks and Mark Norton Schatz, eds., *Between North and South: A Maryland Journalist Views the Civil War, the Narrative of William Wilkins Glenn, 1861–1869* (Rutherford, N.J.: Fairleigh Dickinson University Press, 1959), pp. 82–83.

37. Gaddy, "William Norris," pp. 174–75.

38. Pember to Mrs. J. F. Gilmer, 16 April 1864, in Bell I. Wiley, ed., *Phoebe Yates Pember: A Confederate Woman's Story* (St. Simons Island, Ga.: Mockingbird Books, 1959), p. 140.

39. Norris to Benjamin, 7 March 1865, Ryder Collection of Confederate Archives, Tufts University, Medford, Mass.; Gaddy, "William Norris," p. 184.

40. Gaddy, "William Norris," p. 185.

41. Davis quoted in Ibid., p. 186.

42. Fremantle, *Three Months in the Southern States*, p. 202.

4

Tactical Intelligence in the Army of Northern Virginia

Intelligence is for commanders. That phrase is sometimes used among military intelligence personnel to remind themselves that the most important user of intelligence is the decision maker. Unless the commander's needs for information are met there is not much point in collecting information for the amazement of the intelligence specialists on a staff.

Before the emergence of the modern military staff, a commander was personally responsible for assembling the information needed to plan his strategy, just as he was responsible for assembling the troops and the military matériel needed to carry out his campaign. Assembling the necessary intelligence frequently made the difference between a successful commander and a failure. Later, staff officers began to take on some of these tasks, and today many specialists are needed to do them.

Robert E. Lee's service in the Mexican War provided him with extremely important personal experience in the value of intelligence and the techniques of collecting it. Few people realize that a large part of Lee's pre-Civil War military reputation was based on his performance in intelligence-related assignments.

As an engineer captain on the staff of General John E. Wool in northern Mexico in 1847, Lee conducted a series of reconnaissances that resulted in the location of the main enemy forces. He was later transferred to the staff of General Winfield Scott, commander of the main expedition against the city of Mexico. Again he conducted several successful scouting expeditions. One of these ventures found Lee lying under a log on which Mexican soldiers were sitting. Such experiences no doubt gave him a deep emotional appreciation for the importance and danger of intelligence work.

On several of his assignments Lee discovered routes through unknown country that enabled the U.S. Army to outmaneuver the Mexicans. At the battle of Churubusco in August 1847, Lee was particularly successful in finding a route through terrain believed to be impassable. Use of this route was decisive in the battle.[1]

When in April 1861, Lee became a general officer, he faced the need to organize a staff. The first member of Lee's staff was Walter Herron Taylor, who on 31 May 1861 was nominated captain and assistant adjutant general, and who served with Lee throughout the war. As military staffs had developed up to 1861, the adjutant of a command was usually the key staff officer. In addition to the adjutant, a general's staff normally consisted of aides-de-camp, a quartermaster, a commissary, a surgeon, an engineer, and an ordnance officer. Later in the war many general officers added a signal officer to their staffs and several also had chaplains. If the work for one of the functional positions was especially burdensome, the load might be eased by the appointment of one or more assistants.[2]

No provision was made for two of the most important functions of modern military staffs—operations and intelligence. Many commanders doubtless discussed operational plans with members of their staff and found that one officer was more useful than the others in originating ideas and in helping to flesh out concepts. Such a person might be appointed as an extra adjutant or as an aide to free him from the duties of the functional positions.

Assisting in the collection of intelligence meant that a staff officer must have the commander's trust and that he must have some knowledge of intelligence techniques. During the Civil War, much of the training came on the job through experience and by word of mouth from the commander himself. Sometimes, however, schools in intelligence techniques were organized to help raise the level of expertise. One such school operated by the Confederate government is described in Chapter 6, below.

In the British army of the nineteenth century the quartermaster was the staff officer traditionally responsible for providing secret intelligence to the commander. The normal activities of quartermaster agents were a good cover for such work. They had money at their disposal and needed to go many places and consult with a variety of people in the procurement of equipment for the army. In the Crimean War of 1854, however, British intelligence had failed. In the aftermath of the war, responsibility for the secret intelligence function was transferred to the Adjutant General's Department.[3]

General Lee's headquarters maintained a register of correspondence received, which was listed in a series of "entry books," some of which have survived in Record Group 109 in the National Archives. At first documents were numbered in sequence from 1 to 10,000, but this system did not conveniently match the size of the blank books available, so a separate number series was used for each book. In addition, registers for sets of special correspondence were maintained.

The first book used to record correspondence received by the Virginia forces was large and runs from 1 to 2090, reached on 16 July 1861. Special collections are listed in the remainder of the book. One series recorded letters from Jefferson Davis, the secretary of war, heads of bureaus, general officers, judge advocates, and the like. Another series recorded telegrams received. This book may have been brought along by Lieutenant Colonel Taylor, who served with Lee in both Virginia and Confederate forces.[4]

Different officers served on General Lee's staff at various times, but the archives contain a list of his staff at one moment during the war. On 19 August 1863 the horses of the staff of the Army of Northern Virginia were appraised so that the owners might be reimbursed in case of loss. The left-hand column in the following list gives those officers' names as they were entered in the appraisal.[5] In the right-hand column we have identified their roles on Lee's staff.

General [sic] R. H. Chilton	Chilton carried the title of chief of staff for a time and looked after confidential matters for General Lee, many of which were of the sort normally handled by an inspector general. He later served with the adjutant and inspector general in Richmond.
Major W. H. Taylor	Although formally designated as aide-de-camp for a time in 1863, he was normally the principal assistant adjutant general and the man who most nearly functioned as a modern chief of staff.
Major C. Marshal	Another assistant adjutant general who was listed as an aide-de-camp in 1863. He handled some intelligence-related matters as well as other subjects.
Lt. Col. T. R. R. Talcott	Also listed as an aide-de-camp in 1863, he was an engineer officer of northern birth. In 1864 he became commander of the First Confederate Engineer Regiment.

Maj. C. S. Venable	Listed as aide-de-camp but later an assistant adjutant general, he seems to have handled some intelligence matters, including correspondence with scouts and agents behind enemy lines.
Col. A. L. Long	An artillery colonel, he was listed as military secretary in 1863.
Lt. Col. B. C. Baldwin	Chief of ordnance
Lt. Col. R. G. Cole	Subsistence department
Lt. Col. J. L. Corley	Chief quartermaster
Capt. W. D. Harvie [sic]	Lieutenant Colonel Edwin J. Harvie had served with Lee and then joined General Joseph E. Johnston. We have not identified Captain W. D. Harvie.
Capt. H. L. [sic] Young	An assistant adjutant general, he later became judge advocate general.
Lt. Col. E. Murray	Assistant adjutant and inspector general. A graduate of West Point in 1841, he had served as lieutenant colonel of the Ninth Virginia Infantry but was dropped in the reorganization of May 1862. He may have come to Lee's staff initially to work with Lieutenant Colonel Lay as manager of the espionage net in Washington.
Capt. Sam Johnson [sic]	Engineer officer Samuel Johnston
Maj. Clark	Not identified

These officers, with the assistance of an undetermined number of clerks, handled 4,135 documents between 10 April and 3 September 1863. That means that in addition to helping General Lee fight the battles of Chancellorsville and Gettysburg, and being on the move a good part of the time, the staff handled almost 30 documents per day. Most probably concerned administrative detail and did not include the volume of correspondence dealing with intelligence.

Apparently by accident Major Charles Venable saved several hundred intelligence reports received by the headquarters of the Army of Northern Virginia during 1863 and 1864. These documents are now in Venable's papers in the Southern Historical Collection in the Library of the University of North Carolina at Chapel Hill. About 50 percent of them are addressed to General

Robert E. Lee by name or as "General." About 20 percent are addressed to Lieutenant Colonel Walter H. Taylor, and 6 percent are addressed to General J. E. B. Stuart. A few are addressed to other members of the staff and to Generals Fitzhugh Lee, Wade Hampton, and John Imboden. These documents in the Venable Papers and other information tell us the major sources of information used by General Lee in planning the operations of his army. Among the most important of these sources were clandestine agents reporting directly to Lee's headquarters. A particularly interesting report, signed "B," appears to be in the handwriting of Marylander Walter Bowie. It is an extremely accurate account, dated 27 April 1864, of the forces and strategy that General Grant expected to employ in the Wilderness campaign, which opened 4 May 1864. It was clearly written for General Lee's personal use.[6] Some agents, including those organized by General Winder, reported to the commander of the Department of Richmond. Others reported to the Confederate government and may have been employed by the president, the secretary of war, the secretary of state, or one of the president's staff. Their messages in some cases appear to have been delivered to Richmond by the Confederate Signal Corps. Copies were sent to General Lee if the recipients felt the reports contained information of use to him. In addition to forwarding information supplied by others, the Signal Corps also observed enemy activity and reported anything that seemed noteworthy. Prisoners of war were a good source. Information from prisoners usually came from the units making the capture, but the provost marshal system that delivered them to Richmond sometimes made supplementary reports.

An important responsibility of the cavalry was to keep the army posted on the whereabouts and activity of enemy units. Sometimes the information was collected by direct observation by cavalry units or patrols. The majority of the information, however, was supplied by a group of cavalry scouts, many of whom seem to have reported personally to General Stuart and after his death to General Hampton or General Fitz Lee. Among the most successful of these scouts were Frank Stringfellow, Channing Smith, T. Sturgis Davis, and John S. Mosby, during his early career. Lee and Stuart maintained a busy correspondence concerning where scouts should be placed and what they reported. Another important intelligence-gathering group was the Thirty-ninth Battalion of Virginia Cavalry. This battalion was commanded by John Harvie Richardson of Richmond, a prewar militia officer and author of a

Confederate infantry manual, who had served as lieutenant colonel and colonel of the Forty-sixth Virginia Infantry Regiment. In September 1862 he was commissioned a major and assistant adjutant general and was ordered to report to Colonel Shields, who commanded General Winder's Camp of Instruction near Richmond. Shortly thereafter, Richardson appeared as the commander of the Thirty-ninth Battalion, which furnished couriers, scouts, and escorts for Generals Jackson and Richard Ewell. In 1864, the battalion was working with Lee near Petersburg. Apparently it was organized and trained specifically to conduct intelligence-related activities.[7]

The engineers made maps and did personal reconnaissance to assess the effects of terrain on military operations. In the course of this work they also made direct observations of enemy activity. Stonewall Jackson used the engineers as an essential part of his combat decision process. It is not clear that General Lee, a former engineer officer, used them to the same extent, but he showed a great deal of interest in their work and had his own personal collection of terrain maps. Mosby's Rangers provided a great deal of information on Union activity in northern Virginia and in the Washington area. Originally Mosby reported to General Stuart, but after Stuart's death in May 1864 he reported directly to Lee.

In this array of intelligence activities the cavalry scouts played a particularly important role. Not only did they provide much valuable information, but they were trained in observation and experienced in operating behind enemy lines. As a result, they were frequently used in other clandestine activities. Stringfellow, for example, was eventually commissioned in the Signal Corps and was to operate in Washington on behalf of the Confederate government. Thomas Nelson Conrad of the Third Virginia Cavalry was sent by Jefferson Davis to get independent information on Union activities in April 1864 and later was involved in the operation to capture President Lincoln.

General Lee's headquarters was also supported by the Provost Guard, a provost marshal battalion that played a key role in the handling of prisoners. This battalion was originally known as the First Virginia Battalion and was commanded by Major David B. Bridgeford. The organization was assigned on 4 June 1863 to serve temporarily on provost marshal duty, but the temporary assignment lasted for the duration of the war.[8] This battalion not only provided the guard for General Lee's headquarters, but it also acted as the focal point for the collection of prisoners captured by the

Army of Northern Virginia. Bridgeford maintained contact with the Confederate prisons in Richmond and also supported minor intelligence operations.

Lee's personal involvement in clandestine operations is proved by a note in his own handwriting: "Mr. Channing M. Smith served in the Cav. of the Confederate Army and was one of Gnl. J E B Stuart's most trusted scouts. He was frequently sent in charge of detachment parties, to watch the enemy gain information of his movements etc. and always acquitted himself well. He sometimes acted under my special direction, I found him active, bold, faithful & intelligent in the discharge of his duties & very reliable." The note is signed simply "R E Lee."[9] It is clear evidence that Lee sometimes gave instructions directly to the agent who was to carry them out.

Smith wrote several pieces about his wartime experiences for the *Confederate Veteran,* and his compiled service record in the National Archives gives more detail. In the operation under General Lee's personal direction, Smith and several other scouts worked behind Grant's lines in the spring of 1864. His later assignment to Mosby seems to have been worked out by Lee and Mosby personally, and Smith was promoted to lieutenant in Lee's Provost Guard battalion in January 1865 while he was with Mosby.[10] This assignment appears to have been one of convenience to satisfy the paper requirements for promotion. Clearly, while with Mosby, Channing Smith was involved in some task of personal interest to General Lee.

Another example of Lee's personal involvement with the collection of intelligence is found in his correspondence with Secretary of War Seddon. In December 1862, he sent Captain E. Pliny Bryan of the Signal Corps into Maryland to watch the Potomac River from that side. Abruptly the Confederate War Department ordered Bryan to Charleston, South Carolina, for duty as a signal officer without coordinating the assignment with Lee. Lee complained but was overruled. In March 1863, Lee summarized the effect of Bryan's loss on his team: "Some of my best scouts are absent; one was killed . . . two have been captured, and Captain Bryan, of the Signal Corps, whom I had sent into Maryland to watch the river on that side, was without my knowledge . . . ordered to General Beauregard in Charleston."[11] General Stuart may have been the nominal commander of these men and spent a good deal of time recruiting, training, and caring for them, but Lee's interest in them was personal and strong.

It is not clear how intelligence reports were analyzed by Lee's staff. Walter Herron Taylor, Lee's adjutant, paid a great deal of attention to them, but he did so to many other things as well. It may well be that there was no single "intelligence" officer short of General Lee himself. Rather, intelligence analysis might have been one of the major duties of several officers, including Taylor and Venable.

Lee showed an appreciation for many of the critical aspects of intelligence work. He was very much aware of the importance of security, as indicated by the following quotes:

> Secrecy so essential to success.

> Directions by telegraph for the movement of troops . . . [should] be sent in cypher.

> Commit nothing to the telegraph on the subject and keep the matter secret.[12]

Lee also demonstrated a sound understanding of how to use information from diverse sources to confirm or modify a developing picture of enemy activity. Commenting on a report received from an agent in Washington, he said, "Although I think his statement very much exaggerated, yet all accounts agree that Hooker has been reinforced." On another occasion he wrote, "The information from the signal officer in Maryland telegraphed to me by Genl. Cooper is confirmed by the scouts on the Potomac."[13]

The Confederates seem to have had a pretty clear idea of the extent to which the Union tracked Confederate order of battle, but they do not seem to have followed Union order of battle with equal attention to detail. The Union and Confederate armies were not organized along parallel lines. The latter had field armies along geographic lines (Army of Northern Virginia, Army of Tennessee, and so on). Each army, if large enough, might be broken down into two or three loosely organized corps, but the main subdivision was the division. The Union army, on the other hand, had a total of twenty-five infantry corps and four cavalry corps. Each corps was made up of two or three small divisions, but the corps was the more important tactical unit.

As a result of Union emphasis on the corps, the Confederates tended to keep track of the Union corps rather than smaller units.[14] Furthermore, General Lee and many of the senior Confederate officers knew personally most of the men who became corps commanders in the Union army. It would have been relatively easy, therefore, for them to carry a mental picture of the Union organization by corps and the capabilities of the various corps.

It also seems clear, however, that somebody on General Lee's staff kept track of the regiments furnished by the various states. On 7 July 1864 Lee wrote to Jefferson Davis giving his evaluation of Union strength and intentions: "It is possible that some of these men may belong to regiments to be discharged, of which 68 regiments go out this month.[15] I do not know how many belong to Grant's Army, but I believe all from Maine, Mass., Vermont, Conn, NY, MD and several from Ohio, Indiana, and Penn."[16]

It would have made sense for the Confederacy to keep track of Union military activity at the state level. The Confederacy believed that the individual states were the major political element, and except for regular army units, regiments were recruited and organized by the states, not by the federal government. Furthermore, by the judicious use of agents and the review of newspapers, a good deal of information could be collected on the status and strength of the regiments being organized without having to wait until they turned up on the field of battle. This information, with the help of reports from well-placed contacts in Washington, kept Lee and the Confederate government reasonably well informed of Union strength.

Notes

ABBREVIATIONS

NA National Archives
OR U.S. War Department, *The War of the Rebellion: A Compilation of the Official Records of the Union and Confederate Armies*. 128 vols. Washington, D.C.: U.S. Government Printing Office, 1880–1901.
ORN U.S. Navy Department, *Official Records of the Union and Confederate Navies in the War of the Rebellion*. 30 vols. Washington, D.C.: U.S. Government Printing Office, 1894–1914.
RG Record Group

1. Douglas Southall Freeman, *R. E. Lee*, 4 vols. (New York: Charles Scribner's Sons, 1935), 1:255–58.

2. This paragraph is based on an analysis of the staff structures preserved in a book of staff appointments prepared by the Confederate War Department, Chap. 1, vol. 99, RG 109, NA. Freeman, *R. E. Lee*, 1: Appendix I-4, lists the members of Lee's

staff at different times throughout the war. Freeman tries to distinguish between "personal" staff and a "general" staff, but Confederate records do not reflect such a distinction.

3. Personal communication from a senior British intelligence officer, 12 November 1982.

4. Chap. VIII, vol. 232, RG 109, NA.

Record of correspondence received at Lee's headquarters. Table gives estimate of approximate time covered by the missing books.

Number Series	National Archives Description	Begin Date	Begin No.	End Date	End No.
1st		1862*		5 Dec. 1862*	
2nd	Chap. 7 Vol. 356	5 Dec. 1862	#1	24 Feb 1863	9,800
	Chap. 2	24 Feb. 1863*	#9801*		10,000
3rd	Chap. 2 Vol. 86	1 Mar. 1863*	#1*	10 Apr 1863	5,099
4th	Chap. 8	10 Apr. 1863	#1	3 Sept 1863	4,135
5th	Chap. 2 Vol. 87	3 Sept.	#1	27 Jan 1864	3,789
6th	—	27 Jan. 1864*	#1*	Fall 1864*	?
7th	—	Fall 1864*	#1*	April 1865*	?

*Estimate

5. Ibid., vol. 355, p. 522.

6. Passes for travel on the Virginia Central Railroad issued in Richmond show that Venable was in Richmond in November 1863 and again in January and February 1864. On 5 January 1864 he returned to headquarters on the same train that carried Walter Bowie to Charlottesville. Venable may well have been responsible for conferring with intelligence personnel in Richmond at regular intervals to keep them posted on General Lee's needs for information. To get back to Maryland, Bowie may have used the overland route through Colonel Mosby's area of operations rather than the Signal Corps route across the Potomac.

7. Compiled Service Records of the individuals mentioned and of the Thirty-ninth Battalion of Virginia Cavalry, NA.

8. *OR*, Ser. 1, vol. 51, pt. 2, p. 721.

9. A photocopy of the note is owned by Mrs. Lucy Welling Boss of Laurel, Maryland, a granddaughter of Channing Smith. The original was in the possession of a relative of Mrs. Boss who has died. She does not know who has it now.

10. Chap. I, vol. 128, p. 520, RG 109, NA.

11. *OR*, Ser. 1, vol. 25, pp. 622–23, 691.

12. R. E. Lee, *The Wartime Papers of R. E. Lee,* ed. Clifford Dowdey and Louis H. Manarin (New York: Bramhall House, 1961), pp. 693, 398, 658.

13. Ibid., pp. 441, 593.

14. The Army of Northern Virginia issued a circular on 7 April 1864 ordering that when captured, Confederate soldiers might give their names and identify their companies and regiments but should not reveal the identity of the brigade, division, or corps to which they were assigned (ibid., p. 693).

15. These were regiments enlisted in 1861 for three years.

16. Manuscript Collection, No. 22737, Virginia State Library and Archives, Richmond.

5

Prisoners of War
and the Protection of Richmond

The Confederate systems for handling Union prisoners of war and for defending the capital evolved initially under the direction of sixty-one-year-old Brigadier General John H. Winder, a West Point graduate and member of a distinguished Maryland family. Winder had been an instructor at West Point when Jefferson Davis was a cadet, and this relationship played a part in the establishment of Winder's role.

On 19 April 1861, shortly after President Lincoln announced his intention to restore the Union by force, a violent confrontation took place between the people of Baltimore and Union troops on their way to Washington. The following day, Winder resigned his commission in the U.S. Army. He immediately offered his services to the state of Maryland, but the state government was too preoccupied with the issue of secession and the activities of Union troops to form a state defense force. As a result, Winder went south and offered his services there.

Before the war, Winder had been stationed for a time in North Carolina, and Major General William B. Martin, adjutant general of state forces, sent Winder a commission as colonel of the First Regiment of North Carolina Infantry, which he apparently did not accept. Winder had also continued to search for a position with the Confederate government in Montgomery, Alabama, and in Richmond. On 21 June 1861, just as he was getting ready to leave Richmond for North Carolina, Winder received a message asking him to call on President Jefferson Davis before his departure. At the meeting Davis presented Winder with an appointment as a brigadier general in the Provisional Army of the Confederate States.[1]

115

Winder's initial assignment was that of provost marshal of the city of Richmond responsible for maintaining military order in the city and its environs. Supervising the conduct of individual soldiers while they were in Richmond and checking passes to make sure that each soldier was on legitimate business and not a deserter were important parts of this job. The hunt for deserters involved a police function, which led to the establishment of a prison system. Richmond was too near the potential battle area to be an ideal place for a major prison. On 8 July 1861 Secretary of War Leroy P. Walker asked the governor of North Carolina if there were a suitable site for a prison in that state.[2] The prison system that was eventually established in Richmond was not ideal, but when a prison was finally established in North Carolina, the system in Richmond was too embedded to be dissolved.

Other duties were thrust upon Winder in the hurry of preparations for war. On 16 July he was designated to take command of the Camp of Instruction near Richmond, which had been established originally by the state of Virginia at the Richmond Fairgrounds northwest of the city, where the VMI cadets were brought to help whip into shape the newly activated regiments of Virginia volunteers. This appointment was a hint of the broader responsibilities he was to assume as head of the main security apparatus in the capital of the Confederacy.

On 21 July the Confederacy emerged from the First Battle of Manassas with about a thousand Union prisoners. Since it is a duty of a provost marshal to care for military prisoners, Winder was responsible for finding a place to keep these men. It took some time to move them from Manassas to Richmond, and in the interim Winder rented a warehouse at Twenty-first and Main streets in Richmond as a temporary holding area. On 30 July he ordered Colonel Charles Dimmock to furnish guards for this prison,[3] but soon thereafter he rented a building at Nineteenth and Cary streets from the ship chandler firm of Libby & Co. The prisoners were moved into this building, which became the notorious Libby Prison at which prisoners of war were held throughout the Civil War. In this early period prisoners were handled without much system and with considerable leniency. They could send letters so long as they were unsealed and free of "party" matters. They were also allowed to send representatives on parole into the city to purchase food and other items.[4]

In addition to handling prisoners, the provost marshal was responsible for the security of the capital, and this involved being on the lookout for Union spies, which led to the use of detectives to investigate suspected individuals. To guard against penetration by Union agents, the provost marshal attempted to control the movements of individuals into and out of Richmond by issuing "passports" or passes authorizing the bearer to pass through the checkpoints around Richmond. These functions were necessary in a wartime capital such as Richmond, but they did not sit well with many freedom-loving Virginians. Furthermore, the issuance of passports led to a jurisdictional dispute with persons in the Confederate War Department who felt that their superior positions in the government hierarchy should give them overriding authority to decide who came and went.

To carry out his various investigative functions Winder recruited a staff of detectives and other functionaries to help administer the passport system, the prisons, and other areas for which he was responsible. Because Winder was from Maryland and knew the family background of many Maryland refugees in Richmond, and because Union spies might base themselves in southern Maryland, Winder tended to employ Marylanders in his organization. Some of these people were from Baltimore; some were former policemen in that city. The stress of wartime constraints and the involvement of strangers caused considerable ill feeling among the citizens of Richmond. By November 1861, Winder's people were being referred to as "plug uglies," a reference to the prewar Baltimore street gangs.[5]

It seems clear that the Confederate government supported Winder's efforts. On 21 October 1861 the Department of Henrico was established with Winder as its commander.[6] He thus became the principal military authority over the county in which Richmond was located. As a department commander he had much broader responsibility than he had as provost marshal, but he still served as the provost marshal of Richmond and was in charge of the Camp of Instruction, the military prisons, the presidential guard, several hospitals, and the defense of Richmond.

The Union still held Fortress Monroe at the tip of the peninsula between the James and York rivers. The most immediate threat to Richmond was the possibility of an attack up the peninsula. Federal troops had already tried a sortie from Fortress Monroe, which was stopped at the Battle of Bethel on 10 June 1861.[7]

Although General Magruder was stationed at Yorktown with a small army to block Union advance up the peninsula, Winder's primary concern was the immediate defenses of Richmond. Late in

1861 the Wise Legion, organized by former governor Henry A. Wise and temporarily under the command of Colonel Lucius Davis of the West Point Class of 1833, was ordered to report to Winder.[8] He stationed Wise's force on the left bank of the James about eight miles below Richmond at a point where the river turned between high bluffs. The high ground provided a good site for artillery, and the course of the river would give the artillery a good field of fire. The bluff on the south bank was known as Drewry's Bluff and that on the north as Chaffin's Bluff. Wise's Legion made its headquarters at Chaffin's Farm, the home of the owner of the property on the left bank, and began to organize defenses.

About this same time the Camp of Instruction was informally renamed Camp Winder. Its main purpose at this point appears to have been to complete the organization and training of artillery units which the various states had assigned to the Confederate government. Presumably many of these artillery units ended up in the new fortifications around Richmond.

In the meantime, the Confederate military prison system had been developing rapidly. For a time Libby was the only prison; Union officers were held on the top floor and enlisted men on the ground floor. The Confederate guards attempted to enforce some order upon a vigorous and uncooperative prison population, and prisoners were sometimes shot for leaning out of the windows,[9] but the war had not yet turned into the deadly business that it later became, and the guards were not uniformly firm enough or disciplined enough to be entirely successful in keeping order.

Lieutenant George Emack of Beltsville, Maryland, was an officer of the guard at Libby during the first half of 1862. He was disliked by the prisoners because he tried to enforce regulations, and he was known as a "Yankee killer" because he had stabbed a Union guard when escaping from Maryland to join the Confederacy. In letters to his family, however, he claimed to have been carefully correct in his discipline of the prisoners.[10]

When prisoners from the Battle of Balls Bluff in October 1861 were added to the population, Libby became crowded. Occasionally civilians or Confederate soldiers accused of crimes were also held there, adding to the confusion. It was clear that another Confederate military prison was needed. On 2 November 1861, the Confederate government bought a structure known as the "Old Cotton Factory" at Salisbury, North Carolina, and began to convert it into a prison. On 9 December, the first prisoners transferred from Libby arrived there. One prisoner described a transfer that occurred a few weeks later. The prisoners were taken in a group under a guard commanded by Lieutenant Emack with one of General Winder's detectives named Meyer in overall control.[11] ("Meyer" was probably Phillip Cashmeyer, one of Winder's senior detectives.)

The problem of confusion and overcrowding at Libby was further alleviated by the acquisition of another building at Eighteenth and Cary streets, a block away from Libby. This building became known as Castle Thunder and was used to house civilians accused of disloyalty, Union deserters, and Confederate military offenders.[12] Castle Thunder seems to have had a special status. In addition to its guard force it had a small force of detectives and clerks detailed by the provost marshal, and it was used by S. S. Baxter, the commissioner appointed to resolve cases of alleged disloyalty.[13]

A large island in the James River named Belle Isle was another holding area for prisoners. The remaining enlisted men from Libby were moved to Belle Isle in 1862, and Libby was used only to house officer prisoners. Prisoners were sometimes kept at Belle Isle for only a short time and then sent on to Salisbury or other locations. There was no proper shelter on Belle Isle, and the men suffered from the cold in wintertime.[14]

In January 1862 Major George Gibbs, commandant at Libby, was transferred to head the new prison at Salisbury, and Captain A. C. Godwin assumed command. In February 1862, a Richmond newspaper listed the following in addition to Godwin as the officers of the guard force at Libby: "Lieutenant G. W. [sic] Emack of Maryland, Lieutenant E. A. Semple, Lieutenant E. C. Mohler, Lieutenant T. J. [sic] Turner, Lieutenant E. W. Ross, of Richmond, Clerk, and Captain Warner, Commissary."[15] This group included the eventual long-term commander of Libby, Thomas P. Turner of King George County, Virginia. His family was well connected in the Northern Neck (his grandmother was a Washington), and he had been a member of the Class of 1862 at VMI. In 1860 he left VMI and entered West Point but resigned and returned to Virginia to become a lieutenant of Virginia forces in May 1861. Presumably he was assigned to the Camp of Instruction because of his military training, and there he came under General Winder's jurisdiction. On 7 April 1862 Captain Godwin was promoted and replaced by Turner as commander of Confederate prisons in Richmond.[16] He held that position, finally being promoted to major, until the end of the war. He was clearly an efficient officer who was hated vigorously by many of his prisoners.

Out of the original confusion in the handling of prisoners of war a tough but rational system evolved. When prisoners were captured they were usually interrogated, or "examined," by the capturing unit. The actual interrogation was sometimes performed by the regimental or brigade adjutant, or an aide, but often it was done by the brigade commander himself. On some occasions the division commander or even a corps commander would participate in this process.[17] Any information divulged by the prisoner would thus be immediately available to those who were best equipped to evaluate and use it. After interrogation, prisoners were turned over to the provost marshal of the army engaged. In the Army of Northern Virginia, the provost guard responsible for handling prisoners was commanded by Major David Bridgeford. Bridgeford in turn sent the prisoners to Richmond or turned them over to local provost marshals who sent them on to Richmond. One of these local officers was Major Cornelius Boyle, provost marshal and commander of post at Gordonsville, Virginia, who acted as a collector and forwarding agent for prisoners of war.[18]

In Richmond the prisoners were taken first to Castle Thunder or to a building nearby where they were held for a few hours and classified as prisoners of war, Union deserters, Confederate deserters, civilians, and so on. Presumably, the delay provided the prisoners with an opportunity to desert to the Confederacy, in which case they were held at Castle Thunder with other Union deserters while those classified as prisoners of war were sent on to other prisons—the officers to Libby and the enlisted men to Belle Isle.

On their way to their next location, however, the men were taken to the nearby Pemberton building, where they were placed at one end of a long room. Across the center of the room was a row of tables. The men were brought individually to the tables, where they were searched and examined again. Nearly everything in their pockets was confiscated. Occasionally a friendly interrogator would allow one of them to keep some special item, but usually everything was taken.[19]

The prisoners felt that they were being robbed, and they made considerable efforts, often successfully, to hide money from confiscation. Their fears, however, were based on a misunderstanding of the Confederate system. The letters, receipts, pictures, pipes, pocketknives, official papers, watches, and other personal items taken from prisoners were eventually turned over to Captain Charles Morfit, the prison quartermaster, for safekeeping. Presumably this material would be returned to the prisoners when they were released, except that in the circumstances of war the man might be released before the personal items could be given to him. Furthermore, many prisoners died in prison. By the end of the war a considerable quantity of prisoners' property had accumulated in Richmond.[20]

It might seem strange to make such an effort to consolidate and store the minutiae of a soldier's pocket, but this store of material might be invaluable to an intelligence officer who wished to establish a new identity for an agent. The agent could be outfitted with items from northern sources and provided with all the trappings of a new identity, including letters from home. An agent thus equipped might easily operate in the North so long as he stayed away from units recruited in his adopted locale.

Money was also handled very carefully. All funds over $20 were confiscated unless the soldier could prove that the money was his personal property. The assumption was that more than that amount must belong to the U.S. government and subject to seizure (the same rule was followed by the Union in handling Confederate prisoners).[21] The remaining money was turned over to Captain Morfit, who opened an account in the prisoner's name. Morfit kept careful records and converted greenbacks and specie in whatever manner was most advantageous to the prisoner. Late in the war, however, as part of a general effort by the Confederate government to support the value of its own currency, Morfit was directed to exchange prisoners' money for Confederate dollars on a one-for-one basis. During the course of his captivity a prisoner could draw money from his account for approved purposes such as additional food. Upon his release, the remainder of the money due the prisoner was returned to him.[22] (During the classification and "examination" process, prisoners whose behavior or background suggested that they might be influenced to switch allegiance were separated from the others. This process of switching sides began fairly early in the war.)

There were many allegations that the Confederates deliberately mistreated their prisoners. This idea was supported by appalling mortality statistics on Belle Isle and at Andersonville.[23] There is no question that on many occasions rations were meager and sanitation poor. There is also no question that the training and discipline of the troops assigned to guard the prisoners were frequently poor. In spite of these lapses, it seems clear that it was not Confederate government policy to mistreat prisoners of war. Most of the ills cited by former prisoners were the result of poor training, poor discipline, and a lack of adequate resources, not of a deliberate policy.

It is apparent, however, that after the initial era of relatively friendly feelings, the Confederates adopted a policy designed to make their prisoners uncomfortable. The prisoners were treated with a tough hand, and infractions of rules often met such punishments as "riding a rail" and "bucking and gagging." These disciplinary measures were not likely to inflict bodily damage, but they made the victim very uncomfortable, and they had the beneficial effect of making many prisoners more cooperative than they would have been otherwise. Prisoners' cooperation sometimes took the form of volunteering to perform skilled labor outside of the prison walls. Sometimes they even became willing to switch allegiance.

As early as 1862 Union prisoners were joining the Confederate forces.[24] This process continued with varying intensity throughout the war but saw its greatest results toward the end. The opening of the prison at Salisbury, North Carolina, relieved the congestion in the Richmond prisons. On 22 March 1862, for example, the morning report for the Richmond prisons showed 572 prisoners on hand. General George B. McClellan's drive up the Peninsula below Richmond, which began on 4 April, created a new influx of prisoners. By 10 April the number in Richmond had risen to 725.[25] The prisoner population continued to increase steadily thereafter. Many of the newcomers were sent to Salisbury and other locations as soon as they had been processed through the system in Richmond. The problem of congestion came to an abrupt end, however, with the Dix-Hill cartel on the exchange of prisoners, signed on 22 July 1862. The next day Colonel Robert Ould, a former assistant secretary of war, was named as the Confederate commissioner of exchanges, and within a few weeks the number of prisoners was greatly reduced.[26]

From July 1862 to October 1864 the prisoners at Salisbury were mainly civilians and Confederate convicts.[27] Prisoners captured in battles in the east after July 1862 were held in the Richmond prisons or in places like Danville until enough of them accumulated to justify a shipment on the flag-of-truce boat. They were delivered to the Union at City Point on the lower James River, and newly released Confederate prisoners were accepted and taken back up the river to Richmond. The men on both sides were under parole not to rejoin the combat forces until their names had been matched with somebody from the other side and they had been informed officially that they had been exchanged.

The exchange system was not a very efficient way to handle large numbers of men. Gradually the number of prisoners grew faster than the exchange system or the prisons in Richmond, Danville, and elsewhere could move them. By 16 December 1863 the morning report showed 10,528 prisoners in Richmond.[28]

Since many prisoners were being taken by the Army of Tennessee as well as by the Army of Northern Virginia, it was decided that a new prison should be built in Georgia to take the excess prisoners captured in both areas. On 21 November 1863, General Winder's son and aide, Lieutenant W. S. Winder, was ordered to Georgia to select the site for a prison. Eventually a stockade was constructed at Andersonville, Georgia. Known officially as Camp Sumter, this stockade became the notorious Andersonville Prison, which received its first Union prisoners in February 1864. Large numbers of prisoners from the Wilderness and the fighting around Atlanta ended up at Andersonville. In the meantime the exchange process became bogged down in political jockeying and prospects of relieving congestion by this route ended.[29]

On 25 August 1864 the Confederacy stopped sending prisoners to Andersonville, and there was a good deal of shifting of prisoners from spot to spot until it was decided to reopen Salisbury to Union prisoners of war. On 5 October 1864, Salisbury, under the command of Major John H. Gee, began to receive Union prisoners again. In the next five months more than ten thousand prisoners were sent there.[30]

On 21 August 1864 the adjutant and inspector general issued General Order 65, which spelled out a new policy of encouraging enemy prisoners, particularly aliens, and most particularly Irish Catholics, to enlist with Confederate forces. In their postwar memoirs, Union prisoners indicated that shortly thereafter Confederates disguised as prisoners circulated among them attempting to persuade them to join the Confederacy. In late 1864 Colonel Zebulon York established a camp about three miles west of the prison at Salisbury to which prisoners enlisting were taken to be trained and organized into Confederate units.[31]

After the war the U.S. government compiled a list of prisoners who had sworn allegiance to the Confederacy based on the records of Salisbury prison. It is hard to know exactly how many individuals are represented on the list because a man might appear as John Albert Doe, John Doe, and J. A. Doe, all referring to the same person. The list shows the man's unit, but that is not too useful in reducing the ambiguity because many units were recruited in the same locality and had several men with the same last names. With allowances for double counting, however, the list contains something over two thousand names.[32] Most of the men were of Irish extraction.

Of 2,072 names on the list believed to be unique, nearly half (48 percent) were from units recruited in New York. The next largest group was from Pennsylvania (15 percent), followed by Massachusetts (9 percent), the border states (6 percent), New Hampshire (4 percent), the regular army (4 percent), with the remaining 13 percent coming from twelve other states, including the District of Columbia. The men from border states might have been natives of those states and suffered from ambivalent loyalties. Men from the eastern seaboard may have been recent immigrants with little inherent loyalty to the Union. Men from the regular army and from other states in the North may have been immigrants, or they may have been opportunists. Many of the men may have enlisted with the full intention of deserting and rejoining the Union at the first opportunity. There are reports of such happening, but Colonel York's "Galvanized Yankees," as they were called, gave a good account of themselves in defending the Yadkin River bridge against General George Stoneman's cavalry in April 1865.[33]

In summary, it would appear that the Confederate handling of prisoners of war deprived the Union of several thousand soldiers and made a modest addition to Confederate manpower. There is no way of knowing how many Union prisoners agreed to serve as Confederate agents on their return north, but undoubtedly some did. In addition to direct recruitment, the Confederacy also exploited the exchanges to plant its own agents under assumed identities.

The best-documented example of the Confederate use of exchanges to plant persons of interest to the Confederacy is described in a letter from Robert Ould to General Winder on 17 March 1863: "A Flag of Truce boat has arrived with 350 political prisoners. General Barron and several other prominent men are among them. I wish you to send me at 4 o'clock Wednesday morning all of the military prisoners (except officers) and all of the political prisoners you have. . . . Tell Capt. Turner to put down on the list of political prisoners the names of Edward G. Eggling and Eugenia Hammermaster. The President is anxious they should get off. They are here now, this of course between ourselves."[34] Captain Turner, of course, was the commandant of Libby Prison and could enter the names of persons chosen by the Confederacy on the list of prisoners. These persons could then mix with the prisoners on the exchange boat and would be carried into Union territory with them.

Ould maintained good working relationships with most of his Union opposite numbers and played an astute game in the manipulation of exchanges. He declared himself strongly opposed to special exchanges, saying that all prisoners should be treated equally, but he was constantly engaged in the arrangement or execution of special exchanges even through the period in 1864 and 1865 when the Union was ostensibly not participating in exchanges. Some of these special deals involved the return of the bodies of Confederates who had died in the North, and others involved the repatriation of specific individuals who had good political connections or who might be needed for some specific reason.[35]

During the evolution of the system for handling prisoners of war General Winder was deeply involved in several other important intelligence-related activities. The headquarters at Chaffin's Farm used by General Henry Wise became very active in maintaining a watch on Union activity. Scouts and agents were sent beyond Confederate lines, and information collected was forwarded to General Winder. Chaffin's Farm was well located to be used as a forward base from which to launch scouts or agents into enemy territory.[36]

Lieutenant Colonel John M. Maury, commander of the artillery on Chaffin's Bluff, eventually emerged as the coordinator of information coming from Wise's people and from Confederate Signal Corps sources across the James. Maury was a former officer in the U.S. and Confederate navies who had worked on underwater mines with his cousin Matthew Fontaine Maury in the early days of the war. When first assigned to Chaffin's Bluff he had commanded the naval battery, which may have included an array of mines in the James. He may already have established a system of watchers on the river to alert him to the approach of U.S. naval vessels. Later, after he switched to the army, his role as coordinator of information could have grown out of such an activity.[37]

General Winder needed a staff to help him carry out his many-faceted intelligence work. In addition to handling prisoners of war, he was involved in counterintelligence against Union spies, in the lookout for Confederate deserters, and in collecting information on Union activity that threatened Richmond. The surviving records do not show the size of his staff in the early days of the war, but comments in the press and in the letters and diaries of contemporaries indicate that it was large enough to generate considerable controversy. Rosters for his staff in 1863 and 1864 have survived, which with the accounts of the quartermasters yield some useful information.[38]

At first General Winder was held in high repute in spite of the negative public relations aspects of his counterintelligence work. In the spring of 1862 his staff helped to uncover a Union spy ring operating for the Union detective Allan Pinkerton. The leader of the spy ring, Timothy Webster, was hanged on 29 April 1862.[39]

Criticism of Winder continued, however, and on 1 April 1863 the Department of Richmond was established under Brigadier General Arnold Elzey, another Marylander and a graduate of the West Point Class of 1837.[40] The new department was apparently intended to take over the defensive aspects of Winder's job and to develop them more actively. Its creation diminished Winder's power and may have involved some aspect of Maryland politics as well. Winder was not without friends, however. On 15 and 23 April 1863 a group of twelve Confederate senators wrote letters to President Davis urging Winder's promotion to major general.[41] These men could understand the necessity that underlay some of the irritating measures Winder's office sponsored, but Davis apparently did not want the Confederate government to appear to champion these measures and chose not to act on the senators' recommendations.

The further decline of Winder's influence is suggested by a comparison of his rosters for 1863 and 1864. In the earlier year there were ten civilian employees in his office, nineteen at Castle Thunder, including nine detectives, and sixty-eight in the provost marshal's office, including twenty-seven detectives. About a year later, the number of civilian employees had shrunk to nine in Winder's office, six at Castle Thunder, including three detectives, and thirty-one in the provost marshal's office, including fourteen detectives. This radical shift in manpower may reflect in part the pressure to get men out of the bureaucracy and into the army, but it also suggests that in 1864 Winder did not have the prestige or influence to resist such pressure.[42]

Another insight into the functioning of Winder's staff is given by the accounts of Major John H. Parkhill, Winder's quartermaster. Parkhill's accounts charge expenditures to various funds. In 1863 the detectives charged their expenses almost entirely to a fund called "Arresting Deserters." This seems to have been a catch-all citation covering general operations of the detective force. Beginning in 1864 Parkhill began to distinguish between charges to "Arresting Deserters" and those to "Special Service."[43]

The term "Special Service" was frequently used by the Confederates to refer to irregular or clandestine operations. The term "Secret Service" was usually restricted to espionage or covert political activity. The terms, however, do not appear to have been rigorously defined, and there may well have been some overlap in their use.

Of the seventeen detectives remaining under Winder in 1864, five of the provost marshal detectives and all three of those at Castle Thunder charged their expenses to "Special Services"; five of the provost marshal detectives charged their expenses to "Arresting Deserters," and four charged to both accounts. This allocation suggests that the detectives may have been divided according to the cases they handled. Winder's detectives may have been active in a broader range of clandestine tasks than was previously believed to have been the case.[44] Winder's detectives carried shield-shaped silver badges with the letters "C.S. Detective" engraved on the face. The term hints at a broad jurisdiction.[45]

In the winter and spring of 1864 a minor scandal broke out in Richmond when Winder's men arrested an "Austrian" visitor named Orazio Lugo de Antonzini. "Dr. Lugo," as he was known, had been widely entertained by prominent Confederates and had served as a consultant to the Confederate Ordnance Bureau. On his arrest, however, he was found to have in his possession maps and other military information not appropriate to his ostensible status as a visitor.[46]

Lugo's arrest was the result of sound work by some of Winder's detectives, but it also showed that it was possible for a potential Union agent to get access to important information, which probably did not help the reputation of Winder's organization. There is no way of knowing what influence this incident may have had, but on 5 May 1864 the Departments of Henrico and Richmond were consolidated as the Department of Richmond under the command of Major General Robert Ransom, Jr.,[47] and General Winder was reassigned.

Ransom was a West Point graduate of the Class of 1850—thirty years later than Winder—and had a good combat record. He had been active in collecting intelligence on the enemy's threat to Richmond and obtained a remarkably good picture of Union plans for the spring campaign of 1864. It was probably expected that he would be able to handle Winder's responsibilities with more vigor and less friction with the public. But General Ransom did not last long as the head of the Department of Richmond. On 13 June 1864, Lieutenant General Richard S. Ewell, a former corps commander in the Army of Northern Virginia and recovering from wounds, relieved him. Shortly thereafter, Ransom went off to serve as chief of cavalry under General Early during his raid on Washington in July 1864.[48]

General Ewell was assisted by Brigadier General William M. Gardner of the West Point Class of 1846. Gardner seems to have taken over Winder's duties in supervising prisons and for a time was designated as commandant of post in Richmond, which gave him authority over various administrative activities.[49] Ewell worked hard to organize the reserves of Richmond and the local defense forces to reinforce the city's defenses. General Grant's move from frontal attacks in the Wilderness to siege warfare around Richmond and Petersburg made the threat to Richmond more immediate and more constant.

On 29 September 1864 the Union launched a surprise attack on the fortifications at Chaffin's Farm and captured Fort Harrison, the principal defense in the area. Union troops were unable to exploit their success, and the Confederates were unable to dislodge them by counterattacks. The resulting stalemate was to last throughout the remainder of the war.[50]

Lieutenant Colonel Maury was captured in the attack on Fort Harrison, and General Lee moved his headquarters to Chaffin's Farm to give that section his personal attention. On 20 October Lee's eldest son, George Washington Custis Lee of the West Point Class of 1854, was promoted to major general and put in command of a new division to defend the Chaffin's Farm region. This division was made up of a brigade of veteran troops under the command of Brigadier General Seth Barton, a brigade of the Virginia reserves under the command of Brigadier General Patrick T. Moore, another officer of Anglo-Irish background, and a brigade of artillery troops armed with muskets commanded by Colonel Stapleton Crutchfield, a former professor at VMI.[51] After about a month General R. E. Lee decided that the defense at Chaffin's Farm had been strengthened enough and the major threat lay elsewhere. He sent his staff back to the Petersburg area and left Custis Lee to take over the headquarters at Chaffin's Farm.[52]

On 25 May 1864 General Winder was relieved of duty in Richmond and assigned to the Department of North Carolina and Southern Virginia. He stayed at this assignment until, on 21 November, he was appointed commissary general of prisoners, responsible for the custody, care, discipline, and administration of all prisoners east of the Mississippi.[53] This position was apparently created in an attempt to handle the problem of too many prisoners, a problem created in large part by the Union decision in August 1864 to stop the exchange of prisoners.

Winder struggled with this unmanageable task until on 7 February 1865 he died at Florence, South Carolina. He was replaced for a short time by Brigadier General Gideon Pillow, who saw most of the prisoners repatriated when exchanges were resumed on 16 February 1865. On 24 March 1865 Pillow was replaced by Brigadier General Daniel Ruggles, who served as commissary general of prisoners until he surrendered in May 1865.[54]

Notes

ABBREVIATIONS

NA   National Archives

OR   U.S. War Department, *The War of the Rebellion: A Compilation of the Official Records of the Union and Confederate Armies.* 128 vols. Washington, D.C.: U.S. Government Printing Office, 1880–1901.

ORN   U.S. Navy Department, *Official Records of the Union and Confederate Navies in the War of the Rebellion.* 30 vols. Washington, D.C.: U.S. Government Printing Office, 1894–1914.

RG   Record Group

1. The document, dated 21 June 1861, is in John Winder Papers, Southern Historical Collection, University of North Carolina, Chapel Hill.

2. Louis A. Brown, *The Salisbury Prison: A Case Study of Confederate Military Prisons, 1861–1865* (Wendell, N.C.: Avera Press, 1980), p. 16.

3. Winder to Dimmock, 30 July 1861, Winder Papers. Winder signed as "Brigadier General and Inspector of Camp."

4. William C. Harris, *Prison Life in the Tobacco Warehouse at Richmond* (Philadelphia: George W. Childs, 1862), p. 31.

5. John B. Jones, *A Rebel War Clerk's Diary,* ed. Howard Swiggett, 2 vols. (New York: Old Hickory Book Shop, 1935), 1:91; see also Alfred Hoyt Bill, *The Beleaguered City: Richmond, 1861–1865* (New York: Knopf, 1946), pp. 96–97.

6. Henry Putney Beers, *Guide to the Archives of the Government of the Confederate States of America* (Washington, D.C.: General Services Administration, 1968), p. 268.

7. Documents relating to the Battle of Bethel are in *OR,* Ser. 1, vol. 2, p. 77–104.

8. Special Order 254/4, Adjutant and Inspector General's Office, 1861 Series, bound volumes by year in library of NA.

9. Harris, *Prison Life*, p. 33.

10. Ibid., pp. 122–24, 28, 29. Emack's letters are in the possession of his niece, Ellen Emack, of Hyattsville, Md.

11. Harris, *Prison Life*, p. 87; Brown, *Salisbury Prison*, p. 34; Charles Cornell Gray Diary, entry for 15 May 1862, Southern Historical Collection, University of North Carolina.

12. William B. Hesseltine, *Civil War Prisons: A Study in War Psychology* (New York: Unger, 1930), p. 247; Gray Diary, entry for 14 May 1862; Chap. IX, vol. 250, RG 109, NA.

13. File entry 29, vol. 54, RG 249, NA; *OR*, Ser. 2, vol. 2, p. 1403. Beers, *Guide to the Archives*, pp. 249, 256, locates some of Baxter's correspondence which illustrates his activities.

14. On 23 September 1864, Captain Charles Morfit, the brigade quartermaster, was still trying to get tents and planks to provide shelter on Belle Isle (Chap. IX, vol. 232, RG 109, NA).

15. Harris, *Prison Life*, p. 28. The list of guards at Libby Prison is in a clipping from an unidentified paper in the possession of Ellen Emack.

16. Alumni Archives, Virginia Military Institute, Lexington; Thomas P. Turner, Compiled Service Record, NA.

17. Many prisoners mentioned being questioned by Confederate officers, and a number of letters by senior Confederates refer to information from prisoners. John C. Babcock to Major General Humphreys, 8 July 1864, *OR*, Ser. 1, vol. 40, pt. 3, p. 75, refers to a Union prisoner who was interrogated in 1864 by General Richard S. Ewell.

18. Cornelius Boyle, Compiled Service Record, NA.

19. Some prisoners reported success in smuggling in greenbacks or persuading their interrogators to allow them to keep an item of special interest. Most, however, complained bitterly of being "robbed" of all their possessions. The U.S. Army Historical Center at Carlisle Barracks, Pennsylvania, has an extensive collection of personal accounts by sour prisoners of war.

20. Letters sent by Captain Clarence Morfit, Chap. IX, vol. 232, RG 109, NA. On 26 March 1864 he reported soldiers' effects worth $69,613.72, including watches, chains, rings, trinkets, and valuable papers.

21. Hesseltine, *Civil War Prisons*, p. 50.

22. Captain Clarence Morfit letters, dated 28 November 1863, Chap. IX, vol. 232, RG 109, NA.

23. Hesseltine, *Civil War Prisons*, p. 138; U.S. Christian Commission, *Record of the Federal Dead* (Philadelphia, 1865).

24. Gray Diary, entry of 20 April 1862.

25. Prison Morning Report, Ryder Collection of Confederate Archives, Tufts University Library, Medford, Mass.

26. Brown, *Salisbury Prison*, p. 60; Hesseltine, *Civil War Prisons*, p. 69.

27. Brown, *Salisbury Prison*, pp. 62–64.

28. Ryder Collection.

29. Hesseltine, *Civil War Prisons*, pp. 135–232.

30. Brown, *Salisbury Prison*, p. 70.

31. Jones, *Rebel War Clerk's Diary*, 2:268–69; Brown, *Salisbury Prison*, pp. 90–91.

32. Records of the Commanding General of Prisons, Entry 136, vol. 13, RG 249, NA.

33. Brown, *Salisbury Prison*, p. 153.

34. Entry 135, vol. 106 1/2, RG 249, NA.

35. Letter Book, Chap. IX, vol. 245 1/2, RG 109, NA.

36. Letters Received by the Department of Richmond, Chap. II, vol. 236, RG 109, NA.

37. John M. Maury, Compiled Service Record, NA.

38. Miscellaneous Records, Department of Richmond, Entry 29, vol. 54, pp. 2–64, RG 249, NA; Expenditures of Major John H. Parkhill, Chap. V, vol. 248 1/2, RG 109, NA.

39. Allan Pinkerton, *The Spy of the Rebellion* (New York: G. W. Carlton, 1883), pp. 501–60; James D. Horan, *The Pinkertons* (New York: Crown, 1967), pp. 103–5.

40. Arnold Elzey, Compiled Service Record, NA.

41. John H. Winder, Compiled Service Record, NA.

42. Miscellaneous Records, Department of Richmond, Entry 29, vol. 54, RG 249, NA.

43. Expenditures of Major Parkhill, Chap. V, vol. 248 1/2, RG 109, NA.

44. Ibid.

45. One such badge is preserved in the Confederate Collection of the Maryland Historical Society, Baltimore. It was worn by Confederate detective John S. Hammond of that city.

46. Meriwether Stuart, "Dr. Lugo: An Austro-Venetian Adventurer," *Virginia Magazine of History and Biography*, (July 1982): 339–58.

47. Robert Ransom, Jr., Compiled Service Record, NA.

48. Special Order 137, paragraph 32, Adjutant and Inspector General, Richmond, 13 June 1864, *OR*, Ser. 1, vol. 40, pt. 2, p. 646; Robert Ransom, Jr., Compiled Service Record, NA.

49. William M. Gardner, Compiled Service Record, NA.

50. Richard J. Sommers, *Richard Redeemed* (Garden City, N.Y.: Doubleday, 1981), pp. 448–49.

51. Stapleton Crutchfield, Compiled Service Record, NA; Virginia Military Institute, *Register of Former Cadets* (Lexington, Va.: Virginia Military Institute, 1939).

52. McHenry Howard, *Recollections of a Confederate Soldier* (Baltimore: Williams & Williams, 1914), p. 353.

53. Special Order 84, Adjutant and Inspector General, Richmond, 21 November 1864, General Order 2, Headquarters, C.S. Military Prisons, Columbia, S.C., 5 December 1864, both in Isaiah White Papers, Duke University Library, Durham, N.C.

54. Daniel M. Ruggles, Compiled Service Record, NA.

6

Partisans and Irregular Warfare

The idea of irregular warfare seems to appeal to many Americans. It has a romantic aura about it, but the romantic notion is largely based on ignorance of the training and discipline required for such a form of warfare to be successful. Contrary to the popular idea that it involves an uprising of the masses as "amateurs at war," partisan warfare has a long history as a body of technical military lore studied and practiced by American soldiers. Many schoolchildren have read that the American colonists understood how to fight the Indians and the French on the frontier whereas the British regulars did not. What is not generally known is that the first modern textbook on the subject was written by a Frenchman between 1757 and 1760. In the latter year an English translation of *The Partisan, or the Art of Making War in Detachment* was published in London, having been translated by "an officer in the Army" who felt that his British comrades should understand the kind of war the French were planning to wage against them.[1]

By the time of the American Revolution, irregular warfare against the British army in the American colonies seemed to be a logical tactic for the Americans to employ, for it was the tactic of the small against the large. A new edition of *The Partisan* was published in Philadelphia in 1776 and dedicated to General George Washington. Washington probably studied the text because a copy of it was listed in the inventory of his library made after his death.

Despite the well-deserved reputation of Daniel Morgan and Francis Marion (the Swamp Fox) as leaders of irregular forces, it was actually General "Lighthorse Harry" Lee who provided the main partisan force employed by Washington against the British. It was only logical, therefore, that Lighthorse Harry's son Robert E. Lee should be aware of both the value of partisan warfare and the discipline, training, and skills needed to carry it out successfully.

The French textbook described partisans as a body of light troops, numbering from one hundred to two thousand, who operated apart from the main army. Their mission was to provide security for the main army on the march, protect the main army's encampment or base area, reconnoiter the countryside and the enemy, raid enemy posts and convoys, and form ambushes. In short, partisans were to use every available strategy to harass or disturb the enemy.

The text recommended that a partisan force should be made up of both infantry and cavalry in a ratio of six mounted to four foot soldiers. Companies were to be headed by a captain with two lieutenants, two sergeants, and sixty-five privates, if infantry, or fifty privates, if mounted. The commander of the partisan force was urged to be energetic, to secure faithful and intelligent spies, and to keep the commanding general fully and promptly informed. He was also advised to take great care to avoid being observed by the enemy and to keep no deserters but to send them on to the main army.

Two themes run throughout the text—the need for good discipline and the importance of careful preparation and planning. To the author of *The Partisan*, irregular warfare should not be left to amateurs. It could be successfully carried out only by those who were willing to acquire the skills of dedicated professionals. We do not know today whether Harry Lee read *The Partisan*, but he was noted for the discipline he instilled in his organization and for the careful planning that normally preceded his operations.

When Union armies began to occupy southern territory in 1861, it was only logical that the idea of irregular warfare should arise. Companies of guerrillas or partisan rangers were formed in several states. Initially there was no regularity or system involved in those efforts. In many cases, they were an outlet for enthusiasm and a refuge from discipline. Irregular warfare seemed to attract those persons who abhorred discipline and system, yet it was only by good discipline and trained leadership that the idea could be made to work.

The early partisan companies caused a great deal of trouble and criticism. General Henry Heth's letter of 2 April 1862 from western Virginia to the governor of Virginia is a good example:

Governor: I feel it my duty to inform you of certain facts arising from the organization of the irregular force known as "rangers," authorized by an act of the Legislature of Virginia. The companies of this organization which have come under my observations are simply organized bands of robbers . . . many of them . . . are notorious thieves and murderers, more ready to plunder friends than foes. . . . The effect of this organization upon the volunteering has been very injurious . . . a guerilla force without being closely watched becomes an organized . . . band of robbers. Properly managed in small parties they are very efficient. . . . A guerilla chief should be able to enforce obedience and command the respect of his associates. . . . This organization has become a loophole through which hundreds are escaping draft in fact all service.[2]

In the spring of 1862, the Confederate government made a serious effort to put the irregular warriors on a more regular basis. It was announced that henceforth the captains of partisan ranger companies would be commissioned by the War Department and that the organization would have to be approved by the general commanding the department in which it was to serve and by the governor of the state in which the men were to be recruited. Furthermore, the men would have to agree to serve for three years or the duration of the war, and there had to be at least sixty men in a mounted company or eighty men in an infantry company.[3]

During late spring of 1862, interest in creating these new units ran high. By September, however, the War Department had lost interest and was declining to approve additional companies. It is possible that some of the old evils cropped up in the new organizations, but the main reason to discourage the effort was probably the need to put more manpower into the regular line units and to discourage its diversion to other purposes.

The partisan units attracted unusual personalities, and some of these men made outstanding contributions both to Confederate intelligence and to irregular operations. Among the first was Richard Henry Thomas of St. Mary's County, Maryland. Thomas was impressed with Garibaldi and the Italian fight for freedom and had his name changed legally to Zarvona to capture the aura of the Italian example. He persuaded Governor Letcher of Virginia to provide arms and money and began to organize a unit at Tappahannock on the Rappahannock River, known variously as the Maryland Guerrilla Zouaves, the Potomac Zouaves, or the Zarvona Zouaves.[4]

On 28 June 1861, Zarvona, disguised as a woman, took passage at Baltimore on the steamer *St. Nicholas*. At the mouth of the Potomac, he and about fifteen associates brought out concealed weapons and took over the ship. In the next few hours, they captured some other smaller ships in the bay and sent them up the Rappahannock to Fredericksburg. Zarvona had hoped to capture a Union gunboat but could not find one while the element of surprise was in his favor.

As a reward for his exploit, Governor Letcher commissioned Zarvona a colonel in the Virginia forces. Shortly afterward, however, Zarvona tried the same tactic on another vessel and was captured and imprisoned. Although his unit continued to operate from Tappahannock for some time, without its original leader and without a larger organizational sponsor it did not thrive. Later in 1861, its men were taken into the newly formed Forty-seventh Virginia Infantry Regiment, and the idea of raiding in the Potomac and Chesapeake Bay was abandoned temporarily.[5]

Other partisan units were established in Virginia. A company was raised in the Prince William-Stafford County area between Washington and Fredericksburg. This company was originally under Captain William G. Brawner and later Captain James C. Kincheloe. In May 1864, it was incorporated into the Fifteenth Virginia Cavalry Regiment but was later disbanded because the men would not serve as regular cavalry. Another partisan unit brought into the Fifteenth Virginia Cavalry was the company of Captain T. Sturgis Davis, who had recruited a mixed group of Virginians and Marylanders.

By far the most famous of the partisans in northern Virginia was John Singleton Mosby, the commander of the Forty-third Battalion of Virginia Cavalry.[6] He was famous because he was successful, and he was successful because he was smart, lucky, and a good leader who usually followed *The Partisan's* prescription of good discipline and careful planning. Mosby is usually thought of as a guerrilla leader, and it is true that his men lived with farm families scattered over a wide area of northern Virginia and collected as units only to train or to perform specific missions. But contrary to the typical guerrilla fighter, Mosby's men were regular soldiers fighting in the partisan manner, and Mosby's Rangers were officially known as the Forty-third Battalion of Virginia Cavalry.

The guerrilla image is enhanced by the numerous successful small raids that Mosby's men carried out on Union forces and lines of communications. One of his troopers claimed that although more than a thousand men served in Mosby's battalion, there were never more than three hundred together for any one operation. Yet these men were reported to have captured more than two thousand Union soldiers, twenty-three hundred horses, and a thousand mules. A large quantity of federal property was also destroyed or captured, including wagons, trains, and $173,000 in greenbacks.[7]

Mosby was so adept at escaping Union attempts to capture him that a large area in Fauquier and Loudoun counties in northern Virginia became known as "Mosby's Confederacy." His survival, however, owed as much to his skill at military tactics as to his partisan techniques. *The Partisan* had recommended in the mid-eighteenth century that the saber be used as the main mounted weapon instead of a lance or sword because several of the enemy could be injured in a few moments by slashing with a saber, but the penetrating weapons, though deadly, had to be extracted from each victim, and this delay reduced the total damage that could be done. In the 1860s the saber was still regarded as essential for cavalrymen. For many years, carbines and pistols had also been carried, but in the days of the flintlock they were clumsy and unreliable weapons. The repeating revolver had recently come on the scene, but its value was not yet fully recognized.

Mosby saw the virtue in being able to fire several shots at close range and armed his men almost exclusively with pistols—two per man. He then taught them how to shoot rapidly and accurately from moving horseback. With this skill instilled, he had his men charge the enemy cavalry regardless of the numerical odds so they got too close for the enemy to use carbines. When the Union troopers drew their sabers to meet the Confederates, they found that each gray-clad trooper could deliver twelve accurate shots while the Yankee sabers were still waving in the breeze. As a result, Mosby's men repeatedly shot their opponents out of the saddle and won skirmish after skirmish against superior numbers.[8]

The tactical superiority that Mosby's Rangers maintained over their Union opponents made it possible for Mosby to operate more or less at will, so long as he avoided the main Union forces. He maintained a Confederate presence in northern Virginia, where he was able to keep in touch with events in the Washington area and prevent the Union from gaining control of the countryside.

At the beginning of the war, Mosby was a twenty-seven-year-old lawyer in Washington County in southwestern Virginia. He had spent some time in jail for a shooting scrape at the University of Virginia but eventually persuaded his prosecutor to sponsor him in reading for the bar. When the war began, he joined the Washington Mounted Rifles, which became part of the First Virginia Cavalry, and served both as adjutant and as a scout.[9] This combination of administrative and reconnaissance skills is unusual, but it would have been good background for somebody with an intelligence mission. His performance as a scout established him in General Stuart's confidence, and he came to Lee's attention in 1862 when he brought word of the shift in the federal effort from the Peninsula to northern Virginia. In December 1862, after the Union and Confederate armies clashed at Fredericksburg on the Rappahannock, the Union army occupied winter quarters between the Rappahannock and the Potomac, and most of the Confederates went into winter quarters in the area south of the Rappahannock in Caroline County.

In his memoirs, Mosby said that Stuart decided to relieve the Christmas boredom by taking his cavalry to raid the Union land communication routes with Washington. They got as far as Dumfries and captured some Union wagons and supplies. Some time earlier the Confederate cavalry had received a shipment of new revolvers. These had been parceled out to the various units, and Mosby's unit got six, with Mosby as one of the lucky recipients. On leaving Dumfries, Stuart left Mosby and six men behind to "operate on the enemy's outposts." This may have been the beginning of Mosby's education in the value of a six-shooter. Mosby's performance in these operations was apparently so successful that on 24 January 1863 Stuart sent Mosby and fifteen men to northern Virginia to try to set up partisan operations. General Lee appears to have been personally interested in this operation. When Mosby submitted his formal application for government recognition of the unit, Lee approved it in spite of the general disenchantment with partisans that had resulted from the experiment of 1862.

On 23 March 1863, Lee's adjutant, Walter Herron Taylor, sent a letter to Mosby through Stuart with the news that President Davis had appointed Mosby captain of partisan rangers. Taylor added, "The General Commanding [Lee] directs me to say that it is desired that you proceed at once to organize your company with the understanding that it is to be placed on a footing with all troops of the line."[10] Stuart endorsed the letter and forwarded it to Mosby. Mosby had started off under very favorable sponsorship.

There was a small misunderstanding about the interpretation of Lee's instructions, but within a few days Mosby had been promoted to major. He had wasted no time in getting organized and starting operations. On 9 March 1863, Mosby and thirty-nine men had infiltrated the village of Fairfax Court House about fifteen miles from Washington and captured a Union brigadier general, two captains, thirty privates, and fifty-eight horses. This raid made Mosby a popular hero, but a fight a few weeks later was much more significant because it demonstrated the superiority of Mosby's mounted tactics.[11]

On 31 May 1863, Mosby and 69 men were surprised while mounting up in the morning by about 150 men from the First Vermont Cavalry. The Union cavalrymen were so confident of success that they closed a gate behind themselves to make sure Mosby could not get away. Even though many of Mosby's men were unprepared, the few already mounted charged the Union cavalry and in the ensuing fight drove them several miles down the road. Several of the Union soldiers were trapped by the closed gate. Union casualties were 9 killed, 15 too badly wounded to be moved, and 82 prisoners. Mosby lost 1 man killed and a handful wounded.[12]

During the remainder of 1863 Mosby continued his small unit operations, collecting intelligence and putting pressure on the Union security system. He crossed into Maryland for some of those operations, but after the Confederate army returned from Gettysburg his operations were more often directed toward the overland communications between Washington and the Union forces north of the Rappahannock.

In August 1863, A. R. Boteler, the onetime U.S. and Confederate congressman who served as a civilian aide to General Jackson and later to General Stuart, wrote to Secretary of War Seddon that he and Mosby had discussed the possibility of using the newly developed percussion "torpedoes" on the Orange and Alexandria railroad lines. Mosby seemed interested in the idea, and Stuart suggested that Mosby be furnished with an expert in their use. In the same letter, Boteler passed on a request by Mosby that the recent permission granted to Edward P. Castleman to raise a partisan company in nearby Clarke County be revoked. Mosby apparently felt that Castleman's operating standards were not high enough and that inept operations so close to him would interfere with his own success.[13] By the end of the year, Mosby's Rangers had grown in number and were organized into three companies. On 1 April 1864 he added Company D to the organization, on 1 August Company E, and on 13 September Company F.[14]

In the North Mosby was referred to as a guerrilla and regarded by many as a bandit, but this was an erroneous notion that may have helped to prevent the Union from dealing with him effectively. His soldiers were not local farmers who worked during the day and went on raids at night. Rather, they were regularly enlisted soldiers, organized into units recognized by the Confederate government.

The men of Mosby's Forty-third Battalion of Virginia Cavalry were quartered in small groups in the farmlands of Fauquier and Loudoun counties. Mosby established a time and a place for a roll call or sent out couriers if no time had been designated previously.[15] Once assembled, the men engaged in training or went off on raids—sometimes in a single unit but more frequently in smaller groups.

On 22 June 1864 Mosby formally established the bounds of "Mosby's Confederacy"—the area in which his men were allowed to move when not on duty. The area covered about 250 square miles from the Blue Ridge in the west to the Bull Run Mountains in the east and from the Plains and Marshall in the south to Aldie and Snickersville in the north.[16] Mosby further decreed that if a man missed two roll calls he would be sent back to the main Army of Northern Virginia. Most of the men with Mosby greatly preferred his style of living and fighting, and the threat of expulsion was enough to make them toe the mark.

In 1864 Mosby supported General Early's raid into Maryland, and then when Early returned to the Shenandoah Valley and General Philip Sheridan took over the force opposing him, Mosby tried to keep Sheridan's supply line disorganized. In early October the federal authorities decided that the railroad from Manassas to Front Royal should be reestablished.[17] With good rail connections to Front Royal, Sheridan could move his base from Winchester at least twenty miles toward the south, thereby gaining an advantageous position and shortening his supply line.

During October Mosby hit at the railroad repeatedly, as well as continuing to raid in the Shenandoah Valley and outside of Washington. By mid-November the Union generals decided to give up the attempt to restore the railroad, and the rails were moved to be used on the railroad between the Potomac and Winchester. At the end of this campaign, Mosby reported that his men had captured or killed about six hundred Union soldiers at a loss of about twenty-five of his own.[18] Several times the Union sent large forces through Mosby's base area in an attempt to round up his force. None of these operations was successful.

In the midst of this important fight to keep the Union from reestablishing the railroad to Front Royal, Mosby made a move that was very much out of character. Up until that time he had concentrated on raids in areas where there would be a direct benefit to the Confederate army. But in late September 1864, he sent Lieutenant Walter Bowie of F Company, a Marylander, with twenty-five men on a mission with the ostensible goal of going to Annapolis to capture Maryland Governor Augustus Bradford. There are some puzzling aspects of this operation. For one thing, a captive Governor Bradford would have no real effect on the prosecution of the war. More, the plan had little prospect of success.[19]

Three men named Walter Bowie served in the Army of Northern Virginia. Two were Virginians from Westmoreland County. The other Walter Bowie, the one of interest here, was born in Prince George's County, Maryland, on 25 June 1837, the son of Walter William Weems Bowie, a prosperous lawyer-planter. He grew up on his father's plantation, Eglington, near the present town of Bowie. Perhaps to distinguish him from his father, he was known as Wat Bowie.

When the Civil War started, Bowie was a young lawyer at the county seat, Upper Marlborough. A picture of him made after he joined Mosby shows him with a handlebar mustache and a Van-dyke beard. On 1 May 1861 Bowie enlisted in Company C, First Regiment of Virginia Artillery; on 23 September 1861 he was appointed captain in the Provisional Army of the Confederacy. At around this date he was pulled from military duties and assigned to clandestine activities in Maryland.

Bowie was good at clandestine work, but he left tracks here and there. On 3 February 1862 he wrote to Judah P. Benjamin, Confederate secretary of war, offering to set up a secret courier route through lower Maryland to deliver northern newspapers and publications to Richmond in a timely manner.[20]

Bowie's luck ran out on 14 October 1862. A tip by an informant led to his arrest at the home of T. B. Cracroft, near the Patuxent River in lower Prince George's County. He was locked up in the Old Capitol Prison in Washington and charged with being a spy. With the help of some well-placed bribes, he escaped on 17 November 1862. In early 1863 he was in Baltimore to buy paper, which was in short supply in the Confederacy. The paper was confiscated but Bowie slipped away. He did not go far. The federals traced him to the home of a family connection, John H. Waring, who lived at Bald Eagle, a plantation on the Patuxent River southeast of Upper Marlborough. At two o-clock in the morning of 24 May 1863, the house was surrounded by heavily armed detectives. After sunrise

Bowie walked out, carrying a water pail and wearing the dress of a black nurse, Peggy. He wore a red bandana on his head, and his face had been blackened with carbon from the bottom of a wash kettle. A detective became suspicious as a result of a chance remark by a stableman. Bowie dropped the water pail and ran amid a flurry of shots. He got away.

In accounts published after the war by members of Mosby's command, Bowie is mentioned for his skill and daring. He regularly led small parties into Montgomery County, Maryland, to harass Union troops and gather intelligence for the Army of Northern Virginia. He used the alias "Captain Mitchell" in some of these operations.

If Mosby actually intended to capture Governor Bradford at Annapolis, he picked the right man for the job. Bowie was cool and resourceful. He and his twenty-five men left Fauquier County about 27 September on a route that took them through Stafford County and to the Potomac River in King George County. They made bivouac on the Tennant farm near Lieutenant Charles Cawood's Signal Corps camp.[21]

There was a problem. Bowie could find no way to ferry all his men and the horses across the river into Charles County, Maryland. To seek an answer, he and two of his men crossed the river to scout the area around Chapel Point and Port Tobacco. An ardently pro-Confederate citizen helped solve the dilemma. He told Bowie that a small contingent from the Eighth Illinois Cavalry was quartered at the county courthouse in Port Tobacco. They had horses. Accordingly, Bowie decided to cut the size of his raiding party to seven men and himself. He sent back across the river for the additional men and ordered the others to return to Mosby. At 8:00 on the night of 2 October, Bowie and his seven men filtered into Brawner's hotel in Port Tobacco. Here they drank with numerous blockade runners and waited until well after midnight. Then they walked over to the nearby courthouse, captured the sleeping Union cavalrymen, saddled up eight horses, and rode off into the night. The *Washington Evening Star* for 3 October 1864 reported this incident on the front page.

Bowie and his men pushed on until sunrise and holed up for the day, possibly on the farm of Dr. Samuel Mudd.[22] They reached the Bowie home, Eglington, at 4:00 the next morning. They spent the day there, eating and resting. Brune Bowie, Walter's younger brother, was there recuperating from a war wound. He decided to join them. That night the party, now nine in number, camped near

Hardesty's store at Collington. Bowie left them there, saying that he was going into Annapolis. When he returned, he reported that the mission was canceled. Governor Bradford was too well guarded. Before they left the bivouac on the evening of 6 October, a new recruit was added, Thomas Belt. Now ten in all, they set out through Montgomery County for the upper Potomac River, intending to cross at an obscure ford. Just before midnight they reached the tiny Quaker village of Sandy Spring. They came upon a well-stocked little store. Bowie decided to raid it.

Two Quakers, Richard Bentley and Alban Gilpin, owned the store. Gilpin lived in a house behind the store with his nephew and two store clerks. Bowie's men aroused and captured them. The raid went off smoothly. One of the raiders, James G. Wiltshire, even stripped the new boots from the feet of Alban Thomas, a clerk. Unnoticed, however, one of the clerks, Arthur Stabler, slipped out a window. He began spreading news of the raid. As the raiders rode off, he fired at them from behind a gate. At first light a posse of seventeen men from the village was in hot pursuit. Couriers were sent for Union cavalry at Rockville. At 8:30 in the morning the searchers came upon Mosby's men unexpectedly, sleeping in a pine grove three miles north of Rockville.

There was much shooting and dashing about. The only casualties were one horse, shot in the eye, and Walter Bowie. William H. Ent, a carriage maker, was concealed behind a small pine. As Bowie came riding by, he fired at him with a double-loaded shotgun. The buckshot hit Bowie in the face and head. That ended the battle. The civilians had enough and retired. The wounded Bowie was carried to a nearby farmhouse and left in the care of his brother, Brune. He died there about noon, 7 October 1864. Brune was captured. The remainder of the party made it back to Virginia safely.

Most historians have accepted the view that Mosby sent Bowie into Maryland to capture Governor Bradford. But the timing of Bowie's raid leaves many unanswered questions. Captain Thomas N. Conrad and his action team left Richmond for Washington on 17 September 1864 to explore ways to capture President Lincoln. Sergeant Mountjoy Cloud, a member of Conrad's team, was sent by the upper Potomac River route to advise Mosby of the plan and to secure his cooperation. Thus his visit with Mosby would have come a few days before Bowie and his twenty-five men set out for King George County. In fact, Bowie entered Charles County, Maryland, on the heels of Conrad's team. Perhaps Bowie was to conduct a probe to test how a small group of men might move through hostile territory with a captive. There is no way now to learn the precise connection between Conrad and Bowie.

After being wounded on 14 September 1864, Mosby met with General Lee,[23] the first of at least three such meetings. This timing in connection with Mosby's operations may be significant. Could it have been the genesis of Bowie's trip into Maryland?

Up until the time of General J. E. B. Stuart's death in May 1864, Mosby had reported directly to him. After that date he reported directly to Lee, probably primarily because the main Confederate army was farther away from Mosby's territory and the cavalry corps was frequently operating on its south flank, where it would have been very difficult for Mosby to get reports to Stuart's successor. Also, Major Cornelius Boyle, the provost marshal at Gordonsville, was in contact with Lee's headquarters by telegraph and rail. Mosby had often sent prisoners and information to Richmond through Major Boyle. Finally, Lee appears to have been personally interested in Mosby's work and found his operations and information useful and important.

On 29 October 1864, Lee wrote an informal letter to Mosby in which he said that it would be difficult to replace the artillery Mosby had recently lost. He urged Mosby to continue his attacks against the Manassas Gap Railroad and cautioned him to be extra careful that new recruits were reliable.[24]

This letter, plus the records of the personnel of the Forty-third Virginia Cavalry Battalion, indicates that Mosby's Rangers were being strengthened. Among other men added to the Rangers, about 40 cadets from the Virginia Military Institute joined his force during the last year of the war.[25] Included in this number were about 30 who had fought with the Cadet Corps at the Battle of New Market on 15 May 1864. (At the end of July 1864, there were only 432 former cadets serving in the Confederate armed services. Thus nearly 10 percent of the men who had had some military training at VMI were in Mosby's unit.) Another measure to improve the conditions of Mosby's organization appears to have been to provide him with an experienced signal officer.

Mosby's Rangers were the most successful unit to emerge from the Confederacy's experiment in organizing and controlling irregular warfare. The Confederate government itself, however, sponsored various irregular operations. One of the more widely known of the men involved in these efforts was John Taylor Wood.[26]

Wood was a nephew of Jefferson Davis's first wife and a grandson of former President Zachary Taylor. He graduated from the U.S. Naval Academy in 1853 and served in the U.S. Navy until 1861. After some agonizing, he took his family south after the First Battle of Manassas and joined the Confederate navy. He first commanded batteries at Aquia Creek on the Potomac and then was named to command the aft gun on the CSS *Virginia*, the ship that was the model for many of the Confederacy's ironclads. Following the famous battle with the USS *Monitor* on 9 March, the *Virginia* was finally blown up by her crew on 11 May 1862 when Norfolk was evacuated and the vessel could not be gotten up the James River to safety. Wood and the crew of the *Virginia* were then sent to Drewry's Bluff on the James, below Richmond, where he turned in a superior performance of aggressive defense when the Union navy tried to go upriver to attack Richmond.

After the conclusion of the Peninsula campaign of 1862, Wood got permission to create a new type of raiding force organized around boats mounted on wagons that could carry the boats to a launching point of Wood's choosing. On 1 October 1862, he left Richmond on his first raid, which resulted in the destruction of a Union schooner in the Potomac off Popes Creek, Maryland, on 7 October. Within a week Wood's force made a second raid in the Chesapeake from Matthews County, Virginia, where it captured and burned a merchant ship loaded with nitrate.

Before Wood could find an appropriate opportunity to organize a new raid, Jefferson Davis appointed him a presidential aide with a commission as a colonel of cavalry. Since Davis had the power to cross-commission selected officers from the various services, Wood thereafter was both a navy and an army officer and used whichever rank was appropriate for the specific assignment at hand.[27]

After recommending improvements in the defenses of Wilmington and Charleston, Wood organized another raid into the Chesapeake area in August 1863. He captured two gunboats from the U.S. Navy's Potomac River Flotilla, the USS *Satellite* and the USS *Reliance*, as well as several merchant ships.

In January 1864 Wood began a new operation under verbal orders from President Davis, which eventually became a joint army-navy attack on New Bern, North Carolina, under the command of General George Pickett. Wood loaded his boats at Richmond and took them down the James and up the Appomattox to Petersburg, where they were loaded onto flatcars and taken by rail to Kinston on the Neuse River above New Bern. The operation as a whole was not a success. Wood's men captured and destroyed the USS *Underwriter,* one of the largest Union gunboats in the area, but General Pickett decided to abandon the expedition in early February 1864.

In the spring of 1864, in response to complaints from some inhabitants of the Northern Neck about their defenseless position and fear of an impending invasion by Union forces, General Lee wrote to his son Brigadier General G. W. C. Lee, one of the president's aides:

> I think the best thing we can do is to destroy the boats in the St. Mary's River . . . I am confident that Col. Wood, if he can procure the means, can accomplish it. I have sent down to procure accurate information about them if possible. Colonel Wood might do the same. I can furnish volunteers from the 9th Virginia Cavalry, who are acquainted with the shores of the Potomac, and who are now on the lower Rappahannock. Captain Fitzhugh of the 9th VA Cavalry, the officer who destroyed the enemy's steamers on Cherrystone Creek, on the Eastern shore of Virginia I have no doubt could join him with some of his men.[28]

The efforts to acquire information about the area around the St. Mary's River seem to have generated other ideas. On 9 June 1864, an unidentified agent in southern Maryland wrote to Major Norris of the Confederate Signal Corps: "We think it all important that a diversion should be made either to capture or release our prisoners at Point Lookout or a raid upon Washington with a view to the destruction of the military supplies and public property, or both at the same time would certainly be better, if the necessary troops can be spared at this time. There is not a troop stationed in our county or Prince George at this time. We therefore infer that the garrison at Point Lookout must be weak."[29]

Further discussion of this operation apparently led Lee to conceive a broader and more decisive operation. On 26 June 1864 he wrote to Jefferson Davis:

> Great benefit might be drawn from the release of our prisoners at Point Lookout [less than ten miles from the St. Marys River] if it can be accomplished. The number of men employed for this purpose would necessarily be small, as the whole would have to be transported secretly across the Potomac where it is very broad, the means of doing which must first be procured. I can devote to this purpose the whole of the Marylanders of this army, which would afford a sufficient number of men of excellent material and much experience, but I am at a loss where to find a proper leader. As he would command Maryland troops and operate upon Maryland soil it would be well that he should be a Marylander. Of those connected with this army I consider Col. Bradley T.

Johnson the most suitable. . . . Such a body of men under an able leader, althought they might not be able . . . to capture Washington, could march around it and cross the Potomac where fordable. . . . The operations on the river must be confided to an able naval officer, who I know will be found in Colonel Wood. . . . With relation to the project of Marshall Kane [former police commissioner of Baltimore, who had been working with General Winder's office on some unknown project involving Maryland] if the matter can be kept secret, which I fear is impossible, should General Early cross the Potomac he might be sent to join him.[30]

On 29 June, Lee wrote again: "The success of Genl. J. E. Johnston, announced in this morning's journals, besides its general good effect, will favor Early's movement. If it could be united with a release of the prisoners at Point Lookout the advantages would be great. I believe the latter only requires a proper leader. Can one be found? There will be time to shape Early's course or terminate it when he reaches the Potomac, as circumstances require."[31]

At this juncture the plan was still to take troops across the Potomac to carry out the operation. Shortly thereafter, however, it was suggested that one or more blockade runners from Wilmington be used to ferry the attacking force. This new plan would create surprise, provide an opportunity to carry more troops and heavier armament than could be ferried clandestinely across the Potomac, and provide a means to evacuate some of the personnel rapidly if need be.

On 3 July, Lee wrote to Davis:

I had the honour to receive last eve by the hands of Col. Wood your letter of the 2nd Inst: & to learn from him the arrangements made to release the prisoners—. . . I think we cannot with safety attempt any communication with the prisoners . . . neither in my opinion would it be safe to throw across the Potomac any party. . . . I send today an officer to Gen. Early to inform him that an effort will be made to release the prisoners about the 12 Inst: & if successful he will certainly know it through Northern Sources. In that event, if circumstances permit he must send down a brigade of Cavy with Genls Gordon and Lewis to command & lead around Washington the prisoners.[32]

Lee's words indicate that the idea of using blockade runners had been developed in Richmond, possibly by Davis and Wood. The officer Lee selected for the highly sensitive task of oral instruction to Early was his own son Robert, who delivered his message to Early in Maryland on 8 July. Early promptly ordered General Bradley T. Johnson to attack Point Lookout from the land side at daylight on 12 July. Once the prisoners were freed, Johnson was to take command and march them to a rendezvous with Early at Bladensburg, just outside Washington. Johnson protested that he could not carry out existing orders to cut communications north of Baltimore and reach Point Lookout by the time indicated, but Early told him to try.[33] Early appears to have misinterpreted Lee's instructions; Lee's letter to Davis indicated that Early was to act *after* he heard of a successful landing by the raiding party about 12 July. A few days later, after Johnson had reached the outskirts of Washington, Early canceled the order. Meanwhile, on 3 July, a party of about 130 marines and 150 seamen left Richmond for Danville and proceeded to Greensboro and then Goldsboro, North Carolina, finally reaching Wilmington on 6 July.[34]

On 5 July 1864 Major James D. Ferguson, General Fitzhugh Lee's adjutant, recorded in his diary: "General Custis Lee and Colonels Wood and Cox dine with us on their way to Stony Creek."[35] Lee's cavalry division was guarding the Weldon railroad south of Petersburg and the visitors seem to have been the command group on its way to Wilmington. At Wilmington, two blockade runners, the *Let-Her-Be* and the *Florie*, were prepared for the expedition.[36] After some delay in getting the arms for the freed prisoners, the ships finally pulled away from the dock on 9 July.

On the same day, John Tyler, son of former President John Tyler, wrote to Major General Sterling Price, commanding the Arkansas District: "The plan is that he (General Early) shall seize Baltimore and hold it with his infantry while his cavalry proceeds to Point Lookout to liberate our prisoners there concentrated to the extent of near 30,000. In the meanwhile, Captain Wood, of the Navy, proceeds from Wilmington with five gunboats and 20,000 stand of arms for the same point by water."[37] On the same day, J. B. Jones, Confederate War Office clerk, wrote in his diary: "We have a rumor today of the success of a desperate expedition from Wilmington, N.C. to Point Lookout, Maryland to liberate the prisoners of war (20,000) confined there and to arm them."[38]

With these rumors floating around Richmond, it is no surprise that on the tenth, Jefferson Davis felt compelled to send the following message to Wood: "Telegram of yesterday received. The object and destination of the expedition have somehow become so generally known that I fear your operations will meet unexpected obstacles. General R. E. Lee has communicated with you and left your actions to your discretion. I suggest calm consideration and full comparison of views with General G. W. C. Lee, and others with whom you may choose to advise."[39]

The *Florie* and the *Let-Her-Be* had reached Fort Fisher, at the mouth of the Cape Fear River, when they were signaled to stop to receive this message. The decision apparently was made to abort the operation.[40] The Union moved many of the prisoners out of Point Lookout on 7 July. On 18 July, days after the project had been canceled, the commander of a U.S. ship at Point Lookout reported that he had learned that "800 sailors and marines, under John T. Wood, left Richmond on the 7th and 8th of July, to man two armed blockade runners at Wilmington, N.C. for the purpose of attempting the release of prisoners confined here."[41]

On 14 July Major Ferguson wrote in his diary: "General Custis Lee, Colonels Wood and Cox and Captain Hobart of Blockade runner and several other Englishmen from Wilmington stop a short time with us—furnish us with a good lunch and we have ambulances for them to go to Petersburg."[42] The party was apparently on its way back to Richmond for a postmortem on the operation. Colonel Cox was doubtless Fleet William Cox, lieutenant colonel of the Fortieth Virginia Infantry and a graduate of the Virginia Military Institute in the Class of 1849. He had lost an eye at Chancellorsville, but he was from Westmoreland County, Virginia, and knew the lower Potomac region.[43] Captain Hobart was Charles Augustus Hobart-Hampden, a son of the earl of Buckinghamshire. He had served in the Royal Navy and commanded Queen Victoria's large steam yacht, the *Victoria and Albert*. In 1863 and early 1864, he had been captain of the *Don*, one of the fastest blockade runners in the business, with a British crew many of whom were formerly of the Royal Navy. Captain Hobart's role in the operation is not clear. From his own writings he is known to have commanded two blockade runners and to have visited Richmond in the company of Custis Lee, where he met both Jefferson Davis and Robert E. Lee. The blockade runners he commanded were the *Don*, which was captured by the Union Navy on 4 March 1864, and the *Condor*, which made her maiden voyage in September 1864. Clearly, he was in command of a different ship in July 1864 but was sufficiently sensitive to omit its name.[44]

The *Florie* was described elsewhere as a "light gossamer craft with three funnels" with big tubular boilers as the only strong and heavy articles aboard. She was painted a dull lead-gray color and had practically no rigging. Crows' nests were mounted on the masts, and she blew off steam under water to avoid making a noise to attract the U.S. Navy at night. Hobart described an unnamed new command as a "very fast paddle-wheel vessel . . . just strong enough to stand the heavy cross sea in the Gulf Stream."[45] This description does not fit the *Condor*, which was an iron vessel, but it would fit the *Florie* or the *Let-Her-Be*, which was shown in a sketch done in Wilmington harbor by Confederate engineer Lieutenant B. Lewis Blackford as a long, low, side-wheel steamer. The command group sailed on the *Let-Her-Be* and then returned to Richmond with Hobart, so it is likely that he was in command of that vessel. If Hobart commanded one of the ships involved in the Point Lookout raid, that involvement could have made him sensitive about implied British cooperation with the Confederacy and been the reason he did not mention the incident in his postwar writings.

Shortly after the abortion of the Point Lookout operation, Wood took command of the *Tallahassee*, a new, ultra-fast blockade runner that had just been taken over by the Confederate government and armed as a commerce raider. During August 1864 Wood took her on a highly successful cruise to and from Halifax, in the course of which he captured and destroyed twenty-nine ships flying the Union flag. In spite of his success, after his return to Wilmington at the end of August 1864, the *Tallahassee* was renamed and turned over to another commander, and Wood returned to his duties as a presidential aide.

Wood led no more dashing raids against the Union. According to diarist Jones, he was busy for some time in the autumn of 1864 planning a naval (amphibious?) operation involving both Generals Lee and Beauregard. The involvement of those two players suggests that the planned raid was aimed at the coast of North Carolina or the forces attacking Charleston, South Carolina. Wood was later involved in some of the planning for the unsuccessful sortie of the Confederate James River Squadron in January 1865. At the end of the war, Wood escaped to Cuba and finally settled in Halifax, where he became a Canadian subject. It was years before he visited the United States, and his reluctance to return may have stemmed from fear that he might be punished for his involvement in irregular operations.

Wood, however, was not the only amphibious raider in the South. Another partisan or irregular warfare activity sponsored by the Confederate government involved Captain John W. Hebb. The Hebbs lived in southern Maryland and the District of Columbia before the Civil War, but John Wise Hebb enlisted in the Second

Louisiana Regiment in New Orleans on 9 May 1861.[46] On 22 June 1861 he was transferred to the Seventh Regiment of Louisiana volunteers, but no record of him serving with that regiment has been found. In early 1862 he was a second lieutenant in the Twenty-fourth Battalion of Virgina Partisan Rangers. This unit operated in northern Virginia, and Hebb lost a horse killed in action near Culpeper Court House on 12 July 1862. On 5 January 1863 the unit was disbanded and many of the men were transferred to other units. Hebb was listed as belonging to Company B of the Fifth Virginia Cavalry, but most of the men assigned to the company failed to serve with it.

Hebb appears to have changed from army to navy partisan work in early 1863. The operations of his group are described in some detail in two short journals kept by brothers from southern Maryland and published in 1867 in the *History of the United States Secret Service* by the Union counterintelligence agent General Lafayette C. Baker, but their significance has been overlooked.[47]

The authors of the journals were James R. Milburn and Charles W. Milburn, natives of southern Maryland. From the journals the following sequence can be pieced together. The brothers crossed the Potomac into Northumberland County, Virginia, on 23 July 1863 and made their way to Richmond on foot. On 27 July, the day after they arrived in Richmond, they called on General Winder and got a pass that allowed them to move freely about the city. They also called on "Mr. Barton," probably Major William S. Barton, who was working for Winder at this point (he had established the first clandestine courier route through southern Maryland in 1861).

On 30 July the brothers went by rail to Weldon, North Carolina, and from there to Buffalo Springs in Mecklenburg County, Virginia, arriving the next day. Buffalo Springs was the location of a small resort that advertised the corrective powers of a series of mineral springs. At the springs hotel the brothers were assigned to room 49 in what was locally known as "Rowdy Row." Apparently the young men who habituated that part of the resort were noted for enjoying their stay. The Milburns remained at the resort until 28 August, when they returned to Richmond.

While at the resort the brothers were apparently taught how to write reports in the form of personal letters. At least, they both wrote letters to the same nonexistent persons on the same days, a technique used by Confederate agents in other circumstances. Cryptic remarks in the journals suggest that they may also have been taught observation and other techniques of the spy.

One may surmise that the brothers attended a four-week school for clandestine operations. A remote resort would be a suitable place for such a school. Neither brother mentioned an instructor, but Mecklenburg County was the home of Randolph-Macon College, which had closed because the war had drained off some faculty and most prospective students. It is possible that some remaining faculty were employed as instructors in the school at Buffalo Springs. This notion is supported in a roundabout way by the fact that after the war Randolph-Macon College purchased and moved into the hotel and resort at Ashland, Virginia, which may also have been used by Confederate intelligence personnel.

After returning to Richmond, the Milburn brothers were enlisted into the Confederate (volunteer) navy and on 2 September left Richmond on the Richmond, Fredericksburg, and Potomac Railroad. One brother reported traveling in a group headed by Captain Hebb, and the other noted that his group was headed by Walter Bowie (probably the Bowie from VMI). Both groups left the train at Milford and then marched east, through Caroline County, to Layton's ferry on the Rappahannock, where they crossed to Leeds and then went north five miles to the plantation of a Mr. Rust on the Potomac. The Rust plantation was in what is now the northern part of Colonial Beach, Virginia.[48] It lies between Rosiers Creek and Mattox Creek, where a Confederate Signal Corps camp was located. This camp appears to have been the main base for the naval partisans. One group, however, moved to the Nomini River, twenty miles down the Potomac. From there they moved to southern Maryland and then to Sharpes Island and Tilghman Island in the Chesapeake.

On 2 November Captain Hebb was captured and imprisoned in Maryland. The record of his imprisonment by the provost marshal of Baltimore says that Hebb was an acting master's mate in the Confederate Navy, for which he had been recruiting within federal lines, and that he had been secreting arms for the use of privateers.[49] Hebb escaped on 26 December 1863 and apparently rejoined his men in Virginia. James Milburn was captured about 15 February 1864 in Maryland. The other brother moved to Mathias Point with Walter Bowie. They contacted Lieutenant Cawood of the Signal Corps and Mr. Hooe at Waterloo on the Potomac, about three miles upriver from Mathias Point. On 13 September 1863 Bowie and eight men crossed into Maryland. Milburn and another group crossed into Maryland on 19 September. On 22 September Milburn got orders from Bowie to return to Virginia, which he did on the following day, accompanied by two escaped prisoners from Point Lookout.

In November, Charles Milburn was in Baltimore and took passage on a steamer to West River. From there he went overland to Herring Bay, where he apparently got a small boat. He tried to sail from there down the bay to Virginia but was forced ashore near Cove Point, just above the mouth of the Patuxent, where he was captured.

From these journals we can draw several conclusions about Captain Hebb's naval partisans. Some of them had training in clandestine operations, making it possible for them to play a wide variety of roles behind enemy lines. Although there was Union opposition, it was possible for trained Confederate partisans to live and move through southern Maryland for extended periods of time.

The examples of Mosby, Wood, and Hebb show that the basic precepts of the eighteenth-century textbook *The Partisan* still held true. Good discipline and careful prior planning made irregular warfare a useful tactic. Many Confederate irregular warfare units did not have the required discipline or skilled leadership, but in the cases outlined in this chapter, the organizations had official sponsorship at various levels in the Confederate government. Mosby operated with close attention from General Lee; Wood had the blessings of Jefferson Davis, the secretary of the navy, and Lee; and Hebb had the backing of General Winder's organization. With such official control, the respective irregular warfare activities could be used to play a positive role in operations of special interest to the Confederate government. More than anything else, however, these cases illustrate the extent to which senior members of the Confederate establishment involved themselves directly in the conception and direction of irregular operations.

Notes

ABBREVIATIONS

NA   National Archives
OR   U.S. War Department, *The War of the Rebellion: A Compilation of the Official Records of the Union and Confederate Armies.* 128 vols. Washington, D.C.: U.S. Government Printing Office, 1880–1901.
ORN   U.S. Navy Department, *Official Records of the Union and Confederate*

Navies in the War of the Rebellion. 30 vols. Washington, D.C.: U.S. Government Printing Office, 1894–1914.

RG   Record Group

1. The Library of Congress copy of this book could not be found. The copy used here was that belonging to the Virginia State Library. The names of the author and translator are not known.

2. *OR,* Ser. 1, vol. 51, pt. 2, p. 526.

3. Confederate Secretary of War to E. A. Banks, 23 April 1862, M-524, RG 109, NA.

4. John Letcher, "Colonel Richard Thomas Zarvona," *Confederate Veteran* 22 (September 1914): 418. Another version of the Zarvona-Letcher relationship, varying in some important details, is in the John Letcher Papers, Box 103, George C. Marshall Research Library, Lexington, Va.

5. Lee A. Wallace, Jr., *A Guide to Virginia Military Organizations, 1861–1865* (Richmond: Virginia Civil War Commission, 1964), p. 172.

6. For more on Mosby, see Virgil Carrington Jones, *Ranger Mosby* (Chapel Hill: University of North Carolina Press, 1944); and Kevin H. Siepal, *Rebel: The Life and Times of John Singleton Mosby* (New York: St. Martin's Press, 1983).

7. Channing M. Smith, *Confederate Veteran* 31 (September 1923); John S. Mosby, *The Memoirs of Colonel John S. Mosby,* ed. Charles Wells Russell (Bloomington: Indiana University Press, 1981), p. 321. In his memoirs, Mosby corrected the figure of $168,000 given in his first official report of the raid.

8. For Mosby's emphasis on the pistol, see John S. Mosby, *Mosby's War Reminiscences* (Boston: George A. Jones, 1887), pp. 89, 105; and John W. Munson, *Reminiscences of a Mosby Guerrilla* (New York: Moffett, Yard, 1906), pp. 23–25.

9. Mosby, *Mosby's War Reminiscences,* p. 10.

10. *OR,* Ser. 1, vol. 25, pt. 2, p. 856.

11. Mosby's capture of General Stoughton is described in John Scott, *Partisan Life with Col. John S. Mosby* (New York: Harper & Bros., 1867), pp. 43–53; and James J. Williamson, *Mosby's Rangers* (New York: Sturgis and Walton, 1909), pp. 33–46.

12. See Mosby, *Mosby's War Reminiscences,* pp. 104ff.

13. *OR,* Ser. 1, vol. 29, pt. 2, pp. 653, 654.

14. Scott, *Partisan Life with Mosby,* p. 209.

15. Williamson, *Mosby's Rangers,* p. 18.

16. Ibid., p. 175.

17. *OR,* Ser. 1, vol. 43, pt. 2, p. 258.

18. Ibid., p. 918.

19. A more complete account of Walter Bowie and his Civil War activities was given in a lecture by James O. Hall on 23 March 1983 at the Friends Meeting House, Sandy Spring, Maryland, to a largely Quaker audience. A copy of this lecture is on file with the Montgomery County Civil War Round Table, Rockville, Maryland.

20. Walter Bowie to Judah P. Benjamin, 3 February 1862, Letters Received, Confederate Secretary of War, File 10287-B-1862, RG 109, NA.

21. James G. Wiltshire was one of the twenty-five men who accompanied Bowie on this raid into Maryland. Wiltshire's well-written and detailed account appeared in the *Baltimore American,* 1 July 1900, p. 29.

22. A former slave, Rachel Simms, testified 25 May 1865 at the trial of Dr. Samuel A. Mudd. She recalled Bowie being there but thought it was "last summer."

See Benn Pitman, *The Assassination of President Lincoln and the Trial of the Conspirators* (1865; rpt. ed. Philip Van Doren Stern. New York: Funk and Wagnalls, 1954), p. 170.

23. Mosby, *Memoirs*, p. 374.

24. Lee to Mosby, 29 October 1864, Manuscript Collection, No. 21767, Virginia State Library, Richmond.

25. Virginia Military Institute, *Register of Former Cadets* (Lexington, Va.: Virginia Military Institute, 1939).

26. Most of the information on John Taylor Wood is taken from Royce Gordon Shingleton, *John Taylor Wood: Sea Ghost of the Confederacy* (Athens: University of Georgia Press, 1979).

27. Ibid., p. 69.

28. R. E. Lee to G. W. C. Lee, 7 April 1864, Charles Marshall Papers, Southern Historical Collection, University of North Carolina, Chapel Hill. Fitzhugh was actually a member of the Fifth Virginia Calvary.

29. *OR*, Ser. 1, vol. 51, pt. 2, pp. 1000–1001.

30. Ibid., vol. 37, pt. 1, p. 767.

31. R. E. Lee, *The Wartime Papers of R. E. Lee*, ed. Clifford Dowdey and Louis H. Manarin (New York: Bramhall House, 1961), p. 811.

32. R. E. Lee, *Lee's Dispatches: Unpublished Letters of General Robert E. Lee, CSA, to Jefferson Davis and the War Department of the Confederate States of America, 1862–1865*, ed. Douglas Southall Freeman and Grady McWhiney (New York: Putnam, 1957), pp. 269–71.

33. Bradley T. Johnson, *Maryland*, vol. 2 of *Confederate Military History*, ed. Clement A. Evans (rpt. Secaucus, N.J.: Blue and Grey Press, n.d.) p. 126; John C. Brennan, "General Bradley T. Johnson's Plan to Abduct President Lincoln," *Chronicles of St. Mary's* 22 (November–December 1974): 413–24.

34. Ralph W. Donnelly, *The History of the Confederate States Marine Corps* (Washington, N.C.: Privately printed, 1976), p. 78.

35. James D. Ferguson Diary, Munford-Ellis Papers, Thomas Munford Division, Duke University Library, Durham, N.C.

36. Donnelly, *History of the Confederate States Marine Corps*, p. 79.

37. *OR*, Ser. 1, vol. 40, pt. 3, p. 759.

38. John B. Jones, *A Rebel War Clerk's Diary*, ed. Howard Swiggett, 2 vols. (New York: Old Hickory Book Shop, 1938), 2:246.

39. *OR*, Ser. 1, vol. 40, pt. 3, p. 761.

40. Donnelly, *History of the Confederate States Marine Corps*, p. 81.

41. *OR*, Ser. 1, vol. 5, p. 467.

42. Ferguson Diary, 14 July 1864.

43. F. W. Cox, Compiled Service Record, NA; Virginia Military Institute, *Register of Former Cadets*.

44. Hamilton Cochran, *Blockade Runners of the Confederacy* (Indianapolis: Bobbs-Merrill, 1958), pp. 122–23, 137, 142; Captain Roberts [C. Augustus Hobart-Hampden], *Never Caught* (Carolina Beach, N.C.: Blockade Runner Museum, 1967), pp. 44–48; U.S. Navy Department, *Civil War Naval Chronology* (Washington, D.C.: U.S. Government Printing Office, 1971), pt. 6, p. 222.

45. Cochran, *Blockade Runners*, pp. 267–68, Roberts, *Never Caught*, p. 44.

46. John Wise Hebb, Compiled Service Record, NA.

47. Lafayette C. Baker, *History of the United States Secret Service* (Philadelphia: Privately printed by Lafayette C. Baker, 1867), pp. 185–90.

48. Westmoreland County, Virginia, Land Record, County Offices, Montross, Va.

49. John W. Hebb, Compiled Service Records (both army and navy), NA.

7

The "Department of Dirty Tricks" and the Secret Service

Despite the eventually fatal imbalance of resources between the two warring sides, the Confederacy held one advantage at the outset: its enemy commenced the war with no secrets. Having played a vital role in the establishment, organization, and running of the federal government, southerners brought with them the knowledge of whatever techniques and instrumentalities for waging war had been considered or employed by the United States government. Confederate leaders had held positions that gave them access to knowledge: Davis had been secretary of war and chairman of the Senate Military Affairs Committee; Cooper, adjutant general of the U.S. Army; Mallory, naval affairs specialist and for the decade before the war, chairman of that committee of the Senate. The Confederacy also had the advantage of the underdog—the inclination to innovate, to try new and unorthodox methods, to employ strategies and tactics to compensate for imbalances, such as the tactics of partisan or guerrilla warfare on land and at sea. Finally, the Confederacy had men of genius in certain areas. Matthew Fontaine Maury, internationally famous as an oceanographer—"Pathfinder of the Seas"—was perhaps the closest the federal government had to a chief scientist. Gabriel James Rains of North Carolina, West Point Class of 1827 (a year ahead of Jefferson Davis), was an infantry "light colonel" of distinguished service. The two shared a fascination with explosive ordnance.[1]

Maury was serving in Washington, D.C., in the 1840s when Samuel Colt (inventor of the revolving pistol identified with his name) was trying to interest the government in his submarine explosive battery, an advanced system for electronic detonation of

155

"mines." Whether Maury was directly involved with the highly secretive Colt remains unknown, but his professional interests would surely have drawn him indirectly into knowledge of what Colt was about and perhaps even to observation of Colt's dramatic demonstration in the Potomac in 1844.[2]

The Civil War brought Maury back to his native Virginia, and a natural concern with the defense of its extensive seacoast prompted his interest in mine warfare. He became a member of Governor Letcher's Advisory Council on 23 April 1861, just three days after his resignation from the U.S. Navy, and a little more than two months later, on 7 July, the U.S. Navy had its first encounter with Confederate mines in the waters of the Potomac.

In the interim, Maury, encouraged by Confederate Secretary of the Navy Mallory, had gone immediately to work to demonstrate the effect of a submarine mine against a surface ship. Preferring to use electricity to detonate the mines but frustrated by a lack of insulated wire, he turned to percussion and the use of a mechanical striking system set off by contact or remotely by a cord. His invention was demonstrated to an initially skeptical, then shocked and persuaded group of state and Confederate officials at the Richmond waterfront in June.[3] Given a title, office, and funding, Maury went to work with zeal, tackling the James River first.

During this same time the USS *Pawnee*, a patrol steamer, encountered "torpedoes" moored in the Potomac.[4] The responsible party was another former naval officer now in the Confederate navy, Lieutenant Beverly Kennon, Jr. Whether working with Maury or independently, Kennon emerged as an expert on mine warfare. Others, too, came to assist Maury or to learn from him. Lieutenant Isaac N. Brown, CSN, followed Maury's guidance in planning a system of electric torpedoes to assist General Leonidas Polk's defense of the Mississippi River.[5] Lieutenant William L. Maury, a relative, and Lieutenant Hunter Davidson joined Maury's Submarine Battery Service, when Maury set up shop as the Bureau of Special Service in a building at Ninth and Bank streets, a few doors from the Signal (and Secret Service) Bureau of the War Department.[6] In June 1862 Maury was sent to England, where research and development opportunities occupied him throughout the war. Hunter Davidson replaced him with a civilian, R. O. Crowley, as his "electrician," and to Davidson, whose name deserves to be better known, goes the credit for translating Maury's ideas into practice.[7]

Concurrent with the riverine defense systems, fears of being outnumbered and hard-pressed prompted a similar recourse by an infantry officer, Brigadier General Gabriel J. Rains, who had long held an interest in explosive ordnance. (In the Seminole War he had experimented with what today would be termed antipersonnel mines, composed of buried artillery shells.) Serving on the Peninsula during the spring of 1862 under General Magruder, Rains participated in Magruder's brilliant delaying action against the slow advance of McClellan, and he had a few tricks of his own to add to Magruder's *opera bouffe*. He instructed some of his men in devising pressure-sensitive fuses for shells and planted them on the lines of approach to the evacuated Confederate lines around Yorktown.

The resultant explosions were all out of proportion to Union losses. Rains met a storm of protest from his foes and even from his new commanding officer, General James Longstreet, who joined northerners in condemning this dastardly, immoral, if not illegal, method of waging war. Rains staunchly defended his action, although he admitted that some of his men might have gone beyond his intentions in applying inventions in prankish ways ("booby traps," they were called in a later war). He appealed directly to the War Department with an endorsement from his immediate superior, crusty D. H. Hill, that "in my opinion all means of destroying our brutal enemies are lawful and proper."[8]

Secretary of War George Wythe Randolph, grandson of Thomas Jefferson, rendered a masterful opinion. Without unduly offending Longstreet or undercutting his authority, he preserved Rains and Rains's innovativeness for the Confederacy. His views also provide an insight into the thinking of confederate officialdom on the moral aspects of waging war:

Whether shells planted in roads or parapets are contrary to the usages of war depends upon the purpose with which they are used.

It is not admissible in civilized warfare to take life with no other object than the destruction of life. Hence it is inadmissible to shoot sentinels and pickets, because nothing is attained but the destruction of life. *It would be admissible, however, to shoot a general, because you not only take life but deprive an army of its head.*

It is admissible to plant shells in a parapet to repel an assault or in a road to check pursuit because the object is to save the work in one case and the army in the other.

It is not admissible to plant shells merely to destroy life and without other design than that of depriving your enemy of a few men, without materially injuring him.

It is admissible to plant torpedoes in a river or harbor, because they drive off blockading or attacking fleets.[9]

Finally, Randolph concluded, "As Generals Rains and Longstreet differ in this matter, the inferior in rank should give way," adding quickly, "or, if he [Rains, the junior officer] prefers it, he may be assigned to the river defenses, where such things are clearly admissible." Rains, eager to pursue mine warfare, jumped at the invitation, and Randolph welcomed him to Richmond, adding "Rains' Torpedo Service" (officially, the Torpedo Bureau) to the circle of bureaus of the War Department.[10]

Although the lines of demarcation were not always clear, even during the war, and they have been thoroughly blurred and confused by later writers, there were two distinct Confederate organizations at work developing mine warfare, one under the Navy Department (Davidson) and one under the War Department (Rains).[11] Both organizations, the Navy's Submarine Battery Service and the War Department's Torpedo Bureau, were authorized by Congress in an act of October 1862 that also provided for secret services.[12] Riverine operations were an ever-present area of overlap or potential conflict of responsibility in the division of effort based on water and land use or between subterra and submarine torpedoes, as they were described. But in a service in which men such as John Taylor Wood held dual commissions, sailors manned artillery pieces in land fortifications, and army men captured ships, what was important, as Lee once remarked, was not who got the credit as much as who took action.[13] Traditional rivalry between the army and navy, however, was ingrained, and not all were as unparochial as Lee.

There was yet another distinction between the two organizations, apart from their departmental or service allegiance: Davidson specialized in electrical control systems, whereas Rains preferred mechanical devices. Davidson and Crowley apparently viewed themselves as scientists of war and tended to consider Rains and his instruments of destruction as beneath them. Going beyond traditional army-navy standoffishness, the bureaus tended to keep each other at arm's length, although in the field, where there was more than enough work for both, there was a more tolerant and even cooperative atmosphere among subordinates. The assignment of naval Lieutenant Brown to General Polk has already been noted, and both naval and army officers served Beauregard in devising defensive (and even offensive) schemes around

Charleston and along the South Carolina, Georgia, and Florida coasts. Weak batteries, poor insulation, and shortages of wire plagued the electricians, making some, like Rains, prefer mechanical devices.[14] Both types suffered from inferior or water-dampened powder, tidal disruption, primitive minesweeping, and malfunctioning firing mechanisms, and both types lost effectiveness if they were spotted or informed on—and possibly even from sabotage. Still, the damage sustained on land and water was considerably greater than that normally attributed to mines, the number planted was greatly in excess of that generally encountered in the histories, and funding for mines was increasing. The unmeasurable factor was the effect on enemy morale, the psychological warfare aspect of these weapons of destruction. Silent, deadly, impersonal, and devoid of compassion, torpedoes tended to replace "black horse cavalry" and "masked batteries" as fearsome and unnerving to the enlisted ranks. As one writer later expressed it, torpedoes "attack both matter and mind."[15]

In August and September 1863, official arrangements were made in Richmond to dispatch mine warfare experts to the field under orders from the Engineer Bureau (presumably serving as cover for the Torpedo Bureau) and at the direction of Secretary of War Seddon:

I have the honor to send you the following list of men, who, by the wish of the honorable Secretary of War, are to be employed in your department on the special service of destroying the enemy's property by torpedoes and similar inventions, vis: John Kirk, Charles Littlepage, John Silure, Robert Cruzebaur, E. Allen, W. D. Mille, and C. Williams.

These men should each be enlisted in and form part of an engineer company, but will, nevertheless, be employed, so far as possible, in the Service specified above, and, when the public interests in your judgment require it, details of additional men may be made, either from the engineer troops or from the line, to aid them in their particular duties. Their compensation will be 50 per cent of the property destroyed by them by the use of torpedoes or of similar devices. Beyond this, they will be entitled to such other reward as Congress may here after provide.[16]

A similar letter went to General Joseph E. Johnston, commanding the Department of the West.[17] It listed E. C. Singer, J. D. Brannan, R. W. Dunn, B. A. Whitney, D. Bradbury, James Jones, C. E. Tracy, J. R. Fretwell, and L. C. Hirschburger. On 15 September 1863, also acting under Seddon's approval, Colonel Rives amended the assignments, notifying General Smith that Singer, Dunn, and

Fretwell would be coming to him (instead of Johnston), along with one F. M. Tucker, a total of eleven specialists in torpedo warfare.[18]

Beauregard seems to have been the most willing of all the Confederate generals to try innovations in warfare, especially if they promised compensation for his lack of manpower. Although Major Norris of the Signal (and Secret Service) Bureau had no responsibility for torpedo warfare, he had been on the Peninsula with Magruder and Rains and doubtless shared the opinion of Rains and D. H. Hill about the propriety of such weapons. In a semiofficial letter of 3 October 1863 to Beauregard (with whom Norris maintained a closer relationship than the disparity in rank would suggest), Norris mentioned that some new developments in torpedoes were forthcoming and that great things were expected of them.[19] But an officer nominally of the Signal Corps was indirectly Norris's greatest contribution to Beauregard—Captain E. Pliny Bryan. Born near Surratt's tavern in Prince George's County, Maryland, and a neighbor and friend of Charles H. Cawood of the Secret Line, Bryan was a prosecessionist in the Maryland legislature when the war started, and when Union troops moved to arrest those legislators, he crossed the Potomac to offer his services to Virginia and the Confederacy.[20] Native to the Potomac crossings, he was quickly involved in espionage and reconnaissance, and he had learned signaling from Alexander. His ability to penetrate Union territory to gain intelligence brought him to the attention of General Lee, who personally employed him as a spy.[21] But Bryan was not content with such passive forms of warfare as intelligence, and he became perhaps the most skilled army practitioner in the application of mine warfare. Conflicting orders between Lee and Beauregard, the former seeking to use him as a spy and the latter as a demolitions expert, show his versatility and reputation. Demolitions won out, and Bryan served for a year along the coast and waterways from Florida to the James in Virginia, inflicting heavy damage to the Yankees and impeding their progress. It was a terrible blow to this shadowy side of the Confederate war effort when, in September 1864, E. Pliny Bryan contracted a fatal case of yellow fever.

A navy counterpart of Bryan was Lieutenant Beverly Kennon, Jr. Kennon was involved with torpedoes from the outset, and to him goes the credit for the first encounter the U.S. Navy had with these new instruments of destruction. Kennon devised and set afloat in the Potomac barrel buoys, from which were suspended containers of gunpowder with waterproof fuses. The *Pawnee*, patrolling the

Potomac, encountered these on 7 July 1861. Whether Kennon was acting independent of Maury's early efforts or under his guidance has never been settled, but Kennon became the best-known navy torpedo operator. In an early display of army-navy cooperation, General Leonidas Polk, who was building river defenses along the Mississippi in the summer of 1861, had had a navy lieutenant, Isaac N. Brown, assigned to his staff. Brown was an old navy associate of Maury and aware of Maury's ideas, and he may have prompted Polk to request Secretary of the Navy Mallory to dispatch Maury personally to supervise the effort on the Mississippi. Instead, Kennon was sent from New Orleans, where he was on ordnance and torpedo duty, and he and Brown set up "the first combat electric mine station to be established in America and, probably in the world."[22] These mines were concealed in the water and set off by closing a telegraph key from a hidden location along the riverbank. They became the model for application in Virginia and elsewhere, when insulated wire and galvanic battery supplies permitted.

"Spar torpedoes," demolition charges placed at the end of a pole and delivered against the side of a ship by launch or boat, were a logical evolution of mine warfare. Impatient when wary foes hesitated to approach their devices, aggressive Confederates plotted ways of taking the torpedoes to the enemy, changing from defensive to offensive applications. (An earlier, more primitive form of the offensive approach was simply to float mines downstream with the current, but once released, such devices were out of control.) Spar torpedoes were a forerunner of submarine boats.

Other inventors, both citizens and members of the services, contributed their ideas for torpedoes, and cooperation between citizens and government officials encouraged such inventors. Two Texans, E. C. Singer, a gunsmith, and Dr. J. R. Fretwell, both of whom were mentioned in the Engineer Bureau order of August–September 1863, collaborated in the development of a pressure or spring-actuated firing device for torpedoes. Their invention produced a quantity of torpedoes second only to those of Rains. Army Captain Francis D. Lee, an engineer under Beauregard at Charleston, perfected a chemical fuse, and Major Stephen Elliot turned a sawed-off musket into the firing mechanism for a torpedo. A more advanced idea than a musket was an electrical torpedo developed by Captain of Engineers M. Martin Gray and Lieutenant Charles G. DeLisle at Charleston. It was intended that the iron hull of a ship would complete the electrical circuit inside and detonate the mine.[23]

"Horological bombs" (we would call them "time bombs" today) were developed by several men, among them Kennon-trained Master Zedekiah McDaniel of Kentucky and Francis M. Ewing of Mississippi, members of the Submarine Battery Service at Vicksburg, who worked with Kennon himself, and Lieutenant Isaac Brown and John Maxwell, an Irishman from St. Louis. Captain Thomas E. Courtney perfected one form of torpedo that was far ahead of its time. Cast of iron in the irregular shape of a lump of coal and painted black, it was a self-contained explosive charge with a fuse, intended to be placed in the coal supply of a ship. President Davis personally examined and approved the device and kept one (inert, one would imagine) in his office as a souvenir paperweight. Working with Courtney was John Maxwell, inventor of the time bomb. This team also produced a torpedo similar to the lump of "coal" in a stick of wood—perhaps targeted against the wood-fired locomotives of the time.[24]

In August 1863 Courtney was authorized in the District of Arkansas, Trans-Mississippi Department, to raise a secret service corps of up to twenty men; the order did not specify their mission.[25] That December he broadened his horizons and proposed to President Davis that a separate secret service corps be set up, particularly for use on the inland waterways of the Mississippi Valley, but even going outside the Confederacy, into the North, the West Indies, and to Europe. A bill to authorize such an enterprise was drafted by Courtney, passed by Congress, and signed by Davis on 17 February 1864.[26] The organization was to consist of twenty-five men, and the War Department was to provide the necessary chemicals to produce the bombs. Compensation was to be reckoned up to 50 percent of the value of destruction accomplished, to be paid in 4 percent bonds. Courtney's secret service corps was intended to make use of the coal, stick, and time bombs he, Maxwell, and others had developed. Because of their secrecy and the emotion raised by admission of involvement with this highly controversial form of warfare, members tended to remain mute about their accomplishments, even well after the end of the war. Some explosions aboard ships—such as the one that destroyed General Benjamin F. "Beast" Butler's luxurious headquarters steamer, Greyhound, on the James on 27 November 1864 (almost taking the lives of Butler, Rear Admiral David Dixon Porter, and Major General Robert C. Schenck, who were aboard)—have the hallmarks of their work. But a well-recorded exploit is that of the City Point bombing that came close to removing Grant, Meade, and their headquarters staff from the scene.[27]

On 9 August 1864 Maxwell and R. K. Dillard unobtrusively entered the massive Union supply base at City Point, Virginia. They carried with them a clockwork bomb devised by Maxwell, which contained twelve pounds of powder. Bluffing his way successfully, Maxwell saw to it that the "captain's box" was taken aboard one of the barges tied up at a City Point wharf and stored below deck. He and Dillard then retired to a convenient observation post on a bluff and sat back to await the results. What happened an hour later exceeded their expectation. Powder, artillery shells, ammunition, and other forms of ordnance and implements of war were touched off, and the resultant explosions became an enduring memory for all those present. Maxwell was temporarily in shock; Dillard was permanently deafened. Destruction boggled the minds of those who later tried to describe it. The human incidents better captured the force of the explosions—a half-mile from the scene, bayonet-first in the ground, was the musket of a guard; an exchanged Confederate prisoner of war, awaiting return to his lines, was killed; Grant wrote to General Henry W. Halleck in Washington that "every part of the yard used as my headquarters is filled with splinters and fragments of shell," and his escape was a near miracle. Some measure of the destruction is offered by the very rough estimate that it took 58 lives, wounded 126, and inflicted $4 million in loss of supplies and government property. The immediate northern reaction was exactly what the southerners must have hoped for—they thought it was an accident on an ordnance barge. "It is probable we shall never know how the accident occurred," reported the chief quartermaster. The truth came out two months after Appomattox, when Halleck informed Secretary of War Stanton: "I have just received the original official report of John Maxwell, of the rebel secret service, of the blowing up of the ordnance stores at City Point last year. It appears from this report that the explosion was caused by a horological torpedo placed on the barge by John Maxwell and R. K. Dillard, acting under the direction of Brig. Gen. G. J. Rains and Capt. Z. McDaniel. I have ordered the arrest of these persons, if they can be found."[28]

Captain McDaniel was the Kentuckian whom Kennon had trained as a member of the Vicksburg Submarine Battery Service in August 1862. He and a colleague, Francis M. Ewing, claimed credit (and compensation) for destruction of the *Cairo* in a celebrated incident recalled in this century by the raising of this ironclad.[29] Their claim for compensation (one-half of the estimated value of the *Cairo*, or $76,726.30) was never paid, in part because they had kept their device a secret from the government, which was contrary to Confederate law, and in part because they were simply "doing their duty." But on 29 February 1864 McDaniel was made captain of Company A, Secret Service, under Superintendent Rains of the Torpedo Service. Records preserved in the National Archives show Joseph C. Frank as first lieutenant and a roster of some twenty-six men in Company A.[30] Their dispositions, circa September 1864, show ten men in Richmond, eight inside enemy lines; three in Mobile; two each in Augusta, Lynchburg, and en route; and one in Pittsylvania County, Virginia, awaiting orders. Although the designation "Company A," sometimes associated with McDaniel's unit, implies at least one other company, contemporary secrecy, the intentional destruction of secret service records, and the fragmentary nature of preserved records make it difficult to be precise about the organizational relationships at a given time. In any event, both Courtney's efforts and those of McDaniel (including Maxwell, who evidently worked at times with both men) fell under the orders of Rains's Torpedo Service.

As torpedoes (mines or bombs) were both offensive and defensive weapons of the Confederacy and, in more compact forms, lent themselves to sabotage and covert warfare, so other weapons and tactics were employed in similar ways. These ranged from direct attack to the tools of the arsonist. As one pursues indignant reports from Union authorities, a name crops up repeatedly (or perhaps it seems that way because of its peculiarity)—Minor Major. Major, or Majors, as the name also appears, operated in the Mississippi Valley, and his specialty was fire. He and his colleagues, all evidently candidates for the gallows if captured and identified, were civilians organized into a strike force by a former Missouri editor, Judge Joseph W. Tucker, sometime in 1863.[31]

Having already established his reputation with General Polk, Major and Thomas L. Clark were sent by that officer to Richmond with a letter of recommendation of 27 February 1864.[32] President Davis referred them to the secretary of the navy, who, in turn, sent them to Seddon. They were identified as "two of the principal persons who have been engaged in destroying boats on the western rivers" (which is doubtless the reason Davis thought first of Mallory's jurisdiction), and through John Bullock Clark, Sr., a member of Congress from Missouri, they requested a private and confidential interview with Seddon. Their purpose was not revealed beyond that, but it is reasonable to infer that they sought authorization and some form of funding or compensation for their proposed mission.

Tucker had broached his plans for covert warfare to Seddon the previous December, and on 14 February 1864 he addressed the following letter to the secretary:

> *Mr. Seddon:* I beg your permission to write a few words, after the style of a plain unofficial, but earnest man, writing to a man of practical wisdom.
>
> I feel, as intensely as it is possible to feel, the vital necessity of striking hard blows now, and striking at as many points, and in as many ways as possible, so as to aid our cause and save our country.
>
> I have perfected my plans, and distributed my men, with means improvised for the purpose, (since the government has not as yet paid our force any money) and between the *1st and 15th of March*, on *the same day*, I propose to destroy the enemy's transports, arsenals, navy yards, stores, etc. in accordance with the outline of the plan I gave you in December.
>
> I beg that this plan be borne in mind as *one link* in the chain of testimony in favor of our force, *on the same day at all points*, we mean to strike effectually, so as to exert an influence upon the spring campaign.
>
> Hon. John B. Clark did me the kindness to advise me by letter that the Senate had passed a bill—he did not state its provisions—which might aid in facilitating my plans, which he supposed would also be passed by the House. This led me to conclude it was the bill which you informed me in our latest interview you would propose and submit to the Military Committee, for the purpose of putting this *secret service* upon a systematic and legal footing: and then would give me those facilities which I asked, in some *written propositions* submitted at your suggestion.
>
> Mr. Seddon, please do me the kindness to take *ten minutes* of your over taxed time, and give me the commision, or order, or direction, or authority, or recognition, which will enable me to prosecute this work vigorously and systematically; and *I promise you to render a good account of our labors.*
>
> I visit my family for a few days, with whom I have spent *one week* in *two and a half years.* I shall be much gratified to receive your orders; and for twenty days to come, my address will be "Hebron, S.C."—with great respect &c &c[33]

The bill referred to was "to organize bodies for the capture and destruction of the enemy's property, by land or sea, and to authorize compensation for the same." It had been working its way through the two houses in secret sessions and finally passed the House on 9 February and the Senate on 12 February 1864. It included the establishment of a Secret Service fund of $5 million, $1 million of which was set apart for Canadian operations, to be disbursed by Secretary of State Benjamin, and is the same legislation noted earlier which resulted in Seddon's order to Thomas E. Courtney.

The demonstrations Tucker planned for March cannot be identified as having taken place—perhaps they were delayed or found to be unnecessary to impress Seddon. In any event, if federal counterintelligence reporting can be believed (and a Union agent had identified Tucker as leader of the "steam-boat burners" in December 1863), Tucker received his desired authority from Seddon and set to work in the Mississippi Valley. An indication of what transpired is provided in a confession by one of his men, Edward Frazor, who was captured and imprisoned in St. Louis.[34] He claimed to have met with Seddon in the summer of 1864 in company with "Clark" (probably John B.) acting as his intermediary. Frazor, it seems, was in Richmond seeking compensation for their activities. Seddon sent him to Benjamin, who studied the claims overnight, had Frazor verify them the next day, and then offered $30,000 in greenbacks (federal currency). Frazor declined; Benjamin said he would study the matter further. (These delays suggest that Benjamin, whose office was on the floor below President Davis's in the old Customs Building in Richmond, was consulting with someone else.) Benjamin's next offer was $35,000 as a down payment, with $15,000 on deposit, payable in four months if a claim for destruction of federal medical stores in Louisville in 1863 could be verified. Frazor then went to Benjamin's office to sign the receipt and, while there, was sent for by Davis. Accompanied by Benjamin, Frazor went to the president's office and, according to his statement, underwent a detailed and penetrating questioning about his ability to take out a specific target: the "long bridge" in Nashville, an important railroad center for the North. Davis's purported questioning was that of an experienced operator: did Frazor know the target, what would be the best approach to it, would Frazor undertake the mission, what assistance would be required from Davis? Benjamin set $400,000 as the pay for the accomplishment of the mission, then, upon Frazor's acceptance of the task, gave him a draft for $34,800 in gold payable in Columbia,

South Carolina. Clark then obtained twelve or more passes from Seddon.

The party—six in all—left Richmond, drew the money, and set out for Memphis. At Mobile they were arrested by Confederate authorities but released after General Richard Taylor, the area commander, communicated with Davis. They continued to Memphis, where they separated and went about their mission. By January 1865, federal authorities were receiving reports of their identities and whereabouts, and in February, thanks to an informant, one William Murphy, ten of the team were arrested by the provost marshal in St. Louis, where Frazor decided to talk in late April 1865. He told his captors that Judge J. W. Tucker of Mobile was the "chief of this service under the Secretary of war," with Minor Majors [sic] "next in rank to Tucker, and chief of this service in Union lines." The Honorable John R. Barrett of St. Louis was said to be in charge of "land operations." (Barrett was a former congressman from Missouri, who had been in Europe in 1863—supposedly on business—where he conferred with Confederate commissioners James M. Mason in London and John Slidell in Paris. He had been arrested in 1864 as a member of the Order of American Knights but subsequently released.) Sixteen others were identified as part of Tucker's operation, including Isaac Elshire, Robert Loudon, and Thomas L. Clark, and an impressive list of boat burnings in August–September 1864 was attributed to their efforts. The Union official reporting on Frazor's testimony noted that during the course of the war, more than seventy steamboats owned in St. Louis had been destroyed by fire, only nine of them "by rebels in arms." "And," he added, "there can be little doubt but the greater portion of the balance were fired by the above or similar emissaries of the rebel government." Writing its opinion in mid-May 1865, the Bureau of Military Justice of the U.S. War Department made much of the official and personal involvement of Benjamin and Davis in sanctioning the operations, "illustrating the fact that Davis and other leaders of the rebellion have been the principals in this and other similar detestable and treasonable enterprises executed by men who were merely their hirelings."[35]

Although better documented than some other Confederate secret missions, the Tucker operation was but one, and it was centered in the Mississippi Valley. Elsewhere we describe the efforts directed out of Canada (where Minor Major sought financial assistance from Thompson) and other "cloak-and-dagger" activities.

The scope of Confederate "unconventional warfare" conducted by uniformed soldiers and sailors, secret agents, and free-lancers brings up the question whether all this activity was coordinated. Apart from the personal involvement of men such as Davis, Benjamin, and Seddon with their retentive memories, the answer would probably be "not very well."

Notes

ABBREVIATIONS

NA   National Archives

OR   U.S. War Department, *The War of the Rebellion: A Compilation of the Official Records of the Union and Confederate Armies.* 128 vols. Washington, D.C.: U.S. Government Printing Office, 1880–1901.

ORN   U.S. Navy Department, *Official Records of the Union and Confederate Navies in the War of the Rebellion.* 30 vols. Washington, D.C.: U.S. Government Printing Office, 1894–1914.

RG   Record Group

1. The classic biography of Maury is Francis Leigh Williams, *Matthew Fontaine Maury, Scientist of the Sea* (New York: Harcourt, Brace and World, 1963), with a charming companion piece for the young reader, *Ocean Pathfinder*, by the same author (New York: Harcourt, Brace and World, 1966). A concise sketch of the work of Rains and his younger brother, George Washington Rains, a fellow West Point graduate and ordnance specialist who manufactured gunpowder for the Confederacy, is the "The Rains Brothers," in Burke Davis, *Our Incredible Civil War* (New York: Holt, Rinehart and Winston, 1960), pp. 62–69. See also G. J. Rains, "Torpedoes," *Southern Historical Society Papers* 3 (May–June 1877): 255–60.

2. See Philip K. Lundeberg, *Samuel Colt's Submarine Battery: The Secret and the Enigma* (Washington, D.C.: Smithsonian Institution Press, 1974), p. 31.

3. Richard L. Maury, *A Brief Sketch of the Work of Matthew Fontaine Maury during the War, 1861–1865* (Richmond: Privately printed, 1915), pp. 6–8. The writer was Maury's son and collaborator in some of these early experiments.

4. Milton F. Perry, *Infernal Machines: The Story of Confederate Submarine and Mine Warfare* (Baton Rouge: Louisiana State University Press, 1965), pp. 3–4. U.S. Navy Department, *Civil War Naval Chronology* (Washington, D.C.: U.S. Government Printing Office, 1971), pt. 1, p. 19, credits the USS *Resolute* as being the first unit to encounter Confederate torpedoes, 7 July 1861.

5. Isaac N. Brown, "Confederate Torpedoes in the Yazoo," in Robert Underwood Johnson and Clarence Clough Buel, eds., *Battles and Leaders of the Civil War*, 4 vols. (1884–88; rpt. New York: Castle Books, 1956), 3:580.

6. *The City Intelligencer: or, Stranger's Guide* (Richmond, 1862), p. 19.

7. R. O. Crowley, "The Confederate Torpedo Service," *Century Magazine*, June 1898, quoted in Philip Van Doren Stern, *Secret Missions of the Civil War* (Chicago:

Rand McNally, 1959), pp. 207–18; Hunter Davidson, "Electrical Torpedoes as a System of Defence," *Southern Historical Society Papers* 2 (1876): 1–6.

8. Longstreet did not "recognize it as a proper or effective method of warfare." See G. Moxley Sorrel to Rains, expressing Longstreet's views, *OR*, Ser. 1, vol. 4, pt. 3, pp. 509–10.

9. Ibid., p. 510; emphasis added.

10. Ibid., p. 608. Longstreet later changed his mind. His order of 8 March 1865 at Petersburg calls upon his chief of artillery, Brigadier General E. P. Alexander, to "have some sensitive shells placed along the abatis in front of our lines . . . so that should the enemy advance and endeavor to pull [the abatis] away, they should explode and destroy any further attack" (*OR*, Ser. 1, vol. 46, pt. 2, p. 1293).

11. "Those [torpedoes] generally intended for use on land naturally fell into the hands of the War Department, while electrical torpedoes for use under water came within the province of the Navy Department," according to Confederate electrician R. O. Crowley, "Confederate Torpedo Service," p. 209.

12. Perry, *Infernal Machines*, p. 31.

13. Lee to Ewell, 11 July 1864, *OR*, Ser. 1, vol. 40, pt. 3, p. 764, concerning the mining of the James River: "There seemed to be some conflict of authority between the subterra and the submarine departments. . . . It matters little which department wins the credit, provided the work is well done."

14. A European officer in Confederate service as an engineer, Viktor Ernst Rudolph von Scheliha, lieutenant colonel and chief engineer, Department of the Gulf, provided a scientific appraisal of the Confederate experience in his *A Treatise on Coast-Defence* . . . (1868; rpt. Westport, Conn.: Greenwood Press, 1971). Von Scheliha (p. 231) considers Rains's friction fuse superior, but his knowledge of what the Confederate navy was doing with electricity seems limited.

15. Perry, *Infernal Machines*, p. 159.

16. A. L. Rives to Kirby Smith, 20 August 1863, *OR*, vol. 22, pt. 2, pp. 973–74.

17. *OR* editors' note, ibid.

18. Ibid., p. 1017.

19. Norris to Beauregard, 3 October 1863, in Jefferson Davis Norris Papers, Alderman Library, University of Virginia, Charlottesville. Similar evidence of Norris's awareness of, and willingness to involve his men in, the use of torpedoes is contained in his letter of 8 March 1864 to the secretary of war, in which he remarks on the Courtney bomb and volunteers his men for "a simultaneous distribution of the shell of Capt. Courtney in a great number of places in the enemy's lines" (Letters Received, Confederate Secretary of War, Microcopy 437, NA).

20. E. Pliny Bryan, Compiled Service Record, NA.

21. *OR*, Ser. 1, vol. 25, pt. 2, pp. 622, 626; in the latter case, Lee to Seddon, 14 February 1863, Lee mentions Bryan among "some of my best scouts."

22. Perry, *Infernal Machines*, p. 11.

23. Ibid., pp. 43, 50–55, 442.

24. Ibid., pp. 32, 130–33. See also *Military Collector and Historian* 11 (1959): 7–9, for a description of the Courtney device. The inventor's name appears variously as -enay, -ney, -nay. On Maxwell, see John W. Headley, *Confederate Operations in Canada and New York* (New York: Neale, 1906), p. 244.

25. Special Order 135, paragraph 6, Headquarters of Arkansas, Little Rock, 18 August 1863, *OR*, Ser. 1, vol. 22, pt. 2, p. 970.

26. Perry, *Infernal Machines*, pp. 135–36; *ORN*, Ser. 1, vol. 26, p. 190.

27. The official report of the team, John Maxwell to Captain Z. McDaniel, 16

December 1864, is in *OR*, Ser. 1, vol. 42, pt. 1, pp. 954–55, with endorsements by McDaniel, Company A, Secret Service, to Brigadier General Rains and Rains to the secretary of war, ibid., p. 956. See also Morris Schaff, "The Explosion of City Point," quoted in Stern, *Secret Missions*, pp. 231–35.

28. Grant to Halleck, 9 August 1864, *OR*, Ser. 1, vol. 42, pt. 1, p. 17; Halleck to Stanton, 3 June 1865, ibid., vol. 46, pt. 3, p. 1250.

29. Virgil Carrington Jones and Harold L. Peterson, *U.S.S. Cairo: The Story of a Civil War Gunboat* (Washington, D.C., 1971).

30. McDaniel's Company, Secret Service, Compiled Service Records, NA.

31. *OR*, Ser. 1, vol. 48, pt. 2, pp. 194–96; see also ibid., vol. 43, pt. 2, p. 934.

32. Letters Received, Confederate Secretary of War, Microcopy 599, reel 7, frames 0174–76, NA.

33. Ibid.

34. *OR*, Ser. 1, vol. 48, pt. 2, pp. 194–95, contains the details.

35. Ibid., pp. 196–97.

8

Confederate Operations in Canada

When Confederates looked to the North, they saw beyond their Yankee enemy a friend and possible ally. Canada stretched along the unguarded northern frontier of the United States. Its people included English-speaking citizens whose families had left the United States eighty years earlier because of their hostility to the Yankees and French citizens whose families had fought the Yankees for generations. These people and their fellow British subjects in Nova Scotia and New Brunswick were administered and garrisoned by representatives of a British nation that was officially neutral but supported or tolerated many of the efforts of the Confederacy. The Confederates, however, tended to overlook the existence of many friendly cross-border ties with the North and a basic Canadian antipathy to the institution of slavery.

Not only did the human and political atmosphere in the British provinces of North America seem favorable to the southern cause, but their geographic features made them attractive as a place from which to conduct clandestine operations against the United States. The Canadian rail net provided rapid transportation from Quebec to Windsor, Ontario, parallel to the U.S. border. It was augmented by the ship transportation available on the Greak Lakes, the St. Lawrence River, and the canals around Niagara Falls. This transportation net made it possible to move people and equipment rapidly from one point of entry into the United States to another. A clandestine group operating from the vicinity of Toronto could move speedily against almost any point from Detroit to Maine.

Any clandestine operator attempting to work against the United States would be bound to recognize the opportunities provided by

171

this combination of friendly people, a tolerant government, and advantageous geography.[1] As the Civil War progressed, a number of situations arose that made it desirable for the Confederacy to exploit these factors: the need to move people and dispatches between the Confederacy and Europe via British-owned territory; the need to procure abroad and bring into the Confederacy materials in scarce supply; the existence of a large antiwar element in the North that needed support and leadership; the presence of large numbers of Confederate prisoners-of-war in makeshift prisons not far from the northern border of the United States who might be helped to escape; the presence in Canada of escaped Confederate prisoners, stragglers, or sympathizers who found it expedient to take refuge in Canada and constituted an asset that might be actively employed on behalf of the Confederacy; and the need to support other clandestine operations in the United States designed to reduce its warmaking power.

As soon as one or more of these needs was turned into an active Confederate operation, another situation was created that required additional clandestine support. That was the need to keep abreast of the status of British and provincial policy toward the Confederates in that area and to influence both population and officials to think well of the Confederacy. In other words, Canada itself was a target for clandestine operations so that it might be used in support of operations against the United States.

Fortunately, we can trace much of the Confederate clandestine activity involved in pursuing these various goals. Some of the information is in official records, some in memoirs of participants or other publications, and some in the official reports of the U.S. consuls and consular agents stationed at various points in British North America.[2] Many specific details are missing, but the broad outline is fairly plain.

The problem of moving people and dispatches developed early. The Confederates sent James M. Mason and John Slidell as commissioners to England and France respectively. On 8 November 1861, an American warship stopped the British *Trent* on which they were passengers and took them prisoner. A diplomatic tempest resulted that caused their release and eventual arrival at their respective destinations. The affair also raised tension between Britain and the United States to the point that British troops in Canada were reinforced against a possible outbreak of war. The incident caused joy to the Confederates and put the Union representatives in Canada on the alert. Mason and Slidell had been given instructions on 3 September 1861, before their departure, and R. M. T. Hunter, the Confederate secretary of state, sent them further instructions on 8 February 1862. But when Judah Benjamin succeeded Hunter as secretary of state in March 1862, the Confederate government still had received no official information from either man. Neither arrived at his post until 30 January 1862.[3]

The U.S. consul in Quebec reported on 25 December 1861 that persons carrying "treasonable" dispatches were passing through the city.[4] These could hardly have been diplomatic dispatches, but they might well have included correspondence connected with Confederate efforts to evade the Union blockade or to other Confederate agents in Europe.

The U.S. consul in Halifax reported the first arrival of a blockade runner at that port on 6 August 1861. It was a schooner from New Bern, North Carolina, and was traveling under British registry. The consul had never heard of New Bern and suspected that the British registry was a convenience to protect the southern ownership of the vessel. Later that month the consul reported that there were many southerners in Halifax and they were working very hard to create a favorable impression on the people of the city.[5]

By the end of 1861, there was enough Confederate activity in Canada to cause concern on the part of various Union officials. In December, the U.S. consul in Quebec wrote that he needed a confidential agent to help him, and in January, the U.S. consul in Montreal hired Henry Howes to replace a New York City detective who had been stationed at Island Pond, Vermont, a convenient checkpoint on the railroad near Montreal.[6] One Confederate sympathizer in Montreal at about this time was Patrick Charles Martin, a New Yorker who had lived in Baltimore for many years. He may have been involved in anti-Union activity in Baltimore in early 1861 and seems to have moved to Canada in 1862 to escape Union retaliation. He later participated in several Confederate clandestine operations, one involving John Wilkes Booth.

The U.S. consul in Montreal reported in February 1862 that during the previous months there had been many southerners in Toronto, but that most of them stayed for a relatively short time. He estimated that about twenty southerners resided there permanently. They seemed to be concentrated in the Rossin House, one of the leading boardinghouses of the city.[7] One of the southerners at the Rossin House was William L. McDonald, who became one of the leading Confederate agents in Canada.

On 6 February 1862, the U.S. consul in Montreal commented to Washington that aid to the enemy from Canada was exaggerated except for that passing through the mails. It was not long, however, before the aid became more plentiful. In early April, the consul in Halifax reported that the *Consul* of Liverpool, a British ship of 1,040 tons, was in the harbor loaded with sheet iron and waiting for a favorable opportunity to run the blockade.[8]

It quickly became obvious that Halifax was a key to the Confederate use of British territory in North America. The pattern for ships was to go from Britain to Halifax, then to Bermuda or Nassau, and then into Wilmington, North Carolina, Charleston, South Carolina, or Savannah, Georgia. For people the route was more varied. From one of the blockaded southern ports they might go to Nassau or Bermuda and from thence to Halifax or in a few cases directly to British ports. There were alternative routes, however. Southerners might cross the Potomac into southern Maryland and then go to Baltimore. From there they might go by train to Buffalo and Niagara Falls or through New York City to Montreal. Another variant was to go down the Shenandoah Valley to the Baltimore and Ohio Railroad at or near Harpers Ferry. From there they could go to Baltimore and follow the first route, or they could go to Wheeling, where they had the choice of going to Buffalo or to Detroit or to lake ports in between. At either point the Canadian railway system would take the traveler to Point Levis, opposite Quebec, from where one could, in the warm half of the year, take a ship direct to Europe. The remainder of the year ice on the St. Lawrence prevented departures by sea, but the traveler could follow the railroad to its end at Pointe du Loup and then take a ten-day trip overland through New Brunswick and Nova Scotia to Halifax. If one were daring enough to risk arrest, it was possible to travel by rail from Quebec to Portland, Maine, and then take a two-day sea voyage to Halifax. In the West, one could pass into Confederate-controlled territory on the Mississippi River and go up the river to St. Louis or Cincinnati and then by rail to Detroit to the Canadian railroad net at Windsor across the river in Ontario. From then on the traveler could follow the same routes as those who entered at Niagara Falls or Montreal.

The need to look after ships putting into Halifax on their way to the Confederacy, and to look after travelers, made it necessary for the Confederates to establish an organization there. They employed the firm of B. Weir and Co. as their agents and Weir and

Alexander Keith, a British subject, engaged in a wide range of activities on behalf of the Confederacy.[9]

By mid-1862, Confederate couriers were exploiting these various routes with increasing frequency. On 2 July 1862, the U.S. consul in Halifax reported that a courier carrying Confederate dispatches had sailed for Europe on the *Africa*. On 15 August 1862, the consul in Montreal reported that Confederate couriers were passing through that city. On 27 August 1862, the consul in Montreal reported that a note from London indicated that a Confederate courier was due to arrive on the next steamer.[10]

August 1862 saw some other developments with considerable significance for Confederate clandestine operations. In that month, a wealthy expatriate Georgian, Robert Edwin Coxe, came to Canada from Europe and moved into a house in St. Catharines, a town on the Welland Canal a few miles inland from Niagara Falls. In that same month, George N. Sanders of Kentucky met former Governor Charles S. Moorehead of Kentucky at the Clifton House, a popular hotel on the Canadian side of Niagara Falls.[11] Sanders had lived in Europe for several years before the Civil War and doubtless knew Coxe during that period.

Sanders had acted as a political agent on behalf of the southern wing of the Democratic party for many years. His main effort in Europe seemed to have been to encourage the development of republican movements to focus attention on the defects of the monarchies so as to divert attention away from the defects of the American slaveowning democracy. In the course of those efforts he had supported Garibaldi and other republican revolutionaries and opposed Napoleon III and other autocrats. He had a mixed reputation among less daring politicians, but there is no question that he was well informed, imaginative, and willing to take the initiative to influence events.[12] Coxe and Sanders will reappear in the story of Confederate operations in Canada. Their presence in the same area at the same time in 1862 may have had special significance for later events.

On 25 August 1862, the U.S. consul in Quebec reported that Sanders had sailed on the *Luna* for Europe carrying dispatches from Jefferson Davis. During his stay in Quebec, Sanders had an interview with an important official of the government who happened to be a friend of the consul. Over a period of several weeks, the consul was able to elicit considerable information about this interview and its bearing on Sanders's mission.[13] The consul was also responsible for starting a story that cropped up when Sanders's name was mentioned. He reported that Sanders had entered Canada at Niagara Falls and that he had crossed the suspension bridge to Canada disguised as a miner carrying a carpetbag full of tools. This story has been distorted until some writers have had Sanders going to meet Horace Greeley in 1864 in the same disguise.

According to the consul's information, Sanders had said that his mission was to offer both Britain and France future rights of free trade with the South in return for current financial aid. He mentioned that eventual conditional emancipation of the slaves might be part of this package. Sanders also described the South's effort to arm itself and apparently was successful in convincing the Canadian official that the Confederacy was in good shape. He went on, however, to say that the Confederacy had made plans to rescue the border states and recover lost territory. He said that the prosouthern elements were "now completely organized for an uprising" in Maryland, Kentucky, and Tennessee. Cincinnati, Ohio, was to be the focus of an attack by a secret force being assembled in Kentucky.[14]

Sanders's bragging is pertinent to some of his later activities, but his trip had another purpose that he did not mention. He wished to arrange for the construction of several iron ships to be used as raiders and needed to come to a satisfactory financial understanding with bankers of England. These arrangements did not work out as well as Sanders had hoped, and he returned quickly to the Confederacy. On 20 September, he sailed from Ireland, and by late October he was in Richmond.

On 28 October 1862, Sanders was given a contract to carry Confederate dispatches to Europe by a special courier service,[15] apparently as a shortcut instead of the longer routes through Canada and by way of the blockade runners. When coming back through Halifax, Sanders had apparently arranged for a fast schooner to meet a secret rendezvous on the Chesapeake Bay shore of Virginia to ship dispatches by this schooner directly to Halifax for forwarding to Europe.

Unfortunately for Sanders, he was betrayed by the son of an old friend, and his own son Major Reid Sanders was captured. The major was speedily exchanged, but traveling with the traitorous friend, he tried to carry Secretary Benjamin's dispatches through the blockade out of Charleston. Again, he was betrayed, and Reid Sanders was captured for the second and last time on 4 January

1863. The dispatches were published by newspapers in the North, causing Benjamin great distress.[16]

The personal misfortune did not deter George Sanders. On 20 February 1863, the U.S. consul in Halifax reported that Sanders had sailed for Europe carrying dispatches.[17] These may have been the dispatches received by John Slidell on 19 March 1863.

After experimenting with various ways of sending dispatches, Benjamin finally settled on a new arrangement. On 9 May 1863, he wrote to Slidell telling him to send his dispatches on blockade runners. Those were fast ships, the system by now was well organized, and it avoided the longer and often trickier crossing of the North from Canada to the Confederacy. Benjamin later commented that these arrangements were highly successful.[18]

Sending dispatches by the blockade runners was working smoothly by 1863. The U.S. consul in Halifax mentioned ships that might be engaged in blockade running and tried to keep abreast of news on these ships sent by U.S. representatives in Britain, Bermuda, and Nassau, but most of the action had shifted from Halifax to Bermuda.

Also in 1863 there was some interesting traffic to England. George Sanders and four unidentified Confederate passengers sailed on the *Edmund Hawkins* in February. On 25 March the Reverend Kensey Johns Stewart resigned his post as chaplain in General Winder's command in Richmond and went to England, ostensibly to arrange for the publication of prayer books for the Confederacy. He was joined in London by the Reverend Stephen F. Cameron, who later worked with Stewart in clandestine operations in Canada. In late June or July 1863, Lewis Sanders, George Sanders' son and aide, was in Halifax, probably on his way to or from England. He was later active in Confederate clandestine activity in Canada.

On 7 May 1863, the consul in Halifax reported that William Cornell Jewett had sailed to England on the *Arabia*. Jewett was an ardent advocate of a negotiated peace, and his ostensible purpose for the trip was to persuade Her Majesty's government to play the role of mediator between the North and the South. Jewett returned to Quebec on 18 September 1863, and the consul reported that he was carrying dispatches for the rebel government. Kensey Johns Stewart returned to Richmond sometime in the late summer, but in October 1863 his brother-in-law Cassius F. Lee reported that

Stewart was living in Guelph, not far from Toronto and Hamilton, Ontario.[19]

Letters from Stewart, writings by Judah Benjamin, and statements of others prove that Stewart was in the Confederate Secret Service. If he received training in clandestine operations, it most likely occurred during his visit in England. It is possible that during 1863 Stewart, Cameron, Jewett, and others were trained by the British or by Confederate instructors using England as a sanctuary area.

As the war progressed, exchanges could not always be arranged fast enough to keep up with the volume of prisoners taken. Furthermore, official policy toward exchanges varied from time to time. As a result, substantial numbers of prisoners began to accumulate on both sides. In the North, some prisoners needing special attention were kept at Fort McHenry in Baltimore, at Fort Delaware in Delaware, at Fort Lafayette in New York, and at Fort Warren in Boston Harbor. Many more, particularly officers, were sent to Johnson's Island in Sandusky harbor off Lake Erie. A large number of the men captured in the West were imprisoned at Fort Douglas in Chicago, at Camp Morton in Indianapolis, at Camp Chase in Columbus, Ohio, and at a number of other locations in Illinois. The proximity of Camp Douglas and Johnson's Island to Canada and the Great Lakes made them inviting targets for Confederates operating from Canada. Like good soldiers in many a prisoner-of-war camp, the Confederate prisoners on Johnson's Island organized themselves to manage their housekeeping effort and to put themselves in a position to take advantage of any opportunity to find freedom or to damage the enemy. By mid-1862, they were reported to be organized with a general in command, an adjutant, and other key appointments.[20]

In February 1863, Lieutenant William H. Murdaugh, CSN, conceived the idea of raiding Lake Erie by capturing by surprise the USS *Michigan*, the only U.S. warship on the Great Lakes. He obtained Navy Department approval of the idea but could not get permission from Jefferson Davis, who feared the effect such action might have on Confederate interests in Great Britain.[21]

On 21 September 1863, Major Y. H. Blackwell, CSA, a recently exchanged officer, wrote to the Confederate secretary of war forwarding an unsigned letter from Brigadier General James J. Archer, a prisoner on Johnson's Island. According to Archer's letter, "We count here 1,600 prisoners, 1,200 officers. We can take the Island, guarded by only one battalion, with small loss, but have no way to get off. A naval officer might procure in some way a steamer on the lake and with a few men attack the Island and take us to Canada."[22]

This letter seems to have stirred Richmond to immediate action. Murdaugh's scheme was approved and amended to include the rescue of the prisoners on Johnson's Island. On 21 October 1863, exactly one month after the date of Major Blackwell's letter, the U.S. consul in Quebec reported that twenty Confederates had arrived who had recently landed at Halifax on the *Robert E. Lee*. This ship, as the *Giraffe*, had been used by Confederate agent Benjamin F. Ficklin in some of his early blockade-running operations. These included shipping Austrian rifles to the Virginia Military Institute, which the cadets later used to good effect against Union General Franz Sigel at the Battle of New Market. In 1863, Confederate Secretary of War Seddon took over the *Giraffe* for the War Department and changed her name to *Robert E. Lee*.

On 1 October 1863, the commander of the prison at Johnson's Island reported that the prisoners were talking about making an attempt to escape. To forestall such plans, he asked that the guard be reinforced and that the USS *Michigan* be anchored off the island. This surge in activity among the prisoners suggests that they had already been contacted by Confederate agents to prepare them for the rescue operation.[23]

By 28 October, the *Michigan* had been moved to Sandusky, and the commander of the prison wrote that he believed that her presence had averted a fight with the prisoners. He was sure that 24 October had been selected as the date for the escape attempt. In view of other information, this early a date for the escape does not seem likely. Perhaps the commander got it through inadvertent leakage from the prisoners or perhaps it was part of a war of nerves against the guard force. A few days later the military commander at Detroit reported that he had heard there was to be an attack on Johnson's Island and that the Confederates had bought a boat in Montreal for this purpose.[24]

On 13 November the U.S. consul in Quebec reported that he had heard that the southerners in Canada were planning an expedition against the United States. He had questioned the Canadian government and been told that its agents and detectives had found no substance to the rumor.[25] This was a case of the right hand not knowing what the left was doing, or of the British authorities playing a game, because on 11 November, Secretary of War Stanton had wired the governors and mayors in the Great Lakes states that he had been notified by the British minister in Washington that the governor-general of Canada had reported the discovery of a plan to invade the United States. Reinforcements had been promptly sent to Johnson's Island and other possible target areas.[26]

A few days later, the Union had reports that rebels who had left Windsor to join the raid were returning to that city;[27] and the state of Ohio began on 17 November to dismiss some of the militia called up for the emergency. On 13 November, an unattributed statement was published in a Montreal paper, which said, in part:

> The Washington government having refused to continue the exchange of prisoners of war under the cartel, sent the southern officers accustomed to a tropical climate, to Johnson's Island. . . . It was in fact, an attempt to commit murder without publicly incurring the odium of slaughter. In these circumstances the Confederate Government determined to make an attempt to rescue the doomed officers, and for this purpose an expedition was fitted out, consisting of 36 officers, under the command of one who had distinguished himself in similar daring enterprises, and 300 men. The officers embarked at Wilmington, North Carolina, in the Confederate steamer *Robert E. Lee,* and landed at Halifax. The cotton and tobacco brought by that steamer as freight, were sold to furnish the funds required, amounting to about $110,000. The men came overland through the states in small parties to the general rendezvous. . . . The intention was to surprise the Federal garrison on Johnson's Island, liberate the prisoners, and forward them by Halifax to Nassau or Bermuda. . . . Any further operations on the lakes were left to the discretion of the officer in command, whose orders were stringent and preemptory to avoid a breach of British neutrality.[28]

This statement sounds as though the Confederates running the operation in Canada had decided that the best way to stay in the good grace of Canadian public opinion would be to make a clean breast of the matter.

After his return to the Confederacy, Lieutenant Robert D. Minor, the second in command of the operation, wrote a full account of it to Admiral Franklin Buchanan of the Confederate navy. According to Minor, twenty-two men were sent on the *Robert E. Lee.* They met former Baltimore police marshal George P. Kane in Montreal and with the help of Kane and Patrick C. Martin, with whom Kane was living, set to work to organize their attack. They informed the prisoners of the approximate date of their attack by using a personal ad in the *New York Herald*—"a few nights after the 4th of November." They scouted the Sandusky area and were delighted to find the *Michigan* anchored near Johnson's Island. They bought two small nine-pounder cannon and dumbbells as a substitute for cannon balls. One hundred navy Colt revolvers were purchased along with other weapons and equipment. They had been promised 180 men to help with the raid, but only 32 arrived in time to take part. They intended to ship all the arms on the same ship on which the party would travel, disguised as laborers on their way to Chicago. At the appropriate moment they would capture the ship and collide with the *Michigan* by "accident." They would board and capture the ship and turn her guns on the Johnson's Island guard camp to force its surrender. They would then commandeer all ships in Sandusky harbor to take the released prisoners to Canada. The party had assembled at St. Catharines on the Welland Canal prepared to board ship when they heard of Stanton's message warning of the raid. That caused them to abort the operation.[29]

On 18 and 19 November the Canadian papers published various versions of the story of the planned raid on Johnson's Island. Beginning on 19 November, the U.S. consul in Quebec was able to identify a number of the Confederates involved in the operation as they passed through Quebec on the way to Halifax and their return to the Confederacy. These included some of the men who had come in on the *Robert E. Lee.* It seems clear that the numbers published on 13 November were an exaggeration. A larger number of men could not have gone back through Halifax without being detected, and only a few dozen were observed. The remainder must have stayed in Canada or returned to the Confederacy overland.

Minor gave the organization of the raiding party, which was commanded by Captain John Wilkinson, a Confederate naval officer who made a brilliant record as a blockade runner both before and after this operation. The party also included W. B. Ball, colonel of the Fifteenth Virginia Cavalry, and Lieutenant Colonel W. W. Finney, formerly of the Fiftieth Virginia Infantry, both of whom went as acting masters' mates. Finney had been a longtime friend and partner of B. F. Ficklin, who first procured the *Robert E. Lee* for the Confederacy. They had graduated from the Virginia Military Institute a year apart and later worked together in organizing the Pony Express.

Most of the officers for the raid seem to have come in on the *Robert E. Lee* and were from the eastern part of the Confederacy. The supposed three hundred men infiltrated in small groups, however, probably came from the western part of the Confederacy and entered Canada via the Windsor route. It is possible that someone such as General Daniel Ruggles was organizing that end of the operation and that the Confederates were taking their men up the Mississippi River and then inside Union lines. Many Confederates who participated in clandestine operations in Canada were from states along the Mississippi River.

The Confederates embellished history by circulating the story that several armed blockade runners under the Confederate flag had been sent to Canada to carry the expedition on the raid, attempting thus to play down accusations of violation of Canadian neutrality while at the same time frightening residents of the American lake ports with thoughts of Confederate raiders.[30]

Confederate operations to free their prisoners of war in the North must be seen in the context of other Confederate activities in the northern United States. In due course, these operations became entwined with the operations in Canada.

When Abraham Lincoln carried the election of 1860, he was a clear victor in the northern states, but those states also contained several hundred thousand voters who were opposed to him. In fact, many of those who voted for Lincoln had voted the Democratic ticket only four years before. As the situation grew more tense in the early months of 1861, people in the North tended to fall into two opposing camps—those who favored the use of coercion to bring the seceded states back into the Union and those who favored a national convention to work out a constitutional compromise that would lead to reunification without war. When war finally broke out, many of the latter group dutifully supported their government, but many remained disenchanted with Lincoln and not merely because of the war; he was a Republican and they were Democrats. The reality of politics at the state and local levels was a strong influence on many people.

As soon as the Confederate government had settled in its new capital of Richmond and survived the opening stages of the war, Jefferson Davis began to investigate the condition and state of mind of the opposition in the North. The leaders of the Confederacy had nearly all been Democrats at some point in their political careers, and many of them had friends and longtime allies among the Democrats of the northern states.

In early 1862 Davis sent a young captain from Missouri, Emile Longuemare, to contact key people in the Democratic party in the northern and western states about their feelings toward the war. He found many of them anxious to get out of the war and to revive the Democratic party. He reported their feelings to Davis.

Before the war there had existed a secret society known as the

Knights of the Golden Circle. This organization had elaborate oaths and rituals and was intended to strengthen the feeling of brotherhood among those opposed to the Republicans. It was now moribund. Many of its members were in the South, and the northern Democrats were suffering low morale as a result of their defeat by the Republicans. Jefferson Davis and his chief advisers decided that the opposition in the North needed to be organized and encouraged and that a revived secret society might be a useful device to bring unity and direction to the opposition. Captain Longuemare was therefore sent back into Union territory to see if he could effect a rebirth of the Knights.

He went first to familiar territory in Missouri, and there in early 1862, in a building at the corner of Fifth and Market streets in St. Louis, the first meeting was held of the new Order of American Knights. This organization had strict rules of secrecy, no records were to be kept, and messages were to be transmitted orally. There were various degrees of membership in the order, and it contained an "inner circle" whose members were called Sons of Liberty.

The ostensible purpose of the Order of American Knights was to save the Democratic party, but its true purpose from the Confederate point of view was to organize noncombatants in the North and turn them into a military force that could operate in the rear of the federal army. The order was organized by state, county, and township, and each township chapter was urged to organize and arm itself for defense against persecution by the federal government.[31]

P. C. Wright, an attorney who had moved to St. Louis from New Orleans, was the operating head of the organization. H. H. Dodd became the head of the Indiana organization, Charles L. Hunt of the Missouri chapter, and James A. McMasters of the New York element. Judge Joshua Bullit of the court of appeals was the head of the Kentucky organization.[32] The Kentucky wing was regarded by the Confederacy as a critical part of the movement because direct military support might be provided in Kentucky, which could be given military help in return. This may well have been the movement that George Sanders referred to when he passed through Canada in August 1862.

In that same month, a grand jury in Indianapolis reported that treasonable secret societies were being formed in Indiana, and in September 1862 there were disorders in Indianapolis that were blamed on those secret societies. The Order of American Knights continued to grow. By June 1863, some of the township chapters in

Indiana were reported to be armed and drilling.[33] In July 1863, there were massive riots in New York City to protest the draft. They were widely blamed on the defunct Knights of the Golden Circle at the time, but later scholars have tended to ignore or play down such a connection. The New York draft riots, however, were exactly the sort of activity that the Confederacy sought to encourage through the Order of American Knights. The organization's connection with the draft riots may have been more than casual.[34]

In contemplating a military action such as the raid on Johnson's Island, the Confederates doubtless received some help from local sympathizers in the form of information and the spreading of rumors. That raid, however, seems to have been organized so that most military action would be carried out by Confederates. As time went by, other opportunities arose for action that could be performed by the Order of American Knights, which was growing more and more powerful. Its political chief was Clement L. Vallandigham, a congressman from Ohio who had lived for a time in Maryland and was hostile to the war and to the policies of the Republican administration. Vallandigham was defeated for Congress and for the governorship of Ohio and was charged with treason by the federal government. In 1863, he was sent across the lines into the Confederacy.[35]

On 7 July 1863, the U.S. consul at Halifax reported that Vallandigham and "Captain Hartsteen" (H. C. Hartstene, commander, CSN) had arrived from Wilmington and promptly left for Canada. On 14 July, Vallandigham and a party of associates left Montreal for the Clifton House at Niagara Falls on a special train after having been entertained royally by the provincial premier, the president of the railroad, and "William Robinson of Manchester."[36] The British apparently were extending special courtesy to a man who might someday be a political power in the United States. In 1863, he might well have been regarded as a successor to Lincoln in case of a serious Union defeat. In August 1863, Vallandigham and his wife made a short visit to Quebec, where he was introduced to Parliament and lavishly entertained. On 25 August, he left Quebec to return to Canada West to be closer to his sympathizers in the United States.

By 1863, Confederate clandestine operations in Canada had matured to the point that the organization could support the oceangoing, blockade-running operation at Halifax. It could also arrange for the movement of supplies from Canada to Halifax for transshipment to the Confederacy. It could provide assistance to the Copperhead movement led by the Order of American Knights, and it could carry out individual operations. But the apparatus could not yet provide all the support and managerial talent necessary to handle the large group of men brought in for the Johnson's Island rescue operation. That operation appears to have overwhelmed the resources of the Confederate agents resident in Canada during 1863. Furthermore, the officers brought in to carry out that operation appear to have been sent back to the Confederacy before the majority of the men were quartered and given directions, leaving the mop-up job to an apparatus not trained, organized, or budgeted to handle it. In addition to the soldiers left over from the Johnson's Island operation, Morgan's raid, which ended in Ohio in late July 1863, resulted in a number of soldiers evading capture or escaping and making their way to Canada in the autumn and winter of 1863–64. Many of Morgan's men were active in Confederate operations in Canada.

At about this time, the Confederates undertook their most radical clandestine operation. It was a serious attempt at what we would now call biological warfare. Much of the operation is well documented because it became public knowledge before the end of the war, and British and American investigators and courts left records of their investigations.

The central figure in the operations was Dr. Luke P. Blackburn of Woodford County, Kentucky. Dr. Blackburn was born in 1816 and graduated from Transylvania University in 1835. He began the practice of medicine in Lexington, Kentucky, and in 1846 moved to Natchez, Mississippi, where he became an expert in the treatment of yellow fever. He toured Europe in 1857, making a study of European hospitals. By the time of the Civil War, he was one of the leading authorities in the United States on yellow fever.

When the Civil War broke out, Dr. Blackburn served for a time as a civilian aide on the staff of General Sterling Price. On 13 May 1863, he applied for the post of medical inspector serving under Colonel George B. Hodge, General John C. Breckinridge's assistant adjutant and inspector general. There is no record of what happened to this application.[37] Hodge was an influential Kentucky politician who later became a brigadier general and in the closing months of the war served as commander of the District of Southwestern Mississippi and Louisiana.[38] This is the area where General Ruggles had served earlier in the war. It is possible that Hodge inherited the territory because he, like Ruggles, had been involved in clandestine operations.

The next record of Blackburn is his presence in Canada in November 1863. There he recruited one Godfrey J. Hyams, a former resident of Arkansas, to carry out an important task in the spring of 1864. According to a statement made by Hyams to the Union authorities on 12 April 1865, he was to wait in Toronto until he received instructions from Blackburn. On 10 May 1864, Blackburn wrote from Havana instructing Hyams to go to Halifax and report to Alexander Keith. Financed by William L. McDonald of Toronto, Hyams went to see H. G. Slaughter, the chief Confederate agent in Montreal, who arranged finances for his trip to Halifax. Hyams and a young man named W. W. Haynes traveled overland to Halifax, arriving on 22 June 1864. Keith had Hyams stay at the Farmer's Hotel and told Hyams he was expecting word from Dr. Blackburn. The doctor finally arrived on the *Alphia* from Bermuda on 12 July.[39]

Hyams learned that C. H. Huntley, who later became one of the St. Albans raiders, knew of Hyams's mission. Hyams also saw Dr. Blackburn with men named McGregor and Hammach from New Orleans, who also seemed to be privy to the operation. It developed that Hyams's task was to unload several trunks from the *Alphia* and arrange to transship them to Washington, Norfolk, and New Bern, North Carolina, the last two places being under federal occupation. The trunks were filled with clothing and bedding presumably infected with yellow fever. Dr. Blackburn wanted Hyams to take a special valise with "elegant" infected shirts in it as a present to President Lincoln, but this Hyams refused to do.

Hyams arranged to smuggle the "infected" trunks into Boston and had them shipped to Philadelphia, where he collected them and on about 10 August 1864 placed them in the hands of an auctioneer at the corner of Ninth Street and Pennsylvania Avenue in Washington. He was unable to deliver any of the material to Norfolk or New Bern because of military operations that prohibited civilian travel and arranged for a sutler going there to deliver the material intended for those areas.

Hyams was back in Canada on 13 August 1864. At Hamilton he met Clement C. Clay and James P. Holcombe, Confederate commissioners in Canada, apparently by accident, and they congratulated him on earning "an independent fortune." On 16 August he was visited by Blackburn and Lieutenant Bennett Young. Blackburn was scheduled to leave Toronto the next day to go to Bermuda to help put down the yellow fever epidemic there. The epidemic in Bermuda was so severe that it had caused the blockade runners to move their main base of operations back to Halifax. For several months in 1864, as many as six or seven runners would be in Halifax at one time.[40]

Blackburn spent over a month in Bermuda, helping the British doctors fight the epidemic. When a patient died he bought the bed clothes and bedding of the departed and stored the material in a trunk. When he left in October to return to Canada, he left seven trunks full of "infected" material in storage with the declaration that he would send for them in the spring of 1865.[41] Blackburn believed that yellow fever was contagious and that its outbreaks came in hot weather in locations where there were extended periods of hot weather. Therefore, Washington was believed to be a good target area, but Boston would not be. Blackburn believed he was using the best scientific knowledge available to attack the enemy with a deadly disease.

Blackburn does not appear to have been a monster. He had a good reputation as a physician and after the war served as governor of Kentucky. His involvement in this yellow fever operation, however, is indicative of the intensity of hatred for the enemy that pervaded the Confederate government at this stage of the war. It also suggests that strong emotions may have prevented the Confederates from thinking as deeply as they might about the consequences of some of their operations.[42]

On 25 January 1864, the U.S. consul at Halifax reported that former police marshal of Baltimore George P. Kane, Dr. Blackburn, and Major Wistor or Wister (an escapee from Johnson's Island) were expected to arrive in the next two or three days. He said they were planning to run the blockade and all of them had been involved in the Johnson's Island "rescue plot." Blackburn was presumably on his way to Havana to collect "infected" clothing, but Kane was on his way to Virginia. On 15 February he was being serenaded by well-wishers at his hotel in Richmond.[43]

In Richmond, Kane told the Confederate government that there were an estimated four hundred Confederate soldiers in Canada who needed to be repatriated. Their number included men who had escaped from Union control, either in or on their way to prisoner-of-war camps. There probably were also a few strays who found their way to Canada for a variety of peculiar reasons, but it is probable that the majority had been sent to Canada for the Johnson's Island operation in 1863 but had not yet been able to return to their original units. Most of these men were probably in Ontario, and the existing Confederate organization did not seem to have the funds or other resources to get so large a group organized and back to the Confederacy.[44]

Secretary of State Benjamin was in the process of sending off to Halifax a commissioner to represent the legal interests of the Confederate government in the case of the *Chesapeake,* a ship captured and taken into Halifax by Lieutenant John C. Brain, whose letter of marque appeared to have been issued illegally. Benjamin had chosen as commissioner Professor James P. Holcombe of the University of Virginia. Holcombe was also given the task of organizing the repatriation of the four hundred Confederates believed to be in Canada.

On 24 February 1864, Benjamin gave Holcombe $8,000—$5,000 to be used for expenses and $3,000 as his salary for six months' service. Holcombe was briefed on the repatriation problem and told to use B. Weir of Halifax to help solve it. He was also told that a letter of credit for $25,000 was being sent to Liverpool to provide emergency funds and admonished to tell the British authorities what he was doing. The Confederate government apparently wanted to maintain credit for observing British neutrality.[45]

By late March, Holcombe had reached Halifax, where he quickly discovered the weakness of the Confederacy's claim to the *Chesapeake.* He did not seriously begin to work on the problem of expatriates until April. On 28 April 1864, he wrote to Benjamin that he had not done much about them yet but that he was sending an agent named Cromwell to Windsor to bring back forty or fifty men reported to be there.[46]

Even after this letter, Holcombe did not put much vigor into his efforts to organize the return of the Confederate soldiers. This lapse may be explained by a report from the U.S. consul in Montreal in June, who wrote that Holcombe was accompanied by a "vixen" named Stansbury.[47] This person cannot be firmly identified. A Captain Smith Stansbury was the commander of the Confederate Ordnance Depot at Bermuda, and it is possible that Holcombe's companion might have had some connection with him.

On 27 May 1864, Holcombe wrote to Benjamin that he would now spend full time on the returnee problem. He felt sure that Kane had overestimated the number of men involved. At that time twelve of them were in Halifax of whom nine were scheduled to leave that day. These, he said, were men from General Morgan's command. There were only about a hundred left to be taken care of. On 8 June 1864, the U.S. consul at Halifax wrote that ten escaped prisoners had reached Halifax the day before from Canada and that several others had left Halifax about two weeks earlier. Presumably, these were the men Holcombe had mentioned to Benjamin.[48]

The new commissioners to Canada, appointed by Jefferson Davis in the spring of 1864, Jacob Thompson and Clement C. Clay, reached Halifax on 19 May after a sixteen-day journey from Richmond. Their arrival may account for Holcombe's belated renewal of interest in his task on behalf of the returnees. Thompson and his secretary, W. W. Cleary, left Halifax for Canada two days after their arrival, but Clement Clay stayed on in Halifax until 30 May.

Of the two commissioners, Thompson was the senior, and he considered himself a representative of the Confederate government, specifically the president and secretary of state. He had control of a large sum of Secret Service money—on the order of $1 million, a tremendous sum for that time—and believed that he was authorized to spend it only for the purposes that had been spelled out to him by Davis and Benjamin. He could support a military operation if it had a clear political aspect such as the participation of the Order of American Knights. He could not support a military operation purely for military purposes. Clement Clay represented the Confederate War Department but had to get his money from Thompson. The latter's rigid view of his authority led to some bickering and ill-feeling between the two men, but in general they seem to have made a strong effort to overcome their differences.

Clay was an aggressive man, eager to find ways of getting at the Yankees. He probably spent his time in Halifax learning what he could from Weir, Holcombe, Keith, and other knowledgeable people in the area. By this time, Confederate soldiers were trickling into Halifax, and Clay may have felt that their presence provided an opportunity that should not be overlooked.

One of the returnees he met was a young soldier of the Eighth Kentucky Cavalry Regiment, Bennett H. Young. Young had been captured with General Morgan in July 1863 but had escaped from Camp Douglas in Chicago and made his way to Canada near the end of 1863. The two seem to have become immediate friends. Young believed that it would be possible to launch raids into the United States from Canada to give northerners a taste of the anguish the Union armies were bringing to the South. Clay was so impressed by Young that he wrote to Benjamin and Seddon recommending that they approve Young's ideas.[49] Young sailed from Halifax in early June and in Richmond on 16 July 1864 was promoted to first lieutenant and assigned to duty behind enemy lines. The officials in Richmond had found him as impressive as Clay had.[50]

There is no direct evidence of a connection between Clay and another group of soldiers from the Mississippi Valley, but the timing is suggestive. In July 1864, the U.S. consul in St. John's, New Brunswick, reported that a group of twenty or thirty Confederates were preparing for a raid into Maine. When the consul learned that the bank at Calais, Maine, was to be a target, he wrote directly to the cashier of the bank. This message seems to have arrived on 16 July, within an hour or two of the actual attempt, and the raiders found their target alert and defended. In the course of the affair, four of the Confederates were captured, including their leader, Captain William Collins, formerly of the Fifteenth Mississippi Infantry Regiment, who claimed to have served as a scout for General Polk.[51]

Collins was an Ulsterman who had lived in New Brunswick, then in New York, and finally in the South. His formal military service in the South had been in the Mississippi-Louisiana area, and he had dropped out of the official roster in 1862.[52] One of the men captured with Collins was a Union deserter named William Daymond, who appears to have been a Union spy. The others were Francis X. Jones of the First Missouri Infantry Regiment and "Phillips," probably Private J. C. Phillips of the Ninth Louisiana Infantry.[53] Collins and Jones both served in Confederate secret service work during 1863 and came to Nova Scotia separately in 1864.

The captive raiders were brought to trial and sentenced to three years in prison for conspiracy—not as captured soldiers. Suddenly, in early September 1864, Jones appears to have decided to tell all. His information was so sensational that Judge L. C. Turner, the judge advocate of the Union army, was sent to Maine to interrogate him. Jones said the raid on Calais was a small part of a much larger plan that involved the landing of Confederate troops on the coast of Maine. Fifty topographic engineers had been sent to Maine in the spring to map the coast and prepare for the landings. The landings were to be accompanied by raids on the border towns of New England by Confederates in Canada. Part of the preparation for the operations was to be a cruise up the coast by the Confederate raider *Tallahassee* to paralyze local shipping. To direct Union attention elsewhere, there were to be a series of raids in Illinois and Iowa.

Judge Turner was impressed by the details of the story, particularly the mention of the *Tallahassee*, which had raided the coast of New England in August 1864 while the prisoners were being held incommunicado. If Jones could not have learned about the actual raid, he must have known before he was captured on the Calais raid in July that the voyage of the *Tallahassee* was planned. If that important detail were true, then other details could also be true.[54] This one item that stunned Judge Turner may prove instead to have been deliberate misinformation. The CSS *Tallahassee* did not exist until the blockade runner *Atlanta* was given that name on 23 July 1864.[55] Jones could not have known that she was to raid the coast of New England before he was captured on 16 July.

Jones's story is also suspicious because he went into great detail concerning the clandestine Confederate organization that was to carry out the series of raids. He mentioned several known Confederate agents, including Alexander Keith of Halifax, who resided outside the United States. He also mentioned several agents who were operating in the North, including Major Dudley Harris in Portland and Colonel J. D. Martin in Boston.

Judge Turner was told that during the previous two months somebody had called at the post office in Portland several times for mail addressed to Major Dudley Harris. We have been unable to find any such person among the Compiled Service Records in the National Archives. It is probable either that the person did not exist or that the name was an alias. It would be easy enough for the Confederates to have somebody impersonate Harris at the post office to support Jones's story. We were successful in finding a record of Colonel J. D. Martin of the Twenty-fifth Mississippi Infantry Regiment, but we also found that he was killed on 3 October 1862.[56] Perhaps somebody was using a name familiar to him whose owner he knew could not be found by the Union.

Jones's story was a masterpiece, but there appear to be many reasons to doubt its veracity. It would seem to be more likely that the Confederates decided to take advantage of the failure of the Calais raid and to use one of the prisoners as a channel to insert a piece of disinformation into Union thinking. Somehow, they probably arranged for Jones to be coached on his story. Since he would have to undergo cross-questioning, his story would have to be consistent, and it would make sense to use real names when possible or names Jones could remember easily. Jones appears to have said nothing that was true that the Union did not already know. Nobody on the Confederate side would be likely to be damaged by his tale.

Some of the activities of Clement Clay after he left Halifax might shed some light on this operation and the mysterious Major Dudley Harris. Clay left for Halifax on 30 May and arrived at Montreal about 10 June with Holcombe in tow. The latter reported to Benjamin on 16 June that ten or twelve more returnees were on their way to Halifax. Weir was running the line to forward the men from Halifax, and "discreet" persons in Montreal, Norfolk, Hamilton, St. Catherines, and Windsor would start the returnees on their way. On 17 June, the U.S. consul in Halifax reported that thirty or forty former prisoners had arrived there from Canada with aid from the Confederates. Some of Collins's men may well have been drawn from this stream of returnees.[57]

Canada was beginning to fill with top Confederate agents. In February 1864, the U.S. consul in Halifax had reported the arrival there of Beverly Tucker, formerly the U.S. consul in Liverpool.[58] Tucker had served as a Confederate agent in Europe during the early part of the war and then returned to Richmond. Now he had been sent to Canada, ostensibly to arrange for the shipment of supplies to the Confederacy. He met Clay and Holcombe in Montreal when they arrived in June. Another first stringer was George N. Sanders, who arrived in Canada on 1 June.

At some point in June or July 1864, Clay reestablished contact with an old acquaintance, Robert Edwin Coxe, who had moved into a house at St. Catharines, Ontario, in August 1862. If one were choosing the location for a headquarters from which to conduct clandestine operations against the North, it would be hard to find a better place than St. Catharines. It was near the center of the Canadian rail net and close to Buffalo, New York, which was centrally located on the American railroad system. In addition, Niagara Falls, twelve miles away, was an ideal location for meeting secret agents and as a letter drop for secret messages.

At Niagara there were a number of hotels and the village of Clifton catering to the tourists who came to see the falls. The Clifton House was a reasonably large and luxurious hotel, but one of the smaller hotels, the Table Rock House, shared a building with the Barnett Museum. The museum was open seven days a week and had a constant stream of visitors who signed a guest register. After the Civil War, the museum and hotel fell into the same hands, and the registers of both museum and hotel are still in the possession of the Niagara Falls Museum.

From an examination of these registers, it is obvious that both were used by Confederate agents. Robert Coxe visited the museum as early as September 1863, and one possible Confederate courier

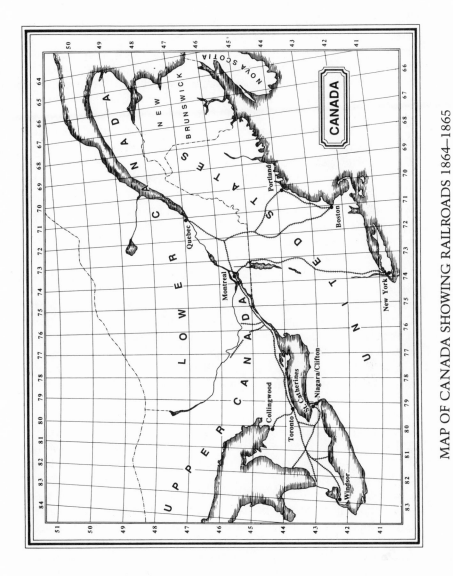

MAP OF CANADA SHOWING RAILROADS 1864–1865

visited it at least twenty-one times in fifteen months. It would have been very easy for a courier or other agent to visit the museum and sign the register, thus reporting his presence to a local agent, who could inspect the register at frequent intervals. Meetings or exchange of messages could follow in accordance with previously arranged procedures. With St. Catharines less than an hour away by train or two or three hours by horse, Confederates living at St. Catharines could meet visiting agents or northern Copperheads among a crowd of strangers in which they would not be noticed. At the same time, the visitors would not know the permanent location of the Confederates they met.

The ideal characteristics of this arrangement make it worth speculating that Coxe may have been deliberately sent to St. Catharines to establish a base for more active Confederate secret operations against the North. Coxe may also have known George Sanders and Beverly Tucker during his stay in Europe before the war. Tucker moved into the Coxe house in June, and Clay moved in during July 1864. It seems likely that Coxe was an active agent on behalf of the Confederacy.

About 6–8 July 1864, Coxe and his family went to Poughkeepsie, New York, to visit Mrs. Coxe's family, and before the end of July they went to Cape Elizabeth near Portland, Maine, where they stayed until 15 September, when Coxe moved the group to North Conway, New Hampshire. This small town was on the rail line between Portland and Canada so it would have been easy for Coxe to move in either direction as required.

The timing of Coxe's stay in Maine is most interesting. It is possible that he was the missing "Major Dudley Harris" and the man who masterminded Private Jones's fabulous story about the raid on the coast of Maine. In a letter to Clay written from North Conway on 26 September, Coxe said that he had been keeping Beverly Tucker informed of his activities. This suggests that Tucker may have been Coxe's principal contact in the Confederate clandestine apparatus.[59]

During October, Coxe took his family back to Poughkeepsie and left them there while he returned to Canada, arriving in St. Catharines about 5 November 1864.[60] While Coxe was at Poughkeepsie, John Wilkes Booth was reported to have been observed at Newburgh, New York, just fourteen miles away, on 16 October.[61] Newburgh would have been a good place for the two to meet if Coxe did not want his clandestine contacts to get too close to his family. Booth left New York for Montreal the next day, and it is possible that he was seeing Coxe for last-minute instructions concerning where and when he was to make the right contact in Montreal.

While the Confederate apparatus in Canada was being reinforced, the Copperhead movement in the North had been growing. In the summer of 1863, John Hunt Morgan, the Confederate cavalry general from Kentucky, used one of his young officers, Captain Thomas H. Hines of the Ninth Kentucky Cavalry Regiment, to contact members of the Order of American Knights to discuss support that group might give to a Confederate raid across Ohio. In July, Morgan crossed into Indiana and turned east into Ohio. Eventually, on 26 July, he was forced to surrender in eastern Ohio, not far from the Pennsylvania border.[62]

Morgan and his officers were not treated as prisoners of war but instead were incarcerated in the Ohio State Penitentiary as if they were criminals. This situation, however, may have worked to Morgan's advantage. In October, Morgan and six of his officers, including Captain Hines, escaped from the prison and made their way back to the Confederacy. It is possible that money and local political influence may have been of help in this escape, which would have been harder to arrange if Morgan had been in a prison controlled by the military.

Once in the Confederacy, Hines was sent back into enemy territory to assess the strength of the Order of American Knights and the possibility of using them to attack Union forces from within. He came back to Richmond in February 1864 with a generally favorable report and then went off to Kentucky to visit his fiancée. At that point, the Dahlgren raid occurred, and he was called back to Richmond on an emergency basis.[63]

In March 1864, the armed strength of the Order of American Knights was represented to be 340,000 men out of a total membership estimated to be about half a million in the northern states.[64] Those were rational figures derived by a responsible official, but they did not take into consideration the willingness of the individuals to be shot at. Furthermore, the Knights' idea of a well-drilled unit was one that drilled once or twice a month. As a true military threat they were something of a joke, but in 1864 neither the Union nor the Confederacy knew that, and as a political force they formed a black cloud in the Union sky.

On 14 March 1864, Hines was ordered to go to Canada to operate from there with the Order of American Knights to bring on an uprising in the North. On 16 March, Hines's orders were amended to have him report to commissioners who were to be put in charge of clandestine operations in Canada. At that date, the senior commissioner had not yet been selected.

Whereas Hines's earlier work with the Copperheads had been under War Department jurisdiction, he was now operating under State Department auspices. The Signal Corps, however, trained him in cipher operations.[65] The change in jurisdiction probably reflected the increased importance of this activity in the eyes of the Confederate government.

The generous budget given to Jacob Thompson had not yet been allocated, and the War Department gave Hines $5,000 and a quantity of cotton at Memphis to be sold across the lines to get the money to finance the start of his operation. At about the same time, General Ruggles of the "Special Branch" in Mississippi was ordered back to Richmond for reassignment. Hines reported to General Polk's headquarters in the Department of Mississippi and East Louisiana for consultations and arranged to sell the cotton for $70,000. He appears to have returned to Richmond for a short stay and then proceeded across northern territory to Canada, reaching Toronto on about 20 April 1864.

In Richmond, Ruggles had his son Mortimer appointed as his aide. On 16 May they left Richmond to return to General Polk's headquarters, where Ruggles was placed in charge of reserve forces in southwest Mississippi and East Louisiana.[66]

About the time Hines returned to Canada, R. C. Bocking, a "dutch" chemist from Cincinnati, came to Windsor to spend two weeks in consultations with the Confederates. Bocking had developed his own formula for a superior quality of the incendiary "Greek Fire." He had also developed a number of ingenious explosive devices, some with delayed-action fuses. Bocking apparently agreed to manufacture these devices and to have them implanted in boats on the Ohio and Mississippi and in other likely targets. He was to receive 10 percent of the estimated value of the destruction he caused.[67] This agreement was in keeping with new legislation concerning secret service actions against the enemy passed in the winter of 1864. It is possible that Hines brought with him from Richmond the information on this new inducement for sabotage.

Pending the arrival of the commissioner, Hines must have gone to work reestablishing contact with the Order of American Knights. P. C. Wright and Captain Longuemare had transferred their activities to New York City, but the same leaders continued to operate in Indiana and other states in the Midwest.

When Thompson and W. W. Cleary, his secretary, arrived in Canada, Thompson stayed for a short time in Montreal but sent Cleary on to Toronto, where their "permanent" office was to be established. Hines appears already to have lined up key Copperheads for interviews with Thompson. Presumably Thompson began the process in Montreal and continued to work on it in Toronto.

At about the same time that Thompson reached Montreal, George N. Sanders arrived from Europe. Judging from the statement of H. H. Stewart mentioned in the previous chapter and a subsequent statement by Sanders, his participation in the Canadian operation was arranged by Davis, but Thompson appears to have been somewhat uncomfortable to have such an active helper. While Thompson was seeing the leaders from the Order of American Knights, Sanders went off to visit Vallandigham at Windsor. Thompson promptly followed.

Clement Clay arrived in Montreal on 10 June, just as Thompson was preparing to leave Toronto for Windsor. Clay and Holcombe stayed on in Montreal for several days. Holcombe was working on the returnee problem and taking short visits to see his "vixen" at a country hotel outside of Montreal. Clay was presumably being briefed by knowledgeable Confederates in Montreal. It was important that he understand what had happened during the aborted Johnson's Island rescue operation in 1863. Many of the people involved were probably in Montreal and could discuss the event and the lessons learned with Clay.

On 25 June, the U.S. consul in Montreal reported that "in the last day or two" Clay had received dispatches, which he kept constantly with him and which appeared to interest him greatly.[68] These might have been letters from Thompson, Sanders, or other active Confederates concerning plans for future operations.

One operation took place almost immediately. In accordance with the Confederate government's declared objective of seeking a negotiated peace, in July 1864, William Cornell Jewett persuaded Horace Greeley, the powerful Democratic editor of the *New York Tribune*, to act as a channel to President Lincoln in an attempt to arrange a peace conference at Niagara. This maneuver caused considerable tense discussion among the various participants. Sanders acted as the chief operator on the Confederate side with Clay and

Holcombe standing by at Niagara to take advantage of any opportunity that arose. They urged Thompson to join them, but he seemed to be busy with his Copperhead friends and other projects and remained aloof from this operation.[69] Lincoln apparently felt that the Union was too strong to need to negotiate with the Confederates and not strong enough to do so successfully. As a result, the peace talks fell through on the excuse that the Confederate commission was not specifically empowered to negotiate a peace. This was a fairly petty procedural objection and caused some comment favorable to the Confederates when the news of it got around.

In the meantime, Hines and Thompson had been hard at work trying to arrange for the Copperheads in the states of the old Northwest Territory to take action. Shipments of arms had been arranged to equip the conspirators, and the leaders had screwed up their courage to act, but Union authorities had penetrated several of the components of the Order of American Knights, or the Sons of Liberty as it was now often called. Several key members of the order were arrested and some of the arms shipments were intercepted. These actions generated enough pressure on the conspiracy to force postponement of the date for action. First, 15 June had been selected as the date, but that had been switched to 16 August. Early in August the date was changed to 29 August. At this point, however, there occurred one of those small actions around which great historical events sometimes revolve.

In late 1863, P. C. Wright had enlisted in the American Knights the editor of the *Indiana Sentinel*, Joseph J. Bingham, who also was chairman of the Indiana State Committee of the Democratic party. Bingham had favored any idea that sounded like good politics for the Democrats and was not an ardent supporter of the war, but he paid little attention to the detailed activities of the Knights. Finally, on 2 or 3 August 1864, H. H. Dodd, one of the leaders of the Knights, called on Bingham and briefed him on the planned uprising. According to Dodd, there was to be a simultaneous release of the prisoners from Johnson's Island, Camp Chase in Ohio, Camp Morton in Indianapolis, and Camp Douglas at Chicago. At the same time, the government stores in Louisville were to be seized. These events were to take place on 16 August.

Bingham also heard independently that some of the members of the American Knights were selling their crops for ready cash and making other preparations for action. He was alarmed at the prospect of untrained men becoming involved in a dangerous business and called together all the leading Democrats in Indiana whom he could contact on short notice. On 5 August they met with Dodd and other leaders of the American Knights and extracted from them a promise that the uprising would not take place.[70]

Because the American Knights claimed to be acting for the Democratic party, they could not afford to go ahead with an activity that the party had disowned. The Indiana Knights, however, did not repudiate their own beliefs. They still kept contact with the Knights in other states and continued to talk to their Confederate contacts about action against the Union. Vanity, if nothing else, would not let them tell the reason behind their new reluctance to act, but if the Knights of Indiana dragged their feet, their central position made it impossible for the other states to act without them.

The Confederates sent a team of sixty-two men from Canada to Chicago to be ready to help liberate the prisoners at Camp Douglas on 29 August, but although Chicago was full of armed Copperheads the Confederates could never get the Copperheads to act. Excuses were made that more military support was needed, and the date was finally postponed to coincide with the elections in November.[71] The Confederates were frustrated but kept trying. It seems apparent, however, that after 5 August 1864, the Knights never had any serious intention of starting a fight. They were willing to use talk about an uprising for political ends and to pry more money out of the Confederates, but they were not willing to act. The Confederates sent another party to Chicago in November to support their final effort there, but several of their leaders were arrested and the undertaking fizzled.[72]

After the failure at Chicago in August, part of the Confederate effort was diverted to attempt again to free the prisoners at Johnson's Island. This operation was managed by Thompson, and it would appear that in keeping with his jurisdiction over political matters, it was to be a joint operation of Confederates and Copperheads.

The key, as in 1863, was the USS *Michigan*. As long as this ship was nearby there was no hope of using Lake Erie to free the prisoners. Vessels of more or less comparable size, however, had been captured elsewhere by the Confederates through the use of boarding parties. It was felt that with surprise, the *Michigan* could also be captured in the same manner.

Charles H. Cole was assigned by Thompson to make friends with the officers on the *Michigan* so he could work from the inside. Acting Master John Yates Beall of the Confederate volunteer navy was assigned to capture a civilian vessel on Lake Erie to use to bring the boarding party alongside the *Michigan*. Ohio members of the American Knights were organized to support the operations from the landward side.

Beall was a neighbor of Alexander Boteler, Edwin Gray Lee, and Daniel Lucas of Jefferson County, Virginia (now West Virginia). All of these men figure elsewhere in this book. In the summer of 1863, he had been engaged in a campaign of attacks on Union shipping in Chesapeake Bay.[73] Beall had attended the University of Virginia and had many friends and relatives in high places in the Confederate government. He was widely regarded as a young man of great promise.

Beall and a party of twenty Confederates were successful in capturing the *Philo Parsons*, a lake steamer, on 18 September and were prepared to use her to attack the *Michigan*. They learned, however, that the crew of the *Michigan* was expecting the attack, and Beall's crew refused to offer battle.[74]

This lapse of courage did not stop the Confederate plan for operations on the Great Lakes. They arranged for the purchase of a lake ship, the *Georgian*, and had cannon made at Guelph, Ontario, to arm her. With Union prodding, the Canadian authorities kept a close watch on these matters, and the delays caused by the scrutiny and the coming of winter prevented the *Georgian* from ever being used.[75]

The Union heard that John Yates Beall was managing the Confederate activity at Guelph and pressured the Canadians to arrest him. Bennett Burleigh, who was actually superintending the activity, was arrested by Canadian authorities who thought they had arrested Beall. Burleigh did not reveal his identity, and it was some time before the mistake was discovered. Burleigh had been Beall's second in command on the *Philo Parsons*, and the Confederates made strenuous efforts to defend him. Papers were produced to prove that he was acting as an authorized agent of the Confederate government; and Jefferson Davis wrote a letter on his behalf. He was finally turned over to the United States for trial but escaped and after the war became a famous journalist.[76]

Clement Clay's protégé, Lieutenant Bennett H. Young, returned to Canada from Richmond to begin the program that he and Clay had discussed at Halifax. Even though Clay was interested in "retribution" raids on the United States and theoretically was not responsible for the paramilitary activities of the American Knights, he allowed Young to participate in the clandestine expedition to Chicago sponsored by Thompson. After this foray fell through, Young reported back to Clay and was sent to study Burlington and St. Albans, Vermont, as possible targets for a raid.

On 8 September, Thompson wrote to Clay about several operational matters and mentioned that "retaliating raids" such as those contemplated by Clay and Young "embarrassed" him.[77] Clay may have been concerned enough at Thompson's embarrassment to search for some more palatable target. He sent Young to Ohio to determine whether the prisoners at Camp Chase might be freed by a raid of Confederates from Canada, presumably without counting on Copperhead assistance.

Young seemed to feel that the job could be done with thirty men, and he went to work to recruit and organize such a party. Clay supplied Young with operating money, and Young began to organize and train his group. On 6 October, however, Young reported that he had not been able to recruit enough men of the right quality for the Ohio raid, and he and Clay decided that St. Albans, Vermont, should be the first target.[78] They seemed to expect that the purpose of the raid would be to burn the town and rob the banks in the process. Destruction of the town would be direct retaliation for damage done by the Union army in the South, and any money obtained from the banks would help with Confederate operating expenses in Canada. St. Albans in flames would clearly be an act of war and not a mere robbery.

Clay appears to have authorized the St. Albans raid as a swan song. He apparently had already made up his mind to leave Canada and return to the Confederacy. On 11 October, Weir at Halifax wrote to Clay, responding to a query concerning the best way to get back home through the blockade.[79]

Before Clay could leave, however, Young and twenty men raided St. Albans. They conducted the foray in a well-organized manner, but the Greek Fire they used did not work well and the town was not burned. They took in excess of $200,000 from three banks and got back across the border into Canada. The failure to burn the town made the raid look like nothing more than a large-scale bank robbery, and there were massive repercussions.

Fourteen of the raiders were imprisoned by Canadian authorities and about $90,000 confiscated from them. The others managed to avoid capture. Presumably they had the rest of the money taken from the St. Albans banks. The captive raiders immediately sent a telegram to George Sanders telling him of their plight and asking for his help. On 22 October 1864, Clay gave Sanders $6,000 for the defense of the raiders. Sanders turned $5,500 of this over to his son Lewis, who took charge of overseeing the diet of the prisoners and working with their defense counsel. George Sanders used the raid as the excuse for threats that the Confederate campaign was only beginning, and he launched a series of operations designed to influence opinion in Canada and help free the raiders.

The story of the St. Albans raid and the machinations to free the captured raiders has been told at length elsewhere. It took several months and numerous trips by clandestine couriers between Canada and Richmond, but eventually all of the raiders were freed and the money confiscated by the Canadians returned to them.[80]

In late September 1864, Lieutenant Colonel Robert M. Martin and Lieutenant John W. Headley of General Morgan's command arrived in Canada under orders to assist Jacob Thompson in his campaign against the North. After the failure of the uprising scheduled for 29 August, early November was picked as the time for the next effort, to coincide with the presidential election in the North. In addition to the expedition sent to Chicago, Martin and a team were sent to New York to work with Captain Longuemare and James McMasters, leader of the American Knights there, to bring about simultaneous action. In spite of considerable effort by Longuemare and McMasters, the New Yorkers could not be persuaded to act.

In frustration over much talk and no action, the Confederates finally decided to take matters into their own hands and strike for their cause. They collected bottles of Greek Fire and rented rooms in several New York City hotels. On 25 November 1864 they set fires simultaneously in twenty-two hotels and in a passageway of Barnum's museum. They made a technical mistake, however. To delay discovery, they carefully closed up the hotel rooms after setting the fires. As a result, the fires did not get enough oxygen to get a good start. Most of them went out or were put out before much damage resulted. The Confederates caused a sensation in New York but accomplished little else.[81]

Shortly thereafter, the Confederates in Canada heard that seven Confederate general officers, prisoners of the Union, were to be moved from Johnson's Island to Fort Lafayette in New York on 15 December 1864. Thompson quickly organized a group to intercept the train and release them. The operation failed, however, and John Yates Beall and a companion were captured before they could get back to Canada.

Beall and his companion were taken to Fort Lafayette in New

York, where the companion turned state's evidence and Beall was tried and convicted as a guerrilla and a spy. He was sentenced on 8 February to be hanged and was executed on 24 February 1865 before any serious steps could be taken to intervene on his behalf.[82]

The reaction of the British authorities in Canada to the St. Albans raid and the increasing prevalence of Union detectives operating in Canada put severe limitations on Confederate clandestine operations. They were further constrained by the Confederate government, which seemed to be undertaking a different strategy. Secretary of State Judah Benjamin wrote to Jacob Thompson in December 1864:

> I have now to inform you that from reports which reach us from trustworthy sources we are satisfied that so close espionage is kept upon you that your services have been deprived of the value which is attached to your further residence in Canada. The President thinks, therefore, that as soon as the gentleman arrives who bears this letter . . . it will be better that you transfer to him as *quietly* as possible all of the information that you have obtained and the release of funds in your hands and then return to the Confederacy.[83]

The "gentleman" was Brigadier General Edwin Gray Lee.

The Confederate government apparently was not satisfied with the conduct of the campaign from Canada and wanted to give it a new direction under fresh leadership. Lee was a young lawyer who had experience in both troop warfare and clandestine operations. His most recent assignment had been as chief of reserves in the Shenandoah Valley District in Virginia. His headquarters was at Staunton, and he may have had other duties relating to the clandestine route that ran from Richmond to Staunton by rail and then by road down the Valley to the Baltimore and Ohio Railroad near Harpers Ferry. Once on the railroad, agents could go west to Wheeling and from there to Detroit, Erie, or Buffalo. Or they could go east to Baltimore and then north to Buffalo, New York, or Boston. By either branch they could eventually reach Canada.

The Reverend Dr. Kensey Johns Stewart's wife was E. G. Lee's aunt, and Lee apparently had been an early supporter of the idea of an attack on the prison at Elmira, New York. Cassius Lee, one of the early Confederates in Canada, was E. G. Lee's uncle. Jefferson Davis and Judah Benjamin may have felt that Lee would manage clandestine affairs in Canada with more military realism and less internal friction than Thompson and Clay had done.

At the time of Benjamin's letter to Thompson, many of the Confederate personnel active in 1864 were in prison or otherwise out of action. P. C. Martin had drowned in a shipwreck in November 1864. Stewart and his group apparently never came to Union attention. The senior people in the Confederate apparatus, George and Lewis Sanders, Beverly Tucker, and W. W. Cleary, continued to work with Jacob Thompson. Much of their attention was devoted to helping the various people in prison, but plans continued to put the *Georgian* into action in the spring. Title of the *Georgian* was transferred to George Taylor Denison, a relative of Confederate Colonel George Dawson, and William "Larry" McDonald of Toronto was reported to be working to get her ready for operations in the spring.[84]

George Sanders kept in contact with leading Democrats in the North. Others continued to work with the Copperheads, and an effort was made to organize them for another attempt at an uprising to occur about the time of Lincoln's inauguration in March 1865.[85] Sanders mentioned his mission in a letter to Jefferson Davis on 7 March 1865 in which he reported on his nine months of effort in Canada. It apparently arrived in Richmond shortly before the evacuation, where it found its way into the hands of a Union journalist, who published it in the *New York Herald* on 8 July 1865.

In this letter, Sanders said that Davis had approved Sanders's suggestion that he go to Canada to try to form an alliance with the Democrats in the North with a view to working out a "satisfactory adjustment" with the government in Washington. In other words, Sanders was to try to heal the split in the Democratic party that had allowed the election of a Republican president in 1860. Northern and southern Democrats, united, could recover control of the country. When Thompson found out about Sanders's mission he commented to Clay that Sanders "has come from abroad Europe to do what he says he did not know we were intended to do, and he had gone on to do it." Thompson was annoyed because his target was also northern Democrats.

Jefferson Davis does not appear to have helped clarify this problem of conflicting jurisdiction. In effect, he had three separate programs running in Canada at the same time: Sanders working on the northern Democratic politicians; Thompson working on the northern Copperheads; and Clay trying to organize military action to free Confederate prisoners, stimulate a Copperhead rebellion, or conduct raids against U.S. territory. All three campaigns were related and overlapped, but they had distinct features that separated them.

Sanders was working with upper-class politicians who would have been frightened by the working-class Copperheads who were Thompson's main target. In fact, Davis may have encouraged the Copperhead movement in part to frighten the politicians into action. Clay's efforts were more technical and seem to have been designed to support the other efforts and help the general Confederate war effort by creating alarms and drawing northern attention to the Canadian border. This overlap of effort may have been the result of long-distance mismanagement, but if it were intended it would be a tribute to the sophistication of Davis's strategy and indicative of the time and effort he devoted to covert activity.

Throughout the winter of 1864–65, a constant campaign was conducted to keep the Union nervous about its northern border. A series of rumors and reports about planned rebel raids was fed to the various U.S. consuls. The consul at Halifax heard that the Confederates had organized a special group of three to four hundred men to raid steamers on coasts and lakes. Headquarters of this new organization was said to be in Havana with "squads" at Nassau, Vera Cruz, California, and elsewhere. Lieutenant Brain of the *Chesapeake* affair was reported to have been in Halifax in connection with this organization. Other reports mentioned Oswego, New York, as a target, and the *Tallahassee* was reported to be active off northern ports again.[86] Although many reports of this nature might have been generated by individual rumor mongers, the campaign had a consistency that suggests Confederate inspiration and organization.

Other operations appear to have been more sophisticated. For example, on 23 January 1865, the U.S. consul at Halifax reported that he had received a letter from D. H. Hazen of Pittsburgh which informed him that a Confederate officer in Halifax wished a pardon from the U.S. government. Later he wrote that the officer had information on Confederate plans for operations along the Canadian border which he would be willing to reveal if he could be promised a pardon. On 31 May 1865, the consul wrote to the State Department asking for favorable treatment for a former Confederate, Simon E. Adler, who had requested a pardon and who "on three occasions has given me information of importance to the Government." The information imparted by Adler was not identified specifically, but during the time in question, the consul had reported that the Confederates were planning a raid by six hundred men and blockade runners were being converted to armed raiders to support an attack on the U.S. coast by Confederate ironclads. None of this information was true, but it was similar to that received by other U.S. consuls. Adler appears to have been "fed" to the consul in Halifax.[87]

Lieutenant Headley later wrote a book about his experiences and told about some other operations that had occurred before his arrival in September. From information in his book and elsewhere it is possible to get some idea of the Confederate manpower involved in the clandestine campaign in Canada. From a list of those to whom weapons were issued for the operation, Headley printed the names of the sixty-two men who were sent to Chicago in August 1864. Some of the names were garbled at some point between the man who issued the ordnance and the printer, but most can be identified. Headley also printed the names of the crew of the *Philo Parsons* who refused to continue the operation against the USS *Michigan*, those of the St. Albans raiders, including the seven who were never captured, and those of men involved in several other operations.

A comparison of Headley's list with the names known from the Calais raid and other operations leads to several conclusions. Although, because some of the names seem to be garbled, we cannot be sure of the exact number, it is clear that the total strength of all of these operations was not much over one hundred. Young drew ten members of his St. Albans group from the sixty-two who had gone to Chicago. To avoid the appearance of violating Canadian neutrality, Young claimed to have recruited his team while on the Chicago operation and to have planned the raid while in U.S. territory. It is obvious that he also recruited people elsewhere. There was no overlap between the Chicago group and the group that captured the *Philo Parsons*. The second Chicago operation in November 1864 drew heavily from personnel involved in the first Chicago operation. Aside from Beall and Burleigh, the personnel for the *Georgian* and other later operations was different from the Chicago group. Thirty-six names on the first Chicago list did not appear on any other list, but Headley said that when the group in Chicago dispersed, twenty-eight of them chose to go home instead of returning to Canada. Of the other eight names, one man was later reported to be active as a courier between Confederate elements in Canada.

To the number of men accounted for here it is necessary to add those who were active with William "Larry" McDonald and his explosives "factory" at Toronto. Headley also said the Confederates had a farm outside of Toronto where the sixty-two men bound for Chicago assembled. This was probably a training, storage, and holding area, and several men may have been occupied in operating it. Aside from one man possibly identified, only the men captured from the Calais raid are known. Altogether, however, this group would not likely add more than another twenty-five or thirty to the one hundred who have been identified.

As we have seen, the Confederates never had a chance to cause a serious revolt in the Union rear, but they kept alive the threat of an uprising, kept governors nervous and the population alarmed, and were able to hold away from the front substantial numbers of troops that otherwise might have been released by the states. When the resources expended are compared with the results, Confederate operations in Canada were an outstanding success.

The operations that were conducted from Canada tell us much about the Confederate organization there and allow other inferences to be made. We know that the Confederates had a number of well-educated and experienced men in Canada working on clandestine operations. They were often assisted by Confederate soldiers—some escapees, others assigned to the Canadian operation by the Confederate government. They spent a great deal of money on clandestine operations. They could carry out more than one operation at a time. They could continue to carry out clandestine operations while the commissioners were preoccupied with political efforts to free the St. Albans raiders. Some of their operations were assisted by persons resident in the United States. They received help from time to time from individual British or Canadian officers or citizens. Although their operations were not always successful (and we know the most about those that failed), some were conceived with considerable daring and sophistication.

We can therefore infer that the Confederates had a reasonably large and efficient clandestine organization in Canada, probably dating from sometime in 1862 and growing larger and more sophisticated as the war went on. The Confederates had arrangements in Canada for training and maintaining personnel and for procuring arms and safe areas for planning and running operations. Although some operations against the North were run from Confederate territory, Canada was the main operational field station for many important clandestine operations in the North. In view of these attributes of the Confederate clandestine organization in Canada, it is not surprising that it played a role in the operation to take President Lincoln as hostage.

Notes

ABBREVIATIONS

NA   National Archives

OR   U.S. War Department, *The War of the Rebellion: A Compilation of the Official Records of the Union and Confederate Armies.* 128 vols. Washington, D.C.: U.S. Government Printing Office, 1880–1901.

ORN   U.S. Navy Department, *Official Records of the Union and Confederate Navies in the War of the Rebellion.* 30 vols. Washington, D.C.: U.S. Government Printing Office, 1894–1914.

RG   Record Group

1. Two historical works are particularly useful in tracing Confederate relations with Canada: Oscar A. Kinchen, *Confederate Operations in Canada and the North* (North Quincy, Mass.: Christopher, 1970), and Robin W. Winks, *Canada and the United States: The Civil War Years* (Montreal: Harvest House, 1971).

2. General Records of the Department of State Consular Correspondence, T series microfilm, RG-59, NA.

3. Robert Douthat Meade, *Judah P. Benjamin* (London: Oxford University Press, 1943), pp. 247–48.

4. Dispatches from U.S. Consuls in Quebec, 25 December 1861, T-482, reel 9, General Records of the Department of State Consular Correspondence, RG 59, NA.

5. Dispatches from U.S. Consuls in Halifax, 1861, T-469, reel 10, ibid.

6. Dispatches from U.S. Consuls in Montreal, January 1862, T-222, reel 4, ibid.

7. Dispatches from U.S. Consuls in Montreal, 4 February 1862, ibid.

8. Dispatches from U.S. Consuls in Montreal, 6 February 1862, ibid.

9. Dispatches from U.S. Consuls in Halifax, T-469, reel 10, ibid., and numerous other references, including General E. G. Lee Diary, Southern Historical Collection, University of North Carolina, Chapel Hill.

10. Dispatches from U.S. Consuls in Montreal, 27 August 1862, T-222, reel 4, RG 59, NA.

11. M-599, reel 6, frames 0380–81, ibid.; Investigation and Trial Papers Relating to the Assassination of President Lincoln, RG 153, NA.

12. T. M. Armstrong, ed., *The Biographical Encyclopedia of Kentucky* (Cincinnati, 1878), 2:538–41.

13. Dispatches from U.S. Consuls in Quebec, T-482, reel 9, RG 59, NA.

14. Ibid.

15. Meriwether Stuart, "Operation Sanders," *Virginia Magazine of History and Biography* 81 (April 1973): 157–99.

16. Ibid.

17. Dispatches from U.S. Consuls in Halifax, 20 February 1863, T-469, reel 10, RG 59, NA.

18. Meade, *Benjamin*, p. 249.

19. Cassius F. Lee to Charles H. Lee, 4 November 1863, Vertical Files, Lloyd House, Alexandria Public Library, Alexandria, Va.; Dispatches from U.S. Consuls in Quebec, 18 September 1863, T-482, reel 9, RG 59, NA.

20. Charles E. Frohman, *Rebels on Lake Erie* (Columbus: Ohio Historical Society, 1965), p. 46.

21. Minor to Buchanan, 2 February 1864, *Southern Historical Society Papers* 23 (1895): 283–90.

22. Frohman, *Rebels on Lake Erie*, p. 38.

23. Ibid., p. 39.

24. Major William S. Pierson to Colonel Hoffman, 28 October 1863, in ibid., p. 39.

25. Dispatches from U.S. Consuls in Quebec, 13 November 1863, T-222, reel 4, RG 59, NA.

26. Frohman, *Rebels on Lake Erie*, p. 40.

27. Ibid.

28. Dispatches from U.S. Consuls in Montreal, T-222, reel 4, RG 59, NA.

29. Minor to Buchanan, 2 February 1864, *Southern Historical Society Papers* 23 (1895): 283–90.

30. This information was based on several reports in Dispatches from U.S. Consuls in Montreal, T-222, reel 4, RG 59, NA.

31. Mary K. Maule, "A Chapter of Unwritten History," typescript, n.d., Western Reserve Historical Society, Cleveland, Ohio.

32. Benn Pitman, *The Treason Trials in Indianapolis* (Cincinnati: Moore, Wilstack, and Baldwin, 1865), p. 325.

33. Ibid., p. 49.

34. For the New York draft riots see Adrian Cook, *The Armies of the Streets* (Lexington: University Press of Kentucky, 1974); James McCague, *The Second Rebellion: The Story of the New York City Draft Riots of 1863* (New York: Dial Press, 1968).

35. *Biographical Directory of the American Congress, 1774–1971* (Washington, D.C.: U.S. Government Printing Office, 1971).

36. Dispatches from U.S. Consuls in Halifax, T-469, reel 10, RG 59, NA. Vallandigham was seen off at Wilmington, North Carolina, by Major Norris of the Signal (and Secret Service) Bureau (David Winfred Gaddy, "William Norris and the Confederate Signal and Secret Service," *Maryland Historical Magazine* 70 [Summer 1975]: 175).

37. Luke P. Blackburn, Compiled Service Record, NA.

38. Ezra J. Warner, *Generals in Gray: Lives of the Confederate Commanders* (Baton Rouge: Louisiana State University Press, 1959), pp. 138–39.

39. Statement made by Godfrey W. Hyams at Hamilton, Ontario, 12 April 1865, Records of the Office of the Attorney General, NA.

40. Dispatches from U.S. Consuls in Halifax, T-469, reel 10, RG 59, NA. Several reports during the summer of 1864 refer to blockade runs to Halifax.

41. Letters from H. H. Emmons to the Attorney General, 22 April 1865, Records of the Office of the Attorney General, NA.

42. The Reverend K. J. Stewart wrote to Jefferson Davis on 30 November 1864 that the yellow fever project had "no other effect than to disgust good men and anger the Almighty" (Chap. VII, vol. 24, pp. 58–65, RG 109, NA).

43. Dispatches from U.S. Consuls in Halifax T-469, reel 10, RG 59, NA; a

clipping from a Richmond newspaper in George N. Sanders Papers, RG 109, NA, carries on its back a news item describing a serenade welcoming Kane to Richmond.

44. Benjamin to Holcombe, 24 February 1864, *Southern Historical Society Papers* 7 (1879): 99.

45. Ibid.

46. Holcombe to Benjamin, 28 April 1864, ibid.

47. Dispatches from U.S. Consuls in Montreal, 21 June 1864, T-222, reel 5, RG 59, NA.

48. Holcombe to Benjamin, 27 May 1864, *Southern Historical Society Papers* 7 (1879): 139.

49. Clay to Benjamin, 2 November 1864, *OR*, Ser. 1, vol. 48, pt. 2, pp. 914–17.

50. Bennett H. Young, Compiled Service Record, NA.

51. William Collins, Compiled Service Record, NA. The backgrounds of the raiders are reported in considerable detail in Mason Philip Smith, *Confederates Downeast* (Portland, Me.: Provincial Press, 1985).

52. William Collins, Compiled Service Record, NA.

53. J. C. Phillips, Compiled Service Record, NA.

54. Files of Investigations by Levi C. Turner and Lafayette C. Baker, 1861–66, Turner-Baker Papers, M-797, reel 1223, file 4026, NA.

55. Royce Gordon Shingleton, *John Taylor Wood: Sea Ghost of the Confederacy* (Athens: University of Georgia Press, 1979), p. 121.

56. J. D. Martin, Compiled Service Record, NA.

57. Holcombe to Benjamin, 16 June 1864, *Southern Historical Society Papers* 7 (1879): 293; Dispatches from U.S. Consuls in Halifax, T-469, reel 1, RG 59, NA.

58. Dispatches from U.S. Consuls in Halifax, T-469, reel 10, RG 59, NA.

59. Coxe to Clay, 26 September 1864, Clement C. Clay Papers, Duke University Library, Durham, N.C.

60. Mrs. Robert Edwin Coxe to Clement Clay, 31 October 1864, ibid.

61. *New York World*, 21 April 1865.

62. For an insider's account of Morgan's raid, see Basil W. Duke, *A History of Morgan's Cavalry* (1867; rpt. Bloomington: Indiana University Press, 1960), pp. 407–62.

63. James D. Horan, *Confederate Agent* (New York: Crown, 1954), p. 71.

64. Report of Judge Advocate General Holt in Pitman, *Trials for Treason at Indianapolis*, p. 326.

65. Horan, *Confederate Agent*, p. 72.

66. Chap. IX, vol. 43, Incidental and Contingent Expenditures, 18 March 1864, RG 109, NA; Daniel Ruggles and Mortimer B. Ruggles, Compiled Service Records, NA.

67. Pitman, *Trials for Treason at Indianapolis*, p. 108.

68. Dispatches from U.S. Consuls in Montreal, 25 June 1864, T-222, reel 5, RG 59, NA.

69. Kinchen, *Confederate Operations*, p. 80.

70. Pitman, *Trials for Treason at Indianapolis*, pp. 97–103.

71. Kinchen, *Confederate Operations*, pp. 66–70; John W. Headley, *Confederate Operations in Canada and New York* (New York: Neale, 1906), p. 228.

72. Kinchen, *Confederate Operations*, pp. 149–55.

73. Horan, *Confederate Agent*, pp. 153–57.

74. Kinchen, *Confederate Operations*, p. 112; Headley, *Confederate Operations*, pp. 250–51.

75. Dispatches from U.S. Consuls in Montreal, T-222, reel 6, RG 59, NA.

76. Various episodes in Burleigh's story were reported by the U.S. Consul in Montreal (Dispatches from U.S. Consuls in Montreal, T-222, reel 6, RG 59, NA).

77. Thompson to Clay, 8 September 1864, Item 22, Clement C. Clay Papers, RG 109, NA.

78. Headley, *Confederate Operations*, p. 258.

79. Weir to Clay, 11 October 1864, Clay Papers, Duke University Library.

80. Headley, *Confederate Operations*; Kinchen, *Confederate Operations*; and especially Winks, *Canada and the United States*; see also Oscar A. Kinchen, *Daredevils of the Confederate Army* (Boston: Christopher, 1959), pp. 72–74.

81. Headley, *Confederate Operations*, pp. 274–76.

82. Ibid., pp. 357–69.

83. Benjamin to Thompson, 30 December 1864, containing "extract" of letter dated 6 December 1864, untitled MS, believed to be the work of the Reverend Stephen F. Cameron, in the Museum of the Confederacy, Richmond.

84. Dispatches from U.S. Consuls in Montreal, T-222, reel 6, RG 59, NA.

85. Ibid.

86. Ibid.

87. Ibid.

9

The Beginnings of Central Intelligence

Previous chapters have outlined some of the secret Confederate activities aimed at damaging the enemy, and others have dealt with various means by which the Confederates collected information. It is obvious that several different Confederate organizations were involved in espionage, but their individual organizational structure and responsibilities are difficult to define.

The activities of Rose Greenhow and her associates in 1861 have been so well publicized that one is led to view her as a distraction from an effective covert apparatus in place in Washington. The work of the Signal Corps and other espionage nets, including that of Walter Bowie, were described in Chapter 6. General James Longstreet and his associate General Gilbert Moxley Sorrell both wrote about a spy named Harrison who was assigned to them by the secretary of war in 1863 and who provided Longstreet with some very useful information. Subsequent investigation by one of the present authors has determined that this man was Henry Thomas Harrison of Tennessee and Mississippi.[1] He not only served Longstreet, but he also worked with General D. H. Hill in North Carolina and later in the New York area. He had been commissioned as a second lieutenant early in the war but was soon put on detached service and assigned to various duties by the secretary of war.

Another member of the War Department Secret Service was James H. Fowle, who was interrogated by a special congressional committee in 1866. According to his testimony, Fowle enlisted in the Seventeenth Virginia Infantry but was injured accidentally and sent home to recuperate. When he returned to duty on 16 May

1863 he was detailed for duty with the Signal Corps "and then put in the Secret Service." On 19 September 1864, Fowle was assigned to Sergeant Harry Brogden's Signal Corps camp in Westmoreland County. Later he was transferred to work for Secretary of State Benjamin.

In the course of his testimony, Fowle distinguished between the War Department Secret Service, to which he was assigned by the Signal Corps, and the State Department Secret Service, to which he was detailed in January 1865. He said that John Williamson Palmer, a correspondent for the *New York Tribune*, who wrote dispatches under the name "Altamount," was an agent of the Confederate War Department. He also named as Confederate agents John Harrison Surratt and Augustus Howell.[2]

From these fragments and the evidence in the preceding chapters it seems clear that by 1864 Confederate clandestine activities had grown in number and complexity. There was a War Department Secret Service and a State Department Secret Service. There was an Army Torpedo Bureau and a Navy Submarine Battery Service, both engaged in developing new weapons to use against the enemy. Various army and navy partisan operations were ongoing, and several Secret Service companies were taking the war to the enemy. In Canada there was an ambitious operation to focus the activities of northern Copperheads against the Union government, and the Copperheads themselves were involved in developing and using secret weapons. The Army of Northern Virginia and others had an aggressive espionage effort under way, and the residue of General Winder's organization in Richmond appears still to have been active.

As President Davis and his various collaborators struggled with an extensive program of clandestine operations in the late summer and autumn of 1864 it must have become obvious that a formal, centralization system was needed. Secret legislation was drafted to establish the needed machinery—the Bureau for Special and Secret Service.

On 28 September 1864 John B. Clark and A. H. Conrow, congressmen from Missouri, wrote a joint letter to the secretary of war in which they said:

> The undersigned would respectfully express their beliefs that the organization of a Bureau of Secret Service if placed under the charge of a qualified officer would result [?] greatly to the advantage of the country by damaging the enemy in various ways perfectly legitimate in civilized warfare—in ascertaining the plans of the enemy and misleading him as

to ours—in encouraging inventions and a proper assistance in operating them and in regulating the manner of obtaining proof of damage and in protecting the Government from various frauds now perpetuated upon it and in protecting the deserving.[3]

This is a clear statement of the classic goals of a clandestine organization plus some unique duties. The classic items were to ascertain the plans of the enemy, mislead him as to one's own plans, and, damage him by clandestine means. To these were added the somewhat unusual but sensible tasks of encouraging the development of new weapons and assessing the damage caused—an important task because the Confederacy rewarded its entepreneuers of sabotage based on the value of the object destroyed.

The remainder of the letter is devoted to advocating the appointment of one Lieutenant Colonel Robert S. Bevier as the chief of this new organization. Bevier had commanded a Missouri infantry battalion but in 1864 was on detached service in Richmond. Clark and Conrow apparently were aware of plans being formulated to create the new bureau and wanted to have their man considered early.

This interpretation is supported by Clark's later role in the passage of legislation creating the bureau, an unprecedented act that was not paralleled in America until World War II. The heart of the bill "to provide for the establishment of a Bureau for Special and Secret Service" is clearly stated:

There is now no efficient system for the encouragement, development, or application of new inventions, or secret agencies for the defense of the country . . . it has been shown that by individual exertion, and private enterprise, many useful inventions have been made which would be greatly beneficial to the common defense, were they regularly and systematically applied. . . . There is now no department authorized under existing laws to experiment upon and reduce to system the operation of new and destructive modes of warfare, or for the efficient direction of secret agencies.[4]

The drafters of this bill were doubtless impressed by the ingenuity shown by southern inventors in designing and developing new cannon, ironclad ships, underwater mines, and submarines, as well as in providing an arms- and ammunition-producing industry where none had existed before. Many of the ideas developed might not have been the first of their kind under the sun, but overall new ideas and the new applications of old ideas made a great impression on those responsible for conducting the war.

The drafters were aware of the many contributions made by

secret agents and the successes achieved by irregular warfare operations. They must also have been aware, however, of the many operations that had gone wrong because they were not properly planned and conducted. One reason why such operations were not as effective as their authors had hoped was because no central, coordinating mechanism had been established. The only real coordinating apparatus was the inside net consisting of Davis, Benjamin, and Seddon with help from General Bragg; the commissioners in Canada; Davis's aides; General Lee and his headquarters; the army and navy torpedo operations; General Winder and his detectives and prison administrators; Robert Ould; and William Norris's Signal (and Secret Service) Bureau. This group was able to acquire much useful intelligence, but operational coordination was minimal and ad hoc.

On 30 November 1864, in secret session, Clark submitted the bill to establish the Bureau of Special and Secret Service in the House of Representatives. The bill was referred to the Committee on Military Affairs, which reported it to the House on 30 January 1865.[5] The matter was apparently considered important because Clark asked for and obtained approval to have the regular schedule of business set aside so that his bill might be read. There is no way of knowing how much the bill was reworked between 30 November and 30 January, but the initial draft must have been prepared for Clark by somebody who knew the facts about Confederate Secret Service and who had Jefferson Davis's confidence.

The bill, known as HR 361, came to the floor of the House again during a secret session on 25 February 1865 for its final reading. Two minor technical amendments proposed by John Perkins, Jr., of Louisiana were approved. J. T. Lynch of North Carolina then proposed an amendment that would have caused the bureau to report to Robert E. Lee as commanding general of the army instead of to the president. This appears to have been an anti-Davis maneuver, not a quarrel with the substance of the bill. The amendment was defeated, and the bill passed the House by a vote of thirty-four to twenty-six.[6]

On 25 February 1865, HR 361 was read in the Senate in secret session and referred to the Senate Committee on Military Affairs. On 6 March 1865, again in secret session, Louis T. Wigfall of the Committee on Military Affairs reported the bill without amendment. It was passed by a vote of ten to eight.[7] This narrow margin again seems to have been caused by anti-Davis feeling rather than by concern for the provisions of the bill.

The text of the bill is interesting for what it tells of the Confederate intelligence effort as it had existed, as well as for plans for the future. The principal provisions of HR 361 were as follows:

1. The bureau was established to examine, experiment with, and apply warlike inventions and to direct secret agencies. There were to be a chief of bureau and a Board of Examiners to consist of three members with competent scientific and mechanical experience. The president could determine the rank of these persons and could assign serving officers or make appointments from outside the services as he deemed best.

2. The bureau was to examine inventions, plans, and enterprises for offensive or defensive warfare and to cause to be tested by actual experiment those approved by the president of the Board of Examiners. Once an invention, plan, or enterprise was approved, the bureau was responsible for its efficient application. For this purpose, it would have the authority to make contracts for the construction or purchase of all necessary devices, materials, and implements. All other departments and bureaus were to honor requisitions when to do so would not injure the other branches of the public service. The bureau could employ agents and experts and should abide by the regulations of the Engineer Bureau that were "not inapplicable."

3. The Board of Examiners was responsible for approving projects and candidates for appointment except that the president might override a negative decision by the chief of the bureau, and the bureau must act on those projects assigned to it by the president using any of the secret service funds approved for the bureau.

4. The chief of the bureau, subject to the approval of the president, could employ secret agents for service in the Confederate states or within the enemy's lines, or in any foreign country. He was also authorized to organize a system for the application of new means of warfare and to organize Secret Service agencies as needed to obtain the objectives of the bureau.

5. Under the bureau there was to be a Polytechnic Corps to consist of a chief of corps with the necessary number of commanders, captains, first lieutenants, and second lieutenants as well as noncommissioned officers and men. Pay would be the same as for corresponding grades in the Engineer Corps.

6. Members of the Polytechnic Corps would be assigned from other branches or requisitioned by the chief of the bureau or recruited directly in the same manner as other branches of the military. The number of officers from other branches fit for active service was not to exceed twenty and a similar number could be made up of officers not fit for field service. The number of noncommissioned officers and men fit for service could not exceed two hundred. In addition, others might be detailed temporarily as needed and personnel could also be recruited from those not fit for field duty.

7. The chief of the bureau could contract for purchase or license of inventions subject to the review of the president or a Board of Examining Officers and in the case of inventions resulting in awards for destruction of enemy property authorized by the act of 21 April 1862, the cost of purchase of the inventions should first be deducted from the award.

8. The bureau could hire clerks, draftsmen, and others unfit for field duty with the same pay as the Engineer Bureau.

9. "The companies and parties now irregularly organized for the application of submerged or other defense and known as torpedo corps and for the construction and use of new warlike inventions or for Secret Service should if approved by the President, be incorporated into and form a part of the organization contemplated by this act." The secretary of war had to approve exemptions from military service.

10. Compensation for enemy property destroyed would be according to the act of 21 April 1862 (the procedure for adjudicating claims was described).

11. A majority of the Board of Examiners would determine the value of enemy property destroyed.

12. Department commanders were to control the time and place of operations carried out by the new bureau.

13. Awards could be paid in currency instead of bonds.

14. Inventors in the service of the Confederacy were allowed to collect awards.

15. Correspondence on claims settled and pending must be turned over to the Secret Service Bureau, subject to the decision of the president as to what service should be placed under the control of the bureau.

The rationale behind this bill reflected the realization that new weapons, devices, and operations to hurt the enemy must be kept secret to provide for maximum effect. They could be best developed, kept secret, and used effectively if kept in the hands of a group of skilled professionals who had both the technical and the

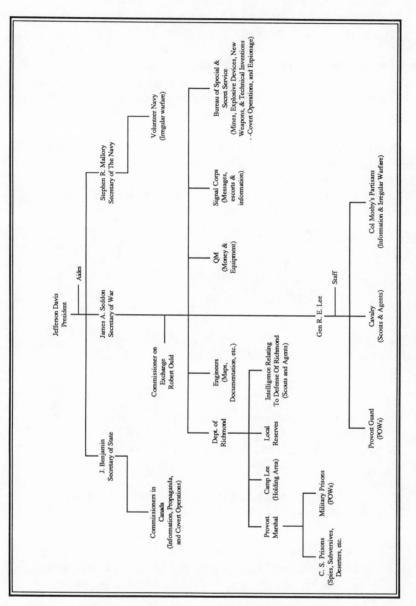

PRINCIPAL ELEMENTS OF THE CONFEDERATE
GOVERNMENT INVOLVED IN INTELLIGENCE WORK—1865

operational training to apply them effectively. Therefore, the new organization should be made up of men having a good technical background who knew how to conduct clandestine operations. Incentive was to be encouraged by monetary reward. The idea of paying a government employee to develop a good idea was in keeping with the idea prevalent at the time that a person was allowed to make money out of damage inflicted on the enemy. The new element was that the government would furnish the capital and the talent to turn an idea into a practical system. In the past this stage had often been left to private initiative.

HR 361 was enacted into law too late in the war to have much effect, but it is interesting to examine how it might have been implemented and to see if there is any evidence to indicate how far it was carried into effect.

Robert Ould would have been a logical choice to head the new Special and Secret Service Bureau. He had been district attorney in Washington, D.C., and appears to have been a man of considerable personal competence. He served as assistant secretary of war, then commissioner of [prisoner] exchange. He seems to have had Jefferson Davis's confidence, and his experience with the prisoner exchange must have kept him in touch with many aspects of clandestine operations.

The single most qualified person to serve on the Board of Examiners was probably Matthew Fontaine Maury. He had been in England since 1862, but in 1865 he left to return to the Confederacy with a considerable quantity of special material for torpedoes and other devices. Possibly his return was in connection with an assignment to the new organization. The war ended before Maury reached the Confederacy. Another logical member of the examining board would have been Brigadier General Gabriel Rains, head of the already existing Torpedo Bureau, which would have been included in the new Secret Service Bureau.[8] Rains had been particularly successful in developing antipersonnel mines. Davis might logically have drawn one or more members from the academic world. A logical choice from Virginia Military Institute might have been Colonel Thomas H. Williamson, professor of engineering. Williamson was a former West Pointer and had served as an engineer of the Confederate army in northern Virginia in 1861 before he returned to his academic duties. A possible candidate for chief of the Polytechnic Corps would have been John Taylor Wood. He was a graduate of the U.S. Naval Academy, had taught at Annapolis, and had an outstanding career in the Confederate service as a leader of amphibious raids. He may even have been the staff officer who helped to draft the legislation.

There is no indication of how the bureau was to relate to Confederate operations in Canada, but by late 1864 the civilian commissioners appear to have been considered no longer effective, and General E. G. Lee may have been sent to Canada in December 1864 in part to take control of the operations that were to be continued under the new bureau.

The handling of prisoners of war was to remain the primary responsibility of General Winder and his successors as commissioner general for prisoners. Exploitation of the prisoners as potential agents and as sources of information and identity material might well come under the new bureau, however. Winder and Generals Bradley T. Johnson and Daniel Ruggles, who handled the prisoner-of-war system in the final months, all had some association with clandestine operations and would have understood how to cooperate in such matters.

The buildup of Mosby's Rangers that took place in late 1864 could also have been related to the formation of the Secret Service Bureau. It is possible that the Confederacy planned to expand operations in the Mosby style behind Union lines under the eye of the new bureau.

The references to the Engineer Bureau in HR 361 show some coarse similarities between it and the new organization. Both activities involved the application of scientific knowledge to combat against the enemy. In that sense it would be logical to use the Engineer Bureau as a model in solving bureaucratic problems such as the pay and rank given for certain skills. The bill does not indicate whether the bureau should remain secret, but the references to the Engineer Bureau suggest an intention to use it as the cover for the Secret Service Bureau.

In many respects, the idea underlying the Special and Secret Service Bureau was very sophisticated. Nothing like it was to be developed in the United States until World War II, and even then the marriage between technology and clandestine operations was not as complete as it might have been under the Confederate system. It is unfortunate that the Confederate experience has been buried in archives. Their ideas were based on practical experience and might have provided a useful precedent for the resolution of similar problems in the twentieth century. In a sense, the Special and Secret Service Bureau was to combine operations that today are handled by the Defense Advanced Research Projects Agency and the Clandestine Services of the Central Intelligence Agency.

As sophisticated as the idea of the new bureau may have been, it still left unresolved one of the important problems that modern American intelligence legislation has tried to solve. The Confederate system made no provision for the coordinated analysis of information about the enemy. Each major user of information was left to do his own analysis. Apparently, the officials and officers receiving the information were thought to be the best qualified to evaluate it. That was doubtless true in many situations, but it prevented Confederate intelligence from playing the role of objective analyst, unbiased by policy involvement, that is one of the goals of modern American intelligence.

In reading the chapters that follow, it is important to keep in mind that during 1864 and 1865, while ambitious clandestine operations were being organized, the leaders of the Confederacy were also working to improve the institutions supporting such operations and that their ideas are reflected in the provisions of HR 361. Hardly the product of a death rattle from a defeated nation, the act looked to the future just as did other measures taken in Richmond at that time. The Confederacy, with four years of experience, was girding its loins as never before, preparing for the spring offensive of 1865, in which all available weapons, conventional and unconventional, were intended to play a part.

Notes

ABBREVIATIONS

NA   National Archives

OR   U.S. War Department, *The War of the Rebellion: A Compilation of the Official Records of the Union and Confederate Armies.* 128 vols. Washington, D.C.: U.S. Government Printing Office, 1880–1901.

ORN   U.S. Navy Department, *Official Records of the Union and Confederate Navies in the War of the Rebellion.* 30 vols. Washington, D.C.: U.S. Government Printing Office, 1894–1914.

RG   Record Group

1. James O. Hall, "The Spy Harrison," *Civil War Times Illustrated*, February 1986, p. 18.

2. Benjamin Butler Papers, Library of Congress; David Winfred Gaddy, *Maryland Historical* Society *Magazine* (to be published summer 1988).

3. Letters to the Secretary of War, M-437, reel 124, RG 109, NA.

4. Investigation and Trial Papers Relating to the Assassination of President Lincoln, M-599, reel 4, NA; A Docket of Bills Referred to the House of Representatives Committee on Military Affairs, Chap. VII, vol. 20, p. 82, ibid.

5. Journal of Open and Secret Sessions of the House of Representatives, Chap. VII, vol. 7, p. 95, ibid.

6. Ibid., p. 121.

7. Journal of Open and Secret Sessions of the Senate, Chap. VII, vol. 7, p. 169, ibid.

8. Toward the end of the war, General Henry Grey asked that Captain Zedekiah McDaniel of the "Torpedo and Secret Service Corps" be assigned to him. Special Order 73 of 28 March 1865 ordered McDaniel to report to General Grey, "commanding on the Mississippi River." Before leaving his base at Lynchburg, Virginia, McDaniel was to be relieved by a "competent officer" of the Torpedo Bureau. This episode may indicate that the legislation was being implemented.

PART TWO

Using the Machinery against President Lincoln

10

Portents

The old terrorist John Brown prophesied grimly in a little note written on 2 December 1859, just before he was hanged at Charles Town, Virginia: "I, John Brown, am now quite certain that the crimes of this guilty land will never be purged away but by blood."[1] The abolitionist raid at Harpers Ferry on 16 October of that year was but one of the portents of things to come. It was a watershed, an end to any hope that the political process between the North and the South could reach accommodation. A realist, Senator William H. Seward called it the "irrepressible conflict."

News of the John Brown raid set off alarms all over the South. Idle talk turned to serious planning for secession and war. With a strong military tradition, an expectation of foreign aid, and a superior intelligence network, southern leaders believed they could achieve independence. As in all great social or economic upheavals, fanatical elements were prepared to strike at the symbols of opposing thought and power. Abraham Lincoln was such a symbol. He was in danger of assassination from the day of his election until he was shot by John Wilkes Booth at Ford's Theatre on the night of 14 April 1865.

Before Lincoln left Springfield for Washington, he was warned of plots against his life. A few such letters expressed fear that he would be poisoned, a reference to the popular suspicion that Presidents William Henry Harrison and Zachary Taylor had suffered such a fate. Major David Hunter wrote about an assassination plot by young Virginians. Joseph Irwin reported that "border ruffians" were saying Lincoln should be killed. Horace White called Lincoln's attention to a *Chicago Tribune* story that said $40,000 had been raised in a hotel in New Orleans to hire assassins.[2]

Washington was in an uproar. Senator Seward, soon to be secretary of state, wrote to Lincoln that the city was in a state of great unrest with "apprehensions of possible disturbance and disorders connected with your assumption of the government." The next day Seward wrote Lincoln again about a plan by dissidents to seize the capital on or before inauguration day. He wanted Lincoln to come early and unannounced. This view was supported in a letter by Joseph Medill of the *Chicago Tribune*.[3]

Senator Seward's sensitive antennae had picked up some of the schemes aimed at blocking Lincoln's inauguration. One was to take the city by force. Another was to stir up bloody demonstrations on a scale calculated to cause a complete breakdown of authority. Still another was to prevent the constitutional ceremony of counting the electoral votes. Senator Louis T. Wigfall of Texas allegedly suggested kidnapping President James Buchanan so that Vice-President John C. Breckinridge could take over and settle things in the South's favor.[4] Seward was particularly concerned about the power vacuum. Buchanan was indecisive, and his advisers were badly split. Worse, General Winfield Scott, who commanded the army, was old and tired. He could muster but a tiny force to keep peace in Washington. The city teemed with ardent secessionists at every level, public and private. Each day brought word of additional pro-Confederate militia units being formed in the area. The elements of a coup d'état were in the making.

Lincoln declined Seward's suggestion to come early and unannounced. It turned out to be the right decision. There were no disorders, and the electoral votes were counted without incident on 13 February 1861. Still, it could have gone the other way. The margin for error was thin.

On 26 January the House of Representatives directed its select committee to look into the clamor. Pointedly, these instructions exempted the legislative branch from the inquiry: "Resolved, That the select committee of five be instructed to inquire whether any secret organization hostile to the Government of the United States exists in the District of Columbia; and, if so, whether any official or employees of the Federal Government in the executive or judicial departments are members thereof."

The testimony began three days later. In all, twenty-four men came before the committee. Among them were the mayor of Washington, James G. Berret; General Winfield Scott; Colonel Charles P. Stone, inspector-general of the District of Columbia militia; Dr. Cornelius Boyle, head of the Washington branch of the bitterly anti-Lincoln National Volunteers; Jacob Thompson, secretary of the interior; Enoch Lowe, former governor of Maryland; Thomas H. Hicks, the incumbent governor of Maryland; and two Baltimore members of the National Volunteers, Cipriano Ferrandini and Otis K. Hillard.

A main theme in the testimony was the question of Lincoln's safety. As if seen through a glass, darkly, the portent of 14 April 1865 was there. The testimony droned on until 13 February, the day the electoral votes were counted. The committee report with testimony of witnesses was published the next day. The committee was unanimously "of the opinion that the evidence produced before them does not prove the existence of a secret organization here or elsewhere hostile to the government, that has for its object, upon its own responsibility, an attack upon the Capitol, or any of the functions of government."[5] In this astonishing report, the committee was obviously "whistling by a graveyard." Perhaps the operative words in the document were "secret organization." In any case, organizations violently opposed to the government abounded in Washington and in nearby Maryland and Virginia. The people involved made little effort to conceal their intent to destroy the Union and to occupy Washington by force, if necessary.

After a nostalgic little speech at the station, Lincoln left Springfield for Washington on the morning of 11 February 1861. There were two reports of attempts on his life while he was aboard a train en route. The *Lafayette* (Indiana) *Journal* reported on 18 February that a derailer had been placed on the tracks just outside State Line, Indiana. It was found by accident and removed a short time before the train carrying Lincoln arrived at that tiny railroad junction. The train would not have been derailed, however; planners of his trip had taken just such an incident into account. Pilot engines were assigned to run just ahead of his train to see that the tracks were clear. A more sensational account was published in the *Syracuse* (New York) *Journal* on 23 February. A reporter for this newspaper interviewed unidentified members of the Lincoln party during a brief stop there on 18 February. He was told that a "grenade of the most destructive character" was found in a carpetbag just after the train pulled out of Cincinnati. The story went on to state that the grenade was set to explode in fifteen minutes. According to this account, the device was disarmed and disposed of. Norman B. Judd and Ward H. Lamon, who were with the Lincoln party, later discounted these newspaper accounts.

Even before Lincoln left Springfield for Washington, a distant storm was gathering in Baltimore. The secession drumbeat in that city was incessant: Maryland must go with the South! At the lower levels, the solution was ugly: Lincoln would be killed when he came through the city on his way to Washington. This talk of assassination reached some trained and attentive ears and resulted in Lincoln's dramatic secret passage through Baltimore during the early morning hours of 23 February. The story of this journey is almost incredible.

In the late summer of 1860, William Byrne, a prosperous Baltimore businessman, organized the paramilitary National Volunteers to work for the election of John C. Breckinridge. Breckinridge carried Maryland. After the election, Byrne expanded the organization, and it became the focus of the Maryland movement to prevent the inauguration of Lincoln. A branch of the National Volunteers was set up in Washington under Dr. Cornelius Boyle. Among the members of Byrne's organization was Otis K. Hillard, a native of Richmond. Another was Cipriano Ferrandini, a fiery Baltimore barber. Because of their activities, Boyle, Hillard, and Ferrandini had all been called before the select committee in early February.

Byrne was in the top leadership of the clandestine Knights of the Golden Circle, but his rank is unknown. Ferrandini's commission in the Knights refers to him as "Captain, Company B, Maryland Regiment." The commission is dated 8 August 1859 and signed by George Bickley, who headed the organization.[6] Hillard was undoubtedly a member, but documentary proof is lacking. The inner circle of the National Volunteers appears to have been drawn from trusted members of the Knights of the Golden Circle.

The plan to kill Lincoln in Baltimore was simple enough. Lincoln and his party were scheduled to pass through the city on 23 February. His special train from Harrisburg, Pennsylvania, using the Northern Central Railroad, was due to arrive at the Calvert Street station at about noon on that date. From this station, Lincoln would pass by carriage through crowded streets to the home of a railroad executive to have lunch. In the press of a hostile crowd, he was to be shot by multiple assassins who would escape in the resulting confusion.

There was just one hitch: Lincoln's special train from Harrisburg to Baltimore was on time, but he was not on it. He had already arrived in Washington and was at Willard's Hotel. Lincoln's decision to change travel plans had its origins in January 1861, when Samuel M. Felton, president of the Philadelphia, Wilmington, and

Baltimore Railroad, received information that the pro-Confederate apparatus in Maryland intended to isolate Washington by burning the bridges north of Baltimore and by sinking the train ferry on the Susquehanna River. Felton retained the famous Chicago detective Allan Pinkerton to protect his property. By 3 February Pinkerton was in Baltimore with his most experienced detectives: Timothy Webster (who was later hanged in Richmond as a Union spy); Harry W. Davies; Charles D. C. Williams (possibly an alias); Hattie W. Lawton; and the iron-nerved Kate Warne.

Pinkerton secured office space at 44 South Street and set up cover as a broker under the name John H. Hutcheson. The people who came and went were not customers but detectives. Within days he had evidence of a plot to kill Lincoln in Baltimore. With Felton's approval, he turned his principal attention to this plot.

By 9 February Pinkerton and his detectives had identified Virginia-born Otis K. Hillard as a party to this plot and had information implicating the National Volunteers. Alarmed by the threat to assassinate Lincoln in Baltimore, Pinkerton sent a warning letter to his Chicago office with instructions to deliver the letter to Norman B. Judd, a close friend. Judd was on the train with the Lincoln party, en route to Washington. A Pinkerton agent from Chicago, William H. Scott, caught up with the Lincoln entourage at Cincinnati and handed Pinkerton's letter to Judd at breakfast on 13 February. After reading the warning, Judd remarked to Scott that he had been "looking for this." Judd decided not to reveal the assassination warning to Lincoln or others in the party, pending additional specific details promised by Pinkerton.

As the Lincoln train steamed eastward, Pinkerton and his detectives probed the pro-Confederate activities in Baltimore. Detective Harry W. Davies was assigned to Hillard, and these two became almost inseparable. Davies wrung the dissolute Hillard dry. The two even went together to visit Madame Annette Travis's bordello at 70 Davis Street.

One of Pinkerton's office neighbors at 44 South Street, a broker named James H. Luckett, was "worked" by Pinkerton himself. Luckett arranged a meeting between "Mr. Hutcheson" (Pinkerton) and the Corsican barber Cipriano Ferrandini at John Barr's saloon on South Street. Also present at this meeting was William H. H. Turner, clerk of the Baltimore Circuit Court. Luckett introduced them as "Captain Ferrandini" and "Captain Turner." Undoubtedly the titles referred to commissions in the Knights of the Golden Circle. Ferrandini told Pinkerton enough to confirm his fears:

there was a serious plot to kill Lincoln when he came through Baltimore. Accordingly, he sent another warning letter to Judd, which reached him at Buffalo.

As the bits and pieces of the plot were put together, Pinkerton's view hardened. He decided to recommend that Lincoln change his travel plans and come through Baltimore secretly and at night. On the morning of 18 February he directed Kate Warne to take the 5:10P.M. train to New York. He gave her a letter addressed to Judd and a letter of introduction to Edward S. Sanford, the telegraph and express magnate. Sanford had influence if needed to open doors in the right places.

Mrs. Warne saw Judd in her room at the Astor House at about 7:30 P.M. on 19 February. Pinkerton's letter stated firmly that Lincoln must change his travel plans. Judd wanted to show the letter to others and call in the New York City police, but Mrs. Warne talked him out of that idea. Wait, she said, and talk it over with Pinkerton in Philadelphia on 21 February. Sanford came in toward the end of this discussion and promised to help. Mrs. Warne returned to Baltimore on the next train to convey the understanding to Pinkerton. Up to this point, Judd was the only member of the Lincoln party to be told of Pinkerton's discoveries.

At around seven in the evening of 21 February Pinkerton and Felton met with Judd in room 21 of the St. Louis Hotel in Philadelphia. Felton explained why Pinkerton came to be on the job in Baltimore to protect his railroad. Pinkerton went into details of the assassination danger, mentioning Hillard, Ferrandini, and the National Volunteers. He then offered his proposal. Would Lincoln agree to leave Philadelphia for Washington on the late train that night, together with Pinkerton and Mrs. Warne, and go through Baltimore secretly?

Judd was convinced, but he could not speak for Lincoln. He asked Pinkerton to come with him to the Continental Hotel and lay the matter before Lincoln. After some difficulty in making arrangements, the conference got underway at 10:15P.M. in Judd's room. Only Lincoln, Judd, and Pinkerton were present. Lincoln flatly refused to leave Philadelphia that night. He was, he said, committed to raising the flag at Independence Hall the next morning and to addressing the Pennsylvania legislature at Harrisburg in the afternoon. After these functions, if Pinkerton and Judd still thought the Baltimore situation was critical, he would consider changing his travel arrangements.

In anticipation of a positive decision, Pinkerton explained his plan. The key element was secrecy. A special train would be ready at Harrisburg. The telegraph line to Baltimore would be cut and other lines would be closely watched. At dusk Lincoln would slip away from the hotel and leave on the special train for Philadelphia, where Pinkerton would be waiting with a carriage to take him across town to board a sleeping car attached to Felton's 10:15P.M. train for Baltimore. Pinkerton had checked it out and there was no problem in Baltimore. The practice was to use horses to draw the sleeping cars from the President Street station over a connecting line to the Camden Street station. The sleeping cars would then be hooked to the regular Baltimore and Ohio train scheduled to arrive in Washington at 6:00 A.M. Lincoln would not be exposed. The heavily armed Pinkerton and Kate Warne would provide protection from Philadelphia to Washington.

Lincoln said he most certainly would have to tell Mrs. Lincoln about the plan so that she would not worry. He also thought she would insist that Ward H. Lamon come along with him to provide added security. The matter was left to be decided the next day. With that the conference broke up at 11:00 P.M., and Lincoln went back to his own room. Here he found an unexpected visitor from Washington, Senator Seward's son Frederick—and more bad news about conditions in Baltimore.

Young Seward's trip to Philadelphia was the result of an investigation by detectives sent to Baltimore by John A. Kennedy, superintendent of the New York City police. These men, David S. Bookstaver, Thomas Sampson, and Eli DeVoe, arrived in Baltimore on 1 February. Using aliases, they quickly penetrated the secessionist apparatus. Their instructions were to report secretly to Colonel Charles P. Stone, an aide to General Winfield Scott in Washington.

Acting independently, Kennedy's detectives picked up much the same information as Pinkerton's men and came to the same conclusion. An attempt would be made on Lincoln's life if he came through Baltimore openly as scheduled. Accordingly, on 21 February Bookstaver took the 4:15 A.M. train from Baltimore and went directly to see Colonel Stone at his office. Stone heard him out and prepared a summary of the conference for Scott. Scott decided to send Stone up to the Capitol to confer with Senator Seward about a course of action. It was almost noon when Stone finally located Seward and gave him the summary, together with a little note from Scott.

Seward's private sources had been sounding the same alarm

about danger to Lincoln in Baltimore. Now it was confirmed. It was agreed that Seward's son Frederick would leave for Philadelphia on the next train out, carrying Stone's summary, Scott's note, and a letter from Seward to Lincoln.[7] The plan was to persuade Lincoln to come through Baltimore unannounced and at night. Thus Seward and Pinkerton were in agreement, although each had come to the same view through separate investigations.

When Lincoln got to his room after the conference with Pinkerton and Judd, Frederick Seward was waiting for him. Lincoln read the documents brought by Seward and asked many questions. In the end he told Seward, in effect, that he would sleep on it. The next morning Seward was given the answer: Lincoln would come to Washington unannounced. Seward sent a code message to his father to let him know this decision.

The rest was pure cloak and dagger. After dinner at the Jones House in Harrisburg on the evening of 22 February, Lincoln, Ward H. Lamon, and Governor Andrew G. Curtin slipped out by a side door and went by carriage to the special train waiting on a back siding. Lincoln and Lamon boarded the train and the governor went home. The train pulled out for West Philadelphia at 6:00 P.M. Other trains on this route were sidetracked.

Pinkerton, who remained in Philadelphia to run the operation, had planned effectively. The telegraph wires from Harrisburg to Baltimore along the right-of-way of the Northern Central Railroad were cut and grounded. Secure people were placed in the Harrisburg and Philadelphia telegraph offices to see that no word leaked. A watch was established in New York to stop all telegraphic messages about Lincoln's movements.

Pinkerton was waiting in a carriage at the West Philadelphia station to take Lincoln and Lamon on to the Philadelphia, Wilmington, and Baltimore Railroad station. Kate Warne met them there with tickets for four berths in a sleeping car. Lincoln was almost literally smuggled aboard. The train pulled out of Philadelphia for Baltimore at 10:55 P.M. Upon arrival at the President Street station in Baltimore at 3:30 A.M., Mrs. Warne left the party. The rest of the trip was uneventful. The sleeping cars were uncoupled and pulled over the connecting line to the Camden Street station and connected to the early morning Baltimore and Ohio train for Washington. Just after 6:00 A.M. on 23 February, Lincoln, Lamon, and Pinkerton arrived in Washington. They were met at the station by Congressman Elihu Washburne, whom Seward had sent to meet them. They all took a carriage to Willard's Hotel.[8]

Although some historians question the existence of an active conspiracy to assassinate Lincoln in Baltimore, the bits and pieces add up. The conspiracy was real. The participants were highly motivated, and they meant business.

Lincoln had been in office but six weeks when word of danger to his life was brought to him by the English actress Jean Davenport, who was married to Colonel Frederick W. Lander. On the evening of 18 April 1861, Miss Davenport, accompanied by an older woman, called at the Executive Mansion and asked to see the president about a matter concerning his safety. Lincoln had retired for the night. John Hay, a presidential aide, was only too happy to interview the lady, whom he remembered wistfully from his "stage-struck salad days." After some blushing and hesitation, Miss Davenport said that she had just met a young friend, a dashing Virginian, who was in the city to buy a saddle. In a moment of indiscretion, he told her that he and six others, including a daredevil named Ficklin, would shortly do something that would "ring through the world." There was more, much more, which she put together as a plot to assassinate or capture Mr. Lincoln. Would Mr. Hay please warn the president? Still a bit stage-struck, Hay agreed. He went in to tell Lincoln, who was in bed. Lincoln sat up in bed to hear Hay tell of Miss Davenport's visit. Hay wrote in his diary for that day that Lincoln's only response was a grin.[9]

The Ficklin mentioned by Miss Davenport has never been identified. Major James R. O'Beirne, however, one of the most active officers engaged in the hunt for those involved in the assassination of Lincoln in 1865, got a tip that a well-known rebel, Benjamin F. Ficklin, had come up from Richmond and had been seen in a Washington hotel. Ficklin was described in this tip as having the appearance of a "refined pirate."[10] Arrested on 16 April, two days after Lincoln was shot, Ficklin denied any connection with the assassination. Major O'Beirne was not convinced but lacked proof. Ficklin was released from custody on 16 June 1865.

A few days after Miss Davenport's warning, one Camille La Valliere De Kalb turned up in Richmond with an enterprise taken from the Guy Fawkes episode, celebrated in English history. On 19 June 1861, he sent a note to the Confederate secretary of war in which he pointed out that the United States Congress would soon reassemble and that the Capitol was "undermined." De Kalb and Walker met the next day. In this conference De Kalb proposed to blow up the Capitol "at a time when Abe, his mirmidons, and the Northern Congress are all assembled together." If his plan worked he wanted a colonel's commission and $1 million. Walker put De Kalb off on the ground that he was a stranger. After the conference, De Kalb wrote a letter to Walker in which he gave some of his background and explained how he planned to proceed. Apparently another conference was arranged, to be attended also by Judah Benjamin. There the record stops. In any case, De Kalb did not bring the Capitol tumbling down around Lincoln's ears.[11]

As the war progressed, threats to Lincoln's life increased. They came in speeches by "Peace Democrats," in letters to the president, and in Copperhead editorials. Some were direct, some veiled. By 1863, the Copperhead press was replete with editorials that fell just short of openly advocating his assassination. These editorials became more virulent in 1864 and early 1865. An undated 1864 clipping from the *Beaver Dam* (Wisconsin) *Argus* was blunt: "History shows several instances where people have only been saved by the assassination of their leaders, and history may repeat itself in this country. The time may come when it will be absolutely necessary that the people do away with such rulers the quickest way possible." The *LaCrosse* (Wisconsin) *Democrat,* commenting on the coming election, put it this way on 20 August 1864: "And if he is elected . . . for another four years, we trust some bold hand will pierce his heart with dagger point for the public good."

A favorite gambit of the Copperheads was to appeal for a new Brutus or a new Charlotte Corday. References to the fates of Caesar and Jean Paul Marat were frequent.

Threats to Lincoln from dissidents in the North were matched by dangers to his person from Confederates. Abduction was considered. Major Joseph Walker Taylor, a cousin of Jefferson Davis's first wife, was wounded during the siege of Fort Donelson but escaped capture on 16 February 1862. While recuperating in Louisville, he conceived a plan to go into Washington and capture the president. He came alone in civilian dress. Later he boldly attended a reception at the Executive Mansion, where he was presented to Lincoln as "Mr. Taylor of Kentucky." For some time he watched the president's movements. In the early summer, he laid his plan before President Davis. In the only published account of this episode, in the *Confederate Veteran* (April 1903), Davis allegedly rejected the abduction scheme on the ground that Lincoln might be killed. Reading between the lines, one surmises that Davis did not object to abduction as such but that any resulting injury to Lincoln would prove counterproductive by arousing public opinion in the North and in foreign countries.

Plans to capture Lincoln continued to crop up at various levels in the Confederate army. After the Battle of Gettysburg, there was a rash of such talk, including some assassination proposals. That such schemes were just below the surface of official sanction is evident in a stray comment by Colonel Walter H. Taylor, an aide to General Robert E. Lee. On 8 August 1863, Taylor wrote to his future wife, Elizabeth Saunders, who lived in Richmond. In this letter he told of a conversation he had with a citizen of Hagerstown, Maryland. Taylor included the tantalizing words: "had a great mind to tell him . . . that we had a private plot to kidnap old Abe and needed." The following portion of the letter is missing. The comment may have reflected irritation rather than serious intent. Still, the subject must have been discussed in Taylor's presence.[12]

The day after Taylor wrote to Miss Saunders, Private Robert Stanton, Company D, Fifth Texas Infantry, wrote from camp near Fredericksburg to Confederate Secretary of War James Seddon. He sent his letter through Captain James Pleasants, an ordnance officer in General John B. Hood's division, to whom Stanton was detailed as an artificer. Stanton asked Seddon's approval of a plan to "remove at once and forever those persons who fill high places in the North." Seddon replied on 17 August telling Stanton to forget such ideas: "The laws of war and morality, as well as Christian principles and sound policy forbid the use of such means."[13] Apparently Private Stanton's letter had its origin in talk making the rounds in camp. Obviously, it was sent with at least the tacit approval of Captain Pleasants.

On 17 August 1863, Sergeant Henry Clay Durham, Company I, Sixty-third Georgia Infantry, wrote to President Davis asking that he be furnished "three to five hundred men" to go North and assassinate Seward, Lincoln, and others. According to John B. Jones, Davis "referred the letter without notice to the Secretary of War." The letter ended up unanswered in the files of the Confederate War Department and was discovered there when the captured archives were searched for evidence to incriminate Davis in the assassination of Lincoln.[14] According to family records, Durham died in Tennessee after the war.

It is obvious that men such as Stanton and Durham were not of a caliber likely to be entrusted by Confederate authorities with anything approaching direct action against Lincoln. But such men did exist in the Confederacy. One was Colonel Bradley T. Johnson. During the winter of 1863–64, Johnson planned to take two hundred picked cavalrymen and make a lightning raid on the Soldiers' Home, where Lincoln regularly stayed in the summer months. The plan was to cross the Potomac River above Washington, dash to the Soldiers' Home, which was located in a rural area outside the city, and carry off Lincoln.

With General Wade Hampton's approval, Johnson began gathering and equipping the raiding party. He soon found himself operating in an area commanded by General Jubal Early. Early pulled him off the project, saying that as soon as Union General David Hunter could be driven off, he would beef up the raiding party and perhaps command it himself. But a fateful bullet ended the scheme. General William E. Jones was killed in battle on 5 June 1864, and Johnson was shortly assigned to his brigade with a promotion to brigadier general. Further, the plan had obvious defects since the raid would have been carried out without firm knowledge that Lincoln would be at the target location. It is likely that the plan was abandoned when it was fully explored. After the war, and with General Johnson's approval, Major W. W. Goldsborough told of this planned abduction in a book published in 1869, *The Maryland Line in the Confederate Army*. Goldsborough repeated the account in a revised version published in 1900.[15] Johnson himself wrote an excellent article in which he explained in detail how the abduction of Lincoln was to be carried out in June 1864. Lieutenant C. Irving Ditty, First Maryland Cavalry, confirmed Johnson's account in testimony given on 9 February 1877 before a congressional committee.[16]

Such an attempt could not have been seriously considered without the sanction of top Confederate authorities. General Wade Hampton would never have given his approval to Johnson without clearing the idea with Secretary of War Seddon and probably with General Robert E. Lee and President Davis. The political and military consequences of abducting Lincoln would have been enormous. The Confederate government, it seems, had undergone a change of heart in the spring of 1864 after the Kilpatrick-Dahlgren raid on Richmond. By then, direct action against Lincoln himself was not unthinkable.

On 16 March 1864, Seddon ordered Captain Thomas H. Hines to Canada to organize the Copperheads in Indiana, Ohio, Illinois, and adjoining states into armed rebellion against the Lincoln administration.[17] In a report to Seddon, sent in cipher on 1 June 1864, Hines laid out the assassination theme: "The State governments of Indiana, Ohio, and Illinois will be seized and their executive heads disposed of."[18] Hines had never been squeamish about shedding Yankee blood. Almost literally he had in mind severing some executive heads. Evidence presented at the treason trials at Indianapolis in late 1864 put the head of Indiana Governor Oliver Morton high on the list.

President Jefferson Davis's letterbook contains copies of identical notes dated 27 May 1864, thanking two Confederate agents for an effective secret service mission behind enemy lines.[19] These two men, Captain Thomas Nelson Conrad and Sergeant Daniel Mountjoy Cloud, were soon to become principals in yet another scheme to kidnap President Lincoln, with the full approval of Seddon. Conrad's mission to Washington is discussed at other points in this narrative. But it is inconceivable that Seddon would have approved and supported Conrad's mission without first clearing it with Davis.

Even before Conrad left Richmond for Washington on 17 September 1864 to explore the possibility of capturing Lincoln, an attempt was made on the president's life. Former Private John Nichols, Company K, 105th Pennsylvania Volunteers, related the incident in the *Cincinnati Enquirer* for 15 August 1885. His unit had been assigned to guard the Executive Mansion and the Lincoln summer domicile at the Soldiers' Home. Nichols was on duty at the Soldiers' Home one night in August 1864. The president was expected shortly. Nichols heard what he described as a rifle shot followed by rapid hoofbeats approaching. It was Lincoln riding alone and without his usual tall hat. Nichols and his corporal searched for the hat and found it near the gate to the grounds. There was a bullet hole through the crown. Lincoln ascribed the shot to some "foolish gunner" and said it was not intended for him. He requested absolute secrecy about the event. Nichols told the reporter: "After that the president never rode alone."

Nichols' memory of this attempt on Lincoln's life at the Soldiers' Home was confirmed by Ward Hill Lamon in a little book, *Recollections of Abraham Lincoln,* based on Lamon's notes and edited by his daughter Dorothy Teillard. Teillard placed the shooting incident in August 1862, obviously an error as to year. As Lamon recorded it, Lincoln told him of the shooting in a rather humorous fashion when he returned to the Executive Mansion the next morning. Except for the year, the account agrees with that of Private Nichols.[20]

Lamon had always been solicitous of Lincoln's safety. Now he became almost fanatical. At 1:30 A.M. on 10 December 1864, he wrote a somewhat intemperate letter to the president offering his resignation as United States marshal for the District of Columbia. Lincoln ignored the resignation. Lamon's outburst was triggered by Lincoln's attendance that evening at Grover's Theatre with Senator Charles Sumner and a "foreign diplomat." The attraction was the German Opera Company's performance of Meyerbeer's *Les Huguenots*. Lamon wrote with emphasis: "You are in danger." Neither Sumner nor the diplomat (possibly the Marquis de Chambrun) "could defend himself from an assault from any able-bodied woman in this city." He reminded Lincoln that he had provided police for duty at "your mansion." In short, Lincoln should use the protection provided and not go out unguarded.[21]

Toward the end of November 1864, another Confederate soldier offered to go north "to rid my country of some of her deadliest enemies by striking at the very hearts blood." This man was Lieutenant Waldeman Alston, Company G, Eleventh Kentucky Cavalry. Alston had been captured during General John Morgan's famous raid across the Ohio River. He escaped and made his way to Canada. On his way back to the Confederacy, he contracted yellow fever in Bermuda and was later hospitalized at White Sulphur Springs, Virginia. Here, with time on his hands, he decided to write to President Davis and offer his services. Burton Harrison, Davis's private secretary, endorsed the letter: "Reply refd by direction of the President to the Hon. Secty of War." The letter ended up unanswered in War Department files.[22] Clearly a sick and bitter former prisoner of war was not thought capable of such an undertaking.

George W. Gayle, a prominent attorney of Cahawba, Alabama, had his own notion of how to rid the world of Abraham Lincoln, William H. Seward, and Andrew Johnson. He placed an advertisement in the *Selma* (Alabama) *Dispatch* on 1 December 1864 asking citizens of the Confederacy to contribute $1 million to procure the assassination of these "cruel tyrants."[23] The advertisement turned out to be very expensive for Gayle. He was arrested at his home on 25 May 1865 and brought to Washington, where he was lodged in Old Capitol Prison on 21 June. He was released 5 July.

These are but some of the many portents of the threats and plots against President Lincoln's safety. That he lived to learn of the surrender at Appomattox Court House is almost a miracle.

Notes

ABBREVIATIONS
NA   National Archives
OR   U.S. War Department, *The War of the Rebellion: A Compilation of the Official Records of the Union and Confederate Armies.* 128 vols. Washington, D.C.: U.S. Government Printing Office, 1880–1901.
ORN   U.S. Navy Department, *Official Records of the Union and Confederate Navies in the War of the Rebellion.* 30 vols. Washington, D.C.: U.S. Government Printing Office, 1894–1914.
RG   Record Group

1. For the full text, see Jules Abels, *Man on Fire* (New York: Macmillan, 1971), p. 365.

2. The warnings mentioned in this paragraph are contained in letters to Lincoln quoted by David C. Mearns, ed., *The Lincoln Papers*, 2 vols. (Garden City, N.Y.: Doubleday, 1948). Fear that Lincoln would be poisoned is shown in letters from R. S. Bassett, Lawrence, Kansas, 17 October 1860, 1:293, F. R. Shoemaker, Chester, Pennsylvania, 17 October 1860, 1:294, and A.H.W., Haverhill, Massachusetts, 1:306. The assassination plot by young Virginians is mentioned in a letter from Major David Hunter, Fort Leavenworth, Kansas, 20 October 1860, 1:295–96. The reference to "border ruffians" saying Lincoln should be killed is in a letter from Joseph Irwin, Columbus, Indiana, 12 November 1860, 1:307. The story about $40,000 being raised to hire assassins is in a letter from Horace White, Illinois Republican State Central Committee, Chicago, 11 December 1860, 2:336.

3. Both Seward and Medill thought Lincoln should come to Washington earlier than planned. Seward's letter to Lincoln, 28 December 1860, is on microfilm reel 12, item 5406, Lincoln Papers, Library of Congress. Medill's letter to Lincoln, 31 December 1860, is on the same reel, item 5511.

4. "The Diary of a Public Man," *North American Review,* August 1879, entry for 28 December 1860, pp. 38–39. The diarist is thought to be Samuel Ward, brother of Julia Ward Howe, who wrote the lyrics for "The Battle Hymn of the Republic."

5. U.S. Congress, House of Representatives, *Alleged Hostile Organization against the Government within the District of Columbia*, Report 79, 36th Cong. 2d sess., 14 February 1861.

6. William Byrne's membership in the Knights of the Golden Circle is disclosed in his letter, marked "Confidential," of 10 October 1860, to Dr. Cornelius Boyle, Washington, D.C. The holder of this letter does not wish to be identified. Cipriano Ferrandini's commission in the Knights of the Golden Circle is in the possession of Dr. Cipriano Respess, Richmond, Va.

7. The three communications mentioned are in the Lincoln Papers, Library of Congress, and have been copied in microfilm reel 17. All are dated 21 February 1861. Colonel Stone's summary of the information furnished by Bookstaver is item 7427; General Scott's letter to Senator Seward is item 7436; and Senator Seward's letter to Lincoln is item 7438.

8. For a more complete account of Lincoln's midnight journey, see excerpts from Pinkerton's record book in Norma B. Cuthbert, ed. *Lincoln and the Baltimore Plot* (San Marino, Calif.: Huntington Library, 1949). Additional details are found in Allan Pinkerton, *History and Evidence of the Passage of Abraham Lincoln from Harrisburg, Pa., to Washington, D.C.* (Chicago: Republican Press, 1868). Other details

are in Frederick W. Seward, *Reminiscences of a War-Time Statesman and Diplomat* (New York: G. P. Putnam and Sons, 1916), pp. 134–39.

9. John Hay, *Lincoln and the Civil War in the Diaries and Letters of John Hay*, ed. Tyler Dennett (Westport, Conn: Negro Universities Press, 1972), p. 2, entry for 18 April 1861.

10. Investigation and Trial Papers Relating to the Assassination of President Lincoln, Microfilm M-599, NA, has many scattered references to the arrest of Benjamin F. Ficklin. For the "refined pirate" description, see reel 7, file 51, frame 0220.

11. For the De Kalb account, see U.S. Congress, House of Representatives, *Assassination of Lincoln*, Report 104, 39th Cong., 1st sess., 28 July 1866, pp. 21–22.

12. Taylor-Saunders Letters, file 28114, Miscellaneous Confederate Papers, Virginia State Library, Richmond.

13. Stanton to Seddon, 9 August 1863, Letters Received, Confederate Secretary of War, file 518-S-1863, RG 109, NA, Seddon's response was sent 17 August 1863.

14. For a reference to Durham's letter to Davis, see John B. Jones, *A Rebel War Clerk's Diary*, ed. Howard Swiggett, 2 vols. (New York: Old Hickory Book Shop, 1935), 2:24.

15. William W. Goldsborough, *The Maryland Line in the Confederate Army*, was first published in 1869 by Kelly, Piet & Company, Baltimore, and revised in 1900 by Goldsborough with the aid of George Booth. The most recent edition was published in 1983 by Butternut Press, Gaithersburg, Maryland. Johnson's plan to capture Lincoln appears in all editions and on pp. 203–8 of the Butternut Press version. Also see John C. Brennan, "General Bradley T. Johnson's Plan to Abduct President Lincoln," *Chronicles of St. Mary's* 22 (November–December 1974): 413–24.

16. See Bradley Johnson, "My Ride Around Baltimore in Eighteen Hundred and Sixty-Four," *Cavalry Journal*, September 1889, pp. 250–60. Former Confederate C. Irving Ditty, who was to have commanded a cavalry company in this operation, confirmed Johnson's account in testimony before a congressional committee investigating the Hayes-Tilden election controversy. See U.S. Congress, House of Representatives, Miscellaneous Document 42, 44th Cong., 2d sess., 1 February 1877, p. 275.

17. The letter, Seddon to Hines, 16 March 1864, was published in full in James D. Horan, *Confederate Agent* (New York: Crown, 1954), pp. 72–73.

18. Hines to Seddon, 1 June 1864, copy in Thomas H. Hines Papers, Margaret L. King Library, University of Kentucky, Lexington.

19. Jefferson Davis, *Jefferson Davis, Constitutionalist: His Letters, Papers, and Speeches*, ed. Dunbar Rowland, 10 vols. (Jackson: Mississippi Department of Archives and History, 1923), 6:261.

20. Ward Hill Lamon, *Recollections of Abraham Lincoln*, ed. Dorothy Teillard (Cambridge, Mass.: The University Press, 1895), pp. 260–70.

21. Ibid., pp. 274–75.

22. Alston's letter is reproduced in Benn Pitman, *Assassination of President Lincoln and the Trial of the Conspirators* (1865; rpt. ed. Philip Van Doren Stern, New York: Funk and Wagnalls, 1954), p. 52.

23. Ibid., p. 51.

This picture of four Confederate agents was taken about 7 July 1864 near the Table Rock Hotel on the Canadian side of Niagara Falls. From left to right: George N. Sanders, Captain John B. Castleman, Colonel George St. Leger Grenfell, and Captain Thomas H. Hines. Courtesy Colonel William Banning, a descendant of George N. Sanders

Confederate Colonel William Norris, Commissioner of Exchange, 1865; and Major and Chief, Signal Bureau and Secret Service Bureau, 1862–1865. From the collection of David Winfred Gaddy

Confederate Brigadier General Edwin G. Lee, Montreal, 1865; he was sent to Canada in December 1864. Courtesy Notman Photographic Archives, McGill University, Montreal

Confederate Colonel John S. Mosby, 1865. Cook Collection, Valentine Museum, Richmond

11

Dahlgren's Raid
and Its Aftermath

By the winter of 1864 everybody in the South had lost relatives or friends in the struggle to escape the clutches of Yankee "tyranny." The great harvest of death in the battles of 1862 and 1863 had made the men in the Confederate army particularly aware of the cost of pursuing the southern ideal of liberty. A great religious revival had swept the army, and issues of moral right and wrong were intimately entwined with the emotional need to find a justification for the human sacrifices the war was causing.

At the same time, determination and faith in an ultimate victory remained strong. The Confederacy had survived nearly three years, won great victories, invented new ways of fighting, and had powerful armies in the field under the leadership of men who, by and large, were trusted to lead them wisely.

The institutions of the Confederacy had begun to mature. There was no longer a scramble to create organizations where none had existed before. In the world of clandestine warfare the Confederate Signal Corps was a going concern, intelligence flowed from Washington to Richmond, the Torpedo Bureau was making the rivers and harbors hot for the Union navy, the cavalry scouts were veterans, and Mosby had learned how to create ever more confusion in the enemy's rear. This atmosphere of veteran confidence and moral righteousness was shaken by an event of relatively minor military importance which caused a fundamental change in the attitude of the Confederate leaders toward their opponents.

On 28 February 1864, a force of about four thousand Union cavalry embarked on a raid behind Confederate lines intended to capture Richmond and release the prisoners of war in Libby and

241

Belle Isle prisons. This raid was under the command of Brigadier General Judson Kilpatrick, but it was fated to be remembered in history as Dahlgren's raid.[1]

The Union populace was disturbed at reports of the mistreatment of prisoners of war in the South, and in early February 1864 several prisoners broke out of Libby Prison and reached Union lines. Their stories of conditions in the Richmond prisons aroused public feelings to an even higher pitch. Lincoln felt pressure to demonstrate that the prisoners were not being forgotten and that the Union was pursuing the war with vigor. As a result, he seems to have intervened directly in the planning of a military operation.

Kilpatrick seized this opportunity to lobby for approval for a raid intended to go around the flank of the Army of Northern Virginia, stationed along the Rapidan River, and attack Richmond directly. He felt that by rapid movement he could outdistance pursuit and overcome the poorly manned defenses of Richmond before they could be reinforced. He appears to have gone over his supervisors' heads and won Lincoln's personal approval for the scheme.

As a condition in the plan approved by Lincoln, Kilpatrick was asked to take with him cavalry Colonel Ulric Dahlgren, the son of Admiral John A. Dahlgren, whom Lincoln greatly admired. Ulric had lost a leg in the Gettysburg campaign, but he was anxious to get back into the war, and he felt that on horseback his wooden leg would not be a hindrance. Kilpatrick apparently left much of the detailed planning of the raid to Dahlgren, which, in view of the association of Lincoln and the elder Dahlgren, later reinforced the southern belief that the operation was personally sponsored by Lincoln.

When the raid got under way on 28 February, the Union cavalry slipped across the Rappahannock above Fredericksburg past the right flank of General Lee's army. Dahlgren, leading about five hundred men in an independent command, headed west and south to cross the James River from above Richmond. At that time Richmond was virtually undefended from the south, and he would have had easy access to the prisoners on Belle Isle from the south side of the James River.

Kilpatrick with the main body of troops headed generally south to attack the defenses of Richmond from the north. It was anticipated that the few defenders of Richmond would be drawn to meet Kilpatrick's main body and that a simultaneous attack across the James from the south by Dahlgren would find Richmond wide open.

The project was plagued with bad luck from the very beginning. Bad weather delayed both groups and prevented them from communicating as planned by signal. Couriers sent with messages were captured by the Confederates. Word of the raid spread, and numerous groups of Confederates scurried to interfere.

When Dahlgren finally reached the James River, he found the water much higher than usual and his guide—a black man provided by Union intelligence—could not find a place to cross. Dahlgren was convinced that he had been betrayed and hanged the guide on the spot. With no other reasonable course available, he chose to go down the northern bank of the James to attack Richmond from the west.

In the meantime, Kilpatrick reached the Richmond defenses on the north side and tried to break in, but he found resistance much greater than he had expected. He fought for several hours, but not hearing any noise from an attack by Dahlgren on the south, he gave up the attempt and began to slip around Richmond moving down the Peninsula toward the safety of Fortress Monroe and General Butler's forces.

Dahlgren reached the western defenses of Richmond at dark a few hours after Kilpatrick had abandoned his attack on the north. Dahlgren was met by the Richmond city battalion of reserves under the command of General Custis Lee. The clerks and beardless youths made a good showing, and in the darkness and confusion the tired troopers of Dahlgren's party could make no headway against them.

Dahlgren led his force around Richmond to the north and tried to get around the Confederates chasing Kilpatrick. During the night of 2–3 March 1864 his group broke into two segments, and Dahlgren was ambushed in King and Queen County and killed while leading the smaller segment.

On the morning of 3 March several papers were found on Dahlgren's body and taken to Richmond, where they caused a tremendous uproar. The papers included the draft of an address that he apparently meant to read to his officers and men: "We hope to release the prisoners from Belle Island [sic] first, and having seen them fairly started, we will cross the James River into Richmond, destroying the bridges after us and, exhorting the released prisoners to destroy and burn the hateful city, and do not allow rebel leader Davis and his traitorous crew to escape." Also among the papers was a special order stating, "The men must keep together

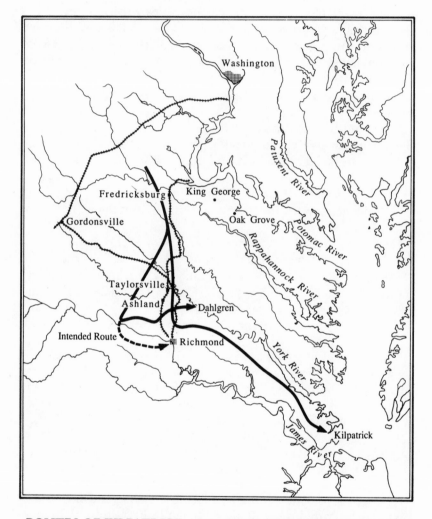

ROUTES OF KILPATRICK AND DAHLGREN FEB.–MAR. 1864

and well in hand, and, once in the city, it must be destroyed and Jeff Davis and his Cabinet killed."[2]

The ferocity of these statements sounded a new note in Union policy toward the war, but it was not unexpected to a growing body of opinion in the South. Most southerners blamed Lincoln for the war, but there were many who felt that his intentions were even more diabolical. They believed he was bent on destroying the South and that the atrocities committed by Union troops were the result of a deliberate Union policy of savagery. The word *genocide* was not as widely used in the 1860s as it is today, but many of the emotions associated with it were felt when Lincoln's policies were mentioned.

Many in the Confederacy came to believe that the best way to combat the evil policy of the Union administration would be to hold the Union officials individually and personally accountable for the actions of Union troops in the South. Lincoln was looked upon as the tyrant who set the policy.

The Dahlgren papers provided the spark for this group in the South to advance its cause and pressure the Confederate government for a more vigorous counterattack. As an example, the *Richmond Examiner*, already anti-Davis, found this an excellent opportunity to attack the conduct of war and at the same time to urge a policy of retribution: "If the Confederate capital has been in the closest danger of massacre and conflagrations; if the President and the Cabinet have run a serious risk of being hanged at their own doors, do we not owe it chiefly to the milk-and-water spirit in which this war has hither to been conducted?" The paper continued: "To the Washington authorities we are simply criminals awaiting punishment, who may be hanged or who may be pardoned. In their eyes our country is not ours, but theirs. The hostilities which they carry on are not properly war, but military execution & coercion." As policy it asked: "What then, would we practically suggest? First, to put to death all 'raiders' caught in the fact; secondly, to insist upon the most scrupulous carrying out of retaliation for murders, robberies, and other outrages, with the most punctual exactitude."[3]

The *Richmond Sentinel* took direct aim at Lincoln. Its 5 March editorial on the Dahlgren papers reads in part: "Let Lincoln and Kilpatrick remember that they have bidden their subordinates give no quarter to the Confederate chiefs. Perhaps even a Scotch cap and a military cloak will not prevent a just and stern vengeance from overtaking them." The reference to the Scotch cap and the military cloak was a scarcely concealed threat of retaliation by assassination. To understand this, one must go back to the famous plot to assassinate Lincoln in Baltimore in February 1861. Lincoln was widely abused in the press for his undignified entry into the capital. Joseph Howard, a reporter for the *New York Times*, fictionalized this journey in his newspaper by saying that Lincoln was disguised "in a Scotch plaid cap and a very long military cloak."

The Confederate editorial opinions about the Dahlgren papers cannot be dismissed as mere bombast. The Confederate leaders knew that these papers had been found on Dahlgren's body and they had them in hand. More, their excellent intelligence apparatus in Washington would have been dense in the extreme if it had not picked up the various stories floating around that both Lincoln and Stanton were involved in planning the raid. As many researchers have learned, newspaper editorials are often the first draft of history.

At first Jefferson Davis was inclined to dismiss the matter, but the feeling of frustration and the need to strike back at a devilish foe were widely shared in the South. No responsible executive could ignore the feeling. The Confederate government would have to comply with or defuse this emotion. Its initial reaction was to order the execution of the prisoners taken from the raiding party, but cooler heads prevailed. Then steps were taken to learn what lay behind Dahlgren's words. General Lee wrote to Union General George G. Meade asking whether Dahlgren's words reflected U.S. government policy. Meade, who had kept himself well insulated from the planning and conduct of the raid, disavowed any official U.S. support for the policy expounded by Dahlgren.

General Kilpatrick claimed to have read papers similar to those quoted by the Confederates but without the offensive language. There was a general outcry of "forgery" in the North, but the Confederates had photographic reproductions of the papers circulated to the Union and to foreign governments. In the surviving photographs the papers appear to be genuine, and a study of the timing involved indicates that it would have been extremely difficult for the Confederates to have fabricated such convincing material in so short a time.

In a sense, however, the genesis of the papers was not the real issue. The real issue was that Southerners thought they reflected the personal attitude of President Lincoln and that the Confederate government felt considerable domestic pressure to seek retribution for the atrocities that sprang from Lincoln's policies. The Dahlgren raid was not the first of its kind. On 6 February 1864, just three weeks before the Kilpatrick-Dahlgren expedition, Brigadier General Isaac J. Wistar of the Union army led a force of cavalry intending to enter Richmond from the northeast. Wistar's force included part of the District of Columbia cavalry unit commanded by Lafayette C. Baker, the Union counterintelligence expert. According to a note from General Butler to Wistar, his instructions were to relieve Union prisoners, destroy public buildings and commissary stocks, and capture some of the leaders of the rebellion. Wistar's raid was aborted on 7 February when he discovered that a key bridge over the Chickahominy River was heavily defended and that the Confederates appeared to have been waiting for him. It turned out that the Confederates had been given advance information of the raid.

Wistar's raid was believed to have had Lincoln's personal approval, else why would District cavalry be involved, and the similarity of Wistar's orders to those carried by Dahlgren convinced the Confederates that the head of the federal government had adopted a policy of ad hominem attack.[4] The problem of what to do in this situation seems to have taken a great deal of time and discussion during the following months. In mid-March there was a big meeting of senior Confederate generals in Richmond, which lasted for several days. There would have been many items for such a group to discuss, but it could hardly have avoided considering how to respond to the Dahlgren raid.

President Davis appears to have been diverted from the routine business of his office for some weeks. For example, from 6 March to 8 April, no officers were recommended for promotion to general. This was an unprecedented gap in the flow of recommendations that came from Davis's office. We do not know the details of what went on in the decision-making levels of the Confederate government during this period, but from subsequent events we can draw some useful inferences.

The Confederate government did not have to conceive actions to take in retribution from thin air. Several suitable ideas had been under discussion for some time. One of these was to exploit the peace sentiment among the Copperheads in the North in the hope of political action favorable to the South or revolt in the most disaffected northern states. Another was to raid Union prisons to free the Confederate prisoners of war. This idea was an obvious response to the Dahlgren raid. Still another idea that had been suggested on several occasions was to capture Lincoln and bring him back to Confederate territory for a personal confrontation with the victims of his policies. It would have been something like a Civil War version of a war crimes trial. This scheme was particularly appealing to those who were concerned with issues of morality, who saw Lincoln as the personification of evil and accountable for his deeds.

The idea of exploiting the Copperheads had been under discussion for some months with Captain Thomas H. Hines, the young Kentucky cavalry officer who had escaped from prison in Ohio with General John H. Morgan in October of 1863. Hines had gone to visit his fiancée in Kentucky and was recalled to Richmond on an emergency basis in early March 1864. The recall may have been in response to the need for a reaction to the Dahlgren raid, or the timing may have been fortuitous, but it appears to have fitted in with a broader decision to conduct serious clandestine operations from Canada.

On 25 March 1864, Confederate Secretary of State Judah Benjamin wrote to the Honorable H. H. (Sandy) Stuart at Staunton, Virginia. The letter was marked "Confidential." Benjamin asked: "Would it be in your power to come to Richmond as promptly as possible on a matter of great public interest? The President and myself are desireous of conferring with you in person, as the subject is too delicate for correspondence. I need scarcely say that it should not be known that you come on any but your own private business."[5]

Stuart was a former member of the U.S. Congress and a former secretary of the interior. He had opposed secession but was regarded as intelligent, capable, and knowledgeable. After the war, writing about the visit to Richmond, he said that in a confidential interview Benjamin had explained that he and Davis had determined to send a team of operatives to Canada. They would be directed by a "Commissioner," and their mission would be to foster "by means of a secret service" the peace sentiment understood to be active in the border and northwestern states. Benjamin concluded that he and Davis had agreed that Stuart should be in charge of the enterprise. Congress had deposited £3 million in London that would be at his disposal. Stuart declined the mission, partly on personal grounds and partly because he felt that Benjamin did not understand the true strength and nature of the peace sentiment in the North. He added that the commission was later formed, "composed of Jacob Thompson of Mississippi, C. C. Clay of Alabama, and J. P. Holcombe, Professor of Law at the University of Virginia, who undertook the work which had been tendered to me. They went to Canada with Mr. [George N.] Sanders as their agent, but were able to effect nothing."[6]

Stuart's judgment that the commission was ineffective was overly harsh. It had considerable influence though not as great as the Confederate government had hoped. The commission had been in the planning stage for some time. Stuart had been sounded out in January 1864 concerning his feeling about serving the Confederate government and had indicated his willingness. The Richmond conferences in March had probably resulted in a decision to go ahead with the scheme.

The choice of George Sanders as the principal agent of the commission indicated, however, that there might be more to the mission than fostering peace sentiment. Sanders was a radical republican activist who had supported Garibaldi and other revolutionary movements in Europe and who had even advocated the assassination of Napoleon III. His credentials as a democrat and a lover of (white) freedom were impeccable, but his willingness to foster peace sentiment from a post in Canada would be open to serious question. He was not a man to sit idle when action could be taken.

One authoritative glimpse at the activity of Confederate intelligence personnel at a moment when retaliation for the Dahlgren raid must have been on many people's minds survives in a pass to Libby Prison for 30 March 1864.[7] It was signed by General John H. Winder, and it authorized B. G. Burley, John Maxwell, and Daniel Lucas to visit Libby Prison to interrogate prisoners from the Purnell Legion captured on the Eastern Shore of Virginia—that part of Virginia on the east side of Chesapeake Bay.

What is interesting about this pass is the association of the men in the group, for each is well known for his involvement with Confederate clandestine activity. All three had been associated with Edwin Gray Lee in 1863 in a naval raiding party operating in the Chesapeake Bay. Later, in September 1864, Burley was associated with John Yates Beall, another member of the 1863 group, in an attempt to capture the USS *Michigan* in Lake Erie. On 9 August 1864 Maxwell planted the bomb that blew up General Grant's supply docks at City Point, Virginia. Later in the year, when E. G. Lee was made a brigadier general and sent to Canada on a secret service mission, Daniel Lucas was one of his principal assistants.

Jacob Thompson, who ultimately headed the commission, had also been a member of the U.S. Congress and a secretary of the interior. In addition, in the early part of the war he had recruited a partisan unit in Mississippi. His background and character seem to have been more in keeping with action than with "fostering." Thompson's principal colleague, Clement C. Clay, had also earned a considerable reputation as a senator from Alabama. In reading his biography, however, one notes that he was not averse to a fight. He may have been a politician and not in the best of health, but he was willing to take personal action when he felt it was called for. According to Thompson, the final instructions given to him by Jefferson Davis were to respect the neutrality of Canada; try by all diplomatic means to gain a peace; failing to arrange a peace, to adopt measures to cripple and embarrass the military policy of the federal government; and avoid transgressions of the laws of war.[8]

In the meantime, Captain Hines had been launched on his mission to Canada, and General Daniel Ruggles, a man experienced in clandestine operations, was ordered on 22 March to return to Richmond from his post in Mississippi. Ruggles visited the headquarters of the Army of Northern Virginia and may have been briefed in Richmond on the planned activities in the North. Ruggles was in Richmond until 16 May, when he left to return to the Army of Tennessee. General Polk then put him in command of reserves in Louisiana and Mississippi.[9] That post would have put him along the Mississippi River, where agents could be infiltrated into Union lines and headed for Canada or the Midwest. In the case of Ruggles, as in that of Edwin G. Lee in Virginia, the Confederacy used men to command the reserves who did not have the stamina for field service. It was an assignment that would use their experience and ability yet leave them relatively free to engage in additional activities such as sponsoring covert activities.

The Confederate government gave top priority to organizing the effort in Canada, but the idea of capturing Lincoln seems to have remained alive. Several persons associated with Confederate clandestine operations might have been involved in the planning for this effort. A number of these were from Maryland.

First, there was General Winder, who commanded the Department of Richmond and who had an active clandestine program as part of his operation. Second was George P. Kane, the former commissioner of Baltimore police. Kane had worked hard to help Maryland secede and had been arrested for his pains. After release from prison in 1862, he escaped to Canada and then in 1864 traveled to Richmond to work with Winder. Winder was relieved of his position in Richmond in May 1864 and sent to North Carolina, but

Kane stayed on and was mentioned by General Lee in June 1864 as being involved in a secret operation that might require his presence in Maryland.[10]

The third was Colonel, later Brigadier General, Bradley T. Johnson, an aggressive Maryland officer with a great deal of political interest and influence. He was able to persuade the Confederate government to create, for a time, the Maryland Line, an organization of Maryland troops in the Confederate army. It did not last long because it did not have the continuous manpower needed to keep it alive, but it was a great political coup, recalling the Revolutionary War formation of Marylanders and thereby appealing to their patriotism and support of a second revolution.

In the first months after the Dahlgren raid, several different schemes to capture Lincoln may have been discussed. Jefferson Davis, however, was no longer automatically disapproving such ideas. In other words, the Confederate government had not yet found a satisfactory plan to capture President Lincoln, but the atmosphere was now more tolerant of those who developed such plans.

It is likely that those in Richmond who were planning further clandestine operations felt that the capture of Lincoln might be worth attempting at some future date and did not want to forestall the operation through a misguided, unsuccessful attempt. An enlarged apparatus was being set up in Canada to conduct clandestine operations in the North. It would have men trained in clandestine operations who could probably create better opportunities to capture Lincoln.

Direct, personal retribution might still be possible.

Notes

ABBREVIATIONS

NA   National Archives

OR   U.S. War Department, *The War of the Rebellion: A Compilation of the Official Records of the Union and Confederate Armies.* 128 vols. Washington, D.C.: U.S. Government Printing Office, 1880–1901.

ORN   U.S. Navy Department, *Official Records of the Union and Confederate Navies in the War of the Rebellion.* 30 vols. Washington, D.C.: U.S. Government Printing Office, 1894–1914.

RG   Record Group

1. For a description of the raid, see Edward J. Longacre, *Mounted Raids of the Civil War* (New York: A. S. Barnes, 1975), pp. 225–57.

2. Photographic copies made by the Confederates of several of the Dahlgren papers are in Records of the Adjutant General's Office, 1780's–1917, Entry 721, Serial 60, RG 94, NA. These were recopied under ultraviolet light and were reproduced in James O. Hall, "The Dahlgren Papers," *Civil War Times Illustrated*, November 1983, pp. 30–39.

3. John M. Daniel, *The Richmond Examiner during the War* (New York: Frederick S. Daniel, 1868), pp. 176–77.

4. Butler to Wistar, 4 February 1864, Benjamin F. Butler, *Private and Official Correspondence of Gen. Benjamin F. Butler*, ed. Jesse Ames Marshall, 5 vols. (Norwood, Mass.: Plimpton Press, 1917), 3:373–74; Lafayette C. Baker, *History of the United States Secret Service* (Philadelphia: Privately published by L. C. Baker, 1867), pp. 199–200; *OR*, Ser. 1, vol. 33, pp. 145–48.

5. Manuscript Collections, Virginia State Library and Archive, Richmond.

6. Alexander F. Robertson, *Alexander Hugh Holmes Stuart, 1807–1891* (Richmond: William Byrd Press, 1925), pp. 206–8.

7. Pass, 30 March 1864, Ryder Collection, Tufts University Library, Medford, Mass.

8. James D. Horan, *Confederate Agent* (New York: Crown, 1954), p. 86.

9. Daniel Ruggles, Compiled Service Record, NA.

10. Lee to Davis, 26 June 1864, in R. E. Lee, *The Wartime Papers of R. E. Lee*, ed. Clifford Dowdey and Louis H. Manarin (New York: Bramhall House, 1961), p. 808.

11. Bradley T. Johnson, *Maryland*, vol. 2 of *Confederate Military History*, ed. Clement A. Evans (rpt. Secaucus, N.J.: Blue and Grey Press, n.d.), p. 123.

12

Enter John Wilkes Booth

John Wilkes Booth was born 10 May 1838 at the family farm near Bel Air, Maryland. He was the ninth child of the famous English actor Junius Brutus Booth and Mary Ann Holmes. These two had come to the United States from the island of Madeira aboard the ship *Two Brothers*, landing at Norfolk on 30 June 1821. Junius left behind in England a lawful Belgian wife, Adelaide, and a two-year-old son, Richard.

The two traveled around wherever Booth could find acting engagements. Their first child, Junius, was born at Charleston, South Carolina, on 22 December 1821. A second child, Rosalie Ann, was born 5 July 1823. With two young children there was need to settle down. On 4 June 1824, Junius purchased a tract of unimproved farmland in Harford County, Maryland, some twenty miles northeast of Baltimore. The deed from Robert Hall shows that Booth paid $733.20 for a thousand-year lease, with ground rent at one cent each year.[1] A rickety log cabin was moved onto the property. With alterations and additions, this became the home where seven of the other eight Booth children were born. Joseph was born in Baltimore.

With a wife in London who stood to inherit, Junius may have felt apprehensive about his property in Harford County. In a deed of trust made on 25 April 1833, he named his actor friend Edwin Forrest trustee for Mary Ann Booth, "maiden name Mary Ann Holmes," and their children.[2]

Junius sought to keep Adelaide in ignorance of his new life. Apparently she learned of her husband's second family through London newspaper accounts or through her son, Richard, who had come to Baltimore from London in 1842. A woman scorned, she sailed from Liverpool on 31 October 1846 for New York. Upon

253

arrival in Baltimore, she wrote to her sister Therese on 17 December 1846, saying that her lawyer would fall on Booth's back "like a bomb."[3] Later Adelaide filed for divorce charging adultery. This Junius admitted in his response. He could hardly do otherwise, since Mary Ann had borne him ten children. The divorce was granted on 18 April 1851.[4] Junius and Mary Ann were married in Baltimore on 10 May 1851.[5] Their son John was thirteen on that day. When the embittered Adelaide died in Baltimore on 9 March 1858, her son, Richard, placed a notice in the *Baltimore Sun* giving her name as Madame Marie Christine Adelaide Booth.[6]

Acting took Junius from home frequently, leaving Mary Ann and the children at the farm. This isolation and the need to provide educational opportunities for the children persuaded Junius to buy a townhouse at 62 North Exeter Street in Baltimore. He paid John H. Eng $1,480 on 26 September 1845 for a ninety-nine-year lease on the property, with ground rent of $47.50 each year. A mortgage was made to John Latrobe for $820.[7]

John Wilkes Booth's schooling cannot be pieced together with certainty. It is known that he was a student at the Bel Air Academy in Harford County; at Baltimore under Susan Hyde and Martin Kerney; at St. Timothy's Hall, Catonsville; at Milton School for Boys, Philopolis; and at Bland's Boarding Academy, York, Pennsylvania.[8] In later years he was remembered as an indifferent student. Still, he learned to organize his thoughts. His "To whom it may concern" letter, written in late 1864 to justify a plan to kidnap President Lincoln, is direct and forceful.[9]

While at St. Timothy's Hall, Booth became friendly with Samuel B. Arnold, son of a prosperous Baltimore baker. When this friendship was renewed in the late summer of 1864, Arnold agreed to join Booth's action group with the object of carrying President Lincoln off to Richmond as a prisoner.

The records of St. Timothy's Episcopal Church show that John Wilkes Booth was baptized by the rector, Libertus Van Bokkelen on 23 January 1853. No record of confirmation has been found. There are unverified reports that in the last year or so of his life, Booth flirted with Catholicism. In any case, when he finally was buried in Green Mount Cemetery in Baltimore on 26 June 1869, the services by the Reverend Fleming James were Episcopalian.

John Wilkes Booth was left fatherless at fourteen. Junius Brutus Booth made his final appearance at the St. Charles Theater in New Orleans on 19 November 1852. Then he headed home aboard the river steamer *John S. Chenowith.* The first day out he became ill and died on 30 November, just before the vessel docked in Louisville. He was buried in the Baltimore Cemetery. Edwin Booth purchased, in his mother's name, lots 9 and 10, Dogwood Area, Green Mount Cemetery, Baltimore, on 13 June 1869. Bodies from the farm and from the Baltimore Cemetery were reinterred there on 14 June. Ultimately, seven of the ten Booth children were buried in this plot.[10] Only Henry Byron, Edwin, and Junius Brutus, Jr., are buried elsewhere.

The acting career of John Wilkes Booth got off to a shaky start. His first formal role was on the evening of 14 August 1855, when he took the part of Richmond in *Richard III* at the Charles Street Theatre in Baltimore. He was just seventeen. He was untrained, and the performance showed it. Through his future brother-in-law John S. Clarke, he was hired in stock at the Arch Street Theatre in Philadelphia. He was listed as "J. B. Wilkes." The season began 15 August 1857 and closed 19 June 1858. Booth appeared regularly in minor roles. He did not always do well. Other actors complained that he flubbed lines and missed cues.

But Booth's prospects were looking up when the season closed. Edwin Booth asked him to appear with him as Richmond in *Richard III* at the Holliday Street Theatre in Baltimore on 27 August 1858. John T. Ford, who owned this theater, was a partner with George Kunkel in the Old Marshall Theatre, Richmond, Virginia. Perhaps with a push from Edwin, Kunkel signed John Wilkes Booth in stock for the 1858–59 season. He remained with Kunkel in Richmond for two seasons, 1858–59 and 1859–60, billed as "J. B. Wilkes." Booth was generally well received by Richmond audiences. He was learning his trade. More, he was learning something else: in the festering sectional dispute that led to the Civil War, he became almost fanatical in his belief that the South was in the right.

A subversive pro-South secret society, George W. L. Bickley's Knights of the Golden Circle, was attracting thousands of members around the country just before the war. Apparently Booth became a member in Richmond. Samuel K. Chester, who acted with Booth there, told federal investigators on 28 April 1865 that he thought Booth joined a "society" in Richmond in 1858 or 1859. George Wren, another actor who had been with Booth in Richmond, told investigators on 19 April 1865: "There is no question in my mind that he was a Knight of the Golden Circle and a very prominent man in it."[11]

A turning point for Booth may have come on 16 October 1859.

At eleven o'clock that night, John Brown and his abolitionist followers crossed the Potomac River railroad bridge from Maryland to begin their bloody raid on Harpers Ferry, Virginia. Local militia soon trapped the raiders in the small engine house. The action ended when a contingent of marines commanded by Colonel Robert E. Lee stormed the building just after dawn on 18 October and captured those left alive.[12] Booth was determined to be involved on the fringes of this sensational event. Somehow he made it.

In his famous "To whom it may concern" letter, Booth wrote: "When I aided in the capture and execution of John Brown . . . I was proud of my little share in the transaction." His part was slight. The Richmond Grays were ordered to take a train on 19 November, to Charles Town, Virginia, to perform guard duty pending the execution of Brown. The best evidence is that Booth borrowed part of a uniform and talked his way aboard the train. He was not a member of this unit. Upon arrival at Charles Town from Harpers Ferry, Booth was given duties and allowed to remain. A correspondent for the *Baltimore American* reported seeing him there on 24 November.[13] A similar dispatch was filed by a reporter for the *New York Tribune*. Booth told his sister Asia that he had been in Charles Town when Brown was hanged.[14] Others also placed him there, including George W. Libby, who had been a member of the Grays. Whatever George Kunkel thought about Booth leaving the theater shorthanded, he took his errant young actor back when the Grays returned to Richmond on 5 December 1859.

The 1859–60 season at the Old Marshall Theatre closed on 28 May 1860. Booth and a fellow actor, J. W. Collier, arranged a benefit performance for themselves on 31 May. This time Booth did the fifth act of *Richard III* as J. Wilkes Booth, the name he used later as a star.

The apprenticeship was over. That fall Booth agreed to star with Matthew Canning's company in a tour of the South. The company opened on 1 October 1860 at Columbus, Georgia, with Booth as Romeo and Mary Mitchell as Juliet. He was billed as "John Wilkes." Newspaper accounts used his correct name. All went well until the evening of 12 October. Booth and Canning were practicing with a pistol at Cook's Hotel when Canning attempted to let the hammer down. It slipped and the weapon discharged. The *Columbus Enquirer* for 16 October reported that Booth received a "flesh wound in the thigh."[15]

Apparently the wound was more serious than first believed.

Attendance lagged without Booth. To keep up interest, Canning kept promising that Booth would return shortly. But Booth did not appear until the last night, 20 October, when he recited the funeral oration of Marcus Antonius over the body of the murdered Caesar. The company went on to Montgomery, Alabama, without Booth. He was well enough to join them on 26 October. The following Monday he performed as Pescara in Richard Sheil's 1817 tragedy *The Apostate*, which became one of his favorite roles. He was billed as "Mr. John Wilkes." Booth's last appearance in Montgomery was on 1 December with Maggie Mitchell. This time he was billed as "J. Wilkes Booth." Shortly thereafter he left for Philadelphia to see his mother and sisters. Asia Booth Clarke wrote from that city on 16 December 1860 to a Baltimore friend, Jean Anderson: "John Booth is home. He is looking well, but his wound is not entirely healed yet: he still carries the ball in him."[16]

During his stay in Philadelphia, Booth prepared a lecture for delivery before an undisclosed audience in Pennsylvania. This plan may have been triggered by the secession of South Carolina on 20 December 1860. The copy of the lecture in the Players Club library in New York is in his hand. With it is Edwin Booth's note: "This was found long after his death, among some old playbills & clothes in my house." It is a remarkable document, a passionate statement of southern views. In some ways the wording is prophetic of Booth's part in events to come.[17]

Booth was now ready to challenge better-known actors as a star. The star system was simple enough: theater managers brought in "name" performers for limited engagements. They were supported during the run by members of the theater's own stock company. The top billing, along with a substantial share of the proceeds, went to the star. Because of summer heat, seasons generally ran from early September until mid-June.

The *Rochester Union and Advertiser* for 21 January 1861 announced that Booth and the Irving sisters (twins, Henrietta and Maria) would open there that evening with Booth as Romeo and Henrietta as Juliet. One critic wrote that both leading players "won warm applause." It was a successful beginning, closing on 2 February.

From Rochester, Booth went on to Albany and the tiny New Gayety Theatre on Green Street. He opened on 11 February as Romeo, this time with Annie Waite as Juliet. On the second night he was Pescara in *The Apostate*. His athletic acting almost canceled the engagement. During the last act he fell on the sharp end of his dagger, inflicting a deep wound under his right arm, which kept him off the boards until the following Monday, 18 February, when he repeated his role as Pescara.[18] That night Albany had a distinguished visitor at the Delavan House. Abraham Lincoln stopped there en route to his inauguration in Washington. Perhaps Booth saw Lincoln, perhaps not.

Booth was back for two more runs at the New Gayety Theatre that season. After the last engagement closed on 26 April, he again had trouble with a sharp point. This time the volatile Henrietta Irving sought to carve him up with a dirk. In a fuss that had the classic ingredients, dalliance and alcohol, she came into his room at Stanwix Hall and slashed his arm. She then retired to her own room and stabbed herself, inflicting a superficial wound. One newspaper reported the cause of this minor bloodletting as "disappointed affection, or some little affair of that sort."[19]

The 1861–62 season for Booth opened at Detroit on 11 September 1861. Now becoming established as a star, Booth received generally good reviews in the press. From Detroit he went on to appear in ten other cities, including Cincinnati, Indianapolis, St. Louis, Chicago, Baltimore, New York, and Boston. He closed in Louisville on 1 July 1862.

When the 1862–63 season began, Booth stopped off at Lexington, Kentucky, for two nights before beginning a two-week stand at Louisville, where he was popular. Then followed bookings at Cincinnati, Chicago, St. Louis, Boston, Philadelphia, Washington (at Grover's National Theatre and the Washington Theatre), closing out at Cleveland 3 July 1863. He was usually advertised as "J. Wilkes Booth, Tragedian." To be a "tragedian" in those days, Shakespeare was de rigueur. That season Booth did *Richard III* at least twenty times. Where Edwin Booth's silky delivery made him an ideal Hamlet, John Wilkes Booth's less temperate style fitted him equally well to be the villainous Richard Crookback. Audiences loved it. To book him was to fill the house.

When Booth was in St. Louis at Ben Debar's theater for a two-week engagement beginning 22 December 1862, his ardent pro-Confederate sentiments got him into difficulties with the federals. Lieutenant Colonel Henry L. McConnell, then provost marshal, Department of Missouri, told of the incident in a statement to the War Department on 24 April 1865. Booth had been heard to say that he wished the "whole damned government would go to hell," or words to that effect. After being arrested and fined, he took the oath of allegiance.[20]

Booth began the 1863–64 season, his last, at Boston on 28 September 1863. After a series of short runs in various New England cities and in Brooklyn, he came to Ford's Theatre in Washington on 2 November for a two-week stand. On Monday, 9 November, he appeared in the double roles of Phidias and Raphael in *The Marble Heart*. In the audience that evening were President and Mrs. Lincoln and several guests. They were seated in the fateful box (combined boxes 7 and 8, upper tier, audience right), where some seventeen months later Booth would shoot the president. John Hay, one of the president's secretaries, was there. He wrote of the performance: "Rather tame than otherwise."[21]

From Washington, Booth went directly to Cleveland. He had something on his mind beyond an engagement at John Ellsler's Academy of Music: he wanted to get rich by investing in the Pennsylvania oil boom. While in Cleveland he had time to work out a tentative understanding with a friend, Thomas Mears, and with Ellsler, to form a partnership to buy leases near Franklin, in Venango County, and drill for oil. They decided to call their venture the Dramatic Oil Company. Mears was to explore the possibilities and draw up the partnership agreement. Booth was to furnish most of the capital. Ellsler wrote years later that he and Booth agreed to go to Pennsylvania as soon as each had finished the season's theater activities.[22]

Beyond the theater and oil, Booth had another commitment. At some point, possibly in mid-1863, he was drawn into Confederate clandestine operations. His passion for the South, his ability to travel and observe, and his ready acceptance in various levels of society made this involvement almost inevitable. Acting made a good cover, as Asia Booth Clarke noted in her beautifully written manuscript, which was held in England for many years in the Farjeon family, descendants of the famous English comedian Joseph Jefferson. The manuscript was finally published in 1938 under the title *The Unlocked Book*. Clarke tells of Booth's confession to her that he was engaged in smuggling drugs to the South, particularly quinine. And he admitted more than Asia put into words; the implications ran deeper. Looking back sadly, she wrote: "I now knew that my hero was a spy, a blockade-runner, a rebel! I set these terrible words before my eyes, and knew that each one meant death."[23]

A possible reference to Booth's drug smuggling emerged in the interrogation of Henry C. Higginson in Washington on 25 April 1865. Higginson had been a private in Company K, Nineteenth

Illinois Volunteers. He was captured at Chickamauga on 20 September 1863 and brought as a prisoner to Richmond. One of General John H. Winder's tough Baltimore detectives, a man named Ritchie, was assigned to the prison as a guard and to extract useful military information from prisoners. With Higginson this became a two-way street. Ritchie became somewhat friendly with Higginson and a bit too talkative. One day the conversation got around to the theater and actors. Ritchie mentioned the name J. Wilkes Booth and said: "We find him a firm friend." Later Ritchie bragged about the aid the South was getting from the North and displayed a letter, dated as Higginson remembered it, Louisville, December 1863, around the twelfth. The letter was signed "J. Wilkes." It said a man named Perkins was bringing a load of medicine down the Kanawha Valley. Whether "J. Wilkes" was J. Wilkes Booth was not stated.[24]

For some reason not fully understood, Booth accepted an engagement at the Union Theatre in Leavenworth, Kansas. It was a near disaster. He opened on 22 December 1863. Already it was bitterly cold and snowing. After his last appearance, Booth took a steamer up the ice-filled river to St. Joseph, Missouri. There he found that the blizzard had closed down the Hannibal and St. Joseph Railroad. There were huge drifts everywhere; nothing moved for days. He holed up in the Pacific House, almost out of cash. There was no alternative but to send theater manager Ben Debar a telegram saying he could not make opening night in St. Louis on 4 January 1864.[25]

Booth described his predicament at St. Joseph in a letter to John Ellsler from Louisville on 24 January 1864. He was down to his "last cent." To raise money he arranged to do dramatic readings at the local auditorium, Corby's Hall, on the evening of 5 January 1864. Before a shivering audience he did several bits from Shakespeare and recited "The Shandon Bells," Lord Tennyson's "The Charge of the Light Brigade," and James Whittaker Watson's tearjerker, "The Beautiful Snow," which, considering the surplus of snow, was appropriate in a perverse way.[26]

In his letter to Ellsler, Booth wrote that the recital netted him $150, which he used to hire a sleigh to take him across the plains: "*Four days and nights* in the largest snow drifts I ever saw."[27] Actually some part of the trip from St. Joseph to St. Louis must have been by train. In a letter by the actor Edwin Adams to "Dear Reakirt," 17 April 1865, Adams told how he met Booth at Louisville in January 1864 and heard him "boasting over a very long and tedious journey from Leavenworth in a sleigh to St. Louis—and after having threatened the conductor's life who had stopped his train on account of the great depth of snow, and that by placing a pistol at his head made him continue his journey."[28]

The blizzard cost Booth all but four nights of his St. Louis engagement. From there he went on to Nashville for two weeks at Wood's Theatre, opening on 1 February 1864 in *Richard III*. In Nashville he met Governor Andrew Johnson and his secretary, William A. Browning. After Lincoln's assassination, this chance acquaintance with Johnson was circulated by Johnson's enemies with lurid tales of debaucheries with Booth. And there were even darker hints of their collaboration in the murder of Lincoln.[29]

Booth's next engagement was at Cincinnati. He arrived sick, reportedly with a severe cold. The first night, 15 February, he substituted *Othello* for *Richard III* thinking the lighter role would be less taxing on his voice. His part in *The Robbers* on 17 February was taken by a substitute. Somehow he struggled through the run, which ended on 26 February. But the nagging voice problem would not go away. It was with him when he opened at the St. Charles Theatre in New Orleans on 14 March. The *New Orleans Times* for 19 March noted that a "severe hoarseness" marred his efforts. This affliction held on, and Booth was forced to cancel two performances. Again, as at Cincinnati, he managed to complete the engagement, closing on 3 April with *Richard III*. Some experts have attributed his hoarseness to a lack of training in how to project without strain, and a few writers have expressed the opinion that he could not long have continued on the stage.

Relaxed and confident after a three-week rest, Booth opened at Boston Museum on 25 April 1864 in *Richard III*. On the whole, the press notices were favorable although one critic noted a voice problem. When he closed on 28 May 1864, with a matinee performance of *The Corsican Brothers*, his career as a traveling star was over. He performed but three more times, in benefits. The first was in New York on 25 November 1864, with his brothers Edwin and Junius, in *Julius Caesar* to raise money for the Shakespeare statue in Central Park. He agreed to appear on 20 January 1865 at Grover's Theatre, Washington, in *Romeo and Juliet* with Avonia Jones. It was her benefit night. Booth's last performance was in *The Apostate* at Ford's Theatre, Washington, on 18 March 1865. This was a benefit for an old friend, John McCullough.

After Booth closed out at the Boston Museum, he left for the Pennsylvania oil region. Earlier in 1864 he and his partners, John

Ellsler and Thomas Mears, had acquired rights to three and one-half acres of the Fuller farm near Franklin. Booth brought in an old friend, Joseph Simonds, to manage their venture, the Dramatic Oil Company. Henry Sires was hired to drill a well, called the "Wilhelmina" after Mears's wife. Booth was a romantic figure around Franklin. After the death of Lincoln, there was a spate of reminiscences about his activities there.[30]

Evidently Booth was in and out of Franklin several times during June. He registered at the McHenry House in Meadville, Pennsylvania, on 10 June and again on 29 June, probably to make railroad connections. It is unlikely that he had any knowledge of the inscription cut with a diamond on the window of room 22 at the McHenry House. Booth did not occupy this room. The scrawl reads: "Abe Lincoln Departed This Life August 13th 1864 By The Effects of Poison." Nobody knew when this message was scratched on the pane of glass or who did it. There has been much speculation.[31]

The *Cleveland Leader* for 1 July 1864 noted Booth's arrival at the Waddell House the day before. Where he went from Cleveland has not been learned although he probably returned to Franklin. On 26 July Booth registered at the Parker House, Boston. His presence there would have gone unnoticed except for newspaper accounts about the testimony of Godfrey Hyams (alias J. W. Harris) at the Lincoln assassination conspiracy trial on 29 May 1865. Hyams testified that he had been hired by Dr. Luke Blackburn, a refugee from Kentucky living in Canada, to bring clothing belonging to yellow fever victims from Halifax to Washington. Dr. Blackburn mistakenly believed that yellow fever could be transmitted by contact with infected clothing.[32]

Cordial Crane, an official of the Boston Custom House, saw the Hyams account in a newspaper and noted that the trunks had been shipped from Halifax through the port of Boston. He decided to take a look at hotel registers in the city to see if "Harris" had been a guest in late July or early August 1864. He did not find "Harris," but he did find J. Wilkes Booth on the Parker House register for 26 July 1864 along with three men from Canada and one from Baltimore. Crane's suspicions were aroused. He copied the entries and sent a letter dated 30 May 1865 to Secretary of War Edwin M. Stanton. He listed the names "Charles R. Hunter, Toronto, CW [Canada West], J. Wilkes Booth, A. J. Bursted, Baltimore, H. V. Clinton, Hamilton, CW, R. A. Leech, Montreal." In his letter to Stanton, Crane wrote that he sent the "names as a remarkable circumstance that representatives from the where named places should arrive and meet at the Parker House at about the time Harris was on his way from Halifax with his clothing." Crane put the emphasis in his letter on "Harris" and the supposedly infected clothing. No investigation was made into the other names on the Parker House register. After all, Booth was dead and the War Department already had information about the "yellow fever plot." Crane's letter was filed and not followed up.[33]

Now, more than a century later, the gathering at the Parker House can be construed differently. It has all the earmarks of a conference with an agenda. The inference is that agents of the Confederate apparatus in Canada had a need to discuss something with Booth. Capturing Lincoln? Within a few weeks Booth was in Baltimore recruiting others for just such a scheme and had closed out his Pennsylvania oil operations. The inference becomes stronger as a result of a careful search of records in Toronto, Baltimore, Hamilton, and Montreal. No trace of Hunter, Bursted, and Leech was found. Thus the names appear to be aliases.

The man using the name "H. V. Clinton" did turn up in a not unexpected place. Such a man registered at the St. Lawrence Hall, Montreal, on 28 May 1864. Instead of listing himself as from Hamilton, CW, he gave his home address as St. Louis, Missouri. He was back at the St. Lawrence Hall on 24 August 1864, again entering his name on the register as "H. V. Clinton, St. Louis."[34] A thorough search of St. Louis records for the 1850–70 period was made. "H. V. Clinton" was not found. Examination of other entries on the registers of the St. Lawrence Hall revealed that St. Louis was frequently given as a place of residence by Confederates. It was a shallow cover, giving the flavor of being neither North nor South. Beginning in early 1864, the St. Lawrence Hall was increasingly used as a headquarters for Confederate agents in Canada.

Around the middle of August 1864, Booth came to Baltimore and took a room at Barnum's Hotel. The purpose of this visit was to obtain trusted recruits for a plan to capture President Lincoln. He sent for twenty-four-year-old Michael O'Laughlen, a boyhood friend, who lived with his widowed mother at 57 North Exeter Street, across from the Booth townhouse. O'Laughlen had been in Company D, First Maryland Infantry, CSA. He had once been a member of the Knights of the Golden Circle.[35] At the same time, Booth sent for twenty-nine-year-old Samuel B. Arnold, another boyhood friend with whom he had attended school at St. Timothy's Hall, Catonsville, Maryland. Arnold had served in Company

C, First Maryland Infantry, CSA, until he was discharged for disability. Later he went back south and worked as a civilian, returning to Maryland in February 1864.

Arnold arrived at Booth's hotel room a little before O'Laughlen. Over drinks and cigars, the three talked of old times. Then Booth got down to business. The federals had stopped exchanging prisoners of war and the South was running out of manpower. Booth proposed that they join in the plan to capture Lincoln while he was en route to or from the Soldiers' Home on the outskirts of Washington, where he lived until the cold weather set it. Booth pointed out that Lincoln often went unguarded. It should be easy. A captive Lincoln in Richmond could then be used as a hostage to force the renewal of the prisoner exchange. Arnold and O'Laughlen agreed to become parties to the plan.[36]

The implications of what Booth told Arnold and O'Laughlen at Barnum's Hotel that day have been overlooked. Booth came there with precise information about Lincoln's habits and movements. He knew that Lincoln disliked the trappings of a military guard and that he often went to the Soldiers' Home without them. Yet, so far as can be learned, Booth had not been in Washington since November 1863 when he last performed at Ford's Theatre. This suggests that intelligence was being fed to him. Also, Booth's Soldiers' Home scenario was in principle the same as that proposed earlier by Bradley Johnson to Wade Hampton and Jubal Early. And it corresponds exactly with the plan approved by Seddon, who sent a group under command of Captain Thomas N. Conrad to Washington in mid-September 1864 to explore possibilities.

When Conrad was on assignment in Washington, he holed up at the old Van Ness mansion near the White House. This was the home of Thomas Green, who was married to Anne Lomax, a sister of Confederate General Lindsay Lomax. Green was a Confederate source, a "sleeper" burrowed deep underground by years in the city. Both Green and his wife were arrested on 18 April 1865, on suspicion of complicity in Lincoln's assassination. When their house was searched, detectives found a volume of Shakespeare's plays, opened at the point where Hamlet holds the skull and says, "Alas, poor Yorick!"[37] This evidence, if nothing else, kept the Greens in Old Capitol Prison until 3 June.

Booth was not operating in a vacuum. But those in the "cell," Booth's action group, were never told who on the outside was involved; only that people were there, ready to help. Booth kept things properly compartmentalized.

With Arnold and O'Laughlen committed to the enterprise, Booth went on to New York. About two weeks later he wrote to Arnold saying that he was "laid up" with erysipelas of the arm. Asia Booth Clarke told of this illness in her book but did not fix the date. As soon as he was well enough to travel, Booth went to Franklin, Pennsylvania, to dispose of his oil investments. Through his agent, Joseph Simonds, he had a series of complex conveyances drawn up. His one-third interest in the Alleghany River property was divided two ways, one-third to Simonds and two-thirds to his brother Junius Brutus Booth, Jr. The stock in the Pithole Creek operation was given to his sister Rosalie. In his 13 May 1865 testimony at the conspiracy trial, Simonds said that these transfers were completed on 27 or 28 September 1864. Booth left the area immediately, and Simonds never saw him again. According to Simonds, Booth's oil interests were "entirely closed out," and his losses amounted to some $6,000.[38]

It was not necessary to do anything about the valuable property in Boston, which Booth had purchased earlier in the year. It was in his mother's name. But many things remained to be done. A trip to Montreal was essential. There were people to see in that city. Besides, his theater wardrobe had to be taken to Montreal for shipment through the blockade to some port in the South. Booth fully expected to go south himself soon—with a captive Lincoln.

Booth was in Newburgh, New York, on 16 October 1864 and crossed the Hudson River about noon.[39] It is interesting to note that Robert E. Coxe, a wealthy southerner, was then with his family in Poughkeepsie, a few miles up the river. Coxe was a close friend of Clement C. Clay and provided the house in St. Catharines, Ontario, used by Clay and others as a headquarters for Canadian operations. Suspected of being involved in Lincoln's assassination, Coxe was arrested by order of Secretary of War Stanton and questioned on 10 May 1865. Nothing came of it.

One day is missing in our knowledge of Booth's journey to Montreal. He was in Newburgh around noon on Sunday, 16 October, and he did not check into the St. Lawrence Hall in Montreal until Tuesday, 18 October, at 9:30 P.M.. He was given room 150.

Notes

ABBREVIATIONS

NA   National Archives

OR   U.S. War Department, *The War of the Rebellion: A Compilation of the Official Records of the Union and Confederate Armies.* 128 vols. Washington, D.C.: U.S. Government Printing Office, 1880–1901.

ORN U.S. Navy Department, *Official Records of the Union and Confederate Navies in the War of the Rebellion.* 30 vols. Washington, D.C.: U.S. Government Printing Office, 1894–1914.

RG   Record Group

1. HD 407, Harford County Land Records, Bel Air, Md.

2. HD 16–97, ibid.

3. F. A. Burr, "Junius Brutus Booth's Wife Adelaide," *New York Press,* 9 August 1891.

4. Box C-166, Chancery Records, 1847–51, Baltimore City Hall, Baltimore.

5. Carded marriage entries for Baltimore, Maryland Hall of Records, Annapolis.

6. Adelaide's tombstone in the New Cathedral Cemetery, Baltimore, reads in part: "Wife of Junius Brutus Booth Tragedian."

7. AWB 357–265, Baltimore Land Records, Baltimore City Hall.

8. James W. Shettle, "J. Wilkes Booth at School," *Dramatic Mirror,* 26 February 1916, pp. 3, 5; Father Robert L. Keesler, "The Education of John Wilkes Booth," 2 February 1977, MS, copy in the Booth file, Surratt Society, Clinton, Md.

9. Booth's undated "To whom it may concern" letter is in Records of the U.S. Department of Justice, Attorney General's Papers, RG 60, NA. For security, the document has been placed in what is called the "Treasure Vault."

10. Records of Green Mount Cemetery, Baltimore. Two of the Booth children buried at Green Mount died in England, Henry Byron Booth (d. 1837) and Asia Booth Clarke (d. 1888).

11. Statement of Samuel K. Chester, Investigation and Trial Papers Relating to the Assassination of President Lincoln, reel 4, frames 0140–70; statement of George Wren, M-599, reel 6, frames 0491–96, NA.

12. For a full discussion of John Brown's Harpers Ferry raid, see U.S. Congress, *Select Committee of the Senate Appointed to Inquire into the Late Invasion and Seizure of the Public Property at Harper's Ferry,* Senate Report 278, 36th Cong., 1st sess., Serial 1040, 15 June 1860.

13. Quoted in *Richmond Enquirer,* 29 November 1859.

14. Asia Booth Clarke, *The Unlocked Book* (New York: Putnam, 1938), p. 113.

15. Knowledge of the scar on Booth's thigh would have been useful for identification at the autopsy aboard the *Montauk* on 27 April 1865. There was no reference to it.

16. Clarke to Anderson, 16 December 1860, File ML-518, Peale Museum, Baltimore.

17. Directors of the Walter Hampden Memorial Library, Players Club, New York, have yet to publish the document. Permission to quote from it could not be obtained.

18. H. P. Phelps, *Players of a Century: A Record of the Albany Stage* (Albany: McDonough Co., 1880), pp. 324–27.

19. For one account, see *Madison (Indiana) Courier,* 10 May 1861. The date of the

stabbing incident varies in published versions, but the best evidence is that it happened on the evening of 26 April 1861. The location of the wound is also given differently. One report has it above an eye, another has it on an arm. Booth's two Albany wounds were not mentioned in the autopsy on 27 April 1865.

20. McConnell did not date this incident, and the oath of allegiance has not been found. The only time McConnell's tenure as provost marshal coincided with Booth's presence in St. Louis was in the period 22 December 1862 through 3 January 1863. See M-599, reel 4, frame 0074, and McConnell's service record, M-405, reel 88, NA.

21. John Hay, *Lincoln and the Civil War in the Diaries and Letters of John Hay*, ed. Tyler Dennett (Westport, Conn.: Negro Universities Press, 1972), p. 118, entry for 9 November 1863.

22. John A. Ellsler, *The Stage Memories of John A. Ellsler*, ed. Effie Ellsler Weston (Cleveland: Rowfant Club, 1950), pp. 122–31.

23. Clarke, *Unlocked Book*, pp. 113–270.

24. Higginson's statement is in M-599, reel 2, frames 0162–69, NA. Higginson's uncertain recall of the Ritchie discussion precluded adequate research. Booth was in Cleveland in late November and early December 1863.

25. In the "Dear Kim" letter Booth wrote from St. Joseph to Leavenworth on 2 January 1864, he told how he got to St. Joseph in "a sea of troubles." A wagon ran over and crushed his "best friend," which he described as his flask. A copy of this letter is in the Charles C. Hart Autograph Collection, Library of Congress.

26. The *St. Joseph Morning Herald* for 5 January 1864 announced the program for Booth's dramatic readings at Corby's Hall, and the next edition reported how it went. "The Beautiful Snow" is about the remorse of a young prostitute who thinks of her lost virtue as she watches the white snow falling.

27. Booth to Ellsler, 24 January 1864, MS 2875, John A. Ellsler Papers, Western Reserve Historical Society, Cleveland.

28. Edwin Adams's letter is in M-599, reel 2, frames 0059–62, NA.

29. On the afternoon of 14 April 1865, Booth left a little card for Johnson at his hotel, the Kirkwood House. It read: "Don't wish to disturb you. Are you at home? J. Wilkes Booth." The Radical Republicans used this note against Johnson, ignoring the point: Booth wanted to know that Johnson would be there so that the assassin, George A. Atzerodt, could murder him at ten o'clock that night. See M-599, reel 15, frame 0312, NA, for this card.

30. Hildegarde Dolson, *The Great Oildorado* (New York: Random House, 1959), pp. 145–76.

31. Despite what Mary McHenry wrote to the adjutant general from Philadelphia on 26 December 1879, Booth was not in that hotel on 13 August 1864. See correspondence, M-599, reel 7, frames 0082–90, NA. S. D. Page, the hotel clerk, wrote to Secretary of War Edwin M. Stanton on 25 April 1865, with the hotel register before him, that Booth had been a guest only on 10 and 29 June 1864. The text of his letter is in Ernest C. Miller, *John Wilkes Booth—Oilman* (New York: Exposition Press, 1947), pp. 72–75, n. 74.

32. Hyams named other Confederate agents in Canada who knew about or were involved in the "yellow fever plot," including Clement C. Clay and James P. Holcombe. Another Confederate agent in Canada, the Reverend Kensey Johns Stewart, wrote to Jefferson Davis from Toronto on 30 November 1864 urging that this form of warfare be stopped (Chap. VII, vol. 24, pp. 58–65, RG 109, NA).

33. Crane to Stanton, 26 July 1865, M-599, reel 3, frame 0153, NA.

34. Copies of the St. Lawrence Hall registers for 1863 through 1865 were secured from the Archives of Canada, Ottawa. Unfortunately, the entries show only date of arrival, not length of stay.

35. After he was arrested in Baltimore on 17 April 1865, O'Laughlen admitted to Thomas Carmichael, marshal of police, that he had once belonged to the Knights of the Golden Circle. Union Sergeant Samuel Street, who grew up with O'Laughlen and Booth, confirmed this. See M-599, reel 4, frames 0198–99, and M-599, reel 6, frames 0286–89, NA.

36. See Samuel B. Arnold, *Defence of a Lincoln Conspirator* (Hattiesburg, Miss.: Book Farm, 1943), pp. 18–19. A copy of Arnold's confession is found in Letters Received by the Office of the Adjutant General (Main Series), 1861–70, M-619, reel 458, frames 0305–12, NA. The original of the confession has been lost.

37. See M-599, reel 3, frame 1268, NA.

38. These transactions are traced in Miller, *John Wilkes Booth*, pp. 76–77; nn. 90–96.

39. *New York World*, 21 April 1865.

PART THREE

*A Desperate Plan
to Win the War—
No Holds Barred*

13

Development of a Plan

At the end of July 1864, the Confederacy's prospects looked very good. Grant, with superior numbers, had been defeated repeatedly in the Wilderness campaign, and far from "fighting it out on this line if it takes all summer," he had been forced to abandon the northern approach to Richmond. General Early and a powerful Confederate army had just rattled the gates of Washington and now occupied the Shenandoah Valley. John B. Hood, a fighting general, stood between Atlanta and Sherman. General Richard Taylor had defeated a major Union expedition west of the Mississippi River. The ports of Mobile, Savannah, Charleston, and Wilmington were still in Confederate hands. The North was war weary, and the Democratic party appeared ready to nominate a "peace" candidate to oppose Lincoln in the November election.

The leaders of the Confederacy had good reason for optimism. They were so elated, in fact, that they may have become blinded to the residual strength and determination in the North. On 8 August 1864, the consistently proadministration *Richmond Sentinel* published a long editorial that may have reflected the thinking of Jefferson Davis and his colleagues. The *Sentinel* suggested that the war was nearly over. The Union leaders were not yet willing to admit defeat, but there was little they could do but prolong the agony. This view may seem bizarre in light of subsequent history, but it is important to recognize that it was held by men high in the Confederate government.

Although it may seem absurd to posit a defiant Confederate high command still expecting success in 1864–65 (in the face of the modern conventional view of the crumbling, exhausted Confederacy), this interpretation is consistent with the recent study

271

Why the South Lost the Civil War, in which the authors note the propensity of southern leaders to seek military solutions to military reversals, the inability of the North to defeat the South on the battlefield, and the decisive importance of morale to both sides, with each seeking to boost morale through military success. The authors of that book, however, were unaware of the scope and daring of Davis's orchestration of covert operations and military planning for the last year of the war. Moreover, because secrecy was so necessary to the realization of the plan, neither could the people of the Confederacy take heart from the gamble and set aside growing defeatism, both on the home front and in the trenches. Only the planners and, within the limits of their need to know, the soldiers, sailors, and civilian actors involved, could share the thrill of the hunt and the prospect of success.[1]

In this context, the old idea of capturing President Lincoln seemed particularly attractive. If Lincoln were removed from the leadership, the Union will to fight on might collapse. That was an even more important reason than mere retaliation for the Dahlgren raid. The two ideas, retribution and disrupting the enemy government, may have reinforced each other. One idea satisfied emotional needs and the other answered the need for a logical justification.

As a result of this reasoning, the leaders of the Confederacy decided to explore the possibility of capturing Lincoln. That does not mean that the Confederate government actually decided in 1864 to carry out such a scheme. Governments are seldom so foolhardy as to commit themselves irreversibly to risky courses of action. One may begin to plan several alternative courses and, by building checkpoints into the planning, cancel those that appear questionable and foster those that develop favorably.

The decision to plan for the operation to capture Lincoln was, in mid-1864, probably no more than a decision to make a plan. The operation might be useful as a political and propaganda measure or in helping persuade the U.S. government of the futility of attempting to restore the Union by force, but it might never be carried out. The people charged with the planning, however, had to take it seriously. It might be an essential operation at some future date, and it provided them with a good opportunity to make a personal contribution to the winning of the war.

Like military operations, clandestine operations normally begin with a concept developed by an individual on the basis of information available. Obviously, an operation cannot be based on a par-

John Wilkes Booth. Courtesy
Harvard Theater Collection

Abraham Lincoln.
Courtesy National Archives

John Harrison Surratt, Jr. He fled Canada in 1865, then went to Rome and enlisted in the Papal Zouaves. Courtesy of National Archives

Dr. Samuel A. Mudd. Courtesy National Park Service

Thomas H. Harbin (alias Thomas A. Wilson), a Confederate agent who reported directly to President Jefferson Davis and was deeply involved in the Booth operation. From the picture collection of Colonel Julian Raymond, courtesy of Walter Burke, Ft. Myers, Florida

Samuel Cox, Sr., owner of "Rich Hill," Charles County, Maryland, where John Wilkes Booth and David Herold stopped around midnight 15 April 1865. Picture courtesy David Rankin Barbee Collection, Georgetown University, Washington

Confederate agent Thomas A. Jones at his home near La Plata, Maryland, about 1890. Jones fed and protected John Wilkes Booth and David Edgar Herold from 16 April through 21 April 1865, and furnished the small boat they used to cross the Potomac River to King George County, Virginia. Courtesy National Park Service

William Rollins, Port Conway, King George County, Virginia. He furnished vital information to the federal cavalry pursuing Booth and Herold and guided the cavalry to Bowling Green, where Willie Jett was captured at the Star Hotel. Contrary to most accounts, Rollins did not operate the river ferry.

A Military Commission composed of nine Union officers was convened on 9 May 1865 at the old penitentiary on the grounds of the Washington Arsenal (now Fort Leslie J. McNair) to try eight people on a charge of conspiring with John Wilkes Booth and others to murder President Lincoln. The specification listed the names of the accused as follows: David E. Herold, Edward Spangler, Lewis Payne, Michael O'Laughlin, Samuel Arnold, Mary E. Surratt, George A. Atzerodt, and Samuel A. Mudd. All were found guilty on 30 June. Herold, Payne (actually Powell), Atzerodt, and Mrs. Surratt were sentenced to death by hanging. Arnold, O'Laughlin (his name was really O'Laughlen), and Mudd were sentenced to life in prison. Spangler (his first name was Edman, not Edward) was given a six year sentence. The hangings took place on the penitentiary grounds on the afternoon of 7 July 1865. Left to right in this Gardner photograph, the hanging bodies are: Mrs. Surratt, Powell, Herold, and Atzerodt. Courtesy Library of Congress

ticular behavior pattern or a particular piece of geography if the planner does not know they exist. It is interesting, therefore, that several reported schemes to capture President Lincoln had some common elements. The Bradley Johnson scheme, the plan described by Thomas Nelson Conrad, and the plan actually used by John Wilkes Booth all involved capturing Lincoln on the outskirts of Washington at or near his summer residence at the Soldiers' Home. A small group would escape rapidly, carrying the captive Lincoln. The Conrad and Booth plans specified escape through southern Maryland.

If all of these plans were scions of the same concept, the person who originated it must have been familiar with Lincoln's custom of spending summer nights at the Soldiers' Home; he must have known the geography of the area around the Soldiers' Home well enough to be confident that it would be feasible to capture Lincoln there, and he must have known the surrounding roads well enough to know that it would be possible to get from that locality into southern Maryland without running a great risk of being intercepted.

Following this same line of reasoning, it seems clear that the person who conceived the plan that Booth tried to implement must also have been familiar with the terrain and people of Charles County, Maryland, and he must have known that it would be possible to find a suitable location and reception for a landing in King George County, Virginia. Doubtless many people knew each of the individual parts of the puzzle, but in that day of poor roads, how many people would have known all of them? Given the poor state of mapping, it is doubtful that even the mapmakers in the Confederate War Department or in the Army of Northern Virginia would have known them all.

In view of the scarcity of people with the requisite knowledge, it is interesting that we know of two men to whom most or all of these things would have been familiar. In view of their positions during 1864 it is possible that one or both of these men may have conceived the basic outline of the operation to capture Lincoln.

Benjamin Ogle Tayloe, son of John Tayloe III, was the Harvard-educated son of one of the richest families in the United States. For many years he lived in a house, which is still standing, on the east side of Lafayette Square in Washington, D.C. From that location he had a good view of the comings and goings at the White House. He was also active socially and knew all the well-to-do people who lived in the vicinity. The Tayloe family came from the Northern

Neck of Virginia, and Ogle Tayloe, as he was known to his friends, was descended from a governor of Maryland on his mother's side. With this family background it is hardly surprising that he had strong southern sympathies.

One of Ogle Tayloe's possessions was the Petworth plantation in the rural part of the District of Columbia, north of the city of Washington and next door to the Soldiers' Home. He also owned the Nanjemoy plantation, a large piece of land on the west side of Nanjemoy Creek in Charles County, Maryland. This was the creek in which Booth's party hid a large boat that they intended to use to take President Lincoln across the Potomac.

On the Virginia side of the Potomac in King George County, Ogle's nephew John Tayloe V lived at Clifton, now called Chatterton, in sight of the mouth of Nanjemoy Creek. Nearby were Boyd's Hole and the camps of the Confederate Signal Corps, specialists in transferring information and people across the river and down to Richmond safely and secretly. Thus Benjamin Ogle Tayloe could have had in his head all of the geographic and personal knowledge necessary to conceive the operation to capture Lincoln.[2]

One other man known to be connected to Confederate clandestine operations shared most of this knowledge with Ogle Tayloe. He was the Reverend Kensey Johns Stewart, an Episcopal clergyman. Stewart was descended from a governor of Delaware and was married to Hannah Lee, a first cousin of Robert E. Lee.

In 1839 Stewart served as rector of the Rock Creek Episcopal Church in the District of Columbia. This church is located next to Petworth Plantation and across the street from the future location of the Soldiers' Home. Stewart doubtless knew Ogle Tayloe during this period. He probably traveled through his parish by horseback and was familiar with the roads north and east of Washington.

From 1855 to 1860 Stewart served as rector of St. Paul's Episcopal Church in King George County, Virginia.[3] John Tayloe V and his family may have been members of the congregation. Nanjemoy Creek was visible from Stewart's rectory. John Tayloe V had at one time owned property in Charles County across from Clifton and near his uncle's Nanjemoy property. Perhaps coincidentally, one of the original parcels of Tayloe's Nanjemoy plantation was known as "Tusculum," and after the Civil War, Reverend Stewart wrote a long narrative poem entitled "Tusculum."

Either Stewart or Ogle Tayloe was familiar enough with the main geographic elements of the area to have conceived the operation. Certainly, working together they could have done it.

It is also possible that the plan to capture Lincoln may have originated in Canada during the winter of 1863–64. P. C. Martin and George P. Kane had worked together to help organize the expedition to rescue the Johnson's Island prisoners in November 1863. Both men were from Baltimore and strongly pro-Confederate. They could have conceived the idea of capturing Lincoln as a hostage and discussed it with other Confederates in Canada, including Stewart, who had the geographical knowledge necessary to flesh out the concept. When Kane went to Richmond in February 1864, he may have taken the idea with him. After the Dahlgren raid the climate for so radical an action was more favorable.

On 26 June 1864 Robert E. Lee wrote to Jefferson Davis: "With relation to the project of Marshal Kane, if the matter can be kept secret, which I fear is impossible, should Genl. Early cross the Potomac, he [Kane] might be sent to join him [Early]."[4] One may infer that Kane's project was the capture of Lincoln.

Tayloe and Stewart both had personal connections with people involved in Confederate clandestine activity. In addition to his inherited property in Virginia, Maryland, and the District of Columbia, Tayloe had acquired large holdings in Alabama. As might be expected, Senator and Mrs. Clement C. Clay of Alabama were among his social acquaintances. Clay, of course, was one of the Confederate commissioners in Canada. Thomas Nelson Conrad wrote that when he was in Washington during the war he used as a safe house the home of Thomas Green. Green's wife was a cousin of Ogle Tayloe, and Tayloe helped the Clays and the Greens at the end of the war when both families were in trouble with the federal government. Conrad also wrote that he watched Lincoln's movements from Lafayette Square. Ogle Tayloe's writings state that he had observed Lincoln from his home.[5] Did Conrad watch Lincoln from behind a tree in the park or was he comfortably behind a window in Tayloe's house?

Although Tayloe was a strong southern sympathizer, he stayed in Washington throughout the war. Already in his sixties, he was too old to be tempted by service in the field. Given his social and economic position in Washington, he could hardly have avoided knowing Rose Greenhow and William T. Smithson, who were known Confederate agents. He doubtless also knew Judah Benjamin, Lucius Quintius Washington of the Confederate State Department, and Robert Ould. He also knew the Lee family. With all of these contacts and his strategic location, it would be logical that some Confederate operative would have thought of exploiting his sympathy and access on behalf of Confederate intelligence.

Stewart's relationship to Confederate operations is more clearly established. Early in the war, while helping out in a church in Alexandria, Virginia, Stewart was arrested at the altar for failing to pray for the president of the United States. Once released, he fled to Richmond (on crossing into Confederate lines he provided a fairly detailed report of useful military information observed on his way south)[6] and was appointed a chaplain to the Sixth North Carolina Infantry Regiment. He served in the field through much of the heavy campaigning of 1862 and made at least one trip through the lines into Maryland. In late 1862 he was transferred to General Winder's organization in Richmond and served as chaplain in the hospital for Union prisoners of war.[7] One of the duties a chaplain in such a position might perform would be to try to spot sick prisoners who might be potential candidates for recruitment as agents for the Confederacy.

Rather suddenly on 25 March 1863, Stewart resigned his chaplaincy and went to England, ostensibly to get a special edition of the prayer book printed for use in the Confederacy.[8] Stewart stayed in London for a considerable period and spent his time writing a geography textbook for use in southern schools.[9]

It is tempting to speculate that Stewart's trip to England was a cover and that he was trained in clandestine operations either by the British or by Confederates using England as a safe area. In his geography, Stewart acknowledges the help of the Reverend Robert Gatewood, who later became head of the Confederate army's Intelligence Office. This office dealt with information on the welfare of individual soldiers and not with military intelligence, but Gatewood provided a cover for Thomas Nelson Conrad and may have done the same for Stewart.

Stewart appears to have returned to the Confederacy and then proceeded to Canada. A letter of 4 November 1863 from his brother-in-law Cassius Lee, who was living in Canada, mentions that Stewart had a post in a church near Guelph, Ontario. This, however, may have been deliberate misinformation originated by Stewart or by Cassius Lee to cover Stewart's actual work. A Dr. Stewart was pastor of the Episcopal church at Guelph, but his name was Edward Michael Stewart and he had been there since 1850.[10]

Beginning in the latter part of 1864, there is considerable information to tie Stewart to Confederate clandestine operations. According to an autobiographical account, Stewart left Canada in September 1864 and went to Baltimore, where he purchased five yards of rubberized cloth. From Baltimore he went by train toward Washington, but at Annapolis Junction he switched trains and then got off at the next station on the line to Annapolis.[11]

Stewart then went to the house of the "Rev. Mr. S.," probably the Reverend Dr. Harvey Stanley, rector of Holy Trinity Church at Collington, Maryland. Stanley was a strong supporter of the southern cause and helped many Confederates traveling through Maryland. Stewart's visit might have coincided with Walter Bowie's trip through southern Maryland. A neighbor of Stanley's drove Stewart to the banks of Nanjemoy Creek, where he made a fourteen-foot basket boat from his rubberized cloth and a framework of saplings.

After various adventures with nature and Union gunboats, he crossed the Potomac, landing on the shore of King George County near a house called Waterloo, which was several miles below his intended landing point. The cliffs along the river were difficult to scale, and he finally found his way to the Tennant house, near Charles Cawood's Signal Corps camp. He then sent a message to General Lee saying that he would stay at Cedar Grove, the home of Dr. Richard Henry Stuart. While with Cawood's group he appears to have heard the story of Walter Bowie and his party capturing the Union cavalry outpost at Port Tobacco. He did not mention Bowie's death, however, which suggests that this event, which occurred on 7 October, had not yet been reported to Cawood's organization.

The next day, probably the ninth or sixteenth of October, he delivered a sermon from his old pulpit at St. Paul's Church in King George County. In due course he received a reply from General Lee asking him to visit Lee at his "earliest convenience." Stewart then went to Richmond and called on Jefferson Davis. According to the autobiographical account, Stewart discussed with Davis a project to aid northern prisoners of war in Andersonville Prison. The next day he visited General Lee for several hours. Lee reported Stewart's visit in a letter to Jefferson Davis, which makes it clear that Stewart discussed a clandestine project with Davis and that Davis wanted Lee's view on the matter. Stewart apparently was to see Davis after conferring with Lee. Lee wrote to Davis as follows:

> Mr. Stringfellow has just handed me your note enclosing one from Mr. Stewart—Mr. S. said upon your advice he had come to consult me upon a project he had in view, especially as to its morality.—I gave him opinion as far as I understood it & thought from what he said he had not determined to undertake it, but that it would depend upon an interview

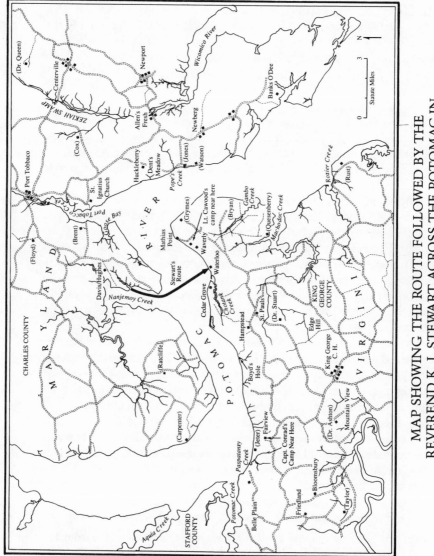

MAP SHOWING THE ROUTE FOLLOWED BY THE
REVEREND K. J. STEWART ACROSS THE POTOMAC IN
EARLY OCTOBER 1864.

he would have with you I know so little of Mr. S. that is his capacity for such an undertaking as he intimated rather than explained that when Mr. Stringfellow first came to me I told him, as I have written to Genl Fitz Lee, that I could give him no advice or recommendation as to his course—He must make up his own opinion as to what he should do—Col: E. G. Lee has just called on me on the same subject, having been referred to me by Mr. Stewart—As Mr. S. told me, what I very well knew, that his project must be kept a profound secret, I could neither explain it to Mr. Stringfellow or Col: Lee even as far as he had unfolded it to me—In fact I have not a high opinion of Mr. Stewarts Discretion, & could not advise any one to join him in his enterprize. I had inferred that his companions were to be taken from Canada, until I got a note from Genl Fitz Lee, asking if he must send some half dozen of his men to Mr. S.—To take a party of men from here seems to me to ensure failure & I could not recommend it. I supposed he would make up his mind as to what he would do & arrange his party in his own way.—I have had nothing to do with it—I return Mr. Stewarts letter.

He added a postscript: "Upon reperusal of your note I perceive you ask my advice—I do not think Mr. Stuart by his habits life etc. qualified for the undertaking he proposes—It was on this account that I could not advise others to join him. He may be an entirely different man from what I suppose him & the best fitted for the business, but I do not know it—I know nothing of the means or information at his disposal & can form no opinion as to his probable success."[12]

Two important points emerge from this letter. First, Lee was being asked to pass judgment on the morality of a project proposed by a minister. Stewart must have felt the need for reassurance that others would interpret his proposal as right and just. Second, although General Edwin G. Lee and scout Franklin Stringfellow were both aware of part of the project, neither knew its full extent. It is also clear that the project would need manpower and that Stewart was lobbying for such support, possibly cavalry scouts, from General Fitzhugh Lee.

After seeing General Lee, Stewart apparently visited Edwin G. Lee in Staunton. He then returned to Canada using the Signal Corps route through King George County. Instead of using the Signal Corps boat, however, he and a companion procured another boat and rowed from Chotank Creek, near Dr. Stuart's home, back to his starting point in Nanjemoy Creek.[13] He later found hospitality at the nearby house of "Judge B," probably Judge George Brent, who lived on high ground between Nanjemoy and Port

Tobacco creeks. From there he returned to Canada by way of Washington and New York.

Stewart appears to have arrived in Canada in late November 1864. He visited Jacob Thompson and told him that he had been given a draft on Thompson for $20,000 in gold but that the draft had been lost in the turmoil of his trip to Canada. Thompson advanced him $500 in gold and wrote on 3 December to Secretary of State Benjamin asking for verification of Stewart's story. In the meantime Stewart had written to Jefferson Davis from Toronto on 30 November 1864 explaining about the lost draft and asking that an ad be placed in a New York paper to signify that Thompson should honor Stewart's request for funds. Another letter to Davis followed on 12 December, full of sermonizing and gratuitous advice on how clandestine affairs should be managed.[14] In one of these letters Stewart mentioned "Conrad," perhaps Thomas Nelson Conrad. From these letters it would appear that Stewart felt that Davis had put him in charge of raids into the United States and that he had a veto on clandestine operations conceived by others.

Stewart's autobiographical article discloses that at least part of his mysterious project was a raid on the federal prison for captured Confederates at Elmira, New York, to be led by "Gen E. Gray." This was probably an alias for General Edwin Gray Lee, who used the alias "W. Gray" in correspondence with Judah Benjamin.[15]

According to Stewart, "A sufficient number of picked men were waiting orders in Canada for this service, all of whom, armed with revolvers, were to be sent to Elmira as recruits for the U.S. regiment at that place." An agent documented as a British subject was sent to reconnoiter the prison, and he reported that the project was feasible. It was expected that, once free, the prisoners could be organized and would fight their way to meet a raiding force sent from Virginia to help them escape. Presumably, arms for the freed prisoners could be sent to Elmira or some nearby location and concealed. This plan could account for E. G. Lee's interest in Stewart's project, but there does not seem to have been anything of questionable morality in it that would cause Stewart to seek General Robert E. Lee's opinion.

A number of the Confederates who were aware of the project to capture Lincoln explained that their motive was to use Lincoln as a hostage to bring about the freedom of Confederate prisoners of war. Given Stewart's interest in prisoners, the capture of Lincoln for this purpose might have been another part of his project.

Stewart may have conceived the idea of capturing Lincoln, but if he did, it seems clear that the idea had outgrown him. Possibly he retained an interest in it and continued to contribute ideas and information, but he was clearly not in charge of it, and judging by his letters to Jefferson Davis, he would not have made a very good leader for such an operation. Regardless of who conceived the idea, George P. Kane would have made a better advocate for the plan than Stewart.

John Wilkes Booth appears to have been recruited as an action agent in Washington. Before Booth could be put to work on the Lincoln operation, however, it needed to be worked out in much more concrete form. Somebody, possibly Kane, Tayloe, or Stewart, had put together a broad concept of how the operation might be done, but was the concept feasible? For example, what were Lincoln's routine movements? Was he guarded? Did he ever go to remote areas without a guard where it would be easy to capture him? Was it feasible for a small group to take Lincoln through the guards around Washington? Once out of Washington, could a small armed group move through nominal Union territory to an area where Lincoln could be put under Confederate control? How should the party cross the Potomac and where?

To answer these questions it would be necessary to send somebody to Washington who knew what information was needed, who could be trusted, and who could have a good chance of obtaining the information without getting caught. One candidate for the job appears to have occurred to Davis or somebody near him. This was Thomas Nelson Conrad, chaplain of the Third Virginia Cavalry Regiment.

Thomas N. Conrad, a Virginian by birth, was educated for the ministry at Dickinson College, Carlisle, Pennsylvania. Here his roommate was another Virginian, Daniel Mountjoy Cloud. After graduation, Conrad became a lay preacher and principal of Georgetown Institute, District of Columbia. After the war started, he did not hide his Confederate sympathies. A closing exercise for his students was held on 27 June 1862 in the lecture room of a Methodist church in Georgetown. An arrangement was made for the Marine Band to play. Conrad instructed the band director not to play "national tunes" and to wind up with "Dixie." A bit miffed, the director complied. The next day the *Washington Evening Star* reported on the event, noting that some people thought that Reverend Conrad should have been arrested. They did not have long to wait.

Major William E. Doster, Washington's provost marshal, had

been watching Conrad. On 2 August 1862, Doster had Conrad arrested and lodged in Old Capitol Prison, charging him with recruiting for the Confederate army. A month later Conrad was released on parole pending exchange. The federals were happy to be relieved of the difficult reverend, a decision they would come to regret. He was exchanged and reached Richmond on 23 October 1862.[16] Almost immediately he was drawn into Confederate clandestine operations. As cover he was appointed chaplain of the Third Virginia Cavalry on 30 September 1863. His active employment, however, was as a member of the unique group of cavalry scouts employed by General J. E. B. Stuart. From time to time these scouts undertook special missions not sponsored by their parent organizations. B. F. Stringfellow, for example, delivered a message to a foreign embassy in Washington, D.C.[17]

In April 1864, the Union was preparing for a major campaign against the South. Grant had taken over the Army of the Potomac and General Ambrose Burnside was training a new army corps near Annapolis, Maryland. To meet the anticipated offensive, the Confederates needed to know whether Burnside's corps was intended to reinforce Grant or the Union forces under Butler in the Tidewater area below Richmond. The Confederacy had too few troops to cover both areas adequately, and it would be risky to wait for the event and then adjust the disposition of forces.

Conrad says that President Davis ordered him to go to Annapolis to find out what mission General Burnside's corps was preparing for. His unit roster carried him as detailed to "secret service" for May and June 1864. On 25 April 1864, Conrad wrote a letter to General Braxton Bragg, seething with righteous indignation.[18] Bragg was acting as President Davis's principal military assistant at that time, and elsewhere Conrad mentions having been sent by Bragg on a mission for Davis. In this letter, Conrad complained that the men in the Signal Corps camp on Mattox Creek had not helped him get across the Potomac. The Signal Corps replied that Conrad did not have the necessary passes. In late April 1864, Captain Conrad was still a bit naive in dealing with the Signal Corps. Whoever sent Conrad on the mission should have gotten passes for him from the secretary of war and the chief of the Signal Corps, but he himself apparently did not know the proper procedure, and his conduct did not assure future cooperation from the Signal Corps.

Conrad says that he found no evidence that Burnside's troops were being prepared for any other purpose than to reinforce Grant. He reported that observation and stayed until the vanguard of

Burnside's force had reached Washington on its way to join Grant.[19] He then returned to Richmond and presumably was sent back to his parent unit.

In his book *A Confederate Spy*, Conrad said he fraternized with South Carolina officers in General Wade Hampton's cavalry when he was in camp. Actually, they were Maryland officers. These officers had a pet project: to go into Washington and abduct President Lincoln. They knew that Lincoln lived at the Soldiers' Home in the summer and fall and that he often went back and forth without escort. Why not intercept him and carry him off to the Confederacy? According to Conrad, he put the proposition to Secretary of War Seddon, who approved.[20]

On 9 August 1864, the Adjutant and Inspector General's Office in Richmond issued Special Order 187. Paragraph XII of that order directed: "Rev. Thomas N. Conrad, Chaplain, Third Regiment Virginia Cavalry, will report to Chaplain R. Gatewood, of the Army Intelligence Office, for temporary assignment to duty."[21]

The Army Intelligence Office handled tasks that today are done in part by the Red Cross and in part by the chaplains.[22] It was logical to assign a chaplain to that office, and it provided a plausible reason to send Conrad to Richmond. The Army Intelligence Office was in the same block as President Davis's office and only about two blocks from the War Department, but Conrad apparently never had any connection with it, and the orders may have been merely a cover to get him away from his unit.

Confederate records show that Conrad was paid for four days for forage for a horse in Richmond for 12 through 15 September 1864.[23] In *The Rebel Scout*, Conrad describes going to Richmond, where Davis gave him two letters, one to Secretary of War Seddon and the other to Secretary of State Benjamin. As a result of the letters, he was placed on the rolls of the "Secret Service Department" so that he "could draw gold" for his trip across the lines. The letter to Benjamin apparently authorized the money. The letter to Seddon enabled Conrad to "get papers and outfit." He was not going to repeat the mistake of April 1864 by going on a mission without proper preparation and documentation.[24]

Conrad requested the assistance of Sergeant Daniel Mountjoy Cloud, his Dickinson College roommate, with whom he had previously worked in clandestine operations. Secretary Seddon issued the necessary order on 1 September 1864, placing Cloud on "detached service," a common device in such cases.[25] The date of Cloud's orders suggests that Conrad arrived in Richmond long before 12 September. It is possible therefore, that he was engaged in staff work—planning or training—that prepared him for his final instructions and arrangements in Richmond.

Planning for the mission got under way promptly. A team was assembled in Richmond. Its composition, in addition to Conrad and Cloud, is revealed by entries in a passbook kept to show names of people leaving Richmond, who authorized the trips, and destinations. The passbook shows that on 17 September the secretary of war authorized the departure of Conrad, J. J. Norton, L. H. Henry, and G. Edmondson for Milford, Virginia.[26] Milford is a station on the Richmond, Fredericksburg and Potomac Railroad, located in Caroline County near Bowling Green. Confederate agents coming from Richmond usually left the train there for other means of transportation to the Signal Corps camps along the lower Potomac River. The trips were authorized by Major Isaac Carrington, the Richmond provost marshal.

Writing many years later, Conrad could not remember the correct first name of Norton. He called him "Edwin" in one place and "Edward" in another. Although this is speculative, the man may have been John J. Norton, who enlisted at Harpers Ferry on 1 June 1861 as a private in Company D, First Maryland Infantry. Very little can be learned about him from Confederate records, but a postwar publication implies that he was from Maryland.[27]

The "L. H. Henry" in the passbook entry is Lemuel H. Henry, who was employed before the war by the Treasury Department in Washington. He enlisted at Alexandria on 22 April 1861 as a private in Company E, First Virginia Infantry. Henry was discharged on 14 May 1862 and later worked in various unexplained capacities for the Confederate government. After the war he returned to Washington; his name appears in city directories through 1890.

"G. Edmondson" is Gabriel Edmondson, who was born in Washington. He enlisted as a private in Company F, Forty-first Virginia Infantry, on 10 June 1862. Seriously wounded at Sharpsburg on 17 September of that year, he spent the next month in a hospital. After his release he was detailed to the Confederate navy. Somehow he met Colonel Edwin G. Lee, who was impressed with him. When Lee was en route to Montreal to take over the Confederate apparatus there from Jacob Thompson, he sent a communication dated 15 December 1864, from Nassau, to Secretary of War Seddon requesting that Gabriel Edmondson of the "signal corps" be sent to him in Canada.[28] Apparently this did not happen, for the twenty-four-year-old Edmondson was paroled at Winchester, Virginia, on 28

April 1865. He returned to Washington but is not shown in city directories after 1866.

Conrad mentioned Edmondson as a member of his Washington team on page 84 of the typescript that later became his book *A Confederate Spy*. This reference was in connection with Conrad's plan for a massive breakout of Confederates from Old Capitol Prison. Edmondson's name was edited out of the published version and an alias was substituted.

Sergeant Daniel Cloud's name was not found in any of the extant Richmond passbooks. As will be seen, he went by the "upper Potomac," so his most likely route out of Richmond would have been over the Virginia Central Railroad to Gordonsville.

Two days before Conrad's team left for Washington, Seddon provided Conrad with the following order: "Lt. Col. Mosby and Lieutenant Cawood are hereby directed to aid and facilitate the movements of Captain Conrad."[29] Somebody was being very careful that there would not be a mix-up like that of April 1864. All key players should be aware that Captain Conrad was on important business. The cooperation of Cawood, the senior Signal Corps officer in the Northern Neck, would be important to any operation that required crossing the Potomac and sending messages to Richmond.

Mosby's Forty-third Battalion of Virginia cavalry was operating in northern Virginia. Mosby was known primarily as a leader of partisan operations, but he had an important mission as a collector of intelligence on Union activity, and judging from his postwar correspondence, he seems to have been aware of the Confederate program of clandestine operations. In this case, it appears that he might have been called on to cooperate in Conrad's operation, and Seddon wanted him to be aware that the government was very interested in Conrad's mission.

Conrad had no sooner received his copy of Seddon's note, however, when he wrote his own note to the secretary: "I leave for the lower Potomac, my friend and co-partner Captain [sic] D. M. Cloud, for the upper Potomac. I am compelled to ask therefore for a copy of the orders given me on yesterday for him inserting his name instead of mine in them. He was my co-laborer in our former enterprise."[30]

From Conrad's use of the term "lower Potomac" and "upper Potomac," it is apparent that he was to notify Cawood, and Cloud was to notify Mosby. Perhaps Cloud was to enter Washington through Montgomery County, north of Washington, and would have to have cooperation from Mosby as Conrad needed cooperation from Cawood.

On 10 January 1865, Conrad wrote from King George County, Virginia, to Seddon: "I received from the Honorable Secretary of State, Mr. Benjamin, last September, four hundred dollars in gold which yielded me $1,000 in northern funds. This has borne the expense of five of us for four months, (including two horses) averaging fifty dollars a month, therefore . . . I would be obliged if the Honorable Secretary would, at his pleasure, remit a draft."[31]

From this series of records, and interpreting Conrad's stories in their light, it would appear that in September 1864 he was assigned by senior Confederate officials to a secret mission of some importance.[32] Whether Conrad's mission was exploratory or intended for action, Seddon's approval and support had to mean that Davis was informed. The enormous political and military implications of a captive Lincoln would have made any other course by Seddon unthinkable.

While Conrad was in Richmond involved in discussions with Benjamin and Seddon, something seems to have perked up Seddon's spirits. On 14 September, one of his War Department clerks, John B. Jones, noted in his diary: "Mr. Secretary Seddon appears to be in very high spirits today, and says our affairs are by no means so desperate as they seem on the surface."[33] Is it possible that Seddon's attitude reflected the covert planning for Conrad's mission?

By 12–15 September 1864 the euphoria of early August had evaporated. General McClellan had been nominated as the Democratic candidate for president in the North, but he had disavowed the peace platform of the Democratic party. The Confederate defenses of Mobile Bay had been defeated, and Atlanta had fallen to Sherman. Grant was trying to extend his lines around the southern flank of Petersburg to cut off the Confederate supply routes leading to the Richmond area, and Sheridan and a strong army were active in the northern part of the Shenandoah Valley. These were not irrecoverable disasters for the Confederacy, but they must have forced Davis to make a realistic assessment of the strategic situation.

If the Confederate army were to defeat the enemy, serious planning was necessary, and such planning clearly required the best talent available. Lee was not one to sit in the trenches around Richmond and Petersburg hoping to win by discouraging Grant. The Confederacy would have to create a situation that would allow it to win. Lee had done the trick once already. During the Wilderness campaign he had led Grant into one of the most perfect military traps ever created. At the North Anna River, he had Grant's army divided into two wings that could not support each other, and Lee was in a position to use his entire army to destroy one wing at a time. Unfortunately for the Confederacy, fate interfered in the form of illness, and Lee could not provide the personal leadership that would have made the trap work.[34]

The North Anna situation, however, is important as background for the task now facing the leaders of the Confederacy. How could they break out of the stalemate around Richmond? What maneuver would provide them with a winning opportunity?

The problem was now much greater than it had been in the Wilderness. There, the constant maneuvering created numerous combinations of positions. Around Richmond the trenches inhibited such opportunities. Furthermore, planning for a winning opportunity was complicated by the need to defend in the existing situation. The day-to-day battles were desperately important. It was necessary to get as much flexibility as possible to be in a position to exploit an operation that might result from long-range planning, but the condition and location of specific units were constantly being changed by the effects of the day-to-day fighting, and the need for flexibility caused further attrition as efforts were made to strengthen and optimize the position of the lines. It was a planner's nightmare, and the war was being fought in an era when the art of planning complex military operations was not fully developed.

As General Lee's failure to implement his North Anna plan showed, staffs were not organized to function smoothly without the personal involvement and decision making of key leaders. The development of the plan to break out of the stalemate was, therefore, inescapably, a personal concern of President Davis, his secretaries of state and war, and General Lee. They were all busy men, and they must have had professional help in developing the plan.

The exact organization of the Confederate planning effort is lost in the darkness of missing records and time long past. Any attempt to reconstruct the probable organization is further confused by measures taken by the Confederates to protect the security of the operation. The Confederate government was well aware that the Union had an active intelligence effort of its own, and the Confederates probably used an array of cover stories and notional assignments to account for the activities of key people actually involved in the planning effort.

It seems clear that during the period of 12–15 September, Davis, Benjamin, and Seddon all spoke with Conrad. They talked with other people as well. Lee came up to Richmond from his headquarters in Petersburg on the afternoon of 12 September and stayed for three days.[35] A few days after Lee's return to Petersburg, Mosby came to see him for the first of at least three planning sessions.[36] This visit provided an opportunity for Lee to tell Mosby about Conrad's mission and of his duty to support Conrad and to discuss Mosby's own role in the operation.

Several other people who later were involved in the Confederate Secret Service could have been in Richmond at the same time to participate in the discussions. George Sanders had left Canada for Richmond before 12 September; Clement C. Clay mentioned his departure in a letter of that date to Benjamin.[37] Daniel Bedinger Lucas, a cousin of Edwin Gray Lee, of Jefferson County, Virginia, had been "military secretary" to former Governor Wise in the early days of the Civil War. In the spring of 1864, Lucas and E. G. Lee were both in Richmond, and in December Lucas left Richmond to join Lee in Canada.[38]

Colonel Edwin Gray Lee had been a successful infantry officer, but he suffered from tuberculosis and had left combat service. Since that time he had been involved in a paramilitary operation in the Chesapeake Bay along with his neighbor John Yates Beall and Daniel B. Lucas. In May 1864, Lee was assigned to command the Virginia reserve forces in the Valley District and had moved to their headquarters at Staunton. He was only a few hours away from Richmond by train and could easily have attended a conference in Richmond in September. On 23 September he was promoted to brigadier general and in November was designated to go to Canada as a commissioner to take over much of the responsibility for covert operations that Jacob Thompson and Clement Clay had held.[39] There is no proof that any of these people met with Davis et al. during September 1864, but their later associations are suggestive, and the opportunity seems to have existed.

The *Richmond Sentinel* published an article on 16 September 1864 which probably reflected the substance of some of the discussions of the previous three days. It pointed out that the south flank of the Confederate position was the critical area for future fighting and that the main Union aim would be to push past that flank to cut the Confederates off from rail lines that supplied them from the south and west.

There was no indication of the strategy that would be adopted to deal with this situation, but it is important to realize that the Confederate leaders recognized their critical strategic problem more than six months before it happened and that they recognized it in conjunction with what was probably a discussion of how to capture Lincoln. This does not mean that they did not have other alternatives in mind. If they built up too much strength in the south at the expense of their northern flank, Grant could always reverse his field and attack Richmond directly as he tried to do at the end of September 1864. There was also the possibility of a negotiated settlement with the Union. Horace Greeley's abortive peace negotiations of July 1864 with Clay and Sanders had shown that there was a strong sentiment in the North to accept a settlement, and no matter how much the Confederates hated Lincoln, they would doubtless have been happy to swallow their hatred if they could buy peace by doing so. On balance, however, they probably expected Lincoln to continue to be difficult to negotiate with and recognized that in the end, the problem of the southern flank would have to be solved.

There were three logical ways of meeting this Union threat. One would be to hold in position and try to defeat each Union attempt to extend the line. A second way would be to allow Grant to move to the south and then try to cut him off from his bases on the James River. A third would be to leave Richmond and Petersburg and try to outrun the Union army.

The first course was the obvious one to follow in the short term. It still left open the other two options, but it would not defeat Grant in the end. The second course might result in a major defeat for Grant if it could be properly staged, but it was much harder and riskier from a purely military standpoint than the third course. From a political standpoint, however, the third course was the least desirable. It would mean abandoning Richmond, and it might mean the loss of most of Virginia. Given Virginia's investment of men, resources, and leadership in the Confederacy, and particularly in the Army of Northern Virginia, there would undoubtedly be political opposition to the evacuation of the Richmond-Petersburg lines and a question about the willingness of Virginians to abandon their homes and fight in North Carolina.

In September 1864, it was too early to decide which should be the ultimate solution. It must have occurred to the Confederates, however, that the capture of Lincoln could provide useful leverage in any of the alternatives. With Lincoln as a captive, they might be able to use him as a hostage to stop further penetration of Confederate territory. It was a way of forcing Lincoln to negotiate (to the extent that one can negotiate with a hostage), and his absence from Washington might strengthen the peace party. At the very least, his absence would disrupt normal decision making, which might help the Confederates militarily. There was every reason, therefore, to continue to investigate the feasibility of a covert operation to capture him.

There is another indication that General Lee may have been thinking of a breakout strategy as early as September 1864. On 3 October, Jed Hotchkiss, the mapmaker of General Early's army in the Shenandoah Valley, sent Lee a copy of a map of southeastern Virginia. Hotchkiss had borrowed maps from Lee on earlier occasions, and they had previously discussed mapping problems. Hotchkiss does not say so, but the map was probably sent in response to a request from Lee, who may have been searching for a map that covered his area of interest at a suitable scale. It would appear that Lee was not satisifed with any of the maps he may have found, for on 1 November, Hotchkiss recorded that his men began work on a map of Southeastern Virginia for the Engineer Bureau.[40] The Engineer Bureau in turn may have been responding to Lee's desires.

Hotchkiss later referred to two separate maps—one of eastern Virginia and one of southeastern Virginia—both for the Engineer Bureau. He also mentioned that one of his men was working on a map of Virginia at a scale of fifteen miles to the inch.[41] That is a scale of almost 1/1,000,000. It is a good scale to use for fixing a broad geographic pattern in one's mind, but it is not very useful for most tactical planning.

Several times during the winter, Hotchkiss mentioned that his men were working on one or more of these maps for the Engineer Bureau. On 18 March 1865, Hotchkiss was in Richmond and spoke to General Jeremy Gilmer, the head of the Engineer Bureau, about publishing "my map."[42] Two days later, printer Charles Ludwig sent Gilmer an estimate for making a lithographic copy of a map approximately five feet by four feet in size.

At a scale of 1/250,000, such a map would have covered Virginia from the Atlantic to past Danville and Roanoke and from the North Carolina border to Harpers Ferry. Since most Virginians thought of Virginia as including West Virginia, this might have been the map of eastern Virginia that Hotchkiss's draftsmen were working on over the winter (not the map of southeastern Virginia mentioned earlier).

Captain Albert H. Campbell, chief of the Army of Northern Virginia's topographic engineers, demurred at Ludwig's estimate and recommended that the map be reproduced by photography at one-fourth the cost of lithography.[43] Campbell did not mention it, but photography would also have been faster and more accurate. Campbell added that if several thousand copies of the map were needed, lithography would prove to be cheaper. This suggests that a relatively small number of copies would be needed. A hundred copies or fewer would probably have satisfied the needs of the Army of Northern Virginia for a map at a scale of 1/250,000.

In writing about his own activities at this point, Conrad was careful to be titillating but to stay within the bounds of the "official" line of the postwar Confederacy—that Davis had nothing to do with any plan against Lincoln. Conrad claimed that Seddon's note to Cawood and Mosby was issued at his request to make it possible for him to get emergency assistance for a scheme which he and his associates had conceived. According to Conrad, they thought that it would be a good idea to capture President Lincoln and in late September 1864 set about the attempt.[44]

In *A Confederate Spy* Conrad described his work on the scheme to capture Lincoln.

Ten days after securing the order for the War Department at Richmond [presumably this would have been about 25 September 1864], I had reached Washington safely and began to reconnoiter the White House. . . . I had to ascertain Mr. Lincoln's customary movements first. . . . LaFayette Square only a stone's throw north of the White House entrance was the very place I needed as vantage ground. Partially concealed by the large trees of the park, I found no difficulty in observing the official's ingress and egress, noting about what hours of the day he might venture forth, size of the accompanying escort, if any: and all other details. . . . Hours and days of watching were necessary before I learned that he usually left the President's quarters in the cool of the evening on pleasant days, driving and accompanied in his private carriage, straight out Fourteenth Street to Columbia Road then across to the high elevation. . . . We [unidentified] had to determine at what point it would be most expedient to capture the carriage and take possession of Mr. Lincoln; and then whether to move with him through Maryland to the lower Potomac and cross or to the upper Potomac and deliver the prisoner to Mosby's Confederacy for transportation to Richmond. To secure the points necessary for reaching a proper conclusion about all these things, required days of careful work and observation. . . . Having scouted the country pretty thoroughly . . . we finally concluded to take the lower Potomac route.[45]

At this same time, Walter Bowie was leading his detachment through southern Maryland with the ostensible purpose of capturing the governor of Maryland.

According to his story, Conrad and his friends were going to try to seize the president while he was in his carriage on his way to his summer residence in the Soldiers' Home north of Washington. They were frustrated when the president unexpectedly turned up with a cavalry escort. There is no independent evidence of this attempt. Conrad felt that the capture of President Lincoln was feasible and that the best escape route was through southern Maryland.[46] Presumably he reported information consistent with that view. His reports, those of K. J. Stewart, and the results of Walter Bowie's expedition into southern Maryland should have been available to the Confederate authorities by the end of October 1864. Presumably, these pieces of information would have been encouraging to those responsible for the Lincoln operation. The next steps would logically be the organization of the escape routes and the development of the action groups. Geography dictated that it be a three-part effort. Two parts, organization of the route north of the Potomac and organization of the action team, would have to be carried out by Booth and others assigned to help him—possibly under the supervision of the Confederate apparatus in Canada. The organization of the escape route south of the Potomac could be carried out by the Confederate government itself.

In planning an escape route through southern Maryland, there were two obvious strategies to follow. One was to get to the Patuxent River at the nearest point where it was wide enough and deep enough to hold a proper sized sailboat. From there, several options were available as the final destination. The Union navy was busy in the York and the James, but the Rappahannock was still nominally in Confederate hands, and the action party could be landed in the vicinity of Urbanna on the south bank, where it could head westward overland toward Richmond. The other strategy was to head south through Charles County, Maryland, cross the Potomac, and keep on south toward Richmond more or less along the path of the modern Route 301.

The Patuxent strategy would have the advantage of getting the action party off the roads sooner. It would also give the party some flexibility in choosing a landing site and would provide a means of transportation if anyone were too injured to ride on horseback. Its worst feature was that the action party would have to travel seventy or eighty miles overland after landing in Virginia.

The Potomac strategy provided the more direct route. Further, it had the least exposure to the Union navy and had the advantage of connecting with the railroad at Milford. It would make sense to develop both routes because circumstances at the time of action might make one more desirable than the other.

During the time that the Confederate government was launching Conrad to reconnoiter the situation in Washington, another activity was getting under way which seems to have been directly involved in the preparation for the capture of Lincoln. If an action party were to land on Virginia's shores with a captive Lincoln, it would not do for it to get lost for want of a map, and if troops were to guard the escape route, they would need maps to plan their operations.

This other activity centered around First Lieutenant B. Lewis Blackford, a topographic engineer. On 21 August 1864, Special Order 196 of the Adjutant and Inspector General's Office in Richmond directed him to report to Captain Albert H. Campbell. He settled his accounts in Wilmington on 27 August and reported to Campbell in Richmond on 1 September.

Campbell's instructions to Blackford on 2 September were to "proceed as soon as possible with your party to resume the Survey of Stafford County. . . . After completing Stafford secure as much as possible of the County of Prince William, and Fauquier as far north as the Orange and Alexandria Railroad."[47] According to these instructions, he would have to map a strip about ten miles wide of the counties bordering Stafford on the north, in addition to a substantial amount of Stafford County itself at a time when our sense of history tells us the activities of the Army of Northern Virginia in this area were ended.

The party was plagued with sickness and other difficulties but worked through September and most of October. Blackford reported that he had personally sketched the Potomac coastline because he did not want the Potomac River Flotilla to spot his crew working with chains and plane tables. Union troops apparently searched for the party on several occasions without finding it. On 25 October, Campbell wrote to Blackford, "As soon as you complete Stafford move down and commence a survey of King William County commencing on the main roads at least one-half mile in Caroline. . . . Gen. Gilmer is still anxious about Stafford." On the same day, Campbell wrote a personal letter to Blackford in which he said that General Walter Husted Stevens, chief engineer of the Army of Northern Virginia, wanted four engineer officers assigned to him, including Blackford. The other three could be spared, but Blackford could not be released until the survey of Stafford was finished.[48]

On 31 October 1864, the Topographic Department of the Army of Northern Virginia sent Blackford a no-nonsense message: "On completing your map of Stafford report with it, in person, to these Headquarters."[49] Blackford finished his map of Stafford and reported to Richmond, but he was not assigned to General Stevens. Instead, his party was ordered on 7 November to survey King William County, and Blackford left Richmond the next day. Lieutenant Charles Cawood of the Signal Corps camp in King George County was in Richmond at this same time, possibly to participate in discussions about the escape route. On 9 November 1864 he was issued a pass in Richmond which permitted him to travel back and forth between Richmond and King George County. Within a few days, Blackford was back in Richmond, for the passports issued in Richmond show that he left again on 22 November 1864, headed for Hanover.[50] Blackford's crew of fifteen represented 20 percent of the total work force of the Topographic Department during November 1864, clearly making this a high priority task.[51]

The work appears to have been finished by 21 February, for on that date Blackford was sent back to the Army of Northern Virginia Topographic Office and later worked on the Pittsylvania County region, where Danville, Virginia, is located. He was paroled with the engineers of the Army of Northern Virginia at Appomattox in April 1865.[52]

Conrad's letter of 15 September 1864 to Secretary of War Seddon shows that in mid-September there was a plan for Conrad's associate Mountjoy Cloud to organize an operation similar to Conrad's on the upper Potomac—presumably on the stretch of river above Washington between Montgomery County, Maryland, and Loudoun County, Virginia. If this were being considered as an alternative escape route for the action party with a captive Lincoln, it would make sense for the action party to be escorted and defended by Mosby's Rangers.

The party would have had to move from Loudoun County south to Gordonsville, the railroad junction northeast of Charlottesville. From that point it could be moved by rail to Hanover Junction, a few miles from the hotel at Ashland. Alternatively, the party could have continued to Richmond by rail and then returned by road to Ashland if that were desired.

The weak point in such a route was the long trek from Loudoun

County to Gordonsville. If the Union forces knew or could guess the route, it would be fairly easy to send troops down the railroad toward Orange or down the Potomac to Aquia Creek and then overland through Stafford County toward Culpeper or Orange. To forestall such a move, the Confederates would have had to be prepared to move a blocking force into Stafford or Fauquier counties quickly to delay the Union pursuit. Such a plan could account for Blackford's original instructions to map both Stafford County and those parts of Fauquier and Prince William lying south and east of the railroad.

By late October, however, there would have been time to receive Conrad's reports on his reconnaissance of Washington and southern Maryland and the after-action report of Bowie's party as well as Stewart's report. Other reports from Mosby and from Mountjoy Cloud on the route above Washington could also have been received. These reports may have indicated that the lower route was preferable. This could have led to a change in the directions to Blackford to finish Stafford County, forget the area in Fauquier and Prince William, and prepare to work on the key portion of the southern route—King William County.

One other piece of information bears on Blackford's knowledge of the operation. One of the survey books used in King William County was an excellent leather-bound book that Blackford had "inherited" from a fellow engineer, Captain William H. James, in Wilmington.[53] The endpapers of the book are covered with sketches and scribbles. One is a handsome sketch of a blockade runner, *The Letter B* (the ship's real name was the *Let Her Be*). Another is a cartoon of a beardless Lincoln (Lincoln grew his beard after the election of 1860, and after that date few pictures of him were published in the South). Across the cartoon somebody had written "A Lincoln" three times—alongside, somebody had written "A Lincoln President—President in United States"—and then in larger script, "Abram Lincoln 'Chief Nigger'." Possibly this was nothing more than a young man's musings about the enemy head of state, but it could also indicate an awareness of the purpose of the survey.

In sum, there is firm and detailed evidence that a high-priority effort was under way in late 1864 and early 1865 to prepare maps of areas that logically could have been used to bring a captive President Lincoln to Virginia. There is no indication of an alternative explanation for this mapping effort.

Notes

ABBREVIATIONS

NA   National Archives

OR   U.S. War Department, *The War of the Rebellion: A Compilation of the Official Records of the Union and Confederate Armies.* 128 vols. Washington, D.C.: U.S. Government Printing Office, 1880–1901.

ORN   U.S. Navy Department, *Official Records of the Union and Confederate Navies in the War of the Rebellion.* 30 vols. Washington, D.C.: U.S. Government Printing Office, 1894–1914.

RG   Record Group

1. Richard E. Beringer, Herman Hattaway, Archer Jones, and William N. Still, Jr., *Why the South Lost the Civil War* (Athens: University of Georgia Press, 1968), see esp. pp. 297–98.

2. A large collection of Tayloe family papers is in the Virginia Historical Society, Richmond.

3. Robert McMurdy, "The Reverend Kensey Johns Stewart" (biographical note at class reunion, 1887), *Washington and Jefferson Historical Collection* (Washington, Pa., n.d.); Parish records of St. Paul's Parish, King George County, Va.

4. R. E. Lee, *The Wartime Papers of R. E. Lee,* ed. Clifford Dowdey and Louis H. Manarin (New York: Bramhall House, 1961), p. 808.

5. William Watson, *In Memoriam: Benjamin Ogle Tayloe* (Washington, D.C.: Privately printed, 1872), p. 180.

6. *OR*, Ser. 1, vol. 11, pt. 3, pp. 428–29.

7. K. J. Stewart, Compiled Service Record, NA.

8. G. Maclaren Brydon, "The 'Confederate Prayer Book,'" *Historical Magazine of the Episcopal Church* 17 (1948): 339–42.

9. K. J. Stewart, *A Geography for Beginners* (Richmond: J. W. Randolph, 1864).

10. Cassius F. Lee to Charles H. Lee, 4 November 1863, typescript, Letters of Mrs. Cassius F. Lee of Menokin Farm, vertical file, Lloyd House, Alexandria Public Library, Alexandria, Va.; Archival Secretary of the Anglican Church of Canada to Tidwell, 9 July 1982, author's files.

11. K. J. Stewart, "Adventures of the Doctor," *Southern Magazine* 8 (January–June 1871): 407–13, 526–36, 727–34.

12. Lee to Davis, 25 October 1864, in Robert E. Lee, *Lee's Dispatches: Unpublished Letters of General Robert E. Lee, CSA, to Jefferson Davis and the War Department of the Confederate States of America, 1862–1865,* ed. Douglas Southall Freeman and Grady McWhiney (New York: Putnam, 1957), pp. 302–4.

13. A relic of this crossing is a map of King George County hanging in the office of the King George county clerk. On its back is the notation "St. Paul's Rectory, November 1859." At that date Stewart lived at the rectory. Penciled on the map are the locations "Stuarts Wharf" and the house of William Henry Harrison Cawood, a relative of Lieutenant Charles Cawood, who had married one of the Hooe girls. This Cawood may have been the man who helped Stewart cross the Potomac. The map was presented to the county by A. H. Morgan, a twentieth-century owner of Cedar Grove, the Stuart house on the Potomac.

14. Chap. VII, vol. 24, pp. 58–65, RG 109, NA.

15. E. G. Lee to Mr. Secretary, 15 December 1864, Pickett Papers, M-13744, reel 6, frame 002785, Library of Congress.

16. S. S. Baxter to Secretary of War, 30 October 1862, Letters Received by the Confederate Secretary of War, M-437, reel 36, file 1415-B-1862, NA.

17. R. Sheperd Brown, *Stringfellow of the Fourth* (New York: Crown, 1960), p. 268.

18. Thomas Nelson Conrad, *A Confederate Spy* (New York: J. S. Ogilvie, 1892), p. 56; Thomas Nelson Conrad, Compiled Service Record, NA; Conrad to Bragg, 25 April 1864, Jefferson Davis Papers, Duke University Library, Durham, N.C.

19. Conrad, *Confederate Spy*, p. 60.

20. Ibid., p. 69.

21. Special Orders issued by the Confederate adjutant and inspector general are printed by number by year of issuance in bound volumes in the Reading Room Library in the National Archives.

22. Henry Putney Beers, *Guide to the Archives of the Government of the Confederate States of America* (Washington, D.C.: General Services Administration, 1968), p. 233.

23. Thomas Nelson Conrad, Compiled Service Record, NA.

24. Thomas Nelson Conrad, *The Rebel Scout* (Washington, D.C.: National Publishing Company, 1904), pp. 94–97.

25. Carded CSA Compiled Service Records, M-325, reel 74, shows Fourth Sergeant D. M. Cloud as "on detached service by order of Sec. of War since Sept. 1, 1864."

26. Book 131, covering the period 9 March–16 December 1864, Chap. IX, RG 109, NA.

Capt. T. N. Conrad	Ord Secty War	V Maj C	Milford, VA
J. J. Norton	"	"	"
L. H. Henry	"	"	"
G. Edmondson	"	"	"

27. Daniel D. Hartzler, *Marylanders in the Confederacy* (Silver Spring, Md.: Family Line Publication, 1986), p. 235.

28. Miscellaneous Confederate Papers, M-13744, reel 6, no. 2785, Library of Congress. Materials found to date yield no record of his service in the Signal Corps.

29. This order is quoted in Conrad, *Confederate Spy*, p. 70, and in *Rebel Scout*, p. 119.

30. Conrad to Seddon, 16 September 1864, Letters Received by the Confederate Secretary of War, 1861–65, M-437, reel 124, frame 275, RG 109, NA.

31. Ibid., reel 146, frames 294–301.

32. Conrad, *Rebel Scout*, p. 119.

33. John B. Jones, *A Rebel War Clerk's Diary*, ed. Howard Swiggett, 2 vols. (New York: Old Hickory Book Shop, 1935), 2:282.

34. Douglas Southall Freeman, *R. E. Lee*, 4 vols. (New York: Charles Scribner's Sons, 1935), 3:356–58.

35. Walter Herron Taylor to Bettie Saunders, 12, 18 September 1864, MS File 28114, Virginia State Library, Richmond. The original letters are in the Kirin Memorial Library in Norfolk, Virginia.

36. John S. Mosby, *The Memoirs of Colonel John S. Mosby*, ed. Charles Wells Russell (Bloomington: Indiana University Press, 1981), p. 374.

37. C. C. Clay to Judah Benjamin, 12 September 1864, *Southern Historical Society Papers* 7 (1879): 338–43.

38. J. E. Norris, *History of the Lower Shenandoah Valley* (Chicago: A. Warner, 1890), pp. 597–99; *Richmond Sentinel*, 2 May 1864.

39. E. G. Lee, Compiled Service Record, NA; Beall to Lee, 20 July 1863, William Nelson Pendleton Papers, Southern Historical Collection, University of North Carolina, Chapel Hill.

40. Archie P. McDonald, *Make Me a Map of the Valley* (Dallas: Southern Methodist University Press, 1973), pp. 234, 242.

41. Ibid., pp. 242, 244.

42. Ibid., p. 262.

43. Ludwig to Gilmer, 20 March 1865, Campbell Endorsement, Miscellaneous Papers of the Confederate Engineer Department, File entry 27, RG 109, NA.

44. Conrad, *Confederate Spy,* pp. 68–71.

45. Ibid., p. 72.

46. Ibid., pp. 68–74.

47. Engineer Department Sketch and Cash Books, File entry 26, RG 109, NA.

48. Ibid.

49. Ibid.

50. Record of Passports Issued, Chap. IX, vol. 131, RG 109, NA.

51. Engineer Department Sketch and Cash Books, File entry 26, RG 109, NA.

52. Lewis E. Blackford, Compiled Service Record, NA.

53. Engineer Department Sketch and Cash Books, File entry 26, RG 109, NA.

14

Organization in Virginia

The geography exploited by the Signal Corps to protect its routes to Washington could also be exploited to make a clandestine Potomac River crossing with a fair guarantee that it would not be interrupted by the Union navy. It was one thing, however, to dodge a routine patrol of the Potomac River Flotilla and a radically different task to escape from determined pursuers. On the route through southern Maryland there were two main threats from pursuit. One, of course, was horseback pursuit on the heels of the action party. Once that party was afloat, however, there would not be much to worry about from direct pursuit. Boats were hard to find in Maryland, and it would take a while to organize a river crossing in the wake of an action party.

More alarming was the possibility of a steamer pursuing the action group downriver from Washington with troops on board intending to land in Potomac Creek, Boyd's Hole, or a number of other possible landing sites along the shore of King George County, Virginia. The danger area ran from the mouth of Potomac Creek to the mouth of Chotank Creek. Farther east was Mathias Point and Lieutenant Cawood's Signal Corps camp. If the Federal forces landed there, the signal unit could provide an alarm, and since the Potomac curved to the north, a landing there would be farther away from the Lincoln party's route. The ten miles of coast between Potomac Creek and Chotank Creek formed the critical area that needed to be protected against hostile landings

On the Patuxent-Urbanna route, the main threat would be pursuit by the Union navy. Fast boats and shrewd captains could easily dodge the Union navy in the Chesapeake, but the Union navy had a good enough success record to make Confederate planners nervous. The odds of a successful escape by this route could be enhanced by laying a defensive mine field in the mouth of the Rappahannock to let the action party through but catch its pursuers.

The Confederates had laid mines in the Rappahannock earlier,[1] but it had not been a priority effort, and when the mining parties were broken up by the Union navy no effort had been made to continue the operation. Now, however, there was a need for mines that might have the necessary high priority.

The Confederacy had never been able to afford to fortify the shore of King George County, and it was not likely that the necessary assets could be found in 1864 or 1865. Furthermore, this was a clandestine operation, and obvious fortification would only advertise the Confederate interest in the area. It appeared to be a situation in which underwater mines could be used profitably. Mines laid before the likely landing areas and observed by a screen of pickets could slow down a hostile landing operation and provide information to a central point. There, a small mobile reserve could be used to delay pursuit further while Lincoln was rushed to Milford Station. Mines would provide an important addition to the safety of both escape routes.

At Milford, it would be necessary to keep an engine and one or two cars standing by for immediate departure. This would require modest cooperation from the railroad authorities, but since the line to Milford was kept open in part to support the signal route, that did not seem to be an insurmountable additional burden.

Clandestine operators had constantly to be on guard against security leaks. For this reason the operations were usually separated into compartments with nobody in one compartment aware of what was going on in another. In this case, the railroaders were probably told that the train was needed to support the arrival of special contraband goods smuggled through enemy lines or some similar tale.

Once the plan had reached this level of detail, the planners in Richmond had to make specific arrangements. They had to arrange for the laying of mines, which would require a clear directive and high priority from the highest levels in the government. Once the mines were in place, it would be necessary to provide troops to man the pickets along the Potomac, provide a mobile reserve, and guard the railhead at Milford Station. Additional troops would be needed near Urbanna to protect the landing site there and screen the area from Union raids out of Fortress Monroe or Grant's lines around Richmond.

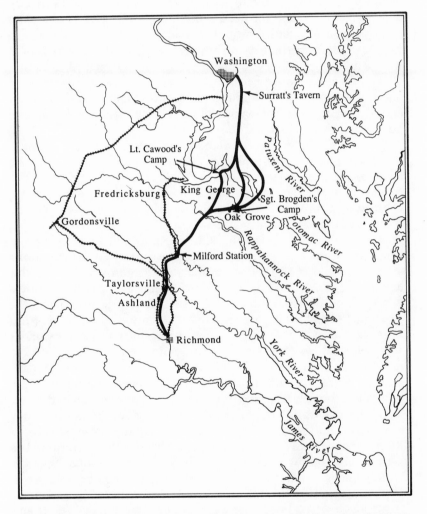

THE "SECRET LINE" OF THE CONFEDERATE SIGNAL CORPS

From a security standpoint, the plan seemed acceptable. The men laying the mines, the pickets, and the guard force near Urbanna could be told that the Yankees were planning a raid on the area and that the mines were meant to ambush the raiders. Union forces had already conducted several raids in the Northern Neck. This explanation, therefore, was perfectly plausible. The troops near Urbanna would not need much of a cover excuse. It was an exposed position, and it would be logical for the Confederacy to keep a small force there as a trip-wire and as a cadre around which to assemble local reserves. The presence of troops at Milford Station could be explained because of the importance of the station to communications with Richmond. There would be no apparent connection between them and the troops at Urbanna and along the Potomac in King George County.

To begin to implement the plan for the covert operation, it would be necessary to select people for several key positions and to make additional arrangements. The key positions would include the managers of the covert portion of the operations in King George County, Virginia, and in the vicinity of Urbanna; the man to lay the mine fields; and the commander to organize the troops providing security for the operation. In addition, it would be necessary to brief the Signal Corps personnel on essential elements of the scheme and position them to provide maximum support without destroying their ability to carry out their normal important duties. It would be necessary to arrange sufficient priority to get the personnel to lay the mines and divert the mines themselves from other locations where important military operations were under way. It would also be necessary to obtain the cooperation of key military authorities to make it possible to get the personnel for the security force without dislocating military plans and without tipping off federal intelligence to the existence of a special operation.

Rail transportation might prove essential to get the capture party out of the northern part of Virginia as rapidly as possible, and Richmond was only three hours by rail from Milford Station. The action party might well arrive with no advance notice and with Union troops in pursuit. In such a case, there could be no thought of having to wait while a locomotive came up from Richmond.

Although we do not know who actually commanded the troops in the field, the ranking man overseeing the military part of the operation appears to have been George Washington Custis Lee, Robert E. Lee's oldest son. The younger Lee was a graduate of West Point with a reputation for brains and good staff work. He had served as an aide to Jefferson Davis and in 1863 had been promoted to brigadier general and placed in command of the reserve forces in Richmond.[2] He continued to carry out special assignments of interest to the president, such as monitoring the preparation of John Taylor Wood's aborted raid on Point Lookout.[3] His main role in the capture of Lincoln seems to have been to make the troops available as a security force to guard the escape routes from the Virginia border to the vicinity of Richmond.

We do not know who first conceived the idea of the security force, but it was a brilliant one. The Union intelligence people had a sophisticated system for keeping track of Confederate order of battle, and the absence of several regiments from their normal stations would have been noticed by Colonel George H. Sharpe, chief of the Bureau of Military Information, Grant's intelligence specialist, within a matter of days or a week or two at the most. The unexplained absence of several units from their normal location would have immediately raised questions in the minds of the Union command, and efforts would have been made to find them and explain their current activity. In other words, if the Confederacy wished to keep its preparations for the capture of Lincoln secret, it could not afford to take regiments out of line to guard the escape route. Nevertheless, a considerable number of reliable troops were needed for the task.

The answer to this dilemma was both simple and elegant. It apparently was decided to draw from regiments recruited in the areas to be guarded. In that way, the troops could live at home and be supported by the local economy. The regiments themselves were to be moved to a portion of the line where their numbers would not be obvious. Once in position, the regiments would be left in the line, but large numbers of individuals would be sent home on leave. Once at home, the men would be organized into provisional units and put to work patrolling the area.

G. W. C. Lee's main role, therefore, seems to have been to assemble the right regiments at the right part of the Confederate lines where they could be stripped of manpower without the enemy noticing. It was a move that might well have been resisted by the regular commanders of brigades and divisions, whose success depended on having enough men on hand to win battles.

To get Custis Lee into the proper position to play his role in the operation it would be necessary to put him in command of regular troops instead of only the reserve forces. The easiest way to do that would be to make him a major general and put him in command of a division. As it happens, G. W. C. Lee's promotion to major general on 20 October 1864 was something of an anomaly.

One of the most important tasks for those managing any military establishment is that of selecting its general officers. In the Confederate government, the selection and promotion of generals was a constant chore for Jefferson Davis and his secretary of war. In total, 429 officers were selected by the Confederacy for promotion to general.[4] The number of officers selected tells us something about the workload carried by Davis and his secretary of war. The identity of the generals also tells us something about the problems that were of primary concern to the Confederate government from time to time. It was customary for Seddon and Davis to concern themselves with short ad hoc lists recommended by the various army commanders.

In this continuous grind of the promotion mill in 1864, there appear to have been two curious pauses. There were no promotions from 6 March to 8 April 1864. The gap coincided with the aftermath of Dahlgren's raid. Dahlgren was killed on the night of 2–3 March, and his papers were first published on 5 March. Presumably the promotions announced on 5 and 6 March were already decided. Thereafter, Davis and Seddon were probably too busy with the reactions to the raid and decisions about Confederate courses of action to pay attention to the routine of promotions until on 20 April they seemed to have gotten back into the normal routine.

On 20 September 1864, a normal list of combat generals was selected. On 23 September E. G. Lee, the commander of reserves in the Shenandoah Valley, was promoted. Thereafter, there were no further promotions until 20 October, when G. W. C. Lee was promoted to major general. On 27 October Moxley Sorrel, Longstreet's chief of state, was made a brigadier general, and on 1 November Cavalry General Thomas L. Rosser was promoted to major general and William Hay Fitzhugh Payne was selected to command a brigade of cavalry in Fitz Lee's division.

Thus, from 20 September to 1 November, only three general officers were selected or promoted, and all three were men with staff rather than combat backgrounds. Although Davis was out of Richmond for part of this time, the change in the flow of promotions clearly suggests that during late September and October 1864, Davis and Seddon were giving their attention to something other than the promotion of combat generals. The promotion of the two Lees during this period suggests that their attention may have been devoted instead to the planning of clandestine operations. This was exactly the time when Thomas Nelson Conrad was in Washington observing the movements of President Lincoln and Walter Bowie was operating in southern Maryland. It was the time when much planning would have had to take place to allow some of the events of the following December and January to occur.

On 16 October 1864, General Lee asked General William N. Pendleton, his chief of artillery, to make a thorough inspection of the defenses in the Chaffin's Farm sector. General Pendleton noted in a letter home that they were in good condition.

On the same day Lee and Davis had a long meeting, which involved a look at the defenses and ended at night with both men at Lee's headquarters at Chaffin's Farm. Presumably Pendleton could have made a verbal report of his inspection to them and may have been included in some of their discussions.

It was only natural that both Davis and Lee would have been interested in the defenses at Chaffin's. Slightly over two weeks earlier, those defenses had been assaulted in strength by the Union. In view of the role played by troops assigned to this sector in later phases of the operation against Lincoln, however, it is tempting to think that the basic concept for their use was already being developed. It is possible that this was the meeting between the two men, mentioned in Lee's letter to Davis on 25 October, in which the two discussed Kensey Johns Stewart and his proposed clandestine operation.

Pendleton's involvement would be normal in a strictly military sense, but he turned up again in early December, when Davis, Seddon, Mosby, and General E. G. Lee may have been discussing clandestine operations in preparation for the latter's departure for Canada. It is possible that General Robert E. Lee could have used Pendleton as his liaison with the clandestine operation. Lee trusted Pendleton, and the latter's status as an Episcopal minister would have been convenient if Lee were concerned about questions of the ethics involved in the operation.

At the same time, Pendleton might have been most willing to associate himself with an operation that, in his eyes, would have resulted in righteous judgment against a supreme evildoer. Pendleton's feelings about Lincoln could not have been very good, and they probably worsened as time went by. Pendelton felt strongly enough about the issues of the war to serve in uniform as a fighting soldier instead of in his religious capacity. In June 1864, the houses of several of his close friends and neighbors were burned by Union troops while General Hunter's forces occupied Lexington. Pendleton's house escaped destruction, but his family was outraged at the conduct of the federal forces. In September 1864, Pendleton's only son, Lieutenant Colonel "Sandy" Pendleton, was mortally wounded at the battle of Fisher's Hill in the Shenandoah Valley. Doubtless Pendleton was well aware that Sandy's life was at risk, but knowing such a fact rationally is not nearly so strong an influence as feeling the actual loss. In December Pendleton's ailing civilian brother, with whom he was very close, died as a result of his treatment at the hands of Union troops. He was living in the Northern Neck and was arrested and forced to walk to Fredericksburg in the winter weather. With this background, it would not be surprising to find that Pendleton shared the views of Stewart, Cameron, Gatewood, and other Episcopal ministers concerning Lincoln's guilt.

In October 1864, General Lee asked for Lieutenant Jed Hotchkiss to come from General Early's army in the Shenandoah to see him at his headquarters outside of Richmond. On the twenty-third, Hotchkiss traveled by train to Richmond and reached Lee's quarters at 11:00 P.M. For several hours, Lee questioned Hotchkiss about recent events in the Valley (the Battle of Cedar Creek had been fought a few days before) and discussed other undisclosed matters. Hotchkiss spent the next day inspecting the fortifications from Chaffin's Bluff just north of the James River to Fort Gilmer. On the twenty-fifth, he toured the lines again with General Ewell and reported to Lee again, presumably on the results of his survey.[5]

That area had been threatened when Union forces captured Fort Harrison on 29–30 September, but the lines had been strengthened since then and Union attention had turned elsewhere. Presumably General Lee wanted to get another expert opinion on the condition of the fortification in that section without making a big to-do about it.

On Sunday, 23 October 1864, General Lee spent a large part of the day in Richmond. About that time he appears to have had a discussion with the Reverend K. J. Stewart about a mysterious project. On 25 October he wrote a letter to Jefferson Davis commenting somewhat adversely on Stewart's ability to carry out the project in question.[6] On the same day, in a letter to his wife, he mentioned Custis Lee's health but not his recent promotion.[7]

The segment of the line inspected by Hotchkiss was eventually taken over by Custis Lee as commander of a new division. It was the sector occupied by the units that were to furnish most of the manpower for the force guarding the escape routes. The basic decisions about the establishment of that security force appear to have been made in late October 1864. On 24 October, General Wade Hampton, the successor to J. E. B. Stuart as commander of the Cavalry Corps, wrote to General R. E. Lee concerning the strength of the corps and measures that might be taken to improve it: "The Ninth Virginia [Cavalry Regiment] is already full, though many desire to join it still. As many men will be retired from disability from the regiment soon, I respectfully recommend that authority may be granted to Col. Beale [commander of the Ninth Virginia Cavalry] to receive additional recruits so as to fill his regiment to the maximum."[8] On the surface, this sounds as if there had been a medical survey of the troops in the Ninth and that many had been found to be unfit for service. There is, however, no evidence of such a survey and no indication in the service records of the individuals in the regiment that many of them were unfit for duty.

The letter probably meant that in late October 1864 it was contemplated that the men would be sent home to man the security force under the cover of a physical disability. As it turned out, it appears that they were sent home on leave instead. This had a less final ring to it and would allow the individuals to return to duty when their special assignment was finished.

On 5 November 1864 the Confederate War Department submitted a voucher to the Treasury Department for $250,000 to be issued to Captain George Barksdale, a quartermaster paymaster in Richmond. The voucher cited "Pay of the Army" as the purpose of the funds and stated as justification: "These funds are needed to pay officers and soldiers arriving at the post [Richmond] and going on furlough and who cannot be detained."[9] This voucher was without precedent. Barksdale most recently had been engaged in the payment of returned Confederate prisoners of war. The sum was sufficiently large to have covered the payroll of about fifteen hundred officers and men for a period of six months. The justification quoted above almost exactly describes the procedure actually followed in setting up the security force.

It was apparently decided to put Conrad in charge of the covert operations part of the King George–Milford route. He had already been involved on the Maryland side and thus would know something of the conditions where the action party would be operating when it reached the Potomac. Davis trusted him, and his background as a chaplain would give him moral authority as well.[10]

As a second in command, Conrad was given Lieutenant Mortimer B. Ruggles, son of Brigadier General Daniel Ruggles, who had commanded the Virginia forces in the Fredericksburg area in 1861.[11] The Ruggles home was Friedland, a large house less than four miles from the camp Conrad established on the Potomac shore. Ruggles was also related to the Hooes, one of the leading families of King George County. He could be of considerable help in any matter involving the local population. He had been an aide to his father but resigned that position with the declared intention of joining Mosby's Rangers.[12]

Two experienced officers of the Signal Corps were also assigned to Mosby's command, and the timing and location of their assignments suggest that their skills were needed because of the role the partisans might be called on to play in the capture of Lincoln. General Longstreet's signal officer, Captain Jacob H. Manning, was sent to Mosby's headquarters in Loudoun County, Virginia, and Lieutenant James Carey was sent to the portion of Mosby's battalion stationed in the Northern Neck.[13]

To understand the probably significance of Conrad's camp in the total operation, it is necessary to establish its approximate location. He consistently refers to it as being near Boyd's Hole, a landing site for a ferry between Virginia and Maryland in the colonial period. The Potomac between Mathias Point and the mouth of Potomac Creek, where the river bends to the north, is bordered on the Virginia side by a sandy bluff or hills about 100 to 120 feet in height. In some places the land drops steeply to the water, in other places the hills sit back a few hundred yards from the water. The hills are cut by a few small creeks whose mouths provide shelter and an access route through the hills for people coming ashore in small boats. Boyd's Hole is one of the larger of these creek mouths, but it was not big enough to support any sizable amount of traffic, and its use was dwindling. Its physical layout and relative isolation would have made it an excellent location for an unobserved landing by the action party and a captive Lincoln.

In general, the hills along the Potomac were not thickly populated. A few large houses sat either on the water's edge or high on the hills, where they could get a good view. There were a few small farms, but the area was relatively isolated from the main roads and the main population of King George County.

Conrad's naming of Boyd's Hole as the location of his camp merely used the best-known name in the area. Boyd's Hole could have been the planned landing place, but it could not have been the exact location of Conrad's camp. Elsewhere in his writings, he says that he could exchange signals with Lieutenant Cawood, which means he was in the high ground somewhere near Boyd's Hole. Nearby was Clifton, the home of John Tayloe V and John Tayloe VI, who figure elsewhere in this book.

At this location, it would have been fairly simple to build an observation platform in the trees from which one could see up the Potomac for several miles. From this same location, it also would have been possible to see the knoll behind Cawood's camp on Mathias Point. One purpose for locating a camp in this particular area would be to extend the range of the Confederate observation system that reported the approach of Union gunboats. This would enhance the safety of the crossings from both Cawood's and Sergeant Brogden's camps. Observation at that location would also give warning to mine-laying parties in the river below. Not only could Conrad warn Cawood of ships coming down the river, but Cawood could alert Conrad to ships coming upriver. In that way, mine-laying parties could work in daylight and pull for shore when an enemy was sighted. The gunboats would find only an empty river.

Compared to the Nanjemoy–King George–Milford route, overseen by Conrad, there is very little direct information available on the Patuxent-Urbanna route aside from the work by Lieutenant Blackford and his mapping party. A likely candidate to be involved in this route, however, appears to have been Lieutenant Colonel Fleet William Cox, formerly of the Fortieth Virginia Infantry Regiment.

As described in an earlier chapter, Cox was a native of Westmoreland County and a VMI alumnus of 1849, a classmate of Benjamin F. Ficklin and Robert Gatewood. In the early days of the war, he had been stationed in King George County and, because he had a sweetheart in Maryland, he had become involved with the clandestine passage of mail across the Potomac. In 1863, he lost an eye at the Battle of Chancellorsville and thereafter did not serve in normal troop duty.

When the expedition to free the prisoners at Point Lookout was organized in 1864, Cox went with Colonel John Taylor Wood, the commander of the project, as an observer for General Bragg. He therefore had had some experience with clandestine operations and was familiar with the Chesapeake area involved in the Patuxent-Urbanna route.

Cox formally retired to the invalid corps on 2 February 1865, which may have been a way to justify his presence in the Urbanna area. He was paroled in Northumberland County on 12 May 1865 but was promptly arrested and held in prison until 28 June 1865 because he had commanded a small group of Confederate irregulars operating in the Northern Neck (possibly a reference to the security force).[14]

The choice of the man to install the mine fields fell on Lieutenant Beverly Kennon, Jr., son of Commodore Beverly Kennon, who was killed in 1844 in the accidental explosion of a gun on board a ship in the Potomac. In 1842, the elder Kennon had married for the second time. His bride was Britannia Peter, the daughter of one of the richest families in the District of Columbia and a cousin of Mrs. Robert E. Lee. The family owned Tudor Place, which still stands in stately splendor in the midst of Georgetown. After her husband's death, Mrs. Kennon continued to live in Georgetown as a widow lioness of Washington society.[15] The younger Kennon was raised by his mother's relatives in Norfolk rather than by his stepmother in Georgetown, but it is interesting to note that Mrs. Kennon was a friend of the family of Confederate General Lindsay Lomax, whose sister was the wife of Thomas Green, who provided a safe house for Conrad on some of his visits to Washington.[16] Kennon had been in Richmond in August 1864.[17] There is no evidence concerning his activity at that time, but he was available if planning for the mine fields were under way that early.

As a result of the move of Grant's army to the lines around Richmond and Petersburg in May and June 1864, the Confederate government apparently decided to mine the James River as part of an overall scheme of defense. The laying of mine fields would help the small Confederate James River Squadron prevent the Union fleet from moving closer to Richmond.

On 7 July 1864, General Gabriel J. Rains chief of the Confederate Torpedo Bureau—the army organization responsible for laying mines—wrote to Davis: "Pursuant to instruction I have the honor to state that two light boats, about twenty-five feet long, such as could be carried on a wagon truck, four wagons to carry the boats and torpedoes, and the inclosed detail of men, adept in this business, with twelve oarsmen, are required to prosecute successfully our enterprise against the enemy in the James River."[18] According to these figures, two boats could be expected to lay mine fields large enough to shut the James River, and each boat would be manned by six oarsmen with additional crew to handle the mines.

Shortly afterward, the mining operations began under the command of Captain E. Pliny Bryan of Maryland. He overcame various logistical problems to start operations on 14 July, but four days later he reported that his group had been interrupted by a Union vessel and that he had lost two boats and twelve torpedoes.[19]

This disaster and Bryan's untimely death on 30 September 1864 apparently caused the Confederates to give up temporarily their plans to mine the James River. On 10 October 1864, however, President Davis met with General Rains.[20] One result of this meeting was a decision to train army personnel to use "subterra" mines and employ mines aggressively against enemy land forces, presumably to avoid a repetition of the recent loss of Fort Harrison. Decisions also appear to have been made at about this time to proceed with the plan to mine the James River and to approve General Lee's recommendation that Mosby's Forty-third Battalion of Virginia Cavalry should be furnished with mines and trained to use them behind enemy lines.

The mining of the James River was assigned to Lieutenant Beverly Kennon. On 29 October 1864, the commander of the Confederate James River Squadron directed the CSS *Virginia* to furnish Kennon with men to lay torpedoes. The work apparently proceeded without undue delay. On 7 December, the Confederate navy advised the army that as of 4 December, Kennon had emplaced a field of seventeen spar torpedoes and had located a large electric torpedo in another position.[21] This appears to have concluded Kennon's work on the James River.

In the meantime, on 22 November 1864, Commander Foxhall A. Parker, commander of the Union Potomac River Flotilla, reported that he had been informed on "undoubted Authority" that Kennon had been appointed torpedo officer for the Rappahannock and neighboring rivers.[22]

The time was now approaching when it would be necessary to begin to lay the mine fields to guard the escape routes. To piece the story together, it is necessary to go back to the accounts contained in the various versions of Conrad's story and try to connect them with events that are documented by other sources.

The Union appears to have had a secret line for the passage of information, agents, and sympathizers that ran from Richmond to the vicinity of Fredericksburg and from there through King George County to the ships of the Potomac River Flotilla. One of the principal people passing information through this line was Samuel Ruth, superintendent of the Richmond, Fredericksburg, and Potomac Railroad—the very line that would have to carry a captive

President Lincoln to Richmond. In the Fredericksburg area a former town policeman, John Timberlake, and Isaac Silver, a farmer in Stafford County, appear to have been the main Union agents.[23]

A glimpse of the operations of this line is contained in a letter dated 10 November 1864 addressed to Lieutenant Colonel T. S. Bowen of the Union Army:

> A scout has just arrived who left the house of our Agent at twelve oclock last night. He reports as follows:
>
> The enemys Cavalry is scouring the Country, in the vicinity South of Fredericksburg. for Conscripts and all taken are being sent to Early, who is now at New Market. We could learn nothing as to number of troops sent to reinforce Early. The rebels are taking up the rail road iron between Fredericksburg & Aquia and removing it to Hamiltons Crossing.
>
> This scout, McEnearny expresses his mortification that he is unable to furnish any satisfactory intelligence, but says nothing can now be obtained from the "Old Man", he being so closely watched that he dares not make any effort to learn of the enemys movements. He—McEnearny—is of the opinion that a new line of communication should be established—that known as the "upper route" would be best—and thinks it would be advisable to engage the services of a young lady, now living at Fredericksburg I believe, who has formerly been employed in the secret service with the Army of the Potomac. The scouts having been seen last night by a small body of rebels do not deem it safe to return upon another trip before next Saturday week.[24]

The "Old Man" is probably Silver, who was fifty-five years old. The "young lady" may have been Frances Byrd Turner Dade, the twenty-five-year-old widow of Lucien Dade, who had inherited Spring Hill about eight miles east of Fredericksburg and Boyd's Hole, a farm located near Conrad's camp on the shore of the Potomac.[25]

If indeed Frances Dade was the person in question, and if the Union did try to recruit her for a new assignment, it proved to be bad luck. Captain Conrad apparently was alerted to the existence of the Union line. Conrad appears to have gone to Richmond to discuss the matter with Seddon. Uncovering the line might well create problems in King George County, an area that should not be brought to the undue attention of the Union if the Lincoln operation were to be carried out. Seddon, however, seems to have directed Conrad to inquire further into the matter.

Seddon's diary-keeping clerk, John B. Jones, entered in his diary the text of a letter on 19 December. To maintain some semblance of security, Jones omitted the names of the author and addressee:

A letter from Mr. —— to—— dated Richmond, December 17th, 1864, says: "I have the honor to report my success as most remarkable and satisfactory. I have ascertained the whole Yankee mail line, from the gun boats to your city, with all the agents save one. You will be surprised when informed, from the lowest to the highest class, the agents in your city, and most likely in your department, have yet to be discovered. This is as certain as what we have learned (his arrest, I mean), for the party in whose hands the mail is put coming from your city is known to us; and we have only to learn who gives him the mail, which can be done upon arrest, if not sooner, to know everything. What shall be done with the parties (spies, of course) when we are ready to act? If you ever intimate that trials are tedious, etc. the enemy seize citizens from some neighborhoods as hostages, when their emissaries are disturbed. I will dispatch, if it be authorized, and that will end the matter. The lady I spoke to you of is the fountainhead. What to do with females troubles me, for I dislike to be identified with their arrest."

I request that a good boat, with three torpedoes, and a man who understands working them, be sent to Milford to report to me at Edge Hill. Let the man be mum on all questions. I could meet him at Milford If I have the day (distance is twenty-five miles), with a wagon, to take him, torpedoes, and boat to the point required. I must be sure of the day."

Have the following advertisement published in Monday's papers:

"*Yankees Escaped $1000 Reward*—A Yankee officer and three prisoners escaped from prison on Thursday night, with important matter upon their persons. The above reward will be given for their detection." Let me hear from you through Cawood's line, upon receipt of this.

Respectfully, etc.——[26]

The letter was clearly from Conrad, and Seddon replied promptly. The text of the reply is given in *A Confederate Spy*, but Conrad apparently misdated the letter 20 December 1862. It read: "The officer instructed by the Secretary of the Navy to take up the boat and other articles required by you, has just reported himself as ready to proceed to Milford. I have directed him to go up the day after tomorrow, which will be next Thursday, as that, I presume will be the earliest day at which you can receive notice and have the wagon, etc., to receive him and his articles. Make every effort not to disappoint or delay him, as his presence here is important. Wishing you all success in your operation."[27] If one takes the text as genuine, "the day after tomorrow . . . Thursday," fits December

1864, not 1862. The text, of course, fits the sequence of events in 1864.

Lieutenant Beverly Kennon was the man selected to bring the torpedoes to King George County. On 8 December 1864, Kennon had drawn sixteen hundred pounds of gunpowder, one hundred detonators, and barrels to carry the powder from the Naval Laboratory in Richmond. The record notes that these items were to be used "for torpedoes." The standard "buoyant" torpedo used by the Confederacy carried eighty pounds of powder and five detonators. Kennon had drawn enough explosives to fill twenty such torpedoes. The navy's Torpedo Service built the body of the mines, the Naval Laboratory furnished the powder and detonators, and experts from the Torpedo Service then carried the bodies and the explosives to the point of use, where they would place the powder and detonators in the mines just before they were anchored in the water. These field-work locations were the "torpedo factories" that were found on shore on several occasions by Union scouting parties.[28]

On 22 December, the day Seddon had told Conrad to meet the train at Milford, the Naval Laboratory issued 150 pounds of powder in two barrels to be used for torpedoes. This issue was not directly identified with Kennon, but the date suggests that he might have drawn additional powder for the torpedoes to be used in Conrad's spy-fishing expedition.[29]

Seddon's planned timing for the meeting of Conrad and Kennon did not work, however. Kennon arrived, not on 22 December but on 24 December, and Conrad was not there. The Richmond, Fredericksburg, and Potomac Railroad paid its station crew $100 to work over Christmas, presumably to unload Kennon's gear, but Conrad had probably decided to spend Christmas elsewhere. The charge for unloading Kennon's mines at Milford clearly should have been paid by the Confederate government, yet in the records of the railroad there is no indication of the purpose for which the work was performed.[30] Judging from the surviving railroad records, there must have been an arrangement between the railroad and the government by which the railroad would be privately reimbursed for services the government did not wish to have on record.

Conrad and Kennon apparently did not follow through with Conrad's original idea to use "torpedoes" to disrupt the Union spy organization. In July 1865, Kennon wrote two moderately incoherent letters to the commander of the Potomac River Flotilla telling him that two torpedoes were buried in the yard of a house near the mouth of Potomac Creek.[31] A boat crew from the USS *Delaware*, led by Lieutenant J. H. Eldridge, located the mines and recovered them on 13 July 1865.

The officer who recovered the mines described them as "made of sheet copper, with a concave [sic] head and pointed at the lower end somewhat in the shape of nun buoy, about 2 feet 6 inches in length, and sufficiently large to hold 80 lbs of powder. At the lower end is a socket, by means of which the torpedo is attached to its anchor." The description goes on in considerable detail and outlines the buoyant torpedo widely used by the Confederates as an antiship mine.[32]

On 1 January 1865, Kennon sent a telegram to Seddon from Port Royal saying that he and Conrad had met and were proceeding to the Potomac. Clerk Jones noted in his diary for 4 January 1865 that "Lt. Beverly Kermon [probably a mistaken transcription of Kennon] writes from the Rappahannock that 'thus far (to Jan. 1st) our movements (in connection with Captain T. N. Conrad) are perfectly secret.' The next day he was to go to the Potomac. What has the Secretary sent him there for?"[33] Jones was aware of the 17 December letter asking for torpedoes, but he may not have seen Seddon's reply, and without knowing about that letter, he might not have been able to connect Kennon with that request. The original of Kennon's message in the National Archives agrees with Jones's rendition.

The mines recovered by Eldridge may have been two of those brought by Kennon on 24 December. It is possible that the torpedoes taken to the Potomac by Kennon were part of the group of twenty for which he drew powder on 8 December. Some of them may have been intended for the Potomac in any case, which would explain Seddon's readiness to approve Conrad's request. The ad hoc scheme might have involved placing a mine or two in places that would not be appropriate at a later date, but boats and other gear brought for this small operation could be used later for the main mining operation.

The change in plans for the torpedoes, however, may be explained in part by the following entry in Jones's diary: "A voluminous correspondence is going on between Mr. Conrad (secret agent to arrest disloyal men endeavoring to cross the Potomac) and Mr. Secretary Seddon. Mr. Foote, arrested by their great skill, has applied, indignantly, for a writ of *habeas corpus*. Thus, the time of our great dignitaries is consumed removing molehills, while mountains are looming up everywhere."[34]

Henry S. Foote was a former U.S. senator from Mississippi and a long and bitter enemy of Jefferson Davis. He served in the Confederate Congress as a representative from Tennessee and was a constant critic of the Confederate government. He tried to cross the Potomac into Maryland near Sergeant Brodgen's Signal Corps camp on 24 December 1864. When he was unable to cross, he went overland toward Washington through King George and Stafford counties, where he was arrested in early January 1865 and brought back to Richmond. On 17 January 1865, the Confederate Congres ordered him released. Later a majority of the Congress voted to expel him, and he was allowed to go North.[35] Since Foote passed close to Conrad's location, this may have enabled Conrad to alert Richmond. Foote's arrest may have diverted Conrad from his other activities for a time.

During the period that Kennon was beginning his mine-laying operation, the Confederates sent two detectives disguised as escaped Union officers up the "rat line" to the Potomac. Conrad intercepted them in King George County, and they revealed the details of the Union line's operation.[36]

With Foote out of the way, the Confederates proceeded on 20 January 1865 to arrest one F. W. E. Lohmann, a Richmond associate of Samuel Ruth. On 23 January they arrested Ruth himself. At about the same time, Silver and Timberlake were also arrested. The Union line from Richmond to the Potomac was thereby destroyed, but, unfortunately, the extent of Confederate knowledge of Union activity was also revealed. A suspicious Union intelligence officer might have concluded that the Confederates were particularly concerned about Union activity in the King George area. Such a suspicion, once aroused, could lead the Union to be especially watchful of that area. How could the Confederacy keep the Union line out of action but allay suspicion at the same time?

Long after the war, Ruth revealed the step that may have given the Confederates an escape from their dilemma. He made discreet inquiries among his captors to discern if it might be possible for him to buy his freedom. In due course he was informed that for a certain sum he could win his release. Ruth did not reveal the judge to whom this bribe was paid. Judge S. S. Baxter in Castle Thunder was in charge of cases of treason and disloyalty, and he or one of his assistants might have been the person involved. This event seems to be fairly well documented. What could it mean?

We have no reason to question the loyalty of Baxter or his assistants to the Confederacy or to suspect their honesty. Even the most venal person in this situation, however, would have been rash to accept a bribe. Ruth was a highly placed member of the Richmond business world. He had been uncovered by an agent who seemed to be a favorite of Jefferson Davis. Furthermore, the secretary of war was personally involved in the case, and the president might also have been consulted about it. Any man who took a bribe and released a prisoner in such a case on his own authority would be doomed for trouble. It is far more likely that Ruth's inquiry was reported immediately to Seddon or Davis or both.

The inquiry presented an excellent solution to the Confederates. Let Ruth pay a bribe and think he had bought his way out. He could then be released feeling that the Confederacy was not particularly interested in him or his past activities. In carrying out this course of action, the Confederates brought Mrs. Dade down from King George County to testify against Ruth and his cohorts. The hearing was postponed until 1 February 1865, and when it occurred, Mrs. Dade seemed to have forgotten what she had known earlier. She denied knowing anything about Ruth, and he was released. The Richmond papers were almost unanimous in giving this story a big play and pointing out that Ruth was a highly respected person and above suspicion.[37] Presumably the hearing had been delayed to allow time for Mrs. Dade to learn the new testimony that she was to give concerning Ruth.

Ruth appears to have believed that his release was the direct result of his bribe, and he continued to act as the superintendent of the Richmond, Fredericksburg, and Potomac Railroad. The Union rat line, however, no longer operated in King George County, and Conrad was free to turn his attention to his primary mission— preparing for the reception and forwarding of a captive President Lincoln. The Union did not forget Mrs. Dade, however. On 17 April 1865, the Potomac River Flotilla captured Conrad and sent him to prison in Washington. The same ship that captured Conrad then proceeded to Boyd's Hole and sent a party ashore to arrest Mrs. Dade.[38] They had an old score to settle with her.

While Conrad had been preoccupied with Foote and the Union rat line, Kennon had been busy with his torpedoes. We know that he left two buried near the mouth of Potomac Creek. These were probably intended to ambush the Union naval vessel meeting the rat line, but the arrest of the various members of the line destroyed the opportunity for an ambush. Conrad wrote in *A Confederate Spy* that the secretary of war had sent him a boat that was so large it could not be hidden properly. As a result, it was found and destroyed by a patrol from a ship of the Potomac River Flotilla. He added that the supplies also included a number of torpedoes and that "Lt. Kenyon [sic] who brought the outfit" helped them line the "creeks and coves of the vicinity" with explosives. In *The Rebel Scout* Conrad wrote that the mines were placed in the "two creeks nearest our quarters, which were among the largest on the Virginia shore," and added that they were picked up by the U.S. Navy after the end of the war. "Lt. Kenyon" was obviously Beverly Kennon.[39] Presumably the "two creeks" would have been Passapatanzy Creek and Chotank Creek, the major streams on each side of Boyd's Hole.

On 4 January the USS *Don* captured two torpedoes and two barrels of powder on the south shore of the Rappahannock about six miles from its mouth. We do not know that these were Kennon's torpedoes, but on 11 January, Kennon drew another 280 pounds of powder for torpedoes and on 12 January 1965, Lieutenant Daniel Trigg, CSN, was designated to command a party detailed from the Confederate ships *Virginia, Fredericksburg,* and *Richmond* for "special duty."[40]

From Conrad's description, the mines must have been placed fairly close to shore, outside of the main shipping lane. This would make sense because the mine field had to be defensive in nature. It could not have been intended to interfere with the main channel because, without an adequte force to watch it, the mine field would have been easy to sweep as soon as it was discovered. There would be no Confederate force in the area strong enough to defend the mine field from a serious attack.

Kennon and his sailors must have worked at the mine fields for some time. Presumably, they began with the first good weather, after the middle of January. ("Good" weather is considered to be a day with no snow, rain, sleet, or wind and a maximum temperature above 40°F.) According to the records of the U.S. Naval Observatory in Washington, this was probably Tuesday, 17 January. The following Friday, 20 January, was also probably a good day. Ten days of bad weather followed, but 30 January began four good days in a row. The tenth and eleventh of February were also probably good days. A very cold spell intervened from 17 to 24 February. There was then a streak of good weather, which was broken on 25 and 26 February and 2 March by rain. Between 17 January and 3 March, there was a total of twenty days when the weather may have been good enough to permit mining. This would have given time enough to plant a respectable mine field. A list of the officers of the James River Squadron prepared in Feburary 1865 shows Lieutenant Trigg and Midshipman Bartlett N. Johnson as still being on "expedition" with Kennon.[41]

In early March, the commander of the Potomac River Flotilla reported that landing parties of seventy-five men each had skirmished with "Mosby's Guerrillas" in Chotank Creek on 3 March and in Passapatanzy Creek on 5 March. In the latter site, they found and destroyed a large boat with rowlocks "muffled for night service."[42] The nearest Mosby guerrillas at that time were the men of Company C quartered in Westmoreland County, at least fifteen miles from the location of these skirmishes. (Most were actually at the far end of the county.) Both Mosby's men and Kennon's sailors were armed with pistols, and in all probability the men from the Potomac River Flotilla had been exchanging shots with the sailors in Kennon's group or with men from the security force for the Lincoln party's escape route. One boat was probably operating in the Rappahannock. The other boat operated out of the Passapatanzy and apparently was destroyed before it had completed its mission. It was necessarily a good-sized boat if it was being used to plant mines and carried a crew of eight or ten men. In all probability, this was the incident described by Conrad when he told of the destruction of the large boat provided by Secretary Seddon.

The Potomac River Flotilla's sweep on 3–5 March anticipated a larger operation which sent several boats from the flotilla up the Rappahannock on 6–7 March to launch a raid on Hamilton's Crossing a few miles from Fredericksburg. A large quantity of tobacco had been accumulated there, presumably for shipment through the blockade, and this raid destroyed the tobacco. No attempt was made to hold territory, however, and the Northern Neck reverted to its normal condition as a quasi no-man's-land. This condition was disturbed by two further incursions in March. One by Union soldiers at Kinsale, in Westmoreland County, was driven back by the vigorous and unexpected opposition of Mosby's men, and on 16–18 March a force of sailors landed in Mattox Creek at the opposite end of Westmoreland County and destroyed several boats and a "supply base."[43] Presumably, this latter raid involved Sergeant Brogden's camp and may have caused him to cease operations temporarily.

From reports of the Union navy concerning the presence in the Rappahannock area of "marines" from the ships of the James River Squadron, it would appear that in mid-March Kennon's group was planting mines about six miles above the mouth of the Rappahan-

nock.[44] This was the approximate location of the torpedoes captured by the Union navy in early January 1865.

Unfortunately for Kennon, the Union navy was watching the
Rappahannock closely in March and doubtless kept the mine-
laying team from making much progress. In any case, the Kennon
expedition ended its work near the end of March, and the sailors
rejoined their ships. After the ships were scuttled upon the evacuation of Richmond, the sailors became part of the naval contingent
in General Ewell's corps. Several of them were captured with that
corps at the Battle of Saylor's Creek on 6 April. Kennon was
purportedly with the remainder of the Army of Northern Virginia
at Appomattox Court House on 9 April.[45]

While Conrad and Kennon were worrying about a mine field,
John Wilkes Booth and others in southern Maryland had been
organizing their escape routes through that area. The key to one
escape route was a large boat hidden in Nanjemoy Creek in Charles
County, Maryland. The mouth of Nanjemoy Creek lay directly
opposite Chotank Creek. Boyd's Hole was only about three miles
upstream. On the west side of Chotank Creek was the main home
of Dr. Richard Henry Stuart, and on the east side was the home of
Dr. Abram Barnes Hooe. This is the area explored by Kensey Johns
Stewart in early October 1864.

Both were leading citizens of King George County. As mentioned
in Chapter 3, in December 1864, the Confederate Adjutant and
Inspector General's Office made an investigation of the Signal
Corps in the Northern Neck. (Conrad's camp was not among them
and therefore was not part of the regular Signal Corps.) Dr. Stuart
and Dr. Hooe were among the four local citizens interviewed concerning the conduct and reputation of Signal Corps personnel.

From Boyd's Hole or from Dr. Stuart's dock, there were connections by road to the ferry at Port Royal and from there to the
railroad at Milford Station about twenty-five miles as the roads of
1865 lay. With a fresh team of horses, President Lincoln's carriage
could have traveled that distance in five or six hours.

The escape boat was kept in Nanjemoy Creek. A neighbor was
Judge George Brent, whose house sat on the top of a 150-foot ridge
between Nanjemoy and Port Tobacco creeks, about a mile from the
Potomac. It has a spectacular view of the Potomac as far as Potomac Creek. The road that the Lincoln party would have to follow
to reach the boat led near the Brent farm. There is a local tradition
that Confederates used the Brent location as a signal station. There
is no indication that it was tied into Lieutenant Cawood's signal

system, but it is possible that the action party intended to exploit its visibility to the Virginia shoreline.

When the Lincoln party reached the vicinity of Nanjemoy Creek, a signal could have been made from the hill where Brent lived to alert the organization on the Virginia shore to expect the captive and his escort. If the mines were not already activated, they could have been activated at that time and horses harnessed to haul Lincoln's carriage. The escort party could have been prepared and a messenger sent ahead to Milford Station to get steam up in the locomotive waiting there. Brent's location would have been visible to most of the pickets along the shore of the Potomac. Therefore, most elements of the party along the Potomac could have received the alert simultaneously. The soldiers manning the pickets could have been told that the signal meant that the enemy raid was about to start. Only the persons at the landing need know the real meaning of the signal.

There is no direct evidence of the escape route via the Patuxent. Its existence must be inferred from other information—Lieutenant Blackford's mapping operation, Confederate soldiers guarding the route from Urbanna to Ashland, Booth's action on his escape from Washington, and Dr. Mudd's possible role in the plan. These items will be discussed in greater detail below. One other item that may be connected with the Patuxent route comes from the activities of an acting master in the Confederate navy named John Clibbon Brain.

Brain was born about 1840 in Gloucestershire, England, of a "good" family.[46] He was brought to America by his father in the late 1850s and developed an adventurous spirit at an early age. A less charitable view was that he developed many of the talents of a confidence man. He was arrested in Michigan City, Indiana, in September 1861 as a Confederate spy. He had so many different stories to explain his activities that it is difficult to establish what he was really doing at this stage of his career. He claimed British citizenship, however, and was released in Feburary 1862.[47]

Brain seems to have enlisted in the Confederate army shortly thereafter and was then transferred to the navy, which acquired many of its seamen by retraining men furnished by the army. He served on the CSS *Jamestown* and then in a naval battery on shore. From that dull routine he seems to have worked his way into clandestine activities in the North and in Canada. In the course of these activities, he acquired a fair amount of money by working a confidence game which involved the sale of subscriptions to a nonexistent railway guide. He visited relatives in England briefly and returned to America, where he organized a party -of Confederate sailors and was given letters of marque as a privateer. (These letters of marque appear to have been spurious. Perhaps Brain was the victim of a confidence game.) In December 1863, Brain and his party captured the SS *Chesapeake* and took her into a Canadian port, where she was recaptured by the U.S. Navy.

The *Chesapeake* affair involved some complicated diplomatic issues, but it made Brain something of a popular hero in the South. After a fling at blockade running through Wilmington, North Carolina, Brain and his party captured the SS *Roanoke* and took her to Bermuda. From there he returned to Richmond in time to serve briefly in the attempt of the Confederate navy to go down the James River on 23 January 1865.

After the war, Brain said that he left Richmond on his next assignment on 27 February 1865. This assignment resulted in the capture of a fast schooner, the *St. Mary's*, off the mouth of the Patuxent River in southern Maryland early in the morning of 1 April 1865. Brain was reported to be using a yawl when he captured the *St. Mary's*.[48] Brain took the *St. Mary's* to the Bahamas and then to Jamaica and eventually burned her at sea.

After his return to the United States, Brain spent some time in prison for piracy and then devoted much of the remainder of his life to exploiting his credentials as a hero of the Confederate navy. Nobody has ever connected Brain to the assassination of President Lincoln, but the timing and geography of his last mission are suggestive.

If the Confederate navy had to supply a boat to carry Lincoln and the action party from the Patuxent to the Rappahannock, Brain might have appeared to be an ideal choice as its skipper. The Confederate navy may not have been aware of the questionable side of Brain's character, knowing him as a man who had successfully captured two enemy ships and had experience in clandestine operations. With such a background, he might have seemed a logical choice for a clandestine assignment that required seamanship and might involve some fighting.

If Brain and his party were to provide an escape boat in the Patuxent, the party could have gone by rail to Milford and then overland to Sergeant Brogden's camp near Oak Grove. From there they could have gone to the Maryland shore, where an agent such as Captain William L. Sheirburn of Newport, Maryland, might have arranged to provide them with a boat in the Patuxent. Sheirburn owned several work boats in the Potomac and was identified in a Confederate cipher message along with Thomas Jones as a contact of the Signal Corps system in Maryland.

An alternative would have been for Brain to take one of John Taylor Wood's wagon-mounted whaleboats, or something like it, and sail from Urbanna in the Rappahannock to the Patuxent. A yawl rig would have been appropriate for a whaleboat. The shores of the Patuxent were not heavily populated, and there were several places near Aquasco in Prince George's County and near Patuxent City in Charles County where a boat and party could remain hidden for some time. The most direct route to these locations from Washington led past Surratt's tavern and Dr. Mudd's house. In either alternative, Brain and his party could have been in a boat in a hiding place in the Patuxent as early as 3 or 4 March 1865. This timing fits Booth's efforts to capture Lincoln in early to mid-March.

While Kennon was collecting his sailors to battle ice and cold winds to lay mines in the Rappahannock and the Potomac, Conrad wrote his 10 January letter to Seddon asking for more money to support his operation. This letter started a chain reaction in Richmond which clearly established the personal involvement of President Davis, Secretary of State Benjamin, and Secretary of War Seddon in supporting Conrad's operation.

The first record of the reaction to Conrad's request for money appears to be a letter from Benjamin to Seddon on 16 January 1865: "I return your two notes about Secret Service funds, one with the endorsement of [the] President—there is but one way in which these funds can be given you—it is necessary to address to the President a request that you be furnished with the money, and the exact sum must be stated so that you can draw a requisition—The money will then be furnished *you* by me for the use of your subordinates—if you prefer not to leave your receipts on file in my Department, they will be returned to you on your replacing them with the receipts of the subordinates to whom you transfer the money."[49] In other words, Benjamin was telling Seddon that he could issue money only if the president personally approved the uses for which it was intended. This is a tutorial on procedure, and it underlines the fact that no clandestine project got funds without the personal approval of Jefferson Davis.

There is no record of Seddon's request for funds for Conrad, but there is a copy of a request that he made on 16 January to President Davis for Secret Service funds for the use of General William J.

Hardee, one of the Confederate commanders facing General Sherman. This was probably one of the notes returned by Benjamin. Seddon undoubtedly wrote the request to Davis for money for Conrad because the Confederate Department of War files contain the following letter to Seddon from disbursing clerk William J. Bromwell on 25 January: "I have the honor by direction of the Secretary of State to inform you that the gold for General Hardee and for Mr. Conrad, requested in your letter of the 18th instant to the President, is now ready and will be held subject to your order."[50] It is clear that Seddon did request money for Conrad from Davis and that Davis personally approved the request. There can be no doubt that Davis also approved Conrad's mission.

It seems likely that Conrad was in Richmond to collect his funds. In a letter to the president from Conrad dated merely January 1865, he said: "I have had the honor of making three successful trips to Washington upon secret service for our government. The first trip I had the honor to report to your Excellency, the second and third to the Honorable Secretary of War. I am now anxious to devote myself wholly to this field of labor." Conrad continued, describing his success in recruiting sources in Washington and how he would recruit young men to form a "club," which would organize sources in each military department in Washington to collect information on military movements. He said: "Heretofore, I have been acting for the War Department on special trips on special occasions. I wish now to resign my chaplaincy and to devote myself exclusively and wholly to this field." At the bottom of the letter he added a note in pencil: "Could the President be seen tonight. I have to leave on tomorrow. T.N.C."[51] It is possible that Conrad was in Richmond as a result of the arrest of Samuel Ruth. He may have been brought to town to help settle the matter of how to handle the Ruth case with a minimum of disruption to the plan to capture Lincoln. It is also possible that he was there because of the maturation of the plan to capture Lincoln.

In this letter Conrad says that he had made three trips to Washington. Presumably, the first was in April 1864, when he was working on the Burnside problem. The second would have been in September 1864, when he set up his special information net, and the third may have been the trip referred to in the 10 January 1865 letter. The first trip for Seddon is probably the one Conrad described in *A Confederate Spy* as being devoted to planning to capture Lincoln.

In reviewing the correspondence involving Davis, Seddon, and their agents, Conrad and Kennon, it is worthwhile recalling that the officials were giving personal attention to the matter during a time of great turmoil. General Hood threw away his army in frontal attacks at Franklin and Nashville, Tennessee, and news of the magnitude of this disaster arrived in Richmond in late December. Davis's administration was under heavy political attack, and as early as December there was talk of Seddon's resignation as a result of this pressure. He did finally resign on 1 February 1865. In addition to the political pressure, there was constant pressure to look after the needs of the army in the trenches around Richmond and Petersburg.

In addition to all these unsettling influences, General Sherman had cut loose from his supply line in Georgia and had marched to Savannah. Although the loss of Savannah was a blow, and the South was outraged by the conduct of his march through Georgia, there were many in Richmond who regarded his move as an opportunity for the Confederacy. If Sherman could be caught where he could not be reinforced, he might be defeated, and if one of the Union's two major armies were defeated, there was a good chance that northern war weariness would lead to a negotiated settlement of the conflict.

With all of these influences at work, Davis and Seddon could not devote much time to covert operations. That they did devote as much effort to Conrad and Kennon as the correspondence shows would indicate that they considered the matter to be of some importance.

On the basis of the evidence reviewed so far, it would appear that the decision to mount an operation to capture President Lincoln must have been made early enough to enable the selection of key members of the organization to begin by late July or early August 1864. By early October, the detailed information on the president's movements and guards and the layout of Washington needed for further planning must have begun to flow from Conrad's network.

By late January 1864, the mining operations must have been far enough along for Kennon to estimate a "ready" date. This means that the general outline of the action plan must have been in existence for weeks or months. The time had come for the Confederate government to decide if the operation should be carried through and if it were successful, how it would be exploited.

Notes

ABBREVIATIONS
NA   National Archives
OR   U.S. War Department, *The War of the Rebellion: A Compilation of the Official Records of the Union and Confederate Armies.* 128 vols. Washington, D.C.: U.S. Government Printing Office, 1880–1901.
ORN   U.S. Navy Department, *Official Records of the Union and Confederate Navies in the War of the Rebellion.* 30 vols. Washington, D.C.: U.S. Government Printing Office, 1894–1914.
RG   Record Group

1. *ORN,* Ser. 1, vol. 5, p. 429; see also Chapter 7, above.

2. G. W. C. Lee, Compiled Service Record, NA.

3. Jefferson Davis, *Jefferson Davis, Constitutionalist: His Letters, Papers and Speeches,* ed. Dunbar Rowland, 10 vols. (Jackson: Mississippi Department of Archives and History, 1923), 6:287; see also Chapter 6, above.

4. Ezra J. Warner, *Generals in Gray: Lives of the Confederate Commanders* (Baton Rouge: Louisiana State University Press, 1959).

5. Archie P. McDonald, *Make Me a Map of the Valley* (Dallas: Southern Methodist University Press, 1973), p. 241.

6. Robert E. Lee, *Lee's Dispatches: Unpublished Letters of General Robert E. Lee, CSA, to Jefferson Davis and the War Department of the Confederate States of America, 1862–1865,* ed. Douglas Southall Freeman and Grady McWhiney (New York: Putnam, 1957), p. 302.

7. R. E. Lee, *The Wartime Papers of R. E. Lee,* ed. Clifford Dowdey and Louis H. Manarin (New York: Bramhall House, 1961), p. 865.

8. *OR,* Ser. 1, vol. 42, pt. 3, p. 1162.

9. Requisitions on the Treasury Department for Funds, Chap. IX, vol. 84, RG 109, NA.

10. K. J. Stewart to Davis, 30 November, 12 December 1864, Chap. VII, vol. 24, pp. 58–65, RG 109, NA. See Richard E. Beringer, Herman Hattaway, Archer Jones, and William N. Still, Jr., *Why the South Lost the Civil War* (Athens: University of Georgia Press, 1986), pp. 82–102, for a discussion of the importance of religion in the South's attitude toward the war.

11. Thomas Nelson Conrad, *A Confederate Spy* (New York: J. S. Ogilvie, 1892), pp. 102–7.

12. M. B. Ruggles, Compiled Service Record, NA.

13. Jacob Hite Manning and James Carey, Compiled Service Records, NA; see also Evelyn Ward, *Children of Bladensfield* (New York: Viking Press, 1978), pp. 106, 121, for a description of Carey's stay in the Northern Neck.

14. Fleet William Cox, Compiled Service Record, NA.

15. *Records of the Columbia Historical Society* (Washington, D.C., 1901), 4:240.

16. Conrad, *Confederate Spy,* p. 51.

17. James D. Ferguson, Diary, Munford-Ellis Papers, Thomas Munford Division, Duke University Library, Durham, N.C.

18. *OR,* Ser. 1, vol. 40, pt. 3, p. 747.

19. Ibid., pt. 1, p. 795.

20. Ibid., vol. 42, pt. 3, p. 1181.

21. *ORN,* Ser. 1, vol. 11, pp. 748, 777.

22. Ibid., vol. 5, p. 493.

23. Meriwether Stuart, "Samuel Ruth and General R. E. Lee," *Virginia Magazine of History and Biography* 71 (1963): 91.

24. George K. Leet to Bowen, 10 November 1864, Miscellaneous Records of the Army of the Potomac, Boxes 8–13, RG 343, NA.

25. King George County Deeds and Wills, King George County Court House, King George, Va.

26. John B. Jones, *A Rebel War Clerk's Diary*, ed. Howard Swiggett, 2 vols. (New York: Old Hickory Book Shop, 1935), 2:358. This advertisement was published in the *Richmond Enquirer*, 20 December 1864. We have been unable to find it in any other issue.

27. Conrad, *Confederate Spy*, p. 38.

28. "Ammunition Record of the C.S. Naval Laboratory," WH-1975-122, Washington Headquarters Museum, Newburgh, N.Y.; *ORN*, Ser. 1, vol. 5, pp. 575, 429, 430, 497.

29. "Ammunition Record of the C.S. Naval Laboratory."

30. Records of the Richmond, Fredericksburg and Potomac Railroad, December 1864, Virginia Historical Society, Richmond.

31. *ORN*, Ser. 1, vol 5, p. 577.

32. Ibid., p. 575.

33. *OR*, Ser. 1, vol. 46, pt. 2, p. 1000; Jones, *Rebel War Clerk's Diary*, 2:376.

34. Jones, *Rebel War Clerk's Diary*, 2:388.

35. Howard C. Westwood, "Henry Foote Skedaddles," *Civil War Times Illustrated*, December 1981; p. 38.

36. Thomas Nelson Conrad, *The Rebel Scout* (Washington, D.C.: National Publishing Company, 1904), pp. 134–38.

37. Stuart, "Ruth and Lee," pp. 96–98.

38. Log of USS *Don*, Records of the Bureau of Naval Personnel, RG 24, NA.

39. Conrad, *Confederate Spy*, p. 39; Conrad, *Rebel Scout*, pp. 140–41.

40. *ORN*, Ser. 1, vol. 11, pp. 793–94.

41. Ibid., vol. 12, p. 187.

42. Ibid., vol. 5, pp. 520–21.

43. *OR*, Ser. 1, vol. 46, pt. 2, pp. 891, 901, 954 (there are also various accounts of this skirmish in local histories and in Ward, *Children of Bladensfield*, p. 108); *ORN*, Ser. 1, vol. 5, p. 535.

44. *ORN*, Ser. 1, vol. 5, p. 534.

45. Morning Reports of the Old Capitol Prison in Washington, D.C., RG 383, NA. Kennon is not listed in the index to vol 15 of the *Southern Historical Society Papers*, which attempted to list all men paroled at Appomattox. It is possible that he later claimed to have been paroled there or used a forged parole form.

46. David Hay and Joan Hay, *The Last of the Confederate Privateers* (New York: Crescent Books, 1977), pp. 5–11.

47. *OR*, Ser. 2, vol. 2, pp. 711–13.

48. Hay and Hay, *Last of the Confederate Privateers*, p. 153; U.S. Navy Department, *U.S. Civil War Naval Chronology, 1861–1865* (Washington, D.C.: U.S. Government Printing Office, 1971), pt. 5, p. 73.

49. Letters Received by the Confederate Secretary of War, M-437, reel 146, frames 294–301, RG 109, NA.

50. Ibid.

51. Jefferson Davis Papers, Duke University Library.

15

The Action Team

In Chapter 12 we left John Wilkes Booth in room 150 at the St. Lawrence Hall, Montreal. He signed in at 9:30 P.M. on 18 October 1864. There is no way to learn the names of all those persons Booth saw during his ten-day stay. The city had a growing contingent of Confederates of many hues. Some were well fixed and lived with families in rented houses. Others lived in hotels. The less affluent lived in cheap boardinghouses. There were also former prisoners of war scrounging for meals and a bed. And, of course, there were others, hard-eyed and secretive, often using aliases, who came and went on mysterious Confederate business. The common thread was a fanatical hatred for all things Yankee.

The St. Lawrence Hall was the unofficial Confederate clearinghouse and headquarters in Montreal. Here one could pick up the latest war news, get mail from home, meet friends, and conduct whatever business was at hand. When Booth registered there he dropped into a milieu of "Little Richmond." He must have felt at home.

Booth's Montreal visit is usually noted in historical accounts without analysis. To assume that Booth went to Montreal merely to ship his theatrical wardrobe through the blockade to the South is naive in the extreme, like believing in leprechauns. Federal detectives investigating Lincoln's assassination did not believe it for a moment. They were certain that Booth went there in connection with a conspiracy aimed at Lincoln. From Samuel Arnold's confession they had evidence that the plan to capture Lincoln had been conceived at least six weeks before Booth's Montreal trip. From Joseph Simonds they knew that Booth closed out his oil operations in late September. But knowing something and being able to prove it with competent evidence are not the same. The federals could not quite put it together.

Pressed by Stanton to get on with a trial, Judge Advocate General Joseph Holt adopted a tactical approach: he would downplay schemes to kidnap Lincoln and focus on the assassination. This strategy had merit because any attempt by armed men to capture Lincoln could have ended in his death. In any case, Holt and his advisers simply rolled everything into one conspiracy—to assassinate—and asserted that its origins were in Canada and Richmond. The trial strategy was flawed by questionable testimony on key points, which allowed the Confederates and their Copperhead allies to launch an effective disinformation campaign after the war. It would have read as follows: "John Wilkes Booth? Not one of ours, certainly. An actor fellow wasn't he? Obviously a madman. Everybody knows that the death of Lincoln was the worst thing that could have happened to a defeated South. And look at the trial testimony of Sandford Conover (Charles A. Dunham), Godfrey Hyams, Dr. James B. Merritt, and Richard Montgomery. Perjury, rank perjury."[1]

Repeated ad infinitum this became truth. It obscured the Confederacy's plans—legitimate acts of war—to make Lincoln a prisoner and Booth's role in one such plan. Thus an old political ploy became useful: cover one transgression by denying a different one.

No evidence has been found to show that Booth met with either Jacob Thompson or Clement C. Clay during his Montreal visit. These two were in Quebec City on 14 October seeking an interview with Governor General Lord Monck. He refused to see them. They planned to leave there the next day.[2] They would, of course, pass through Montreal, Thompson en route to Toronto and Clay en route to St. Catharines. Clay was back in St. Catharines by 19 October. Thompson arrived at the Queens Hotel in Toronto on 21 October. Where he was from the time he left Quebec on 15 October and the time he arrived back in Toronto has not been learned.[3]

Shipping a theatrical wardrobe does not take ten days. Federal investigators therefore wanted to know who Booth saw in Montreal and what they talked about. The trail was cold, local citizens were largely uncooperative, and the police were hostile. The investigation came up short. Now, after more than a century, researchers are in a better position to collect the bits and pieces, to study the background of the protagonists, and to evaluate.

There is solid evidence that Booth was in personal contact with two Confederate agents during his Montreal visit. They were Patrick C. Martin and George N. Sanders. Martin, a native of New York, had been a Baltimore liquor dealer. A letter in the War Department files, dated 24 July 1862, protested government dealings with his firm and described him as "an uncompromising rebel of the 19th of April notoriety." One unconfirmed report is that he got into further difficulty with the federals because of an act of piracy on Chesapeake Bay.[4]

Most likely Martin was recruited by the Confederates as a blockade runner because of his earlier experience at sea. Regardless, he arrived in Montreal in the late summer of 1862 and immediately set up operations to buy and ship contraband to the South, plying small vessels between Montreal and Halifax. Later this trade expanded to oceangoing traffic.

Federal detectives intercepted a letter from Baltimore, dated 12 December 1862, intended for a refugee in Montreal. One comment questioned Martin's integrity: "How do you like Mr. Martin? Keep a sharp lookout. I have been informed by several persons he is slippery and not as fair as he might be."[5] Apparently federal detectives were also keeping a sharp lookout for Martin, but there was no way they could reach him in Montreal.

Martin continued to extend his contraband operations and arranged a loose partnership with Alexander Keith, Jr., of Halifax. There are numerous references to Martin in Confederate records and in the *Official Records of the Union and Confederate Navies*. Three documents refer to him as "Capt. P. C. Martin," presumably as the master of a ship rather than as one holding rank in the Confederate service.[6]

That Martin was an insider in the Confederate apparatus in Canada is made clear in a report dated 2 February 1864 by Captain Robert D. Minor, CSN, to Admiral Franklin Buchanan. Captain Minor had been sent to Canada with twenty-two men and a plan to capture the federal gunboat *Michigan* on Lake Erie and free the Confederate prisoners at Johnson's Island. The scheme failed. Captain Minor's lucid report explained in detail what actions he took and why the attempt had to be abandoned. He also commented:

> Finding Marshal Kane and some of our friends in Montreal, we set to work to prepare and perfect our arrangements, the first object of the plan being to communicate with the prisoners on Johnson's Island, informing them that an attempt would be made to release them. This was effected through a lady from Baltimore, a Mrs. P. C. Martin, then residing with her husband and family in Montreal, and whose husband did all in his power to aid us in every way.[7]

Booth arranged for Martin to ship his theatrical wardrobe to Halifax and on south. Martin's chartered vessel, *Marie Victoria*, a seventy-three-foot schooner built in 1858, left Montreal with cargo about 18 November 1864, bound for Halifax. Some two weeks later she foundered in a storm and ran aground near Bic, Quebec. Presumably all hands were lost in the icy waters of the St. Lawrence River, including Martin. Mrs. Martin was listed in a later city directory as a widow. Portions of Booth's wardrobe, badly damaged by salt water, were recovered from the wreck when salvage operations were undertaken in the spring of 1865.[8]

Booth and Martin had much more to talk about than shipping a theatrical wardrobe. There was the plan to abduct Lincoln. Martin had connections with the Confederate underground in Maryland. He gave Booth a letter of introduction to William Queen, an elderly physician who lived on the edge of the Zekiah Swamp some six miles south of Bryantown, in Charles County. The expectation was that Dr. Queen would assist Booth by lining up local support and escape routes through the area. The cover story was that Booth had an interest in buying land. Martin's letter of introduction set off a chain of events that almost sent Dr. Samuel A. Mudd to the gallows.

In Montreal Booth was also intimate with Kentuckian George Sanders. They were made for each other: each was fanatical in his southern sympathies, each held strong republican views, and each looked upon Lincoln as a bloody tyrant. In addition, Sanders had a record of advocating political assassinations.

In late 1853, President Franklin Pierce appointed Sanders to be consul in London. Without waiting for confirmation, Sanders left for England and took up his consular duties. In London he soon became closely associated with refugee European radicals, including Giuseppe Mazzini, Felice Orsini, Lojos Kossuth, Giuseppe Garibaldi, and Andre Ledru-Rollin. On 14 February 1854, the Senate refused to confirm Sanders as consul.[9]

Despite Senate rejection, Sanders remained in London and continued his revolutionary activities. He was deeply impressed by Mazzini's "theory of the dagger," that is, tyrannicide is justified. Increasingly Sanders made Napoleon III a target. In a biographical sketch of Sanders, written after his death, a longtime associate, William Corry, put it this way: "In London Mr. Sanders fulminated an extraordinary letter advising the killing of Louis Napoleon, by any means, and by any way it could be done."[10] With others, Sanders became directly involved in a plot to assassinate Louis

Napoleon, which culminated in the Frondí affair, fully explored in a scholarly book by Amos A. Ettinger.[11]

After Sanders returned to the United States, he continued to advocate Mazzini's theory of the dagger. He spoke at a meeting in New York on 22 September 1855, held to celebrate the French republic of 1792. The *New York Herald* reported this meeting on the front page the next day and quoted Sanders as saying he was of the Ledru-Rollin school, he was for death to tyrants, and he was for the guillotine and "would work it by steam, by G——."

Sanders was still urging political assassinations when he came to Washington to monitor a high-level conference convened on 4 February 1861 to explore ways to avert civil war. In the "Diary of a Public Man," Sanders is mentioned in the entry for 28 February. Here the diarist reported a discussion he held with President-elect Lincoln at Willard's Hotel: "I told him, what I believe to be perfectly true, that the worst stories all originate with men like George Sanders of New York . . . they have been telling wonderful stories of conspiracy and assassination."[12]

Together with Clement C. Clay and James P. Holcombe, Sanders sought to arrange a peace conference in early July 1864 at the Clifton House on the Canadian side of Niagara Falls. The idea was a good one, intended to embarrass Lincoln and influence the November election. Lincoln avoided any commitment, and the conference never took place. General John A. Dix, who commanded in New York, however, sent the head of his secret service, Colonel Ambrose Stevens, to the Clifton House in civilian clothes. Colonel Stevens found the hotel filled with Confederate agents, Copperheads, and peace Democrats. He reported to General Dix that one of the Confederate peace commissioners was urging a plan to assassinate Lincoln just before the November election to disorganize the Republicans and cause electoral chaos. General Dix came to Washington to inform Lincoln of this plot. On Lincoln's orders the matter was hushed up on the ground that publicity would do more harm than good.

A correspondent for the *New York Times* interviewed Colonel Stevens on this subject shortly after the war, but the story was not published in the *Times* until 30 December 1880. The Confederate peace commissioner who advocated assassinating Lincoln was not named in the article, but it could only have been George Sanders.

A whiff of Sanders's "electoral chaos" idea came out in a 28 December 1886 letter written by Edward H. Wright, a former military aide to General George B. McClellan, to George T. Curtis, a political associate of McClellan. Both Wright and Curtis were concerned that an attempt would be made to damage McClellan's reputation by implicating him in a scheme to assassinate Lincoln. Wright told Curtis in the letter that he had been asked to meet secretly with Allan Pinkerton in Baltimore on 28 October 1864, just before the election. Pinkerton told Wright that he was acting on Lincoln's instructions and that there was a conspiracy by friends of McClellan to assassinate the president. Wright was outraged by this assertion. In effect, Pinkerton gave Wright the message, "Call it off or else!" Colonel Stevens, it seems, was having the last word.[13]

When John Wilkes Booth arrived at the St. Lawrence Hall in Montreal on the evening of 18 October 1864, George Sanders was staying at the Ottawa Hotel in that city. The two must have met promptly. Various people saw them together frequently. Their discussions, however, were interrupted by the famous Confederate raid on St. Albans, Vermont, on 19 October.

Caleb C. Wallace, one of the raiders, was captured the next day and lodged with others in the jail at St. Johns, a few miles south of Montreal. Wallace managed to send a telegram to Sanders at the Ottawa Hotel saying: "We are captured. Do what you can for us."[14] Sanders went to St. Johns on 23 October. When he returned on 25 October, he did not check in at the Ottawa Hotel. Instead, he checked into the St. Lawrence Hall and was given room 169. Booth was in room 150.

By the time federal investigators got around to checking Booth's association with Sanders in Montreal, the trail was cold and the witnesses were scattered. Further, the Canadian police were uncooperative and Canadian citizens were not enthusiastic about appearing before the military commission sitting in Washington. But three credible witnesses were found and gave testimony: Hosea B. Carter, who lived in New Hampshire; John Deveny, a Marylander, who had known Booth in the past; and William E. Wheeler of Chickopee, Massachusetts.[15] Others furnished similar information to investigators but were not called as witnesses. Charles A. Dunham, alias Sandford Conover, was probably truthful when he testified that he saw Booth and Sanders together, but his outright perjury in other matters renders his statement suspect.

There is no way to reconstruct what took place between Sanders and Booth in Montreal. Sanders would have been bitter. His son Major Reid Sanders, a prisoner of war, had died at Fort Warren, Boston, six weeks before.[16] Given Sanders's manipulative skills and his history of advocating political assassinations, he probably would have encouraged the plan to kidnap Lincoln but suggested that Lincoln deserved killing.

To cover contingencies, Booth went to the Ontario Bank in Montreal on 27 October 1864 to make some financial transactions. He deposited $455 and then purchased a bill of exchange in the amount of £61 12s 10d. With proper identification, this bill could be cashed anywhere. Testimony about these transactions was given at the conspiracy trial on 20 May 1865 by Robert Campbell, first teller at the bank. Campbell was uncertain, but he thought Booth was introduced at the bank by "Mr. P. C. Martin." His business in Montreal completed, Booth left the next morning for New York.

In early September 1864, while Booth was busy with preliminary plans and recruiting his boyhood friends, O'Laughlen and Arnold, a parallel scheme was being developed in Richmond. Confederate Secretary of War James Seddon was preparing to send a team of agents to Washington to explore ways to capture Lincoln. This mission has the flavor of a feasibility study. Seddon's team was headed by Captain Thomas N. Conrad.

Here we are faced with difficulties in appraising the Booth and Conrad missions. Did the Confederate apparatus in Canada approve Booth's operation without checking with authorities in Richmond to see if it cut across other plans? There is no way to be certain. Possibly poor communications resulted in the Confederates initially having two teams with the same plan. But whether Conrad's mission was exploratory or for action, it was not pursued. Booth's mission continued and was supported. It would almost seem that Conrad handed the initiative to Booth. Conrad was in Washington when Booth arrived at the National Hotel on 9 November 1864, and he was still there when Booth left for New York on 16 November. In his book *The Rebel Scout*, Conrad fixed the date of his return to King George County, Virginia, as 24 November [17]

Booth did not tarry long in New York after he got back from Montreal. While there on 29 October 1864, he signed a document relating to the final disposition of his Pennsylvania oil properties.[18] Then he left for Baltimore and Washington, to deliver Patrick C. Martin's letter of introduction to Dr. William Queen in Charles County, Maryland. John C. Thompson, Dr. Queen's son-in-law, testified at the conspiracy trial that Booth was brought to the farm from Bryantown by Dr. Queen's son Joseph about dusk on a Saturday in the "latter part of October last, or some time in November following." This was probably Saturday, 12 November.

The next morning Booth went with Thompson and Dr. Queen to St. Mary's Catholic Church, Bryantown, to attend mass. Here Thompson introduced Booth to Dr. Samuel A. Mudd. Dr. Mudd normally would have attended services at his own church, St. Peter's, near his home. St. Mary's is some eight miles from St. Peter's. It has been speculated that Dr. Mudd came to St. Mary's by appointment to meet Booth. It was a fateful meeting for the young physician.

On 16 November Booth deposited $1,500 in Jay Cooke's Washington bank.[19] This may have been his own money or it may have been furnished by the Confederacy. That same day he left for New York to rehearse with his brothers Edwin and Junius for the play *Julius Caesar,* to be presented at the Winter Garden Theatre on the night of 25 November in a benefit performance to raise money for the Shakespeare Statue Fund.

The play was interrupted briefly by a fire alarm at a nearby hotel, the Lafarge House. A group of Confederates from Canada had attempted to burn New York City by setting fires in various hotels. The Confederate incendiaries were commanded by Lieutenant Colonel Robert M. Martin, Tenth Kentucky Cavalry, who had been sent to Canada by Secretary of State Judah P. Benjamin.[20]

And here we must digress by looking ahead. In one of those surprising historical asides, the paths of Robert M. Martin and John Wilkes Booth crossed. Martin was arrested in October 1865 at his father's Kentucky home and lodged in a military prison at Louisville. He was placed in a cell with two errant Union soldiers, Privates Alfred W. Wheels and Hugh Shaw. The prisoners became friendly and talkative—Martin too much so for his own good. In a series of rambling discussions with Wheels, some of which were overheard by Shaw, Martin admitted trying to burn New York and told of other daring exploits. More important, he spoke knowingly about the assassination of President Lincoln. Wheels informed the prison commandant, and the matter soon came to the attention of Judge Advocate General Joseph Holt in Washington, who sent an assistant, Colonel William M. Dunn, to interrogate Wheels and Shaw. Wheels was questioned on 30 November 1865 and Shaw the next day.[21]

Wheels and Shaw may not have fully understood the import of Martin's ramblings or remembered imperfectly and out of sequence. Still, two basic points come through: while in Canada, Martin was involved in discussions of action against Lincoln on 4 March 1865, and Martin knew John Wilkes Booth.

Whatever plans Martin and his group had for Lincoln on inauguration day, the date was circulated among Confederates and Copperheads in January and February 1865. A rash of reports hinted that "something great" would happen on 4 March. An example is found in a report by Union Captain Levi Wells to Secretary of War Stanton on 25 May 1865. In January Wells had boarded briefly with a strongly southern lady, Martha Hunter, at Martinsburg, West Virginia. In discussing rebel prospects, Mrs. Hunter said, "We will see after the 4th of March." Another time she told Wells, "Our prospects will look better after the 4th of March." Mrs. Hunter's son, Major Robert W. Hunter, was then a member of the Virginia legislature and on the staff of General John B. Gordon, Army of Northern Virginia.[22]

Wheels and Shaw both recalled Martin saying he knew John Wilkes Booth. According to Wheels, Martin said he drank with Booth in Toronto. Certainly Martin had the opportunity to meet Booth. Martin and his arson squad came to New York in late October 1864 and left for Toronto on the evening of 26 November. Booth arrived in the city on 16 November. He was still there on 27 November, when he and his brothers Edwin and Junius were photographed together in their *Julius Caesar* costumes.[23] Booth then went to Philadelphia for a few days. After this his movements are unknown until he checked back into the National Hotel in Washington on 12 December. There was ample time for him to make a trip to Toronto and good reason for him to go there for consultations.

Based on the statements of Wheels and Shaw, Martin was brought from Louisville and imprisoned at Fort Lafayette in New York to await trial. The matter dragged on without trial, and he was finally pardoned by President Johnson in 1866. Martin was very lucky. Two of the men under his direct command in New York underground activities were captured, tried, and executed: John Yates Beall was hanged at Fort Columbus on 24 February 1865, and Robert Cobb Kennedy was hanged at Fort Layfayette on 25 March 1865.

While in New York between 16 November and 12 December, Booth secured two seven-shot Spencer carbines, three pistols, ammunition, daggers, and two sets of handcuffs. Spencer carbines were not easy to acquire, so he must have had support in procuring them. On his way back to Washington, Booth dropped off much of this arsenal with Samuel Arnold in Baltimore.[24]

Now Booth had something on his mind besides capturing Lincoln. On 17 December he checked out of the National Hotel and went to Baltimore. He brought back a nineteen-year-old prostitute, Ellen Starr (alias Ella Turner and Fannie Harrison), and installed her in a "house" at 62 Ohio Avenue in a red-light district known locally as "Hooker's Division."[25] At that time the bordello was kept by Ellen's sister Mrs. Mary Jane Treakle (alias Molly Turner). In a somewhat humorous side note, the Washington provost marshal prepared a listing of bawdy houses in the city. There were seventy-three for whites, thirteen for blacks. He ranged them on a scale of first to fourth class, with a few others rated as "low" and "very low."[26] If it was any comfort to Booth, Molly Turner's brothel was rated first class. Booth must have found Miss Starr's charms enduring. Upon his return with her from Baltimore, he did not obtain a room at the National Hotel.

By 20 December Booth had more pressing business than continued dalliance with Ellen Starr. Word had come that he was needed elsewhere. That morning he left by stage for Bryantown where he again spent the night with Dr. William Queen.[27]

The next day Booth met Dr. Samuel Mudd by appointment at Montgomery's tavern in Bryantown. Dr. Mudd had arranged for an experienced Confederate Secret Service agent, Thomas H. Harbin (alias Thomas A. Wilson), to come up from his post in King George County, Virginia, to meet with Booth. Dr. Mudd knew Harbin well because Harbin had once been postmaster at Bryantown. He introduced Booth to Harbin for "private conversation." They took an upstairs room. As Harbin told it over twenty years later, Booth was very theatrical. But one question was paramount: was Harbin prepared to assist in capturing Lincoln? The answer was yes.[28] Obviously Harbin had the approval of his superiors in Richmond.

Subsequently Harbin was instrumental in enlisting George A. Atzerodt, a Port Tobacco carriage painter and blockade runner, into the scheme. In a confession published in the *Baltimore American* on 19 January 1869, Atzerodt said: "Harborn was in it first; he came for me with John Surratt during the winter." In his unpublished confession dated 1 May 1865, Atzerodt turned it another way: "Thos. Holborn was to meet us on the road and help in the kidnapping."[29]

After the conference with Harbin, Booth went home with Dr.

Mudd and remained overnight. The next morning the two walked across a field to look at some horses owned by Mudd's neighbor, George Gardiner. Booth settled for a one-eyed horse for which he paid $80. He bought a saddle and bridle at Bryantown, rode the horse to Washington, and checked back into the National Hotel. The next day, 23 December, Dr. Mudd came to Washington with a relative and put up at the Pennsylvania House. That evening he met Booth by appointment at the National Hotel.[30] The two set out for Mary E. Surratt's boardinghouse so that Dr. Mudd could introduce Booth to her son, John H. Surratt, Jr., a young courier on the Confederate Secret Service line through Maryland. On the way, they met Surratt in company with Louis J. Wiechmann, one of Mrs. Surratt's boarders. The four went to Booth's room for talk and drinks. What transpired in the hotel room is disputed, but Surratt soon became a key figure in Booth's operation. It is not unreasonable to conclude that Mudd, Harbin, or both advised Booth that Surratt would be a useful addition to the team.

The chronology Dr. Mudd sought to establish in his statement to Union Colonel H. H. Wells on 21 April 1865 does not fit the records of Booth's stays at the National Hotel.[31] It is not hard to see why. Dr. Mudd could not afford to admit he met with Booth on his second visit to Charles County, particularly because this might somehow disclose that he had introduced Booth to Harbin, a known Confederate agent, to further the action plan. So Dr. Mudd adjusted the chronology to telescope provable events into three successive days: meeting Booth at church, Booth staying the next night in his home, and going with Booth the following morning to buy the horse. Then he added the lie that nearly cost him his life: "I have never seen Booth since that time until Saturday night" (Mudd meant before dawn Saturday morning, 15 April). His story came apart when Louis Wiechmann testified at the conspiracy trial that he had been present at the meeting in Booth's room at the National Hotel. Fortunately for Dr. Mudd, the meeting with Harbin at the Bryantown tavern was not revealed until years later.

Booth left Washington on 24 December to be with his family in New York for Christmas. On his way back he stopped at Baltimore to arrange with Samuel Arnold to buy a horse and buggy and to ship the weapons on to Washington. While in Baltimore, he collected the rent on the Harford County farm, signing the receipt on 30 December. The next day he checked into the National Hotel. It was time to get the operation rolling.

The one-eyed horse was moved into William Cleaver's stable on

New Year's Day. Shortly thereafter, Arnold and Michael O'Laughlen brought the horse and buggy over from Baltimore. They stabled the horse at Naylor's and took a room at a hotel. Later they found accommodations with Mary Van Tine on D Street.

The meeting in Booth's hotel room on 23 December now paid off. John Surratt, who had taken a job with the Adams Express Company on the thirtieth, gave up this employment on 13 January 1865 to devote full time to capturing Lincoln. He did not bother to come back for the balance of his wages.[32] Surratt was energetic, he knew every back road in southern Maryland, and, more important, his work as a Confederate courier put him on the inside. He knew the right people and was trusted by them.

Surratt had an appointment to meet Thomas Harbin on 14 January at Port Tobacco, then the county seat of Charles County, Maryland.[33] This tiny village was situated on an old canal that ran into the lower Potomac River, with secluded creeks and inlets all around. It made it an ideal haven for blockade runners and Confederate agents coming and going. Surratt and Harbin were there to buy a boat suitable for carrying a captured Lincoln across the river into Virginia and to recruit an experienced blockade runner into the scheme. Surratt purchased a large boat owned by Richard Smoot and James Brawner for $250. He paid $125 of this amount to Judge Frederick Stone, to be held in trust until the boat was used, with the balance to be paid later.[34] The boat was turned over to George Atzerodt, who concealed it in Goose Creek and later in a tributary to Nanjemoy Creek under the care of two other blockade runners, Charles and George Batemen.

Word went out that the proposed capture of Lincoln needed a fearless recruit. The man chosen was Private Lewis Thornton Powell, Company B, Forty-third Battalion of Virginia Cavalry (Mosby's Rangers). Powell came into a Union encampment at Fairfax Court House, Fairfax County, Virginia, on 13 January 1865. Under the alias Lewis Paine, he applied to the provost marshal there, a Lieutenant Maguire, to protect him as a civilian refugee from Fauquier County. It must have been a gem of a story. Maguire accepted it and sent "Paine" along to headquarters in nearby Alexandria. At Alexandria he took the oath of allegiance and was discharged from custody. One of the documents involved described him as having "dark complexion, black hair, blue eyes, height six feet one and a half inches." Powell, now Paine, sold his horse in Alexandria and left for Baltimore.[35]

News of Powell's arrival in Baltimore must have reached Booth or Surratt quickly. Surratt and Louis Wiechmann went to Baltimore on the evening of 21 January and checked into room 127 at the Maltby House. In questioning Wiechmann at Surratt's trial in 1867, the prosecution sought to establish that Surratt was in Baltimore to see "Payne"—that is, Powell. The point was made even though Wiechmann testified that he did not know who Surratt saw there. The response to one question is revealing:

> Q.Now proceed to state what occured while you were there.
> A. On the morning of the 22d Surratt took a carriage and said he had $300 in his possession, and that he was going to see some gentlemen on private business, and that he did not want me along.[36]

Within days of his Baltimore trip with Wiechmann, Surratt went to Richmond and met with Secretary of State Judah P. Benjamin. According to the testimony of stableman William Cleaver, Surratt hired a horse from him on the stormy evening of 25 January 1865, saying that he was going to help someone "across the river."[37] It was a quick trip. A squib in the *Daily Morning Chronicle* for 2 February shows that Surratt checked into the National Hotel in Washington the previous day. Evidence about this trip to Richmond came out in the 25 May 1866 testimony of a former Confederate Secret Service agent, James H. Fowle, before the Boutwell Committee. This committee had been set up in the House of Representatives to investigate the assassination of Lincoln. At several points in his long testimony, Fowle placed Surratt in Richmond in January or February 1865. One such exchange relative to Surratt is as follows:

> 876. Q. When was he in Richmond?
> A. He was in Richmond about January or February. They told me so when I got back.
> 877. Q. Was Surratt the secret agent of the State Dep't; if not, what Dep't did he belong to?
> A. I think the State Dep't but I will not swear to it. Each agent was kept to himself; we did not know about the other. Mr. Benjamin told me that Surratt was there, and Quinton Washington told me.
> 878. Q. When did they tell you that?
> A. When I got back on the 2nd or 3rd of March. They told me he had been there since I came over.[38]

The chronology in other parts of Fowle's testimony leaves no doubt that he had been in the North from 18 November 1864 until he returned to the Confederacy on 27 February 1865. George

Atzerodt rowed him over to the Virginia shore from Port Tobacco along with Augustus Howell, another agent, and the courier from Canada, Sarah Slater. When Fowle reported to Benjamin a few days later, he was told that Surratt had been in Richmond recently. Fowle left Richmond for New York City on 18 March and was there when Richmond fell and General Lee surrendered. Thus he could not have seen Benjamin after 18 March 1865. For whatever it means, Colonel John S. Mosby was also in Richmond at the time of Surratt's visit there.

We do not know absolutely why Surratt went to Richmond in late January 1865 to confer with Benjamin. But it is not hard to draw a logical conclusion. Booth's scheme to capture Lincoln was well along in planning. The action team had been rounded out when Lewis Powell reported in from Mosby's command. The boat was in hand for use in crossing the Potomac River, and an experienced boatman, George Atzerodt, had been recruited by John Surratt and Thomas Harbin. Now there were loose ends to tie up with Benjamin. First, it was necessary to know whether the Confederate Signal Corps camps along the lower Potomac were alerted and ready to receive a distinguished captive, Abraham Lincoln.[39] Then, too, there must be assurance that an adequate military screening force was in place to interdict pursuit once the Potomac River was crossed.

Sometime in January, John Surratt added a recruit to the team. He was David Edgar Herold, a twenty-two-year-old pharmacy clerk and a former student at Georgetown college. Herold lived in Washington near the Navy Yard with his widowed mother and sisters. He was an enthusiastic bird hunter and spent a great deal of time at this sport in the lower counties of Maryland. He became acquainted with Surratt as a result of frequent visits at the Surratt tavern in Prince George's County. After Mary Surratt opened her Washington boardinghouse in November 1864, Herold renewed his friendship with John Surratt.

The Washington action team had been assembled: Booth, Surratt, Powell, Herold, Atzerodt, O'Laughlen, and Arnold. But what of the "others unknown" mentioned in the charge and specification upon which the conspiracy trial of 1865 was based? Assistant Secretary of War Major Thomas T. Eckert visited the *Montauk* and the prison several times to quiz Powell, who responded: "All I can say about this is, that you have not got the one-half of them."[40]

One of those in Powell's uncaught other half was Thomas H. Harbin. The federal net was spread too late to pick him up. He appeared at Ashland, Virginia, on 28 April 1865 and secured a formal parole as a member of Company B, First Maryland Cavalry. There is no confirmation that Harbin was ever in this unit, but he urgently needed a parole in hand. At this point Harbin disappeared without a trace. Some five years later he turned up as a clerk at the National Hotel in Washington, a job he held until he died on 18 November 1885.

During his years at the National Hotel, Harbin often talked with friends about his wartime activities as a Confederate agent. Some of these reminiscences were published in a Chicago newspaper shortly after his death. Harbin said he had called himself Wilson and reported directly to Jefferson Davis. He explained that he escaped to Cuba and then went on to England, where he remained for several years.[41] This was a wise move. Harbin was too deeply involved in the Booth operation to feel safe from the hangman.

Notes

ABBREVIATIONS

NA   National Archives

OR   U.S. War Department, *The War of the Rebellion: A Compilation of the Official Records of the Union and Confederate Armies.* 128 vols. Washington, D.C.: U.S. Government Printing Office, 1880–1901.

ORN   U.S. Navy Department, *Official Records of the Union and Confederate Navies in the War of the Rebellion.* 30 vols. Washington, D.C.: U.S. Government Printing Office, 1894–1914.

RG   Record Group

1. For examples of how skillfully the Confederate apparatus in Canada handled the issue, see F. A. St. Lawrence, *Testimony of Sandford Conover, Dr. J. B. Merritt, and Richard Montgomery* (Toronto: Lovell & Gibson, 1865), and Rev. Stuart Robinson, *Infamous Perjuries of the "Bureau of Military Justice" Exposed* (Toronto: N.p., 1865). Both pamphlets are in the Library of Congress.

2. Clay to Beverly Tucker, 14 October 1864, quoted by Oscar A. Kinchen, *Confederate Operations in Canada and the North* (North Quincy, Mass.: Christopher, 1970), Appendix VII, pp. 231–32.

3. St. Lawrence, *Testimony*, p. 61. St. Lawrence secured an affidavit from Henry Winnett, bookkeeper at the Queens Hotel, Toronto, concerning Thompson's periods of residence there. This shows that Thompson arrived back on 21 October 1864. An entry in Clay's check record shows he paid a Mrs. Coles $60 on 19 October 1864. See Clement C. Clay Papers, Duke University Library, Durham, N.C.

4. Letters Received by the Secretary of War, Registered Series, 1801–70, M-221,

reel 221, frames 0484–86, NA. The date "19th of April" refers to the 1861 attack on Massachusetts troops en route to Washington by citizens of Baltimore. For a reference to Patrick C. Martin's act of piracy on the Chesapeake Bay, see George Alfred Townsend's long story "Thomassen," *New York Daily Graphic*, 22 March 1876.

5. Turner-Baker Papers, M-797, reel 59, file 2276, NA. The letter dated 16 December 1862 is addressed to "Dear Brother" and signed with scribbled initials which appear to be AGC.

6. For example, see *ORN*, Ser. 2, vol. 2, pp. 714, 728, 735; Ser. 1, vol. 15, pp. 374–77.

7. *ORN*, Ser. 1, vol. 2, pp. 822–28. "Marshal Kane" is George P. Kane, former marshal of police, Baltimore, who was arrested on 1 July 1861 by order of General Winfield Scott and imprisoned until released by Stanton on 26 November 1862. He soon fled to Montreal. Later he turned up in Richmond.

8. W. H. Gurley, consul at Quebec, kept the Department of State informed about the salvage of the *Marie Victoria* in a series of dispatches (Consular Reports, Quebec, RG 29, NA). Other references to this subject are in Investigation and Trial Papers Relating to the Assassination of President Lincoln, M-599, reel 7, file 52, beginning at frame 0225, NA.

9. *Washington Evening Star*, 15 February 1854.

10. *Biographical Encyclopedia of Kentucky* (Cincinnati: J. M. Armstrong, 1878), pp. 538–41. This biographical sketch of Sanders was furnished by an old friend, William M. Corry.

11. Amos A. Ettinger, *The Mission to Spain of Pierre Soulé, 1853–1855* (New Haven: Yale University Press, 1932), pp. 316–38.

12. "Diary of a Public Man," *North American Review*, August 1879, entry for 28 February 1861, p. 62.

13. Vol. B-39, reel 60, George B. McClellan Papers, Library of Congress.

14. The telegram appeared in the *Burlington* (Vermont) *Daily Times*, 22 October 1864.

15. Benn Pitman, *The Assassination of President Lincoln and the Trial of the Conspirators*, (1865; rpt. ed. Philip Van Doren Stern, New York: Funk and Wagnalls, 1954), pp. 38–39.

16. *New York Herald*, 6 September 1864.

17. G. W. Bunker, a clerk at the National Hotel in Washington, prepared a memorandum of Booth's stays there, which was in evidence at the conspiracy trial as Exhibit 4. See M-599, reel 15, frames 0260–63, NA (hereafter cited as Bunker memorandum); Thomas N. Conrad, *The Rebel Scout* (Washington, D.C.: National Publishing Co., 1904), pp. 130–31.

18. Joint Claims Deed, Deed Book CC, p. 366, Venango County Land Records, Franklin, Pa.

19. Booth's ledger with Jay Cooke & Company Bank, Washington, is in the Abraham Lincoln Papers, Chicago Historical Society. Seven checks were drawn on this account, three of which are known to be extant: one for $100, made to Matthew Canning, dated 16 December 1864, which was sold to an undisclosed buyer at a Sotheby auction on 28 November 1979; one for $150 cashed by Booth on 7 January 1865, Jay Cooke Collection, Box Jan.–Feb. 1865, Historical Society of Pennsylvania, Philadelphia; and another for $25 cashed by Booth on 16 March 1865, on permanent showcase exhibit, Lewis E. Warren Lincoln Library, Ft. Wayne, Indiana.

20. For the full story, see Nat Brandt, *The Man Who Tried to Burn New York* (Syracuse: Syracuse University Press, 1986).

21. The statements of Wheels and Shaw are in the War Department Collection of

Confederate Records, Union Provost Marshal's File, Prison Records, 1861–65, Fort Lafayette Personal Papers, RG 109, NA.

22. M-599, reel 3, frames 0023–26, NA. During his flight into Virginia, Booth met Major Hunter on 23 April 1865 at the home of Dr. Richard Stuart in King George County. Hunter, recently paroled, was courting Margaret Stuart, whom he later married.

23. The date 27 November 1864 is fixed by an explanatory letter on the reverse side of one of the pictures now hanging in the National Portrait Gallery, Washington, D.C.

24. Samuel B. Arnold, *Defence of a Lincoln Conspirator* (Hattiesburg, Miss.: Book Farm, 1943), p. 20.

25. Ellen Starr was arrested by the Washington police at this address on 15 April 1865. She was questioned and released. Her statement is in M-599, reel 6, frame 0258, NA.

26. Bawdy Houses, vol. 296, Provost Marshal Department, Twenty-second Army Corps, RG 393, NA.

27. John C. Thompson, Dr. Queen's son-in-law, testified at the conspiracy trial that Booth's second visit to the Queen farm occurred about the middle of December 1864 and that he stayed one night (Pitman, *Assassination*, p. 178).

28. Interview in 1885 of Harbin by George Alfred Townsend, *Cincinnati Enquirer*, 18 April 1892.

29. Atzerodt's strong German accent was hard to understand, so when his confessions were taken down in writing, the name Harbin came out as "Harborn" in one and as "Holborn" in another. The unpublished confession of 1 May 1865, clearly authentic, is in private hands.

30. See the affidavit of Union Captain George W. Dutton, 23 August 1865, Pitman, *Assassination*, p. 421.

31. Dr. Mudd's statement of 21 April 1865 is in M-599, reel 5, frames 0212–25, NA.

32. Testimony of Henry R. McDonough, Adams Express Company, *Trial of John H. Surratt*, 2 vols. (Washington, D.C.: U.S. Government Printing Office, 1867), 1:356–57.

33. M. E. Martin, a New York broker, was in Port Tobacco about 7 through 15 January 1865, seeking to cross the Potomac River to consummate a cotton deal in Richmond. While there he talked with both John Surratt and George Atzerodt. See *Trial of John H. Surratt*, 1:215–16.

34. Richard M. Smoot, *The Unwritten History of the Assassination of Abraham Lincoln* (Clinton, Mass.: W. F. Coulter Press, 1908), pp. 8–9. The only known copy of this pamphlet is in the Rare Book Room, Library of Congress.

35. Defenses South of the Potomac, Twenty-second Army Corps, Entry 1465, 13 January 1865, RG 393, NA. Powell's sale of the horse was reported in the *Alexandria Gazette*, 23 June 1865.

36. *Trial of John H. Surratt*, 1:273.

37. Ibid. p. 206.

38. On 30 April 1866 the Committee on the Judiciary, House of Representatives, was instructed to investigate the assassination of Lincoln, with emphasis on any part played by Jefferson Davis. Many witnesses appeared before the committee and lengthy testimony was taken. None of this testimony was included in *Assassination of Lincoln*, Report 104, 39th Cong., 1st sess. A sealed package containing the testimony was turned over to the house clerk and later disappeared. In 1930 the

heirs of former Congressman Benjamin F. Butler discovered the package among his effects and turned it over to the Library of Congress. The package included Fowle's statement, which is now in Box 175, Benjamin F. Butler Papers.

39. Benjamin had anticipated this problem. Sergeant Harry H. Brogden and his entire staff at the Signal Corps camp on the Potomac River in Westmoreland County, Virginia, were transferred to Benjamin's control pursuant to Special Orders 18, paragraph XXX, Adjutant and Inspector General's Office, 23 January 1865. Such orders are in volumes, bound by year, in the National Archives library.

40. Testimony of Thomas T. Eckert on 30 May 1867 before the Judiciary Committee, House of Representatives, *Impeachment Investigation*, 39th Cong., 2d sess., and 40th Cong., 1st sess. (Washington, D.C.: U.S. Government Printing Office, 1867), p. 674.

41. The somewhat garbled Harbin reminiscences are in a clipping from an unidentified Chicago newspaper published shortly after his death, in the Elizabeth E. Atwater Scrapbook, Chicago Historical Society library. The federals learned on 15 April 1865 that Harbin was using the alias Thomas A. Wilson. See Union Provost Marshal's File of Papers Relating to Two or More Civilians, M-416, reel 56, file 15772, NA. He also used this alias when he secured a pass on 21 October 1864 to travel from Richmond to King George County, Virginia. See Richmond Passbooks, Chap. IX, vol. 134, RG 109, NA.

16

Come Retribution

On 8 February 1865, Mary Boykin Chesnut, wife of General James Chesnut, Jr., recorded in her journal that on that date her husband received a message from General Beauregard in cipher.[1] The message was enciphered using as a key the phrase "Come Retribution." This may not have been the first use of the new key, but in January the Confederate government was still using the phrase "Complete Victory," and the new one reflected a different, more apocalyptic attitude on the part of the government. Mrs. Chesnut commented that the phrase "Complete Victory" was for the late forlorn Georgia campaign, indicating that "Come Retribution" represented a new stage in the struggle.

The main cipher system used by the Confederacy was the "Court" cipher. This system used a twenty-six-alphabet matrix as the basic tool. All senders and receivers of cipher messages could have a copy of the matrix without compromising the security of the system. In fact, a person could even construct his own matrix if necessary. The secret part of the system was a key word or phrase that could be committed to memory. This key was written down under the message to be enciphered and repeated until each letter in the message had a letter from the key written under it. The key letter indicated which alphabet in the matrix to use to encipher the letter of text.

If properly used, the Confederate system was reasonably secure. It also had the virtue of being fairly easy to administer in the turmoil of war. The key words or phrases were distributed orally by courier whenever a change was made. The keys were proposed and issued by the Signal Bureau under Major William Norris. There is no indication as to who was the highest authority to give final approval to his choice, but given the work habits of the Confederate government, it is likely that the key word or phrase was used as a slogan and approved by the secretary of war or the president. It had the added purpose of communicating policy attitudes to key persons throughout the army and the government.

The use of the key phrase "Come Retribution" suggests that the Confederate government had made a bitter decision to repay some of the misery that had been inflicted on the South. Bitterness may well have been directed toward persons held to be particularly responsible for that misery, and Abraham Lincoln certainly headed the list.

A review of the events leading up to the decision by the Confederate government shows that it was carefully orchestrated and that it dealt with the adoption of a most audacious plan of military operations. Its timing suggests that part of the orchestration involved the maturation of plans for the covert operation to capture Lincoln.

According to the newspapers, it was widely believed in Richmond in the autumn of 1864 that if Grant could be held off until winter, the Union would be too sick of war to risk the high casualties that would result from continuing the siege into 1865. This euphoria was dampened by Sherman's march from Atlanta to Savannah.

Sherman could now turn north into the Carolinas and threaten Richmond from the South, but there were many Confederates who still saw his move as an opportunity for Confederate victory. His army was still isolated from direct reinforcement on the ground and depended on long sea lines for its support. His widespread columns might yet be cornered and defeated in detail, and such a defeat piled on existing war weariness in the North could well bring an end to the war.

In the meantime, the organization of the covert operation against Lincoln moved forward. Captain Conrad had made the basic reconnaissance in September and early October 1864, and Lieutenant Blackford's mapping assignment was nearly completed. These efforts made it possible for the government to make more detailed plans.

Troops would be needed to protect key points along the route to be followed by the raiding party and to escort the raiders and their captive upon their return. A place would be needed to keep Lincoln that would be secure, preferably isolated, and suitable for the "entertainment" of a high-ranking guest. It would have to be near

Richmond to be accessible to the Confederate government and within the general protection of the Army of Northern Virginia.

In planning for the troops to use in the screening force, it would be logical to think of using men who were native to the region in which they would operate. Men from the counties along the tidewater Potomac and Rappahannock rivers were in several different units, but the main groupings were the Thirtieth, Fortieth, Forty-seventh, and Fifty-fifth Virginia infantry regiments and the Ninth Virginia Cavalry Regiment. Elements from these units had collaborated in driving off a Union attempt to fortify Mathias Point in King George County, Virginia, in 1861, and many of the men had friends, relatives, or neighbors in the other units as well as their own.

The colonel commanding the Ninth Virginia Cavalry was Richard Lee Turberville Beale from Westmoreland County, well connected by family with the "establishment" of the Northern Neck. He had also served one term as a congressman in Washington coincident with the single term of Abraham Lincoln of Illinois.[2] Representing opposing parties in a House of Representatives counting 240 members, Lincoln had been a fairly active speaker but Beale had been a very quiet member of the Committee on the Militia.

The colonel of the Forty-seventh Virginia Infantry was Robert Murphy Mayo, also of Westmoreland County and a neighbor of the Beales. Mayo had graduated from the Virginia Military Institute in 1857 and had known as a fellow cadet Walter Herron Taylor, General Lee's adjutant and principal staff officer.[3]

If the question of who to use was fairly easy to answer, there still remained the question of how to do it. The regiments could not be pulled out of forces around Richmond and sent off together on an expedition to the Northern Neck without drawing unwanted attention. Union intelligence on the Confederate order of battle was good. Spies, prisoners of war, and deserters kept it reasonably up to date, and the absence of the units would be noticed, even if they could get to the Northern Neck without being detected by Union scouts.

There were also problems to be avoided inside the Confederate army. Participating units would have to be placed so their commanders would cooperate with the operation and defenses would not suffer by the absence of the men involved. The answer was to leave the units in the order of battle but to take out selected individuals to form a special task force to perform the screening mission.

There remained the question of where to keep the hostage president. In 1836 and later, the Richmond, Fredericksburg, and Potomac Railroad purchased land adjoining the railroad about fifteen miles north of the city. On this property, the president of the railroad built a dance and picnic pavilion called Slash Cottage. Guest cottages, a hotel, race track, and other recreational facilities were also built for the entertainment of Richmond's citizenry. This became a popular weekend resort, and the Richmond militia companies frequently used it for summer encampments which combined training and social activity. When Henry Clay died at Ashland, his home in Kentucky, the pro-Clay owners of Slash Cottage changed its name to Ashland in his honor.[4] It became a favored retreat for Richmond dwellers seeking to escape the heat of summer and, during the war years, for refugees crowded out of the city.

In all the various cavalry raids around Richmond and the battles of the Wilderness campaign, Ashland escaped serious damage. In 1864 it seemed to fit all the requirements for a possible detention area for President Lincoln. This would not be the first time the Confederate government had made use of Ashland. It had been rented from the railroad in 1861 as the training area for the Virginia cavalry regiments. It had been used as a hospital for Confederate wounded in April and May of 1862 but was abandoned following a Union raid in search of supplies. In December 1862, the railroad made an agreement with the Confederated Telegraph Company to install a telegraph line along the railroad. Up until that time, the nearest telegraph line ran along the telegraph road several hundred yards east of the hotel. As part of the agreement, the telegraph company was supposed to provide for telegraph service for the railroad, but in 1863 and 1864 the railroad was paying for telegraphers at Milford, Hanover Junction, and Ashland.

E. W. Thompson, the telegrapher at Ashland, was with Lee's army when it was surrounded at Appomattox. In the parole list compiled at Appomattox, he was carried as a "Confederate States military telegraph" operator "connected with the Army of Northern Virginia."[5] The railroad had been paying the salary of a military telegraph operator who was associated, geographically at least, with the Confederate Signal Corps route to the north. In a sense, the railroad appears to have been acting as a cover organization for the Confederate government. The telegraphers at Hanover Junction and Milford appear to have remained at their posts, and the telegraph may have continued to work between those points.

It will be recalled that on 12 September 1862, President Jefferson Davis had approved the organization of the spy route to Maryland on a regular basis. The Signal Corps and the Secret Service Bureau, which sponsored the route into Maryland, maintained offices in Richmond to serve the president and the secretary of war, but since their functions involved training people in signaling and cryptography and since they also needed to handle couriers and agents out of the sight of Union spies in Richmond, they may have rented the Ashland Hotel and associated buildings as an auxiliary operating headquarters. The financial files of the Richmond, Fredericksburg, and Potomac stopped recording income in September 1862. Presumably the income figures were held privately to prevent anybody from knowing who was paying the company and the services being paid for. This is especially interesting since Samuel Ruth, who was a Union spy, was the superintendent of the railroad. Perhaps somebody was suspicious of a leak and wanted to be particularly careful about the relationship between the railroad company and the government.

Mrs. William Norris, the wife of Major Norris, chief of the Signal Corps and the War Department's Secret Service Bureau, wrote letters from Ashland on 22 September and 10 October 1862 about the time the company refurbished the buildings.[6] Before that date she had been in Richmond. Her presence there proves at least that the Signal Corps was aware of Ashland and its facilities.

It would have been easy enough to use the hotel at Ashland as a school and headquarters and cover the operation by claiming that it was a rest area for recuperating soldiers. The furniture of the hotel was sold at auction in April 1863, but it is clear from bills for plumbing and other repair work that the place was occupied through much of 1863.

After the Battle of Fredericksburg in December 1862, a number of people from the Fredericksburg area fled to Richmond. Some stopped off at Ashland. Among these were the family of Matthew Fontaine Maury and T. B. Barton, the father of General Seth Barton and Major William S. Barton, who was the post commander at Ashland for a short time in April 1862. Some of the people apparently stayed on at Ashland in the guest cottages on the hotel grounds.[7]

Colonel Beale's possible association with the security force seems to be reflected in his assignments. On 6 January 1865, Beale was promoted to brigadier general, and on 20 January he was assigned to command the brigade of which the Ninth Cavalry was a part.[8] The brigade was part of the division commanded by Major General William Henry Fitzhugh Lee, otherwise known as General Robert E. Lee's son Rooney. The division commander obviously could be counted on to cooperate and keep his mouth shut. During February Beale spent considerable time at home in Westmoreland County "on leave."

On 28–31 January, the staff of the adjutant and inspector general made an inspection of Rooney Lee's division.[9] The head of inspections was General Robert H. Chilton, who had previously been General Lee's chief of staff and who was a personal friend of the Lee family. This inspection would have provided information about the state of training and discipline in the Ninth Cavalry without having to single that unit out for attention.

It was not necessary to inspect the Forty-seventh at this time because that unit had an inspection on 29 September.[10] That was probably a routine inspection because the Forty-seventh had been heavily engaged and had lost one hundred men captured on 19 August. It would be normal to check out a unit in such circumstances to see if it were back up to par. In this case, the inspector gave the regiment fair marks. Its weapons were clean. His main complaint was what he felt to be a casual attitude about military courtesy and forms of discipline. That might seem to be an unusual report for a unit whose commander and nearly half of its officers were from the Virginia Military Institute. It is probable that the VMI graduates, well grounded in conventional military discipline, had found that in working with combat troops, it made more sense to dispense with formal discipline in favor of an informal but tightly knit team spirit, much as had been the case with Mosby, who balanced demands for correct combat performance with informality not normally appropriate to a military organization. Such a situation would have met little understanding from a conventional inspector general.

The cavalry units could be moved easily, and they frequently changed locations. There would be no problem, therefore, in locating the Ninth Cavalry where its manpower could be drawn down without anyone noticing. The infantry units were not as amenable to such change, and the Forty-seventh and other units from the Northern Neck were stationed in the lines south of the James River. It would be difficult to draw large numbers of men out of the units without their departure across the Confederate rear being noticed by many not privy to the operation.

On 20 October 1864, G. W. C. Lee was promoted to major general and ordered to report to General R. E. Lee.[11] On 26 November 1864, Special Order 288 of the Army of Northern Virginia directed him to report to General Ewell, commander of the Military Department of Richmond, for assignment to the command of a division to be formed from the troops occupying the fortification from Chaffin's Bluff on the north bank of the James River to Fort Gilmer, two miles to the north. This stretch of the lines had been the scene of bitter fighting earlier in 1864, which had wound down to a heavily fortified stalemate. It was the area that General Lee had asked Jed Hotchkiss and General Pendleton to inspect.

On 22 December, the brigade, under the acting command of Colonal Mayo, containing the Fortieth, Forty-seventh, and Fifty-fifth infantry regiments, was pulled out of the lines to provide an emergency reinforcement to the Confederate forces at Gordonsville who were thought to be under strong Union attack. As it turned out, the reinforcements were not needed, and General Lee's headquarters took the opportunity to change their location in the order of battle. Colonel Taylor, Lee's adjutant, issued orders on 24 December directing the brigade to report to General Ewell north of the James River on 26 December.[12] A Tennessee brigade was sent to take its place south of the James as part of General Henry Heth's Division. This switch of locations put the Forty-seventh Infantry at Chaffin's Farm, where fortifications were heavily developed and differences in numbers of personnel might not be noticed. It also placed it in the portion of the line to be incorporated into General Lee's new division.

On 26 December, General Ewell wrote to Secretary of War Seddon that General G. W. C. Lee was pleading for more reinforcements and asking if Seddon could arrange to get the VMI Corps of Cadets assigned to Lee's section of the line. Ewell remarked that Custis Lee's "habitual coolness makes his opinion more important."[13] Could Lee have been asking for more men for the trenches because he knew that many would be taken away from this newly assigned brigade? Or did he want to use cadets in the covert operation?

Mayo, like Beale, was an acting brigade commander. On 9 January, Brigadier General Seth M. Barton was assigned as acting commander of the brigade containing the infantry regiments.[14] General Barton was a West Point graduate from Fredericksburg and a relative of Thomas Green, the man who provided a safe house for Conrad while he was spying out Lincoln's movements. His brother William S. Barton was involved in intelligence work for the state of

Virginia and in some of General Winder's covert work. Another brother had attended VMI. General Barton had some bad luck, made some poor decisions, and had some enemies. As a result, he had been released from his previous command in May 1864 and for some months had been out of a command. In the autumn, he was assigned to a brigade of the Richmond defense force, but it is possible that during his unemployment and nominal command of the Richmond brigade he was one of the officers helping to plan the covert operation. In any case, his family undoubtedly knew the Seddons, who were from Fredericksburg, and that relationship plus all of his other connections would indicate that he could be counted on to cooperate and not talk.

General Custis Lee had risen in rank through technical brilliance and high-level staff work rather than through command. Barton's brigade was the only veteran infantry unit in his division. One reason for the creation of the division may have been to provide a benign environment for Barton's brigade so that it could take part in the covert operations without creating a stir. In the surviving Confederate records, the exact status of General Custis Lee's new division seems to be a complete muddle. Even more important, it seems to have been a deliberate muddle.

General James Longstreet commanded the Confederate First Corps, which was responsible for the defensive line north of the James River. On 22 January 1865, two days after Barton was assigned to his new command, Longstreet's headquarters addressed a message to "Brigadier General G. W. C. Lee, Commanding Chaffin's," although Lee had been promoted to major general in October 1864. The message ended, "These orders are sent to you under the impression that you command in General Ewell's absence. If, on the contrary, General Barton commands, will you please transmit them to him."[15] Ewell was the commander of the Richmond Military District, and the troops in Lee's division belonged to the military district rather than to the First Corps, even though they occupied a very important piece of terrain in the sector for which General Longstreet was responsible. It is amazing that Longstreet's headquarters was not aware of the status of this unit, especially since General Lee's headquarters had issued Special Order 8 on 9 January, which spelled out the organization for a division Lee was to command and in which Barton temporarily commanded a brigade.

The status of General G. W. C. Lee's division was clouded further by the belief that it may have had a "special" status. On 2 March,

Longstreet's headquarters sent a message to General Ewell asking: "What number of local troops, in addition to Major General Custis Lee's division, could be relied on in an emergency, and how soon could they be turned out? Of course, it is understood they are alone subject to the call of the Secretary of War."[16] If Lee's division was made up of local troops and only the secretary of war could call out these troops, then perhaps Lee's division too was subject only to the call of the secretary of war. Unfortunately, this ambiguous phraseology was not clarified.

The other main infantry unit recruited in and near the Northern Neck was the Thirtieth Virginia Infantry Regiment, currently a member of Montgomery Dent Corse's brigade in George E. Pickett's division. This division, like the brigade commanded by Colonel Mayo, was originally south of the James River. It also contained the Fifteenth Virginia Infantry Regiment, which had in it a number of men from Hanover County, where Ashland was located.

On 4 January 1865, General Pickett received orders to have Corse's brigade cross the James on the pontoon bridge at Drewry's Bluff before dawn the next morning.[17] Once north of the James, Corse's brigade was sent to occupy Fort Gilmer on the left flank of the troops that were about to be incorporated into Custis Lee's new division. In that location, the Fifteenth and Thirtieth regiments could be drawn down in small increments in the same technique probably used to take personnel of the Fortieth, Forty-seventh, and Fifty-fifth infantry regiments.

Corse's bridgade stayed north of the James until, on 24 February, it received orders to return to the south side.[18] During its fifty-day stay north of the James, a few personnel departing each day could add up to a substantial total. Corse was a highly respected officer, and his brigade was frequently given independent assignments. He had served as a Virginia militia officer in the Mexican War and had lived in California.[19] He probably knew Lee and may have known Davis from his Mexican War service. His brigade was large and could probably stand to have men detailed away better than most.

Once the units destined to take part in the operation to capture Lincoln were in place in the Confederate lines, the chief task was to make sure that they stayed in the Union version of the Confederate order of battle. There was no way to prevent desertions, and deserters were regularly interrogated by Union units that picked them up. The impact of the desertions could be minimized, however, by ensuring that the troops in general did not know anything significant and that there were deserters who told their Union interrogators what the Confederacy wanted them to hear.

The first objective could be attained by removing the chosen men a few at a time and making sure they did not know what operation they were involved in. The individuals could travel through Richmond singly or in small groups and reassemble in their home area, where there were few people to notice and nobody to connect them with their disappearance from the parent unit.

A firsthand account of the technique used in one unit is contained in a diary kept by Lieutenant Cornelius Hart Carlton of Company F of the Twenty-fourth Virginia Cavalry.[20] Carlton's company was recruited originally from King and Queen County, between the Rappahannock and Mattaponi Rivers, and on the route from Urbanna to Ashland.

According to Carlton, his regiment was told on the morning of 30 January that the men were to be furloughed, half for twenty days, and upon their return the second half would go for twenty days. The first group was to take all the horses with it, and the men who stayed behind would fight dismounted.

Carlton left for home on 2 February and had several days of relaxation. On 9 February he received orders from Captain L. W. Allen to organize a five-man team to patrol an area south of the Rappahannock for the next thirty days. The twenty-day furlough appears to have been forgotten, and presumably the other half of the regiment never had its turn.

Carlton made reports to Captain Allen at Taylorsville, on the Richmond, Fredericksburg, and Potomac Railroad between Hanover Junction and Ashland and received further orders from Allen by mail. Taylorsville would have been a logical location for the headquarters of the security force south of the Rappahannock. During February and into March, the men on patrol were rotated to spread the burden. Carlton and his men finally returned to their regiment on 29 March 1865.

The second objective of misleading the federal forces could be attained by persuading wounded, ill, or incompetent soldiers to desert with a rehearsed story. A large number of deserters from the Forty-seventh Infantry and the Ninth Cavalry was listed from the end of January to the end of March.[21]

Although doubtless some of these were real deserters, the coincidence of dates suggests that somebody might have been orchestrating the arrival of many of them into Union lines.

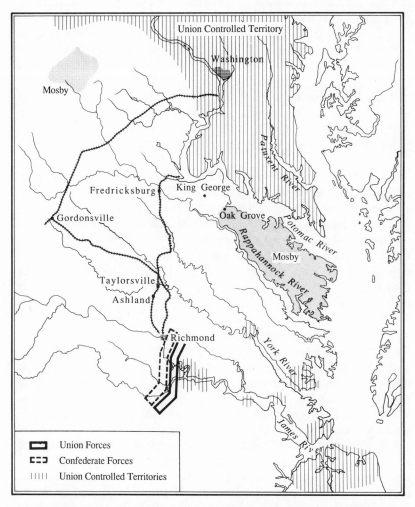

POSITIONS OF UNION AND CONFEDERATE FORCES IN
EARLY 1865

The Twenty-fifth Battalion of Virginia Reserves included in General Barton's new brigade was also known as the Richmond City Battalion. It was made up of men from the business world. Its commander was Lieutenant Colonel Wyatt M. Elliott, a graduate of the Virginia Military Institute and a classmate of General Barton's brother. He had since become an editor of the *Richmond Examiner*. During his battalion's tour in the trenches, he arranged with the Union troops opposite to trade Richmond papers for Washington papers.[22] These papers were brought by steamer from Washington to City Point and could be delivered, through this exchange, in Richmond hours, or in some cases days, before they could be made available through the Signal Corps route via southern Maryland across the Potomac. Union reports quoted remarks made by Colonel Elliott that were repeated by deserters. If somebody was orchestrating the flow of desertions to the Union, it could well have been Elliott.

The Confederate security effort seems to have worked. On 28 March 1865, a Union intelligence report to General Grant said that the Forty-seventh Infantry was a part of Custis Lee's command and was located north of the James.[23] There was no hint that anything unusual was afoot.

While the military screen was being put together, other measures were being taken to prepare for the covert operation. The Confederate commissioners in Canada had been very active in promoting covert operations against the North, and in a strategic sense they had been successful. Thousands of troops that would never see a Confederate were occupied in the North guarding buildings and supplies against attack by the agents of the Confederacy. In a more limited sense, however, the Confederate campaign had been a failure. Almost none of the specific operations launched had achieved its objective. Even the raid on St. Albans, Vermont, one of the few to achieve tactical success, had resulted in a series of diplomatic and legal headaches for the Confederacy.

Jefferson Davis was convinced that more military talent was needed to guide the efforts from Canada, and in December 1864 he sent Brigadier General Edwin Gray Lee to play this role. Lee's military career was a strange one. He had served as an aide to Stonewall Jackson and had commanded the Thirty-third Virginia Infantry Regiment. He resigned because of ill health in December 1862 but returned to duty in 1863 and was assigned to the Torpedo Bureau. From April to June 1863, he was involved with John Yates Beall, the Confederate naval raider, in a covert operation in the

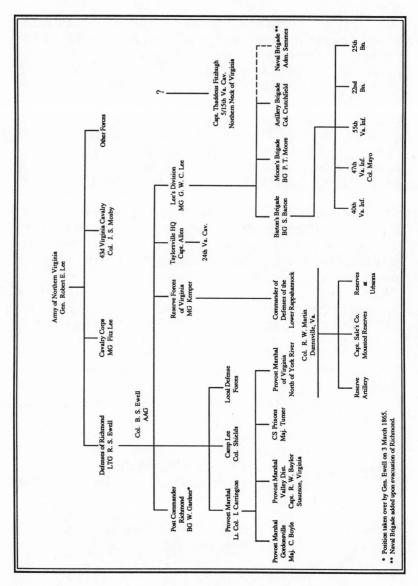

SOME COMMAND RELATIONSHIPS, 1865

Army of Northern Virginia
Gen. Robert E. Lee

Defenses of Richmond
LTG R. S. Ewell

Cavalry Corps
MG Fitz Lee

43d Virginia Cavalry
Col. J. S. Mosby

Other Forces

Col. B. S. Ewell
AAG

Post Commander
Richmond
BG W. Gardner*

Provost Marshal
Lt. Col. I. Carrington

Camp Lee
Col. Shields

Local Defense
Forces

CS Prisons
Maj. Turner

Reserve Forces
of Virginia
MG Kemper

Taylorsville HQ
Capt. Allen

Lee's Division
MG G. W. C. Lee

Provost Marshal
Gordonsville
Maj. C. Boyle

Provost Marshal
Valley Dist.
Capt. R. W. Baylor
Staunton, Virginia

Provost Marshal
of Virginia
North of York River

Commander of
Defenses of the
Lower Rappahannock

24th Va. Cav.

Col. R. W. Martin
Dumsville, Va.

Reserve
Artillery

Capt. Sale's Co.
Mounted Reserves

Reserves
at
Urbanna

?

Capt. Thaddeus Fitzhugh
5/15th Va. Cav.
Northern Neck of Virginia

Barton's Brigade
BG S. Barton

Moore's Brigade
BG P. T. Moore

Artillery Brigade
Col. Crutchfield

Naval Brigade **
Adm. Semmes

40th
Va. Inf.

47th
Va. Inf.
Col. Mayo

55th
Va. Inf.

22nd
Bn.

25th
Bn.

* Position taken over by Gen. Ewell on 3 March 1865.
** Naval Brigade added upon evacuation of Richmond.

Chesapeake Bay area. In May 1864, he was assigned to command Virginia reserve forces at Staunton, Virginia, and in September 1864 he was appointed a brigadier general. His military record was not very well known, and the Confederate Senate failed to confirm him in February 1865.[24] Although Lee's poor health is well documented, his role in clandestine work during his career may account for some of the ambiguity in his known record.

On 5 December 1864 he arrived in Richmond apparently for conferences with the president, the secretary of war, and the secretary of state.[25] Mosby arrived in Richmond on the same day, also apparently to confer with the secretary of war. Both may have been discussing the same project.

Shortly after Mosby returned to his command, he was wounded but a few days later was back on his feet and reorganized his command into two battalions. One he kept under his own immediate command and the other, consisting of Companies C, E, F, and G, he placed under the command of Lieutenant Colonel William H. Chapman and ordered to the lower end of the Northern Neck. The companies were assigned one to a county and scattered in small groups in quarters in farmhouses throughout the area. They were assigned as follows: Company C, Westmoreland County; Company E, Richmond County; Companies F and G, Northumberland and Lancaster counties.[26]

In January and early February, Mosby was back in Richmond again for further discussions. His tactical successes had made him a great popular hero. He was treated as a special guest by the governor of Virginia and was invited to appear before both the Confederate Senate and the Virginia House of Delegates. Colonel Ould took him for a ride to City Point on the truce boat used in prisoner exchanges.

Business mixed with pleasure, however; on 2 February, Mosby met with General Robert E. Lee in his headquarters. The next day, Mosby wrote a partial account of the meeting in a letter to his wife. (The letter was on stationery from the Executive Department of the state of Virginia.) After discussing the personal side of the visit, he mentioned that "Gen. Lee wants me to make a raid here before I return. I am now waiting for the report of some scouts—if I make the raid I should take the companies from the Northern Neck with us."[27] These talks were probably the genesis of the Williamsburg raid on 10–11 February.

Mosby did not mention this raid in his books, and most subsequent writers have ignored it. It occurred out of his customary area and seemed to fit no usually accepted purpose. The Williamsburg raid was led by Captain Thomas W. T. Richards of Company G, which was quartered in Lancaster County, Virginia.[28] He and a small group of rangers stormed into town and chased a large number of Union soldiers into the refuge of Fort Magruder. They killed one Union soldier and captured a few horses. General Edward O. C. Ord of the Union Army of the James asked General August Kautz of the Cavalry Division if the enemy cavalry could be chased off. Kautz begged off on the grounds that Williamsburg was about eighty miles away by road and that a small Confederate force could have easily escaped by the time a pursuit was organized.[29]

On 11 February, Colonel Sharpe, the Union intelligence chief, informed General Meade that a Union spy in Richmond had reported that Confederate forces north of the James had been on an alert on 9 and 10 February.[30]

These activities indicate that General Lee wanted to test the temperature of the Union sensitivity to events north and east of Richmond. He arranged Mosby's raid as a probing action and had the Confederate force in that area nearest to the raid on the alert to exploit or repel any Union reaction. As it turned out, the Union forces were not very sensitive to Confederate activities in that area. They apparently had their minds set on events elsewhere. General Lee and President Davis would have known on the evening of 11 February that the Union was not paying much attention to Confederate activity north of the James River.

The Confederate government took other measures compatible with support for a clandestine operation. Sergeant Brogden was detailed to the Signal Corps unit near Oak Grove in Westmoreland County on 29 June 1864.[31] He took command of the unit responsible for transporting agents formerly headed by Private George Norris. On 12 December, Brogden wrote to the acting chief of the Signal Corps complaining that he was being bottled up by the Union navy and could not carry out his mission to cross the Potomac. He attributed the Union attention to the activities of a group of partisans under the command of a Captain Hebb, who had stayed near his camp and conducted raids into Maryland. The partisans had recently moved on down the river, but the Union navy thought that Brogden's group was responsible. He hoped that Hebb could be told to stop.[32] There is no indication of what happend to Hebb or his unit after Brogden's complaint, but the very absence of information is suggestive. He may very well have been shut down.

On 21 December, Captain J. Louis Smith of the Adjutant and Inspector General's Office reported on a visit he had made to the Signal Corps camps for King George and Westmoreland counties.[33] It is possible that he also had the collateral duty of turning off Hebb's operations, but his report on the Signal Corps camps was a model of inspectoral decorum. He listed the personnel with details on their enlistments, duties, and pay. He also visited leading local citizens such as Charles Mason and Dr. Richard Henry Stuart of King George County, to see if they had any complaints about the Signal Corps personnel. He reported that they had none, although they assured him that any irregularities would have come to their attention.

A month later, on 21 January, Major William Norris, the chief of the Signal Corps, who had been helping run the defenders' signal system during the siege of Charleston, South Carolina, was ordered to return to Richmond to resume his regular duties. On 23 January, Secretary of War Seddon took a blank adjutant and inspector general's form, turned it upside down, and drafted a paragraph that was published the same day as paragraph XXX of Special Order 18. It read: "Sgt. H. H. Brogden, A. W. Weddill [sic], and the men serving with Sgt. Brogden, all of the Signal Corps, are detailed for special service and will report to the Honorable J. P. Benjamin, Secretary of State."[34] This order meant a change of bosses for Brogden and suggests that Benjamin may have been President Davis's chief assistant in overseeing the Lincoln operation.

In the Confederate jargon, the words "special service" indicated a clandestine assignment. This was the period when Benjamin and Seddon were collaborating to get President Davis to approve Secret Service funds for Captain Conrad, and now they were collaborating on another unique and obviously important clandestine activity.

Seddon's specification of Sergeant Brogden's group raises questions. Lieutenant Cawood's group on Mathias Point specialized in moving mail across the river. Brogden's group, however, normally transported people—agents, recruits, refugees, and foreign visitors. Now they might be called on to cooperate in another operation involving the transport of passengers across the Potomac.

All of the actions involving "special service" personnel seemed to be timed to build toward late January or early February as a date when the covert action project would be ready for a decision.

In preparing to present the covert action plan to capture Lincoln for final approval, its authors should have had to make a thorough review of the status of the operation. This final review would have been held before the general strategy review in order for Davis and other key officials to know that the plan was ready to put into action if the strategy review indicated that it could make a useful contribution.

The fragmentary evidence that we have found suggests that the manager of the covert operation would have been ready for such a review in late January or early February. Although Seddon resigned on 1 February, he continued to serve until he was finally replaced by John C. Breckinridge on 7 February. Since he had been intimately involved in the planning, he would probably have participated in such a review.

Good information would be available on the various facets of the covert operations in Virginia, but what about the action itself and the escape routes through southern Maryland? How well were they planned? Clearly, the people doing the actual work would be the best qualified to know the details of these parts of the operation. We have seen in Chapter 15 that John Surratt was in Richmond at about this time. He may have provided firsthand information on the status of the operation north of the Potomac.

In using phrases such as "general strategy review," one is tempted to envision a large room with a long table seating Jefferson Davis, his cabinet, General Lee, and other key commanders, and attended by staff officers with maps, charts, and other technical data. That would make a great scene in film or TV documentary, but it was not Jefferson Davis's style. Large meetings in tense times can get out of hand. Issues were sharp, feelings high, and stakes incalculable. Davis would want to control the decision, and that could be done only by conducting the strategy review as a series of small meetings at which the attendance and the agenda could be tailored to achieve the acquiescence and support required for the chosen strategy. Presumably, these meetings started with less controversial technical matters or covered subjects that were already under Davis's control. The covert operation to capture Lincoln would fall in that category. In January, Davis had called for detailed manpower figures and projections for the War Department[35] and had doubtless discussed the situation at length with both General Lee and Secretary of War Seddon.

The war strategy developed by General Lee and apparently approved by President Davis is well described by Lee's adjutant, Colonel Taylor, in his book *Four Years with General Lee.*

> General Lee was opposed to that policy which designated certain points as indispensable. . . . When it came to a siege, to settle down behind intrenchments . . . besieged, by an adversary with unlimited resources of men and material, he preferred to move out, to maneuver, to concentrate, and to fight.
>
> His policy at Petersburg would have been to unite the greater portion of his army . . . with that under General Johnson [sic], and to fall upon General Sherman with the hope of destroying him, and then, with the united armies, to return to confront General Grant.[36]

Lee's nephew General Fitzhugh Lee wrote a biography of his uncle that describes the plan even more clearly:

> During the winter General Lee had given careful consideration to the question of evacuating Petersburg and Richmond. It was attended with many embarrassments. Richmond was the capital city, the machinery of the Confederate Government was in motion there, and the abandonment of a country's capital was a serious step; there, too, were the workshops, iron works, rolling mills, and foundries, which were so essential. Their loss would be a deprivation; and then, too, there was sorrow in turning away and leaving to their fate the noble women, children, and old men of the two cities, whose hearths and homes he had been so long defending. The question of withdrawal was discussed with Mr. Davis, who consented to it, the line of retreat was decided, and Danville, in Virginia, selected as the point to retire upon. It was determined to collect supplies at that point, so that Lee, rapidly moving from his lines, could form a junction with General Joseph E. Johnston, who on February 23d had been instructed to assume the command of the Army of the Tennessee, and all troops in the Department of South Carolina, Georgia, and Florida. Lee and Johnston were then to assail Sherman before Grant could get to his relief, as the question of supplying his enormous army, moving from its base to the interior, would retard him after the first few days' march.[37]

If this strategy were to be implemented, there was much to do, and nature imposed a critical date by which it must be put into motion. As soon after the winter as the ground had dried enough for large-scale military operations to be feasible, Grant could be expected to take major action to break into, surround, or overwhelm the Confederate positions before Petersburg and Richmond. Depending on the weather, that date would probably occur between late March and late April.

On 1 January 1865, Longstreet had noted the pressure of time in a letter to Lee: "I forward today a letter from General Custis Lee upon the condition, etc. of the command at Chaffin's farm. This command, like many others of our army, seems to be sadly in need of organization . . . we have but about three months left us for this work. . . . I believe that we are better able to cope with [the enemy] now than we have ever been, if we will profit by our experience."[38]

By the time the ground was dry enough for operations, supplies had to be accumulated and stored at the proper locations for the campaign. The manpower situation had to be improved and the troop units prepared for the new round of maneuver. If the operation to capture Lincoln did not result in satisfactory negotiations, it could be turned into an attack on Union command and control. By throwing Washington into turmoil, it might reduce the coordination between Grant and Sherman and enhance Lee's chance of success. Most important, it was necessary to get political support for the abandonment of the key positions in Virginia. The state of Virginia had provided tremendous support to the Confederate cause. Its political leadership, military assets, and technical skills had been essential in creating and continuing the Confederacy. To abandon Virginia to an enemy who had already laid waste much of the South would be a bitter reward. The Virginians could be reconciled only by the logic of the strategy as the only way to break out of the stalemate and achieve ultimate victory. They would have been particularly interested in the capture of Lincoln because a successful operation might make it unnecessary to carry out the military maneuver.

Virginia's position was influenced by its attitude on the manpower question. The Confederacy on the whole had made good use of its manpower. Whites had done the fighting, and black labor had run the economy. Now, however, the supply of white manpower was coming to an end. Over the years, bureaucratic havens for draft dodgers had developed and had withstood many attempts to cut them back. The only obvious way to increase the fighting forces would be to enlist blacks into the Confederate armies.

Lee and Davis favored this action,[39] and they were supported by powerful allies, mainly in Virginia. Needless to say, there were also powerful opponents, including those who might lose economically by forfeiting their slaves and those who would not admit that blacks could make good soldiers. To enlist black soldiers, Davis needed the support of the Virginians, but he might lose that support if he seemed ready to abandon Richmond before it was absolutely necessary. Davis thus had to work his way through a thorny thicket to get Lee into a position to implement his chosen strategy. He seems to have chosen the following tactics: Appointment of General Lee as general in chief would demonstrate that the Virginia "establishment" was still supporting, in fact leading, the Confederate effort. It also had the practical effect of putting both the army in Virginia and the army in Carolina under the control of a single commander. This laudable objective was thus accomplished without calling specific attention to the need to coordinate these two armies for a special maneuver. A replacement was needed for Seddon. Davis and Seddon worked well as a team, but Seddon's departure would allow him to take the blame for past failures and give Davis some relief from his critics. Furthermore, Seddon, as former secretary, would not be likely to snipe at Davis in public. Breckinridge, the replacement, had a good reputation as a soldier and immense political stature as a former vice-president and presidential candidate in the United States. Pressing for black enlistment in the army, though not universally popular, would bring practical military relief, confuse those who regarded the Confederacy as anti-Negro, and possibly make a break in the institution of slavery that might lead to its peaceful demise.

Davis must support General Lee in preparing for the new campaign. He had great faith in Lee's abilities, but the two did not agree on all matters. Lee was able to exploit the situation to get Davis's acquiesence in at least two important areas. One was to replace Colonel Lucius B. Northrop, the head of the Commissary Department, and the other was to rehabilitate General Joseph E. Johnston by making him the commander of all the troops in the Carolinas and neighboring states to the south and west. Supporting the covert operations to capture the enemy president was the final element in this strategy. There was a strong retribution element in the South. Its rationale was that if key personnel in the North could be made personally responsible for the devastation and destruction caused by federal troops in the South, commanders at all echelons would be forced to exert more control over troop conduct and change policies about the destruction of property. With the impending likelihood that Virginia would be abandoned during Lee's campaign of maneuver, this rationale had a special appeal to many Virginians. Even more important, if the Confederacy had physical possession of Lincoln, he could be used as a hostage to guarantee gentle treatment of territory in Virginia evacuated during the new military campaign. The capture of Lincoln would, therefore, impress influential Virginians whose support would be needed to make the entire strategy work.

All of this made good logic from the Confederate point of view, but there was one flaw in the scheme that may not have been perceived adequately when the commitment to the covert action plan was made. If the purpose of the action was to produce a hostage, it would have to be done before the beginning of the maneuver campaign. Once the maneuver had begun, it would be almost impossible to get Lincoln into Confederate-controlled territory. If the purpose of the action was to diminish the ability of the Union to respond to the new strategy, it would have to be done in conjunction with the maneuver. In neither case could the Confederacy really control the timing of the move against Lincoln, for in the final analysis, the timing would be controlled by what the Confederate action agents could cause to happen within the constraints imposed by Union security measures.

In other words, the Confederates might count on the scheme to work, but they could not *make* it work. In fact, they could do very little but hope that the action group could pull it off. Yet the success of some very important Confederate plans would be strongly affected by its success or failure, and in a very important sense, John Wilkes Booth was in charge of the timing of the spring campaign that would make or break the Confederacy. The Confederate trust in large-scale covert actions may have involved some wishful thinking, but it is as likely that lack of experience with covert action was the culprit. Statesmen in Richmond had little opportunity to use such ambitious covert operations and had little basis for judging the claims of those organizing the clandestine effort.

The time during which the general strategy review took place can be narrowed by examining events. Francis P. Blair of Maryland, who was attempting to start negotiations for a settlement of the conflict came to Richmond on 11 January 1865 under the auspices of Colonel Robert Ould, saw President Davis, talked to several leading political figures, and returned to Union lines on 14 January to report to President Lincoln.[40] As a result of his activity, it was decided that the Confederacy would send an embassy to talk with the Union. On 28 January, Davis delegated Vice-President Alexander H. Stephens, Senator R. M. T. Hunter of Virginia, and Judge John A. Campbell, assistant secretary of war, to meet with Union authorities. On 3 February, the Confederate delegation met with President Lincoln and Secretary of State Seward on board the *River*

Queen in Hampton Roads off Fortress Monroe, Virginia. The conference disclosed irreconcilable differences, and Lincoln returned to Washington the next day.[41]

Before the Confederate government could assimilate the news from the Hampton Roads conference, General Grant launched an attack at Hatcher's Run on 5 February to extend his lines around the southern flank of the Confederate position. He was trying to cut across some of the few remaining routes by which supplies could reach Richmond. The fighting lasted until 7 February and ended with the Union forces giving up most of the territory they had occupied initially. There would have been no point in having a strategy review before the results of the Hampton Roads conference were known, and it would have been difficult to get the attention of many who needed to be consulted while the battle was in progress at Hatcher's Run.

In the meantime, other events were moving rapidly. On 23 January, the Confederate Congress named General Robert E. Lee to be the general in chief of the Confederate armies. On 1 February, Secretary of War Seddon resigned. On 6 February, Davis named General John C. Breckinridge as the new secretary of war, and the Confederate Congress confirmed the nomination on the same day. Davis also directed that Lee assume his new duties. Colonel Taylor, his adjutant, had written in his journal on 5 February, "It may be necessary to make very important changes in the campaign, and for this Army to change its position."[42]

Breckinridge was sworn in on 7 February, and one of his first actions was to direct that the chiefs of all the bureaus submit a report on "what means and resources they have on hand, what are their necessities, what impediments, and what their ability for successful prosecution of their business." Similar requests were submitted to General Lee and to other key commanders. Most of the replies came in between 9 and 16 February.[43]

On 8 February, General Lee wrote that his troops around Petersburg had been three days without meat.[44] Upon receipt of Lee's letter, the new secretary of war called in Colonel Northrop, head of the Commissary Department. The colonel handled the complaint with casual disdain, which sealed his fate. His poor performance had been a cause for complaint for some time, but his critics had never managed to get him relieved of his post.

On 9 February, Lee assumed his new duties as general in chief and immediately issued public appeals for the return of deserters and the increase of supplies to the army. On 10 February Jefferson

Davis wrote a note to Lee complimenting him on his new position and inviting him to come to Richmond for a conference: "The knowledge of the activity of the enemy has prevented me from asking you to come here for a conference, which I desire to have with you, and which when circumstances will permit, I hope you will come here to hold."[45]

Lee and Davis appear to have had a series of meetings from 13 to 16 February. On 15 February, Colonel I. M. St. John, the chief of the highly successful Mining and Niter Bureau, was named as the new commissary general. On the same day, diarist Jones reported that General Lee was in town "walking about briskly, as if some great event was imminent."[46] His attitude was apparently the result of the conference of which Davis had invited him. On the sixteenth, Jones reported that Lee was at the War Department again that morning looking cheerful.

On 17 February, Jones had reported the view from northern papers that Grant had attacked at Hatcher's Run because he had heard that Lee was evacuating Richmond and was trying to intercept the retreating army. This had the ring of wishful thinking on Jones's part but may also reflect the extent to which discussions of Lee's new strategy had leaked to the Union. On the nineteenth, Jones noted that President Davis and three of his aides rode past his house that day. He observed, "No one who beheld them would have seen anything to suppose that the Capitol itself was in almost immediate danger of falling into the hands of the enemy; much less that the President himself meditated its abandonment at an early day, and the concentration of all the armies in the Cotton States!"[47] At about the same time, Captain C. M. Blackford of the Adjutant and Inspector General's Office sent his wife to stay at Charlottesville in anticipation of the evacuation, indicating that by that time the decision to abandon Richmond was firm enough for minor functionaries in the War Department to be aware of it.[48]

On 24 February, after a short stay with his command, Colonel Mosby came back to Richmond.[49] Presumably, plans were being coordinated in light of decisions made in mid-February. This may be the occasion mentioned by Mosby in his *Memoirs* when he had dinner with General Lee "about two months before the surrender."[50]

It did not take the Union army command very long to hear of the new decision. On 25 February, General Meade's headquarters issued a warning to the corps commanders: "Everything tends to satisfy the Major General commanding that the rebels contemplate evacuating Petersburg . . . keep your command ready to follow up closely. . . . Deserters are to be examined at once and the result telegraphed."[51]

On 19 February, Jefferson Davis received a message from General Beauregard which caused him concern for the welfare of Confederate operations in the Carolinas. Davis's initial inclination was to send Lee to look the situation over on the ground, but later it was decided to send General Gilmer instead.

On 20 February, Colonel Taylor, Lee's adjutant, wrote: "My orders are to be in marching order. To lose no time, to begin my preparations tomorrow. These instructions apply to army headquarters only. The Army will retain its position still a time longer, but the general-in-chief may soon bid it a temporary adieu and repair to another scene of excitement." Four days later he wrote, "Now that General Johnston has been placed in command of his old army by General Lee, it is not probable that the latter will go to South Carolina—at any rate not immediately."[52]

During the four days between Taylor's journal entries, General Lee was a very busy man. On 21 February, he wrote to the secretary of war: "I have repeated the orders to the commanding officers to remove and destroy everything in the enemy's route. In the event of the necessity of abandoning our position on the James River, I shall endeavor to unite the Corps of the Army about Burkesville [junction of South Side and Danville railroads], so as to retain communications . . . as long as practicable. . . . It was my intention in my former letter to apply for General J. E. Johnston, that I might assign him to duty. . . . I therefore respectfully request General Johnston may be ordered to report to me and that I may be informed where he is."[53] Lee apparently had a strong ally in General Breckinridge, the new secretary of war, for Breckinridge was writing to Lee at the same time saying, "My strong convictions of the absolute necessity of beating Sherman induce me to suggest to you the collection of all available troops from other parts for this purpose."[54]

Johnston, in his memoirs, says that on 23 February at Lincolnton, North Carolina, he received orders from the War Department to report to General Lee for orders and a message from Lee directing him to take command of the Army of Tennessee and all troops in South Carolina, Georgia, and Florida to "concentrate all available forces and drive back Sherman." Johnston also noted that upon assuming command he found that there were rations for sixty thousand men for more than four months in the railroad depots in the triangle formed by Danville, Weldon, and Charlotte, North Carolina.[55] This was the area into which Lee intended to move the Army of Northern Virginia when he left Richmond and Petersburg. If there were any soldiers going hungry, the problem was in the distribution of the supplies, not in their existence.

In fact, the survey of means and resources inaugurated by Breckinridge revealed that a powerful Confederate fighting machine still existed. There were many problem areas—desertions and a shortage of manpower, horses, and transport—but in the essential sinews of war—food, weapons, ammunition, and medical supplies—the Confederacy was in reasonably good shape. The accepted historical view of deterioration in the Confederate army seems to have been based in part on retrospective rationalization of a South "overwhelmed by superior resources."[56]

On 10 February, John B. Jones quoted the ordnance report, which stated that the Confederacy was producing fifty-five thousand rifles per year and seven thousand pounds of powder per day. The powder charge for a twelve-pounder field gun was 2.5 pounds. A pound of powder of appropriate texture could provide for about 140 musket or rifle shots. Thus one days' production could provide for nearly a million shots from rifles or 2,800 shots from a field gun. Daily expenditure was far below those rates, allowing for the accumulation of reserves to support the battles in which expenditures were higher. On 21 February, General Lee reported that there were ten thousand spare arms available to equip returning prisoners of war. Colonel St. John, the new commissary general, later wrote that he had expected to encounter great difficulties in finding food for the armies, but that enemy pressure was the main constraint: "I found the Army of Northern Virginia with difficulty supplied day by day with reduced rations. In other military departments, however, the situation was better; and from several it was still possible to draw a considerable surplus for the Richmond and Petersburg depots, wherever transportation could be procured." By mid-March, great strides had been made in improving the flow of supplies to Lee's army, and by the end of March a special reserve of over 300,000 rations had been assembled in Richmond. In addition, there were 500,000 rations of bread and 1.5 million rations of meat at Danville, Virginia, 180,000 rations of bread and meat at Lynchburg, Virginia, and 1.5 million rations of bread and meat at Greensboro, North Carolina, and vicinity.[57]

Other measures were taken during February to prepare for the new campaign. On 21 February, by Special Order 43, paragraph

XIII, General Rains, chief of the army's Torpedo Bureau, was ordered to report personally to Major General Jeremy F. Gilmer, chief engineer of the forces in the Carolinas. Rains was instructed to take with him a supply of detonators and other technical gear needed to wage a mine campaign.[58] The building of mine fields and barriers would be a logical tactic to employ to delay and constrict the movement of Sherman's army.

A survey was made of the attitude of the soldiers in the trenches around Petersburg toward the enlistment of blacks. On 18 February, General Gordon reported that the officers and men of the Second Corps were "decidedly in favor of the voluntary enlistment of the Negroes as soldiers." On 23 February, General Order 8 instructed generals of reserves to "immediately place upon active duty every man belonging to that class [i.e., reservist] who is not specially detailed or has not been turned over to generals commanding, armies, departments, or districts." On 25 February, General Ewell, who commanded the Department of Richmond, summarized ways to find defensive forces within the city: "There is a reserve force of about 200 reliable men here. There are also about 600 men at the different hospitals organized and armed, which I hope to increase to nearly 1,000. The Negroes at the hospitals wish to join this force. It would require three hours to get the local defense [brigade], nearly 2,000 under arms. McAnerney's battalion (400) could parade in less time. Reserves 200; hospitals 600; cadets [from VMI then in Richmond] 200—1000 could parade within half an hour's notice."[59]

On 26 February, Ewell sent the secretary of war an earlier letter from Lee's staff questioning Lee's desire that the cotton and tobacco stored in Richmond should be removed.[60] Lee apparently wanted to be sure that these commodities were out of Richmond before he abandoned the city to the enemy.

At about the same time, a confidential circular was issued by the War Department. It said in part:

> In addition to the results of personal interviews held with the several chiefs of bureaus of the War Department, they will observe the following general instructions in reference to a possible removal of the Department from Richmond:
>
> Whatever may be indispensibly requisite to the current operations of the Department will be retrieved up to the last moment of safety, the utmost preliminary preparation for removal having first been made.
>
> Whatever may not be deemed thus requisite will be removed without

unnecessary delay to Danville, Virginia, or points on the railroad beyond Danville.[61]

On 24 February, Breckinridge wrote to Lee asking if stores and
archives should be removed immediately or if it was necessary
only to prepare to remove them. The following day, he wrote to
Lee: "I have given the necessary orders in regard to commencing
the removal of stores, etc., but if possible, would like to know
whether we may probably count on a period of ten or twelve
days."[62]

Breckinridge's questions and the general tempo of activity in
February suggest that there was considerable haste in preparations.
It sounds as though some officials thought they may have been
working toward a target date of early or mid-March. That date may
have been influenced by the need to be ready to take advantage of
the condition of the ground when it began to dry out and by the
need to be ready to act when the covert operation delivered President Lincoln into the hands of the Confederacy as a hostage.

The pressure of preparation for the new campaign was so great
that the tension quickly spread to the body politic. On 25 February,
Davis wrote an unusually curt note to Lee: "Rumors assuming to
be based on your views have affected the public mind, and it is
reported obstructs needful legislation. A little further progress will
produce panic. If you can spare the time I wish you to come
here."[63]

Union spies reported that there had been a meeting at President
Davis's house on 26 February, attended by several senior officers
and Governor William Smith of Virginia. They thought that General Lee was also present. Lee may have been there; his adjutant
recorded that he returned to headquarters on 28 February.[64] This
meeting may have been a result of Davis's note to Lee and may have
dealt with the timing of the evacuation of Richmond.

Writing nearly forty years after the war, one of Lee's corps commanders, General John B. Gordon, described an interview with Lee
that probably reflects Lee's attempts to prepare himself for a crucial interview with Jefferson Davis. It was in late February—he
could not recall the exact date. In the discussion, however, Lee
showed Gordon the opinions of General Joseph E. Johnston concerning the strength of the Confederate armies in North Carolina.[65] Johnston received his orders to assume command in North
Carolina in Lincolnton on 23 February. He then traveled to
Charlotte, more than 30 miles away, where he reviewed the situa-

tion with General Beauregard before he wrote his own report to Lee. This report probably could not have been written before 24 February. It does not appear to have been sent by telegraph but by courier riding trains about 250 miles from Charlotte to Greensboro, Danville, Richmond, and then to Lee's headquarters near Petersburg. The trip would require changes in trains along the way because of differences in the width of the track on various parts of the route. The trip from Charlotte to Richmond would probably have taken at least twenty-four hours and might easily have taken forty-eight.

In the course of his conversation with Gordon, Lee said that he would discuss the substance of their conversation with Davis. This latter conversation apparently occurred on 4 March 1865, and the time for this meeting was requested by Lee in a letter to Davis on 1 March. It would appear, therefore, that Lee's conversation with Gordon must have occurred on 25 February or more probably sometime between 28 February, when he returned to his headquarters, and 3 March.[66]

According to Gordon, Lee had him summoned at two o'clock in the morning, and when Gordon arrived at Lee's headquarters he found that Lee had been up all night. Lee was apparently in an agitated state and made Gordon sit down and read through a stack of reports that Lee handed to him in a specific order. Gordon said that when he finished reading he was distressed to find that the difficulties facing the Confederacy were even greater than he had realized. Lee asked Gordon his recommendations as to the course that should be followed. Gordon replied that in his view there were three alternatives, which he stated in order of desirability: (1) negotiate a settlement with the Union; (2) abandon Richmond and Petersburg and join the Army of Northern Virginia to the armies in North Carolina to attack Sherman; (3) fight without delay. Gordon is not very clear on the final point and uses it to help justify the later disastrous attack on Fort Stedman, but his first two points appear to have coincided with those already decided by Davis and Lee. Gordon's reaction may have reassured Lee.

From his actions in February, it would appear that General Lee wanted to keep up a momentum leading toward the big maneuver. He may have feared that the 25 February message indicated a change in Davis's support for the strategy and that the momentum would be lost. The meeting of 26 February may have resulted in a decision to stall the departure from Richmond longer than Lee thought wise. That and the complexity of the work imposed on him might account for Lee's agitation.

Gordon said that after the conference with President Davis on 4 March, Lee told Gordon that Davis was in complete accord with the maneuver plan and had asked Lee why it should not be implemented immediately. Lee had told Davis that it was necessary to wait for the ground to dry out before leaving. That may have been Lee's way of reassuring Gordon without telling him the real reasons for the delay. It would not do to tell every senior officer in the army that the Confederacy could not begin the maneuver until John Wilkes Booth had captured Abraham Lincoln.

Lee apparently did not tell Gordon that he had written to Grant on 2 March seeking to negotiate an armistice and that Grant had begged off on the grounds that he did not have the necessary authority.[67] The only person with whom the Confederates could deal was Lincoln. Jefferson Davis later described his recollections of what may well have been either the conference of 26 February or that of 4 March;

> In the early part of March, as well as my memory can fix the date, General Lee held with me a long and free conference. He stated that the circumstances had forced on him the conclusion that the evacuation of Petersburg was but a question of time. . . . If we had to retreat it should be in a southwardly direction toward the country from which we were drawing supplies, and from which a large portion of our forces had been derived. . . . The programme was to retire to Danville, at which place supplies should be collected and a junction made with the troops under General J. E. Johnston, the combined force to be hurled upon Sherman in North Carolina, with the hope of defeating him before Grant could come to the relief. Then the more southern States, freed from pressure and encouraged by this success, it was expected, would send large reinforcements to the army, and Grant, drawn far from his base of supplies into the midst of a hostile population, it was hoped might yet be defeated.[68]

Davis's memory may have combined recollections of more than one conversation, but it seems clear that there was general agreement on the course that was to be followed. There remained "but a question of time."

The decisions the Confederate government appears to have made during the period January–March 1865 seem to have fallen into a framework of four steps.

First, there was the political decision to refine and redefine the fundamental goals of the Confederacy. Those goals appear to have boiled down to one essential objective—independence. To achieve that objective, the Confederacy was willing to accept a revolution in social, economic, and political organizations—the abolition of slavery—as the price of independence so long as the South could preside over the transition from slavery.

Second was the decision to negotiate with the Union on the basis of the new political goals and, failing the successful conclusion of overt negotiations, to fall back on covert action to seize Lincoln as a hostage. As a captive, Lincoln would be forced to talk to his captors, and negotiations conducted with a captive Lincoln might be far different from negotiations with a President Lincoln on the deck of a Union warship.

Third was the decision concerning the military course that should be followed if the negotiation attempt should fail. Various alternatives were suggested, but there was substantial agreement among men who understood military affairs that Richmond and Petersburg should be abandoned and that the Army of Northern Virginia should be joined to the armies in North Carolina. The main steps in this scheme were fairly clear, and it is likely that supplies were being positioned near Danville and in North Carolina to support this maneuver long before it was accepted as the solution.

Finally, there was the decision that the timing of the military maneuver would be influenced by factors such as weather, the completion of preparations, and other events on the battlefield, as well as by the success of the political negotiations or operations. Successful negotiations might obviate the need for a military maneuver, and the date for the start of the maneuver would have to be postponed until it was clear that negotiations would not produce results. The capture of Lincoln as a hostage was a subsidiary part of this issue, which would require that the military decisions be postponed as long as possible to give the covert operation time to deliver results. At least one other important factor would influence the time of the military decision. That was the related question of military manpower, and that question could be resolved only through positive action by the Confederate Congress to authorize the enlistment of blacks as soldiers in the Confederate army.

Lee might well have wanted to leave Richmond earlier, but to allow time for the covert operation and for the resolution of the manpower question, he may have agreed that it would be safe to delay the departure until mid-April. As it turned out, events in March 1865 made the delay fatal for the Confederacy.

Notes

ABBREVIATIONS
NA   National Archives
OR   U.S. War Department, *The War of the Rebellion: A Compilation of the Official Records of the Union and Confederate Armies*. 128 vols. Washington, D.C.: U.S. Government Printing Office, 1880–1901.
ORN U.S. Navy Department, *Official Records of the Union and Confederate Navies in the War of the Rebellion*. 30 vols. Washington, D.C.: U.S. Government Printing Office, 1894–1914.
RG   Record Group

1. Mary Boykin Chesnut, *Mary Chesnut's Civil War*, ed. C. Vann Woodward (New Haven: Yale University Press, 1981), p. 710.

2. *Biographical Directory of the American Congress, 1774–1971* (Washington, D.C.: U.S. Government Printing Office, 1971): *Congressional Globe*, 1847–48, passim.

3. Virginia Military Institute, *Register of Former Cadets* (Lexington, Va.: Virginia Military Institute, 1939).

4. Robert Bolling Lancaster, *Hanover County, Virginia* (Richmond: Whittett and Shepparson for the Bicentennial Committee for Hanover County, 1976), pp. 63, 64.

5. "Paroles of the Army of Northern Virginia," *Southern Historical Society Papers* 15 (1887): 465.

6. Mrs. Norris to Mother, William Norris Papers, University of Virginia Library, Charlottesville. Dates added through collation and research.

7. Records of the Richmond, Fredericksburg, and Potomac Railroad, January–June 1863, Virginia Historical Society, Richmond.

8. *OR*, Ser. 1, vol. 46, pt. 2, p. 1111.

9. R. L. T. Beale, Compiled Service Record, NA.

10. *OR*, Ser. 1, vol. 42, pt. 2, pp. 1273–74.

11. George Washington Custis Lee, Compiled Service Record, NA.

12. Special Order 316, Headquarters, Department of Northern Virginia, 24 December 1864, in the possession of Hugh MacGill of Hartford, Connecticut, a great-grandson of Mayo.

13. Manuscript Collection, No. 24335, Virginia State Library, Richmond.

14. *OR*, Ser. 1, vol. 46, pt. 2, p. 1025.

15. Ibid., p. 1122.

16. Ibid., p. 1278.

17. Ibid., p. 1014.

18. Ibid., p. 1256.

19. Ezra J. Warner, *Generals in Gray: Lives of the Confederate Commanders* (Baton Rouge: Louisiana State University Press, 1959), p. 63.

20. *Bulletin* of the *King and Queen County Historical Society* 24 (January 1968), no page numbers.

21. Compiled Service Records of the Ninth Virginia Cavalry and Forty-seventh Virginia Infantry Regiments, NA.

22. *OR*, Ser. 1, vol. 46, pt. 2, p. 976.

23. Ibid., pt. 3, p. 237.

24. Warner, *Generals in Gray*, p. 177; Edwin G. Lee, Compiled Service Record,

NA; J[ohn] Y[ates] B[eall] to E. G. Lee, 20 July 1863, William Nelson Pendleton Papers, Southern Historical Collection, University of North Carolina, Chapel Hill.

25. Edwin Gray Lee Diary, 5, 6 December 1864, Duke University Library, Durham, N.C.; Susan P. Lee, *Memoirs of William Nelson Pendleton* (Philadelphia: Lippincott, 1893), p. 378.

26. James J. Williamson, *Mosby's Rangers* (New York: Sturgis and Walton, 1909), pp. 489–93.

27. John S. Mosby to Pauline Mosby, 3 February 1865, Manuscript Collection, Virginia State Library.

28. John Scott, *Partisan Life with Col. John S. Mosby* (New York: Harper & Bros., 1867), p. 466.

29. *OR*, Ser. 1, vol. 46, pt. 2, p. 537.

30. Ibid., p. 525.

31. Harry H. Brogden, Compiled Service Record, NA.

32. H. H. Brogden to Captain William N. Barker, 12 December 1864, Confederate Secretary of War, Letters Received, M-437, reel 146, frames 332–33, NA.

33. Confederate Secretary of War, Letters Received, WD 44-S/65, RG 109, NA.

34. Letters Received by the Confederate Adjutant and Inspector General, 1861–65, M-474, reel 164, frame 0094, RG 109, NA.

35. John B. Jones, *A Rebel War Clerk's Diary*, ed. Howard Swiggett, 2 vols. (New York: Old Hickory Book Shop, 1935), 2:399.

36. Walter Herron Taylor, *Four Years with General Lee*, ed. James I. Robertson, Jr. (Bloomington: Indiana University Press, 1962), pp. 145–46.

37. Fitzhugh Lee, *General Lee* (1894; rpt. Greenwich, Conn.: Fawcett, 1961), p. 354.

38. *OR*, Ser. 1, vol. 51, pt. 2, p. 1056.

39. There are many references to the role of President Davis and General Lee in pushing for the enlistment of black soldiers in the Confederate army. An amusing reaction is found in Jones, *Rebel War Clerk's Diary*, 2:398.

40. Ibid., pp. 395–96.

41. E. B. Long, *The Civil War Day by Day* (Garden City, N.Y.: Doubleday, 1971), p. 633.

42. Taylor, *Four Years with General Lee*, p. 143.

43. "Resources of the Confederacy in February 1865," *Southern Historical Society Papers* 2 (1876): 57–62, 113–28.

44. R. E. Lee, *The Wartime Papers of R. E. Lee*, ed. Clifford Dowdey and Louis H. Manarin (New York: Bramhall House, 1961), p. 890.

45. *OR*, Ser. 1, vol. 46, pt. 2, p. 1227.

46. Jones, *Rebel War Clerk's Diary*, 2:422.

47. Ibid., p. 426.

48. Susan Leigh Blackford, *Letters from Lee's Army*, ed. Charles Minor Blackford III (New York: Charles Scribner's Sons, 1947), p. 277.

49. J. W. Duffey, *Two Generals Kidnapped* (Moorefield, W.Va.: Moorefield Examiner, 1944), p. 18.

50. John S. Mosby, *The Memoirs of Colonel John S. Mosby*, ed. Charles Wells Russell (Bloomington: Indiana University Press, 1981), p. 375.

51. *OR*, Ser. 1, vol. 51, pt. 1, p. 1202.

52. Taylor, *Four Years with General Lee*, p. 143.

53. Lee, *Wartime Papers*, p. 906.

54. *OR*, Ser. 1, vol. 46, pt. 2, p. 1245.

55. Joseph E. Johnston, *Narrative of Military Operations*, ed. Frank Vandiver (Bloomington: Indiana University Press, 1959), pp. 371, 375.

56. See, for example, Douglas Southall Freeman, *R. E. Lee*, 4 vols. (New York: Charles Scribner's Sons, 1935), 3:525, 4:1–4.

57. Jones, *Rebel War Clerk's Diary*, 2:416; *OR*, Ser. 1, vol. 46, pt. 2, p. 1246; St. John to Davis, 14 July 1873, *Southern Historical Society Papers* 3 (1877): 98–99.

58. *OR*, Ser. 1, vol. 51, pt. 2, p. 1063.

59. Ibid., vol. 46, pt. 2, pp. 1251, 1257, 1259–60.

60. Ibid., pp. 1260–61.

61. Ibid., p. 1257.

62. Ibid., p. 1254.

63. Ibid., p. 1256.

64. Ibid., p. 786; Taylor to Bettie Saunders, 28 February 1865, File 28114, Virginia State Library.

65. John B. Gordon, *Reminiscences of the Civil War* (New York: Charles Scribner's Sons, 1905), pp. 385–90.

66. Freeman dates this conversation as occurring on 3 March 1865.

67. Robert Garlick Hill Kean, *Inside the Confederate Government* (New York: Oxford University Press, 1957), p. 203.

68. Jefferson Davis, *The Rise and Fall of the Confederate Government*, 2 vols. (rpt. ed. Bell I. Wiley, South Brunswick: Thomas Yoseloff, 1958), 2:648.

17

Complication and Frustration

On Saturday, 4 March 1865, John Wilkes Booth stood on the Capitol steps in Washington and heard Abraham Lincoln say: "Yet if God wills that [the war] continue until all the wealth piled by the bondsman's two hundred and fifty years of unrequited toil shall be sunk, and until every drop of blood drawn with the lash shall be paid by another drawn with the sword, as was said three thousand years ago, so still it must be said, the judgments of the Lord are true and righteous altogether." For anyone who, like Booth, was already convinced of Lincoln's hostility to the South, these words could only reinforce belief in his implacable enmity. Under the circumstances it is not surprising that the next sentence, so often quoted by the admirers of Lincoln, would fail to make the impression that it does when taken in isolation: "With malice toward none; with charity for all; with firmness in the right as God gives us to see the right, let us strive on to finish the work we are in; to bind up the nation's wounds".[1]

Lincoln, as a good politician, may have thought of the speech as an opportunity to say something for everybody—the first sentence for the hard-line abolitionists and the next sentence for the war-weary in North and South alike. Unfortunately, politics is a bit like the game of bridge; it is difficult to mislead your opponents without also misleading your partner. In Lincoln's case, the effect of his statesmanlike declaration of friendship and tolerance was clouded by a sentence that struck at the survival and family welfare of every southerner who heard or read the words.

It is not surprising that, when the text of the speech reached Richmond during the following week, people were not impressed by the magnanimity of their foe. Rather, they were inspired to

379

increase their efforts toward the moment of victory and retribution.

The decision to leave Richmond to go back to a war of maneuver had cleared the air for many Confederates. It had given them an objective to work toward and positive hope that they could succeed. At the same time, the decision to leave Richmond could not be admitted openly. To inform the public would be to inform Grant, and it was important to create as much uncertainty as possible in the minds of Union commanders. Unfortunately, the public of Richmond could tell from the bustle and scurry that something was afoot and that the outcome might leave the population of Richmond in the hands of the Yankees. As a result, there was a distinct attitude of doom and gloom on the part of many in Richmond. Some historians have seized on this attitude as foretelling the inevitable fall of the Confederacy. Since the Confederacy did fall, their interpretation is self-fulfilling, but it seems far more likely that the attitude of those in the center of decision making was much more optimistic.

In a way, Grant and Lee were working toward a common objective. Grant wanted to surround Lee with Union armies so that he could keep Lee from escaping, and Lee wanted to be in the center of the Union armies so that he could maneuver to strike them one by one. The difference in the Union and Confederate strategies was largely a matter of timing. Lee needed to move before the Union armies got close enough to be mutually reinforcing, and Grant needed to keep Lee from moving so other Union armies could get close enough to finish the encirclement.

One of the clearest official references to the timing of the great maneuver in the surviving records of the Confederacy is contained in a letter of 1 March 1865 from the Confederate secretary of the navy, Stephen Mallory, to Commander James D. Bulloch, the Confederate naval representative in England: "We are upon the eve of events fraught with the fate of the Confederacy, and without power to foresee the result; I can only rely on your good judgment and patriotism to shape the proper course. The coming campaign will be in active operation within fifty days and we cannot close our eyes to the danger which threatens us and from which only our united and willing hearts and arms and the providence of God can shield us. We look for no aid from any other source."[2]

The weather had an important bearing on the question of timing. The average rainfall in March in the Richmond area is 3.7 inches. In April it drops to 3.3 inches, which is the lowest rainfall until

September. Also, in the Richmond area the average date of the last freeze falls between 5 and 10 April.[3] Thereafter, the ground would dry out and the roads would become passable for the supply trains that armies needed for food and ammunition.

In previous years of the war, the opening of the spring campaign had reflected the same combination of factors. In 1862, McClellan had started the ground operations of his Peninsula campaign on 4 April. He was in sandy Tidewater counties, where mud was not the major problem that it was in the Piedmont area, and his troops were near the York and James rivers and could be supplied by water. In 1863, General Hooker had begun to move toward Chancellorsville on 27 April, and Grant had begun the Wilderness campaign on 4 May 1864. In other words, in spite of the unusual rains of the winter of 1865, movement in the Tidewater area occupied by Grant would probably be feasible early in April, but a few miles inland, the mud would be a major obstacle for several weeks thereafter.

Lee had a little more flexibility in picking a departure date. He was planning to move through country occupied by the Confederacy along an operating railroad. Most of his supplies could be positioned in advance to minimize the weight to be carried in his wagons. Grant in pursuit would be moving through hostile country and would have to bring his supplies with him. This requirement would cause him to move slowly until the roads dried out. Lee would have an opportunity to outmaneuver Grant once more.

Grant later summarized his own thinking in his memoirs:

> One of the most anxious periods of my experience during the rebellion was the last few weeks before Petersburg. . . . I was afraid, every morning, that I would awake from my sleep to hear that Lee had gone, and that nothing was left but a picket line. . . . I knew that he could move much more lightly and more rapidly than I, and that, if he got the start, he would leave me behind. . . . There were two considerations I had to observe, however, and which detained me. One was the fact that the winter had been one of heavy rains, and the roads were impassable for artillery and teams. . . . The other consideration was that General Sheridan with the Cavalry of the Army of the Potomac was operating on the north side of the James River. . . . I was therefore obliged to wait until he could join me south of the James River.[4]

The Confederate supply organization headed by General St.John did an amazing job during February and March 1865. The corridor down which Lee expected to move was loaded with supplies. If the Confederate army were to leave Richmond about 10 April, it could expect to move during improving weather, with lightly loaded wagons. It would chew up the same roads that Grant would need to use in his pursuit accompanied by heavily loaded wagons, and for about two or three weeks the roads would continue to inhibit Grant's movements.

That magic date for the exodus, perhaps about 10 to 15 April, became the driving influence for all other measures being undertaken by the Confederates. The military had its preparations to make. Davis had to get the Confederate Congress to pass some key measures and then get out of town, and the government bureaucracy itself had chores to perform—sort records, move money, and decide how to operate in a spartan new environment. If Lincoln were to be used as a hostage, he would have to be in Confederate hands by late March—to try after that time would be cutting it too fine. Thus Booth and his action group must have been under considerable pressure to perform by that date. Doubtless, they were not aware of the reasons for the time pressure, but they must have felt it.

On the Virginia end of the clandestine operation, everything was ready some time during February or early March. The force to protect the escape routes was in place, and the Richmond, Fredericksburg, and Potomac Railroad seems to have had a special train available that may have been the train poised at Milford to take the action party and its captive down to the Ashland area. Since all train crews appear to have been needed for the regular operations of the railroad, other personnel were diverted to train crew duty. A. Searcy, the baggage agent at the Richmond depot, was given extra pay for acting as conductor of a train during February 1865. Sam Minitree, a conductor, was given extra pay to act as the engineer, and Ben Scott was paid $5.50 a day to act as "train hand." Surviving records indicate that he served at least from 22 February to 18 March 1865. The railroad's records covering expenditures for the month of March 1865 would have been filled out and filed in April. Unfortunately, few records filed in April survived, and it is not possible to get a termination date for this special arrangement for a crew for the train.[5]

The presence of the companies of Mosby's battalion wintering in the Northern Neck was fairly overt and well known by the Union. Finding subsistence for the winter months was adequate reason for them to be in that area.

The special security force, however, involved a considerable number of men spread about an area that had received little attention from the Confederate government. It was almost inevitable that somebody would notice their presence, even if their mission remained unknown.

On 1 March 1865, Colonel H. H. Wells, the Union provost marshal at Alexandria, Virginia, just outside Washington, reported that a rebel deserter (an officer) had said that Confederate cavalry had pickets along the south bank of the Rappahannock downstream from the Richmond, Fredericksburg, and Potomac railroad bridge at Fredericksburg. This information was sent as a routine message to the staff of Major General Christopher C. Augur, the commander of the Washington military district. It must have stirred a beehive of interest because three and a half hours later the provost marshal sent Augur a more complete account of the interrogation of the deserter.[6]

According to this message, the first lieutenant providing the information was from a Missouri regiment and had been serving as the commander of train guards on railroads running from Richmond to various points. He apparently deserted while in the neighborhood of Culpeper, Virginia, and traveled south and east along the Rappahannock until he reached Fredericksburg. There he found that the first ford below the railroad bridge was guarded by a detachment from the Fifteenth Virginia Cavalry Regiment. These men told him the remainder of the river was picketed but gave him no indication of its purpose. From that location he traveled north until he fell into Union hands.

The next day this information was circulated to other military commands and interested parties in Washington. On the night of 2 March, Secretary of War Stanton sent a nervous message to Grant: "Have you sent any force toward the Rappahannock. . . . Past disasters from stripping this department of troops repeatedly have made me very solicitous in this matter and apprehensive of a surprise in our defenseless condition." Grant replied immediately with a calm appraisal of this situation:

> If the returns I have of troops in the Department of Washington are anything like correct there need not be the slightest apprehension for the safety of the Capitol. At this time, if Lee could spare any considerable force, it would be for the defense of points now threatened which are necessary for the existence of his army. He would not send off any large body without my knowing it. . . . The fact is, the enemy are reaping such advantages by the way of the Fredericksburg road that they are anxious to avoid attracting attention in that direction. I have ordered a force, mostly infantry, to prepare to go up the Rappahannock, as soon

as transportation can be got for them, for the purpose of breaking up this trade, and shall try to break up the road at the same time.[7]

Grant also asked his own intelligence people to make an extra effort to learn whether any sizable force had left the Confederate lines. General Meade replied on 3 March, reporting the interrogation of seventy-two deserters.[8] The only significant unit missing was Lane's Brigade, formerly Hoke's Brigade of North Carolina troops, and Meade speculated that it had returned to North Carolina.

Grant was overly optimistic about his ability to detect the departure of a "considerable force." It had already left his front, and he was not aware of it.

Major General Winfield Scott Hancock, the commander of the Union Middle Military Division at Winchester, Virginia, was also busy on 2 March. He sent off a résumé of what he knew of the Confederate order of battle to the chief of staff in Washington and asked General Augur for additional information on the enemy in the neighborhood of the Rappahannock. Augur replied: "There is no definite information from the Rappahannock above Fredericksburg. At this point, there is no force excepting guerillas and a few men on furlough. A scout of 500 cavalry has been ordered to the vicinity of Rappahannock bridge to obtain all possible information as to movement of the enemy. It has been reported that he is picketing the river with the Fifteenth Virginia Cavalry, from Fitz Lee's command. Result of the scout will be duly reported."[9]

In other words, while Grant was sending a force up the Rappahannock, Augur was sending another down overland from Washington to the vicinity of Fredericksburg. One of the two should get enough information to reassure Washington of its safety. In this message Augur may have made a classic mistake in military intelligence analysis. Because the one picket actually observed by the deserter belonged to the Fifteenth Virginia Cavalry, it was assumed that all the pickets were from the Fifteenth. That assumption would automatically establish the strength of that cavalry regiment as the top figure for the number of Confederate troops involved. Grant also immediately assumed that the cross-blockade trade through Fredericksburg was the focus of the Confederate activity. That assumption kept the Union forces from looking for alternative explanations. If anybody associated the pickets with the Signal Corps line, that thought was not conveyed to Grant or to the troops involved in the expedition up the Rappahannock.

The troops to go on the expedition were picked with considerable care. The infantry unit selected was Henry's Brigade of eighteen hundred men under command of Colonel S. H. Roberts of the 139th New York Volunteers. Three hundred troopers from the First New York Mounted Rifles (also known as the Seventh New York Cavalry Regiment) under the command of Colonel Edwin V. Sumner were also selected to go along to provide cavalry scouting, protection, and support. Colonel Roberts was given detailed instructions by General Grant on 4 March 1865. He was directed to go up the Rappahannock on transports as far as he felt he could safely do so. At that point he was to debark and proceed overland to capture Fredericksburg, break up the contraband trade, and destroy the railroad as far south as he could.[10]

The expedition headed up the Rappahannock on 6 March and reached Fredericksburg that night. In view of the U.S. Navy's experience with Confederable mines and the previous report about Beverly Kennon being appointed as torpedo officer for the Rappahannock, the ships of the Potomac River Flotilla escorting the expedition were given specific instructions to search carefully in advance of the expedition. At points where electrical mines might be detonated from shore, armed parties were to sweep the shore. The orders went on, "You are to shell as usual all heights."[11]

In the event, no mines were encountered and Lieutenant Carlton's cavalry pickets and others kept themselves well hidden. The expedition captured Fredericksburg without any fighting and destroyed twenty-eight freight cars, eighteen of which were loaded, at Hamilton's Crossing, the first station south of Fredericksburg, burned the stores there, and destroyed the bridge over Massaponax Creek. A few Confederates were sighted on the banks of the Rappahannock on the return trip, but the entire expedition was back at Fortress Monroe on the evening of 8 March.

Colonel Roberts, the commander, filed two messages. In one he reported the significant accomplishments and indicated that he had possible evidence of Union connivance in the contraband trade. In the second he proposed that he return immediately to the Northern Neck and sweep the lower counties to round up "some 500 cavalry . . . living upon the people and ready to collect conscripts and horses for the Confederates." He added, "It will take about five days to do the work well."[12]

Grant immediately ordered Roberts to carry out the recommended sweep and asked the navy to send its ships back up the Rappahannock again to cooperate with Roberts. Roberts, however, found out that the execution of his plan was not as easy as he had thought it would be. On 13 March, he sent an apologetic message from the Maryland side of the Potomac to the headquarters at City Point, Virginia. He had tried landing at Kinsale in Westmoreland County and had been repulsed by Mosby's men: "I regret to report that my expedition to the Northern Neck has not been very successful so far. I find the enemy in stronger force than I expected and superior in cavalry and a perfect knowledge of the country. I can march through the country with my present force, but I should probably lose a good many men, and it would take several days more time. In view of the probable results, I do not feel justified in losing the men and time, without further instructions."[13]

While this expedition was in operation, the Union army received information that might well have been another reflection of the Confederate clandestine task force. On 2 March a prisoner of war reported that Fitz Lee was in New Kent County with a brigade of cavalry. On 7 March, a deserter reported that two hundred rebel cavalry had left New Kent Courthouse for the Fredericksburg area.[14] The Union intelligence people apparently did not connect these reports with the previous report of pickets along the Rappahannock. New Kent County, however, lies between the Pamunkey and Chickahominy rivers just east of Hanover County. A unit stationed there could keep an eye on the extreme right end of the Union line. If the Union forces tried to raid Ashland or to move north overland toward Urbanna, the Confederates would learn of the movement almost immediately. It was a good location for a flanking unit of the security force.

In the meantime, another player was about to enter the scene, and this one man probably did more to cause the failure of Lee's plan than any other. General Philip Sheridan with the main force of Union cavalry was encamped near the northern end of the Shenandoah Valley. Sheridan had a reputation as a fighter who approached his tasks with logic. At a time when most commanders holed up for the remainder of the winter, Sheridan decided he should take the field.

Sheridan had an ideal advantage. The Valley Turnpike was paved, and the cavalry, wagons, and artillery could move southward rapidly for two or three days and leave the turnpike where they would be most likely to surprise the Confederates. Once off the Valley Turnpike, they would be delayed by mud and swollen streams, but of all arms cavalry was best able to cope with such conditions. In any case, Sheridan would have the initiative and the Confederates would be denied their winter rest.

Sheridan was successful in catching General Early and the remains of his army in the Valley at Waynesboro on 2 March. Sheridan captured most of the infantry, artillery, and supplies. The Confederate cavalry was scattered. Sheridan reported this outcome in a message to General Halleck, the chief of staff in Washington, but the message had to go by horseback from Waynesboro to Harpers Ferry for electrical transmission. As a result, the various Union authorities did not know what had happened to Sheridan and his cavalry until 8 March.[15]

General Grant was in the unfortunate position of having to try to guess what had happened to Sheridan by watching what the Confederates in front of him were doing. On 7 March, he was sent a report that General Pickett's division had been pulled out of the line and was at the railroad depot waiting transportation, "it is supposed, for Lynchburg."[16]

That piece of information at least told him that part of Sheridan's plan was working. Sheridan had hoped to be able to cross to the south side of the James so that he would have the flexibility to move across Confederate supply lines toward Sherman or Grant, according to the opportunities presented. The capture of Lynchburg would have been a logical target in that process.

As it turned out, however, Sheridan discovered as soon as he left the Valley Turnpike that the roads were much worse than he had expected. Furthermore, streams were running high and his scouts reported that the James would be very hard to cross. Since he did not have enough pontoons to build a bridge, he abandoned the idea of crossing the James and turned to the east to capture Charlottesville and towns on the north bank of the James. He could still reach Grant, but to do so he would have to swing north and east of Richmond to get behind Grant's lines on the Peninsula. It was a dangerous maneuver. Sheridan would have to move close enough to Richmond to make it possible for the Confederates to attack him in some strength before he was close enough to get help from Grant. Sheridan, of course, did not know that this route would take him right through the middle of the Confederacy's highest-priority clandestine operation.

The Union and Confederate records on Sheridan's passage around Richmond provide an interesting and somewhat mysterious contrast. The Union records report sizable Confederate efforts to intercept Sheridan and indicate that a couple of fairly sharp skirmishes took place. In his memoirs, Grant summarized the episode: "When he [Sheridan] reached Ashland he was assailed by the enemy in force. He resisted their assault with part of his command, moved quickly across the South and North Anna, going north, and reached White House safely on the 14th" (actually the eighteenth).[17]

The Confederate records, on the other hand, make it very clear that the Confederates did not try very hard to stop Sheridan and indicate that no battle took place. How does one evaluate these apparently opposite views?

A few miles from Ashland, the North and South Anna rivers join to become the Pamunkey, which, in turn, helps to form the estuary of the York River at West Point. If Sheridan could stay to the south of this complex of rivers he could eventually reach the James as high upriver as Jamestown or as far down as Fortress Monroe. If he had to stay north he would arrive at White House, a few miles above West Point on the York, and might well need help to reach Grant.

In typical Sheridan style he decided to make a judicious gamble. He sent a screening force south to Ashland to watch for Confederate reaction. If it was not too sharp, he could press on along the south bank of the Pamunkey until he was far enough past Richmond to make it safe to turn south. If Confederate resistance was great, Sheridan could still move his command back across the South and North Anna and continue on toward White House.

The force sent to Ashland was a brigade of George A. Custer's division under the command of Colonel Alexander C. M. Pennington. This brigade arrived in Ashland on the night of 14 March and passed the night without incident. Pennington's scouts reported that Confederate troops under General Longstreet were hurrying north from Richmond to intercept the Union force. Pennington was instructed to send troops as far south of Ashland as the railroad trestle over Royal's (actually Ryall) mill pond. They were to destroy the trestle before returning. This mission was apparently given to a squadron of the First Connecticut Cavalry. This squadron was met by Confederate cavalry. When the Connecticut men charged, the Confederate cavalry evaporated, and a force of Confederate infantry appeared from nowhere to kill Lieutenant Clark and two enlisted men and wound several other troopers and horses. The railroad trestle was not destroyed.

At sundown, another regiment of Pennington's brigade, the Second New York Cavalry, was attacked by Confederate infantry and lost one man killed and an officer and two enlisted men wounded. Twenty-two horses were wounded and had to be abandoned. At about the same time, Sheridan decided to pull back north of the Pamunkey River. All of this is recorded in the after-action reports of General Custer and Colonel Pennington. It is confirmed in some detail by a history of the First Connecticut Cavalry regiment and by General Sheridan's memoirs.[19] From the Confederate side, however, the story is quite different.

When Early was defeated at Waynesboro, Lee was prepared to rush Pickett's infantry division and W. H. F. (Rooney) Lee's cavalry divison to Lynchburg. When Sheridan turned east, Lee's division moved parallel to Sheridan but stayed south of the James River because the flood stage prevented him from crossing just as it had prevented Sheridan from crossing to the south side. Scouts from Colonel Alexander C. Haskell's Seventh South Carolina Cavalry, however, were north of the James and kept Lee informed of the Union movement.

In the meantime, Pickett's infantry was at Manchester, just across the river from Richmond, where it formed a centrally located reserve that could be moved in any direction to meet a new Union threat. In addition, General Thomas L. Rosser, whose cavalry division had been scattered at Waynesboro, managed to reassemble about five hundred of his troopers and took the trail in pursuit of Sheridan's cavalry. By the time Custer's forces reached the Ashland area, Rosser was following about half a day behind Sheridan's force.

The Confederate side of the story is recorded in a series of messages. There is no summary after-action report to put the story all together, but the messages are a good step-by-step account, and General Longstreet's memoirs provide a summary of the events as he saw them.[20]

According to the official records, Colonel Haskell's men reported on 13 March that the Union force was approaching Louisa Courthouse in the next county west and north of Ashland.[21] At this point, Sheridan's intentions were not clear. He could be skirting the Richmond area or he could be planning an attack on Richmond from the lightly defended north and west.

When Longstreet heard of the report, he promptly sent a message to Lee asking if he should get Pickett's division and some cavalry to pursue the Union force. While waiting for a response, he sent Pickett an alerting message telling him to have troops ready to move with cooked rations for three days. Somebody in Lee's headquarters apparently questioned the wisdom of chasing the enemy through Hanover County because Longstreet sent a message to Lee's adjutant, Colonel Taylor, in which he said, "If not pursued the enemy will do very much more damage than he will do if followed. We have many wagons and considerable interests in the country he is going through which, if allowed time, he will destroy." This message appears to have settled the matter, for shortly thereafter Longstreet sent definitive orders to Pickett to start north on the Brook Road the following morning, 14 March. About the same time, Lee advised the secretary of war that Longstreet would start out with Pickett the following morning to intercept the Union force and prevent destruction of property. He also said that Fitzhugh Lee had been instructed to cooperate with Longstreet.[22]

Longstreet and his staff reached Hanover County late on 14 March and waited for Fitz Lee's cavalry to arrive. The next day, Colonel Haskell's scouts reported that another enemy column was moving toward Ashland. Haskell's headquarters was at Yellow Tavern, a few miles north of Richmond on the Brook Road, where J.E.B. Stuart had been mortally wounded the previous year. At 11:05 on the morning of the fifteenth, Longstreet sent a message to Ewell saying that he now believed that the enemy did not threaten Richmond but was concentrated at Ashland. He urged that Lee's cavalry be hurried up so that he could catch the enemy. At 2:00 P.M., Longstreet sent word that the enemy still occupied Ashland but that the Union force seemed to be moving to the right (east). Pickett sent word to Ewell asking him to send information on the location of Fitz Lee's cavalry. In this message he reported that his location was at the Anderson House, "just beyond the crossing of the Chickahominy."[23] This meant that he was in Hanover County about five miles from Ashland.

Diarist John B. Jones reported that twelve hundred men of Lee's cavalry division passed through Richmond at 2:00 P.M. on 15 March and that afterward Lee had telegraphed that he could not find the enemy. On the sixteenth, Jones said, "There was no battle yesterday," and the following day that all local troops had returned to Richmond on the sixteenth.[24] Presumably this reference included Pickett's division.

The Confederate cartographer Jed Hotchkiss kept a journal through most of the war. The entries for March 1865 recount how he accompanied General Rosser on his pursuit of Sheridan's column. Hotchkiss commented that the Union force was "driven out" of Ashland at about sundown on 15 March and that General Rosser's force entered the town at 11:00 that night. He mentioned no battle and no other Confederate force, and it seems clear that Rosser's troopers were not involved in the skirmishes with Colonel Pennington's brigade.[25]

Longstreet's summary of these events in his memoirs says that he waited for Lee's cavalry and a pontoon bridge to arrive. The cavalry arrived late on the fifteenth, but the bridge never did arrive, and Sheridan's force withdrew north of the Pamunkey without hindrance from Longstreet's forces.

This seeming difference in the Union and Confederate records of the incident may be explained in part by considering the situation facing the Confederate authorities at that moment. Most of the work necessary to prepare the army for the new campaign had been carried out. If Sheridan could be kept north of the Pamunkey he might not be able to join Grant in time to help him stop the evacuation of Richmond. The Confederate Congress had, on 13 March, finally passed the legislation making it possible to use black troops in the Confederate army, but implementing instructions still had to be put into effect. The action team in Washington was reported to be ready. It would be difficult or impossible to turn the team on or off depending on Sheridan's location, and Sheridan was about to put himself squarely in the area that was critical to the safe delivery of the team's target. Without considering the capture of Lincoln, the Ashland-Milford axis was very important to the Confederate intelligence effort.

For these reasons Jefferson Davis and company must have wished that Sheridan would go away—anywhere so long as it was away. Furthermore, with the evacuation so close at hand, Lee did not want to get entangled in a major battle with Sheridan that would draw many of his forces northward. That would have put them out of position for the evacuation, which would have to be delayed to return the troops southward once more. Even if he did defeat Sheridan, it would not count as much as if he had defeated Sherman. It was far better to keep one's eyes focused on "Come Retribution" and not be diverted by lesser opportunities.

It seems that somebody in considerable authority on the Confederate side did not favor fighting Sheridan. Longstreet, who commanded the left-flank corps on the Confederate line, was an aggressive soldier and could normally be counted on to find a fight. But he had been in Richmond on urgent business for two nights and a day and did not return to his headquarters until the thirteenth in spite of other hints of Sheridan's approach. Longstreet's relative inaction on 15 March is in keeping with the idea that he was trying to avoid provoking a major battle. He knew the enemy was in Ashland, and he had troops only about five miles away, but he stayed in that position for twenty-four hours and did nothing but make a lame excuse about the lack of a bridge. That does not sound like the Longstreet on whom Lee depended for correct, aggressive military action. The Chickahominy at that point is about spitting distance wide in normal weather, and the Pamunkey is not much wider. It is true that the weather at the moment was soggy, but Longstreet surely could have gotten troops across the Chickahominy.

In all probability, the Confederate troops encountered by Sheridan were from the clandestine security force. It contained both cavalry and infantry and probably had authority to engage in small-scale hit-and-run operations considered necessary for local defense. If Pickett's infantry had repulsed a charge by Union cavalry, there would have been some celebration, even if it did not turn out to be a major operation. If clandestine force troops were involved, nothing would have been said. Any publicity would risk giving away the existence of the security force, which was still a secret matter. Lieutenant Carlton mentioned that his unit fought Sheridan's force on 15 April. The Twenty-fourth Virginia Cavalry may therefore have been the cavalry screen that the First Connecticut Cavalry ran into.[26]

After the action was over, the Union interrogators found a deserter or two who alleged that troops from Pickett's division had been involved at Ashland.[27] Such information does not appear in Confederate records, but it satisfied Union curiosity. It is possible that it, like other themes reported by deserters, was the result of a deliberate Confederate disinformation effort. On the other hand, the Fifteenth and Thirtieth Virginia infantry regiments of Corse's brigade had contributed a substantial number of men to the security force, and they might have been the Confederate troops involved. It is only natural that men on detail would give their parent organization as their unit rather than an ad hoc unit that might not even have a name.

In the meantime, Grant had a very clear idea of how he intended to employ Sheridan to stretch the right of the Confederate line and draw Lee out of position so that Grant would have a chance to attack him before he evacuated Richmond. The handwriting on the wall was clear. Grant's intelligence people were telling him that

Lee was ready to go on short notice. If Sheridan were to be used successfully, time was critical. Grant, therefore, set himself and his staff in motion to minimize that time as much as possible.

By 12 March, Grant was trying to pull Colonel Roberts out of the Northern Neck and use that force to set up a base at White House to enable Sheridan to refit his command as rapidly as possible. When Roberts's plaintive message arrived from southern Maryland on 13 March, however, Grant wired back immediately: "I have sent an officer of my staff with instruction to you. Start immediately and run into York River and await your instructions. The officer who went in search of your command left Ft. Monroe early this morning in Steamer Seneca, and will run in close to the Virginia shore from the mouth of the Rappahannock until he finds you. You may keep your cavalry with you until you join General Sheridan and then send it here."[28]

In effect, Grant laid out in advance the operation he wanted Sheridan to carry out. He then prepared every step of the way to make it possible for Sheridan to carry out the operation as quickly as possible. He had Roberts establish a base at White House to which he sent one hundred thousand rations for men and horses. Grant also sent a large number of remounts to the base so that Sheridan could get his men mounted on sound horses. While that was going on he had other troops prepare a route south from the Pamunkey across a specially prepared bridge over the Chickahominy to a pontoon bridge on the James. Movement of Union troops south of the James was planned so as to leave roads reasonably free from that point on for Sheridan to choose as he saw fit. Grant even had Sheridan send a staff officer ahead to position forage and provisions at those places that Sheridan elected along the entire route from the Chickahominy to Hatcher's Run, the extreme end of the Union line.[29]

Grant's advance staff work was being done during the period 12–14 March, even before Sheridan's flank guard had reached Ashland. Here again Grant and Lee seemed to be agreeing on what they wanted to happen, at least in the short term—both wanted Sheridan to go on past Richmond. Lee wanted to clear the railroad and the area of the clandestine operation.

Grant's wish was getting ahead of reality. On 14 March, Grant wrote to Meade, "Sheridan will be at the White House today. If there is no falling back (of Lee's forces) for four or five days, I can have the cavalry in the right place." He also told Meade to keep his command in condition to be moved "on the very shortest possible notice."[30]

On the fifteenth, however, Grant received a message from a staff officer who had left the White House at 3:00 P.M. that day. The officer had proceeded by steamer directly to Yorktown to get to a telegraph and was reporting at 8:15 P.M. that Sheridan had not yet arrived at the White House.[31] As it turned out, Sheridan did not reach the White House until 18 March. His little foray south of the Pamunkey had delayed his journey. That delay in turn must have given the Confederate intelligence people fits. The route of the action party with President Lincoln had to be replanned with every ripple in the military situation.

About 12 March, somebody in the Confederate government apparently decided there was a need for one hundred VMI cadets. Inasmuch as the cadets belonged to the state of Virginia and not to the Confederate government, it was necessary to get the permission of the governor to borrow them. Somebody of appropriate rank and authority called on Governor William Smith and made the request. On the morning of 13 March, Smith wrote to Colonel J.T.L. Preston, the acting superintendent of the institute: "It is represented to me as very important to have a select corps of one hundred (100) active young men for duty two or three days to be mounted upon gentlemen's horses impressed in this city for the occasion and I am asked for the requisite number from the Corps of Cadets. It is represented that the service is very important and it is particularly desirable to form the proposed command as suggested." Colonel Preston prompt replied: "Our corps is organized as an infantry command, and they are also instructed in artillery. They have never been drilled as cavalry and I could not promise any special efficiency from them on horseback. To make the detail you suggest, would entirely disorganize them as a corps. . . . Allow me to further suggest whether such use as you mention . . . would be in accordance with the limitations which I understand to have been laid down for the character and duration of the service to which the corps should be called."[32]

On 14 March, the *Richmond Examiner* reported that "men dressed in a little Confederate authority were rushing around yesterday, leaping fences, bursting into stables, peering into back yards and houses of private residents, in search of horses to impress for some purpose not made public. . . . Such as they did get it was concluded to return to their owners before the close of the day, either because the number obtained was too trifling to be of any avail, or because the exigency supposed to exist in point of fact existed only in somebody's heated imagination."

On the basis of the coincidence in dates and the mystery surrounding the identity of the people collecting horses, it would appear that the request for the VMI cadets may have had something to do with a covert government action. The main activity of that nature under way at that moment was the plan to capture Lincoln, and the attempt was about to be made. Might someone have decided that it would make an impression on Lincoln to have VMI cadets escort him on his arrival in the Richmond area? Preston, however, had made a wise decision to oppose the use of the cadets for this special duty. Although doubtless most of the cadets could ride well, a good deal of training would be required to turn them into a polished cavalry unit. They did not have such training.

The chances are that the scheme had been abandoned before Preston's letter was received. On the thirteenth, it was becoming clear that Sheridan's force might soon be in the middle of the area through which the cadets would have to travel. Nobody would want to expose them to that risk, and the collection of horses was stopped.

By 17 March, it was known that the Richmond, Fredericksburg, and Potomac railroad bridges over the North and South Anna were down but that rail connection could still be maintained between Ashland and Richmond and between Milford and the site of the North Anna bridge. Presumably, the special train was still at Milford and others could come up from Richmond, but there would still be a gap of about five miles between the two bridges where no train could run.

Also on the seventeenth, the U.S. Navy had a brush with the security force in the upper end of Westmoreland County.[33] Landing parties went up Mattox Creek—one turning up what is today called Monroe Creek behind Colonial Beach, Virginia. Another went up Mattox Creek proper, and a third party plowed through some surrounding countryside. This last group appears to have broken up a Confederate camp, which, judging from the description of its size and location, may well have been Sergeant Brogden's. This group also had a skirmish with fifty Confederate cavalrymen in one group and eight or ten in another. Mosby's Company C was quartered in Westmoreland County and if there had been time could have put fifty men up against the Union landing party, but such an action is not mentioned in the postwar accounts of Mosby's men, who bragged at some length about repulsing Roberts at Kinsale. Furthermore, the Union raid was probably too sudden to allow time to assemble Mosby's scattered troops at the extreme end of the area in which they were quartered.

One of the other Union groups ran into a force estimated to contain three to four hundred infantry. That force was far too big to be a home guard outfit and probably consisted of men from the Thirtieth and Forty-seventh infantry regiments in the security force guarding the Lincoln escape route.

The net effect of the Union raid was to throw another difficulty into the Nanjemoy–King George route. The Patuxent route was also in some question because at that moment Sheridan's troopers were still straggled across King William County. Their presence would force the action party to swing north of the preferred route from Urbanna to Ashland. It would add time and difficulty to the cross-country trip, but it could be done and was probably the safer alternative.

By the end of March, Lincoln was still free, and a review of circumstances by the Confederates would have shown that it was pointless to try at this late date to capture him. At the moment he was not even in Washington. He was at City Point visiting General Grant. It was too slow and difficult a process for Booth to try to put together a new action force. What were needed now were men who would act under discipline and who had been proven in combat. If Lincoln were to be killed instead of captured, the operation should be timed to make it have a maximum impact on the future battle. The best target date would probably be about 10–15 April, the approximate date for the evacuation of Richmond. That would be the moment to disrupt the Union command process.

Other ideas flowed logically from this set of conclusions. If action was not needed until 10–15 April, there was time enough to provide the explosives and explosive experts to Mosby and let him infiltrate a team of picked soldiers into Washington to work with Booth. That would give Booth the professional and disciplined help that he needed.

The decision would also make possible a shift in the Confederate strategy in the Chesapeake. As long as the operation to capture Lincoln was under way the Confederates wanted to keep things quiet in the area through which the action party would have to move with the hostage. Once the scheme was abandoned, however, and emphasis switched to the military maneuver—the abandonment of Richmond and Petersburg to seek a climactic battle in North Carolina—it would be very important to make the

Chesapeake as unsafe as possible for Union shipping. After all, shipping from the bay would support both Grant in the James River area and Sherman in South Carolina.

Although the action in the Potomac, Chesapeake, and Rappahannock had been almost entirely at the Union's initiative in the winter and early spring of 1865, that situation suddenly switched at the end of March. On 1 April Lieutenant Brain and his team captured a fast schooner, the *St. Mary's*, off the mouth of the Patuxent and used it to capture another schooner within a matter of hours. A few days later, another naval guerrilla group captured the steamer *Harriet De Ford* in Herring Bay, a few miles south of Annapolis. She was taken down to one of the rivers in the Northern Neck, where she was stripped and burned with the help of the local populace.[34]

On shore the security force could be disassembled and the troops returned to their permanent units. A few men from the force got back to their units, but most were still in place when the evacuation of Richmond took place on 2 April.

While waiting for the moment to leave Richmond, Lee was very conscious of Grant's efforts to extend the southern flank and knew that Sheridan might well play a key role in that extension. He needed a shrewd maneuver that would hold off the Union for a few days more—ideally he would have liked to prevent Sheridan from reaching the south flank—but in any case he would like to prevent any serious Union actions until mid-April. Once he had started the Confederate army moving, he did not expect to have any problems in outrunning his pursuers.

In searching for the shrewd maneuver, somebody came up with the idea of attacking the Union Fort Stedman, which stood just east of Petersburg. The officers making the proposal thought that they could see additional fortifications beyond Stedman, which, if captured, would cause the Union considerable difficulty in moving troops past that point. Perhaps they could even make it difficult for Sheridan to get his forces to the south flank. If that effect could be achieved, Lee would be almost certain of being able to remain in the trenches until his chosen departure date. Unfortunately, the additional fortifications were not real. They were the result of too little information and too much imagination.

On 25 March, just as Sheridan's troops were leaving the White House, the Confederate soldiers of General Gordon's corps made a surprise attack on Fort Stedman. Initially, it was very successful, but as the attacking column moved into the rear area they did not find the expected fortifications. Instead they found themselves in a trap. The day ended with the Union line restored and several thousand Confederate prisoners of war in Union hands.[35]

It was a serious blow to the Confederates, but it was not a fatal one. On 26 March, when General Lee made his official report to Jefferson Davis on the results of the Fort Stedman fight, he expressed the idea that if the attack had been successful, it might then have been possible to hold Grant with a portion of the Confederate force and combine the remainder with Johnston's army to defeat Sherman. In light of the relative strength of the two forces, it seems that it would have been impossible for Lee to believe such a fairy tale. Instead it seems likely that the report was written for political use in Richmond. Davis could say that it showed that the government did not want to evacuate Richmond and had in fact gone to great lengths to avoid the necessity. Now, however, heroic measures had failed, and it might be truly necessary to evacuate Richmond.[36] Lee could still expect to outrun the Union army. How long the race could be delayed depended to a considerable degree on what Grant would do with Sheridan. During 26, 27, and 28 March the Confederates closely watched Sheridan's progress south. He was in place at Hancock Station near the south flank on 27 March,[37] the day the decision may have been made to blow up the White House.

In preparing to move the Army of Northern Virginia to North Carolina, there was one important deficiency that was almost impossible to overcome in the time available. Large-scale Confederate map coverage of central North Carolina was almost non-existent. Some of the coastal areas had been mapped, but these were not the areas likely to see combat in the coming campaign. It would be impossible to launch a large mapping effort in the middle of January or February 1865 and not have the Union hear about it. That would lend unwanted credence to the rumors about the planned maneuver. More important, however, the job was too big for the existing mapping organizations to do in the time available. Even if the work could be camouflaged and kept secret from the Union, it could not be finished in time to be of use.

One useful shortcut was possible. Since the Confederacy still occupied most of the area in question, it would be possible to measure the distances from point to point in the expected area of operations and publish a table of distances as a handy reference for commanders and their staffs. That information plus the small-scale maps already available would give commanders some idea of the terrain. Furthermore, the Union forces would be relatively worse off because they had no better maps than the Confederates and, initially at least, would not have the table of distances to supplement them.

On 11 March, General Lee sent orders to Lieutenant Blackford, the man who had mapped Stafford and King William counties, to proceed at once to the area in North Carolina below Danville. Blackford was back in Richmond by 25 March.[38] It is possible that other topographers were also at work in North Carolina.

On Tuesday, 28 March, the *Richmond Dispatch* published as a matter of reader interest a table of distances for various points between Richmond and various areas in North Carolina, including Greensboro, Raleigh, Weldon, Goldsboro, and Wilmington. The distances given for points close together seem to be quite accurate when compared with a modern map. The distances for places farther apart seem to be overstated the farther apart they are. That may well have been a function of the curves in the nineteenth-century roads that are no longer present in modern roads. The table of distances would have been a reasonably accurate and useful tool for Confederate officers. Publication in the *Richmond Dispatch* would have made it widely available to them.

On 29 March, Sheridan began to move, pushing toward Dinwiddie Courthouse through the mud, in pouring rain. On the thirtieth, General Pickett arrived with several brigades of infantry to reinforce the Confederate cavalry that was trying to keep Sheridan away from the Confederate flank. On the thirty-first, the rain finally stopped and there was considerable jockeying for position through the mud. By that evening, Sheridan felt that he had Pickett well outside the Confederate defenses and in a position where he might be able to use the Union army's superior numbers to surround and capture Pickett's force. On that same day, however, the Confederates decided that upon the evacuation of Richmond, the ships of the James River Flotilla should be sunk to block the channel. On 1 April, the Engineer Department ordered thirty anchors for pontoon boats to be delivered in ten days. They were to be made of cast iron if they could not be forged within that time.[39] Other recent actions had started the construction of bridges over the Dan and Staunton rivers near Danville, Virginia, and repairs on Goode's bridge over the Appomattox River. Nearly everything was ready for the abandonment of Richmond and the great maneuver toward North Carolina.

On the morning of 1 April, Sheridan had blood in his eye, but

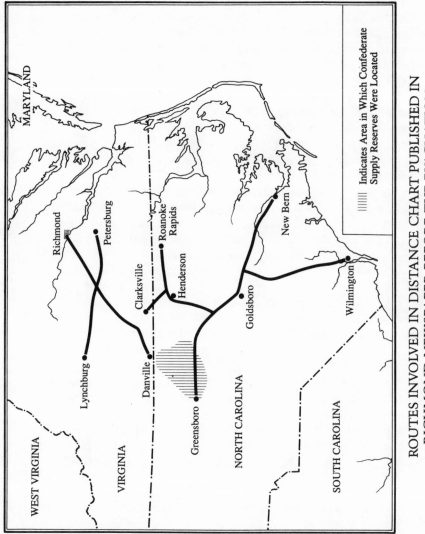

ROUTES INVOLVED IN DISTANCE CHART PUBLISHED IN
RICHMOND NEWSPAPER BEFORE THE EVACUATION

Indicates Area in Which Confederate
Supply Reserves Were Located

Pickett was still holding off the Union force. That was the situation when John Surratt left Richmond to head back to Washington, and it was probably the situation when Lieutenant Harney and his demolition team left Richmond to join Mosby's Rangers in northern Virginia. There was no reason on the Confederate side to think that the campaign would not work, and the attack on the Union leaders played a logical part in that campaign.

Notes

ABBREVIATIONS

NA   National Archives

OR   U.S. War Department, *The War of the Rebellion: A Compilation of the Official Records of the Union and Confederate Armies.* 128 vols. Washington, D.C.: U.S. Government Printing Office, 1880–1901.

ORN   U.S. Navy Department, *Official Records of the Union and Confederate Navies in the War of the Rebellion.* 30 vols. Washington, D.C.: U.S. Government Printing Office, 1894–1914.

RG   Record Group

Chapter 17: Complication and Frustration

1. Abraham Lincoln, *Abraham Lincoln from His Own Words,* ed. Ray Edgar Applien (1942; rpt. Washington, D.C.: National Park Service, 1961), p. 43.

2. *ORN,* Ser. 2, vol. 2, pp. 807–8.

3. U.S. Department of Commerce, National Oceanic and Atmospheric Administration, *Annual Summary 1974, Richmond, Virginia.* The data cover the years 1935–74.

4. U. S. Grant, *Personal Memoirs of U. S. Grant,* 2 vols. (New York: Charles L. Webster, 1892), 2:424–27.

5. Records of the Richmond, Fredericksburg, and Potomac Railroad, February and March 1865, Virginia Historical Society, Richmond.

6. *OR,* Ser. 1, vol. 46, pt. 2, p. 778.

7. Ibid., pp. 782, 781.

8. Ibid., p. 806.

9. Ibid., pp. 796–97.

10. Ibid., pp. 817, 832.

11. *ORN,* Ser. 1, vol. 5, p. 522.

12. *OR,* Ser. 1, vol. 46, pt. 2, p. 891.

13. Ibid., p. 954.

14. Ibid., pp. 781, 880.

15. Ibid., p. 891. Grant, however, heard from Sheridan directly on 5 March (*Memoirs,* 2:427).

16. *OR,* Ser. 1, vol. 46, pt. 2, p. 880.

17. Grant, *Memoirs,* 2:429.

18. *OR*, Ser. 1, vol. 46, pt. 1, pp. 506–7.

19. Custer's report is in ibid., pp. 501–4; Penington's in ibid., pp. 504–8; Philip H. Sheridan, *Personal Memoirs of P. H. Sheridan* 2 vols. (New York: Charles L. Webster, 1888), 2:122.

20. James Longstreet, *From Manassas to Appomattox* (1896; rpt. ed. James I. Robertson, Jr., Bloomington: Indiana University Press, 1960), p. 791.

21. *OR*, Ser. 1, vol. 46, pt. 2, p. 1311.

22. Ibid., pp. 1308–9.

23. Ibid., pp. 1314–15.

24. John B. Jones, *A Rebel War Clerk's Diary*, ed. Howard Swiggett, 2 vols. (New York: Old Hickory Book Shop, 1935), 2:450–51.

25. Archie P. McDonald, *Make Me a Map of the Valley* (Dallas: Southern Methodist University Press, 1973), p. 262.

26. Cornelius Hart Carlton, "Diary," *Bulletin of the King and Queen County Historical Society of Virginia* 24 (January 1968), no page numbers.

27. *OR*, Ser. 1, vol. 46, pt. 3, p. 10.

28. Ibid., pt. 2, p. 954.

29. Ibid., p. 980.

30. Ibid., p. 963.

31. Ibid., p. 994.

32. Smith to Preston, 13 March 1865, Incoming Correspondence of the Superintendent, 1865, No. 304; Preston to Smith, 13 March 1865, Outgoing Correspondence of the Superintendent, 1865, No. 242, Virginia Military Institute Archives, Lexington, Va.

33. *ORN*, Ser. 1, vol. 5, p. 535.

34. Ibid., pp. 540–46.

35. Douglas Southall Freeman, *R. E. Lee*, 4 vols. (New York: Charles Scribner's Sons, 1935), 4:17–19.

36. Robert E. Lee, *Lee's Dispatches: Unpublished Letters of General Robert E. Lee, CSA, to Jefferson Davis and the War Department of the Confederate States of America, 1862–1865*, ed. Douglas Southall Freeman and Grady McWhiney (New York: Putnam, 1957), pp. 341–46.

37. Sheridan, *Memoirs*, 2:125.

38. Blackford to "My Dearest Mother," 12, 27 March 1865, Folder 87, Blackford Family Papers, Southern Historical Collection, University of North Carolina, Chapel Hill.

39. Sheridan, *Memoirs*, 2:154; Jones, *Rebel War Clerk's Diary*, 2:463; Miscellaneous Papers of the Engineer Department, File entry 27, RG 109, NA.

18

Countdown

After spending the holidays in New York with his family, Booth returned to Washington and checked into the National Hotel on the last day of December. The year had wound down and there was Abraham Lincoln still sitting in the Executive Mansion.

The action team was getting a bit restive. As Samuel B. Arnold complained later, Booth was always in motion, but not much seemed to get done. One of the problems was Booth's involvement with women at two levels. The lower level was the young prostitute Ellen Starr, still in residence at 62 Ohio Avenue. At the upper level was the respectable Lucy Hale, daughter of Senator John P. Hale of New Hampshire. The Hales and their two daughters lived at the National Hotel when in Washington. The slightly chubby Miss Hale was starry-eyed about the handsome young actor. Five pictures of young women were found in the flap of Booth's little memorandum book (the famous "diary") after he was shot at Garrett's farm near Port Royal, Virginia. One of the pictures was of Lucy.[1]

Booth checked out of the hotel on 28 January for a quick trip to New York, where he was seen by his actor friend Samuel Chester. Booth was seeking to recruit Chester, who would be useful if a kidnapping attempt were to take place at Ford's Theatre. The Bunker memorandum is garbled as to when he returned to Washington, but it must have been within days. Ellen Starr sent him a plaintive little note on 7 February, addressed to "My Darling Boy" and pleading "for gods sake come." The lady felt neglected.[2]

Before Booth left Washington on 9 February for Philadelphia and New York, he wrote that day to a Boston friend, Orlando Tompkins, asking him to have a photographer there reproduce "a

403

dozen" of his favorite photographs and send them immediately to Edwin's home. In this letter he wrote: "This is very important as there are several parties whom I would like to give one."[3] The suspicion lingers that these photographs were somehow to be used for identification purposes connected with the Lincoln operation.

During this trip, Booth stopped off to see his sister Asia in Philadelphia. He then went on to stay at Edwin's home in New York. His brother Junius was also there. In an undated letter, probably written on 15 February, Junius told Asia Clarke: "John sat up all Mondays night to put Miss Hales valentine in the mail—and slept on the sofa."[4] But Booth's frequent trips to New York obviously had a more serious purpose. Most likely his prime contacts were in that city, and he had people to see in the Confederate network there. An example is an extraordinary letter found among his effects when his room at the National Hotel was searched after Lincoln was shot, which left federal detectives and code experts baffled. The letter was dated "N.Y. 20th Feby/65" and was hand delivered, probably by messenger, to "J. W. Booth, esq." It was signed "J. J. Reford," who described himself as "an old Californian." In part the letter reads:

> I regretted not to have again seen you on Saturday and yesterday could not find out Mr Edwin Booth's house as his name is not in the Directory. As Lewis anxious to have had a conversation with you relative to the order for shipping the horses, as well as the Ile question. With regard to the former may I beg you to find out as soon as convenience will allow if the thing is possible, and if so, write me such a letter as I can show the Gentleman (who wishes to procure the order) and I will go at once to Washington and give the particulars. However, I may say the desire of the owner of the horses is to send them to Paris. He is a *strong Union man* in a good position here.[5]

Clearly this is a loose word code, with padding, meaningful only to the writer and the recipient—that is, "Reford," whoever he may have been, and Booth. Given the advantage of present knowledge of events, an analysis of this letter can at least be attempted. It might run as follows: Reford has been in touch with Lewis Powell in Baltimore and Powell wanted to talk with Booth about some instructions he had received concerning the action plan. Reford also needed a cautious letter from Booth which could be shown to some key Confederate agent in Washington. Reford would go to Washington for this purpose. Reford reminded Booth that the New York man (the control) wanted to take Lincoln to "Paris," a euphemistic designation for Richmond. An extensive search has been made in logical places seeking to identify "J. J. Reford." Nothing was found. The name appears to be an alias.

When Booth was in Philadelphia on 10 February, on his way to New York, he and his sister Asia had their last talk. As she recalled years later, he said: "Let me show you the cipher." He explained that it might be needed to communicate with her about money matters. She refused to consider it. Booth then produced a packet of papers in an envelope, which was placed in the Clarkes' safe. When the envelope was removed from the safe on 18 April, it was found to contain $4,000 in bonds, the documents assigning Booth's oil interests to Junius and his sister Rosalie, an undated letter to his mother, the "To whom it may concern" letter Booth had written in November to justify capturing Lincoln, and another document which Mrs. Clarke burned.[6] John S. Clarke turned the "To whom it may concern" letter over to United States Marshal William Milward, who permitted it to be published in the *Philadelphia Inquirer* on 19 April. Long thought to have been lost, the original was recently discovered in the files of the Justice Department in the National Archives. This document disclosed that Booth had crossed out two crucial words in the final sentence. The sentence appears thus in the original: "A Confederate, ~~at present~~ doing duty *upon his own responsibility.*" What he intended to convey by crossing out the two words, *at present,* is tantalizing.

It is important that Booth wanted Mrs. Clarke to learn how to use a cipher. When Booth's National Hotel room was searched after Lincoln was shot, the officers found among his papers the standard Vigenère alphabetical square used by the Confederates throughout the war to encipher and decipher communications.[7] We do not know the key used by Booth, but it most likely was a special one for his use only rather than one in regular use by the Confederates, such as "Complete Victory." Nor can any message in the captured Confederate records be identified as coming from Booth. An alias would preclude identification in any case. The point here, as federal prosecutors later sought to demonstrate, is that Booth did have a cipher of the official Confederate type and knew how to use it.

Booth returned from New York on 22 February. At some point between that date and 7 April, his path may have crossed that of a former Confederate officer, Lieutenant Colonel James Gordon, later a short-term United States senator from Mississippi. Gordon's postwar admissions concerning Booth are reminiscent of those purportedly made by another former Confederate officer, Lieutenant Colonel Robert M. Martin, while in jail in Louisville. In one sense, Gordon echoes Martin.

Gordon was the son of a wealthy planter who had emigrated from Scotland. His family lived at Lochinvar, Pontotoc County, Mississippi. When the war came he served in various Mississippi cavalry units. Conflicts in the command structure caused Gordon to resign from the Fourth Mississippi Cavalry on 27 June 1863. Jefferson Davis persuaded him to go to England in 1864 to help arrange the purchase of a privateer. Gordon's return was delayed when he contracted yellow fever at Bermuda. He finally reached Wilmington aboard the blockade runner *Blenheim* which steamed blithely into port on the night of 24 January 1865 without the captain being aware that Fort Fisher had been captured by a federal amphibious force on 15 January. The next morning the vessel was taken as a prize, and the crew was removed to Old Point Comfort, Virginia. At Old Point Comfort, Gordon talked his way out on 22 February by telling the Yankees that he was the son of the duke of Argyle and was fleeing from a scrape in Scotland.[8] In a few days he reached New York City, where he was concealed, probably by John Potts Brown, an astute Confederate commercial agent. As Gordon told it later, he went on to Montreal and reported to Jacob Thompson. Entries in the register of the St. Lawrence Hall for 8 March 1865 confirm that Gordon and Robert Brown, giving as their addresses "CSA," were assigned to rooms 145 and 149 at noon.

The relationship between Gordon and Jacob Thompson was close. They had known each other in Mississippi. Further, Gordon had married Thompson's niece Virginia C. Wiley of Oxford, Mississippi, on 7 February 1856. Because of his ties with Jefferson Davis and Jacob Thompson, Gordon was immediately on the inside of whatever the Confederates in Canada were doing or planned to do. Thompson put him to work promptly.

Lieutenant Robert W. Brown, who came to Montreal with Gordon, has been ignored by researchers into Confederate activities in Canada. Born in North Carolina, he grew up in New York City, where his father, John Potts Brown, had moved his prosperous ship-chandlering business from Wilmington in 1846. On 25 November 1856, he married the fashionable Josephine Lovett. To avoid arrest for pro-Confederate activities, Brown fled to Richmond in 1862. There he served on the staff of General John H. Winder and briefly as an adjutant at the infamous Andersonville Prison. In September 1864 he was sent to Canada to join Clement C. Clay at St.

Catharines, Ontario. The fascinating member of the Brown family is Josephine. During the last two years of the war, she served as a highly effective Confederate agent, particularly as a courier. Her story has never been published.[9]

When James Gordon arrived in Montreal, he found a gathering of the clan. Jacob Thompson had checked into the St. Lawrence Hall on 14 February and was still there. George Sanders, Beverly Tucker, William Cleary, and others were in town—many at this same hotel. They were joined there on 11 March by General Edwin G. Lee. Gordon found himself in top company.

Obviously something was in the wind. Instructions were expected from Richmond. The courier, Sarah Slater, arrived in Montreal on 17 March with dispatches from Judah P. Benjamin for Thompson and Lee. Responses to Benjamin were required, and Lee's diary entry for 22 March shows that these were prepared. Mrs. Slater left with them for Richmond.[10]

James Gordon clearly arrived in Montreal on 8 March 1865, in the middle of an important Confederate operation. After the war, in talks with visitors at Lochinvar, he said that while he was in Canada he worked on plans to capture President Lincoln and had met John Wilkes Booth. Although this was known to many people in rural Pontotoc County, it caused scarcely a ripple. In the bitter poverty of the postwar South, who would condemn a plan to capture Lincoln? The first written account, furnished by Gordon himself about 1890, appeared in *Goodspeed's Biographical and Historical Memoirs of Mississippi*, published in 1891, in which he stated flatly that he "formed the acquaintance of J. Wilkes Booth." Even his obituary in the *New York Tribune* for 29 November 1912 contained an oblique reference to Booth.

Gordon was an avid hunter and sportsman and frequently wrote articles for magazines dealing with this subject. This interest led to another published account of his involvement in the plan to capture Lincoln. C. B. Whitford, a contributor to a Chicago magazine, *The American Field: The Sportman's Journal*, interviewed Gordon in New Orleans "some years after the war." Whitford's story was not published until 12 May 1923. In part, Whitford put it this way:

"We knew," said the Colonel, "that we were beaten, and there was a general fear among southern men that the North would impose terms so severe that the already shattered and impoverished South could not meet them. Many plans were discussed in this country and abroad looking to the reaching of a settlement on terms the South could endure. One plan which found favor was to capture Lincoln, take him into the Confederacy, and with him as a hostage, treat for peace. I was party to this plot and did some work to promote it and carry it to a successful conclusion. The venture needed desperate men and the exercise of great caution and skill as well. Somehow the men in the plot became impatient and finally a new conspiracy was hatched which contemplated the killing of Lincoln. With that conspiracy I had no part or sympathy."

Beyond Gordon's admissions, it cannot be established that he met John Wilkes Booth. If he did, where? Washington, Baltimore, Philadelphia, New York, Boston? Booth was in all these places during the six weeks before he shot Lincoln. Except for the entry of 8 March 1865, on the register of the St. Lawrence Hall, Montreal, Gordon's movements are uncertain after he was released at Old Point Comfort, Virginia on 22 February 1865. Whatever the case, Gordon was definite: in Canada he worked on a plot to capture Lincoln, and somewhere along the line he became acquainted with John Wilkes Booth. And there the matter must rest.

On his way back to Washington from New York on 21 February 1865, Booth stopped off at Barnum's Hotel in Baltimore. From there he sent a telegram to "John Wentworth, Esq., National Hotel, Washington." The telegram reads: "I am here. Will you keep promise to-day or tomorrow. Let me know. I cannot stay."[11]

John Parker Hale Wentworth was visiting Washington from California. He was Lucy Hale's first cousin. One speculation about this telegram is that Booth wanted Wentworth to help arrange with Senator John P. Hale to get him an official pass to be in the Capitol stands at the second inaugural of President Lincoln. Such a pass was secured and given to Booth by Miss Hale. What Booth hoped to accomplish by attending the inauguration is uncertain, but one inflated account is that he sought to press his way to the president that day and was restrained by a heroic Capitol police officer, John W. Westfall, who thus saved Lincoln's life. This story is not very convincing.

The matter of being in the Capitol stands at the inauguration did come up in a conversation Booth had in New York on 7 April with an actor friend, Samuel K. Chester. According to Chester, Booth had returned from Boston that day. He was drinking hard and inclined to be loud and belligerent. Suddenly Booth whacked the table with his palm and said, "What a splendid chance I had to kill the president on the 4th of March."[12] In vino veritas?

For a different purpose, it is necessary here to review some of the material in Chapter 13. What was Captain Thomas N. Conrad doing? What evidence is there that he had a working relationship with the Booth team in Washington? In December 1864 Conrad was engaged with Beverly Kennon in mining the lower Potomac River. But on 10 January 1865, he wrote from King George County, Virginia, to Secretary of War Seddon, beginning his letter with the sentence: "Our agents write to me from Washington for funds." Conrad then explained that he had been very frugal with the $400 in gold furnished to him "last September" by Secretary of State Judah Benjamin. Now he needed more money to continue "our labors." A note at the bottom of Conrad's letter reads: "Upon hearing from you I shall leave for Washington unless otherwise ordered by you." Davis instructed Seddon and Benjamin to confer about Conrad's request for money. The jurisdictional problems were worked out. The disbursing clerk, William Bromwell, advised Seddon on 25 January that Conrad's money was ready. A transmittal note shows the amount to be $500 in gold.[13]

It should be kept in mind that Booth was in the National Hotel in Washington beginning 31 December 1864 and, except for two short absences, until 9 February 1865, when he left for New York. He was back in Washington on 22 February. We do not know when Conrad came to Washington after he got the $500 in gold. Apparently he was in the city in early February. A 27 February entry in the diary of war clerk Jones says: "T. N. Conrad, one of the government's secret agents, says that 35,000 of Thomas's army passed down the Potomac several weeks ago."[14]

Conrad's regular contact with the Booth group was probably John Surratt. Conrad let this cat out of the bag when he included a chapter in one of his books defending Mary Surratt and condemning her execution. He wrote that he had known Mrs. Surratt well in peacetime and often stopped at the Surratt tavern on his way to visit his sister or on hunting trips. He came to know "the family" better after the war started because he frequently "took a meal at Surratt's tavern either going or coming and sometimes both." On the same page he added the revealing information: "I was several times invited to go to her house on H Street during my trips, but always declined." Conrad did not say who invited him. The answer is obvious: it was John Surratt. Since Mrs. Surratt did not complete the move from the country tavern to the H Street house in Washington until November 1864, Conrad's "several" invitations to visit there had to come after Booth's operation was well along.[15]

The Confederates did alert their people in the Signal Corps

camps on the Virginia side of the lower Potomac River to be ready to receive a captive Lincoln. One source of information about this came out by accident years later. About 1900 the famous Lincoln collector Osborn H. Oldroyd resolved to write a book about the assassination. He decided it would be useful to take what he called a "walking tour" of the escape route followed by John Wilkes Booth. Oldroyd set out in May 1901. As part of this tour he crossed the Potomac River in a sailboat, intending to be put ashore in Machodoc Creek, King George County. The wind failed, and the fisherman he had hired landed him short of Machodoc Creek. Oldroyd found himself in front of the house of James A. Arnold, a farmer, who also tended a lighthouse on the river.

Arnold, a hospitable man, took Oldroyd around to point out places of interest relating to the movements of Booth. Oldroyd stayed the night and he had long talks with Arnold. He reported one conversation:

> Benjamin B. Arnold, the father of Mr. James A. Arnold, my genial host, died some years ago. Mr. Arnold, Sr., was engaged in the plot to abduct the President, and the part assigned to him was to take charge of Mr. Lincoln on the Virginia side of the river and hurry him to Richmond. When the news of the President's assassination reached the home of Mr. Arnold, which at that time was a few miles further up the river, he expressed his regrets, saying: "I am very sorry the President was shot, but very glad they never succeeded in kidnapping him, for it let me out of a very dirty job."[16]

Oldroyd's account was ignored by historians, perhaps because it ran counter to the accepted belief that Booth acted without Confederate involvement. But what about Benjamin B. Arnold? A search of Confederate records in the National Archives disclosed pertinent information about him.

The name B. B. Arnold is found in two places in these records, both tending to confirm Oldroyd's account. Captain J. Louis Smith of the Adjutant and Inspector General's Office, Richmond, was ordered to inspect portions of the Confederate Signal Corps. He filed his report on 21 December 1864. As an attachment, Smith made a chart of the Signal Corps personnel in the Richmond office and at the two camps on the Virginia side of the lower Potomac River. Private B. B. Arnold is shown as a courier at the King George County camp under Lieutenant Charles H. Cawood. Here he was in precisely the right place and in the right function to assist in moving a captive Lincoln along to Richmond. Further confirmation of his official status as a courier for the Signal Corps is contained in the Richmond passbooks. On 1 August 1864, he was given a pass as a Signal Corps courier to travel from Richmond to King George County. He received a similar pass on 6 December 1864, to travel from Richmond to Milford, the railroad station nearest his camp in King George County.[17]

By the first of March 1865 the action plan was approaching the critical point, so it became increasingly likely that the Confederates would send people to Washington with a "watch or assist" brief. One of these people appears to have been Benjamin Franklin Stringfellow, who was probably the most trusted and effective scout in the Army of Northern Virginia.

Stringfellow was not new in this field. On 16 September 1864, he proposed to kidnap Union General August Kautz in a letter submitted directly to General R. E. Lee. As Stringfellow noted later, Wade Hampton's "great cattle raid" upset the tactical situation so the attempt was not made. But Stringfellow continued to nurse a yen to capture a Union general. Now he raised his sights. On 24 February 1865, he again wrote directly to Lee, this time proposing to kidnap Grant, a formidable undertaking. The letter ended up in the hands of President Jefferson Davis.[18] Davis had something on his mind. He called Stringfellow into his office and laid it out. This was probably 28 February, the date Stringfellow accepted a commission as lieutenant. Davis gave him an assignment that would take him to Washington immediately. The cover was a good one. He was to become a student of dentistry, using the name and papers of a Union soldier from Maryland who had been a prisoner in Confederate hands. Stringfellow left Richmond on 1 March and arrived in Washington on 5 March, the day after Lincoln's second inauguration.[19]

Obviously Grant was not the Washington target. He was at City Point below Richmond and was not expected to be in Washington. Nor was there any need for Stringfellow to gather intelligence about Grant's planned offensive. That was understood all too well by the Confederate leadership. Thus the reason for Stringfellow's assignment must lie elsewhere.

Around 1880 Jefferson Davis wrote to Stringfellow asking for material suitable to include in his memoirs. This query brought a long and cautious response from Stringfellow, dealing almost exclusively with the mission to Washington. Nowhere in this remarkable document does Stringfellow really say what that mission was. It was not necessary to remind Davis—he knew. But the focus on Vice-President Andrew Johnson and President Lincoln is revealing. Stringfellow wrote that he stayed a few days in the Kirkwood House, where Johnson boarded. At another point he told of being "in constant communication with an officer occupying an important position about Mr. Lincoln." And he added that he made this officer a "proposition." While in Washington he frequently saw his future wife, Emma Green, who lived in nearby Alexandria, Virginia.

The dentistry cover worked perfectly. Stringfellow told Davis that he actually obtained a dental license about four weeks after he came to Washington, which he intended to use to permit unhampered travel in the area. For reasons not stated, Stringfellow suddenly abandoned this idea and left Washington on Saturday, 1 April, intending to cross the lower Potomac River into King George County, Virginia. As he explained to Davis: "Leaving the City of Washington by the aid of a person whose name is linked in the history of these last dark days, I went some twelve miles the first evening."

There is no way to identify the person who aided him. But the wording is highly suggestive. John Wilkes Booth left Washington that day "on the afternoon train," as shown in the records of the National Hotel. Stringfellow's reference to "the first evening" would also put his departure in the afternoon. Further, "some twelve miles" is almost the precise distance from downtown Washington to the safe house regularly used by Confederate agents—Mrs. Mary Surratt's country tavern in Prince George's County, Maryland.

Stringfellow was captured in Charles County, Maryland, on Sunday, 2 April, by a patrol from the 238th Provisional Cavalry, Veteran Reserve Corps, based at Chapel Point on the Potomac River. Lieutenant William K. Laverty, who commanded the base, intended to forward Stringfellow under guard to Washington, but Stringfellow escaped on 4 April.

Ultimately Stringfellow made his way to Canada, where he remained for more than a year, despite the charms of Emma Green, who waited for him at Alexandria.[20] A reasonable explanation for this extended Canadian stay is that Stringfellow feared to come home until he felt certain his Washington assignment had not been disclosed to the hated Yankees. He need not have worried. There was no leak.

In February and early March Booth's plans began to go stale. Arnold and O'Laughlen spent increasing amounts of time in Baltimore. Although Booth came back from New York on 22 February, nothing much seemed to be happening. But on 13 March Booth sent a telegram to O'Laughlen in Baltimore: "Don't fear to neglect your business. You had better come at once."[21] O'Laughlen and Arnold took a train for Washington the following day.

On 14 March John Surratt sent an ambiguously worded telegram to Lewis Powell's "control," David Preston Parr, the Baltimore china dealer, requesting that Powell come to Washington.[22] Powell came and put up at Mrs. Surratt's. He almost did not make it. On 12 March he beat up a black maid at Branson's Baltimore boardinghouse. She had him arrested by the federals. Powell again took the oath of allegiance, using his standard alias, Lewis Paine, and talked his way out of jail on the fourteenth in time to be sent on to Washington by Parr. This episode later landed Parr in Old Capitol Prison. George Atzerodt did not have to be sent for. He was at the Pennsylvania House, a fleabag hotel just off Pennsylvania Avenue. And, of course, David E. Herold was in town, living with his mother and sisters at 636 Eighth Street, near the Navy Yard.

Booth had two things planned for the evening of 15 March. First, Surratt and Powell would occupy the president's usual box at Ford's Theatre to see the play *Jane Shore*. Booth had reserved the box (combined boxes 7 and 8) earlier. The purpose was for Surratt and Powell to become acquainted with the layout. After the play, there would be a general planning session in a private dining room Booth had engaged for the night at Gautier's Restaurant, 252 Pennsylvania Avenue.

As cover, it was decided to invite two of Mrs. Surratt's boarders to attend the play. They were seventeen-year-old Honora Fitzpatrick and ten-year-old Mary Apollonia Dean, a student at a Catholic school for girls. It is doubtful if little Miss Dean got the drift of the play. Jane Shore was a fifteenth-century English courtesan, the mistress of Edward IV and several noblemen. When the straitlaced duke of Gloucester became Richard III, he called her a whore and made her do penance by walking the streets in her "kirtle." Anyway, the theater party went off as planned. During the performance, Booth visited the box to talk with his guests.[23]

After the play, Booth's Washington action group gathered in the private dining room at Gautier's for oysters, drinks, cards, and much talk. Present were Booth, Surratt, Powell, Atzerodt, Herold, Arnold, and O'Laughlen. Booth laid out his plan. Lincoln would be taken from his box at Ford's Theatre when he next attended a play there. Arnold objected to this idea as suicidal. By then everyone was a little drunk, and threats were passed between Booth and Arnold. The meeting finally broke up around 5:00 A.M. with nothing really decided.[24]

About noon on 17 March, Booth received word that Lincoln planned to attend a matinee performance of *Still Waters Run Deep*, to be given for sick and wounded soldiers at Campbell Hospital on the outskirts of the city. The cast, headed by E. L. Davenport, was currently appearing at the Washington Theatre. Here was an opportunity! There was much scurrying around to get everyone armed and mounted.

David Herold was dispatched in Booth's buggy to take some of the cache of arms out to the Surratt tavern, about ten miles south of the Navy Yard bridge. The buggy was loaded with enough weapons to fight a small war: two double-barreled shotguns, two Spencer carbines, one pistol, ammunition, a dirk, and a sword. In addition, there was a rope and a monkey wrench.[25]

The hospital was located out Seventh Street near the Soldiers' Home. The action team planned to meet at a restaurant near the hospital. Arnold and O'Laughlen arrived first, then Atzerodt and Powell, and finally Booth and Surratt. They planned to stop Lincoln's carriage as he returned from the play. Lincoln and his driver would be overpowered and handcuffed. The carriage would be used to make a dash through southern Maryland to the Potomac River. Herold would join them on the road with the weapons.[26]

Booth left the others at the restaurant and rode up to Campbell Hospital to check out the situation. There he saw E. L. Davenport and learned that Lincoln was not present and was not expected. Davenport told of Booth's appearance at the hospital some years later in an interview with a reporter for a Chicago publication. The would-be captors returned to the city in disgust. Booth's intelligence was wrong. Lincoln had gone that afternoon to the National Hotel to make a little talk at a ceremony regarding a captured battle flag.[27]

The next night, 18 March, Booth performed on the stage for the last time. He appeared in one of his favorite plays, *The Apostate*, at Ford's Theatre in a benefit for his actor friend John McCullough. On Tuesday, the twenty-first, he took the 7:30 P.M. train to Baltimore, on his way to New York, where he checked into the St. Nicholas Hotel.

The Campbell Hospital fiasco ended any realistic hope of capturing Lincoln. Arnold and O'Laughlen gave up and went home to Baltimore. Powell returned to the Branson boardinghouse in Baltimore and then went on to New York, probably with Booth. Surratt, Atzerodt, and Herold were left in Washington—leaderless.

It is fascinating to speculate why Booth made repeated trips to New York. Certainly he did not go there just to see a favorite prostitute, Annie Horton, or to visit his family. From the bits and pieces, it seems certain that the nerve center of the clandestine enterprise was in that city. Names and connections have proved elusive, but one name stands out: Roderick D. Watson, a well-educated Maryland man from Charles County. Watson had been involved in various Confederate underground activities since the start of the war. He was arrested in Baltimore on 18 March 1864 on suspicion of being a blockade runner, and talked his way out by taking the oath of allegiance. Later he made his headquarters in New York with a mail drop at 178½ Water Street. General John A. Dix, who commanded in New York, had Watson arrested for subversion on 8 May 1864 and confined at Fort Lafayette. He was released on 10 October 1864. Some idea of Watson's insider status with the Booth group can be seen from his letter of 19 March 1865 to John H. Surratt. In this he asked Surratt to come to New York on important business and to respond immediately by telegraph.[28]

While at the St. Nicholas Hotel on this New York visit, something happened to inspire Booth for one more try. On 23 March he dropped into the telegraph office at the hotel and sent a message to Louis Wiechmann at Mrs. Surratt's: "Tell John to telegraph number and street at once."[29] Eliza Holohan, one of Mrs. Surratt's boarders, took the telegram to Wiechmann at the office of the commissary general of prisoners, where he worked. Wiechmann could not understand it. But when John Surratt saw the telegram, it made sense to him. Booth wanted to know the Washington address of the Herndon House, kept by Martha Murray. Powell was to come from New York and board there.

Booth arrived back at the National Hotel, after a stop at Baltimore, on 25 March. At Mrs. Surratt's request, he called on her the next day. Atzerodt was with him. Here Booth learned that the Confederate agent Augustus Howell had been arrested on the evening of 24 March at the Surrattsville tavern. Further, John Surratt had replaced Howell as the escort for Sarah Slater, who was on her way from Montreal to Richmond with dispatches. So John Surratt was not in town.[30]

Sarah Slater was an exotic young French-speaking Confederate agent and courier also known as Kate Thompson. She had passed through Washington several times in February, March, and early

April 1865, spending two nights at Mrs. Surratt's home. George Atzerodt was quite taken with her and mentioned her in his confessions. Once he rowed her across the Potomac River to Virginia. Atzerodt's confession, published in the *Baltimore American* on 18 January 1869, ended up with two surprising sentences: "Mrs. Slater went with Booth a good deal. She stopped at the National Hotel." There were dozens of references to Mrs. Slater at the 1865 conspiracy trial and at the trial of John Surratt in 1867. The federals were certain that she brought communications to the Booth organization from Richmond and Canada. But Mrs. Slater was never found, and her Booth connection was left dangling.[31]

Back in Washington, Booth made an effort to revive the stalled operation. He sent a telegram to O'Laughlen in Baltimore on 27 March: "Get word to Sam. Come on, with or without him, Wednesday morning. We sell that day sure. Don't fail."[32] Booth's intelligence about Wednesday was excellent, but it was dated.[33] O'Laughlen and Arnold were not interested. They did come over to see Booth the following Friday. At this meeting, according to Arnold, the plan was abandoned. In any event, there would have been no chance to capture Lincoln on Wednesday as Booth had anticipated. Lincoln was still aboard the *River Queen* at City Point, Virginia, to be with Grant for the final assault on Lee's army.

Booth's plans for capturing Lincoln were in shambles. On the first day of April he took the evening train for New York. He told George Atzerodt he was going to Canada. Then, on the morning of the fourth, he told members of his family that he was leaving for Boston. According to witnesses quoted in *Boston Sunday Herald*, 11 April 1915, he was seen at various places around the city on 5 and 6 April 1865. The purpose of this trip to Boston is murky, but it has the feel of an appointment with some member of the Confederate apparatus in Canada. Booth returned to New York on 7 April. He was in a black mood. He talked with Samuel Chester that evening and spoke of having "a splendid chance to kill the president on the 4th of March." A decision had been made; now must come opportunity. When Booth checked back into the National Hotel in Washington on 8 April, Lincoln had just over six days to live.

Apart from capturing Lincoln, talk in Booth's group of ways to rid the earth of that tyrant was revealed by George Atzerodt. It is an astonishing account, and it seems to belong at the point when Booth returned on 8 April from New York.

Atzerodt made several rambling confessions. Provost Marshal Henry H. Wells came aboard the *Montauk* on 25 April and took a long statement from him.[34] Atzerodt had also been pleading that he be allowed to talk with his brother-in-law John L. Smith and Maryland Provost Marshal James L. McPhail. Smith was a detective on McPhail's staff. Secretary of War Stanton gave permission for this meeting so Smith and McPhail came over from Baltimore on the evening of 1 May 1865 to see Atzerodt, now in a cell at the old penitentiary on the grounds of the Washington Arsenal. McPhail questioned Atzerodt and Smith wrote down the substance of the conversation as it went along. There is just one problem: the statement disappeared.

That such a statement had been made was revealed in McPhail's testimony of 18 May 1865 at the conspiracy trial. Atzerodt's counsel, William E. Doster, a good lawyer, objected vigorously to any testimony by McPhail concerning a confession taken while his client was in a prison cell and in irons. In the exchange, the judge advocate seemed to lose track of his point, and very little of what Atzerodt told McPhail and Smith got into the record.

The existence of the confession was confirmed by former Assistant Secretary of War Thomas T. Eckert, when he testified before the Judiciary Committee of the House of Representatives, on 30 May 1867. The committee was considering the impeachment of President Johnson. In answer to a question about statements made by "conspirators," Eckert said that a written statement had been taken from Atzerodt by "one of McPhail's men by the name of Smith." Eckert presumed the statement was "in the War Department."[35]

Eckert was speaking with firsthand knowledge. Apparently he had been designated by Stanton to bring Smith and McPhail to the prison on the night of 1 May so they could interrogate Atzerodt. General John F. Hartranft, who was in charge of the prison, reported all this in minute detail to his superior, General Winfield S. Hancock. In his morning report for 2 May, Hartranft wrote that he opened Atzerodt's cell at 8:20 P.M., had the hood removed, and permitted McPhail and Smith to enter. The guard was moved back out of hearing range. Hartranft noted that McPhail and Smith left the cell at 10:12 P.M.[36]

But where was this Atzerodt confession? Contrary to Eckert's presumption, it could not be located in the files of the War Department or elsewhere in the National Archives. In 1977 a member of the Surratt Society was in Connecticut and called on a grandson of Atzerodt's counsel, William E. Doster. He showed her the missing Atzerodt confession and explained that it had been found among

Doster's papers and passed down in the family. The historical importance of the seven-page confession had been overlooked by the Doster family. An arrangement was made later to secure a photocopy.[37] It seems likely that Atzerodt's brother-in-law John L. Smith turned the confession over to Doster for use in Atzerodt's defense. One paragraph reads:

> Booth said he had met a party in New York who would get the prest. [president] certain. They were going to mine the end of the pres. [president's] House near the War Dept. They knew an entrance to accomplish it through. Spoke about getting friends of the prest. to get up an entertainment & they would mix in it, have a serenade & thus get at the prest. & party. These were understood to be projects. Booth said if he did not get him quick the New York crowd would. Booth knew the New York party apparently by a sign. He saw Booth give some kind of sign to two parties on the Avenue who he said were from New York.

The wording of the paragraph leaves few clues to fix a time frame. Further, it weaves in and out with respect to Booth's New York connections who were pressing to "get the president." It is clear that Booth spoke of two separate schemes aimed at Lincoln. Atzerodt knew of these directly from Booth. As Atzerodt told it in the two-hour session with McPhail and Smith, "These were understood to be projects." One of these "projects" was a plan by Booth's New York associates to mine the Executive Mansion to kill Lincoln and others. An entrance had been found on the War Department side for use in planting the explosives. Men had come from New York to explore the project with Booth, and he had discussed it with his Washington action group.

This has the flavor of a contingency plan being developed in tandem with kidnapping: if one did not work, the other would be tried. An expert in the use of explosives was required. There was no such person in the Booth group. One would have to be found and brought in. By some means the word went out to the "wizard war" people in the Confederate Torpedo Bureau under General Gabriel Rains. They had just the man for this work. He was Sergeant Thomas F. Harney, formerly a lieutenant in the Sixth Missouri Infantry.

Harney was a native of Pennsylvania and at one time had been a teacher. He enlisted in the Confederate Army on 1 May 1862 at Corinth, Mississippi. After being severely wounded on 3 October 1862, he returned to duty only to be captured two months later. Harney was held in the Gratiot Street Prison in St. Louis until 2

June 1863, when he was sent to City Point, Virginia, for exchange. He was immediately picked up by General Rains for service in the Strategic Corps and sent to Mississippi to supervise the planting of subterra shells. Rains signed a requisition to furnish Harney a horse, which was delivered to Harney at Brandon, Mississippi, on 12 July 1863.[38]

Subsequent to his exchange, Harney was on Rains's staff and served at various places in the Confederacy where skill in the use of explosives was needed. His assignments took him to Charleston and Mobile in 1864. June of that year found him in Richmond mining the James River. In July he was again sent to Charleston to command forty men assigned to duty with hand grenades. Wherever Harney went, the Yankees suffered casualties and loss of equipment from explosive devices—mines, subterra shells, hand grenades, and innocent-appearing devices that would blow up.

At the end of March 1865, Harney was in Richmond still doing special work with explosives in the Torpedo Bureau. At that point, the Confederates did not expect the collapse of General Lee's lines. There was hope for an orderly withdrawal to join General Joseph Johnston and fight on. The Confederates did not see the war as lost.

A day or so before Richmond was evacuated on 2 April, a party from the Torpedo Bureau was organized under Harney and sent to join Mosby in Fauquier County. Aside from Harney, the others from the Torpedo Bureau have not been identified. At the time Harney and his men left Richmond, John H. Surratt was in the city. He arrived there on 29 March with Sarah Slater, who had come from Montreal with dispatches from Jacob Thompson and Edwin G. Lee for Secretary of State Benjamin.[39] The connection seems obvious; the word was passed to activate the project mentioned by Atzerodt in his confession.

Upon his arrival at Mosby's headquarters, Harney was assigned to Company H, commanded by Captain George B. Baylor. This has all the earmarks of a scratch unit, created on 5 April for the purpose of infiltrating Harney and his special ordnance into Washington. It included men acquainted with the environs of Washington, such as recently promoted Lieutenant James Wiltshire, a Marylander, who had been on the famous raid with Lieutenant Walter Bowie when he was killed near Rockville, Maryland, on 7 October 1864.

A mixed force of about 150 men, mostly from Companies H and D, was quickly assembled under command of Captain Baylor. They left Upperville, Fauquier County, on 8 April and headed in the direction of Washington. Two days later they were at Burke Station in Fairfax County, fifteen miles from Washington. Here they were surprised by a detachment from the Eighth Illinois Cavalry under Colonel Charles Albright. There was a running fight but few casualties. Harney and the three others were captured. On the twelfth the four were brought to Old Capitol Prison in Washington. Colonel Albright's action report of 10 April shows that Harney "brought ordnance to Colonel Mosby and joined his command."

The *Washington Daily Morning Chronicle* for 11 April carried a little story about the Burke Station fight and quoted the prisoners as saying they had joined Mosby "from the army of Lee" a few days before. Harney's name was not mentioned in the account. Whether Booth learned of his capture is speculative. The Old Capitol Prison grapevine was notorious and effective. In any case, Harney and his men did not show up to carry out the project.

Richmond was in Union hands on 3 April. Among the first troops to enter the city were those of Colonel Edward H. Ripley, Ninth Vermont Infantry. In 1907 Ripley published a memoir, *The Capture and Occupation of Richmond, April 3, 1865*. In it, he told that Lincoln had learned that explosives experts from the Torpedo Bureau had left Richmond a few days before with lethal plans directed straight at him. Without realizing it, Ripley had grasped the other end of the Harney mission. Ripley was at his Richmond headquarters on 4 April when an enlisted man named Snyder, from the Torpedo Bureau, came in and begged for an interview on a "very important subject." Ripley was impressed with Snyder, describing him as "more than usually intelligent and a fine-appearing man in uniform." So he granted the interview.[40]

Snyder told Ripley he had a problem of conscience. He felt that the war was over and not another shot should be fired. He was particularly concerned about the safety of President Lincoln, whom he had seen that day walking almost unguarded about the streets of Richmond.

Then Snyder got down to what really bothered him. Ripley recalled Snyder's disclosure as follows:

> He knew that a party had just been dispatched from Raine's torpedo bureau on a secret mission, which vaguely he understood was aimed at the head of the Yankee government, and he wished to put Mr. Lincoln on his guard and have impressed upon him that just at this moment he believed him to be in great danger of violence and he should take greater care of himself. He could give no names or facts, as the work of his

department was secret, and no man knew what his comrade was sent to do, that the President of the United States was in great danger.[41]

Ripley called in his adjutant, Captain Rufus P. Staniels, who took down Snyder's statement under oath.[42] Ripley then sent a note to Lincoln asking for a conference. Lincoln was aboard the *Malvern*, anchored in the James River. By then it was 10:00 P.M. Lincoln responded that same night and set the meeting at 9:00 the next morning, 5 April. Ripley took Snyder with him to the *Malvern*, but Snyder was not permitted to enter Lincoln's cabin. Ripley read Snyder's statement aloud, stressing the danger to Lincoln from men in the Torpedo Bureau. He urged the president to talk with Snyder. Lincoln heard Ripley out but closed the conference by saying "I cannot bring myself to believe that any human being lives who would do me harm."[43]

On 11 April, the day before Harney was put in Old Capitol Prison, Mrs. Surratt was planning to drive out to her country tavern in Surrattsville to transact some business about a debt owed to her by a local farmer, John Nothey. Although there is no direct proof, Booth must have talked with her before she left that day. There was a message to be delivered to her tenant John M. Lloyd. In substance, this message was to get out the arms concealed at the tavern for they would be needed soon. Lloyd testified that Mrs. Surratt told him this when they met by accident just outside Washington. That night Booth and Powell were in the audience when Lincoln spoke from a balcony at the Executive Mansion about his reconstruction plans. Booth urged Powell to shoot Lincoln then and there. Powell refused to take the risk. Later as the two walked around Lafayette Square, Booth told Powell, "That is the last speech he will ever make."[44]

Booth's grim statement expressed the state of his mind on 11 April. Capturing Lincoln was no longer feasible. Richmond was in Union hands; General Lee had surrendered. The project of blowing up the Executive Mansion to kill Lincoln was obviously out—no explosives experts had come to do it. But all was not lost; there were still Confederate armies in the field. Some dramatic action might yet save the Confederacy, and he was the one to do it. This thought was expressed in his famous "diary": "For six months we had worked to capture, but our cause being almost lost, something decisive and great must be done."[45]

Just when the list of those to be assassinated was drawn up is uncertain, but it was probably 12 or 13 April. Three people were on the list: President Lincoln, Vice-President Andrew Johnson, and Secretary of State William Seward. Why Seward? Here Booth evidently had sound advice, based on the premise set out by George Sanders in July 1864: cause total discord in the electoral process. With Lincoln and Johnson both dead, the 1792 statute governing presidential succession would apply. The president pro tempore of the Senate, Lafayette Foster of Connecticut, would act as president until the electoral college provided a new president. Under the law, the secretary of state was required to set this process in motion. The infighting among the Radical Republicans over the selection of a new secretary of state and over control of the electoral college is not hard to envision: monumental confusion and chaos would reign.

The South might regroup and fight on. This must have been on Booth's mind when he talked with a friend, Edward Person, on 13 April. He told Person he had "the biggest thing on his hands that had ever turned up."[46]

This was a time of great joy in Washington. With Lee's surrender, people in the city felt that the war was over. There were plans for an illumination set for the night of 13 April. One wit was quoted in the *Washington Evening Star* as saying that any man caught sober on the streets would be arrested.

It seemed likely to Booth that Lincoln would attend the theater. He planned accordingly. On the afternoon of the thirteenth he dropped in at Grover's National Theatre and asked the manager, C. D. Hess, if he intended to invite the Lincolns to his theater the following night. Hess said he had been thinking about it and this reminded him. He would send an invitation to Mrs. Lincoln. Booth was familiar with this theater because he had appeared there in April 1863 and in *Romeo and Juliet* with Avonia Jones on 20 January 1865. More important, three men who "cased" the Grover's Theatre layout and exits several days before Lincoln was shot were probably Booth associates.[47] There was no problem in securing information at Ford's Theatre; Booth had a close relationship with the Ford brothers. So the bases were covered. He would know soon.

The newspapers had been full of Secretary of State Seward's carriage accident on 5 April. He had suffered lacerations and broken bones and was at his home on the east side of Lafayette Square under constant medical care. Powell was sent around to reconnoiter. On the morning of 13 April, and again the next morning, he spoke through a window to the nurse, Private George Robinson, to ask about Seward's condition. Booth took it further, as was revealed in Atzerodt's unpublished confession: "I overheard Booth when in conversation with Wood [a Powell alias] say that he visited a chambermaid at Seward's house and that she was pretty. He said he had a great mind to give her his diamond pin."

General and Mrs. Grant arrived in Washington on 13 April and were staying at Willard's Hotel. Mrs. Lincoln decided to invite them to a theater party at Ford's the next evening to see Laura Keene in Tom Taylor's comedy *Our American Cousin*. This time Booth's intelligence system functioned perfectly. Somehow he learned of the planned theater party long before Mrs. Lincoln's request to reserve the presidential box was received by James R. Ford at 10:30 in the morning of the fourteenth. Around 8:00 A.M. Booth sent George Atzerodt to check in at the Kirkwood House, where Vice-President Johnson boarded.[48] The Grants sent regrets and left Washington on the evening train to visit their children in New Jersey. Booth was aware of their departure because he saw them in a carriage on the way to the railway station.

That afternoon Booth dropped by to talk with Mary Surratt at her boardinghouse on H Street. This was probably his second visit there that day. He left with her a set of French field glasses to be taken to her tavern at Surrattsville and delivered to John Lloyd. She was also instructed to tell Lloyd to get out the weapons concealed at the tavern because they would be called for that night. Louis Wiechmann drove her to the tavern later that afternoon in a hired buggy. Mrs. Surratt gave the field glasses to the drunken Lloyd and passed on the message about getting out the weapons.

Mrs. Surratt's counsel sought to prove that she went to the tavern to collect money owed to her by John Nothey. She had no appointment with Nothey and did not see him that afternoon. The field glasses and one of the carbines were picked up around midnight, when Booth and David Herold stopped at the tavern in their flight from Washington. The recently discovered Atzerodt confession greatly weakens Mrs. Surratt's Nothey defense. In a pertinent part he said: "Booth told me that Mrs. Surratt went to Surrattsville to get out the guns (two carbines) which had been taken to that place by Herold. This was Friday."

It is not the intent here to describe all the actions of Booth and his group on 14 April. Once Booth had positive information that Lincoln intended to be at Ford's Theatre that night, he spent the rest of the day planning and figuring out logistics. It was agreed that the attacks on Lincoln, Johnson, and Seward would be simultaneous. The hour was set at 10:00 P.M. Powell, with Herold as a street guide, was to go to Seward's home on Lafayette Square and kill him. Atzerodt was assigned to kill Vice-President Johnson at the Kirkwood House. Booth reserved Lincoln for himself.

Notes

ABBREVIATIONS

NA   National Archives

OR   U.S. War Department, *The War of the Rebellion: A Compilation of the Official Records of the Union and Confederate Armies.* 128 vols. Washington, D.C.: U.S. Government Printing Office, 1880–1901.

ORN U.S. Navy Department, *Official Records of the Union and Confederate Navies in the War of the Rebellion.* 30 vols. Washington, D.C.: U.S. Government Printing Office, 1894–1914.

RG   Record Group

1. The five faded pictures are in the files of the National Park Service, Washington, D.C.

2. Investigation and Trial Papers Relating to the Assassination of President Lincoln, M-599, reel 2, frame 0359, NA.

3. Booth's letter to Orlando Tompkins is owned by Richard and Kellie Gutman, Boston.

4. Asia Booth Clarke, *The Unlocked Book* (New York: Putnam, 1938), pp. 198–99.

5. M-599, reel 2, frames 0353–57, NA.

6. Clarke, *Unlocked Book*, pp. 125–27; statement of her husband, John S. Clarke, 6 May 1865, M-599, reel 7, frames 0407–12, NA.

7. Booth's cipher square became Exhibit 7 at the conspiracy trial and is in M-599, reel 2, frame 0174, NA. For an explanation of this cipher square, see Louis A. Sigaud, *Belle Boyd* (Richmond: Dietz Press, 1944), Appendix B.

8. The capture of the *Blenheim* on 25 January 1865 is reported in *ORN* Ser. 1, vol. 2, p. 700. The crew was brought to Hampton Roads, aboard the USS *Alabama* and transferred to the *Rhode Island* on 17 February 1865. James Gordon was listed along with forty-two others. They were all put ashore from the *Rhode Island* on 22 February. See the logs of the *Alabama* and the *Rhode Island*, Records of the Bureau of Naval Personnel, RG 24, NA. The reference to Gordon saying he was the son of the duke of Argyle is from an interview in the *New York Evening Post*, 8 January 1910.

9. Josephine Brown's extensive Confederate clandestine activities are revealed in the Clement C. Clay Papers, Duke University Library, Durham, N.C., in various records in National Archives, and in family papers in the possession of her granddaughter Charlotte Moore, Greenwood, S.C.

10. Edwin G. Lee's diary covers his stay in Canada (Microfilm, Accession 1456, Southern Historical Collection, University of North Carolina, Chapel Hill). For the identification of Sarah Slater as the courier mentioned by Lee, see James O. Hall, "The Lady in the Veil," *Maryland Independent* (Waldorf), 25 June, 2 July 1975.

11. Box 191, Benjamin F. Butler Papers, Library of Congress.

12. Statement of Samuel K. Chester, M-599, reel 4, frames 0142–70, NA.

13. This series of communications is in Letters Received by the Confederate Secretary of War, 1861–65, M-437, reel 146, frames 0142–70, NA.

14. John B. Jones, *A Rebel War Clerk's Diary*, ed. Howard Swiggett, 2 vols. (New York: Old Hickory Book Shop, 1935), 2:436.

15. Thomas Nelson Conrad, *A Confederate Spy* (New York: J. S. Ogilvie, 1892), p. 128.

16. Osborn H. Oldroyd, *The Assassination of Abraham Lincoln* (Washington, D.C.: Privately printed, 1901), pp. 283–84.

17. For Smith's report, see Letters Received, Confederate Secretary of War, 1861–65, M-437, file 44-S-1865, NA. The personnel chart has been detached and is now in Miscellaneous Confederate Muster Rolls, Signal Corps, RG 109, NA; passbooks 131 and 134, Chap. IX, RG 109, NA.

18. Stringfellow to Lee, 16 September 1864, Franklin Stringfellow Collection, MSS 1 St 864a, Virginia Historical Society, Richmond; and Stringfellow to Lee, 24 February 1865, Jefferson Davis Manuscript Collection, document filed chronologically in the collection, Duke University Library, Durham, N.C.

19. Stringfellow to Davis, Stringfellow Collection. This nine-page typescript bears only the date 1880 and was apparently made from a copy kept by Stringfellow. It is one of forty-two items given to the society in 1955 by a Stringfellow descendant, Alice Stringfellow Shultice. The location of the original letter to Davis has not been learned. The typescript is the basic source used here to describe Stringfellow's Washington mission and related movements.

20. The dates of Stringfellow's departure, capture, and escape are derived from his letter of 2 April 1866, written from Hamilton, Ontario, to Emma Green, Stringfellow Collection.

21. Booth to O'Laughlen in Benn Pitman, *The Assassination of President Lincoln and the Trial of the Conspirators* (1865; rpt. ed. Philip Van Doren Stern, New York: Funk and Wagnalls, 1954), p. 223.

22. The Surratt-Parr telegrams, 14 March 1865, are in M-599, reel 3, frames 1046–48, NA.

23. Honora Fitzpatrick testified about this theater party at the conspiracy trial. See Pitman, *Assassination*, p. 121.

24. For a description of the events at Gautier's Restaurant, see Samuel B. Arnold, *Defense of a Lincoln Conspirator* (Hattiesburg, Miss.: Book Farm, 1943), pp. 45–47; also see the statements of Thomas Manning, watchman at Gautier's, and John T. Miles, one of the waiters, M-599, reel 5, frames 0285–94, NA.

25. For a listing of these items, see the testimony of William Norton and John C. Thompson, *Trial of John H. Surratt*, 2 vols. (Washington, D.C.: U.S. Government Printing Office, 1867), 1:510–17. On 18 March 1865, John Surratt and John M. Lloyd concealed the carbines and ammunition between the joists above the Surrattsville tavern dining room. Lloyd's testimony (Pitman, *Assassination*, pp. 85–87) about this was the key evidence leading to the conviction and execution of Mrs. Surratt.

26. Arnold, *Defense of a Lincoln Conspirator*, pp. 47–48.

27. For Lincoln's appearance at the National Hotel, see the *Washington Evening Star*, 18 March 1865.

28. For Watson's arrests, see Turner-Baker Papers, M-797, file 3413, NA, and Selected Records of the War Department Relating to Confederate Prisoners of War, M-598, reel 85, p. 41, Fort Lafayette, NA. The letter to John H. Surratt is in M-599, reel 3, frame 0114, NA.

29. Booth's telegram to Wiechmann is in Pitman, *Assassination*, p. 121.

30. David Barry, who lived near the Surrattsville tavern, had gone with John Surratt and Sarah Slater on 25 March 1865 from the tavern to Port Tobacco where Surratt and Slater intended to cross the river en route to Richmond with dispatches from Montreal. Barry returned the rented team to Washington on 26 March and called on Mrs. Surratt to tell her what had happened. Booth and Atzerodt were at Mrs. Surratt's boardinghouse when Barry came. See Barry's testimony, *Trial of John H. Surratt*, 2:751–54.

31. Hall, "Lady in the Veil."

32. Pitman, *Assassination*, p. 223.

33. Mrs. Lincoln wrote to Senator Charles Sumner on 23 March 1865 inviting him to be the Lincolns' guest on Wednesday, 29 March, for Verdi's opera *Ernani* at Ford's Theatre. How Booth learned of this invitation is a mystery. See Justin Turner and Linda Turner, *Mary Todd Lincoln: Her Life and Letters* (New York: Knopf, 1972), pp. 209–10. The theater party was canceled because Lincoln extended his stay with Grant at City Point, Virginia.

34. Atzerodt's confession to Wells, M-599, reel 3, frames 0596–0620, NA.

35. Eckert testimony of 30 May 1867 before the Judiciary Committee, House of Representatives, *Impeachment Investigation*, 39th Cong., 2d sess., and 40th Cong., 1st sess., 1867, p. 680.

36. Hartranft Letterbooks, Special Collections, Gettysburg College, Gettysburg, Pa.

37. The Atzerodt confession, clearly authentic, was subsequently placed on the market and sold to a Minnesota collector.

38. See Unfiled Papers and Slips Belonging in Confederate Compiled Service Records, M-347, reel 169, NA. In this series the names are filed in alphabetical order.

39. Using the name "Henry Sherman," Surratt checked into the Spotswood House, Richmond, on 29 March 1865 and left on 1 April (testimony of hotel clerk J. B. Tinsley, Jr., *Trial of John H. Surratt*, 2:790–91).

40. Edward H. Ripley, *The Capture and Occupation of Richmond, April 3, 1865* (New York: G. P. Putnam's Sons, 1907), p. 23.

41. Ibid., pp. 23–24.

42. Ibid., p. 24. Snyder's statement of 4 April has not been located in National Archives. He was interviewed again by Ripley on 12 April concerning other secret operations. This statement identified him as William H. Snyder of Co. E, 2nd Virginia Cavalry, assigned to the Torpedo Bureau. See RG 109, Union Provost Marshals' Civilian Files, Snyder, William H. NA.

43. Ibid., p. 25.

44. Eckert testimony of 30 May 1867, *Impeachment Investigation*, p. 674. Powell told this to Eckert, who frequently interviewed him in prison.

45. Booth's little memorandum book is not properly a diary. During his flight after shooting Lincoln, he made two separate entries in this book explaining and defending his actions. The first entry is headed April 13, 14, Friday, The Ides, and the second is dated Friday 21. These entries, containing 701 words, were read into the record, *Trial of John H. Surratt*, 1:310–11.

46. Statement of Edward Person, M-599, reel 6, frames 16–17, NA.

47. Statement of Jane Hickman, M-599, reel 6, frames 0260–62, NA.

48. Testimony of hotel clerk Robert R. Jones, Pitman, *Assassination*, p. 144.

19

Getting Away

Any realistic hope of capturing Lincoln ended when he left Washington on the afternoon of 23 March 1865 aboard the *River Queen* to be with General Grant for the final assault on General Lee's army. The northern press reported Lincoln's trip widely, including the exact time the *River Queen* left Washington and the exact time the vessel docked at City Point on 24 March. Obviously, Confederate intelligence sources knew of Lincoln's arrival and reported it quickly. The *Richmond Sentinel* for 30 March picked up a routine story from the *New York Herald* for 27 March stating that Lincoln was "still with the armies on the James River." The speed with which the Confederate apparatus delivered the *Herald* to Richmond is astonishing.

There was little doubt about Grant's strategy for breaking the stalemate at Petersburg. With superior resources and manpower, he intended to stretch Lee's army to its right until something snapped. Then he would move fast on this flank to destroy Lee's lines of supply. Lee would be forced out of the trenches and beaten in detail during retreat. But Grant had a nagging worry. As he said in his memoirs, "I was afraid, every morning, that I would awake from my sleep to hear that Lee had gone, and that nothing was left but a picket line."[1]

Grant had cause to worry. The Confederates planned to do just that. Years later Jefferson Davis told of this plan:

> The design, as previously arranged with General Lee, was that, if he should be compelled to evacuate Petersburg, he would proceed to Danville, make a new defensive line of the Dan and Roanoke Rivers, unite his army with the troops in North Carolina, and make a combined attack upon Sherman; if successful, it was expected that reviving hope

would bring reinforcements to the army, and Grant, being then far removed from his base of supplies, and in the midst of a hostile population, it was thought that we might return, drive him from the soil of Virginia, and restore to the people a government deriving its authority from their consent.[2]

That the Confederates contemplated such a maneuver circulated in the northern press during March. The *Richmond Sentinel* for 29 March 1865 quoted a Washington newspaper: "The rumor goes further, however, and places Lee at the head of a liberated Richmond army, marching in all haste to unite with Johnston, and fall upon Sherman."

On the first day of April, in a series of bitter fights beginning the day before, Union General Philip Sheridan routed General George Pickett's command on Lee's extreme right. This is usually referred to as the Battle of Five Forks. The area was well outside the fortified zone occupied by the Confederate army. It meant that Sheridan was loose on Lee's flank and had an opportunity to get in Lee's rear if the evacuation of Petersburg and Richmond were delayed any longer. Pickett's division, which Lee had used as a mobile reserve, no longer existed as a military body of any consequence. There was no force immediately available to throw in front of Sheridan to buy more time. Only the remnants of the Confederate cavalry had survived Five Forks. Too few of them were left to stand between Sheridan and the essential supply lines in Lee's rear.

It took Lee until the next day, the morning of Sunday, 2 April, to make a full assessment of the situation. Well before noon, however, he put the evacuation plan in motion. Government officials and other personnel chosen for evacuation left Richmond by train that evening and headed for Danville on the North Carolina border. Officials of the state of Virginia left for Lynchburg. Troops in the District of Richmond went to work destroying military supplies and ammunition not yet shipped out of town.

The most isolated of the Confederate forces were those north of the James River. Included were those of General Ewell and some of General Longstreet's corps. Their departure was well organized, however, and ran smoothly.

About eleven in the evening, the wagons and artillery belonging to Custis Lee's division started for Richmond to cross a bridge over the James River capable of carrying such weight. At about one o'clock on the morning of 3 April, the troops of Crutchfield's and Barton's brigades left the trenches and crossed the James River on a pontoon bridge located behind their positions at Chaffin's Farm. The picket line crossed over the same bridge at daylight.[3]

Custis Lee's division headed toward Amelia Court House, where troops from Richmond and Petersburg would join on the evacuation route. He was followed by the remainder of Ewell's troops, Kershaw's division, and a portion of Gary's cavalry brigade.

On Monday, 3 April 1865, the operations of the Confederate army were still reasonably close to the planned scenario. The troops had left Richmond and Petersburg a week or ten days earlier than expected, but they were now out of the trenches and headed west toward North Carolina. Lee seemed optimistic: "I have got my army safe out of its breast works, and in order to follow me, the enemy must abandon his lines and can derive no further benefit from his railroads or the James River." This, however, was the last moment for optimism.[4]

Most of the special collection of 375,000 rations accumulated in Richmond in February and March had been left behind. It was expected that there would be rations waiting for the army at Amelia Court House. Unfortunately for the Confederates, the planning procedures had broken down. There were no food supplies at Amelia Court House.

Sheridan's aggressive tactics had already put the Confederates in a difficult situation. The race out of Richmond was started with Sheridan's troops much farther forward than Lee had expected when the evacuation plan was drawn up. Without adequate cavalry support, Lee would have had a hard enough time to keep ahead of Sheridan. Now he was forced to wait precious hours at Amelia Court House while the troops vainly foraged for food. The delay was fatal.

Sheridan reached Burkeville ahead of Lee, forcing Lee to keep on west toward Lynchburg, where he had an alternate supply base. This change of plans could not save the Confederate army. Sheridan was traveling light and managed to get far enough ahead to capture rations being sent from Lynchburg.

On 6 April General Ewell's corps, including Custis Lee's division, was caught and surrounded by Sheridan's forces at Saylor's Creek, a few miles east of Farmville, Virginia. Almost the entire Confederate force was captured, including men from Barton's brigade. Officially, of course, Barton's brigade was captured along with the others. In actual fact, a large number of officers and men from the regiments in Barton's brigade were not there. They were at Ashland and points north, left dangling as a "screening force" in an area where a captured Lincoln had been expected to pass en route to Richmond.

After failing to obtain food for his army, and after the debacle at Saylor's Creek, General Lee had no option but to surrender at Appomattox Court House on 9 April 1865.

In the chaos following the evacuation of Richmond and Lee's surrender, direct Confederate action against Lincoln lost its military-political purpose. Most of the machinery remained in place but without guidance. Booth was out of touch and on his own. Harney's mission was already in motion. Even if there had been a disposition to call everything off there was no way to do it. Who was left to act? The Confederate government had collapsed and its leaders were on the run.

The shot fired at Ford's Theatre about 10:15 P.M. on Good Friday found Washington authorities unprepared for a manhunt. In a disjointed way, they recovered quickly. Where the wicked fled, many pursued—but not always in harmony.

Witnesses positively identified John Wilkes Booth as the man who fired that shot. His past association with John Surratt soon became known to city detectives. Shortly after two o'clock that night they raided the boardinghouse of Mary Surratt looking for Booth and Surratt. They came away empty-handed.

John Surratt left Washington for Richmond on 25 March as escort for Sarah Slater, who was carrying dispatches from Montreal for Secretary of State Benjamin. Surratt checked into the Spotswood Hotel in Richmond on 29 March using the alias "Henry Sherman."[5] Benjamin promptly sent him to Montreal as a courier.

Surratt arrived at the St. Lawrence Hall in Montreal on 6 April 1865. General Edwin G. Lee sent Surratt off to Elmira, New York, to survey the possibilities of freeing Confederates in the prisoner of war camp. Surratt was there when he learned that Lincoln had been assassinated. He made his way back to Montreal, where he was concealed in various places by Catholic priests. On 16 September, General Lee and Beverly Tucker arranged passage for Surratt, as "Mr. McCarty," aboard a steamer bound from Quebec to England. Later Surratt went to Italy, where he enlisted in the Papal Zouaves under the alias "John Watson."

Surratt was betrayed by another Zouave, Henry B. St. Marie, whom he had known in Maryland before the war. The problem of dealing with the papacy was delicate, and the Department of State moved with glacial speed. Ultimately, the papal authorities ordered

Surratt's arrest. After a spectacular escape, which had the appearance of being contrived, Surratt was arrested in Alexandria, Egypt, on 27 November 1866. He was placed on trial in Washington in June 1867. The trial ended in a hung jury. Ultimately, the charges were dismissed.

Before noon on 15 April, Maryland Provost Marshal James L. McPhail had solid information about Booth's close association with Samuel Arnold and Michael O'Laughlen. The hunt for them began. Actually, the two had returned home to Baltimore after the attempt to capture Lincoln on 17 March, convinced that the operation was a failure. Booth did entice them back to Washington for a meeting on 31 March, but nothing came of it.

Arnold was arrested on 17 April at Fortress Monroe, Virginia, where he had gone by steamer on the first of April to work as a clerk for a sutler, John Wharton. He readily admitted his part in the plan to capture Lincoln.[6]

O'Laughlen surrendered himself to Baltimore police officer William Wallace on 17 April. Beyond an initial denial, he refused to talk. There is a loose end concerning his presence in Washington on the night Lincoln was shot. O'Laughlen had come to the city with three Baltimore cronies on the afternoon of 13 April. The trial testimony of one of these men, Bernard Early, indicates that O'Laughlen saw Booth in his room at the National Hotel at about 9:00 A.M. on 14 April.[7]

Either Confederate agent Thomas H. Harbin's instincts served him well or he was alerted. At the time Lincoln was shot, Harbin and his partner in clandestine activities, Private Joseph N. Baden, were holed up at the tavern of Austin Adams in the tiny community of Newport in Charles County, Maryland. What they were doing there has raised some historical eyebrows but nobody really knows.

Union Colonel Henry H. Wells was in Bryantown rounding up suspects. On 22 April he wrung out John Lloyd, Mrs. Surratt's alcoholic tenant. Wells learned from Lloyd that Austin Adams might be likely to harbor Booth and Herold at his Newport tavern. Adams and his wife were arrested, along with an employee, James Owens. Wells took a long statement from Owens on 28 April. At the end of the statement, Owens mentioned Thomas Harbin and Joseph Baden. Yes, he knew them. They had come to the tavern "on Tuesday, before I heard of the death of the President." Then he went on to tell Wells that the two, with a man he did not know, had left on Saturday going in the direction of the Potomac River. They gave him five dollars, he said, to row them across a creek.[8]

Lieutenant S. P. Currier interrogated Owens again at Old Capitol Prison in Washington. Owens admitted that he had fibbed to Colonel Wells. Actually, he had rowed Harbin and Baden across the Potomac River and landed them near Mathias Point in Virginia.[9] This makes sense because Baden was attached to Lieutenant Charles Cawood's Signal Corps camp in that area. From other evidence it is likely that the crossing was on the morning of 16 April, a Sunday, rather than the day before. All this set off a bizarre series of events.

Just past 10:00 P.M., George Atzerodt hitched his rented horse at the Kirkwood House and went in to kill Vice-President Andrew Johnson. His courage was not sufficiently screwed up. He got as far as the bar. When he left a few drinks later, he turned his horse into Tenth Street. The frenzied crowd outside Ford's Theatre was a chilling sight. Atzerodt bumbled his way out of Washington, leaving a broad trail. As will be seen, his undoing was the one-eyed horse Booth had purchased from Dr. Samuel Mudd's neighbor in December and Booth's fancy white-trimmed saddle. The horse, equipped with this saddle, had been ridden by Powell at the time he attacked members of the Seward household. However, the immediate cause of Atzerodt's arrest was loose talk at a Sunday dinner.

After leaving the Kirkwood House, Atzerodt rode aimlessly about, first going up to the Capitol and then to the seedy Pennsylvania House at 357 C Street for another drink. Perhaps the horse was an impediment; he returned it to Keleher's stable at about 11:00 P.M. For some reason, he then took the horse car out to the Navy Yard. Two men he knew, Washington Briscoe and John Yates, were on the car. On the way Atzerodt pleaded with Briscoe to let him sleep in his store that night. Briscoe refused. Discouraged, Atzerodt rode the car back downtown and secured a bed at the Pennsylvania House. It was then past 2:00 A.M.

Atzerodt knew a place of refuge, the farm of his cousin Hartman Richter, near Germantown, in Montgomery County, Maryland. He had lived on this place as a boy and had visited there frequently. Only the Richters and a few boyhood friends knew his real name. Others knew him under his alias, Andrew Atwood. He set out for the Richters' early the next morning on foot.

By 8:00 A.M. Atzerodt was in Georgetown. Here he stopped at 49 High Street, where Matthews & Company operated a grocery store. He knew John Caldwell, the manager. Caldwell let him borrow ten dollars, taking a revolver as security. Now back in funds, Atzerodt visited a friendly widow, Lucinda Metz, at 182 West Street.

A stage line ran from Washington to Rockville, the county seat of Montgomery County. Atzerodt was the only passenger that morning when the stage left the Georgetown stop at Cunningham's tavern, High and O streets. Just past Tennallytown, near the District of Columbia line, the stage was halted at the end of a string of market wagons waiting to clear through a military checkpoint at an intersection known as the Forts. The morning wore on, so Atzerodt left the stage and wandered up to the checkpoint. A sutler's store was located nearby. Before long he and the picket sergeant went in to drink cider. No doubt the sergeant and his men had been told to keep their eyes open for suspicious characters. But who would have suspected the clownish Atzerodt?

One of the wagons waiting to clear the checkpoint was owned by William Gaither, a farmer who lived north of Rockville. Atzerodt asked him for a ride. Gaither agreed. When Gaither pulled out that afternoon, Atzerodt was on the seat with him.[10] Atzerodt's escape was as easy as that. The sergeant who drank cider with Atzerodt, however, was arrested and charged with dereliction of duty.

About dark Gaither let Atzerodt off at John Mullican's tavern and blacksmith shop at a road fork three miles north of Rockville. The last drink had been at the sutler's shop, a deplorable condition that could be rectified at Mullican's bar. Properly fortified, Atzerodt set out on foot for Clopper's mill on Great Seneca Creek. He knew the miller, Robert Kinder. The unsuspecting Kinder put him up for the night. Kinder paid a high price for his hospitality. He was arrested on 28 April and did not get out of Old Capitol Prison until 3 June.

On the way to the Richters', Atzerodt dropped by the farm of Hezekiah Metz, who knew him only as Andrew Atwood. Atzerodt was invited to stay for Sunday dinner. Metz had two other guests that day, the brothers Somerset and James Leaman. Young men may not have been a rarity on Sundays after church. Metz had a seventeen-year-old daughter. Somerset Leaman had known Atzerodt from boyhood and was aware that he went by the name of Andrew Atwood. Whether James Leaman knew this is not certain. In any case, they were discreet. They did not tell Metz.

News of the assassination of President Lincoln and the attack on Secretary of State Seward had reached the area, but details were sketchy. Atzerodt let it be known that he had just come from Washington. He was pressed by Metz and the Leamans to tell what he knew. The discussion soon got around to whether General Grant had been killed. Metz had picked up a rumor that Grant had been shot "on the cars." Was this so? Metz understood Atzerodt's answer to be: "If the man that was to follow him followed him, it is likely to be so." There were other comments by Atzerodt along the same line.[11]

After Atzerodt left for the Richters', Metz was troubled. Andrew Atwood knew altogether too much about the tragic events in Washington. He was still troubled when he met a neighbor, Nathan Page, the following Wednesday morning,—19 April. When they got around to talking about the assassination of President Lincoln, Metz repeated to Page the substance of the several suspicious statements made in his presence the previous Sunday by the man he knew as Andrew Atwood. Page thought the situation should be looked into.

Page knew James W. Purdum, a strong Lincoln supporter with close ties to the federal garrison at Monocacy Junction. That afternoon around two o'clock Page visited Purdum at his home north of Germantown and laid out Metz's account to him. Purdum saddled a horse and set out for Monocacy Junction to report the matter to Captain Solomon Townsend, his contact there. On the way he met an acquaintance, Private Frank O'Daniel, Company D, First Delaware Cavalry. O'Daniel had been to nearby Clarksburg to retrieve his overcoat and was on his way back to camp. Purdum asked O'Daniel to carry the message to Captain Townsend and briefed him on the story he had gotten from Nathan Page about the mysterious Andrew Atwood then at Hartman Richter's farm.

Back in camp, O'Daniel hunted up Sergeant George Lindsley and passed Purdum's message on to him. Lindsley took it to Captain Townsend. The situation was made to order for a typical military foul-up. Captain Townsend was skeptical because Purdum had previously sent him some worthless information. So why get in a big stew? This was the recommendation he made to Major E. R. Artman, the post commander. Artman agreed but became increasingly uncomfortable with his decision. By 9:00 P.M. Artman had changed his mind. He ordered Captain Townsend to send out a detail to arrest this mystery man.

The duty fell to Sergeant Zachariah Gemmill, First Delaware Cavalry, and six troopers. This assignment, considered odious at the time, ultimately made them all considerably richer. The information given to Gemmill, which had come from Metz, had been filtered through Page, Purdum, O'Daniel, Lindsley, and Captain

Townsend. When Gemmill left camp at 10:00 P.M. with his men, he thought he was after a man named "Lockwood," supposed to be on the farm of a man named Richter near Germantown. He was to find Purdum, who would sort it all out.

Sergeant Gemmill got lost on the back roads and it was past midnight when he found Purdum's place and got him out of bed. Around four o'clock they finally got to the Richter farm. When Richter came to the door, Gemmill asked him if "Lockwood" was there. Richter got the message: cousin George was in some sort of scrape. He tried to put Gemmill off by saying his cousin had gone to Frederick. Gemmill was too tired for nonsense. He searched an upper bedroom and found three men there. Two were farmhands, the Nichols brothers. The third man seemed to answer the shaky description passed on by Purdum. Gemmill understood this man to say his name was "Atwood." That was close enough.

At that point, Gemmill did not know who he had arrested, so he took the prisoner to the Leaman home in Germantown. The Leamans should know. After much banging and shouting, Solomon Leaman, the father, came to the door. Gemmill asked him if he knew a man named Atwood. Leaman said he did. Is this that man? Leaman identified him as Atwood. Gemmill was being gulled, as he found out later. Solomon Leaman knew very well that Atwood was Atzerodt.

Still rankled by Hartman Richter's evasions, Sergeant Gemmill went back and arrested him too. By noon the weary troopers arrived at Monocacy Junction with the two prisoners. Major Artman quickly established that Atwood was really George Atzerodt, wanted in connection with the assassination of President Lincoln. A long statement was taken down by Lieutenant William Runkel. This statement is presumed to have been lost.[12]

At 11:30 P.M., 20 April, B. W. Leary noted in the log of the monitor *Saugus*, then anchored in the river at the Washington Navy Yard, that he had received two prisoners, "John Ricker" and "John Atzerodtt."

In Washington the night of 14 April was one of anger, disbelief, and horror. Rumor piled on rumor. Cavalrymen dashed about with messages. Doctors tended the wounded at the Seward house on Lafayette Square, while more doctors at the Petersen House across from Ford's Theatre watched helplessly as Lincoln's life slipped away. Secretary of War Stanton sat in the parlor of the Petersen House pulling the government together, issuing orders and reports and taking evidence. Down the same street at police headquarters, Superintendent Almarin C. Richards put his detectives to work.

Major Thomas T. Eckert, who had come to the Petersen House from the Seward home with Stanton, went back to the War Department telegraph office and sent a telegram to General Grant, marked "April 14th, 12 PM 1865," requesting Grant to return to Washington immediately. The telegram reached Grant at Philadelphia as he was preparing to leave for Burlington, New Jersey. Eckert followed up with a 12:40 A.M. telegram to General Marsena Patrick, provost marshal, Army of the Potomac, who was in Richmond.

General Christopher C. Augur, military governor and commander of the Twenty-second Army Corps, kept calm. Around midnight a stream of telegrams from his office began going to outlying commands. Two of these telegrams, both dated 14 April and obviously sent before midnight, were to Brevet Brigadier General William W. Morris, who was in temporary command of the Eighth Army Corps, Baltimore. Both named J. Wilkes Booth as Lincoln's assassin.[13] Contrary to some sensational accounts, the military telegraph lines were operational all night. Service by one commercial line was deliberately interrupted for about two hours. The station manager, William C. Heiss, later justified his action by saying he was keeping plotters from communicating with each other.[14]

More than sixty forts ringed Washington, some of them lightly manned. At critical points these were connected with General Augur's headquarters by telegraph. General Martin D. Hardin, one of Augur's subordinates, began sending telegrams to these forts before midnight, but not all of these communications are extant. One such telegram, marked 12:10 A.M., was sent to Major George S. Worcester at Fort Baker, southeast of the city: "Leave the men at the guns at each fort in your command to remain until daylight. The President and Secretary Seward have been assassinated." General Hardin followed this with another telegram to Major Worcester at 2:30 A.M., which reads in part: "The horse and saddle of the supposed murderers has been found at or near Fort Lincoln Hospital. You will send a mounted patrol along the shore of the East Branch to arrest any one crossing the river by boat."[15] Although neither General Hardin nor Major Worcester was aware of it, Lewis Powell had been riding that horse. It was the one-eyed pacer owned by Booth. The saddle was also Booth's, a fancy one, trimmed in white leather. By 2:00 A.M. the horse and saddle helped

General Augur identify David Herold and George Atzerodt as members of Booth's action team. The sequence of events is almost incredible.

In checking out the situation at Seward's home on Lafayette Square, Booth learned that the injuries Seward had received in the carriage accident were being treated by Dr. Tulio Verdi. Booth and Powell planned for Powell to secure entry into the house by posing as a messenger sent to deliver medicine ordered by Dr. Verdi. David Herold was to wait outside on his rented horse to guide Powell from the city. Powell did not know the Washington streets.

A little before 10:00 P.M., Powell was admitted to the Seward home by a black servant, William Bell. Powell argued with Bell, and later with Frederick Seward insisting that he must deliver the package of medicine to Seward personally and give him Dr. Verdi's instructions for taking it. The delay was more than the fidgety Herold could stand. He deserted Powell and rode away at a good clip, swinging around the Treasury building and back into Pennsylvania Avenue opposite Willard's Hotel.

In the nightmare that followed, five members of the Seward household were wounded, three seriously. Frederick Seward had a fractured skull, the result of being clubbed with Powell's jammed revolver. Secretary Seward had knife gashes on the face and neck; Emerick Hansell, a State Department messenger, was stabbed in the back; Private George Robinson, a nurse, was cut about the head; and Augustus Seward had cuts on his head and left hand.

When Powell ran from the house after this carnage, he mounted Booth's one-eyed horse and turned to his right. That was the wrong way. He rode north past I Street and around into the maze of streets off Vermont Avenue. Powell was soon hopelessly lost. Somehow he managed to reach the Lincoln Hospital area east of the Capitol. He rode the horse hard. Apparently it staggered and fell. A picket found the animal about one o'clock, lame, exhausted, and lathered with sweat. A cavalry search failed to turn up the rider.[16]

After abandoning the horse, Powell hid in a cemetery near the Capitol. Shortly before midnight on 17 April he sought shelter at Mrs. Surratt's boardinghouse. He was hungry, spattered with mud, and carrying a pickax. He wore a makeshift stocking cap cut from the sleeve of a shirt. Powell could not have arrived at a worse time. Federal officers were there to arrest Mrs. Surratt and search the house. They let him in and questioned him about why he was there. He said he had been hired by Mrs. Surratt to dig a gutter. When asked to identify himself, he produced the verification copy of the oath of allegiance he had taken as Lewis Paine in Baltimore on 14 March. The officers were not satisfied and took him under arrest to General Augur's headquarters. William Bell, the black servant at the Sewards', was sent for. He identified Powell as the one who attacked members of the Seward household on the night of 14 April. Powell was delivered to the marines at the Navy Yard. Major Thomas Fields locked him up aboard the USS *Saugus*.[17]

Lieutenant John F. Toffey, who worked at the Lincoln Hospital, brought Powell's horse to General Augur's headquarters, where it was discovered that the animal was blind in one eye. The saddle and bridle were removed, and the horse was taken to a nearby military stable. It was then almost two o'clock. The importance of the horse, saddle, and bridle became known quickly. Just after two o'clock, city detective Charles Stone came to General Augur's office, bringing with him John Fletcher, foreman at Tim Nailer's stable at 299 E Street, just off Pennsylvania Avenue. Fletcher had much to tell General Augur. He was not an articulate man, and the story came out in bits and pieces. It involved a man named David Herold and another man who had recently kept a one-eyed horse in his stable.[18]

At some point, General Augur took Fletcher aside and pointed to the saddle and bridle. Did Fletcher recognize them? Fletcher did, particularly the white-trimmed saddle. They belonged, he said, with the one-eyed horse he had talked about. And who owned this one-eyed horse? Fletcher told Augur that he "disremembered." But he could find out easily. He had the man's name on a card at the stable. Fletcher and detective Stone went after it and handed it to General Augur. The name on the card was George Atzerodt.

As Fletcher told General Augur that night, and later Colonel John Foster, two men came to the stable on the late afternoon of 3 April (actually the first of April). One was riding a light bay and the other a "large brown horse, blind in the off eye." The well-dressed man—the description fitted Booth, right down to the mustache—said he owned the bay and wanted to leave it in livery until sold. Since he was leaving for Philadelphia, the man with him would handle the sale. Fletcher handed the second man a stable card and he wrote his name on it. A few days later the bay was sold. The one-eyed horse remained in the stable until Wednesday, 12 April, when the charges were paid and he was taken away.

Fletcher told General Augur that David Herold and George Atzerodt were acquainted. He knew this because the two had been in his stable together on occasion. Augur may have had to piece Fletcher's account together, but it was worth it.

At about one o'clock on the afternoon of 14 April, Atzerodt brought a dark bay mare into the stable. She was to be put up and fed; Atzerodt would be back for her later. Shortly after Atzerodt left, David Herold came in to rent a horse. He asked for a particular horse, "Charley." Herold paid the rental, five dollars, and requested that the horse be ready at 4:00 P.M. Fletcher set a deadline. The horse must be returned not later than "9 o'clock at the farthest." At 4:30 P.M. Herold came for the horse.

When Fletcher returned from supper between 6:00 and 7:00 P.M., he found Atzerodt waiting. A stable hand had the mare ready to go. Atzerodt paid the fifty-cent livery charge and rode off. He was back in about an hour and asked Fletcher to keep the mare saddled and bridled until 10:00 P.M., when she would be wanted. Without being aware of it, Fletcher had just been given the hour at which three planned assassinations were to be carried out.

It was close to 10:00 P.M. when Atzerodt came back for the mare. He invited Fletcher to a nearby bar for a quick drink. Upon returning to the stable, Atzerodt made a statement Fletcher did not understand: "If this thing happens tonight, you will hear of a present." When Fletcher expressed concern that Herold was still out with the rented horse, Atzerodt responded: "He will be back after a while." As Atzerodt mounted to leave, Fletcher commented that the mare looked "scarish." Atzerodt said she would be "good on a retreat."

Something about Atzerodt's demeanor and Herold's continued absence set off a warning in Fletcher's mind. Was he about to lose Charley in some escapade involving these two? So he followed Atzerodt around the corner to Pennsylvania Avenue and saw him dismount and go into the Kirkwood House. Atzerodt stayed "5 or 6 minutes" and then rode off down D Street into Tenth Street. Puzzled, Fletcher went back to the stable. After fretting a bit, Fletcher walked out to Pennsylvania Avenue again and on up as far as Fourteenth Street. At that time—probably about 10:20 P.M.—he saw Herold riding down Pennsylvania Avenue, coming from the direction of the Treasury. As Herold made the turn around Willard's Hotel into Fourteenth Street, Fletcher shouted at him to "get off that horse." Herold's answer was to use his spurs. The last Fletcher ever saw of Charley was when Herold turned right into F Street. The indignant Fletcher hurried back to the stable. He had an idea Herold and Atzerodt were together, and they might be headed into Prince George's County, Maryland, in the direction of the village of T. B. Fletcher had heard Atzerodt speak of the place. To get there, they would have to cross the Eastern Branch of the Potomac River on the Navy Yard Bridge. Fletcher saddled the fastest horse in the stable and set out for the bridge.

Sergeant Silas Cobb, Company F, Third Massachusetts Heavy Artillery, was in charge of the guard detail at the Navy Yard Bridge. He told Fletcher that two men had just crossed, one of them on a horse such as Fletcher described. Yes, Fletcher could also cross, but he could not come back until morning. Disgruntled, Fletcher rode back downtown. Along the way he stopped at Murphy's stable and was told that Lincoln had been shot and "Secretary Seward is almost dead." After he put up the horse he had been riding, Fletcher sat in front of the stable until 1:30 A.M. People passing by told him that men on horseback had shot Lincoln. Fletcher's suspicions were aroused because of Herold's actions. When Fletcher walked around to Fourteenth Street, he asked a cavalry sergeant if any horses had been turned in. The sergeant sent him to police headquarters on Tenth Street. There Fletcher talked with detective Charles Stone, whom he knew. Stone saw the connection. He took Fletcher to see General Augur.

It must have been well past two o'clock before General Augur had heard enough of Fletcher's story to act on it. Now he had four names to work with: John Wilkes Booth, identified as the man who shot Lincoln; John Surratt, supposedly the man who attacked the Sewards; and two new names, David Herold and George Atzerodt. He knew from Fletcher that two men on horseback had been allowed to cross the Navy Yard Bridge around 11:00 P.M., one of them undoubtedly Herold. Word soon came that the other man who crossed the Navy Yard Bridge told Sergeant Cobb his name was Booth.

Elements of the Thirteenth New York Cavalry had already been deployed in the area around the Navy Yard Bridge. General Augur ordered them to be placed under the command of Lieutenant David Dana, provost marshal at nearby Fort Baker, and sent out into Prince George's County to look for the men who had crossed the bridge. They left before dawn.

John Fletcher got no sleep that night. Acting on information from detective Charles Stone, Superintendent of Police Richards sent his own search party into Prince George's County. They took Fletcher with them.

City detectives got around to the Pennsylvania House on the morning of 15 April, looking for George Atzerodt. From John Greenawalt, the proprietor, they learned that Atzerodt had been a frequent guest in the hotel since 18 March. He had registered again about two o'clock the previous night, along with a man named Thomas. James Walker, the night porter, told the detectives he saw Atzerodt leaving the hotel between five and six o'clock. He was alone. Neither Greenawalt nor Walker knew where he went.

Washington Provost Marshal James R. O'Beirne was uneasy about the security provided the new president. On the night of 15 April he sent one of his military detectives, John Lee, to check on the Kirkwood House, where Andrew Johnson boarded. Lee talked with a friend, Michael Henry, the hotel barkeeper. Henry told him about a rough-looking man who had taken a room the day before. To be on the safe side, Lee took a look at the hotel register and found that "G. A. Atzerodt, Charles County," had been given room 126. Later it was learned that Atzerodt had signed in before 8:00 A.M. on 14 April.[19]

Lee had a hot lead, and he knew it. Together with Henry, he went up to room 126. The door was locked. When the hotel clerk could not find a key, Lee "burst open the door." The search turned up a revolver with spare ammunition and a large knife. Some of the other items were more interesting. A black coat was hanging on the wall. In a pocket Lee found a bank book showing that Booth had deposited $455 in the Ontario Bank, Montreal. There were three handkerchiefs, all marked. The stitching on one indicated that it belonged to Booth's mother. Another was marked "F. M. Nelson." Frederick M. Nelson was Herold's brother-in-law. The third handkerchief was marked "H" in the corner.[20]

If there had been any questions, Lee's finds settled it: Atzerodt, Herold, and Booth were connected. And they must have been together in room 126 at the Kirkwood House. Further proof was provided when Johnson's private secretary, William A. Browning, produced a little card that had been left in his hotel mailbox before five o'clock on 14 April. The card read: "Don't wish to disturb you. Are you at home? J. Wilkes Booth." Booth knew both Browning and Johnson from a Nashville theater engagement in February 1864. The card was probably intended for Johnson and placed in Browning's box by mistake. After all, Johnson was the target to be checked on.[21]

Almost, it would seem, John Wilkes Booth and David Herold each had an appointment in Samarra and each set out to keep it, one with Sergeant Boston Corbett at Richard Garrett's barn in Caroline County, Virginia, and the other with a hangman on the grounds of the old penitentiary at the Washington Arsenal. Their flight from Washington on the night of 14 April 1865 touched off the biggest manhunt in our history. No other manhunt comes close in suspense and drama. Nor has any other left behind so much controversy and so many unanswered questions.

After the Grants decided not to accept Mrs. Lincoln's invitation to the theater, Mrs. Lincoln then asked Major Henry Rathbone and his stepsister, Clara Harris, to accompany them.[22] They arrived late. After they were seated in the presidential box (upper boxes 7 and 8, combined, to the right of the audience), the play resumed. For some reason, city police officer John F. Parker, who was assigned to the Executive Mansion detail, left his post at the outer door to the box. The way was open for Booth.

It was after nine o'clock when Booth took his rented mare out of the little stable he kept in the alley back of the theater. The horse, now saddled and ready, presented a problem. He needed someone to hold her at the rear door of the theater until later. His friend Edman Spangler was too busy shifting stage scenery to do it. Spangler passed the task on to Joseph Burroughs, a boy who did odd jobs about the theater. Burroughs was generally known as "Peanut John" because he had once sold peanuts from a stand in front of the theater.

The planned assassinations were all to take place at ten o'clock. Booth had time to spare. He lounged around the theater lobby and drank in Peter Taltavul's Star Saloon next door. Just after ten o'clock he climbed the stairs to the mezzanine and edged his way back of the patrons to the outer door of the president's box. Lincoln's valet-footman, Charles Forbes, was seated there. Booth showed Forbes a card and was allowed to enter. Once inside the tiny hallway, he jammed a stout length of wood, previously cut to fit, into the acute angle formed by the door and the wall. Facing him were the two inner doors. Lincoln was seated in a rocking chair behind the first door. A small hole had been bored in the door at eye level. At a point when there was loud audience laughter and only one actor, Harry Hawk, was on the stage, Booth opened the door and shot the president in the back of the head. Later he wrote in his famous "diary" that he shouted "Sic Semper" before he fired.[23]

Major Rathbone reacted quickly. He grappled with Booth and received a deep knife wound in the upper left arm. Booth then slid over the balustrade and dropped twelve feet to the floor of the stage. In doing so he became entangled in a Treasury Guard flag which was used to decorate the box. He landed off balance and fractured the fibula in his left leg. Scrambling up, Booth stood on the stage and shouted something. One man thought it was "The South is avenged!" Accounts vary. Booth then ran—limping, some said—across the stage and through a passageway in the scenery leading to the door at the back. Orchestra leader William Withers was in the way. Booth bumped into him and hacked at him with his knife. Then he was gone. It was all over in seconds. But he had been recognized by Withers, J. L. Debonay, an actor, John Buckingham, the theater doorkeeper, and others. There was no question of the assassin's identity.

"Peanut John" was patiently holding Booth's horse in the alley near the door. Booth demanded the horse and then knocked the boy down with the butt of his knife.

Booth reached the Navy Yard Bridge before eleven o'clock. He was stopped by a sentry. Sergeant Silas Cobb, who was in charge of the post, questioned him. He gave his name as Booth and said he was going home to "Charles" (Cobb took this to mean Charles County, Maryland), where he lived near Beantown. Cobb called his attention to the rules: people were not allowed to cross the bridge after nine o'clock. Booth responded that he knew of no such rule; anyway, it was a dark night and he would soon have the moon to ride by. Cobb let him pass.[24] This mistake got him a tongue lashing from General Augur.

Within ten minutes a second man rode up to the bridge on a roan horse. Although Sergeant Cobb failed to identify him at the conspiracy trial, this second man was obviously David Herold, riding Fletcher's missing Charley. In answer to Cobb's questions, Herold gave his name as "Smith" and said he lived at White Plains (a small community in Charles County, Maryland). Cobb asked why he was out so late. As Cobb recalled it, the man used "a rather indelicate expression, and said he had been in bad company." Cobb made another mistake. He let Herold pass.

A short time later, John Fletcher arrived at the Navy Yard Bridge. Sergeant Cobb told him he could cross but could not come back until morning. Fletcher had no desire to be away all night. Fletcher was stubborn, but enough was enough. If Charley were to be recovered, it would have to wait.

At around eleven o'clock Polk Gardiner, a teamster, was coming down Good Hope hill, some two miles out from the Navy Yard

Bridge, when he met a man on a dark horse going up the hill. This man asked if another horseman had just passed ahead. Gardiner said no and drove on. In a few minutes another horseman came up, riding fast. He also asked if another horseman had passed ahead. Gardiner saw the humor of the situation. In describing the scene to investigators, he said the two men seemed to be chasing each other.

Herold caught up with Booth at Soper's hill, in Prince George's County, some eight miles from the Navy Yard Bridge.[25] They stopped briefly to talk with two men whose wagon had broken down and then went on to Mrs. Surratt's country tavern, arriving about midnight. Booth did not dismount. Herold banged on the door and aroused the drunken John Lloyd, Mrs. Surratt's tenant. Herold said, "Lloyd, for God's sake make haste and get those things!"

Herold was referring to two Spencer carbines with ammunition, a set of French field glasses, and two bottles of whiskey. The carbines and ammunition were Booth's, brought to the tavern by Herold on 18 March and concealed in the joists above the dining room by John Surratt and John Lloyd. The field glasses also belonged to Booth. Mrs. Surratt brought them to the tavern, wrapped in a paper package, on the afternoon of 14 April—just a few hours before Lincoln was shot. The whiskey would come from tavern stock. When Mrs. Surratt was there that afternoon, according to Lloyd's testimony, she requested him to have all these items out and ready because they would be called for that night.

Lloyd knew Herold well, but the other man was a stranger to him. But Lloyd had been requested to deliver specific items to parties who would call for them that night. So he went upstairs and brought down one of the carbines, the ammunition, and the field glasses. These he gave to Herold. The man sitting on the horse told Lloyd that he could not carry a carbine because his leg was broken. For this reason, Lloyd did not go back after the second carbine. Herold took a bottle of whiskey out to the man on the horse. After he drank from it, Herold returned the bottle to the bar. As they were leaving, the man with the broken leg offered to tell Lloyd some news. Lloyd was noncommittal. The man then said: "Well, I am pretty certain we have assassinated the president and Secretary Seward." Then they rode off down the road in the direction of the village of T.B. They had been at the tavern no more than five minutes.[26]

Booth and Herold arrived at Dr. Mudd's farm home about four o'clock Saturday morning and left around five o'clock in the afternoon. The account of events on that day comes largely from Dr. Mudd himself.

When Dr. Mudd examined Booth's leg in an upstairs bedroom, he found a simple fracture just above the ankle. In one of his statements, he referred to this bone as the tibia, a mistake in terminology. Actually, it was the small bone, the fibula. He prepared makeshift splints from a "bandbox" and wrapped them in place. Booth's tall boot, cut to be removed, was left in the room.

A bit later in the morning, Booth asked for a razor, soap, and water. These were sent up to him. The famous Booth mustache became a casualty. He shaved it off. Booth also asked about crutches. Dr. Mudd and one of his employees, an elderly man named Best, sawed and whittled a clumsy pair for his use. Booth still had these crutches when he reached Richard Garrett's farm in Virginia on 24 April.

After the noon meal, Dr. Mudd and Herold rode over to Oak Hill, the nearby home of Dr. Mudd's father. Here they sought to borrow a carriage to take the cripple in comfort down to the Potomac River, where, as Dr. Mudd told it later, he could find a boat going to Washington. No carriage was available. Disappointed, the two set out for Bryantown. After a short distance, Herold changed his mind. Dr. Mudd went on alone. He had some small purchases to make. He also had another purpose in going to Bryantown.

Dr. Mudd made two long written statements.[27] Both contain evasions and untruths. He could truthfully say he did not know Herold. But about Booth, Dr. Mudd was in a bind. He could not reveal that he knew Booth when he came to his home on the morning of 15 April. He was already compromised on this point. At St. Peter's Catholic Church the next day, he told Dr. George Mudd and others that the two men were strangers, describing them only as "suspicious persons." This may account for the unlikely story that Booth was wearing a false beard. Nor could Dr. Mudd afford to reveal the full extent of his past associations with Booth. That would have been fatal.

In 1877 Dr. Mudd explained his dilemma to Samuel Cox, Jr., while the two were driving around in a buggy campaigning for the Maryland legislature. He told Cox he recognized Booth when he came to his home on Saturday morning, but Booth said nothing to him about shooting Lincoln. He learned this news when he went to Bryantown that afternoon to mail some contraband letters received from the South. A Union cavalry picket stopped him just outside the village. He was "horrified" to learn from this man that

Lincoln had been assassinated by Booth. His first impulse was to surrender Booth to the military authorities in Bryantown. Upon reflection, he decided to go back and "upbraid" Booth for treachery. This he did. After an impassioned plea by Booth, Dr. Mudd compromised by asking him to leave.[28]

What Dr. Mudd told Cox may be close to the truth. But it was only close. The "impulse" to turn Booth in lasted no longer than it took to consider what Booth might reveal as a prisoner.

Dr. Mudd told Lieutenant Alexander Lovett on 18 April that his Saturday visitors were strangers. He also told Lovett that they asked the way to "Parson Wilmer's" (Reverend Lemuel Wilmer, an Episcopal minister). If followed, this route would place them west of the Zekiah Swamp, going in a southerly direction. Lieutenant Lovett thought Dr. Mudd was deliberately misleading him. In any case, the fugitives did not go that way. Instead, they skirted the swamp back of Mudd's home and made a circuit that took them east of Bryantown. The geography of this area is such that a chance encounter with troopers from the Thirteenth New York Cavalry in Bryantown would be unlikely. As it developed later, Booth intended to reach Hagan's Folly, the home of William Bertle, a secluded farm east of St. Mary's Catholic Church that was used on occasion to shelter Confederate agents. Booth was still working the clandestine apparatus.

On the way to the Bertle place, the pair got lost. They stopped to ask directions from Joseph Cantor, who lived just off the Crackling Town Road, near what is now Hughesville.[29] This helped but not enough. They were still lost when they reached the home of Oswell Swann at nine o'clock. Swann, a black tobacco farmer, lived some three miles southeast of Bryantown and less than two miles from William Bertle.

According to Swann, the two men first asked the way to Bertle's place. Then they asked him to get his horse and take them there. They would pay him two dollars. Before they left, he gave them whiskey and bread. On the way to Bertle's there was an unexplained change in plans. The men asked Swann to take them to the home of "Capt. Cox," for which they would pay five dollars more. Swann knew the way across the swamp. They reached Rich Hill, the Samuel Cox farm, around midnight.

What took place at Rich Hill is disputed. As Swann told it, Cox came to the door with a candle and let the two men into the house, where they remained three or four hours. When they came out to leave, Swann heard one of them say: "I thought Cox was a man of

Southern feeling." Swann helped the lame man mount his horse
and then left for home. He arrived about sunrise. In all, he was paid
twelve dollars. The other side of the story was told by Cox and by a
fourteen-year-old servant girl, Mary Swann. Both maintained that
the two men were turned away at the door.[30]

During the twelve-mile ride to Rich Hill, Swann was threatened
by the "small man" (Herold): "Don't you say anything. If you tell
anybody you will not live long!" Possibly Swann was impressed,
but most likely he kept silent because blacks had learned to avoid
trouble. Subsequent events proved the wisdom of this decision. He
was put in Old Capitol Prison on 27 April and not released until 17
May. But on 23 April, Swann let it slip to a friend, Joseph Padgett,
that the search for Booth and Herold around Bryantown was
useless because they were no longer in the area. Padgett dug the
rest out of him. Then he took Swann to see John Young, a detective
who worked for Colonel Henry Wells in Bryantown. At eleven
o'clock the next night, Samuel Cox was standing before an angry
and implacable Colonel Wells.

What happened at the Bryantown tavern was not pretty. Cox at
first denied that two men had visited him on the night of 15 April.
He was beaten to make him talk, and Colonel Wells warned that he
would "hang him up by the thumbs" if he did not tell the truth. He
gave Cox until four o'clock the next morning to think things over.
Cox got the point. When he was brought back in by guards, Cox
said there was no use denying it: two strangers had come to his
home that Saturday night, but he turned them away at the door.
With this victory, the busy Colonel Wells did not pursue the matter. Cox was sent on to Old Capitol Prison and locked up there on
26 April. There he had time to think things over before he was
released on 3 June.

At Old Capitol Prison, Cox underwent more rough questioning
from Colonel Henry Olcott on 28 April. Olcott took the matter up
to where Cox said he closed the door on his visitors. Then he
dropped it.[31] As it turned out much later, this was a mistake.
Olcott might well have pounded away at Cox about what happened
after that. Olcott's problem was that he lacked a handle to pry Cox
open. There was Swann's statement that the two men rode away
from Rich Hill, complaining that Cox was not a man of "Southern
feeling." True, the federals did pick up some stray gossip about Cox
which should have been exploited. But the full story did not begin
to come out until the early 1880s, after Cox was dead. Then
Confederate agent Thomas A. Jones started talking. Newspaper-

man George Alfred Townsend interviewed Jones in Baltimore and published the account in the April 1884 issue of *Century Magazine*.[32] Jones admitted to Townsend that Cox secreted Booth and Herold near Rich Hill and recruited him to protect and feed them until he could get them across the Potomac River into Virginia. It was a sensational story, but by 1884 Jones was safe from prosecution.

Samuel Cox, Jr., provided additional details in a long letter dated 20 July 1891 to the wife of a former Confederate general, Bradley T. Johnson. Cox confirmed much of the 1884 account given by Jones to Townsend. At one point in this letter, Cox told how Herold and his father's overseer, Franklin Roby, led the horses away to be shot in a bog—an inglorious end for poor Charley.[33]

The rest of the story of how Booth and Herold were concealed near Rich Hill was revealed in 1893, when Thomas A. Jones published his little book, *J. Wilkes Booth*. Jones left no doubt on one point: Cox had flimflammed Colonel Wells and Colonel Olcott. Contrary to what Cox told them, he had cooperated with Booth from the start and promised assistance in getting the two across the river. This brings us back to what happened when Swann, Booth, and Herold came to his house that Saturday night.

Cox knew about the assassination. He told Colonel Olcott he learned of it about dusk on Saturday. The news was brought by a river steamer. Charles County was of the Confederacy without being in the Confederacy. Knowing this, one can speculate almost to a certainty that word was passed around among key members of the underground to be on the lookout for Booth. This is further indicated by the way Jones told of his conversation with Cox early Sunday morning. Cox did not seem surprised by his midnight visitors. In short, the clandestine apparatus was closing ranks as quickly as it could to protect one of its own.

The statement of Oswell Swann is open to a number of constructions. Booth and Herold may indeed have gone into the house and remained three or four hours. If so, the little servant girl, Mary Swann, must have been well briefed. Or Cox could have told Booth to leave and come back after Swann was gone. Perhaps inadvertently, Cox told Colonel Olcott that he did talk with the man who sat on a horse. It could be that detective Young pressured Swann to say that Booth and Herold went into the house. Another possibility is that Young deliberately distorted what the illiterate Swann told him to further some purpose of his own. Even so, Thomas A. Jones put a somewhat different slant on the incident, based on what he had heard from Cox himself.

Whatever the case, Cox agreed to help Booth and did so. Here we must pick up the story as told by Jones in his book.[34] Just after breakfast on Sunday, 16 April, Samuel Cox, Jr., came to see Jones at his home, Huckleberry. He told Jones that his father wanted to see him about some seed corn. Then he added: "Some strangers were at our house last night." Jones had learned from two Union cavalrymen he met on Saturday at Pope's Creek that Lincoln had been assassinated. He recognized instantly that the seed corn story was a ploy and was convinced that the elder Cox wanted to see him about something connected with the assassination.

It was four miles from Huckleberry to Rich Hill. Jones and young Cox reached there about nine o'clock. Samuel Cox met them at the gate. He took Jones aside and the two talked of trivia for a while. Finally, Cox said that two strangers had come to his house "last night," accompanied by a black man. One of the men did not get off his horse. When Cox went out to talk with him, this man wanted assurance that he was Samuel Cox. Then, out of hearing of the others, the man identified himself as John Wilkes Booth, the assassin of Lincoln, and showed Cox the initials, JWB, on his wrist. Booth begged Cox for help, saying that Cox was known for the help and sympathy he had given the Confederacy. Cox agreed to assist and had the overseer, Franklin Roby, take the two off to hide in some thick pines about a mile from the house. They were to remain in hiding until Cox could make further arrangements.

This account, as given by Jones in 1893, may have been overly simplified with events run together. But the flavor comes through that Cox had some reason to believe that Booth might show up and was prepared to handle the situation if he did.

For Cox it all came down to one question: could Jones get Booth and his companion across the river into Virginia? Jones had doubts, pointing out that the area would soon be teeming with Union troops and detectives. He agreed to try. But first he must talk with Booth and reach an understanding about how to proceed.

That Sunday morning he approached the pine thicket cautiously, using a special warning whistle as Cox had instructed. Herold came out, carrying a cocked carbine. After Jones convinced Herold he came from Cox and was a friend, he was taken to where Booth was stretched out on a blanket. An understanding was reached. Jones would visit them every day, bringing food and information.

Booth asked for newspapers. Jones would bring these also, as he could procure them. Meanwhile, they were to sit tight. When the way looked clear, he would take them down to the river and furnish a boat to use in crossing.

The days went by. Jones brought food and newspapers, which did little to add to Booth's peace of mind. He was upset by the emotion of his act. In his pocket he had an old memorandum book for 1864. To pass the time he wrote in it:

> April 13, 14, Friday, the Ides
> Until today nothing was ever thought of sacrificing to our country's wrongs. For six months we have worked to capture. But our cause being almost lost, something decisive and great must be done. But its failure was owing to others who did not strike for their country with a heart. I struck boldly, and not as the papers say. I walked with a firm step through a thousand of his friends; was stopped but pushed on. A colonel was at his side. I shouted Sic Semper before I fired. In jumping I broke my leg. I passed all his pickets. Rode sixty miles that night, with the bone of my leg tearing the flesh at every jump.
>
> I can never repent it, though we hated to kill. Our country owed all our troubles to him, and God simply made me the instrument of his punishment.
>
> The country is not what it was. This forced union is not what I have loved. I care not what becomes of me. I have no desire to out live my country. This night (before the deed) I wrote a long article and left it for one of the editors of the *National Intelligencer* in which I fully set forth our reasons for our proceedings. He or the gov'r—

Booth stopped without completing the sentence. Perhaps he was interrupted by a visit from Jones.[35]

On Friday, 21 April, Jones learned in Allen's Fresh that troops in the immediate area had thinned out, some heading off to St. Mary's County. It was time to act. He reached the hiding place well after dark. The three then set out for Huckleberry with Booth riding the horse. Although the distance was less than three miles, the trip was tedious. Jones took elaborate precautions to avoid trouble. Once safely at Huckleberry, Jones left his charges near the stable and went into the house to get food for them. By then it was past nine o'clock.

The only feasible way to get the crippled Booth down to the river was along a deep ravine. A spring-fed creek wandered along this ravine and into the river through a cut in the cliffs. Jones had instructed his employee Henry Woodland, his former slave, to leave his boat well up this creek. Booth rode the horse part of the way down; Jones and Herold helped him the rest of the way. The boat was there. As a boat it was not much—fourteen feet long with one oar and a paddle.

Booth had a box compass. Jones gave him the heading for Machodoc Creek on the Virginia side. Once there he was to see Elizabeth Quesenberry, who would put him in touch with Thomas Harbin and Joseph Baden. The boat was pushed out into the river, almost two miles wide at that point. That was the last Jones saw of the fugitives.

When Jones mentioned Thomas Harbin and Joseph Baden in his book, he revealed something of the clandestine apparatus working to effect Booth's escape. The word had already gone across the river to those on the other side that Booth was still free and would be sent across as soon as possible. Be ready.

Notes

ABBREVIATIONS

NA   National Archives

OR   U.S. War Department, *The War of the Rebellion: A Compilation of the Official Records of the Union and Confederate Armies.* 128 vols. Washington, D.C.: U.S. Government Printing Office, 1880–1901.

ORN U.S. Navy Department, *Official Records of the Union and Confederate Navies in the War of the Rebellion.* 30 vols. Washington, D.C.: U.S. Government Printing Office, 1894–1914.

RG   Record Group

1. Ulysses S. Grant, *Personal Memoirs of U. S. Grant,* 2 vols. (New York: Charles L. Webster, 1886), 2:424.

2. Jefferson Davis, *A Short History of the Confederate States of America* (New York: Belford, 1890), p. 483.

3. Report by General G. W. C. Lee to Lieutenant Walter H. Taylor, 25 April 1865, *Southern Historical Society Papers* 13 (January–December 1885): 255, relating to the evacuation of Richmond and the debacle at Saylor's Creek.

4. Douglas Southall Freeman, *R. E. Lee,* 4 vols. (New York: Charles Scribner's Sons, 1935), 4:59.

5. Surratt checked into the Spotswood Hotel, Richmond, on 29 March 1865 and left on 1 April (testimony of hotel clerk J. B. Tinsley, Jr., *Trial of John H. Surratt,* 2 vols. [Washington, D.C.: U.S. Government Printing Office, 1967], 2:790–91).

6. The original of Arnold's confession has been lost. A copy is in Letters Received by the Office of the Adjutant General (Main Series), M-619, reel 458, frames 0305–12, NA. The most readable version is in the *Baltimore American,* 18 January 1869.

7. Testimony of Bernard Early, Benn Pitman, *The Assassination of President Lincoln and the Trial of the Conspirators* (1865; rpt. ed. Philip Van Doren Stern, New York: Funk and Wagnalls, 1954), p. 224.

8. Statement of James Owens, M-619, reel 458, frames 0412–15, NA.

9. Currier's notes covering his interview with Owens are in Investigation and Trial Papers Relating to the Assassination of President Lincoln, M-599, reel 4, frames 0228–29, NA.

10. Statement of William R. Gaither, M-599, reel 3, frames 0548–53, NA.

11. Testimony of Hezekiah Metz, Pitman, *Assassination*, p. 149; testimony of James and Somerset Leaman, ibid., p. 152.

12. The story of Atzerodt's flight and capture has been pieced together from numerous entries in M-619, reels 455 and 456, NA. These documents relate to reward claims.

13. Augur to Morris, telegrams, Letters Sent, Department of Washington, Book 22 (pages not numbered), RG 393, NA.

14. Arthur F. Loux, "The Mystery of the Telegraph Interruption," *Lincoln Herald*, 81, no. 4 (Winter 1979): 284–87.

15. Hardin to Worcester, telegrams, Letters Sent, Department of Washington, Book 186 (pages not numbered), RG 393, NA.

16. Testimony of Lieutenant John F. Toffey, Pitman, *Assassination*, pp. 159–60.

17. The log of the USS *Saugus* shows that a prisoner, "Lewis Paine," was brought aboard at 5:00 A.M. on 18 April (Records of the Bureau of Naval Personnel, RG 24, NA).

18. Fletcher's account in the following paragraphs was derived from his testimony and statements: testimony, Pitman, *Assassination*, pp. 145–46; testimony, *Trial of John H. Surratt*, 1:227–31; statement, M-599, reel 5, frames 0414–21, NA; and statement, M-619, reel 456, frames 0299–0307, NA.

19. Testimony of John Lee, Pitman, *Assassination*, p. 144; testimony of hotel clerk Robert R. Jones, ibid., p. 144; and page from the Kirkwood House register, Exhibit 24 at the conspiracy trial, M-599, reel 15, frame 0299, NA.

20. The items found by Lee in Atzerodt's room at the Kirkwood House became Exhibits 9 through 15 at the conspiracy trial. For this list, see M-599, reel 15, frame 0067, NA.

21. Testimony of William Browning, Pitman, *Assassination*, pp. 70–71. The card became Exhibit 29 at the conspiracy trial. See M-599, reel 15, frame 0312, NA.

22. That Booth saw the Grants on the way to the depot was brought out in the testimony of John Matthews, 17 July 1867, before the Judiciary Committee, House of Representatives, *Impeachment Investigation*, 39th Cong., 2d sess., and 40th Cong., 1st sess., pp. 782–88.

23. "Sic Semper Tyrannis" is the motto of Virginia and is generally translated as "Thus will it ever be with tyrants."

24. Statement of Sergeant Silas Cobb, M-599, reel 4, frames 0172–78; testimony, Pitman, *Assassination*, pp. 85–86.

25. From interrogation of David Herold aboard the USS *Montauk* on 27 April 1865, M-599, reel 4, frames 0442–85, NA.

26. Testimony of John Lloyd at the conspiracy trial, Pitman, *Assassination*, pp. 85–87; testimony, *Trial of John H. Surratt*, 1:276–87.

27. Dr. Mudd's two statements are together in M-599, reel 5, frames 0212–39.

28. Samuel Cox, Jr., wrote this account in the margins and blank pages of his copy of Thomas A. Jones's *J. Wilkes Booth* (Chicago: Laird & Lee, 1893). James O.

Hall secured a photocopy of these entries from a Cox descendant. Osborn Oldroyd interviewed Cox in 1901 and secured essentially the same account, which he reported in *Assassination of Abraham Lincoln* (Washington, D.C.: Privately published, 1901), pp. 265–69.

29. The route and the stop at Cantor's abattoir are reconstructed from Herold's interrogation on the USS *Montauk*, 27 April 1865, M-599, reel 4, frames 0442–85, NA, and from an analysis of census records, old maps, and Charles County, Maryland, land records at the courthouse, La Plata.

30. Report by Colonel H. H. Wells giving a summary of his interview with Samuel Cox, M-599, reel 4, frame 0207, NA; statement of Mary Swann, M-599, reel 6, frames 0160–62, NA.

31. Statement of Samuel Cox to Colonel Henry Olcott, Joseph Holt Papers, Library of Congress, Nos. 6769–75.

32. George Alfred Townsend, "How Wilkes Booth Crossed the Potomac," *Century Magazine*, April 1884, pp. 423–32.

33. Samuel Cox, Jr., to Mrs. Bradley T. Johnson, 20 July 1891. A photocopy is in the Cox file, Surratt Society library, Clinton, Md.

34. Jones, *J. Wilkes Booth*, pp. 65–115.

35. The entries in the memorandum book are quoted in full in *Trial of John H. Surratt*, 1:310–11.

20

The Final Curtain

Samuel Cox and Thomas A. Jones had accomplished what they set out to do. Booth and Herold were put out in the Potomac River at about ten o'clock on the night of 21 April. Word had previously been passed to Confederate agents on the Virginia side to be alert for them. Cox and Jones could do no more. Now it was up to the fugitives. But they did not make it across the river that night. Dawn found them back in Maryland, over four miles upstream from where they started. They pulled the little boat ashore on the east bank of Nanjemoy Creek near Indiantown, the home of a Confederate sympathizer, John J. Hughes.[1] In his book Jones mentions the weather conditions and the swell of the Potomac River that night. The U.S. Naval Observatory in Washington was about thirty-five miles away as the crow flies. Its records of weather are compatible with the conditions described by Jones.

Charts of the Potomac River made by the Union navy during the Civil War show that the channels were almost exactly the same as they are today. The Tidal Current Tables published by the National Oceanic and Atmospheric Administration (NOAA) show the tidal velocities at various stages for the mouth of Machodoc Creek, Persimmon Point, a point south of the present highway bridge, the mouth of Port Tobacco Creek, and Maryland Point. The computer at NOAA calculated the times and heights of high and low tide at Mathias Point and Goose Creek inside the mouth of Port Tobacco Creek for several days in April 1865. All these river areas are pertinent to this historical inquiry.

The computer showed that high tide occurred at Mathias Point at three minutes before midnight on 21 April. The *Nautical Almanac*, published jointly by the U.S. Navy and the British Nautical

454

Almanac Office, shows that nautical twilight would have occurred at the latitude of Mathias Point at about twenty minutes after four the next morning. From these various data one can construct a vector diagram of the forces at work on Booth's boat, and it is clear that if Booth steered the course given him by Jones he could not have arrived at Nanjemoy Creek.

Jones gave Booth a compass heading for the mouth of Machodoc Creek on the Virginia side. Presumably this would have been a heading of about 190 degrees magnetic. If he steered this course it would have taken him across the river at a long downstream angle. The route would have taken the boat close to Persimmon Point and then along the Virginia shore to where the mouth of Machodoc Creek opened up to the west.

Complications developed on this route. The USS *Juniper,* a gunboat belonging to the Potomac River Flotilla, had gone to anchor off Persimmon Point at about 10:15 P.M., just after Booth and Herold started across. With fog in the air and the *Juniper* showing only an anchor light, Booth probably did not see the vessel until he was almost upon her. Further, the USS *Heliotrope* passed the *Juniper* at about 11:45 P.M., going upstream. At about that time, the wind, which had been quiet, began to blow from the south. With the river seemingly filled with gunboats and with a contrary wind, a retreat would have seemed the safest course.[2]

A Hughes family account is that Booth and Herold did not come into the house at Indiantown. Hughes treated them kindly and fed them.[3] Hughes may have had second thoughts about his action. One record shows that an unnamed man came into Port Tobacco on 27 April and reported seeing two men, one answering the description of Booth, on Nanjemoy Creek.[4] If Hughes had made this report, it would be disingenuous: he undoubtedly knew Herold.

While in hiding at Indiantown on 22 April, Booth made another entry in his "diary": "After being hunted like a dog through swamps, woods, and last night being chased by gunboats till I was forced to return wet, cold, and starving, with every man's hand against me, I am here in despair. And why? For doing what Brutus was honored for—What made Tell a hero. And yet I, for striking down a greater tyrant than they ever knew am looked upon as a common cut-throat." He went on at some length in this self-pitying mood and then dropped in a thought that would have scared the wits out of his associates in the enterprise if he had expressed it to them: "Tonight I will once more try the river with

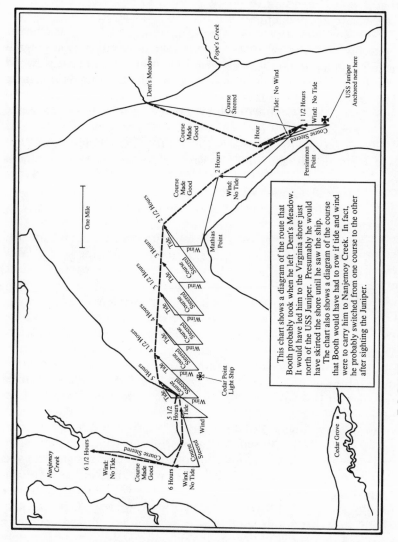

BOOTH'S ROUTE FROM DENT'S MEADOW

This chart shows a diagram of the route that Booth probably took when he left Dent's Meadow. It would have led him to the Virginia shore just north of the USS Juniper. Presumably he would have skirted the shore until he saw the ship.

The chart also shows a diagram of the course that Booth would have had to row if tide and wind were to carry him to Nanjemoy Creek. In fact, he probably switched from one course to the other after sighting the Juniper.

the intent to cross. Though I have a greater desire and almost a mind to return to Washington, and in a measure clear my name— which I feel I can do."

In one of his few concessions to candor, David Herold told his interrogators on 27 April that he and Booth crossed the mouth of Nanjemoy Creek at sundown. This was Saturday, 22 April. It would have been easier to row directly across the river and land below Chotank Creek in the area of Lieutenant Charles Cawood's Signal Corps camp. But Booth could not have been certain that Cawood had been told to expect him, nor could he have known precisely how to reach this camp. Even so, he made a reference probably to Cawood in the hand-drawn calendar in his "diary." In the box for 23 April he entered "Mr C." But Booth had a sure point of contact with the Confederate clandestine organization in Thomas Harbin. So he stuck with the directions given him by Jones, although the route was longer and more hazardous.

They had a long way to go, and the tide was against them for a good part of the trip. The wind was out of the northwest and helped them along. Once they neared the mouth of Machodoc Creek, however, tide and wind combined to push them offshore, and they finally abandoned the attempt and landed on the morning of 23 April near the mouth of Gambo Creek, a smaller stream just north of Machodoc Creek. This put them over a mile from their intended landing point at Elizabeth Quesenberry's place on Machodoc Creek. But they were in Virginia and still free.

Booth was left at Gambo Creek when Herold set out across the fields to the widow Quesenberry's home, the Cottage. He got there about one o'clock in the afternoon. Mrs. Quesenberry was away at the time. While waiting, Herold offered Jones's boat to her daughter as a gift. Upon Mrs. Quesenberry's return, Herold allegedly asked her for a conveyance to take him "up the country." He explained that his brother had a broken leg and was sitting down by the river. According to Mrs. Quesenberry, she refused to help. She did offer food and would send it along shortly. Mrs. Quesenberry then sent for Thomas Harbin and Joseph Baden, which almost has to mean she knew Booth and a companion were expected, and Harbin was the one to handle things. The promised food was prepared, and Harbin took it over to Gambo Creek.[5] There was no problem of identification. Harbin knew Booth from the December 1864 meeting at the Bryantown tavern.

What was said during Harbin's conference with Booth can only be guessed at. George Alfred Townsend interviewed Harbin after the war and included snatches of the interview in his book *Katy of Catoctin*.[6] Booth did complain to Harbin about his broken leg. But there must have been some basic difficulty about a course of action. Booth had a name, Dr. Richard H. Stuart, and he wanted to find him. Whatever Harbin's motives may have been, he agreed to pass Booth and Herold along to Dr. Stuart. Herold was sent with Harbin's blessing to see a nearby farmer, William Bryant, who had horses. Harbin waited. Later that afternoon he told Mrs. Quesenberry the two men were going to Dr. Stuart's and he saw them leaving on Bryant's horses.

Mrs. Quesenberry was later arrested and brought to Washington, although she was not imprisoned. In her statement of 16 May 1865 to Colonel Henry Wells, she lifted the curtain—perhaps inadvertently—on how closely the Confederate clandestine machinery was following Booth's movements through King George County. In her last sentence she said: "I did not report it to any government officer as I had no opportunity to do so, meantime I heard that after they left Dr. Stewart's [Stuart's] they had crossed the Rappahannock at Port Royal and that soldiers were in pursuit." Mrs. Quesenberry probably got this information from Harbin.

Even after General Lee's surrender the Confederate information line from Washington remained in place and operational. Lieutenant Charles Cawood's Signal Corps camp in King George County, Virginia, continued to function. By Sunday, 16 April, news had reached the Northern Neck of Virginia that John Wilkes Booth had assassinated Lincoln. The news was undoubtedly fanned out by courier and over the existing railroad telegraph line at Milford Station in nearby Caroline County. It would have reached the Ashland-Hanover and Gordonsville areas by Monday or Tuesday at the latest. It profoundly changed the situation for Confederate clandestine personnel. No longer would they merely be concerned about embarrassing questions of being involved in a plan to capture Lincoln. Now it was a matter of life or death. The entire Confederate cause would be discredited if the truth became known. If at all possible, this threat must be neutralized.

The clandestine apparatus in Virginia knew within days that Booth was concealed in Charles County, Maryland, and that an attempt would be made to get him over the Potomac River. But the machinery set up to assist in forwarding a captured Lincoln to Richmond was in disarray. Someone with credentials and prestige was needed in King George County to pull things together with a view to getting Booth to safety if he managed to reach Virginia. What if Booth became a Yankee prisoner and decided to talk?

From the bits and pieces, it appears that the man sent to King George County was Thomas Hoomes Williamson. He was not an intelligence officer, but he was admirably suited for the task. Williamson was a professor of engineering at Virginia Military Institute. He came to Richmond in December 1864 when the VMI Corps of Cadets was moved from Lexington to new quarters at the almshouse.[7]

Williamson had a military background. He attended the U.S. Military Academy at West Point but resigned shortly before graduation. He was a lieutenant colonel of militia but was not on active duty in 1865. Williamson knew King George County well. In the early days of the war, he made a strategic survey of the county for the state of Virginia.[8] Williamson served as an engineer officer under Beauregard at the first Battle of Manassas. In 1862 Stonewall Jackson borrowed him from VMI for a few weeks to serve as an engineer officer during the Shenandoah Valley campaign.[9] Above all, Williamson had connections. He was a close friend of General W. N. Pendleton, and he knew General R. E. Lee. At West Point he was a classmate of General Daniel Ruggles, whose son, Lieutenant Mortimer B. Ruggles, was associated with the Conrad spy group. Williamson also knew Colonel Robert Mayo and several other officers then in the Northern Neck of Virginia as part of the security force.

Williamson probably arrived in King George County from Richmond on 19 or 20 April with the intent of finding Booth, if he reached Virginia, and moving him out discreetly. The military security force would be awkward to use for this purpose because of the need for secrecy. Other tools could be used, including trusted civilians. The Signal Corps people were knowledgeable, and the remaining elements of the Conrad group were available. Booth could be identified because Thomas Harbin knew him. Also, Captain Robert Harris Archer was then in King George County. He was from Booth's home territory, Harford County, Maryland, and could be called upon for information if there was a question.

Williamson put up at Mount View, the home of John Temple Taylor, a former VMI cadet and a private in Company B, Ninth Virginia Cavalry. This was an ideal location for Williamson's purposes. Besides, the Taylors were a highly respected family. About all Williamson could do until things were clarified was to make

careful contacts and try to unscramble the rumors and specula-
tions making the rounds. He found the area teeming with Confederates of all descriptions: soldiers awaiting parole whose units
had ceased to exist, soldiers on leave, deserters, paroled soldiers,
and others originally sent there as part of the security force. For
Williamson, this mixed group was more hindrance than help.

That was the situation on the afternoon of 23 April, when
Thomas Harbin watched Booth and Herold ride off with old
William Bryant, headed for Cleydael, the summer home of Dr.
Richard H. Stuart. Most of what happened at Cleydael is known
from the statement of Dr. Stuart, made on 6 May at Old Capitol
Prison to William Wood.[10] Bryant brought Booth and Herold to Dr.
Stuart's about eight o'clock. It was already dark. The man with the
crutches sat on the horse while the other did the talking. He told
Dr. Stuart that they were Marylanders. His brother had a broken
leg, which had been set in Maryland by "Dr. Mudd," who had
referred them to him for further medical aid. He pleaded with Dr.
Stuart to put them up for the night. Dr. Stuart stated that he flatly
refused to help, that he did not know Dr. Mudd, he was a physician
and not a surgeon, and his house was too full to accommodate
more people. He did offer them food, and they came in to eat. At
some point in the discussion, Dr. Stuart was told that his visitors
wanted to "go to Mosby" and needed transportation to Fredericksburg. Dr. Stuart responded by saying, "Mosby has surrendered
. . . you will have to get your paroles." He did tell them that he had
a neighbor with a wagon they might hire. This neighbor was
William Lucas, a free black. Bryant took them on to the nearby
Lucas cabin and left them there.

As far as it went, Dr. Stuart's account is probably accurate. It is
generally supported by the statement of William Bryant.[11] Even so,
a close look at Dr. Stuart's statement is rewarding. He told Wood
that he was suspicious of his two visitors because he had heard on
Tuesday, 18 April, about the Lincoln assassination. The date tells
us that the clandestine apparatus in Virginia had learned quickly
about the assassination. Further, Dr. Stuart knew on 23 April that
Mosby had "surrendered." This is not quite the right word. Actually, Mosby disbanded his organization at Salem, Virginia, on 21
April. What is important is the speed with which this news
reached Dr. Stuart from that distance. It must have come from
someone who was there.

Major Robert Hunter was at the Stuart home, courting Margaret
Stuart, when Booth and Herold came on 23 April. Major Hunter

was interviewed after the war by St. George Coulter Bryan. Hunter said he talked with Booth in Caroline or Essex County in 1865. Booth told Hunter about plans to capture Lincoln and about shooting him.[12] Since Booth was never in Essex County, it must have been in Caroline County, probably on the afternoon of 25 April, when Booth was at the Garrett farm. If Hunter is quoted accurately, we are left to speculate whether Dr. Stuart sent Major Hunter, who had a parole, to check on Booth's whereabouts. One may surmise that Williamson's people had traced Booth to Dr. Stuart's on 24 April and now needed to pick up the trail.

Booth was in a surly mood when he and Herold got off Bryant's horses at the one-room cabin of William Lucas. He used harsh language and threatened Lucas with a knife. The Lucas family moved outside, where they sat for the rest of the night. The next morning there were more threats—Lucas said by the "lame man"—to take their team and wagon. Herold intervened to calm the situation. It was finally agreed that Lucas's twenty-one-year-old son Charley would drive the unwanted visitors to the Port Conway ferry on the Rappahannock River for ten dollars. They left about seven o'clock that morning, 24 April.[13] The wagon pulled up at the Port Conway ferry just after noon.

Booth was outraged at being turned away by Dr. Stuart. He left a sarcastic little note, quoting lines from *Macbeth*, written on a page cut from his "diary," for Lucas to deliver to Dr. Stuart. As an insult to the wealthy Dr. Stuart, he pinned $2.50 inside the rolled-up page to pay for the food received. The note was signed "Stranger."

History has a way of taking odd bounces. Events from the past now began to overtake Booth and Herold. In late December 1864 Lieutenant Colonel William Chapman of Mosby's command was sent to the Northern Neck of Virginia with four companies.[14] Chapman began active recruiting in the Northern Neck, often to the chagrin of other commanding officers, whose men he took. Among those he recruited were William S. Jett, an eighteen-year-old private in Company C, Ninth Virginia Cavalry, who had been wounded on 29 June 1864 and was on detached service as a commissary agent; Absalom R. Bainbridge, a seventeen-year-old private from Company B, Third Virginia Infantry; and Lieutenant Mortimer B. Ruggles, attached to Conrad's spy group and considered by Conrad as his second in command. Jett and Bainbridge went into the relatively new Company G.

Ruggles held rank as an aide to his father, General Daniel Ruggles, although he had not recently been serving as such. On 27

March 1865 he wrote to his father in Richmond asking his permission to join Chapman's battalion. No records have been found to show that he actually enrolled, but in his own account in *Century Magazine* in January 1890, Ruggles stated that he did join Mosby.[15]

On 27 March, Walter Herron Taylor, General Lee's adjutant, wrote to Mosby as follows: "Collect your command and watch the country from the front of Gordonsville to the Blue Ridge and also Valley. Your command is all now in that section, and the General will rely on you to watch and protect the country. If any of your command is in the Northern Neck call it to you."[16] Major Cornelius Boyle, to whom this message was sent, was provost marshal at Gordonsville. It would have taken at least another day for it to reach Mosby by courier.

This note sounds like a warning of the impending evacuation of Richmond. It seems to have no direct relationship to covert actions, except that the failure of plans to capture Lincoln left no future need for part of Mosby's cavalry in the Northern Neck. Lieutenant Colonel Chapman wrote later that in accordance with Mosby's orders, he took the companies under his command out of the Northern Neck on 9 April and reported to Mosby on 13 April. At about the same time, the Union Potomac River Flotilla reported that three hundred of Mosby's men passed through Falmouth on 11 April bound for Fauquier and Loudoun counties.[17]

After Chapman left the Northern Neck on 9 April, Jett, Bainbridge, and Ruggles followed with a group late in getting started. They got to Fauquier County only to learn that Mosby had disbanded his forces. They started back that same day, 21 April, splitting up in King George County on the evening of 22 April. By agreement, Ruggles and Bainbridge were to meet Jett at Bloomsbury, the home of Jett's brother-in-law, on the morning of 24 April. As Jett told it later, they intended to go on down into Caroline County. Just after noon that day, they came upon Booth and Herold at the Port Conway ferry.

Here we are left with the problem of interpreting events with little evidence. Did Ruggles and his two companions receive instructions in Fauquier County to be alert for Booth in King George County and provide support if he were found? Jett said in his statement: "I heard on the day of the disorganization of Mosby's command that the President had been assassinated." Ruggles gave an oblique confirmation in the *Century Magazine* article: "We had heard from United States officers of the assassination of Mr. Lincoln."[18] Clearly these three did not come upon Booth and Herold at the Port Conway ferry in ignorance of what had happened. One crucial question is how and from whom they learned about the assassination in Fauquier County on 21 April. Mosby would have had powerful reasons for wanting Booth to escape—his postwar reputation and his personal safety. After all, he had cooperated with Conrad, he had furnished Lewis Powell as muscle for Booth's action group, and he was instrumental in launching the Harney mission against Lincoln. He or one of his officers could have had a confidential talk with Ruggles. One other possibility exists. There was a narrow period of time during which they could have been briefed by some person in the King George County clandestine apparatus and sent out to look for Booth and Herold. There we must leave it. The episode is suspicious, but proof is lacking.

Much was happening in King George County on 24 April. One such event involved Captain Robert H. Archer and John Tayloe VI, a former lieutenant in the Ninth Virginia Cavalry. Archer had served as a lieutenant colonel in the Fifty-fifth Virginia Infantry but had reverted to captain in a reorganization. He was captured at Gettysburg and exchanged in January 1865. Tayloe had also been a prisoner of war but was released 3 May 1864 because he had resigned his commission and was technically a civilian. Later he claimed to have been given another commission. John Tayloe VI was the grandnephew of Benjamin Ogle Tayloe of Washington. He returned to King George County to live on his father's beautiful estate, Clifton, overlooking the Potomac River not far from Boyd's Hole and near the site of Conrad's camp. Archer joined Tayloe at Clifton about 10 March 1865.

On 24 April these two were involved in some operation that went sour. They were captured on the Potomac River, off Nanjemoy Creek, by the USS *Resolute*. The log of that vessel shows that at twenty minutes after noon "came aboard 2 Rebel officers from Virginia." The two must have been Archer and Tayloe. The prisoners were transferred to the USS *Ella* at 8:15 that evening.[19] Archer and Tayloe were booked into Old Capitol Prison the next day. Tayloe was entered as Taylor and asserted that he was a member of Company C, Partisan Rangers. There is no record that he was ever with any unit of Mosby's command so this appears to be disinformation aimed at diverting attention from some other activity. The entry for Archer was straightforward: "Archer, R. H., Capt. & AAG, PACS." The oddity is that both men insisted they had been paroled.

Later on the same day that Archer and Tayloe were captured, the

USS *Jacob Bell* sighted what was thought to be a flag of truce on the Virginia shore opposite Maryland Point. This would be very near Clifton and Conrad's camp. It was not investigated. Most likely it was a white marker with a red square of the type used by the Confederates to fix the location of a signal station. Communications regularly passed back and forth across the Potomac River.

In analyzing the background of these two men and the circumstances involved, one can speculate almost to a certainty that they had been briefed on the plans to capture Lincoln and stood ready to help. The very location of Clifton is persuasive. Standing on the bank of the Potomac River and opposite the Nanjemoy peninsula on the Maryland side, it was an ideal place to put a captured Lincoln ashore. More, when news was circulated among insiders in King George County that Booth was soon expected to cross the river, Clifton became a likely landing place for him. It seems reasonable to believe that Archer and Tayloe, like Harbin and Baden, would have been alerted to this possibility. Booth's large boat was secreted in a tributary to Nanjemoy Creek in Charles County, Maryland.

The federals soon lost interest in Archer and Tayloe. They were sent over to Alexandria and paroled on 29 April. When the two walked away with their paroles, an excellent chance to fill information gaps in the Booth operation was lost.

Booth and Herold were getting deeper into Virginia. The prospect of escape must have looked better when they reached Port Conway. Once a little village, Port Conway's only occupants on 24 April were an elderly man and William Rollins and his recent bride, Bettie. Rollins lived in a dilapidated building where he had kept a store before the war. Now he made a skimpy living as a farmer and a fisherman. Rollins also had a forwarding function in the Signal Corps line of communication from Richmond to the Potomac River. He had horses.[20]

Booth sat with Charley Lucas in the wagon while Herold negotiated with Rollins. There was talk of finding someone to take them to Orange Court House, but Rollins begged off saying he did not know the way. Herold then asked him to take them to Bowling Green in Caroline County, a distance of about fifteen miles. Rollins agreed to do so for ten dollars. Negotiations finally got down to rowing them across the river to Port Royal. Nothing was settled so Rollins and his helper, a black named Dick Wilson, went out to tend the fishing nets.

When Rollins returned, the wagon had left. He saw three Confederate soldiers talking with Booth and Herold. Rollins recognized one of the men as Willie Jett, whom he had known previously.[21] Although Rollins did not say he knew the other two soldiers, they were Ruggles and Bainbridge. As Jett told it later, Herold began to feel him out. First, he told Jett that his name was Boyd and that his brother, James W. Boyd, was on crutches because of a war wound. Herold soon gave up this tame charade. He bragged to Jett that they were the "assassinators of the President" and told him their true names. Up to that time Ruggles had just been listening. For him, if not for Jett and Bainbridge, everything now fell into place. Here was the man, Booth, who had been the subject of so many discussions and planning sessions with Conrad. If indeed Ruggles and his companions had been instructed to look for Booth and Herold in King George County, then here they were, dumped right into their laps.

An agreement was quickly made to assist Booth and Herold. Rollins was advised that his help was no longer needed. The black ferryman, James Thornton, brought the old scow over from Port Royal and they all crossed, Booth sitting on Ruggles's horse, which, incidentally, belonged to Conrad.

The traditional account is that this party, Booth, Herold, Ruggles, Jett, and Bainbridge, were the only passengers on the ferry that afternoon. But there was another man, Enoch Wellford Mason of the Fifteenth Virginia Cavalry Regiment. This regiment had been consolidated with remnants of the Fifth Virginia Cavalry and unit designations were blurred, so it was sometimes referred to as the Fifteenth and sometimes as the Fifth. Mason, a courier, had been stationed in King George County with elements of this unit as part of the security force created to protect the route to be used in moving a captured Lincoln on to Richmond.

Mason was the only soldier from either the Fifteenth or the Fifth regiment to be paroled at Appomattox. Apparently his courier duties with the forces in King George County put him with Lee's army sometime between 2 and 9 April. Being mounted on his own horse, he could easily have reached home in King George County by 15 April. He was the son of Roy Wiley Mason, a prominent lawyer, who lived about one mile from Mount View, where Williamson made his headquarters with the Taylor family. A map of the Civil War period shows a trail connecting the two houses. In addition, Wellford Mason was the nephew of Charles Mason, who was deeply involved in the operations of the Confederate Signal Corps in that area.

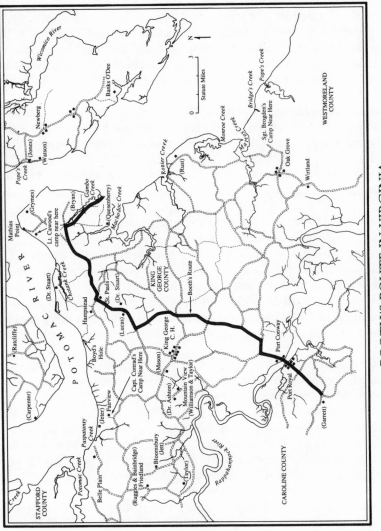

BOOTH'S ROUTE IN VIRGINIA

Booth and Herold had not moved unseen from Dr. Stuart's to the Port Conway ferry. They had gone by way of Mason's mill, Edge Hill, and Office Hall. At Office Hall they stopped for food at the home of William McDaniel. There were eyes everywhere, and the rural telegraph, needing no wires, was beginning to function.

As an old man, Wellford Mason told about crossing the ferry with a live Booth and finding a dead Booth surrounded by Yankee cavalrymen and a curious crowd of civilians when he reached Port Royal on his return trip. In this account, Mason claimed he had gone down to Caroline County on 24 April to buy a wagon and had returned empty-handed. He acknowledged that he knew Ruggles and his associates.[22]

Mason's story about the wagon seems fishy. He crossed by ferry on the afternoon of 24 April and was back at Port Royal on the morning of 26 April before Booth's body was put across the river to the Port Conway side. In other words, Mason was south of the Rappahannock River for almost forty-eight hours. This was ample time for a trained and well-mounted courier to take a message from Williamson or Lieutenant Cawood to the railway telegraph facility at Milford Station, just over two miles from Bowling Green, or even as far as Hanover Junction. Besides, elements of the Ninth Virginia Cavalry were still at Milford Station, left dangling as part of the security force. One must conclude that news about Booth was being spread ahead of him.

Although the gregarious Jett did most of the talking, leadership of the party was clearly with Ruggles, who was experienced in clandestine operations. Booth was the classic hot potato. Ruggles had to find a place for him until he could get through to somebody who knew what to do. Jett suggested the home of the maiden Peyton sisters, Sarah Jane and Elizabeth, in Port Royal as a possible shelter for Booth. They agreed at first. Then they changed their minds because their brother, Randolph, was away that day. Jett knew of a hospitable farmer, Richard Garrett, who lived three miles from Port Royal on the Bowling Green road. With Herold riding double, they set off to try there. Garrett readily agreed to take in the man on crutches, "Mr. James W. Boyd," until his friends could come back for him in a day or so. For his generosity Garrett would pay dearly.

The party, now down to four, left the Garretts' in midafternoon for Bowling Green, Herold again riding double. Jett was anxious to get on to Bowling Green. He was courting sixteen-year-old Izora Gouldman, daughter of Henry Gouldman, who kept the Star Hotel.

But, of course, they could not pass up the Trap, a disreputable tavern a few miles down the road. So they stopped for drinks and to jolly up the four Carter sisters, whose mother ran the tavern. There was talk of visiting Elizabeth Clarke, whose son Joseph had been with Jett and Bainbridge in Mosby's Company G and who was a widow, living on a large farm near Bowling Green. The Carter ladies would later recall this reference to Mrs. Clarke. Upon arrival at Bowling Green, Ruggles and Jett put up at the Star Hotel. Bainbridge and Herold rode to the Clarke farm and spent the night there.

Back in Washington on 24 April the search for Booth and Herold seemed at a dead end. The break came in a series of unlikely events. Major James R. O'Beirne, a Washington provost marshal, assembled a group of detectives and left on the evening of 18 April aboard the steam tug *William Fisher*, intending to scour the Maryland shore of the Potomac River downstream from Port Tobacco. The next morning his detectives began a house-to-house search in the Banks O'Dee area above Cucold Creek in Charles County. Acting on a tip, they called at the home of Richard Clagett. He told detective Michael O'Callaghan that his son had seen men in a boat out on the river early Sunday morning, 16 April, heading across toward the Virginia side. This information corresponds closely with that about Thomas Harbin and Joseph Baden given later by James Owens. It seems almost certain that young Clagett saw these two scurrying back to Virginia.

Major O'Beirne decided to follow up this lead. On 22 April he took his detectives and twelve men from Lieutenant William Laverty's Chapel Point garrison and conducted a search several miles deep into King George County. The trail was too cold by then. On the evening of 23 April he delivered Laverty's men back to their camp at Chapel Point, near Port Tobacco. The next morning he met Samuel Beckwith, General Grant's telegraph specialist and cipher operator, at Port Tobacco. Beckwith was there with two of Colonel Lafayette C. Baker's detectives. In the conversation, O'Beirne told Beckwith about the men seen crossing the river on 16 April. Beckwith immediately tapped into the Chapel Point–Washington telegraph line and sent a cipher message to Major Thomas Eckert at the War Department repeating what he had learned from O'Beirne. The telegram was received at 11:00 A.M., 24 April.[23]

This case of mistaken identity was fatal to Booth and Herold. At the very moment the deciphered telegram was handed to Major Eckert, Colonel Lafayette C. Baker happened to be in his office.

Eckert showed him the telegram. Baker concluded that the men mentioned in the telegram were indeed Booth and Herold and that they were over the river in King George County. He went immediately to see Secretary of War Stanton and asked for twenty-five cavalrymen, a commissioned officer, and a vessel to transport them down the Potomac River to begin the search. Stanton issued the necessary order to General Augur. The order came down through channels to Lieutenant Edward Doherty. Twenty-six troopers from the Sixteenth New York Cavalry fell out for duty, including one who would become famous, Sergeant Boston Corbett.

Colonel Baker assigned two of his detectives to the search party, Everton Conger and Luther Baker. Both had recently been released from active service with the First District of Columbia Cavalry, Conger as a lieutenant colonel and Baker as a lieutenant. Conger was a shot-up veteran, still suffering from his wounds.

At sundown on 24 April, the *John S. Ide*, a propeller-driven steamer of 186 tons, was loaded and ready. The civilian captain, Henry Wilson, pulled away from the wharf and headed down the river. The plan was to debark the men and horses at an abandoned military complex at Belle Plaine on Potomac Creek, in western King George County, forty miles below Washington. At ten o'clock the steamer was tied up at a serviceable wharf. The search would begin in the direction of Fredericksburg and swing around to the southeast.

After General Lee's surrender, Colonel John S. Mosby badly needed information upon which to make decisions. On 12 April he sent Captain Robert Walker to Gordonsville, the duty station of Major Cornelius Boyle, who had been one of Mosby's main channels of information and orders.[24] Lieutenant Channing Smith was sent to Richmond, presumably to make contact with Confederates remaining at liberty in the city.

Lieutenant Smith's mission to Richmond involved some risk, but the federal cork in that bottle was not very tight. He had no difficulty. While in Richmond, Smith managed to see General R. E. Lee shortly after Lee's return from Appomattox on 15 April. In essence, Lee advised Smith that Mosby should disband his organization.[25] News that John Wilkes Booth had assassinated Lincoln was received in Richmond on 16 April.[26] No doubt Channing Smith carried this news back to Mosby, together with Lee's advice.

After Mosby disbanded his organization on 21 April, he and about fifty of his men started for the Richmond area. By 25 April they were camped at Frederick's Hall in Louisa County, between

Gordonsville and Hanover Junction.[27] At this location they were reasonably safe from Union interference. The Virginia Central Railroad was nearby so there was access to a telegraph line. Richmond was within easy reach. Mosby was now in a position to move in accordance with whatever situation developed.

Until he arrived at Frederick's Hall, Mosby had little chance to learn that Booth was loose in King George County. It is, of course, possible that such information reached him at Frederick's Hall on 25 April by telegraph or courier. There is no proof that it did. Assuming that Mosby did receive this information, he would have had strong reasons for wanting to get Booth under his control and out of Yankee reach. Even so, Mosby had no time to intervene effectively. Booth was dead on the morning of 26 April. Mosby's problem was solved; dead men do not tell embarrassing secrets.

There are some dangling threads about Mosby in all this. When Booth and Herold were at Dr. Stuart's on 23 April, they told him they wanted to "go to Mosby," which implies an understanding of some sort. Further, both at the Port Conway ferry and later at the Garretts', there were negotiations about being taken to Orange Court House. After the Yankees moved out in early 1864, Orange County was considered to be Mosby territory.[28]

Mosby left most of his remaining followers in Louisa County and went off to explore the situation in Richmond. John Munson and Cole Jordan were sent into Richmond to gather information and report back to Mosby at a location west of the city. Apparently Mosby also met with former Secretary of War James Seddon, who lived in that area. Before Munson and Jordan returned, Lieutenant Ben Palmer learned from a newspaper that General Joseph E. Johnston had surrendered in North Carolina. The war was over. But Mosby could not afford to fall into federal hands until things cooled off. He began a series of evasive actions that ultimately led to his parole in Lynchburg on 17 June.

The *John S. Ide* was unloaded shortly after ten o'clock on the night of 24 April. Belle Plaine must have looked anything but beautiful to the edgy troopers that night. They feared an ambush. But nothing happened.

The only usable road around a swamp led in the direction of Fredericksburg. About three miles along this road, the command was turned south and struck the Rappahannock River about twelve miles above Port Conway. They then swung to the east along what was known as the River Side Road.

The night was spent rousing sleeping farmers and physicians.

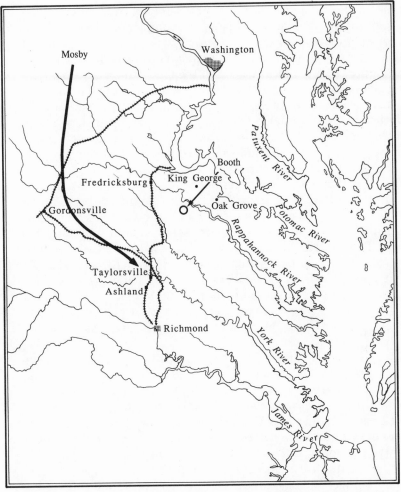

MOVEMENTS OF MOSBY AND BOOTH 23–25 APRIL 1865

Conger and Baker sometimes adopted sly tactics. They pretended to be Confederates separated from two companions, one of whom was lame. Have you seen them, have they been to your house? At times the search was conducted cavalry style, with banging on front doors. Windows were raised to see what the noise was all about. Yankees, damned Yankees! Open up or we will kick the door down! Smelly troopers poking into back rooms and looking under beds, questions about a lame man and a companion. So it went the rest of the night.

Just after dawn on 25 April the searchers reached Bleak Hill, the farm home of Dr. Horace Ashton in the Comorn community near King George Court House. Dr. Ashton was correct and courteous. He had breakfast prepared for the troopers and furnished feed for their horses. About the time breakfast was over, Confederate Captain Murray F. Taylor rode up to Bleak Hill. He had been at the home of Dr. John P. Robb and was en route to his brother's nearby place, Mount View. Captain Taylor had been aide-de-camp to General A. P. Hill and was a tough-minded young officer. In attempting to question Taylor, Conger managed to ruffle his feathers. Taylor fell back on his considerable dignity and pointed to his Appomattox parole. In exasperation, Conger arrested him and took his pistol. Thomas H. Williamson was sent for from nearby Mount View, the home of John Temple Taylor, to vouch for Taylor. At about the same time, Confederate General Charles W. Field rode up. He was staying at the home of his wife's relatives in the area and was on his way to Maryland. Williamson and Field helped smooth things over. Taylor was given back his pistol and released.[29]

In running into Captain Murray Taylor at Dr. Ashton's, Conger's search party had fallen neatly into the web of the clandestine operation working to locate Booth before the Yankees captured him. Williamson now knew the direction and composition of the search party. At that very moment, John Wilkes Booth was preparing to eat a country breakfast at the Garretts'. He had just under twenty-four hours to live.

At Dr. Ashton's it was decided to split the search to cover more ground. Conger and Baker took four men and a corporal and headed down the Rappahannock River toward Port Conway. Lieutenant Doherty took the remainder by way of King George Court House and on to Port Conway. Early in the afternoon the two groups came together at Belle Grove, the home of Carolinus Turner, near the ferry. Turner fed some of the troopers, and the rest got food at another house. Conger went to sleep in the hallway at Belle Grove.

On the way down to the ferry, Doherty and Baker met Dick Wilson, the black who helped William Rollins in the shad fishing. Wilson told Doherty that two men answering the descriptions of Booth and Herold had been there the day before and had crossed the river to Port Royal. Doherty and Baker found Rollins sitting on his front steps. Had two strangers crossed to Port Royal yesterday, a lame man and a shorter one? Yes, they had. They had come to the ferry about noon yesterday in a two-horse wagon driven by a black named Lucas, who lived "upcountry" near Dr. Stuart. One man had a broken leg and carried two crutches. The shorter man carried a carbine. Out came the pictures Colonel Baker had given them in Washington. What about this one? That is the thick-set man who carried the carbine. And this one? That looks like the man on crutches, but he had no mustache. They crossed the river yesterday about one o'clock in the afternoon with three Confederate soldiers. And who were these Confederates? One was Willie Jett.

Here at last was the trail. Doherty sent for Conger. Then he put three men in Rollins's boat with orders to bring the ferry over from Port Royal—at the point of a gun if necessary. It was past three o'clock before James Thornton, the ferryman, began the tedious job of taking the men and horses across, six at a time.

Conger questioned Rollins closely and took a short written statement. This time Rollins identified the pictures more definitely. Again Rollins said one of the three Confederates was Willie Jett. Mrs. Rollins joined in and said the other two were Ruggles and Bainbridge. Then she added a fatal piece of information. Jett was courting the little Gouldman girl at the hotel in Bowling Green and might be found there. Mrs. Rollins kept up with such matters, it seems. A decision was made to push on to Bowling Green to look for Jett. It is ironic that Booth, whose conquests were legion, should come to his end because of a romance. Conger pressed Rollins to come along as a guide. Mrs. Rollins raised a fuss. What would people think? Finally it was agreed that Rollins would go along if placed under highly visible arrest.

By six o'clock the entire command was on the Port Royal side of the river. In answer to questions from curious citizens of Port Royal, the troopers were supposed to say they were going to Fredericksburg. This answer was not very convincing. On the way out of Port Royal on the Bowling Green road, Doherty and Baker thought they saw two or three horsemen on the high ground ahead. They soon disappeared in the twilight. But the fact is, the rural telegraph—the one without wires—was in operation. The search party was being watched. It looks suspiciously as though a screen had been set up around Booth and Herold.

Before noon on 25 April, Herold and Bainbridge returned from Mrs. Clarke's to the Star Hotel, where Ruggles and Jett had spent the night. There is no way of knowing what Ruggles did while in Bowling Green. One good speculation is that he sought someone who could tell him what to do or who would take Booth and Herold off his hands.

Early that afternoon it was decided to go back to the Garretts' and leave Herold with Booth. The attractions of Izora Gouldman were too much for Jett. He would stay in Bowling Green. With Herold riding double, the three started back down the Port Royal road. Once again they stopped at the Trap for drinks and to exchange barroom banter with the Carter ladies. Eight miles away a federal juggernaut was building up at the ferry. Within hours it would hit the Trap.

Herold got off at the gate to the Garrett yard. It would be interesting to know what Ruggles said to Booth or what message Herold brought him. But Ruggles and Bainbridge rode off toward Port Royal, leaving Booth and Herold with the Garretts. One speculation is that Booth told Ruggles he had a deal with John M. Garrett to take them to Orange Court House the next morning. This idea is supported by Garrett's statement to Colonel Lafayette C. Baker.[30] Another possibility—though unlikely—is that Ruggles simply abandoned Booth and Herold. Ruggles probably thought they were secure for a time, and he felt obliged to report back to some person in the clandestine apparatus in King George County. If so, he never got the chance.

At the top of the rise overlooking Port Royal, Ruggles and Bainbridge met a horseman, identified by Ruggles as "a soldier of my command," who told them that Port Royal was full of Yankees searching for Booth. This alarming news caused them to wheel around and ride rapidly back to the Garretts', some three miles distant, to warn Booth and Herold of danger. Ruggles and Bainbridge then had an attack of prudence. They took off to the east in the direction of Essex County.

When Colonel Lafayette C. Baker interviewed John M. Garrett on 20 May 1865, Garrett told him about Ruggles and Bainbridge coming to the farm to warn Booth and Herold about the approaching federal cavalry. As Garrett told it, Booth and Herold immediately started for the woods back of the barn. In a few minutes Herold returned and asked Garrett if he believed federal cavalry was crossing at the ferry. Garrett was doubtful. Just then a young black man named Jim came up from Port Royal. Garrett asked him about the cavalry. Yes, they were in Port Royal when he left. While the three were still talking, the cavalry passed on the road not far from the house, going toward Bowling Green. Garrett then remarked to Herold, "There goes the cavalry now." Herold responded, "Well, that is all."[31]

The leaders of the search party had no interest in the Garretts. They had a hot tip that Jett could be found in the hotel at Bowling Green, and they were following it up. It was already dark when they stopped at the Trap to make inquiries. Conger and Baker went in, followed shortly by Lieutenant Doherty. Later each recalled what took place somewhat differently. At first they got no cooperation. There was a loud clamor from "four or five young women." Finally one of the search party, probably Conger, said they were looking for a man who had committed an outrage upon a girl. This got results. Four men on three horses had been to the tavern the previous afternoon. One of the men was Willie Jett. They had talked of going to Mrs. Clarke's. But no lame man had been in the group. Three of these same men had been back just that afternoon but without Jett. The searchers were in a quandary. Obviously Booth had not gotten as far as the tavern. But Jett was unaccounted for. They must go into Bowling Green after him.[32]

In a joint letter to Secretary of War Stanton on 24 December 1865, Everton Conger and Luther Baker described the scene at the Trap when the searchers left for Bowling Green: "Once more in the saddle, horses exhausted, and men weary, hungry, and sleepy, the command pushed forward and reached Bowling Green between 11 and 12 o'clock." They halted on the outskirts of the town. Half of the men went in with Conger, Baker, and Doherty. They surrounded the hotel, and Doherty pounded on the door. After some delay, a black man let them in by a back door. Mrs. Julia Gouldman, alarmed by the noise, got up to see what was going on. She told her midnight visitors that her husband was away. She was alone in the building except for her children and Willie Jett. And where is Jett? She said he was upstairs in a room with her son Jesse, who was recovering from a war wound.[33]

Jett was hustled down to face an angry trio—Conger, Baker, and Doherty. The questions came thick and hard. Where is Booth?

Where is Herold? The eighteen-year-old Jett was frightened and for good reason. Finally he asked Baker and Doherty to withdraw and told his story to grim Conger. Booth had been left near Port Royal at the farm home of Richard Garrett. Ruggles and Bainbridge had taken Herold back to join Booth. Under arrest, Jett was ordered to saddle up and become a guide. It was past one o'clock on 26 April. Booth had but six hours to live.

Earlier in the day, the situation at the Garrett house had become somewhat tense. Booth was increasingly insistent that he be taken to Orange Court House. John Garrett made a promise of sorts to take him the next morning. But the Garretts had become suspicious of their guests, particularly after the incident of the cavalry. Clearly, the two were running from something serious. The Garretts feared that their horses would be stolen for a getaway. After some discussion, Booth and Herold agreed to spend the night in the tobacco barn. As a precaution, John Garrett and his brother William planned to sleep in a nearby corn crib. After Booth and Herold entered the barn, William locked the door behind them.

Around two o'clock the cavalry arrived at the gate to the lane leading to the Garrett House. Rollins and Jett were left there with a guard. Doherty's instructions were simple: no talking, approach quietly, and when the order is given divide right and left to surround the house. The Garretts all remembered that the dogs started barking. Conger hammered on the door. When Richard Garrett came to see what was happening, a pistol was stuck in his face and the demand was made: "Where are they? Where are your two visitors?" Garrett had a slight speech defect. He was understood to say that they were gone or out in the woods. He was dragged out into the yard with the threat that he would be strung up if he did not start talking.

The uproar aroused John Garrett. He started for the house but was spotted by one of the cavalrymen, who nearly shot him before he could identify himself. Brought before Conger and Baker, he lost no time in telling them the men being sought were in the tobacco barn.

The rest of the story has been told and retold in dozens of books and countless articles. The barn was quickly encircled by the cavalry. John Garrett was persuaded to unlock the door and go in to request Booth and Herold to give up their arms and come out. Booth refused and threatened to shoot him if he came back. A long and dramatic parley followed between Baker and Booth. Finally Conger threatened to burn the barn. Herold had no stomach for this idea and agreed to surrender. He came to the door and was dragged away. Booth continued to be adamant, asking for a fair fight. His performance was pure Booth, theatrical to the end.

An exasperated Conger ordered brush to be piled at a back corner of the barn. Conger lost his composure; he should have waited Booth out and kept up the pressure. Instead he twisted up some hay and set the fire at about three o'clock. The fire spread quickly in loose hay on the barn floor, providing ample light. As the fire spread, Conger watched through four-inch gaps in the vertical plank siding.[34] Booth approached the fire and saw that he could not put it out. He then dropped the carbine he was carrying and turned toward the front of the barn. Sergeant Boston Corbett had also been watching Booth through a similar gap in the planks. He took aim and fired one shot from his cavalry revolver. Booth pitched forward, shot through a neck vertebra. The wound paralyzed him instantly. He was carried out to the yard and then to the front porch of the house. The barn eventually burned to the ground.

Booth appeared to revive slightly so Conger sent to Port Royal for a doctor. Within the hour, Dr. Charles Urquhart, Jr., rode up. He examined Booth and pronounced the wound to be fatal. According to Conger, Booth did manage to say a few words. Once he whispered, "Tell mother I died for my country." Again, on seeing Jett, he asked: "Did that man betray me?" He lingered until a few minutes after seven o'clock.

For Booth, the final curtain had come down.

There were watchful Confederate eyes around the Garrett place. How many and how close they were we shall never know, but the story of William B. Lightfoot, a private in Company B, Ninth Virginia Cavalry, gives a hint. Lightfoot's home was in Port Royal. After the war, he claimed that he returned home after being paroled at Appomattox. On the morning of 26 April he went to the Garretts', where "a shooting had taken place." There he saw Dr. Urquhart examine John Wilkes Booth and heard him pronounced dead.

Lightfoot's story is not quite accurate. The records show that he was not paroled at Appomattox but signed his parole at King George Court House on 2 May 1865. He may already have been in the area as part of the security force originally set up to protect the route to be used to transport a captured Lincoln. He may well have been drawn into the effort to find Booth and escort him out of danger. It would be logical for the clandestine apparatus to send somebody to the Garretts' to find out if Booth was really dead. If so, the problem was solved. There would be no confession. Lightfoot took some risk in going. He had no parole. But the Union cavalry was too preoccupied to notice one stray Confederate.[35]

Notes

ABBREVIATIONS

NA National Archives
OR U.S. War Department, *The War of the Rebellion: A Compilation of the Official Records of the Union and Confederate Armies.* 128 vols. Washington, D.C.: U.S. Government Printing Office, 1880–1901.
ORN U.S. Navy Department, *Official Records of the Union and Confederate Navies in the War of the Rebellion.* 30 vols. Washington, D.C.: U.S. Government Printing Office, 1894–1914.
RG Record Group

1. Indiantown was owned by Peregrine Davis but farmed by his son-in-law John J. Hughes. Herold knew Davis and Hughes and had hunted on the farm. See Herold's statement, Investigation and Trial Papers Relating to the Assassination of President Lincoln, M-599, reel 4, frames 0442–85, NA; also George Atzerodt's statement, M-599, reel 3, frames 0596–0602, NA, in which he said Booth once asked him to be a guide to Indiantown.

2. Log of the USS *Juniper,* Records of the Bureau of Naval Personnel, RG 24, NA. Although some evidence indicates that Booth and Herold started to cross the Potomac River on the night of 20 April, Thomas A. Jones wrote that this was on the night of 21 April. The information on gunboat movements, weather, and tide is more compatible with 21 April.

3. James O. Hall interview with George Carrico Hughes, grandson of John J. Hughes, 21 December 1975.

4. William R. Wilmer, Port Tobacco, Maryland, to Major James R. O'Beirne, Entry 38, RG 110, NA.

5. Statement of Elizabeth R. Quesenberry, M-599, reel 5, frames 0556–59, NA.

6. George Alfred Townsend, *Katy of Catoctin* (New York: D. Appleton, 1886).

7. William Couper, *The VMI New Market Cadets* (Charlottesville: Michie, 1933), p. 11.

8. *OR*, Ser. 1, vol. 2, p. 811.

9. Thomas H. Williamson, "My Service with Genl. Thomas J. Jackson," undated manuscript, Virginia Military Institute Library, Lexington, Va.

10. Statement of Dr. Richard H. Stuart, M-599, reel 6, frames 0205–11, NA.

11. Statement of William Bryant, M-599, reel 4, frames 0095–97, NA.

12. Rough undated and untitled notes by St. George Coulter Bryan including his interview with Major Robert Hunter, in Grennan Family Papers, Mssl G 8855 al79–86, Virginia Historical Society, Richmond.

13. Statement of William Lucas, M-599, reel 5, frames 0144–47, NA.

14. Virgil C. Jones, *Ranger Mosby* (Chapel Hill: University of North Carolina Press, 1944), pp. 243–45.

15. Prentice Ingraham, "The Pursuit and Death of John Wilkes Booth," *Century*

Magazine, January 1890, pp. 443–49. Ingraham interviewed Ruggles about his part in assisting Booth and Herold.

16. Taylor to Mosby, 27 March 1865, *OR,* Ser. 1, vol. 46, pt. 3, p. 1359.

17. James H. Williamson, *Mosby's Rangers* (New York: Sturgis and Walton, 1909), p. 493; *ORN,* Ser. 1, vol. 8, p. 550.

18. Ingraham, "Pursuit and Death of John Wilkes Booth"; statement of Willie S. Jett, M-599, reel 4, frames 0086–99, NA.

19. Log of the USS *Resolute,* Records of the Bureau of Naval Personnel, RG 24, NA.

20. H. B. Smith, *Between the Lines* (New York: Booz Brothers, 1911), pp. 213–14.

21. Statement of William Rollins, Letters Received by the Office of the Adjutant General (Main Series), M-619, reel 457, frames 0550–61, NA.

22. Kate Harvey Mason, "A True Story of the Capture and Death of John Wilkes Booth," *Northern Neck Historical Magazine* 13 (December 1963): 1237–39; Sydnor J. Massey, "A Chapter in the Death of John Wilkes Booth," *Memphis Commercial Appeal,* 23 March 1903.

23. *OR,* Ser. 1, vol. 46, pt. 3, p. 937.

24. Williamson, *Mosby's Rangers,* p. 366.

25. Channing Smith, "The Last Time I Saw General Lee," *Confederate Veteran* 35 (September 1927): 327.

26. *Richmond Whig,* 17 April 1865. The article states that the news of the assassination of Lincoln by John Wilkes Booth was known in the city the previous day, 16 April, and in Petersburg on 15 April.

27. Williamson, *Mosby's Rangers,* p. 398; Compiled Service Records of the Mosby men involved, NA.

28. Statement of William Rollins, M-619, reel 457, frames 0550–61, NA; statement of John M. Garrett, M-619, reel 457, frames 0499–0525, NA.

29. Primarily from the statement of Luther Baker, M-619, reel 455, frames 0665–89, NA.

30. Statement of John M. Garrett, M-619, reel 457, frames 0499–0525, NA.

31. Ibid.; Ingraham, "Pursuit and Death of John Wilkes Booth."

32. Action report of Lieutenant Edward P. Doherty to Lieutenant Colonel J. H. Taylor, Washington, 29 April 1865, M-619, reel 456, frames 0273–84, NA.

33. Joint letter from Everton Conger and Luther Baker to Secretary of War Stanton, 24 December 1865, M-619, reel 455, frames 0691–0703, NA. There are many other sources for the events at the Trap, at the Star Hotel in Bowling Green, and at the Garrett farm. These include statement of Luther Baker on the USS *Montauk,* 27 April 1865, M-619, reel 455, frames 0665–89, NA; Lieutenant Edward P. Doherty's action report, M-619, reel 456, frames 0273–84, NA; statement of John M. Garrett, M-619, reel 457, frames 0499–0525, NA; and testimony of Everton Conger, *Trial of John H. Surratt* (Washington, D.C.: U.S. Government Printing Office, 1867), 1:305–14.

34. The four-inch gaps were described by John M. Garrett, *Trial of John H. Surratt,* 1:304.

35. Notes made by Stanley Kimmel, Stanley Kimmel Papers, University of Tampa Library, based in part on an article in the *Richmond News Leader,* 16 May 1929, p. 15. Lightfoot's Compiled Service Record, NA, was consulted for his parole. Thomas N. Conrad picked up a rumor that Ruggles and Bainbridge were concealed in the woods and saw the shooting at Garrett's farm, which he included in a typescript but softened in his book *A Confederate Spy* (New York: J. S. Ogilvie, 1892), pp. 110–11.

21

Paroled at Ashland

Confederate plans to capture Lincoln and carry him off to Richmond began in 1864 and continued through most of March 1865. John Wilkes Booth was a party to the last such plan. As Booth's operation took shape, it became evident to the planners that a security force should be set up along the route a captured Lincoln must travel from the Potomac River to Richmond. The president's capture would become news almost instantly. Union reaction would be quick and forceful. Cavalry from General Grant's right wing north of the James River could be expected to come pouring across the escape route to interdict the movement of Lincoln's captors and free him. A counterforce capable of delaying such Union efforts was essential. The rest would depend on speedy action.

Booth began to assemble his action team in the early fall of 1864; the final member was Lewis Powell, sent by Mosby in mid-January 1865. Meanwhile, planners in Richmond were looking ahead. In late December 1864, Mosby's Companies C, E, F, and G, under Lieutenant Colonel William Chapman, were moved out of Fauquier and Loudoun counties to the Northern Neck of Virginia. These fast-moving cavalry units were particularly well suited to become part of the security force. As the mid-March target date for the capture of Lincoln came closer, other troops were quietly moved into the area between the Potomac River and Richmond. There had to be enough to do the job, but not so many that they would be seen as a threat. It is doubtful if more than a handful of people at the top knew about the plan and the quiet movement of troops. Certainly the troops themselves had no inkling that they were part of a sensitive covert operation. And as quietly as the security force was assembled, just as quietly did it begin to dissolve after all hope of capturing Lincoln passed in late March.

When Richmond fell and Lee surrendered on 9 April, many of the troops in the security force were left in place, even though their intended function was gone. There was no time for them to rejoin their parent units. Although the size of this force was never formidable, it would have been an embarrassment had the troops been gathered to march out. The solution—probably unplanned—was for everyone to sit tight and await developments. Because the men chosen were from regiments that had been recruited in the area, this was no problem.

The few Confederates involved in the creation of the security force never mentioned it after the war. But the security force left tracks. Our purpose here is to examine some of these tracks and to put together some of the bits and pieces that show its existence.

On 21 April 1865, the First New York Mounted Rifles were sent to occupy Ashland, some eighteen miles north of Richmond in Hanover County. The unit had been all the way around Richmond, participated in a North Carolina raid, and most recently had helped occupy Petersburg. Once the unit reached Ashland, an office was set up to parole Confederate soldiers. This provided a timely opportunity to disband the security force.

The paroles issued by the First New York Mounted Rifles and other Union regiments that moved into the area later are a major source of information about the composition of the clandestine security force. Apparently, each soldier taking parole signed two copies of a dated form giving his name and organization and committing him not to take part in hostilities against the U.S. government or do anything in detriment to the authority of the government until properly exchanged. The form also gave the location of his home.

In addition to the forms, the unit issuing the parole maintained a master log of the paroles issued. This log was a book with each line numbered in series. When a soldier signed a parole, his name, the date, his rank, his regiment or battalion, and his home address were entered in the next blank line. Practices varied from unit to unit, but fortunately, the First New York Mounted Rifles also wrote the serial number of the line of the log book on the copies of the parole. Thus if the log book were no longer available, and few have survived, the serial numbers and dates on the surviving parole forms can be used to reconstruct the overall pattern of paroles issued by a given unit.

For example, more than 305 forms for soldiers paroled at Ashland have been found in the National Archives.[1] From this sample it is possible to estimate that paroles were issued at Ashland as follows:

21 April	35
22 April	33
23 April, Sunday	20
24 April	107
25 April	207
26 April	70
27 April	106
28 April	73
29 April	64
30 April, Sunday	31
01 May	98
02 May	41
03 May	25

Total 910

Thereafter, relatively few paroles were issued at Ashland. In all the total probably ran to about 920 or 930. The men paroled doubtless included many home on legitimate leave, sick, or deserters, but the number is too large and contains too many responsible persons to be accounted for by these explanations alone.

The paroles were slow at first because initially only those soldiers at Ashland or in easy reach were brought in. When General Lee released the cavalry at Appomattox, a substantial part of those remaining with the Ninth Virginia and not already at home appear to have crossed to the northern side of the James and proceeded eastward toward Ashland. Men from the Ninth who were still with the army at Appomattox could thus have been included in the total paroled at Ashland, but the same would not be true for the infantry units.

At first, the number signing their paroles was fairly small. By Monday, 24 April, it was known that Booth was safely in Virginia and that there was still no sign of Union forces on his trail. Troops began to arrive at Ashland in larger numbers on Monday. Presumably many of these men could travel by railroad, at least from Milford to the North Anna.

The list of regiments contributing men to the security force is probably not complete—there are still a couple of nonrandom gaps in the number series reflected in the available samples of paroles at Ashland, which suggests that one or more regiments are missing from those discussed earlier. The regiments that we know, however, have one thing in common: they were recruited originally in the Northern Neck or nearby counties or they were brigaded with units that were primarily from that area. The fate of all the parent regiments can be accounted for in the conventional military history of the retreat from Richmond, but the records show that relatively few of the men were paroled at Appomattox or captured at Saylor's Creek.

While the U.S. cavalry had been chasing Booth, the clock had stood still for the Confederate clandestine operation. Many of the men who could have been paroled at Ashland were held in place waiting to see what was going to happen. On Tuesday, 25 April, 207 men signed their paroles at Ashland, but the next day, the day Booth was killed, only 70 men turned up. In particular, the flow of men from the Thirtieth and Forty-seventh Virginia infantry regiments stopped. These men may have been manning the pickets along the Potomac in King George County, and the Union cavalry was between them and the railhead at Milford. Escorting Booth's body through King George County late on 26 April, Baker reported that he met numerous groups of Confederate soldiers moving toward Port Royal.

The paroles at Ashland for the next few days are especially interesting. On 26 April three men from Mosby's command, plus Colonel Waller of the Ninth Virginia Cavalry and Lieutenant Charles Cawood of the Signal Corps, signed paroles. The next day another Mosby man plus Colonel Mayo and Major Green of the Forty-seventh Virginia Infantry signed their papers.

On 26 April, as soon as the cavalry with its prisoners and Booth's body was out of the way, the flow of men toward Ashland was resumed. The next day 106 men reported for parole. On Friday, 28 April, the First Maryland (U.S.) Volunteer Cavalry took over the post at Ashland from the New York regiment. Among the last parolees to be processed by the First New York Mounted Rifles on 28 April were Thomas Harbin and Joseph Baden.

When the First Maryland Volunteer Cavalry began to issue paroles, it began a new log book and started the number series at the beginning again. Fortunately, again the line number was written on the parole form, and we can reconstruct the pattern of paroles issued. On 28 April, the First New York Mounted Rifles issued only 42 paroles before departing, and the First Maryland issued only 31 after taking over, for a total of 73 paroles issued on that Friday. On Saturday, the number dropped to 64 and on Sunday to 31. On Monday, 1 May, however, it jumped to 98.

On 1 and 2 May, a new development affected the flow of parolees. Union cavalry detachments opened parole offices at the county seats of King George, Westmoreland, Richmond, and Northumberland counties in the Northern Neck and at Bowling Green in Caroline County. Many of the soldiers who would have had to travel to Ashland were now able to take their paroles closer to home. The flow at Ashland dropped to about 25 on 3 May and was a mere trickle thereafter.

Troops of the security force turned up in unit clusters in the various counties. For example, 32 men of the Ninth Virginia Cavalry and 47 men from the Fortieth Virginia Infantry were paroled at Westmoreland County on 5 and 6 May. Thirteen from the Forty-seventh Virginia Infantry were paroled at King George on 1 and 2 May. Seventeen men from the Fortieth Virginia Infantry were also paroled at Northumberland Courthouse on 6 May.

There are a number of other pieces of information that seem to refer to the soldiers providing local security in the area of the escape route. The retirement of Lieutenant Colonel F. W. Cox of the Fortieth Virginia Infantry to the invalid corps is suspicious. He had lost an eye at Chancellorsville in May 1863, but he had been considered able enough to accompany an amphibious raiding task force in mid-1864. He was promoted on 13 February 1865, after his "retirement."[2] He well may have been a member of the security force, with the change in status serving as a cover.

On 11 March 1865, Colonel Robert Mayo, commander of the Forty-seventh Virginia Infantry, wrote to the adjutant and inspector general, that omnipotent functionary to whom soldiers complain, asking that Colonel Mosby be told to stop taking men from that unit.[3] Unfortunately, this letter is missing, and we have only the note recording its receipt. We do not know, therefore, where it was addressed from or the specifics on which Mayo's complaint was based.

The indication of such a letter does tell us, however, that men from the Forty-seventh were being sufficiently exposed to the Forty-third that Mayo was concerned about his men being attracted to the romantic partisan life. Furthermore, since a man had to have a horse to join Mosby, the exposure was probably taking place in the Northern Neck, where the men from the Forty-seventh might be able to get horses at home or from relatives or

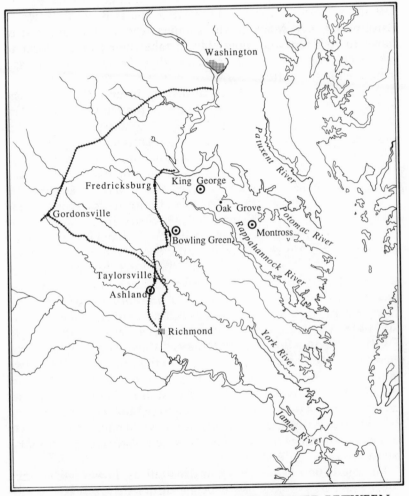

MAJOR SITES WHERE PAROLES WERE ISSUED BETWEEN
21 APRIL–10 MAY TO SOLDIERS FROM REGIMENTS
RECRUITED IN THE NORTHERN NECK

neighbors and join the Mosby companies quartered in nearby counties. It is not likely that men from the Forty-seventh would have had the opportunity to be attracted to service with Mosby while they were in the trenches at Chaffin's Farm.

A few other items in source material from the period must refer to members of the security force. It has been known for many years that there was Confederate cavalry at Milford at the time of the death of John Wilkes Booth, but nobody has investigated what unit it was. By all logic it must have been from the Ninth Virginia Cavalry.

As an old lady, Nannie Brown Doherty wrote about her recollections of the Civil War in King George County. Her father was clerk of the county court, and the Brown family lived about two miles from King George Courthouse. She said:

> A few days after the battle of Appomattox, twelve of our soldiers who belonged to Mosby's command came and asked for a night's shelter. They were on their way to their homes, most of them were far away. Father and mother most gladly welcomed them, but told them we could not give them cots. They said, "let us sleep on the floor anywhere." So here in this room, which was then a sitting room, they slept with pillows under their heads and a little covering, for it was April. I remember the big pots of coffee, and much bread and other things Mother had cooked for their supper and breakfast. We never heard of any of them after they left.[4]

These may have been soldiers left behind when Mosby's companies departed on 9 April, the day of Lee's surrender at Appomattox. More likely, however, they were from the Forty-seventh or Thirtieth Virginia Infantry regiments who had been on picket duty near the Potomac and were now heading for Ashland. Since Mosby's unit was so famous and its stay in the Northern Neck so well known, it was likely that every strange Confederate soldier seen in the area was assumed to be one of Mosby's men.

Doherty did not mention horses, and all of Mosby's men were mounted. One would think that twelve horses around the house would have made almost as much of an impression on a young girl as the men did. When Doherty said that some of their homes were far away and that her family never heard from any of them again, one needs to recall that some of the men from these two regiments lived fifty to one hundred miles from King George County, and in the era of horses and mud roads that was a very long distance. If the soldiers were from close by, they would have stayed at one of their own homes instead of the Brown house.

In the tumult of the search for Booth and his associates, a clear reference to the security force was ignored. On 22 April, General John P. Slough, the military governor at Alexandria, sent a message to the War Department: "Rebel soldiers of the Army of Northern Virginia report that this side of the Rappahannock River there are large numbers of men of that army without paroles; some say many hundreds."[5] If anybody wondered about the significance of this information at the time it was received, Booth's death probably washed away any concern. On 25 April 1865, the *Baltimore American* reported that "there are quite a number of guerilla along the lower Potomac and on the banks of the Rappahannock, near Fredericksburg." This was doubtless a reference to members of the security force who had not yet disbanded.

The existence of the security force is most significant in our understanding of the Confederate role in the attempt to capture President Lincoln and his subsequent death. The Confederates went to great lengths to conceal its creation and dissolved it with equal care. Those few who knew of its creation and the role it was supposed to play went to their graves without revealing its existence. Most of the men in it, of course, did not know its true purpose or dimensions.

Fortunately, the existence of the security force can be established from evidence collected by Union troops at several locations for a completely different purpose—the paroles. The evidence cannot have been fabricated, and though total numbers in the force cannot be ascertained, we have the names of 841 men who could have been in the security force. Even allowing for deserters and those at home on legitimate leave, that is a substantial number and is large enough to produce some fairly convincing statistical extrapolations. In addition, we know from Lieutenant Carlton's diary that some members of the security force had already returned to their parent units before the evacuation of Richmond.[6] Some of them were probably paroled at Appomattox.

Those who are not prepared to accept our analysis of the data relating to the security force can easily present several obvious arguments against it. First, the men paroled at the locations we have studied were all at home for one legitimate reason or another not related to clandestine activity. The Confederate cavalry sent men home to procure new mounts whenever a horse was killed or put out of action. At times, as many as one-third of some cavalry regiments might be at home at any given moment. The answers to this argument are that here soldiers in both infantry and cavalry are involved. Manpower was too scarce to allow so many men to be absent for any but the strongest reasons. By 1865, horses had become so scarce in the Confederacy that cavalry regiments sometimes fought dismounted rather than release men to search for new mounts. The Ninth Virginia had fought dismounted on at least one occasion in the winter of 1864–65. Aside from a few obvious cases, there is no indication that the parolees were ill or had any other personal excuse to be away from duty.

A second argument is that the men paroled were deserters or stragglers left behind when the army evacuated Richmond and Petersburg. They went north of the James to get away from the Union army. The answers to this argument are that there are few reports of stragglers from the units involved. There were many deserters from the army as a whole, but the men paroled in and north of Ashland were from only a few of the regiments from which men might have deserted. In addition, judging from Custis Lee's report of the evacuation of Richmond, there seems to have been no opportunity for men from Barton's brigade to be left behind.

A third argument that could be made is that our parolees were individuals who escaped at Saylor's Creek and made their way home. The answer here seems to be fairly conclusive evidence that Custis Lee's division was so placed that very few, if any, men had a chance to escape from the trap at Saylor's Creek. Furthermore, the cavalry regiments were not involved at Saylor's Creek.[7]

Aside from the statistical evidence and other items that seem to refer to the security force, there is the negative evidence of the lack of specific reference to the units involved during the last six months of the war on the part of men who were members of, or aware of, the existence of the force. Aside from the diary of Lieutenant Carlton of the Twenty-fourth Virginia Cavalry, few diaries or memoirs were written by the men in these units. General Beale wrote a history of the Ninth Virginia Cavalry Regiment, which was published after his death. In it he condensed the history of the last six months of the war into one and a half pages and mentioned only the elements of the regiment that fought on the south flank of Lee's army.

Major Charles J. Green of the Forty-seventh Virginia Infantry wrote a few lines of autobiography for the alumni files at VMI and commented that he had never been captured during the war. He had escaped the surrender at Appomattox because he was "on leave."[8] This was his own cover story. If Green was on leave, he was enjoying this rest in the company of a great many of his fellows from the Forty-seventh. He was paroled at Ashland on 29 April 1865.

Sergeant Dabney Jordan Waller of the Ninth Virginia Cavalry wrote long after the war, "I was on detail service at the time of the surrender, and returned home about three weeks afterward."[9] Inasmuch as he was paroled at Ashland on 29 April 1865, his detail was probably to the security force.

In the 1890s, Samuel Q. Williams of Company D of the Ninth Virginia filled out a souvenir muster record of his Civil War service. After detailing much combat service, he concluded by saying that he was "detailed for special duty with Com. [sic] Maury to put torpedoes in Rappahannock River and as special scout—never surrendered." There is no record of his parole in the National Archives. His memory probably found Maury easier to recall than Kennon, but Maury was in England at the time indicated and Kennon was doubtless the naval officer to whom he was detailed. This memento now hangs on the wall of the old county clerk's office at Lancaster Court House in Virginia.

On 1 August 1865, after the end of the war, Robert E. Lee wrote to Wade Hampton about the closing events of the war. He blamed the disaster at Five Forks on the shortage of cavalry caused by the reinforcements that he had sent with Hampton to the Carolinas during the winter of 1865. He further excused the cavalry who had been left in Virginia by saying, "A large portion of the men who had been sent to the interior to winter their horses had not rejoined their regiments."[10] It is correct that a large portion of the cavalrymen who had been sent home had not returned to their units, but they were in the Northern Neck and along the escape routes rather than in the "interior." General Lee may have been giving a cover story.

We find the evidence of the existence of the security force overwhelming. It involved a large number of men at a time when men were scarce. It was put together in a way to keep its existence secret even from the men who belonged to it, and it maintained a very low profile while on station. When it had served its purpose, it was dissolved as carefully as it had been formed.

By 10 May 1865, the clandestine force had been completely dispersed, most of the men were in their homes, and the Union apparently never learned of its existence. Only the cryptic phrase "paroled at Ashland" remained to remind the veterans that they had won their last battle.

Notes

ABBREVIATIONS

NA   National Archives

OR   U.S. War Department, *The War of the Rebellion: A Compilation of the Official Records of the Union and Confederate Armies.* 128 vols. Washington, D.C.: U.S. Government Printing Office, 1880–1901.

ORN   U.S. Navy Department, *Official Records of the Union and Confederate Navies in the War of the Rebellion.* 30 vols. Washington, D.C.: U.S. Government Printing Office, 1894–1914.

RG   Record Group

1. Figures here and in the following paragraphs are from a search through Compiled Service Records, NA, of the regiments and men involved.

2. Chap. I, vol. 128, p. 58, RG 109, NA.

3. Index of Letters Received by the Adjutant and Inspector General, Chap. I, vol. 73, RG 109, NA.

4. Nannie Brown Doherty, "Some Recollections of the Civil War," *Northern Neck of Virginia Historical Society* 11 (1961): 983.

5. *OR,* Ser. 1, vol. 46, pt. 3, p. 899.

6. Cornelius Hart Carlton, "Diary," *Bulletin of the King and Queen County Historical Society of Virginia* 24 (January 1968): no page numbers.

7. Christopher M. Calkins, *Thirty-Six Hours before Appomattox* (N.p.: Privately printed, n.d.), chap. 1.

8. Alumni file on Major Charles J. Green, Virginia Military Institute, Lexington, Va.

9. Marshall Wingfield, *A History of Caroline County* (Baltimore: Regional Publishing Company, 1975), p. 263.

10. Copy by Thomas Ellis of an excerpt of a letter from Lee to Hampton, Munford-Ellis Papers, Duke University Library, Durham, N.C.

Index